COSIMA WAGNER'S DIARIES

COSIMA WAGNER'S
DIARIES

An Abridgement

Introduced by Geoffrey Skelton and abridged by him from his
translation of the complete *Diaries* edited and annotated
by Martin Gregor-Dellin and Dietrich Mack

Yale University Press
New Haven and London

Cosima Wagner's Diaries were first published in two volumes
in German by R. Piper & Co. Verlag in 1976 and 1977 and in
English, in Geoffrey Skelton's translation, by Harcourt Brace
Jovanovich, Inc. in 1978 and 1980.

This abridgement first published by Pimlico 1994.
Yale University Press paperbound edition published 1997.
Reprinted by arrangement with Harcourt Brace and
Company.

Printed in the United States of America.

Library of Congress Catalog Card Number 96–61144

ISBN 0-300-06904-9

A catalogue record for this book is available from the British
Library.

The paper in this book meets the guidelines for permanence
and durability of the Committee on Production Guidelines
for Book Longevity of the Council on Library Resources.

10 9 8 7 6 5 4 3 2 1

Contents

INTRODUCTION

Cosima, the younger daughter of the composer Franz Liszt, was still the wife of the conductor Hans von Bülow when, on November 16, 1868, she joined Richard Wagner at his home in Tribschen, near Lucerne in Switzerland. From then until Wagner's death on February 13, 1883, the two were never parted, except for a very few days at a time, and Cosima's Diaries, begun on January 1, 1869, provide a continuous and intimate picture of their fourteen years together – first at Lucerne, where, after Cosima's divorce from Hans von Bülow, they were married (on August 25, 1870), and then in Bayreuth in Germany. These were the years during which Wagner completed the huge *Ring* cycle, on which he had been working since 1849, and built the festival theatre in Bayreuth in which to present it. He then went on to write his last work, *Parsifal*, which he produced at Bayreuth only a few months before his death at the age of sixty-nine.

All these events, and many more besides, are dealt with in detail in the Diaries, and there is consequently no need to say anything further about them here. But, in order that the reader can appreciate them to the full, it may be useful to describe the preceding events, which led Cosima, at the age of thirty-one, finally to abandon Hans von Bülow and devote the rest of her long life to Richard Wagner, a man twenty-four years her senior.

When Cosima left her husband and joined Richard Wagner at Tribschen, she was already the mother of four daughters, and another child was on the way. The two elder girls were Hans von Bülow's: Daniela, born in 1860, and Blandine, born in 1863. These two she left at her husband's home in Munich when she parted from him. The two younger daughters, whom she took with her, were Richard Wagner's: Isolde, born in 1865, the year of the first production of *Tristan und Isolde*, and Eva, born in 1867, while he was composing *Die Meistersinger von Nürnberg*. The child as yet unborn when Cosima arrived at Tribschen was to be Wagner's first and only son. Like his sisters, he was named after the work on which Wagner was working at the time of his birth: *Siegfried*.

His 1836 marriage with his first wife, Minna, an actress four years older than he, had been childless. By all accounts Minna was a good-looking woman and an efficient housewife, who coped resourcefully during the lean years when her husband was struggling to establish himself as a composer and a conductor. For her the pinnacle of happiness was reached when, in the early 1840s, he was appointed a conductor at the Dresden opera and brought out in quick succession his three operas *Rienzi* (1842), *Der Fliegende Holländer* (1843), and *Tannhäuser* (1845).

His subsequent involvement in the social revolution of 1849, which forced him to flee to Switzerland to avoid arrest and imprisonment in Dresden, was a shattering blow for Minna, from which she never really recovered. Though she eventually joined him in exile, she became embittered, having no sympathy for his desire to reform the theatre which had provided him with a respectable living, and no belief in the huge work, *Der Ring des Nibelungen*, through which he planned to effect that reform. Wagner was obliged to turn for support to his friends, of whom the staunchest proved to be Franz Liszt, two years older than he. Courageously, in view of the composer's status as a wanted man in Germany, Liszt staged the first performance of *Lohengrin* in Weimar in 1850, and he also did all he could to help Wagner financially and encourage him to work on the *Ring*.

In his increasing estrangement from Minna, Wagner sought solace with other women – first with Jessie Laussot, an English-woman married to a Frenchman in Bordeaux, and then with Mathilde Wesendonck, whose husband, a well-to-do German businessman, had settled in Zurich. It was there, in the little house called Das Asyl in the grounds of the Wesendonck estate, that a jealous scene between Minna and Mathilde virtually brought the marriage to an end in 1858. Wagner, who had suspended work on *Siegfried* to write *Tristan und Isolde*, went off to Venice by himself.

When he had completed *Tristan und Isolde*, he made another attempt to resume his married life, and Minna accompanied him to Paris, where, in 1861, he produced his revised version of *Tannhäuser*. Neither this attempt to repair his marriage nor a subsequent one – in Biebrich, on the Rhine, when he was starting work on *Die Meistersinger* – proved successful; Minna returned to Dresden, and apart from an occasional meeting when he passed through that city, they saw nothing more of each other. Of the two women with whom he shared his life during this period, Friederike Meyer and Mathilde Maier, the second was the more significant; indeed, if his marriage with Minna had ended earlier, it is possible that she might have become his second wife. Both women figure in Cosima's Diaries, as, in fact, do Jessie Laussot and Mathilde Wesendonck.

During that summer of 1862 in Biebrich when he was working happily on *Die Meistersinger*, Wagner received visits from several friends, among them Hans von Bülow and his wife, Cosima. Hans von Bülow had been only sixteen, a promising pupil of Franz Liszt, when Wagner first met him in 1846 in Dresden. Cosima was even younger when Liszt and Wagner paid a visit to Paris in 1853, and Liszt took him to see his three children, Blandine, Cosima, and Daniel. Though he played no personal part in their lives in those early years, Wagner exerted through his music a very powerful influence on the young people, and it was a performance in Berlin, conducted by Hans, of the overture to *Tannhäuser* that finally brought her and Hans together and led to their marriage, on August 18, 1857. They visited Wagner in Zurich during their honeymoon and again a year later, when they were witnesses of the unhappy scenes involving Minna and Mathilde Wesendonck.

Cosima herself was no stranger to domestic trouble and unhappiness. She was the second child of Franz Liszt and the French Countess Marie d'Agoult, and was born on Christmas Day 1837, in Bellagio, Italy, on Lake Como. Her parents, who were never married, separated when she was not quite two years old, and she and her elder sister and younger brother were left in Paris in the care of Liszt's mother, actively discouraged from having anything to do with their own mother, who had by then devoted herself to a literary career under the pseudonym of Daniel Stern. Liszt himself continued to travel through Europe for a number of years, giving piano recitals, but in 1848 he abandoned his career as a virtuoso to settle down in Weimar as Court musical director. Here his companion was Princess Carolyne von Sayn-Wittgenstein, who, like Countess d'Agoult, had a daughter from her previous marriage. Thus Claire in Paris and Marie in Weimar received all the parental care of Countess d'Agoult and Liszt respectively, and the three children of their own union were left to grow up virtually as orphans.

If Cosima had hoped to find in marriage a settled background to her life, she was disappointed. Hans's mother seems to have been unwilling to accept her, and it soon became apparent that Hans himself was not willing to allow her to share his life to the full. The death of her brother, Daniel, from consumption in 1859 was a further grief which much increased her sense of isolation, and her feelings received yet another shattering blow when, later that same year, her sister, Blandine, who had married a French politician, Emile Ollivier, died after giving birth to a son.

Her meeting with Wagner in Biebrich brought them closer together. Indeed, it must have seemed to Cosima, in the period just before and after the birth of her second daughter, Blandine, that her only true friend in the world was Richard Wagner, though his visits to Berlin were rare and fleeting. It was on one of these, as they were driving to a concert to be conducted by Hans, that they at last admitted their love for each other.

However, their activities kept them apart for some time yet. While Cosima continued her life in Berlin as Hans von Bülow's wife and mother of his two children, Wagner moved to Vienna, attempting, with conducting engagements, to earn sufficient money to settle down and finish *Die Meistersinger*. His failure, due in some measure to his own extravagance, brought him to the verge of desperation. He was rescued from it, literally at the last moment, by what he himself described as a fairy story.

In May 1864, at the age of eighteen, a passionate admirer of his ascended the throne of Bavaria as King Ludwig II and immediately sent for him, to offer him generous financial support and complete freedom to write and produce his works in Munich. Wagner, who had been on the point of fleeing to some remote spot to escape his Viennese creditors, found himself all at once in possession of a villa beside Lake Starnberg in Bavaria. After first inviting Mathilde Maier to share it with him as his housekeeper (she refused), he hit upon the idea of asking Hans von Bülow to join him there for the summer, along with his wife and family.

Cosima came to Starnberg in June 1864 without her husband, who was detained a while longer in Berlin by ill health, and it was during this time that Wagner and Cosima's love was physically consummated, as the birth of their daughter Isolde in April 1865 proves.

During this summer visit, Wagner discussed with von Bülow the part the latter might play in the plans he was working out with the young King. These included, as well as new productions of his existing works at the Munich opera, the founding of a music school and (with the help of the architect Gottfried Semper, a friend from his Dresden years) the building of a special theatre in the city in which to present the *Ring*. To begin with, von Bülow was appointed pianist to King Ludwig. He set up house with his family in Munich. Wagner was also living in Munich by that time, and together they brought *Tristan und Isolde* to the stage, Wagner directing and von Bülow conducting.

The period in which Cosima, her husband and her lover were living in close proximity did not last long, for in December 1865, Wagner, having got himself at cross purposes with the government and people in Munich, was forced to leave the city, and he went off to Switzerland.

The death of his wife in January 1866 removed at least one obstacle between him and Cosima, but there still remained von Bülow's reluctance to countenance a divorce. So the subterfuges continued, and were sustained partly for material reasons, since it was important for the fortunes of all concerned not to lose the good will of the young King, on whom Wagner still depended, both for his main income and for the opportunity to complete and stage his works under von Bülow's musical direction.

Cosima helped Wagner choose and furnish a permanent home for himself in Switzerland – Tribschen, a large three-storied villa standing just outside Lucerne on a wooded tongue of land projecting into the Vierwald-stätter Lake – and she was able to pay him frequent visits there on the pretext of taking down from his dictation the autobiography the King had requested him to write, a project he had begun in Munich in July 1865.

Cosima was in Tribschen in February 1867, when she gave birth to Wagner's second daughter, Eva. At that time he had resumed work on *Die*

Meistersinger. Officially, of course, Eva, like Isolde, was the child of Hans von Bülow, but he was this time in no doubt as to who the true father was. In spite of this, he conducted the first performance of *Die Meistersinger* in Munich in June 1868, while Wagner sat in the royal box beside the King.

This was the culminating point of Wagner's personal relationship with Ludwig. Soon afterwards the growing gossip about his venerated composer's scandalous love affair with the wife of his musical director came to the King's ears, bringing disillusionment and a measure of personal estrangement. Cosima's attempts to keep up the fiction of her marriage were now pointless. After a visit with Wagner to Italy, during which their third child was conceived, she returned to Munich only to settle her affairs with her husband; then, along with her two younger daughters, she joined Wagner at Tribschen, never to be parted from him again.

It is at this point that the Diaries begin.

Editor's Note

Since this shortened edition of Cosima Wagner's Diaries is intended for the general reader, my prime aim has been to maintain readability and continuity. Cosima wrote an entry for virtually every single day of the fourteen-year period her Diaries cover, and in reducing the total of one million words to a quarter of that amount, I have found it necessary, not only to omit whole days, but also at times to cut passages within the text of a single day's entry. The recognized way of dealing with such editorial interferences is by the use of devices such as ... and square brackets, but the frequency with which these would occur in the present text could prove such an obstacle to readability that I feel it is kinder to dispense with them entirely. The reader in search of complete authenticity is therefore advised to consult the unabridged version of the Diaries, in which all the rules of scholarship are faithfully observed. I can, however, vouch for it that – apart from the very occasional substitution of 'R.' for 'he' in the interests of clear understanding – every word in this abridgement is Cosima's own (or, to be more exact, my translation of it). So, too, is the punctuation, including the use of ellipses, dashes and round brackets. Square brackets have been used by me to complete where necessary names indicated by Cosima only by an initial, and also clearly to identify literary and other works of which Cosima supplied only the titles.

The footnotes are entirely my own, based for the most part on the notes in the complete edition.

Geoffrey Skelton

1869

Friday, January 1 On Christmas Day, my 31st birthday, this notebook was to have started; I could not get it in Lucerne. And so the first day of the year will also contain the beginning of my reports to you, my children. You shall know every hour of my life, so that one day you will come to see me as I am; for, if I die young, others will be able to tell you very little about me, and if I live long, I shall probably only wish to remain silent. In this way you will help me do my duty – yes, children, my duty. What I mean by that you will find out later. Your mother intends to tell you everything about her present life, and she believes she can do so.

The year 1868 marks the outward turning-point of my life: in this year it was granted to me to put into action what for the past five years had filled my thoughts. It is an occupation I have not sought after or brought about myself: Fate laid it on me. In order that you may understand, I must confess to you that up to the hour in which I recognized my true inner calling, my life had been a dreary, unbeautiful dream, of which I have no desire to tell you anything, for I do not understand it myself and reject it with the whole of my now purified soul. The outward appearance was and remained calm, but inside all was bleak and dreary, when there came into my life that being who swiftly led me to realize that up to now I had never lived. My love became for me a rebirth, a deliverance, a fading away of all that was trivial and bad in me, and I swore to seal it through death, through pious renunciation or complete devotion. What love has done for me I shall never be able to repay. When the stars decreed that events, about which you will find out elsewhere, should banish into isolation my only friend, the guardian spirit and saviour of my soul, the revealer of all that is noble and true, that he should be left solitary, abandoned, joyless, and unfriended, I cried out to him: I shall come to you and seek my greatest and highest happiness in sharing the burdens of life with you. It was then that I left you, my two precious eldest children[1]. I did it and would do it again at any moment, and yet I miss you both and think of you day and night. For I love you all, each with an equal love; in your hearts I seek the refuge for my earthly memory when my time is past, and I would sacrifice everything to you – everything

---

[1] Daniela and Blandine, left in Munich with their father and nursemaid Hermine.

but the life of this one person. Our separation will be temporary, and you are still so small that you will not feel it as your mother does. This is my hope.

Early in the morning the Friend came to greet me and wish me a happy New Year. I am always so overcome by his kindness towards me, in my ever deeper awareness of his greatness, that in his presence I always feel I must dissolve into tears. Afterwards I dressed Loldchen and Evchen prettily (white satin frocks and garlands of roses) and we went to give him our good wishes. Then we had breakfast, after which he went to work as usual (making a fair copy of the second act of *Siegfried*[1] and completing his essay on the Jews[2]. Before lunch (at one o'clock) my beloved read me what he had written. At table he told me more of the range of his essay, and we discussed his position, that is to say, the position of art as laid down by the Jews, which made me see Mendelssohn for the first time as a tragic figure. After the meal he went for his usual walk, after receiving a telegram from the King and another from you. The latter affected him as it did me; my heart was heavy and full to bursting, because you were not here with me, but a glance at him consoled me and gave me courage – I was looking into a happy future. Then I arranged the Christmas tree, which was lit today for the second time. At about five o'clock Evchen and Loldchen, dressed again as angels, came down and found the Christmas gifts which had been kept back. Richard played for them, they danced, and I thought of you, my absent ones, so far away, and once again I watched the merry scene through a veil of tears, yet here, too, these tears were without bitterness. While the little ones were enjoying their supper, he played me the 'Spring Song' from *Die Walküre*[3]. When you one day hear these sounds, my children, you will understand me. I cannot hear them without being transported right away. – We had tea upstairs in my room; I asked my beloved to dictate something to me today (biography[4]) for superstitious reasons (they say that whatever one does on the first day of the year one continues). Although it was an exertion for him, he wanted in his indescribable goodness towards me to do it, and so there emerged two pages about Schopenhauer which for me are beyond all price. At eleven we parted, after once more reviewing the day together and finding it harmonious and good. When he had gone, I sat down at my writing desk to talk to you. The Friend has given me the golden pen with which he wrote *Tristan* and *Siegfried*, and this I consecrate to these communications of mine to you. Thus I signify to you how sacredly I regard this work of a mother's confidences and anxieties; the pen which has traced the sublimest things ever created by a noble spirit shall now be

---

[1] The full orchestral score.

[2] Second, expanded version of *Judaism in Music* (*Das Judentum in der Musik*).

[3] Siegmund's *Winterstürme* in Act I.

[4] Wagner's autobiography *My Life* (*Mein Leben*).

dedicated solely to the depths of a woman's heart. So God bless you, my children, you who are far away, you who are close by, and you lying still unknown within my womb. May your mother's love be a friendly light to you on your path through life! Do not mistake your mother, though you yourselves will never be able to do what she has done, since what Fate has here decreed is something that will not recur. All whom I love are now at rest, and so I, too, will go to my bed. For you and for him my last and friendliest thoughts!

Saturday, January 2 Cheered on opening my eyes by the sight of a rosy sky; the 'foehn' had conjured up its most brilliant colours for the morning display of light. Soon afterwards I was told that Evchen was ill, she had had a bad night. Concern, but no anxiety, for she was cheerful. Richard slightly indisposed but in good spirits. We visit the child, I stay upstairs while he goes to his work (essay on the Jews). Before lunch he reads me the continuation. Great delight in its terseness and pithiness. After the meal a feeling of intense happiness at having found each other. Later – in connection with the biography – I ask him whether I should read Schopenhauer. He advises me against it: a woman should approach philosophy through a man, a poet. I am in complete agreement.

Sunday, January 3 By one o'clock the Friend's essay finished; he reads me the ending (Schumann). The unexpectedly happy and mild mood of this ending. As usual at midday, the Friend takes a walk and I rest, reading Musäus's '*Rothmantel*' on my couch. In the evening to the children; Loldi has hit Evchen, but is good and repentant when I reproach her. – The evening crowned with four cantos from the *Odyssey*. Only distraction during the evening in watching R.'s fine, radiant countenance and delighting in the sound of his voice. – Only shadows over the day: receiving no letter from Munich, and the fact that the Friend entrusted some little service not to me, but to a servant. He does not yet realize how willingly I would do anything for him, the smallest things as well as the largest.

Monday, January 4 Evchen ill again (servants' carelessness!) My great concern about this coupled with some indecision, for it is not easy to make changes in the household. Patience and increased care on my part are called for. A letter from Hermine: the children there are well, they had a merry Christmas; melancholy pleasure in that. – After tea Richard plays for me the Prelude to *Tristan und Isolde*. Deeply moved by it, indeed hardly in control of myself.

Tuesday, January 5 From the moment of rising I was filled with great melancholy; harsh is the dream of life, my children, and in it I seem to myself a stranger. I fight against my depression. A walk in the bright sunshine was a great help to me; from the top of the hill I was enraptured by the ring of snow-capped mountains, which suggested to me a mysterious, unmoving dance. Absorbed long in watching the picture, my spirit heard the music which higher beings reproduce for us in sounds. – The transience of all individual existence, the eternity of the whole, was reflected to me in the blue mirror of the lake. My deep inner strength restored, I summoned the Friend from his work and together we wandered up the hill; the magnificent Mount Pilatus looked like a spectral shadow. – Put the children to bed; Evchen lively, if not yet entirely recovered. Three cantos from the *Odyssey* to finish the evening. The splendid happenings seem like a dream picture to me – so vital and distinct – when the Friend reads them out to me; when I read them for myself, it is as if they were real; but *thus* everything is experienced at a remove. His voice and his manner encompass the immortal work like music. – Sleep well, my children, how your mother longs to see you all united!

Wednesday, January 6 Apprehensive afternoon caused by a visit of the Bassenheims' servants to our servants[1]. Since the former are in contact with Munich, and I can expect nothing but evil from there, I have the feeling that malicious curiosity has driven them here in the worst of weathers to find out whether I and the children are here. My imaginings upset Richard, since there is nothing he can do to help, but he is soon back in good spirits, and I console myself with the thought that in concealing my whereabouts I intended no harm to the world and acted only out of consideration for others.

Thursday, January 7 Richard brought up to me two issues of the *Süddeutsche Presse*, which some impudent person has sent him anonymously; they contained a lengthy article by Fröbel about *Opera and Drama*[2]. I cannot describe the feelings of revulsion that filled me as I read it. May God preserve you, my children, from ever being obliged to see the things you love, honour, and believe in being dragged through the mud. Here there is no question of a contest, in which one courageously faces up to the opponent, not even of a martyrdom joyfully endured in order to bear witness to one's beliefs. This is nothing but a besmirching, which cannot be fought against, and the endurance of which does no good for one's cause. – Richard saw my deep dejection and read the article for himself. At first he took it calmly, for it gave him additional material for his *Judaism in Music* essay. At lunch, however, we sought in vain to dispel the grief which had taken hold of us, all our experiences rose up before us like the ghosts in Shakespeare's plays, and we wondered glumly why every word brought forth only dirt or met with apathetic non-recognition. The whole day remained under a cloud. From town someone brought my Friend the

---

[1] Count Hugo von Waldbott-Bassenheim, a Bavarian court official, and his wife Caroline, who lived in Lucerne.

[2] Dr Julius Fröbel, a friend from Dresden, came to Munich to edit the newspaper *Süddeutsche Presse* at Wagner's invitation, but they subsequently fell out. Wagner's book *Opera and Drama*, first published in 1851, was reissued in 1868.

expected letter from Boni [Blandine]. Also two friendly greetings from afar (M. Muchanoff and Elisabeth Krockow[1]), but I really do not know what to do with these friendships. No one will follow me when he knows whither I have come, and it is only by you that I still want to be loved and understood.

Friday, January 8 Dear Loulou [Daniela] and dear Boni, today is your father's birthday; I wish that he may spend it in a mood of peaceful reconciliation, though there is nothing I can contribute towards it. It was a great misunderstanding that bound us together in marriage; my feelings towards him are today still the same as 12 years ago: great sympathy with his destiny, pleasure in his qualities of mind and heart, genuine respect for his character, however completely different our temperaments. In the very first year of our marriage I was already in such despair over this confusion that I wished for death; many errors arose out of my distress, but I was always able to get a grip on myself again, and your father knew nothing of my sufferings – I do not think he will withhold his testimony that I always stood by him, in suffering as in joy, and that I helped him to the best of my powers. Never would he have lost me if Fate had not brought me together with the man for whom I had to recognize it as my task in life to live or die. I have not a single reproach to make to your father, even if our last years together were hard for me beyond all imagining. I wanted to try combining my former existence with my new life, I believed in the possibility of fusing together all the diverging feelings – abuse and insults proved to me that I was being a fool, and all that remained was for me to make the choice that was no choice. Thus I am now deprived of you, my children, and it worries me greatly, but there is a God who helps.

Today I felt in my womb the first stirrings of the unknown being within me.

Saturday, January 9 A bad night; violent headaches combined with night-mares, worry about the children, dismal thoughts about my mother and father, painful memories of the past, and apprehensions about the children's future. My state of mind reaches the stage of blazing fear. 'Oh, if only I had a sister!' I cry out in the silent darkness. Oh, my children, keep the ring of hearts intact! – I rose, having slept little. The maid has gone for two days to visit her parents, and so I am now spending all my time in the children's room. The children are good and well behaved, I can write and read in their presence; and Eva is now well again.

Sunday, January 10 Slight disappointment that the pen I had sent from New York for R. does not write well. Arrival of the next instalment of Fröbel's

---

[1] Marie Muchanoff (b.1823), Russian-born friend (under her married name of Kalergis) of Wagner and one of the first to recognize his worth, having seen *Tannhäuser* on Liszt's recommendation in Dresden in 1845; she subsequently helped him financially; Muchanoff was the name of her second husband. Elisabeth Krockow (b.1820) was Cosima's friend in Berlin, married to Count Karl von Krockow.

article on *Opera and Drama*. Though R. burned it without reading it, the mere thought of the unworthiness of people is upsetting. The King's silence is also curious and unkind. R.'s great depression in connection with his work, he really feels like abandoning the musical completion of his *Nibelungen* entirely.

Monday, January 11 Eva unwell again; irritation over the way the whole house meddles; I am unjust enough to show R. my irritation. Prolonged sleeplessness is my only excuse for this injustice. He has sent off the essay on the Jews, which makes me apprehensive, yet I did not try to prevent it. Richard at work (*Die Meistersinger* is at last to be staged in Karlsruhe and Dresden). At lunch he said the curse of his life had been poverty and marriage. After the meal I again feel very unwell and go to lie down. Richard is finishing a page of his score; I am glad to see him restored in mood and appearance. It is only when he is out that I am beset by worry and anxiety that we shall not be left in peace; I see us abandoned to misery and malicious scorn. But once he is with me again, my evil thoughts vanish.

Tuesday, January 12 Richard is well – last night we had a moment of strain, because he did not want to dictate to me out of concern for my condition, and I urgently begged him to. But I gave in when I saw his great reluctance and his anxiety, and yesterday evening ended with the first canto of the *Iliad*. After such a moment of discord, however trivial, it is true happiness to exchange kind looks again. At lunch Richard tells me that he has been thinking a lot about his *Nibelungen*, and, he adds jokingly, it has made him feel very puffed up. It makes me happy to see him thinking of his divine work without repugnance. In the evening, dictation; R. started off with great reluctance, but soon began to remember. We parted at about eleven, after having completed four pages.

Thursday, January 14 Restless night, but good morning hours. Richard wakes me with the *Lohengrin* 'Battle Song'[1]. But then he tells me a bullfinch has dashed itself to death on the sides of the bird cage in fright. He bought the little creatures only a few weeks ago; one of them fretted itself to death and would not eat, wasted right away. How sad it is! Kos[2] is also always ill, and does not improve in spite of all our attention.

Friday, January 15 Few worries – perhaps all too few – about Hans; his artistic activities are a source of pleasure to him, my sorrowful detachment from it after the failure of our great undertaking interrupted the flow of this source. How different is R., how utterly he has only me to understand him and to share his isolation from the world! I cannot believe that I shall have to pay for my dedication to him through the alienation of my elder children. Richard is not looking well: is it his inner anxiety or the overcast weather which weighs so heavily on him? The world around us remains

---

[1] Presumably the king's address and chorus in Act III, scene 3.
[2] A pinscher dog, a present to Cosima from Hans von Bülow in 1866.

silent. He asks me whether I am worrying about the children, and he believes that my father has been a bad influence in that matter. Unfortunately I believe so, too. R. is working on his score. Loldi very good, Eva so violent that she hits me. Solitary walk after lunch; the play of sun and mist gives the farther banks of the lake the appearance of a dream vision, the trees, covered with frost, greet me like gentle, friendly ghosts; Mount Pilatus, its peak surrounded by golden clouds, seems like the noble monarch of this dream world. – R. told me during the evening that he loved me above all else in the world, and these words made me immeasurably happy – even if I know it already within my heart without his having to tell me.

Saturday, January 16 Two months ago today I said goodbye to you, children – my heart is heavy when I think of it, and I am without any news of you! In order to get a little sleep I had a warm drink late last night; I went to sleep at once, but soon woke up again and thought of you. R. wished me good morning with the *Meistersinger* theme. The newspapers report that the King is giving many audiences; with a smile we observe that he is at last doing what we long in vain asked him to do! – I am apprehensive about Munich, all this silence; even the painter Lenbach[1], who was always good and loyal to me and promised to write, is silent.

Monday, January 18 Many newspapers came today, much news of musical activities. It all seems a grand muddle. Towards noon R. came up to see me, looking very gloomy; he feels set against completing his work. He began it, he says, at a time when life was to him a fantastic image, and now, when it has been given a basis through me and the children, he feels he could make better use of his powers than writing scores which will never be produced and will mean nothing to anybody. When I replied that times would change, he answered: 'At best they will be terrible, at best they will become puritanical, and my work has no place there. But it would still be a thousand times better than the present situation.' I find this a terrible statement; I feel that there can be no blessing on our bond if the *Nibelungen* remains unfinished. Five times I walked through the entire grounds of Tribschen, dusk fell, sky, mountains, lake stood grey and stiff before me like an impenetrable, threefold wall, and then there rose a sun in my soul, I felt inside me, deep and true, that you would remain by me, my children, whatever the world might do with me. Hardly had this light flared up in me in the enveloping darkness when I heard my name being called; R. had returned home, joyfully bringing me a letter from you. You are well and good and cheerful; your mother in her longing, melancholy happiness blesses you. In his unutterable kindness towards me R. was visibly full of cheer after handing me the letter. – In the evening dictation, four large pages.

[1] The portrait painter Franz von Lenbach (b. 1836) lived in Munich, where he had painted Cosima's portrait.

Tuesday, January 19 I intended last night to go to bed, but did not do so; as I closed the book I was overcome by such sad longing, the children's future seemed to me so dismal, I was so deeply aware that with the growing constriction of my soul I could be of no more help to Richard, that I resolved to go to him in this same midnight hour and tell him that I would go away, that henceforth I would and could live only for you, my children. But I did not do it; to sacrifice my own life and happiness, how happily I should do that; but then I visualized his life, his fate, and collapsed in a faint. When I came to myself I got into bed, and in the morning I could tell R. that I had slept well and – had dreamed of Bismarck[1]. He smiled and told me that he had been thinking – since yesterday – of writing to Countess Bismarck and sending her a copy of *German Art and German Politics*[2]. Perhaps she can influence her husband to take an interest in German art. – I advise him against it, because I anticipate only misunderstanding from such a step. Feeling unwell, I sat down at my writing desk and wrote with great effort to Lenbach concerning my portrait. Yesterday I had a letter from him, asking me to decide what to do about it. In the evening a severe headache, R. reads me [Shakespeare's] *Henry VI*.

Wednesday, January 20 R. once again mentions the letter to Countess Bismarck, I again try to dissuade him, and he gives in. But I do not know if I have done right. He is unutterably good to me. Yesterday evening we had to laugh heartily; he demanded something, I was at first against it, then I came round to it and explained to him how it was that I now wanted to follow his bidding, whereas I had not before; during this explanation he heard me use the words, 'But, *my dear Wagner.*' He mentioned it at first jokingly, and I did not properly understand him, so let it go, but he became increasingly vehement and said it had never happened before that I called him 'my dear Wagner.' At last I understood him, and when I explained that it would never have occurred to me to call him that and he must have heard me wrong, we laughed heartily and long. – After lunch a letter arrives from Esser[3], the musical director in Vienna, saying that the management there intends to stage *Die Meistersinger* in October of next year, that is to say, in two years' time!! Yet Dingelstedt[4] had been in a great hurry with his contract, in which R. was to undertake not to let any fragments from his work be played in Vienna and also to give no other theatre besides the Court theatre the right to produce the opera. So the intention was to suppress *Die Msinger* entirely. Luckily R. was suspicious and did not accept the clause. -- We are quite appalled at this new example of unworthiness.

[1] At that time Chancellor of the North German Confederacy.
[2] Wagner's series of articles in the *Süddeutsche Presse*: King Ludwig's embargo on the final instalment had led to Wagner's departure from Munich and quarrel with Fröbel.
[3] Heinrich Esser, conductor at the Vienna Court Opera 1857–69.
[4] Franz von Dingelstedt, director successively of the Court Operas in Munich, Weimar and Vienna.

Here probably everything is working hand in hand – bureaucracy, Judaism, theatre management (Dingelstedt) and perhaps even the Court.

Thursday, January 21 R. returns from his walk with the news that the article on the Jews is going to be printed. So be it! Then he goes to the children, telling me that he did not ask me to go with him since he had the feeling that this always cost me an effort. And so it is: where I was once used to finding four, I find it painful to see only two. However, the two here are flourishing. Kos on the other hand is ill, very ill; how sorry one feels for such a poor creature!

Saturday, January 23 After lunch a communication from Hans; the *Signale*[1] has printed a biography of him in which it is stated that when Hans was a young man Wagner had befriended him and cared for him like a father, while his own family left him penniless. This seems to have hurt Hans. How petty! I ask R. to write a correction at once in a proper tone of calm, which he then does, sending the draft to Hans. – After tea, conclusion of *Henry VI Part II* and beginning of *Part III*. – Today R. gave me great joy when he told me that he was now so unwilling to write letters because he had resolved to complete his *Siegfried*.

Sunday, January 24 A good night and in consequence a harmonious morning; at the same time thinking out a plan by which I might soon bring the other children to my side, and how I will arrange things generally in the uncertainties and difficulties of the situation. This gives me comfort. Unfortunately R.'s passion for silk materials brought forth a remark from me which I should have done better to leave unsaid, for it produced a bit of ill feeling. Yesterday a carpenter, a plumber, a veterinary surgeon in the house – a singular stirring in my enchanted life; I had to laugh over my own impression and was unable at all to imagine that I would ever again want to visit a theatre or even watch a large number of people moving about. I miss nothing in my seclusion – except the children. – After lunch, in the children's presence, R. plays parts of the second act of *Tristan*. Whether I am becoming increasingly vulnerable or morbidly sensitive I do not know, but there are certain powerful impressions which I can hardly bear any longer. I literally shudder at the power of genius which suddenly lays bare before us the unfathomable secrets of existence, even when there is nothing I cherish and esteem more than this divinely daemonic power.

Tuesday, January 26 Glorious sunshine, the whole countryside dripping with light. Loldi four hours out in the garden today. R. is working on his score and says he could not get through a morning without doing something on it. Cheerful spirits at lunchtime, the sunshine brings smiles to the whole house. Unfortunately, however, as R. is about to go out, a letter comes from Hans which is difficult to understand. He demands from R. the withdrawal

---

[1] *Signale für die musikalische Welt*, a musical periodical published in Leipzig.

of his correction for the *Signale* and reports the visit 'of his wife to Versailles.' R.'s whole appearance alters; he is in an utter frenzy. I understand at once that with the last sentence Hans intends just to let me know what he has told his family[1]. In the afternoon with the children. Returning home very unwell, R. goes to lie down. At seven o'clock, when the children are sleeping, I go outside. The loveliest view of the countryside I have ever seen. Everything blue and silvery, the moon and the stars shining, the mountains glowing, the water glittering, all of it bright, yet veiled. Mood of elevation inside and around me; the unborn child moves in my womb, and I bless it. May it eternally think lovingly of the mother who bore it in love!

Thursday, January 28 Since R. reproaches me for not having been out of doors, I go out when it is already dark; the countryside is wrapped in grey dusk, I feel that the Greek underworld must have looked like this, and I could literally see the forms of its heroes as they wander across the calm grey water and vanish into the mists of the mountains and the clouds. Gradually the sky cleared, a pale star twinkled silently, the first I had seen this evening; 'Greetings, gentle star, guide my fate kindly, shine benevolently on my children.' As I spoke these words the star suddenly disappeared – was it because a tear dimmed my eye or because the emerging moon obscured its little light? – 'Very well, you are as unyielding as all the rest, like them you teach me submissiveness.' Then it came back into sight. 'Are you now appeased? Give me a friendly sign that you will be merciful to my children' – and suddenly I saw Richard standing in front of me: he had been looking for me everywhere, calling out Siegfried's melody to me in all directions! Joyfully I acknowledged the sign; the whole countryside was gleaming, the clouds vanquished by the moon, the underworld atmosphere dispelled. – R. said if only I knew all the things he called out to me when I was not there. Alas, I know that he loves me. – In the evening he dictates to me again, and we part affectionately.

Sunday, January 31 The whole day passes gloomily. R. is weak and very limp, he cannot eat a thing. I in consequence feel deprived of my soul. At midday he says he cannot visualize what would have become of his life if I had not entered it. And if one were to say to him: But if your artistic plans had been carried through, if the King had proved steadfast, then you would not have been so utterly dependent on me? Nonsense! says R., he lives only through me, that had been his feeling from the very first hour. – I suddenly begin to feel unwell and cause him anxiety. He fears that I am undermining my health through my seclusion here. Oh, indeed, my woe is

---

[1] Viz., that Cosima had gone to visit her stepsister Claire Charnacé (b. 1830 to Marie d'Agoult and her husband, Count Charles d'Agoult); Claire was married to Count Guy de Charnacé, and they lived in Versailles.

great, but when I think of the possibility of *Siegfried* I am cured as if by magic!

Tuesday, February 2 After tea, dictation; it appears to me that the year 1858 was the true turning-point in R.'s destiny, and if Frau W[esendonck]¹ had conducted herself well then, all the perplexities up to the appearance of the King could have been spared him. Then my participation in his life would also have been superfluous – even if we should always have loved each other deeply. This feeling makes me despondent. Above all, however, R.'s appearance, which is not good. Bismarck's boastful behaviour in the Chamber ('the reptiles and the miserable dynastic interests') gave R. a lot of joy. He returns to his letter to the Countess. Why do I stop him? It is surely very timid of me.

Friday, February 5 From town R. brought me two lovely camellias – may they flourish; for I shall tend them carefully. And may *Siegfried* also flourish! We are willing, are we not, my children, to bear a little suffering together on that account? My dear, good children! – In the evening we had an interrupted dictation; I did not understand some of it and was foolish enough to say so, which caused a prolonged delay, though no real discord.

Sunday, February 7 Since the weather was fine, R. invited me to go for a walk with him; I did so. For the first time in two and a half months I walked outside the boundaries of Tribschen, with some concern lest I be seen. But I noticed nobody. – In the morning Levi, the conductor², sent a letter reporting the success of *Die Msinger* in Karlsruhe.

Tuesday, February 9 In the course of the morning we discuss our situation, which cannot go on much longer as it now is. I tell R. I should like to write Hans that I could come to the children in Munich for two months and return from there to Tribschen at the beginning of May with all four of them, going on from there to Paris. What I am trying to do is avoid making a commotion, for the sake of the children and the King (that is to say, Richard). Richard, however, can see only one thing – the two-month separation – and will not hear of it. Deep worry in my soul; I really do believe that this way out, in this temporary stage, would be the best. – In the evening I put to R. the question whether our love never appears to him to be wrong; he does not quite understand me and thinks I mean by this what the world considers wrong, the betrayal of a friend; then he says that he knows only one thing – that since the world came into existence no man of his age had loved a woman as much as he loved me. The wrong I meant was not, however, concerned with what other people condemn, but with what it would perhaps be right for us to do according to our own

¹ Mathilde Wesendonck (b. 1828) and her husband Otto (b. 1815) had built a small house (Das Asyl) in the grounds of their villa in Zurich for Wagner. Wagner's love for Mathilde aroused his wife Minna's jealousy, and in 1858 he left the Asyl.
² Hermann Levi (b.1839), conductor in Karlsruhe; moved to Munich in 1872.

conceptions of life and virtue of the highest kind. I would like to receive
my directions from him.

Wednesday, February 10 In a dream I gave birth to a son. As I awoke and
rose from my bed I found my camellia had blossomed; since I had
involuntarily connected it in my mind with *Siegfried*, I am overjoyed. May
the souls of my children blossom as handsomely and as tranquilly! After
lunch played passages from *Siegfried*. He leaves me, saying that, now that I
am with him, he knows what he has lived for, only I should not weep so
much. – I go with Loldi into the garden and reflect on what I have to do.
– I am not arrogant and am always astonished that he needs me, but I
believe with all my heart what he once again said to me today at lunch: that
if I went away, his life and living, his thinking and his thoughts would be
at an end, and for that reason I myself no longer hold to the idea of a
two-month separation. Yet I do not know how to set about getting the
children to me here; no plan seems right.

Friday, February 12 Settled springlike weather, a primrose has already
appeared. In the garden with the children, then a letter from Claire, advising
me to be as considerate to everyone as possible! – In the evening I am
unwell and have soon to take to my bed with a temperature.

Saturday, February 13 After lunch R. tells me he received a letter from the
King in the morning, but had not read it at once or wanted even to mention
it, since he wished to keep his morning free for work. Now he read it out
loud – the same old style of enthusiasm and love. A letter from the King's
secretary Düfflipp[1] was with it, and I started to read this aloud, suspecting
nothing unpleasant. – R. had asked for an advance to be deducted regularly
from his allowance, to settle some outstanding debts. Now he is told by
Councillor D[üfflipp] that Semper's claim (which has now been settled)[2]
and Fr[öbel]'s article on *Opera and Drama* had aroused the King's displeasure, and he would not listen to R.'s request. I told R. that Fr's article might
perhaps have been commissioned expressly to arouse the King's displeasure, so that he would not grant R. a favour, and the people there would
have the amusement of observing his embarrassment. This upsets R. so
much that he becomes quite angry with me. I should indeed have realized
that this subject is an unpleasant one for R., and should not have discussed
it. R. walked off abruptly, and I went in silence – as I had remained
throughout – to my room. The children help to distract me from my sad
thoughts. When they are in bed, R. comes up complaining of great
tiredness. He mentions today's incident and says I should regard all he said
as having been spoken in a fever. I can only press his hand in silence; how
could I ever take upon myself the right to forgive him?

[1] Lorenz von Düfflipp, secretary to King Ludwig II 1866–77.
[2] The architect Gottfried Semper prepared plans for a theatre in Munich for Wagner's works; when the
plan fell through in 1868, Semper put in a claim to the royal treasury for the work he had done.

Sunday, February 14 Yesterday it was windy and dull, today everything glistens, the birds are flitting about, trees budding, mountains, sky and lake are transformed. I find one of my main joys in tending my camellias, a real relationship is developing between these two living things and me, and I would not wish to have many flowers around me. These buds have received quite a few tears today. That is of course foolish, for what is causing me suffering is only the consequence of my situation – whoever steps beyond the boundaries must be prepared to be punished for it, however good his intentions, however difficult to achieve.

Monday, February 15 Kos is being taken to Zurich; he is ill. I have a letter from the children, things are not going well there, Hans's mother is making trouble.

Wednesday, February 17 On waking I hear the strains of the 'Prize Song'[1], the melody which brought Eva into the world and with which R. greeted my birthday (1866). Then R. brings our beautiful child to my bedside, she shines and sparkles, our little Eva! – R. receives from his publishers[2] the proofs of the Jewish article, which gladdens him, for he feared Weber had been intimidated. Presents for the children, meals with the children, much rejoicing. When we drink to Eva's health she is out of her mind with delight, in spite of having nothing to drink herself. Then I say she must go to bed; R. much dismayed, says this strictness is the Catholic side of my nature and that when my pleasure is greatest, I am always ready to renounce it. He is always asking himself how he would fare if I also took charge of him! This made us laugh. In the afternoon a walk with the children, at dusk fireworks in the *salon*. But Evchen is made ill by them; she has a dizzy spell, and I am very much alarmed, but she recovers. In the evening R. reads [Shakespeare's] *Coriolanus* to me in his unique way.

Saturday, February 20 I slept all morning. At lunch R. showed me a letter from Mme Judith Mendès[3], who this summer wrote a very remarkable series of articles about him in the French *Presse*. The letter, too, is very nice and full of buoyant enthusiasm. That pleases us. Afternoon with the children – played the piano. Received a letter from Claire – she advises me to go to Munich.

Monday, February 22 In the afternoon, while R. was sleeping, I thought of the last letter from my father, in which he said to me, 'Passion dies, but the pangs of conscience remain.' What a superficial judgment! As if my coming to R. had been an act of passion, and as if I could ever feel pangs of conscience on that account! How little my father knows me, after all! – How willingly I would give up any sort of joy if I knew but one being to

---

[1] In Act III of *Die Meistersinger*.

[2] J. J. Weber, Leipzig.

[3] Judith Gautier (b.1846), daughter of the French poet Théophile Gautier and wife of the French poet Catulle Mendès (b.1841).

whom I could entrust R.'s isolated life! He is working hard and happily. – My only sorrow is that he does not tell me about some things he writes and receives, for fear of upsetting me. On the contrary: I feel that all things become a game when they are shared.

Tuesday, February 23 Around noon R. brings me the manuscript of the two acts of *Siegfried*. Indescribable joy! As I thank him, he says, 'Everything belongs to you, even before I do it.' – After tea *Twelfth Night*. Very gay mood.

Wednesday, February 24 R. writes to the King (16 pages) and I ink in two pages of the score; I see the notes as sacred runes which take on colour beneath my hand. After lunch R. improvises.

Saturday, February 27 In the afternoon a letter from Hans about the performance of *Tannhäuser* in Munich, enclosing a letter from the King, who had not in fact attended the performance, but all the same writes full of enthusiasm. R. has given me Gibbon[1] (in English) as a present.

Monday, March 1 Snow flurries, 'winter tempests', yesterday Mount Pilatus dispatched a little avalanche, and today the whole country is covered with snow, the skies grey, the water a dirty green. R., however, is busy on his work, may Heaven bless him! Richard says jokingly at lunch that, if he ever completes the *Nibelungen*, I shall deserve an order *pour le mérite*. After lunch the children misbehave; it is difficult to combine bringing up children with an artistic life, but I am determined to succeed.

Tuesday, March 2 At breakfast R. tells me that when anything came between us, it was because we loved each other too much and were too dependent on each other. His good fortune, he calls me! He goes off to work on the song with which Wotan wakes the Wala[2], I to the children. A violent foehn wind is raging outside. After lunch we play duets together on the piano, R. and I get much fun from it. R. says in his exhilaration, 'What a lucky old donkey I am!,' which makes us laugh a lot. In the evening with the children I read Shakespeare's *The Tempest*. A great and sublimely moral impression from it. – Later R. reads me the 3rd and 4th acts of *Antony and Cleopatra*. Well, who would dare to say a single word about that! I am utterly shattered. R. finds something of his *Tristan* reflected in it – inasmuch as it shows a being utterly consumed by love: in *Tristan* time renders it naïve and pure, whereas here it appears in a ghastly, voluptuous setting, yet no less destructively.

Wednesday, March 3 From his walk R. brings home the splendid edition of *Don Quixote* which Mme Viardot[3] has given him. Great joy, for his passion for books grows daily, which leads him to say jokingly that he is well aware

---

[1] Edward Gibbon's *Decline and Fall of the Roman Empire*.
[2] The Wotan-Erda scene which opens Act III of *Siegfried*.
[3] The singer Pauline Viardot-Garcia, whom Wagner met in his early years in Paris.

that I do not approve of it any more than of any other form of passion. In the evening, dictation resumed.

Friday, March 5 Rich. at his work; I with the children; at lunch he talks a lot about Wotan and the Wala. – I tell him I believe that, if his friends knew how he was living and what satisfied him, instead of being pleased they would be angry and would despise me. He thinks that is not so, and that – as long as we demanded no active participation from them – we would find them sympathetic. I find that hard to believe, I do not even expect that in later years, when we are all peacefully at rest, my devotion and love will be remembered with good will – but my children at least shall know me. Snow is falling gently and copiously; it gives solitude a shining aspect; how quiet it is here! When have two beings ever before lived for and in each other, so cut off from the world? – From the post office R. brings back the first copies of his pamphlet on the Jews and a letter from Hermine. The children are fairly well, though Lusch [Daniela] has a cough. Later, dictation, and then discussed with R. my plan to request that the children visit me for a month.

Saturday, March 6 Great delight in the children, who are lively and healthy; yesterday they were sitting opposite each other on the floor of R.'s bedroom and playing. Loldi was putting on R.'s shoe, and Eva brushing her hair with his big brush. R. says he cannot ever forget the sight.

Tuesday, March 9 Since R. is still very much set against dictating, he reads me Shakespeare's *Love's Labour's Lost*. R. is very concerned for me, and I have to tell him how much worse other women in my condition frequently fare, in order to calm him down.

Wednesday, March 10 R. has received a letter from Hans, thanking him for the pamphlet on the Jews (sent to him directly by Weber) and announcing his journey to Vienna, where he is playing at Baron Sina's for 500 florins. The King has commanded *Tristan und Isolde* for May and *Rheingold* for August. Hans is delighted with the pamphlet.

Thursday, March 11 R. works. Then he tells me that Berlioz has died[1]; it brings back to my mind pictures of my childhood.

Friday, March 12 My life as a recluse is now almost ended, since recently, as we drove out, we met Colonel Am Rhyn[2], and when R. saw him again yesterday he had to tell him that I was here, I was expecting the children for Easter and had come early because I should not have been able to travel easily later. However, this will not make much difference to my seclusion, for I am shy of seeing other people. – R. is going through what he composed in the morning and is not satisfied with it, he thinks he has gone too far in the proliferation of his motives. At tea he said that, if he wanted to make things easy for himself, he would, from the moment Wotan says,

---

[1] The French composer Hector Berlioz died on March 8.
[2] The owner of Tribschen.

'*Seit mein Wunsch es will,*' introduce recitative, which would certainly create a great effect, but would put an end to the work as art. Nobody has yet noticed with how much art he has employed all means to prevent the interruption of the flow of melody, while still achieving a romantic effect. – Music, he says, transfigures everything, it never permits the hideousness of the bare word, however terrible the subject.

Friday, March 19 Kos is now really back, but very much changed. R. works, I sit with the children, embroidering. – At this hour of the evening six years ago I was feeling very unwell; unwell and at the same time wretched. How wearily and gloomily I brought my baby into the world, without any assistance; how indifferently did the father greet it! Only Richard, far away, was concerned about me, and I did not know it. How dreary, how empty, how inwardly disturbed was my life at that time! How could I ever thank R. enough for what his love has done for me? At that time I was feeling so wretched that I told nobody that my labour pains had come, and that the baby was already there when they summoned the midwife. My mother-in-law was living in the house, Hans was at home, there were servants in plenty, and I was walking up and down in the *salon* all by myself, wriggling like a worm and whimpering; a cry I could not suppress woke the household and they carried me to my bed, where Boni then crept out. In every home a coming child is a time of joy, but I hardly dared tell Hans that I was pregnant, so unfriendly was his reaction, as if his comfort were being disturbed. I have never told anyone about this before; now I am writing it down – not to complain about Hans (he had many worries on his mind, and he did not know what pleases and what hurts a woman, for I had always kept silent), but because I cannot think without shuddering of that night in Berlin, which serves to make utterly clear to me the subsequent course of my destiny.

Monday, March 22 Hans has written and sends an article from a Catholic paper, in favour of the Jewish pamphlet. I divide the gloomy day between the children, embroidery, and inking in the score. During the night I found myself thinking melancholy thoughts about love: when the sexual emotions play no part, it is surely of a higher nature. Yet I cannot think that a love can be deeper, truer, purer than mine for Richard.

Wednesday, March 24 At midday R. plays me some things (Wotan with Siegfried, powerfully gripping and moving!). At lunch Loldi gives me a shock by becoming suddenly unwell – fearing diphtheria, R. sends for the doctor, but it emerges with considerable certainty that she had drunk something out of the little brandy flask, and that had made her so ill. The doctor tells us in passing that he has read the Jewish pamphlet and he is glad to know the reason for the unceasing acts of enmity. A lady from Zurich had brought the pamphlet with her to read in the train. This amuses us.

Thursday, March 25 After lunch R. suggests that I walk into town with him, and is pleasantly surprised when I agree. So to town with the two children, in gay mood. Stopped for a rest in a hotel, drank coffee and ate cakes, also glanced through newspapers. Then at the post office found a letter from Hermine. It is still undecided whether the children will come – Hans's usual irresolution! Claire writes to me, too, and reports that my mother is again very unwell, a condition calling for profound pity.

Sunday, March 28 R., coming to my room in the morning, says, 'You have now been with me a whole winter, I can hardly believe it; you know nothing of me, have no idea how my heart rejoices when I think of it.' – Yes, our love is a thing of truth in this world of lies and deception. – R. has a letter from Hans reporting on the impact of *Judaism* – the wealthy Jews in Munich are no longer so eager to see Wagner's operas; the theatre management in Breslau has asked Nachbaur[1] to choose a role other than Lohengrin for his guest appearance, since this work cannot very well be played in Breslau just now on account of the pamphlet. – R. writes to his friend Fräulein Meysenbug[2] and mentions me kindly and lovingly. How that touches me! I can hardly say good night to him without tears starting in my eyes – he says we are as happy as lambs; if only there were not those wolves outside!

Monday, March 29 I am shocked at times by my appearance and ask myself if it is so bad on account of my condition, or because I am nearing my end, or just that I am getting older – I believe it is a sign of age. – At midday there arose between R. and myself the question of a change of faith; he said, 'Your father would certainly not object to our relationship if, to make it possible, I were to become a Catholic.' At that I asked him whether in order to marry me he would have become a Catholic, if that had been necessary. He replied that this was a 'devilish' question, he could not even conceive of it. At first I was disconcerted; my immediate feeling was that *I* am giving everything up, religion and all else besides, in order to ally myself with him, but then I understood. A woman may and should sacrifice all for her beloved; a man, on the other hand, can and should have a point from which he neither shifts nor wavers. The whole chapter did, however, bring me into a mood of seriousness; it is difficult to achieve all at once an insight which raises one above the painful realization of the difference between a man's and a woman's love; and since with me everything moves slowly, I spent just about the whole afternoon working on the matter.

Tuesday, March 30 Was with R. at the antiquarian's, then at the post office found a letter from Hermine. In a week I shall see the children again! – In the evening R. unwell, so I contain my joy inside myself. – I had a terrible shock during our walk: suddenly we see Kos in the middle of the railway

[1] Franz Nachbaur, the first Walther in *Die Meistersinger.*

[2] Malwida von Meysenbug (b. 1816), a German political writer, features prominently in the Diaries in later years; Wagner met her in London in 1855.

track fighting with another dog, the train almost on top of him! R. seemed to shoot off like an arrow, and through his running and shouting he rescues Kos, himself escaping only by a miracle – but the sight!

Thursday, April 1 This morning he had a letter from the Berlin Opera, which he did not immediately want to open, expecting something unpleasant as a consequence of his short note in the Jewish pamphlet. But, instead of that, Hülsen[1] informs him very prettily of a production of *Die Msinger* in Berlin and Hanover. – In the evening R. speaks to me about the *Odyssey* and the *Iliad*, smoking and drinking beer. Since the joiners had been varnishing in the next room, all these various smells combine, and I gradually begin to feel dizzy and my head starts to ache; it robs me entirely of my vision and finally of my hearing, too. When I told R. of my condition he became very angry, seeing a reproach in what was only an explanation. He then said many things it would have been better for him not to have said. I up to my room where, feeling upset, I wept. Now I am wondering what would be the best thing to do – whether I should leave his temper to cool down or go to him, quietly explain again what had happened, and soothe him. Hardly had I written this when R. came in to wish me good night. I then went downstairs to him and calmed his fantasies.

Friday, April 2 Richter[2] arrives from Munich with news, much of which is amusing, but there are some unpleasant things, too. Lachner's[3] intrigues are still going on; and Hans has asked to be excused from conducting for several weeks.

Sunday, April 4 R. unwell. The projected production of *Das Rheingold* in Munich[4] distresses him deeply, the means are not at hand, and now things will be forced, his great work cut to pieces – it is a great shame, and I am in deadly fear that dealing with it, even if only from here, will completely rob him of his will to continue his work. – He looks bad and his whole nature is changed.

Monday, April 5 Feelings of great nausea and worries about the redecorations. I spent the day on the sofa, listening to R. going through *Das Rheingold* with Richter, and embroidering. R. himself is very unwell – the trouble has so upset us both. At one o'clock our good Richter made his departure.

Wednesday, April 7 Two telegrams arrive from Paris announcing the great success of *Rienzi* (yesterday was the first performance). A letter from Claire, full of praise for Hans's chivalry in sending the children to me. – How

---

[1] Botho von Hülsen, director of the Berlin Court Opera, also responsible for the theatres in Hanover, Kassel and Wiesbaden.

[2] Hans Richter (b. 1843) came to Tribschen in October 1866 to do copying work on *Die Meistersinger*. A horn player in a Viennese theatre orchestra, he was appointed conductor at the Munich Opera at Wagner's request.

[3] Franz Lachner, conductor in Munich since 1852 and one of Wagner's main opponents.

[4] Ordered by King Ludwig despite Wagner's objection to public performances of it.

willing I am to thank him for it! Played hide-and-seek with the little ones and discovered the first violets. In the evening read Plato's *Laches*. While reading got a fourth telegram, this time from Tausig[1] in Berlin; it reads: 'Huge success of *Lohengrin*, all Jews reconciled, your devoted Karl.' In this way successes mean something. – At supper R. again spoke of his memories of Berlioz and said he would now only praise him, pointing out that his failures were due to the badness of the prevailing musical conditions; yet they were also due to something in himself, his temperament, he had been constrained, and the constraint of his spirit had led gradually to a deterioration in his character.

Thursday, April 8 In Zurich met the children – an afternoon of joy. They are changed and look unwell, though not really ill. A cheerful journey home. R. still run down, though very satisfied with his conference (the machinist Brandt[2] is understanding and inventive). Everyone to bed. Great concern over the note Hermine gave me: Hans is ill, for the most part through annoyance over the eternal torments.

Friday, April 9 R. continually unwell, he does not go to work. Family lunch; Boni very bright, but somewhat affected, Loulou seems nervous. I find the sight of the elder children painful; first, they do not look as well as the younger ones, then I see that their development has lacked my hand. A dark premonition tells me that I shall come to grief on this feeling.

Saturday, April 10 At breakfast R. reads me a letter which he had just received from Hans, who is living there isolated in the midst of the most despicable intrigues. It broke my heart and I spent the whole morning weeping and sobbing and reflecting. In the afternoon I wrote a complete account of things to the King.

Thursday, April 15 In the morning a letter from Hans for Loulou. I again had to weep. R. came, and said it looked as if I would not after all be able to bear my lot. In the garden then, teaching the children in sultry weather. In the afternoon a long visit by Countess Bassenheim, whom I introduce to R. and who deports herself very well. R. looked curiously dignified and respectable during the conversation.

Friday, April 16 My melancholy refuses to budge – in the night I wake up with a start, and in the evening I wonder how things are now with poor Hans. I meant little enough to him – but how hard I find it to withdraw even this little! – In the morning R. greeted me by telling me he had come upstairs because he had suddenly wondered whether I might not be a traditional legend, and he wished to assure himself I was really there! After lunch I finish reading Lewes[3] – and, indication enough of the wretchedness

[1] Karl Tausig (b. 1841), the pianist, a close friend of Wagner's in Zurich while still in his teens.
[2] Friedrich Carl Brandt, Court theatre machinist in Munich and brother of Karl, the *Ring* machinist in Bayreuth.
[3] *The Life of Goethe* by George Henry Lewes.

of the book, afterwards have to look up the dates he mentions in an encyclopaedia. In the evening Loulou dictates to me a nice letter to her father.

Saturday, April 17 With the children as usual. After lunch they go to Countess Bassenheim's, I receive from Claire the news that Mother has been put in a mental home! – A hard month, this.

Wednesday, April 21 Preparations for R.'s birthday. Besides that a lot of furnishing bothers and a new maidservant. In the afternoon a telegram from Claire, 'Some hope, Mother better,' followed by a letter revealing that my mother had been on the brink of death.

Friday, April 23 Hans's mother has taken all sorts of silly precautions with regard to the children, as if I were not looking after them properly – and as if she herself had ever taken good care of her own children, either morally or physically! When Hermine told me about it, I felt like approaching Hans and repudiating her insults, but on reflection I came to the conclusion that, even if I did not deserve the reproaches in this form, I should bear them willingly in return for pain I myself am perhaps causing, however ignoble it may seem.

Sunday, April 25 In the afternoon a letter from Nuitter announcing the agreement of the string quartet, much to my delight[1]. R. surprised to see me in correspondence with his friend.

Friday, April 30 A letter from Hans to Loulou, he has been unwell. Also from Countess Krockow, who wants to visit me. Lusch writes to her father. I sit beside her, embroidering. R. comes in and presses my hand fervently, he is in the midst of his work (*'Heil der Mutter, die mich gebar'*)[2].

Tuesday, May 4 At lunch R. says that in creative work the difficulty is not discovering ideas, but holding oneself in check – all too many things fly into his mind, his agitation and restlessness come from arranging and selecting them.

Saturday, Sunday, Monday, Tuesday, May 8–11 Have written nothing for four days, have scarcely the strength for it, nor the time, for I wanted to get on with my embroidery. A gloomy talk with R. about my confinement. I want it to be far away from here and in secret, for the sake of the elder children, he sees this as a humiliation for him and becomes very bitter. I can understand him and feel painfully for him – and yet it seems to me that here I have a duty in the face of which other feelings must be silenced. From outside notification of honorary membership in the Berlin Academy. Tausig cables the news and begs R. 'for the sake of the good cause' not to refuse it. What does Tausig call a good cause?

Friday, May 14 Loulou dictates to me a letter to her father. R. is concerned

---

[1] In connection with Wagner's approaching birthday; 'Nuitter' was the pseudonym of Charles Truinet, French librettist and translator of Wagner's works up to *Lohengrin*.
[2] 'Hail to the mother who bore me' (*Siegfried*, Act III, Scene 2).

about me and feels I am attempting too much and destroying myself. When he plays the piano in the evening, I am so overcome that I have to sob and pray.

Sunday, May 16 A visit from old Prince Wallerstein[1], who tells me many instructive things about Bavaria (under three kings).

Monday, May 17 R. has a letter from Düfflipp. He claims the evil things in Munich have been put right – God only knows! The King wishes to see R. on his birthday, but R. wants to stay here. At lunch a philologist, Professor Nietzsche, whom R. first met at the Brockhaus home[2] and who knows R.'s works thoroughly and even quotes from *Opera and Drama* in his lectures. A quiet and pleasant visit; at four we drive through light rain into town. R. is preoccupied, since he is not satisfied with his work this morning. In the evening I tell him that I should like my confinement to be away from here.

Tuesday, May 18 R. still sad about our conversation yesterday, I tell him I will do what he thinks right. He writes to the King and says he will not come for his birthday.

Wednesday, May 19 Before lunch R. plays for me what he has written and is delighted that several themes which date from the 'Starnberg days' and which we had jokingly earmarked for quartets and symphonies have now found their niche (*'Ewig war ich, ewig bin ich'*[3]). Great surge of joy at this coming together of life and art. In the evening again considered the question of the birth of the new baby and the presence of the older children; I put consideration for Hans in the forefront; R. consideration for my comfort and well-being.

Friday, May 21 The afternoon passes in the turmoil of preparations. Richter and the Paris quartet[4] have arrived. I to the Hôtel du Lac to discuss everything. Trouble keeping R. at home. The children have their hair done, suddenly R. comes in, sees 'holly' everywhere, rushes out, I tell him the King is here and will be coming to Tribschen tomorrow. R. does not know whether it is serious or a joke.

Saturday, May 22 In the night set up R.'s bust, surrounded by flowers. Early in the morning Richter blew Siegfried's call. Then the children were lined up as heralds of peace, and finally, at 10.30, the Paris quartet. R. very surprised and delighted. In the course of the day they play the B Minor, the A Minor, and the C-sharp Minor Quartets [of Beethoven]. I felt only like weeping. Telegrams from the King and from Hungary. The day goes by like a dream.

[1] Prince Ludwig zu Öttingen-Wallerstein, a Royal Bavarian State Councillor, who lived with his daughter, Countess Bassenheim.

[2] At the home of his brother-in-law Hermann Brockhaus in Leipzig on November 8, 1868; Friedrich Nietzsche (b. 1844) had now been appointed professor of classical philology at nearby Basel University.

[3] These words, in Act III, Scene 2 of *Siegfried*, are sung to the melody with which the *Siegfried Idyll* opens; it is one of the melodies that came to Wagner in 1864 when Cosima visited him in his villa on Lake Starnberg and their love was consummated.

[4] Cosima had engaged the Morin-Chevillard String Quartet (Paris) to play on Wagner's birthday.

Thursday, May 27 Corpus Christi day, proclaimed by cannon shots. The children merry and lively, eager to watch the procession, I pack them off, but spare myself the sight. R. comes to me, looking unwell, and harshly voices his objection to the children's outing. I say nothing and remind him only later that I had sought his opinion the day before, when I told him the little ones wanted to see the procession. R. now goes further and makes the reproach that I am literally killing myself with looking after the children, I am now all mother, and he is losing me entirely. He had been so pleased that I was to occupy the room next to his, but now I have gone to sleep with the children. He cannot reproach me for this, he says, but he feels it painfully. Deeply shattered by his words, I do not know what to say; if he does not feel happy with me, then I deserve his reproaches, and yet I feel I cannot do otherwise; but I shall have to try to arrange things so that nobody will fall short. R. does indeed tell me later that he is very unwell and that this had given rise to his mood. Arrival of flowers sent by the King.

Friday, May 28 Focussed my attention on arranging my twin duties in a way to satisfy all. I hope I have succeeded. The children to be set to work while R. is composing. Then with the children to meet him as he returns from town, after Lusch has dictated to me her letter to her father. In the evening he plays me his divine sketch; these immortal works will give you the answer, my children, when you ask yourselves: What was it Mama loved, for whom did she live?

Tuesday, June 1 How shall I write down this terrible day? In the morning I worked with the children; it did in fact strike me that R. did not go to his *Siegfried* and seemed sad, but I did not ask him why. In the evening he told me he had the day before received a letter from Hans and was wrestling with himself over whether he should go to him. The King has commanded *Tristan* after all – with the two Vogls[1], a veritable disgrace! Now Hans has to conduct the rehearsals; this upsets his nerves, and he begs R. to help him secure his release. The letter is pitiable, and I wish he would go. R. feels nothing good can come of the meeting and is resisting.

Wednesday, June 2 R. writes to Hans that he has decided to visit him if Hans wishes it, and in the meantime expects from him only that, before surrendering the work to the disgrace of such a performance, he should demand his dismissal.

Thursday, June 3 Wrote to the King and begged him to cancel *Tristan*. R. comes to my bed and asks me whether I will live or perish; he would follow

---

[1] *Tristan und Isolde* had not been performed anywhere since the death of the first Tristan, Ludwig Schnorr von Carolsfeld, in 1865, since Wagner thought him irreplaceable. He had at that time a low opinion of Heinrich and Therese Vogl, currently the Court Opera's leading singers, though he later changed his mind.

me, that I must surely know. I get up and pull myself together. [*Continued in R.W.'s handwriting.*] Oppressed feeling of weakness. R. tries in vain to occupy himself with his work. We sat in the garden while the children ate their meal there: R. had sent Loldi to fetch me. He complained about the constraints of his artistic calling – having, by obeying them, to leave his moral inclinations undeveloped: he could do nothing else, otherwise everything would turn out badly; to be a thoroughly moral person demanded complete self-sacrifice. – I [*R.W. started to write 'Cosima', then wrote 'I' over it*] kept silent. Wretched lunch through Lulu's presence, but gradually a cheerful mood. Then garden again. R. reads out Wolfram's poem about the birth of Parzival. Great beauty; much affected. – Worked with Lulu. – R. into town; after putting the children to bed, I go to meet him on his return. At supper I felt sick; I withdrew to the upper floor, to go to the nursemaid. R., who saw in the exertion this put on me a reproach against himself for having, through the renewed and so much delayed rearrangement of the household, put considerable obstacles in my way, lost his head completely and gave way to excessive expressions of his concern. He complained that I continually and, as it seemed to him, with many excuses persisted in ignoring his daily appeals and representations to take possession of the apartment which had at last been put in order for me again, and to make it comfortable for myself. He said this gave him sad feelings of uneasiness, which constantly assailed him and tormented him like the fear of death. I at last won enough control over his ravings to make him listen to me when I explained to him that the reason for my hesitation in moving down to the apartment designed for me was that the proximity of his bedroom to mine (though indeed previously agreed on between us) was embarrassing to me now that the elder children were there. Since this bedroom of his was – as had also already been agreed – in the vicinity of the impending confinement and was to be prepared for the required nurse, I had to admit that I should prefer not to move down until the time for this arrangement arrived. This explanation seemed to surprise R. greatly and to arouse real bitterness in him. He said I should have told him this frankly a long time ago, since in this respect he had been misled concerning my views and my wishes. He became very quiet but, I believe, no less distressed. We parted very sadly.

Friday, June 4 early. R. was up before six o'clock and gave orders that his bedroom should again be moved to the downstairs apartment. [*At this point C.W.'s entries resume.*] When I come down R. hands me this book with the pages he has written in it. I should have preferred him not to have done so. I believe I was given the *coup de grâce* yesterday, and life confronts me as an insoluble enigma to which I intend to give no further thought. I keep the children occupied, rather than concern myself with them, for inside me all is sadness. R. seems unwell, I avoid all reference to yesterday evening – because I wish to say nothing about it. It appears to me like a judgment of God; and it must be borne.

Saturday, June 5 Splendid weather, summer heat. Prof. Nietzsche, the philologist, announces a visit, R. wishes to put him off, I feel it is better that he come. I have still not emerged from my dazed state, I hear everything like a very distant echo, and everything melts away as if in a fog. Long conversation with R.; he believes that I am capable of bearing grudges against him, whereas any harshness from him in fact simply annihilates me. [*Continued from here in R.W.'s handwriting.*] A bearable evening spent with Nietzsche. Said good night about eleven. The labour pains begin. At midnight leave the children's bedroom upstairs and, in order not to awake anybody, carry my bedclothes myself in two journeys down to the lower bedroom.

Sunday, June 6 At one o'clock down to Richard to tell him and to insist that for the time being no fuss be made, that the arrangements for the day be adhered to, and that Nietzsche should stay for lunch with the children. R. throws his dressing gown over me and leads me upstairs to bed. The pains get more frequent; at two o'clock I have Vreneli woken and the midwife sent for. Necessary steps to make the adjoining room ready for the new arrival; but the time adjudged to be not yet so near; I fear the weakness which previously delayed Eva's birth. R. at my bedside in great concern. The midwife arrives after three, to wait in the adjoining room, since I do not wish to speak to anybody. Things appear to quieten down somewhat. R. decides to use this period to get a few hours' sleep in order to strengthen himself for the coming day. He goes downstairs and gets into bed, but is so tortured by restlessness that he gets dressed again and comes upstairs; he rushes in and finds me in the most raging pain, being tended by the midwife. I was startled to see him suddenly standing before me and imagined I was seeing a ghost; I turned away in horror, thus driving him from the room into the open *salon* next door; when he again hears my cries, he rushes in once more, since the midwife has left me alone for a moment; I gripped his arm as I writhed, but signified to him that he should not speak. The midwife returned, R. withdrew again to the neighbouring room; there he remained earwitness to the delivery and heard the cries of the labouring mother. As he hears Vreneli come in and then hears her exclaim in reply to some words from the midwife, 'Oh, God in Heaven!', R. thinks something terrible has happened to me and hastens to the landing to find out from Vreneli as she comes rushing out. But she greets him with a joyful laugh: 'A *son* has arrived!' Her previous exclamation had simply been one of surprise that so little was prepared. Now R. went back into the *salon*: from the unconscious mother he heard little more, yet on the other hand he could clearly distinguish the lusty yells of the baby boy. With feelings of sublime emotion he stared in front of him, was then surprised by an incredibly beautiful fiery glow which started to blaze with a richness of colour never before seen, first on the orange wallpaper beside the bedroom door; it was then reflected in the blue jewel box containing my portrait, so that this, covered by glass and set in a narrow gold frame, was transfigured in celestial splendour. The sun had just risen above the Rigi and was putting forth its first rays, proclaiming a glorious, sundrenched day. R. dissolved into tears. Then to me, too, came from across the lake the sound of the early-morning Sunday bells ringing in Lucerne. He looked at the clock and noticed that his son had been born at four o'clock in the morning. – Just before six o'clock R. was allowed in to see me; he told me of his solemn emotions. I was in a mood of cheerfulness and gladness: the gift which Fate had vouchsafed us through the birth of a son appeared to me to be one of immeasurably consoling value. R.'s son is the heir and future representative of the father for all his children; he will be the protector and guardian of his sisters. We were very happy. The boy is big and strong: they say he weighs two pounds more than other newborn boys. We discussed his name: Siegfried Richard. R. felt an urge to give evidence of his joy throughout the house: he had handsome gifts distributed to all the servants. – From nine o'clock onwards, my hand in R.'s, I was granted my first strength-restoring sleep, even if short, lasting about two hours. At noon R. had to leave me in order to preside over the midday meal with his guest (Nietzsche) and the children. During this time I was given the attention necessary to my condition. At 4.30 R. was relieved of his onerous duties. While the children went for a trip on the lake, we spent the time together, quiet and full of hope. At nine o'clock R. left me so that I could get some rest and he himself recover from his exhaustion in sleep. –

Monday, June 7 Little sleep in the night, much pain: only in the morning some rest. At our first meeting in the morning I could nevertheless give R. reassuring news about my condition. Except for the times in which I had to submit directly to the attentions required by a woman in childbed, R. sat comfortingly at my bedside all day. But at noon he did drive into town to buy a fine watch for Jakob (in the name of his own son Wilhelm); I was satisfied with the purchase and gave the watch to Vreneli, who in her turn took it to her husband to wear. The gift was accepted with touching emotion. – We discussed the relationship we should like to see between Siegfried and the son of our loyal house manager, who is about eight months older: R. said he wished he had at the time insisted on the boy's being named 'Kurwenal'; for he wished that Wilhelm might one day behave towards Siegfried as Kurwenal to Tristan. – There was much of good cheer, of melancholy pride in our talk. I also let the children come to my bedside. The excitement of the younger ones soon exhausted me. On this day I suffered very much: the after-birth pains were significantly greater than at Eva's birth. But I faced the night consoled and with confidence, even though extremely weak, and on the whole it passed so well that I did not call on the nurse even once – and, since for the first time in her life she was able to sleep beside a mother in childbed undisturbed, she was very pleasantly surprised.

Tuesday, June 8 In the morning I was able to greet R. happily and cheerfully. He on the other hand seemed somewhat unwell, for which the thundery atmosphere was mainly responsible, and it made me also very restless and weak throughout the day. Our son is well: R. laughs about his strong fists; his well-shaped head delights us both. We spoke a lot about the significant change he has brought about in our fate. – Hermine had come back on the previous evening. The children were very content to have her with them again. Today R. went down to speak to her and found her, just as we desired, resolved to perform her duties loyally and perseveringly, in accordance with our trust in her. She, too, received a sizable present from R., who also assured her of his willingness to care for her throughout her life if she remained good and loyal. Much of what R. told me helped to put my mind at rest. But in general my condition remained very painful, and in particular my exhaustion and weakness were great. Towards evening R. was in town with the children for quite a while, making purchases. In regard to our son's christening, an attempt is being made to see whether the local Protestant priest thinks he can carry out the sacred task quietly here in the house without attracting the attention of the Catholic clergy. The day came to an end in a mood of mildness and harmony: Siegfried is flourishing, and his mother is glad to be alive. – R. leaves me about ten o'clock, when I at last fall asleep.

Wednesday, June 9 Cheerful, harmonious day. From bed to the *chaise-longue* in the *salon*. R. has his meals upstairs. The children (except Eva) sent off to the Selisberg with Hermine: in the morning much together with them. They leave at five. In the evening pains: too long out of bed. R.'s concern.

Thursday, June 10 Slept little: severe pains. Obliged to lie constantly in an outstretched position. R. unwell and despondent, concerned at my indisposition.

Friday, June 11 Restored by good night's rest (first for a long time!) R. better, too. R. works on *Siegf.* again. Towards midday from bed to the *salon*, on the sofa. There ate with R.

Saturday, June 12 Satisfaction with Siegfried's progress. – R. at work: he intends to finish the sketches in a few days.

[At this point C.W.'s entries resume.]

Sunday, June 13 All hail the day which illumines us, hail to the sun which shines on us! – How shall I, poorest of creatures, describe the feelings with which I again take this book in my hands? . . . When the woman said to me, 'Congratulations, it is a little boy,' I had to weep and laugh and pray. – Preserve him, divinity which gave him to me, that he may be the support of his sisters, the heir of his adored father! Now that my happiness lies so sweetly in reach before my eyes, it seems to me ever more tremendous, more disembodied, I see it hovering, rising up high above all woes, and all I can do is to thank the universal spirit which proclaimed to us through this sign that it is kindly disposed towards us. The day is blazing gloriously, I did not sleep during the night, but all the same feel well. I reflected on a letter to be written to Hans, in which I shall describe my earlier, my present, and my future relationship with him – if he will accept it! May God reveal to me the right things to say in order to help him a little! R. is working, I hear it with bliss; when he comes up to me, he tells me how wonderfully it has turned out that his theme of joy ('*Sie ist mir alles*') fits in excellently as accompaniment to the motive '*Heil der Mutter, die mich gebar*', so that this expression of joy can be heard sounding in the orchestra up to the point where Siegfried himself sings it. Tomorrow he will probably finish his sketch! – Regarded our Siegfried; when R. saw him alone, the child appeared to him as he will once be, reflective and earnest; very moved, he tells me it was as if he had seen the eidolon of our precious boy. God preserve him for us! – R. tells me that my mother heard about the Paris quartet at Tribschen and assumed that the King of Bavaria had arranged for it, so it was no wonder he had no money left to engage Semper; he had enough on his hands with Wagner. We laugh heartily at this pitiful absurdity. 'These poor people think of everything,' says R., 'except that it was the enthusiasm of a loving woman which provided me with this pleasure.'

Monday, June 14 Did not wake up until 6.30 this morning. Saw our boy at once. I dreamed again of R. When he came to me, he said he now knew which little bird it was which, as I had told him, invariably started to twitter all by itself at 3.30 in the morning at the first sign of daybreak: it was Siegfried's bird, which had announced his arrival and now came to inquire after him. – At one o'clock he comes with his sketches in his hand, inscribed 'properly delivered', he says our son is now truly born. It is again divine, this act! – The only thing that distresses me is when R. says he will not live to see our boy's manhood and laments that we did not discover each other fifteen years ago.

Tuesday, June 15 Letter from Richter with the news that Hans has demanded his dismissal on the grounds of ill health! R. already knew. I write at length to Hans in great concern. Final attempt at an understanding.

Thursday, June 17 Today downstairs for the first time and in the garden, with R. to the pigeon house. Smiling reception everywhere! R. asks jokingly in the morning what more Siegfried has in store for him, now that he had already dislodged him from his bedroom. . . . There are lovely flowers in my sitting room, I see nothing but good all around me, yet worry lodges in my heart; I hope, dear children all, that things will be easier for you than for your mother. Surely there will never again be such a poor, bereft being as Hans. He feels so miserable in my absence, and yet I could never make him happy, never even please him. In the evening we discussed, R. and I, the oddly mysterious nature of our alliance. How timid and at the same time rapturous our first approaches, how unpremeditated our first union, how constantly were our unspoken thoughts centred only on renunciation, and how circumstances and people forced us to recognize that our love alone was genuine and that we were utterly indispensable to each other! – 'The spirit of the universe desired me to have a son by you, and so it arranged things; we ourselves were forced to obey, without understanding why.'

Sunday, June 20 Since I was worried that no reply had come from Hans, R. tells me that a letter arrived yesterday. He gives it to me, saying it is very fine. Deep, inexpressible agitation. Probably more because of that than because of getting up, I again feel unwell and have to take to my bed. In the evening the children back from the Selisberg, they are well and lively. They take great delight in Siegfried, who is shown to them. – In spirit now at this performance of *Tristan* in Munich, this dreadful one! At lunch R. and I smiled to think that poor *Tristan*, this night flower of grace, has always been treated like a poisonous toadstool.

Monday, June 21 Still in bed and weak, but worked with the children. In the night I was very worried that Hans might not have been able to get through the *Tristan* performance, and sent a telegram to Richter. The reply reads, 'Bülow came to life during performance, afterwards cheerful, calls of "*Bülow stay*", success tremendous.' R. talks about the work and says that in it the cult of the earth goddess finds true expression; he feels as if he had thrown himself headlong into the paint pots and emerged dripping. He had had to make use of the richest resources of musical expression because the action of the drama is so simple. No one but a musician was in a position to explore such a subject to its very depths and remain at the same time attractive.

Tuesday, June 22 In the afternoon a letter for R. from Hans arrives, a report on the *Tristan* performance. It induces R. to repeat what he said once before to me: 'The King of B[avaria] is all daemon, I have been studying what he does, and he acts by instinct; when he stops to consider, he is lost. Without his even realizing it, his daemon tells him that, if he had gone along with me, had carried out my plans with real boldness, he and I would have gone completely to the dogs. In view of the wickedness and mediocrity of people he does whatever is possible to preserve my works for the world, but I cannot take much pleasure in his activities.'

Friday, June 25 Still wretched nights, reflecting on my situation, my obligations. I got out of bed and was carried by R. into the garden. Great weakness.

Saturday, June 26 I find it easier to get up today, and the day's activities quell my restless thoughts. – Worked with the children in the garden and also ate there. Much pleasure in the flourishing of the little ones; in them I am given the likeness of the greatest happiness; if I did not have the torment of Hans, whose lot could even be compared with mine? How, in blissful innocence, the days pass! No noise from the world reaches us, here love alone rules supreme. I thank the God who gave me this: may He forgive me for having brought suffering to another being!

Monday, June 28 Wanted to get up early, but had another severe haemorrhage and had to remain in bed, to the great dismay of R. who, having risen in good spirits, soon found himself feeling miserable. 'When I think that I shall never again hear a single note of my things, and that I am letting *Das Rheingold* be done without me, where should I find the urge to make music? I do it purely for you.'

Thursday, July 1 The joyful moment of the day was the arrival of Beethoven's portrait, which R. has had copied (from the original, in Härtel's possession). We receive the great man as a friend and benefactor, and R. says we have pleasures which no others have, we lead a life like few others.

Saturday, July 3 Rainy day, and R. would have preferred sunshine for his work, because he has to rewrite (Wotan's last words to Erda, which have turned out too 'idyllic'). We pass the evening in conversation; he is still delighted with the picture of Beethoven: 'That is how he looked, this poor man who gave us back the language men spoke before they had ideas; it was to recover this language of the birds that Man created the divine art. But this is also the reason why a musician such as he is a being for whom there is absolutely no place in society.'

Sunday, July 4 As R. is playing me what he has written, Richter comes in, to our astonishment. Dismal news from Munich, the theatre manager[1] a coward, all the rest so crude that it defies description. Dear good Richter weeps as he recalls his happy days in Tribschen.

Monday, July 5 Dream that I strayed with R. into a gathering of Jews and that I then went out begging with Hans, and stones were thrown at me. R. comes up. I show him the nice letter I received from Claire this morning; that brings us to the question of a divorce. I tell R. that I intend to write to Hans, asking if he wishes me to go to him, to give up everything here, to take just the four children with me, whether he really has the strength to be happy in view of all the stir our relationship has caused; if not, he should consent to a divorce, if only for his own sake. R. says that in this matter he must remain silent. He leaves me and writes to Düffl[ipp] about Hans's position.

Wednesday, July 7 Work everywhere, mine maternal, R.'s magnificent; at noon he calls out to me that he has found it – that is to say, the conclusion

---

[1] Karl, Baron von Perfall.

for Wotan and Erda. After lunch, as I give him my hand, he tells me that the slightest touch from me does him good, no more sympathetic creature exists, but that is also why nobody else can leave me alone! – In the evening R. brings me a letter from Mathilde [Maier][1], she has heard about my fifth child from *Hornstein*[2] and cannot understand why I told her nothing about it!!! R. very annoyed with her, reproaches me for being too weak towards everybody. I reply to her late in the evening, calmly and shortly. But all the same it has again raised a great worry in my mind, since Baron Hornstein lives – of all places – in Munich!

Thursday, July 8 After lunch R. wanted to play something from his sketches, but then did not feel in the mood. I suggested reading his *Parzival* draft[3] and did so amid occasional tears. I could feel deep within myself the purifying and ennobling effect which such sublime things have on us. To R[ichter] it was all completely new, and he listened in great emotion.

Friday, July 9 Sultry. R. unwell. At breakfast he is given a card from Serov (the Russian R. Wagner!)[4] and invites him to join us at table. Serov has in consequence of his Russian national opera been appointed an active councillor of state and bears the title Excellency, about which R. good-humouredly teases him a lot. S[erov] has just seen *Tristan* and *Die Msinger* in Munich and is quite intoxicated by them and also very satisfied with the performances. Before I join them, R. tells him a little about what has happened to us and why he will not go to see *Das Rheingold*; when in the course of it my name is mentioned, Serov cries, '*Quelle femme héroique!*' When R. tells me this, I am utterly astonished, so much have I got used to the thought of just being despised. – The children are well, Siegfried fine; R. was pleased today when Eva brought him his snuffbox as he was composing – 'When a child appears like that one has such an indescribable sense of the grace and sweetness of life.' Today began *Oedipus at Colonus*.

Saturday, July 10 Worked with the children, then received a letter from Mathilde and answered it right away. She wants to know what to tell people when they ask about me. I: 'The truth!' R. is working hard and is in good and cheerful spirits. After lunch to Countess B. with the children. I tell her of the woman who bribed our stableboy to find out things. – Some words of Loldi's, of which I tell R., cause him to suggest that I demand a divorce from Hans – but I cannot now make demands on Hans; I have the strength to suffer, but no longer to wound.

Sunday, July 11 During the morning R. comes up to my room to see

[1] Mathilde Maier (b. 1833), a lawyer's daughter with whom Wagner had a long-drawn-out love affair, beginning in 1862 when he was composing *Die Meistersinger*.
[2] Robert von Hornstein, composer, former friend of Wagner in Zurich.
[3] Prose sketch of *Parsifal*, written in 1865.
[4] Alexander Serov (b. 1820), Russian composer and writer; his opera was *Rogneda*, first performed 1865 in Moscow.

whether I am 'still there'. 'I always believe you will run away.' Then back to his work. I played a Beethoven quartet with R., afterwards went for a walk with him. My grieving about Hans – never expressed aloud – R. guesses, and it makes him sad. He recalls scenes, at which he was present, when Hans struck me, and says he was horrified at the calm indifference with which I had borne this. Very painful feelings.

Monday, July 12 R. comes up with a letter, Judith Mendès announces a visit. For me a letter from Claire, good and affectionate. – In the afternoon, when we wanted to rest, the Serovs arrived with their son. Since the boy understands only Russian, Loldi declares, 'He doesn't know a thing.'

Friday, July 16 One sees the aim is to get rid of the young King. R. thought yesterday evening with great concern about the forthcoming production of *Das Rheingold* – yet again a vast amount of money expended and a pitiful, not to say ridiculous result! All the same, R. does not intend to bother himself about it – how curious the ways of Fate, which fills precisely *this* incapable King with enthusiasm for R.'s works – how curiously terrible! In the evening the Mendès couple (M. Villiers[1] is also with them). She is very remarkable, so lacking in manners that I find it downright embarrassing, yet at the same time good-natured and terribly full of enthusiasm. She literally forces Rich. to play and sing pieces from *Die Walküre* and *Tristan*. When they have gone, R. says to me: 'There are no women left in France – just think of that! My God, what a spirit you are!' he adds. He had noticed that I had been weeping while listening to his recital: 'Yes, for us that is life, we are rooted in it, it is our heart's blood – the others amuse themselves with it, we live it.'

Saturday, July 17 In the afternoon the Mendès couple, I must entertain them. How curious their noisy enthusiasm seems to me! The woman says out loud all the things I believe in my inmost heart; the fact that she can say them aloud makes her seem strange to me. He is highly cultured and both of them thoroughly kind-hearted. They relate how R.'s publisher Schott advertised the translation of the Jewish pamphlet in Paris on the day of *Rienzi*'s first performance; Pasdeloup[2] rushed out in alarm and, as he thought, bought up all the copies. Next day Schott offered him a thousand more copies which he had in stock, at the same price! Who could believe that of a publisher? And again, who was behind it? The last performance of *Rienzi* is reported to have aroused incredible enthusiasm and much presentation of bouquets! R. plays Wotan's farewell to Brünnhilde and several passages from *Lohengrin*. At eleven o'clock they tell us they have not eaten since lunch yesterday. We have nothing in the house, mood of gaiety. Of the movement of the waves in *Das Rheingold* R. says, 'It is, so to speak, the world's lullaby.'

[1] Villiers de l'Isle-Adam (b. 1838), the French poet.
[2] Jules Etienne Pasdeloup, conductor and director of the Théâtre Lyrique in Paris.

Sunday, July 18 Bathing with the little ones, then from two till ten the Mendès couple. She gives me a fan which a Chinese (an academician) has inscribed for her and which in the eyes of the Chinese is worth 100,000 francs; in exchange I have to give her a page of R.'s, which has indeed for me a different worth; I found it hard to part with it, though I do not begrudge it to this remarkable woman. R. regards her and her husband as a real enrichment of our lives, and they are certainly an extraordinary, noble couple. Unfortunately both of them seem in delicate health.

Tuesday, July 20 With the children; only late in the evening the Mendès people, who had been to the riflemen's meeting in Zug. R. was just playing me the last thing he had written when they came in. In the morning I had read some pages of young Villiers's books – little that is edifying, much monstrosity.

Sunday, July 25 Delighted to observe Lulu's progress in piano playing; R. interrupts our practice; talk about the Mendès couple, she a child of Nature, he a highly cultured man, but unfortunately the French character is like a barrier, they put V. Hugo on the same level as Shakespeare. After lunch M. Villiers reads us his play; the same person in whom we could discern no talent has found in real life inspiration for a good play, which he read to us with marvellous skill. Take leave of our excellent friends; when they invite me to come with R. to Paris, to *Lohengrin,* and try to press me, I explain to them that I must make sacrifices in order to prove to another being how earnestly I regard a life which has imposed on me the sad necessity of wounding him. Moved silence. Painful thoughts of Hans and his fate, difficulty in going to sleep. – In the morning a letter from Richter, who has requested his dismissal. He is being asked to stay on, R. answers that he should insist on his dismissal.

Monday, July 26 Costumes for *Das Rheingold* arrived, very silly and unimaginative. After lunch R. writes telling Munich the design of the costumes is as good as nonexistent. In the garden a little. He has received a comical letter from Serov, whose wife seems to have taken umbrage at Judith; to state it briefly, he goes on at length about the French being unfitted to listen to R.'s works, whereas his wife, ah yes, his wife – ! Much amusement over this.

Tuesday, July 27 Awful dream that R. set his head on fire by carelessly turning a gas flame, after that a second, gentler, but all the same melancholy dream about R. In the morning constantly clutching my heart. R. comes up and tells me he had a very bad night with violent pains in the heart! At 5 o'clock he had written to Serov, telling him the French people who so disturbed him had now left, and his music could now proceed as earnestly and gloomily as his wife could wish. – We think with joy of our newly found friends, particularly of her. – Since I am surprised to have received no answer from M[athilde] M[aier], I ask R. whether he has withheld a letter from me; I then find out that a regular exchange of correspondence has been going on, and R. also thinks I was wrong not to have told her of the birth of Siegfried. This unfortunately hurt me deeply; with how much difficulty is self-will broken! When does a human being ever achieve complete renunciation? – Recently R. told me that things had changed between us after all, I was now only earnestly companionable towards him. And yet nothing has changed except that I now want no other joy but to see him happy and in good health and the children flourishing. Years ago, when I received the gift of his love, I was in an ecstasy; I hailed the light as if raised from the dead, I forgot everything I knew and believed in happiness on earth, believed in it and demanded it. Now I know everything again and in consequence am content to go around just like a shadow – and yet, so weak am I, I was hurt today, when all suffering should be welcome to me!

Friday, July 30 While I was asleep, R. came to me and gave me many kisses; I myself do not quite know yet whether this really happened or I just dreamed it. I have renounced all forms of personal joy, may God grant that my beloved and the children are made happy by my silent presence.

Saturday, July 31 R. comes to us and reports that Hans has requested me, through Dr Hallwachs[1], to sign a legal document enabling us to get a divorce. I find it good that it should happen in this way. But the thought that Hans has perhaps been brought to this point by acts of brutality disturbs me. The news appears to make R. happy, and so I, too, feel content, though very solemn. – Visit from Professor Nietzsche; a well-formed and pleasant human being.

Sunday, August 1 R. tells me he has written to Hallwachs, saying that the legal authorization I am required to give cannot be got so easily. R. would like to do it all by himself, in order to spare me the embarrassing details. I tell him the details and the so-called unpleasantness mean nothing to me; if he could free my heart of sad imaginings, I should accept with gratitude, but this he cannot do, and all the rest is a matter of indifference. At lunch Prof. Nietzsche, who is very pleasant and who feels happy at Tribschen. Afterwards accompanied him to Hergeschwyl with the children and R.; he is climbing Mount Pilatus.

Monday, August 2 Heavy rain, housework. Wrote to Claire to ask her to write belatedly to Hans. Suspicion that Hans might have received news of Siegfried's birth in a cruel manner and is offering me divorce as a sort of punishment. R. did not wish to show me Dr. Hallwachs's letter. I beg him never to try to spare me things, since the things I find hard to accept all lie elsewhere than in so-called vexations. I can bear abuse and ignominy and such things more easily in areas where the heart is not involved. Hans

---

[1] The lawyer looking after the divorce suit (not the Munich stage director of the same name).

promises not to try to take advantage of his rights. In the morning with the children, inking in the *Siegfried* score.

Wednesday, August 4 A letter from Judith in Munich. In the evening also, unfortunately, an article by her husband: '*La maison de R. Wagner à Lucerne*'. R. very upset by it. 'The most important thing, my relationship with you and the children, they cannot mention, so they talk about the furniture.' R. completes his sketch of the third act. After lunch with the children in the woods. Glorious weather; the finest summer I can ever remember has produced Siegfried.

Thursday, August 5 R. returns home from his walk, bringing a letter from Dr. Hallwachs. It is true that Hans learned in passing of Siegfried's birth. I regret not having informed him of it personally, R. reproves me for this thought and says it was proper that I did not do this. Heavy feelings, may Hans recover his spirits! – In the evening a Haydn symphony; great delight in its masterliness. – A telegram from Richter reports that they could not get the right singer for Alberich, and he asks whether they might accept the wrong one. R. replies, *Children* and *gentlemen*, do what you will and can, but leave me in peace.'

Sunday, August 8 Serovs for lunch; he a good independent person, she as ugly as the night, interested in women's emancipation, while only yesterday R. and I were expressing our loathing for this so-called up-to-date rubbish. I find it impossible to understand how a woman with a child of her own can ever even consider doing anything beyond bringing up this child, in this field she is the indispensable ruler.

Tuesday, August 10 I am unwell, but can see to the children, since Hermine is in bed. R. at his copying for the King, about whom nothing is heard and who seems literally to have vanished.

Thursday, August 12 Very unwell, the doctor is amazed that with the weakness of my pulse I can still walk about.

Saturday, August 14 Arrival of the *Rheingold* pictures, the costumes have turned out somewhat better. In the afternoon Serov, entertaining conversation with him.

Sunday, August 15 In the afternoon R. plays me his third act, great emotion. 'The kiss of love is the first intimation of death, the cessation of individuality, that is why a person is so terrified by it.'

Monday, August 16 We speak about my father. R. says he first found out through him what Bach is. 'One really cannot blame the world for being unwilling to accept that his gift of virtuosity was for him only of secondary importance. He was born to it – and what have time and duration to do with it?' 'The main thing is that one should be out of the ordinary. In me the accent lies on the conjunction of poet and musician, as a pure musician I would not be of much significance.'

Tuesday, August 17 In the evening Richter. Still troubles in Munich. He has to stick by his resignation. Hans is in Kochel. In bed I remember how incapable he is of living in the country (those terrible holidays in Klampenborg!), and the bad weather on top of it. If only his health would improve!

Tuesday, August 18 Up early; rehearsal with singers[1]. I with the Serovs in the next room. Overwhelming feelings of great melancholy. R. in the evening in a Falstaffian state, as he says, hoarse from choral singing. – To the many bright ideas of the Munich theatre director belongs the commissioning of a prologue for the reopening of the theatre. A prologue for a new stage!! For that reason he has turned down the request of many friends for *Lohengrin*, and instead chooses *Jessonda*[2]! R. telegraphs the King and asks for *Lohengrin* or *Die Meistersinger*.

Thursday, August 19 In the evening a telegram from the King, he will, 'if possible', arrange a performance of *Lohengrin* for his birthday. After lunch we discuss the present comprehensive letter from Hans. He feels my father must have advised Hans against a divorce. I am willing to bear anything and to await things in patience as long as Hans is not put in torment, but all the same I ask R., too, to keep silent.

Friday, August 20 Letter from Judith, full of enthusiasm, I reply and ask her to use the occasion of *Das Rheingold* to make known the reasons why R. is staying away from Munich. In the afternoon R.'s sister Frau Avenarius[3] arrives – he has not seen her for 21 years. When I express my pleasure for R.'s sake and ask him whether she has shown him love, he says with a smile, 'We don't need love, we only need sincerity.'

Saturday, August 21 R. has completed his copying. At lunch the Serovs and Herr and Frau Avenarius, neither of the last two very pleasant, he in particular is terribly crude. Serov shows me an article by Mme Mendès which horrifies me. I do not think we shall be able to have much more to do with these people. R. is extremely hurt. In the evening a visit from Professor Nietzsche, very pleasant as always.

Monday, August 23 R. writes letters and teaches the children, who are now in my sole charge, since I have sent Hermine to Munich to settle some matters there.

Tuesday, August 24 Letter from Marie Muchanoff, she is going to Munich, where she will meet my father, she asks whether I would not see him. This question leads to a conversation with R. from which I learn that he has been forced by a newspaper report to the conclusion that my father dissuaded Hans from his resolve to get a divorce from me! R. is now writing to Marie Muchanoff and giving her an outline of the whole situation, in the hope that she will show this to my father and perhaps cause him to reverse his unfortunate attitude. I also write her a few lines and send

---

[1] I.e., some of those taking part in *Das Rheingold* in Munich.
[2] Opera by Spohr, with which the renovated Nationaltheater in Munich opened on August 25.
[3] Wagner's half-sister Cäcilie, daughter of Ludwig Geyer, married to Eduard Avenarius, a book dealer.

her Hans's last letter to me. I receive a telegram from Hermine: 'Old lady[1] at home, humiliating reception, turned away from the house.' Thus does the good lady avenge herself for the 10 years in which I treated her in such a way that R. was firmly convinced that she did and must love me, and was struck dumb when I once told him, 'The woman is just waiting for an opportunity to do me harm.'

Wednesday, August 25 In the morning a nice letter from Judith Mendès; she is beside herself, the theatre director will not let her into rehearsals of *Das Rheingold*. Still the same old game! R. has telegraphed him (very curtly), he reads the text to me, I beg him to let Richter deal with the matter, which he does. I then write to Judith and tell her what my father has done to me, since she asks whether she should visit him. Meanwhile R. begins on the instrumentation of Act III.

Thursday, August 26 Very friendly letter from Professor Nietzsche, who sends us a lecture on Homer. Again children's day with inking in of score. R. orchestrating.

Friday, August 27 Dire dreams of persecutions. R. comes and says he will on no account let me go to my father, these people were capable of throwing me into a convent like Barbara Ubri (!!!)[2]. My father is now going to see *Rheingold* because he has been officially invited; previously, with *Tristan*, when we asked him to come and everything still gave grounds for hope, he did not wish to.

Saturday, August 28 Richard brought me a letter from the cook in Munich, saying that Hans had gone away, despondent and sad, without saying where. Terrible grief overcomes me, or, rather, bursts forth. I sob, completely possessed by the thought that my true duty would be to die. I remember being told by the botanist that a plant (spurge) would kill a person if he put its poison in an open wound. Continual brooding – oh, children, my children, remember your mother's words, no suffering is so hard to bear as the wrong we do, remember these words, wrought from pain in the most painful of hours! Sobbed the whole morning, uncontrollably. R. very concerned. At midday the Brockhaus family and Prof. Nietzsche, all very kind. I elsewhere. In the afternoon a letter from Judith, she tells me that my father wishes to settle my affairs for me, that he loves me, that Hans has gone away to expedite the matter. The letter did me infinite good, I began to breathe again. Then came telegram after telegram and letter after letter, all reporting that the dress rehearsal of *Das Rheingold* had been appalling, ridiculous to the highest degree, and that stupidity had joined hands with malice to ruin everything. R. telegraphs the King and asks for a postponement.

[1] Hans's mother, Franziska von Bülow.
[2] Correctly Ubryk, a nun recently found in a convent in Cracow, demented after a 21-year confinement in a dark cell.

Sunday, August 29 R. ill with grief about *Das Rheingold.* The telegrams continue: (1) The King – sends thanks for his birthday gift, otherwise nothing! (2) Richter announces his decision not to conduct. (3) Loën[1], the Weimar theatre director, now in Munich, asks whether his conductor [Eduard] Lassen may take over, Perfall is demanding it. R. telegraphs a bravo to Richter, to Düfflipp a demand to put right all the deficiencies, to Loën saying no. In the evening news from Richter, he has really been suspended!

Monday, August 30 R. writes to the King, explains the position to him, and suggests that he go to Munich, to make possible a good performance by Sunday. Great anxiety over this decision; R. says he knows he will return home fit.

Tuesday, August 31 R. teases me because, even though this is the morning of his departure, I still give Loulou a piano lesson, 'in youth love goes under!' At midday letter from the stage director Hallwachs, giving a hopeless account of it all. We consider the possibility of a break with the King if he insists on the performance on Thursday. At four o'clock telegram from the King, he expects the performance on Sunday. Seeing R. off, great melancholy, but pleased that the King had listened to him.

Thursday, September 2 Hermine has seen my father, who is still well disposed towards me. At four o'clock surprise and joy: R. announces his return this evening. With the four children and the two dogs to fetch him; *Rheingold* impossible, the return of Richter to the conductor's desk would be the signal for the resumption of the old witch hunt against us and the King; and besides this the staging of the work is so abominable that the machinist is demanding three months to put it right. But the whole world is said to be in Munich. – Judith sends me a warning against Marie Muchanoff, I regret the confidence I made to the latter. R. well, he is only too glad to be here again!

Friday, September 3 R. telegraphs the King, begs him to cancel the performance, so that the decision will at least come from him. News that the singer Betz[2] has left Munich so as not to have to sing Wotan in such circumstances.... Letter from Hermine, my father has told her Hans is in Berlin. Calmly as I accept all this news, my heart is nevertheless heavy! The warning against Marie Muchanoff also makes me anxious, she has Hans's letter to me, I sent it to her for my father's sake, but is she worthy of this confidence?

Saturday, September 4 To put my fears at rest, R. writes to Marie Muchanoff and asks for the return of Hans's letter. Great melancholy in the evening, life and the world horrify me ever more and more. Played duets with R., a Beethoven quartet.

[1] August Friedrich, Baron von Loën.
[2] Franz Betz (b. 1835), baritone in Vienna, Wagner's first Sachs in *Die Meistersinger.*

Monday, September 6 Siegfried three months old today! Letter from Dr. Hallwachs on Hans's behalf, the petition has been filed, within two months I shall probably be divorced. Mood of solemnity. After lunch letter from Marie Muchanoff, she at last returns the letter from Hans and is coming here the day after next. She also says my father was touched that I wanted to see him, 'but does not wish to create a stir just now'. As if I had either demanded or desired such a thing!! R. also annoyed by this. We drive to the Bassenheims' to report her coming. Terrible thunderstorm. R. returns home alone, I play and read with the children. When I come down, I look for R., he has fallen asleep after bitterly weeping – weeping about the King! We hear nothing about *Das Rheingold*. How can I console him? To weep with him is all I can do! Our mood is melancholy, we play piano duets, that restores our spirits.

Tuesday, September 7 Letter from Judith, very nice and affectionate, reply to her at once. For R. a letter from Peter Cornelius[1], who also now intends to leave the music school; that pleases us, for we had assumed that P.C. was not at all interested in our sufferings.

Thursday, September 9 Inked in score beside the cradle, Siegfried in two versions before me. – Letter to R. from Judith, *Rheingold* postponed, may later be performed for the King alone. Went for a drive with the children, encountered Countess Bassenheim at the railway station, waiting in vain for Marie M. In the end a letter from Marie saying she is coming tomorrow to discuss important matters with me. Stupid, tiresome interference!

Friday, September 10 After parting from me yesterday evening in a very cheerful mood, R. comes up to my room in the morning looking most despondent; it is reported in the newspaper that *Das Rheingold* is now really to be performed within the next fortnight. When we had read in the newspapers that R. had been put off *'ad calendas Graecas'* we had breathed again, thinking the King had come to his senses at last – and now it is to be done after all! Grief over the King's behaviour, rather than the sacrifice of his work, is making R. quite ill. I draft a letter to the King, but R. does not wish it to be sent, he feels he has already said enough. Late in the afternoon Richter arrives. *Das Rheingold* is to be done in a fortnight, with all the roles changed; the singer R. rehearsed for *Loge* is to sing *Mime*, the orchestra has been reduced, etc., etc. The theatre director is bribing newspapers on all sides, and now everyone is happily spreading lies. The members of the orchestra are much put out by all this and by the fact that they are to be directed by the most incapable of all conductors [Franz Wüllner]. But the wretches are within their rights. We discuss with R. the fact that he can only be silent, that his works belong to the King, and if

---

[1] Composer (b. 1824) and one of Wagner's most devoted friends, coming at his invitation to Munich to teach at the newly organized music school.

the latter wishes to use them as mere toys, R. can do nothing to stop him, and there is absolutely nowhere one can look for support.

Saturday, September 11 Contrary to his decision of yesterday, R. produces in the morning a letter to the conductor that horrifies me; I should have preferred him not to send it, but it does him good, for bearing things in silence gnaws at his heart[1]. Worked with the children early in the morning, but then a gathering at Tribschen of Marie Muchanoff, Fräulein Holmès (poetess, composer, etc.)[2], and others besides. The former pains me with various things she tells me about Hans. At midday a very affectionate letter from Countess Krockow. which also affects me, since it concerns my fate. In the afternoon the Brockhaus family, later the Holmèses, father and daughter, and thus till late in the night. Very un-Tribschen-like!

Sunday, September 12 Letter from Düfflipp, nothing really but the same old refrain, the King should not be dragged into it, etc., etc. Richard writes, making another proposal: Eberle[3] as conductor and singers, etc., etc. Meanwhile, together with Richter, I draft a factual account of the situation. I am interrupted by Marie Muchanoff and Countess Bassenheim. Lively conversation, but no pleasure in it. After lunch the *A[ugsburger] A[llgemeine] Z[eitung]* with a shameful article about our affairs and ourselves personally. Really, how wretched these people are! Saying good night to the children, a lot of fun; they play 'dreams', and Boni is especially comical. When shall we return to our Tribschen peace?

Monday, September 13 R. comes up and says he has it in mind to reply to the article in yesterday's *A.A.Z.*, and in fact he drafts out his reply in the morning. Visit from Frl. Holmès, later arrival of the Mendèses! Much pleasure again in Judith. R. is so tired that he can do no more than quickly greet all these good people. – Hermine has returned.

Tuesday, September 14 Richter has left for Paris.

Wednesday, September 15 Long visit from Marie Muchanoff, thoroughly pleasant. She tells me that people blame the Jewish pamphlet on me, etc. Nice people!

Thursday, September 16 Yesterday a letter came from Italy, *Lohengrin* is to be performed in Bologna. – At midday R. reads me a note in the *A.A.Z.* which states that R.'s reply is so vehement that they hesitate to print it. We immediately guess that this is aimed at getting an order from the King to suppress the article. Great annoyance. What to do? Not a single weapon in our hands. R. very downcast.

Friday, September 17 A good day! In the morning a telegram that announces

---

[1] His letter to Wüllner contained the words, 'Hands off my score – that's my advice to you, sir, or may the devil take you! Beat time for glee clubs or amateur choirs.'

[2] Augusta Holmès, French pianist and composer.

[3] Ludwig Eberle, Berlin.

that the article has been printed after all! It looks splendid. Farewell visit to
Marie Muchanoff; she is kind and friendly.

Sunday, September 19 Coffee with Prof. Nietzsche; unfortunately he vexes
R. very much with an oath he has sworn not to eat meat, but only
vegetables. R. considers this nonsense, arrogance as well, and when the
Prof. says it is morally important not to eat animals, etc., R. replies that our
whole existence is a compromise, which we can only expiate by producing
some good. One cannot do that just by drinking milk – better, then, to
become an ascetic. To do good in our climate we need good nourishment,
and so on. Since the Prof. admits that Richard is right, yet nevertheless
sticks to his abstinence, R. becomes angry.

Thursday, September 23 Semper's theatre in Dresden completely burned
down. This made me think of Semper's unlucky star. His great genius
virtually unemployed, his works destroyed! – Following this news we
receive two telegrams reporting the performance of *Das Rheingold* in
Munich. So there it is – it is always the wicked who triumph. My only
consolation is R.'s words: 'I have the feeling that none of it really affects
me, inside I remain unscathed; only when I am not in complete harmony
with you does the ground tremble beneath me.' – In the evening a letter
from Claire. Maman has again become insane!

Friday, September 24 The *A.A.Z.* reports a *succès d'estime* for *Das Rheingold*;
the work is quite happily sacrificed, but the honour of the machinists,
costume designer, director, etc. is saved – on paper, at any rate. I said to
R. that Semper's theatre had gone up in flames in indignation.

Monday, September 27 Lovely day, finest blessings of autumn, I can work
with the children in the garden. In the evening more about *Das Rheingold* in
the newspaper – that it is a lavishly decorated, boring work! In the evening
a long conversation with R. about whether, without saying a word, he
should stop drawing his allowance. Or think only of the completion of the
Nibelungen and give up the fight. I tell him to do what best accords with his
inner feelings, with no thought for the possible consequences. Gnawing
worry for R. – is he now to sacrifice all his works in this way? Deep
melancholy; he says if I were not there it would be the end of him! – It
was my name day today, he gave me flowers, also my father sent a telegram
from Rome! – I can only keep silent.

Thursday, September 30 R. appears to be sketching out *Götterdämmerung*. In
the afternoon R. startles me by informing me that *Kladderadatsch*[1] has now
referred to me, too, and dealt with me in a vulgarly malicious way. (*Cosima
fan tutte.*) I had always maintained to him that *Kl.* would pass over things in
silence, since Dohm was a decent man. R. says I can now see how

---

[1] A satirical periodical in Berlin, whose editor, Ernst Dohm, had been a close friend of Hans and
Cosima von Bülow.

impossible it is for a person to remain decent when he happens to be a journalist.

Saturday, October 2 It says in the newspaper that public demand for *Das Rheingold* has already begun to fall off!! R. in the morning in melancholy mood, but recovered himself in the course of it so much that at midday he could tell me, 'I have something for you, something has arrived' – and then he showed me the beginning of the Norns' scene[1]. At lunch he suddenly says to me: 'No one in this world has proved his courage to me except you. People should at least show respect for that.' I have to reply that I never possessed courage, but only love, which I still have. I know, alas, only too well how slight my strength is!

Thursday, October 7 Birth of the second Stocker child. I assist Vreneli and am terribly moved by the sight of a creature coming into the world. Why are we so badly told in our youth what the world and life are like?

Friday, October 8 R. orchestrates a page of his *Siegfried.* After lunch the arrival of the birds he is presenting to Loulou gives us much, much delight. Unfortunately R. returns home from his walk in a bad humour, and in connection with a letter from Claire he calls me to account in a manner which soon arouses angry impatience in me, for I know quite well that I have never failed him in anything and have guarded his honour more jealously than my own. This impatience, so foreign to my nature, upsets me terribly, and as I write this, my whole body is trembling and quaking, and I feel torn to pieces.

Saturday, October 9 Of course R. realized that he had been unjust to me, and I that his irritability was only the result of the unpleasant impression Claire's letter had made on him (she urges me to be cautious about my marriage contract!). We have to fall into each other's arms without explanations – for anything which serves in the least to separate us is nonsense and madness.

Sunday, October 10 Quiet morning; we discuss peacefully and in detail the question which recently so upset us, and I write to Claire, asking her to attend to my little bit of business, namely to obtain for me the 40,000 francs my mother owes me, so that I can set it aside in an insurance company for the two elder children.

Tuesday, October 12 Lulu nine years old! Grand presentation of gifts – birds, a dress, all sorts of things; she is overjoyed. Children's party with puppet show (me!) and dancing. R. saddens me by claiming to have established through small, unimportant incidents that it would be better not to bring little girls together with boys. I almost reproach myself for having brought into his house as much disturbance as today, and intend to celebrate future birthdays in a different way. It also makes me melancholy that Hans did not send his child a greeting.

---

[1] The opening of *Götterdämmerung.*

Thursday, October 14 A letter from Claire, saying I shall probably not get my little bit of capital! Arrival of a picture of Beethoven – a present from the King of Bavaria. R. put in a very bad mood by it; first, his behaviour, and then this unusable gift.

Saturday, October 16 In the evening *Don Quixote*. R. remarks how C[ervantes]'s genius creates exactly like Nature, and he and Shakespeare belong among the poets in whom, as in Homer, one does not notice the art, while (for example) the Greek tragedies, Schiller, Calderón, seem like high priests, constructing their forms, as it were, out of a thought. The figure of Don Q. is a counterpart of Hamlet, he says, in regard to the mixture of the sublime with the ridiculous. And everything always human.

Monday, October 25 R. comes to breakfast with a letter from the King. All the old expressions of love and rapture, and with them a plea for pardon concerning his behaviour over *Das Rheingold* ('my longing was too great'). Then we read in the *Signale* that *Die Walküre* is being prepared in the Munich Court theatre; so much for the letter: it really is terrible! But we agree that R. is in fact living on his *Nibelungen*, he owes his existence to them, and so one really ought to thank God that a being such as the King has such curious fads in his head and truly wants to see and have the things, though indeed without being able to appreciate their sublimities. R. says: 'He cannot kill the work, I am the only one who can kill it, by breaking with him and not completing it. The fact that he is ruining things now will not detract from the impression when they are one day presented in the way I want, for people still have me to thank for *Tannhäuser* and *Lohengrin*. This great presentation does, however, depend in a general sense on cultural conditions, and if these are not achieved, not even the most consummate performances in Munich would be of any avail. All this is in the hands of Fate. But to reply to all the King's enthusiastic assurances is difficult.'

Friday, October 29 Letter from Dr. Hallwachs; the first legal deed concerning our divorce is on its way. Thick snow outside, much brightness indoors.

Monday, November 1 R. says he has decided to write to the King, saying he cannot write to him. He reads me his letter, which I should have liked to be severer still. During the day, great concern about Loulou and Boni, who have complained of my strictness. I feel shaken to my very soul – are my children really so estranged from me that they repay my love with resentment?

Thursday, November 4 Dreamed of taking leave of Hans; great melancholy. In the morning R. comes up to me, he is concerned about my health, then he says, 'What should we give the first people who congratulate us on our marriage?' I ask who they are. 'The Chaillous' – my tailors in Milan! We laugh. After that a letter from Claire informs me that my mother read the announcement of our marriage in *La Liberté*. I have to write to her, which

I find very uncongenial. 'Oh, your parents,' says R. jokingly, 'your dear papa
— it soon turns out that sitting down to a piano is rather different from
sitting down to life.' — After lunch R. says he wants to write me a letter, he
is too worried about my life, then he lights two candles and shows me a
colossal shotgun in the corner of his room. He will shoot himself with this,
he says, if I do not take care of myself. Much amusement over it, questions
as to where the shotgun came from. 'Well, that is a secret.'

Friday, November 5 A Paris newspaper announces our marriage in very
dignified phrases. R. laughs, embraces me, and says, 'Oh, yes, you are being
gossiped about with me.' Then he takes Siegfried in his arms and plays with
him for a long time; to me he says: 'We shall have to send Siegfried away;
when he is approaching manhood he will have to meet other people, to get
to know adversity, have fun, and misbehave himself; otherwise he will
become a dreamer, maybe an idiot, the sort of thing we see in the King of
Bavaria.' 'But where?' 'With Nietzsche — wherever Nietzsche is teaching —
and we shall watch from afar, as Wotan watches the education of Siegfried.
He will have free meals twice a week with Nietzsche, and every Saturday
we shall expect a report.'

Saturday, November 13 R. wants to write to the King again, to describe to
him all we have been through, then describe all he is to him, what he owes
to him, how without him he would never have been able to get down to
his work, and finally to ask him to have nothing performed for the time
being, to ignore the theatre completely for a while. I ask R. not to send it
yet. In the afternoon visit from Professor Nietzsche.

Sunday, November 14 In the evening R. and Prof. Nietzsche discuss the first
conceptions of language, which R. describes jokingly as talking primitive
philology. (Yesterday evening R. played us the beginning of the Norns'
scene.)

Monday, November 15 Much joy about a box arriving from Milan, R. loves
it best of all when I am wearing new clothes. When I come down to him
towards evening: 'The joy,' he says, 'when you come in like that; you look
like a child.'

Monday, November 22 In the afternoon a letter from the clergyman asking
me to visit his office with regard to my divorce. I decide to go, in order
not to cause any delay in this matter.

Tuesday, November 23 In the morning with R. to the lawyer with the
clergyman's letter, I am dissuaded from going to see him and give up the
intention with pleasure.

Wednesday, November 24 Letter from the lawyer, saying I shall have to
appear before the clergyman after all. In the afternoon some concern that
R. cannot be persuaded to curb his inclinations. (Recently he said *à propos*
of births or procreations, 'The time must be right, the position of the stars
right, that's how it was with me; that it didn't all turn out brilliantly you can

see in my restlessness and the fact that nothing much came of my brother Albert.'[1]

Friday, November 26 Cheerful atmosphere, R. again in working vein: 'At least the Norns' rope has now got into a tangle.'

Saturday, November 27 The Catholic party has won in Bavaria, they are talking of arraigning the ministry and appointing a guardian for the King. R. works on his 'Norns' Song'.

Sunday, November 28 Six years ago today R. came through Berlin, and then it happened that we fell in love; at that time I thought I should never see him again, we wanted to die together. – R. remembers it, and we drink to this day. In the evening I reflected on how love works on us like a Plutonian eruption, it bursts through everything, throws all strata into confusion, raises mountains, and there it is – utmost transformation and utmost law. In the morning R. told me he had always wanted to come to me; now, when he is working on his Brünnhilde, I am constantly before his eyes.

Monday, November 29 I heard something which made me truly glad. Pohl[2] told me that Dohm had fled to Weimar nine months ago because of his debts, so he is no longer editing *Kladderadatsch*. This proves that it was not *he* who permitted those nasty things to be printed about me; that was a relief. Abuse matters little, but what meant much to me was that someone whom I had always known and acknowledged to be a decent person had suddenly become vile.

Wednesday, December 1 R. tries to force himself into working, but it cannot be done, he is unwell, and on top of that we have to suffer the piano tuner. I with the children as usual. In the afternoon R. goes through the third act of *Siegfried* with Pohl. In the evening the biography. – Saying good night, I confess to R. that the presence of any other person makes me sad; everyone who is in touch with the world and brings news of it disturbs the quiet rhythm of our life here, or, rather, evokes a mood of melancholy in me.

Thursday, December 2 Departure of Dr. Pohl.

Tuesday, December 7 Work with the children, R. at his sketches, he complains of feeling constantly unwell. In the evening R. reads me [Laurence Sterne's] *Tristram Shandy*, in which the diatribes against solemnity give me much enjoyment, reminding me of those bigots the Schumannians. Spoke with R. about Mendelssohn. Comparison to a crystal: the *Hebrides* Overture so clear, so smooth, so melodious, as definite in form as a crystal, but also just as cold; such an enormous talent as Mendelssohn's is frightening, it has no place in the development of our music. A landscape painter, incapable of depicting a human being.

Thursday, December 9 In the evening *Tristram Shandy*. Talking of the bust of

[1] An actor-singer who became a stage manager after losing his singing voice.
[2] Richard Pohl, a writer on music and friend, who arrived on a visit on November 26.

[Wilhelmine] Schröder-Devrient[1], which always moves R., he tells me: She was no longer very respectable when I came into contact with her, but for such a person, with that formidable talent, there was only one possible compensation, and that was sensuousness; without this she would have been unable to bear it.

Saturday, December 11 Very nice letter to R. from Prof. N. – R. comes to my bed early in the morning to receive the orders of the day – if I am well, he says, he will dress luxuriantly. He works and is satisfied; in Brünnhilde's scene with Siegfried in *Götterdämmerung* none of the themes from the love scene reappear, because everything evolves out of the *mood*, not the underlying thought, and the mood here is different from that of the *heroic idyll* of *Siegfried*. Joy in the children, their jubilant hubbub on the stairs interrupts our table talk.

Sunday, December 12 R. completes the pencil sketch of the Prelude to *Götterdämmerung*. After tea continued with *Tristram Shandy*.

Monday, December 13 Christmas bits and pieces and work, R. laughs at my being so exclusively occupied with all this. He constantly working, on Siegfried and Brünnhilde as well as his essay.[2]

Wednesday, December 15 Vreneli gave me great pleasure today when she said, 'Now the master knows what he is working for', meaning me and Fidi [Siegfried]. The *Christkind*[3] came, a very poor girl from Bamberg; we intend to dress her nicely, so that she can summon the children after *Knecht Ruprecht*, and then give her presents too. R. works, I very weak; it looks as if my strength will never return, I must just take care that R. never notices how weak I feel. (Letter from Claire, saying my new marriage raises doubts about paying me my capital – whereas my proposal is that it should be invested for me there! Very pretty!)

Saturday, December 18 Arrival of the Order of Iftekhar from the Bey of Tunis, a large silver brooch, which R. immediately puts to use on the roof of the puppet theatre; he does not intend to acknowledge its receipt, since it is too ridiculous to be refused.

Monday, December 20 In the evening, looking at Fidi, R. says he has the glittering eyes of the Wälsungen;[4] that brings us on to *Götterdämmerung*; he shows me some lines in his composition notebook which Brünnhilde should sing in place of '*Selig in Leid und Lust*',[5] and in which the chorus should join; the burning of Siegfried's body to be done as a sort of ritual.

---

[1] Renowned dramatic soprano (1804–60), Wagner's idol and his first Adriano in *Rienzi*, Senta in *Der fliegende Holländer*, and Venus in *Tannhäuser*.
[2] 'On Conducting', which he had begun at the end of October.
[3] The *Christkind* (Christ child or infant Jesus) traditionally places the gifts under the Christmas tree; *Knecht Ruprecht* was in folklore Santa Claus's servant.
[4] The race fathered by Wotan on a mortal woman, i.e., Siegmund and Sieglinde and their son Siegfried.
[5] 'Blissful in joy and sorrow': Wagner's attempt to state through Brünnhilde the moral of the *Ring* at the end of *Götterdämmerung*.

But he has abandoned it – rightly – as not being stylistically in keeping with the whole. 'Such things as final choruses have no place in this work'. – In the evening much enjoyment with *Tristram Shandy*.

Wednesday, December 22 Did not sleep; the cook in Munich writes to Hermine that Hans has been enjoying himself in Florence, but has been ill.

Thursday, December 23 While gilding my apples I am given a letter from Counsellor Bucher[1]. It gave me much joy; I thought he belonged among that group of former friends who paid attention to the malicious things said about me. Now he has written in a friendly tone and with no other motive than to greet me on my birthday; since I think highly of him, I found this sign of life from him extremely welcome.

Friday, December 24 Busy with arrangements. I have painted all the names (of the complete household) and distributed them around the living room. Professor Nietzsche comes in the morning and helps me set up the puppet theatre with Iftekhar on it. R. rehearses *Knecht Ruprecht* and the *Christkindchen*. We begin. I, with the professor in the nursery, invite Loulou to recite 'The Fight with the Dragon', in order to exercize her mental powers; she says it up to 'Thou, lord, must know the chapel well', then Hermine comes in and says she can hear such roaring! Suddenly our *Knecht Ruprecht* appears and roars; terrible alarm among the children, R. gradually pacifies him, he scatters his nuts, cries of delight from the children. While they are picking them up, the *Christkindchen* appears, brilliantly illumined. In silence the whole household follows, I with the children in front; the *Christkindchen* beckons with the tree and wanders slowly down the stairs, disappearing through the gallery. The children, dazzled by the gleaming of the tree and the presents, do not notice the disappearance. After the present-giving I pray with the children in front of the extinguished tree. Professor Nietzsche's gift to me is the dedication of his lecture on Homer. (In the evening *Der bethlehemische Kindermord*[2].)

Saturday, December 25 Loldi came to me, R. had sent her in with a little volume of manuscripts and 32 pages of the printed biography. Very moved, particularly by the former, for R. certainly must have gone to much trouble in acquiring them. Tears. I tell the children that the dolls which gave them the most pleasure came from their father. Family lunch; afterwards read *Parzival* with Prof. Nietzsche, renewed feelings of awe. Then some sublime words from R. on the philosophy of music, which, it is to be hoped, he will write down. – Letter from Lenbach. In the evening passages from the biography. – R. still occupied with his essay on conducting. – Great tiredness.

---

[1] Lothar Bucher, German diplomat and close companion of Bismarck.
[2] A play by Wagner's stepfather, Ludwig Geyer.

1870

Monday, January 3 Have not written in this book for a whole week. Spent most of the time with Prof. Nietzsche, who left us yesterday. Today a letter from my mother, whose health is improving. On January 1, I received some money, which I took as a good omen. R. still very much occupied with his essay. We are now both tired.

Friday, January 7 To town for my money, then to Countess B., who tells me she knows the year will turn out well, since Richard visited her on the first day. – In the evening *Tristram Shandy*, pleasure alternating with dissatisfaction. Talent, but no genius.

Sunday, January 9 In the morning R. gets down again to his composing and sketches the opening to the prologue of *Götterdämmerung*. After lunch, Bayer, the lawyer, who gladdens R. greatly by telling him that once we are married the christening of Fidi will cause no difficulties at all. R. very happy, as if a burden had been lifted from him! In the evening finally laid *Tristram Shandy* aside with a feeling of aversion, and began on [Dante's] *Vita nuova* (pedantically mystical, says R.)

Monday, January 10 Letter from the King, still in the same old style. R. thinks he can use it as a pretext to beg him on no account to produce *Die Walküre* without R.'s aid, and he will suggest producing this as well as *Das Rheingold* for him. When I tell him I would not be able to attend the performances, he says: Then on no account.

Tuesday, January 11 All five unwell today, coughs, colds, etc., great concern. R. also unwell, forces himself to work. When he again says that he finds it unthinkable to produce a work without my being there, I kiss his hand in deep emotion, upon which he laughs and says, 'Now one gets praised for a law of Nature.' In the evening read with R. the letters of his stepfather Geyer, very moved by them. R. says, 'He sacrificed himself for us.'[1]

Wednesday, January 12 Read in the newspaper that the King has commanded *Die Walküre*. A great shock, the urge to resume work utterly killed.

Friday, January 14 Lusch tells me that she dreamed of her father and felt

---

[1] Ludwig Geyer (1778–1821) was an actor, dramatist and portrait painter, who married Wagner's mother fifteen months after Wagner's birth. He was thus the only 'father' Wagner ever knew, and he held him in great affection.

such joy at his arrival that she almost fell out of the window. I feel glad that I am succeeding in keeping her feelings for her father alive. R. works and, when I return home, gives me the first pencilled pages of *Götterdämmerung*, with which I consecrate the little bureau in the corner.

Monday, January 17 Letter from my mother, good and friendly; worked with the children while R. was revising his 'Norns' Song' for the second sketch.

Wednesday, January 19 R. tells me that last night he dreamed he had been a minister at the court of Queen Anne of England and had quarrelled with a Lord Evans (Aha, R. had thought to himself, he doesn't yet know who I am, he still thinks I am a musician!) Much amusement from his description; R. then tells me how happy he is with me, because of me. 'Yes, if only I knew of just a single person who could be in the least compared with you – of whom I could say: "Ah, that was the first draft, that has been brought to fruition in C." The only things I fear are change and illness. I do not appreciate anywhere near enough how happy I am. I do not enjoy it nearly enough. I never want to leave this house again.' How I thank God for this happiness! Who could estimate what such words do to my heart? In the afternoon the three children downstairs, Loldi says, 'The wind talks so much.' –

Thursday, January 20 A letter to Lusch from her father, he was touched by our Christmas festivities.

Friday, January 21 R. at his spinning loom, I with the children; R. pleased with his work: 'It sounds like the fluttering of night birds; everything depends on impressions of Nature, and here in the Norns' scene I can see the tall fir tree near the rock and hear the nocturnal rustling.' After lunch he plays the Norns' scene to me, an inexpressible delight.

Saturday, January 22 At lunch R. informs me that he has received a letter from the lawyer, from which it seems the divorce is being held up; Hans has given no sign of life, and his presence in Berlin is required to complete the matter. I write to Hans's lawyer. Concern that Hans might be upset. I am willing to bear the wretched situation into which I have brought myself, and even the difficulties which arise for Fidi out of the uncertainties, as payment for my priceless happiness! Then I wrote to E[mile] Ollivier[1], who has been attacked in the most despicable manner in the Lower Chamber; thus he will not think it is his advancement which has tempted me to approach him again.

Sunday, January 23 Children's games day! R. calls me the good old mother hen; and truly my whole day is spent in entertaining the children. Only during the afternoon do I take up [Beethoven's] *Eroica* with R.; at one point

---

[1] Cosima's brother-in-law (her dead sister Blandine's husband) was now heading the French government.

in the first movement he gets to his feet, much moved: 'The only mortal who can be compared with Shakespeare!' In the evening he reads me passages from Schopenhauer on love ('Kant spoke of it without practical knowledge'). R. thought it might perhaps repel me, but, on the contrary, I am very moved and uplifted. – R. says, 'Love without children is a sham.' The final essay on conducting arrived today in print.

Monday, January 24 R. reads something to me, for we had a great fright. Fidi fell from the sofa with a loud bump. R. in great agitation; Boni, who was there, laughs; afterwards I ask her why, she says the way he snatched his cap from his head (she shows how). We all laughed a lot, and R. pointed out to me that one must always be gentle with children, for they very seldom poke fun vindictively, but simply yield to immediate impressions.

Tuesday, January 25 Letter from Düfflipp; R.'s suggestions have not been accepted. *Die Walküre* will be performed. Great anguish. At lunch, after having tried in vain to force himself to work, R. says: 'If I did not have you, I should not know why I am on earth at all. I think I should go mad – on the one hand unable to be other than one is, on the other, being not at all to the world's liking.'

Saturday, January 29 Our lawyer comes to see us, he thinks that Simson, the lawyer in Berlin[1], is delaying the divorce out of malice.

Monday, January 31 In the afternoon a visit from the old Prince[2]. He speaks of his childhood – he has served under three Bavarian kings – his father a reigning prince, and now he ends up in Lucerne. R. in agitated mood, much in his sketch is not yet as he wants it. 'I am no composer,' he says, 'I wanted only to learn enough to compose *Leubald und Adelaïde*[3]; and that is how things have remained – it is only the subjects which are different.'

Thursday, February 3 Letters from Prof. N. enclosing his lecture on Socrates[4]. In the evening R. reads me the lecture, which we find very stimulating. 'Beloved music', Socrates's dream, brings R. back to the subject of the musical theme. 'How much more significant does such a theme appear than any spoken thought! Schopenhauer is right: music is a world in itself, the other arts only express a world.'

Saturday, February 5 For R. a lively awakening to work, I with the children. Siegfried's passage down the Rhine, signalled by the extensive theme of the Rhinemaidens, who are glad of his arrival, puts us in fine spirits. R. talks about the song of Siegfried and Brünnhilde, '*O heil 'ge Götter*', and says to me: 'If you only knew what it brought back to my mind! In Magdeburg[5], at the end of a gay Auber overture, my poodle, which had been waiting

---

[1] August Simson was Hans von Bülow's lawyer.
[2] Prince Ludwig zu Öttingen-Wallerstein, Countess Bassenheim's father.
[3] Wagner's first attempt, at the age of 15, to write a full scale drama.
[4] 'Socrates and Tragedy'.
[5] Wagner was conductor in Magdeburg in 1834.

outside for me, came into the orchestra, ran to the bassoon, and sat there quite still, but then he suddenly let out a loud note of lament. Everybody laughed; it affected me terribly, and I can always hear that melancholy song above the merry orchestra.'

Monday, February 7 When I go to R., he plays me the Gibichungs' theme, which came to him in such a clear-cut form that he wrote in down in ink immediately. Great delight in it; conversation about these characters Gunther and Hagen, the latter repulsively mysterious, impassive, curt. On long-lost naïveté: 'All these heroes appeared to me like a gathering of animals, lions, tigers, etc.; they also devour one another, but there is no disgusting convention, court etiquette, etc., mixed up in it – everything is naïve.'

Saturday, February 12 In the afternoon, as we are playing Beethoven symphonies in the old piano-duet arrangements, Prof. Nietzsche arrives. Lengthy conversation about his lecture. Then R. plays us passages from Mozart's *Entführung* and *Figaro*. When Prof. N. remarks that Mozart is said to have invented the music of intrigue, R. replies that, on the contrary, he resolved intrigue in melody. One has only to compare Beaumarchais's (incidentally excellent) play with Mozart's opera to see that the former contains cunning, clever and calculating people who deal and talk wittily with one another, while in Mozart they are transfigured, suffering, sorrowing human beings.

Sunday, February 13 Spent the morning with Prof. Nietzsche, talked of many things. He tells me that Dorn, the conductor[1], has published a book whose whole purpose is simply to denigrate R. I beg Prof. N. to say nothing to R. about it. Lunch with the children. Prof. N.'s departure. – How solitary R. is in this world!

Monday, February 14 R. again at work; fine weather, sleigh ride, a landscape of sugar candy and marzipan. When we return home, a letter from Claire, saying Mama has told her Hans does not want a divorce – this she heard through Mme Ollivier[2]. Besides this, many unpropitious things about my mother. I write to them both and struggle against bitter feelings.

Wednesday, February 16 In the morning went by sleigh into town with Loldi. After lunch the lawyer – he is to write to Florence. The advocate is of the opinion that matters have now gone so far that the whole thing could in fact be settled today or tomorrow. R.'s great annoyance.

Thursday, February 17 Eva's birthday; the 'tune' is played. Great joy among the little ones. After lunch children, fancy-dress party. In the evening a letter from Prof. Nietzsche, which pleases us, for his mood had given us cause for concern. Regarding this, R. says he fears that Schopenhauer's

---

[1] Heinrich Dorn had been musical director in Riga when Wagner was conductor there in 1839.

[2] Emile Ollivier's second wife.

philosophy might in the long run be a bad influence on young people of this sort, because they apply his pessimism, which is a form of thinking, contemplation, to life itself, and derive from it an active form of hopelessness.

Friday, February 18 Today, children, I committed a grave wrong; I offended our friend, and since this is something I wish never to do again, regarding it as the blackest of sins, I use this instance to identify the pitifulness of our human nature. We were speaking of Beethoven's C. Minor Symphony, and I wilfully insisted on a tempo which I felt to be right. That astonished and offended R., and now we are both suffering – I for having done it, he for having experienced wilfulness at my hands. After lunch with the children to Countess Bassenheim, whose hard lot and excellent disposition always touch me.

Saturday, February 19 R. cheerful again; he tells me, 'All I now have in this world is my love for you, that is why, when the least discord arises between us, everything ends for me.' Wrote to L. Bucher and requested him to visit Hans's lawyer, to find out from him what is holding up the divorce.

Sunday, February 20 R. well, working. Children's day, I play, read, sing with them. In the evening, when I give a mock dinner for them, R. plays, amid great delight, [Rossini's] *Gazza Ladra* Overture. Then, for ourselves, we take up Luther's hymn[1] in a cantata by Bach, '*Das Wort sie sollen lassen stahn.*' R. as always greatly moved by it. 'A people which can produce such a thing is a people worthy of respect, and a Jew makes a French opera out of it – that says everything.' And yet – say I – it is these very sounds, desecrated and ignorantly distorted, which have made that opera into a success. 'And Bach is Luther,' R. went on. 'Just look at the calm way in which he writes the boldest, most daring of things.'

Thursday, February 24 Great excitement in the juvenile world – today is the Fritschi procession[2]! We drive to the Hôtel du Lac, have a meal, and from there watch the very pretty procession. In the afternoon R. brings me from the post office a letter from my friend L. Bucher, who assures me that Simson, the lawyer, is an honest man, then a letter from Hans to our lawyer – he intends to go to Berlin at the end of March. It moves me terribly, I can scarcely look at the handwriting. God preserve you, my children, from such emotions!

Sunday, February 27 Sudden arrival of Heinrich Porges[3], who tells us many ridiculous things about musical conditions in Munich. *Tannhäuser* under the 'bungler' Wüllner is said to have been utterly unrecognizable. – Since R. was a trifle vexed, he says, 'Music making makes everyone either stupid or

---

[1] '*Ein' feste Burg*'; Meyerbeer used it in his opera *Les Huguenots.*
[2] Carnival procession held annually in Lucerne.
[3] One of the young disciples (b. 1837) Wagner invited to join him in Munich, writer on music and chorus master.

malicious.' In the evening H. Porges reads us his essay about *Lohengrin*, which contains many very good things.

Tuesday, March 1 R. asks Porges in the manner of Socrates the meaning of the philosophical expressions with which his essay is unfortunately heavily larded. Nothing much emerges from P.'s answers, so then R. explains to him how it is that the Holy Grail can be regarded as freedom. Renunciation, repudiation of the will, the oath of chastity separate the Knights of the Grail from the world of appearances. The knight is permitted to break his oath through the condition which he imposes on the woman – for, if a woman could so overcome a natural propensity as not to ask, she would be worthy of admission to the Grail. It is the possibility of this salvation which permits the knight to marry. The Knight of the Grail is sublime and free because he acts, not on his own behalf, but for others.

Thursday, March 3 I discuss some matters from the past with Heinrich Porges. He makes me very happy by telling me that he has never seen R. so tranquil and so lively as he is now; he is convinced that R. would never have taken up his *Nibelungen* again if this great change in his life had not occurred. This affects me so much that I have to weep. When I tell this to R.: 'Nothing, not a single new note would I ever have produced if I had not found you. Now I have a life to live.'

Saturday, March 5 In the evening *Die Walküre*. When we subsequently talk of the production of these works, I tell R. he should look up the article on *Baireuth* in the encyclopaedia; R. had mentioned this place as the one he would choose. To our delight we read in the list of buildings of a splendid old opera house!

Sunday, March 6 An army doctor in Brunswick has sent some fine sausages! We laugh a lot, for some days ago – thinking of the sausage which Richter brought us when he was looking for a singer for Walther von Stolzing – we had said, 'We shall never find such a sausage again.' This time it is for *Lohengrin*. In return R. sends his portrait with a little verse at the bottom. After lunch *Die Walküre*, in the evening as well (Wotan's scene with Fricka and Brünnhilde). R. says: 'You can understand that I felt the need, after writing these parts of the *Nibelungen*, to leave this element of dreadfulness and to write *Tristan und Isolde* which was, so to speak, just a love scene; indeed, I thought of it as an Italian opera, that is to say, to be sung by Italian singers – and in Rio de Janeiro.'[1]

Tuesday, March 8 R. continues work on his '*Höllendämmerung*' (as the newspapers call it);[2] I with the children. Towards noon a letter arrives from Herr Wesendonck, which makes an unpleasant impression on R. as well as

[1] In 1857, while working on *Siegfried*, Wagner was approached by the Brazilian consul in Leipzig with an invitation from Emperor Dom Pedro II to stage his works in Italian in Rio de Janeiro, and he thought of writing *Tristan* for production there; nothing came of it, however.
[2] 'Twilight of Hell'.

on me. Around Christmas R. had asked him for copies of papers in the family's possession, and instead they sent back the originals. Embarrassed by this, R. wanted to give something in return, and sent the printed proofs of the biography with a long letter explaining its significance. To this Herr W. now replies so clumsily, advising him not to proceed with it in such minute detail, etc., that R. is greatly vexed.

Thursday, March 10 Great alarm at the news, given to R. by Porges, that Düfflipp has written to Hans and asked him to accelerate the divorce! Obviously they cannot cope in Munich with *Die Walküre*, and the King is wishing that R. might return to Munich. Hence this letter, which may perhaps – in view of Hans's character – ruin things for us entirely! I write at once to Düfflipp, expressing my indignation, and send a copy of this letter to *Hans* through my lawyer. – Porges departs; obviously he came with the idea of being chosen by R. to conduct *Die Walküre*.

Monday, March 14 In the *Musikalische Zeitung* there is a report on the performance of *Die Msinger* in Vienna. Among other things the J[ews] are spreading a story around that 'Beckmesser's Song' is an old Jewish song which R. was trying to ridicule. In consequence, some hissing in the second act and calls of 'We don't want to hear any more,' but complete victory for the *Germans*. R. says, 'That is something none of our fine historians of culture notice: that things have reached the stage of Jews' daring to say in the imperial theatre, "We do not want this." '

Tuesday, March 15 R. in cheerful mood, gets down to Siegfried's arrival, which has caused him a lot of work. He did not wish to make something very spectacular out of it, and he has assumed that the introduction will have set the basic mood, that we will know that Siegfried is on the Rhine and that the talk of the Gibichungs is just a parenthesis.

Friday, March 18 Letter from Councillor Düfflipp, saying it is not true that he wrote to Hans about the divorce; God knows who is telling lies.

Tuesday, March 22 Letter to me from Secretary Düfflipp; more *Walküre* machinations, deplorable. R. replies to it, again summarizing his whole life in Munich and simply asking the King at least to have *Die Walküre* performed *privatim*. I write to him as well and finish by considering and summarizing the whole Munich past. I also tell the secretary what a great artistic flowering could mean for Bavaria *now*, when everything is crumbling and chaotic.

Wednesday, March 23 In the morning a letter from the lawyer; Hans is now on his way to Berlin; but he is required to spend a month or two there, and he says he has to be back in Florence on May 1. Well, as God wills.

Friday, March 25 Letter from C. Mendès; success of *Lohengrin* [in Brussels] quite enormous; Richter summoned to the royal box, presented with a golden laurel wreath, etc. Biggest success the second act. Also a letter from a lecturer at the University of Vienna, which says that all the scholars and the whole of Vienna's student body are on the side of *Die Msinger*, whereas the Jews are showing violent opposition.

Thursday, March 31 After lunch with the children, arrival of Richter, who tells us all about the difficulties of his time in Brussels. – Music in the evening; R. plays what he has already composed of *Götterdämmerung*. How happy I feel to be no longer personally of any consequence, deriving my pleasure solely from R.'s good progress and the children's well-being! Richter thinks the children are looking very well.

Friday, April 1 The music so affected me that I could not close my eyes for an instant. I feel extremely weak and 'my mind' is only good for pulling the educational cart (R. told me about a Saxon peasant who once said to him: This dog has *no mind*, he will never pull a cart). In the morning a very nice letter from Frau Dr. Wille,[1] to whom R. sent his pamphlet. She speaks about me in a kind and friendly manner. R. says: 'Why are we so pleased? Is it because we have received some of this kindness, or because it is a revenge for us, or something of that sort? No, certainly not – it is just unalloyed pleasure in a friend who is good and worthy of respect.' – Letter from the theatre manager in Magdeburg: he was present at the dress rehearsal of *Die Meistersinger* in Berlin, the King, the entire Court, and royal guests had been there, the impact profound. – But we learn nothing about the performance.

Saturday, April 2 Telegram from Frau Schleinitz[2]; she speaks of tendentious opposition which is being totally annihilated. I sent our good Richter off with hopes for the future of our Bayreuth venture. Richter told us the King has already appointed his stableboys for the Valkyries, whereas R. wants them to be depicted just as hazy images!

Monday, April 4 Bad start to the day with a letter from H. Porges, who actually wants to arrange discussions between R. and Herr von Perfall about *Die Walküre*. Sorrowful conversation with R. about this. How will it all end? – Children in the garden, I embroider. After lunch R. takes my head in his hands and says, 'You are my last support, my only support.' – Letter from Herr von Gersdorff[3] in Berlin about *Die Msinger*, as in Vienna, Beckmesser's serenade was the cue for the hissers, who were completely crushed, however.

Tuesday, April 5 Still worrying about *Die Walküre*; what to do, what to say, and how to find the will to work in such an atmosphere? R. forces himself,

[1] Eliza Wille (b. 1809), British-born wife of German journalist François Wille, was a friend of the Zurich years, and it was to their estate, Mariafeld, that Wagner fled from Vienna just prior to his 'rescue' by King Ludwig; she was a novelist.
[2] Marie, Baroness von Schleinitz (b. 1842), whose husband Alexander (b. 1807) was Prussian Minister of the Royal Household; a close friend of Cosima, she was to become one of the leading lights in the founding of the Bayreuth festival.
[3] Karl von Gersdorff (b. 1844), a close friend of Nietzsche, but still unknown to Wagner and Cosima at this time.

but with no enjoyment. R. reads in the paper that Hans has given a concert in Milan. Long letter from Councillor Düfflipp: R. should come, but in a *conciliatory* spirit! We go out in splendid weather, encounter close to the house an unknown priest, it is the papal nuncio; concern about Fidi's unchristened state. R. replies to D. in the evening, very calmly and clearly: they must do what they can. Prolonged contemplation (yesterday) of a sunset over the mountains, a lively breeze whipping up the blue lake, the peaks glowing serenely; thus our love amid the world's turmoil, it will glow until death.

Thursday, April 7 R. works and is pleased in the evening; he has completed the Oath and is satisfied. 'The difficulty,' he says, 'was to avoid bringing a new tempo into the scene, everything has to be continuous, but all the same it had to seem significant, like a heavy thundercloud.' He has succeeded wonderfully. 'Dear indispensability,' he called me today – how sweet it is for me to hear what I already know: that he loves me!

Friday, April 8 Letter from Heinrich Porges apologizing for the *Walküre* intervention.

Sunday, April 10 Letter from Richter, who has seen my father in Munich and will travel with him to Hungary. Besides that, horrifying accounts of the artistic state of Munich; but *Die Walküre* is being worked on – by painters and machinists. R. is not well and cannot work, he confines himself to correcting the proofs of his biography.

Wednesday, April 13 In the *A.A.Z.* there is a report on the musical situation in Florence; in it Hans is much praised, and it is said that he has been invited to conduct the Beethoven centennial concerts in Milan. R. writes a poem for the King (*dernier effort!*), he feels it will do good to address him in this way. – Start on *Oedipus at Colonus*.

Thursday, April 14 Working and lunch with the children. Discussion of the letter received yesterday from Const[antin] Frantz[1] concerning *Die Msinger* in Berlin, for which R. had given him a ticket. The letter is anything but pleasing, he thinks it a pity there is so little for the barrel organ in it! Yet I am glad that it came, since he informs me that Daniel's grave is being cared for. To town with R. to fetch Easter eggs. In the morning I say I should be glad to hear old Italian church music as before: 'That will be done in our school in Bayreuth.' 'But in this school,' I say, 'the piano must not be taught, the students must be able to play the piano only well enough to become good musicians, but they will get no training in it in our school, otherwise virtuosity will stifle everything.' 'You are right,' says R., 'but how bold you are!'

Friday, April 15 I discuss with R. my hope that Hans might feel contented in Florence, since he found Germany so uncongenial and Munich in

---

[1] A German political writer of federalist views; he visited Wagner at Tribschen in 1866.

particular insufferable. – Not much joy from outside, our young children are our only consolation and support; but for them, I think, we should be willing to die. 'People imagined all sorts of things about our union, but that it was the result of a tremendous love and that our finding each other was no mere accident – that scarcely seems to occur to anybody.' – R. today in gloomy mood, because he was disturbed during his work and is making no progress. (It is Siegfried's departure with Gunther.) 'At such times,' he says, 'one feels one will never be able to do it.'

Sunday, April 17 Easter joys, Easter sorrows, and dressed Easter lamb. I conceal the eggs and then have to retire, because I feel worn out by even this little exertion. R. comes to me and says, ' "Hagen's Watch" will be colossal.' Towards noon he plays me the glorious piece he has just composed. Letter to R. from the conductor [Gustav] Schmidt in Leipzig, who says that for him, after hearing *Die Ms.* in Berlin, it is no longer just a question, but a duty to art and the public to stage the work in Leipzig. – I had just written to M. Maier when R. tells me she has written to him with news of Hans's distressed condition in Florence, conveyed to her by his mother and sister. I can hardly believe that this is true, for all reports maintain the contrary, but my peace of mind is again shattered.

Thursday, April 21 R. has received a letter from Councillor Düfflipp saying that the King was unpleasantly surprised by his last letter and asks him to choose Heinrich Porges after all. Our *Non possumus* to this. Then R. completes 'Hagen's Watch'.

Friday, April 22 Letter from an unknown enthusiast in Berlin (Lieutenant Schöning); he says the management in Berlin has put *Die Msinger* aside until the autumn, so that passions will have time to cool. Great consternation about this – it means a few Jewboys have achieved their aim. R. is at first depressed, but he soon recovers his spirits, and we enjoy a splendid afternoon in the garden, Fidi beside us!

Sunday, April 24 Overcast weather, spring rain; R. in dull spirits because of it. He writes to Düfflipp to tell him that he feels no bitterness, and his only wish is that the King might get some enjoyment from *Die Walküre*. I am very much alarmed by some of the expressions in this letter, and that in turn worries R. I quickly get a grip on myself – I must remember that for me every sorrow is a blessing and my task is above all not to upset R. Then a happy lunch with the children. But concern hangs heavily over us.

Monday, April 25 Go out after lunch with R., he tells me that in his youth he always dreaded spring, for it meant the theatres would be empty, the audience absent, the poor musical director shown the door. As he is telling me this, a man appears and hands me a court summons. If I do not return to Berlin within four weeks, proceedings for divorce will be inaugurated. Only inaugurated! – In the morning R. sent off a different letter to Councillor Düffl., though I begged him to send the first. But the later one seems to me more suited to both the situation and the man. Letter from Schmidt, the musical director in Leipzig; fee for *Die Msinger.*

Tuesday, April 26 R. began the day with a conversation about the Greek attitude towards love, which we cannot ourselves envisage and which, when it did not degenerate into depravity, produced the highest qualities of aestheticism. 'The adoration of women, on the other hand, is a completely new factor, and one which divides us entirely from the antique world. The ancient Germans respected women as something mysterious, closer to Nature – rather in the way the Egyptians worshipped animals – and, in order to preserve their divinity intact, did not wish to touch them. What this cult has led to today, whereby women since chignons and *bibi* hats have demanded to be adored and from which they derive all this emancipation nonsense – that we already know.' – He goes to work again, for the first time in many days.

Thursday, April 28 Letter from the conductor Levi. ('I respect him,' says R., 'because he really calls himself *Levi* as in the Bible, and not Löwe, Lewy, etc.') He says he has been invited to conduct *Die Walküre,* and he asks for R.'s opinion. R. replies calmly and honestly. – I concerned about I know not what, but happy. I asked R. whether he no longer wrote things down, no diary? 'No, that has stopped, now I enjoy my happiness. I swear to you I am amazed at myself when I see that none of my old confidence has left me, my imagination is perhaps even improved, with the constant urge to create. Whom have I to thank for this?' 'The King of Bavaria,' I interpose jokingly. 'Aha, that is your answer to my recent letter. Believe me, I should have wearily dropped his favour if I had not found you.' – Yesterday, when he was surprised not to have received a letter from Hanover, I said our friend von Bronsart[1] was probably shocked by our relationship. After some reflection he said, 'That people cannot see that we knew exactly what we were doing, since after all I am no trickster and you also had sufficient knowledge of the world; that we braved everything and took it on ourselves in order to belong to each other, that should surely fill them with respect.' 'When I have brought the children up nicely and you have finished the *Nibelungen,* then perhaps we shall be respected.' – In the evening read [Scott's] *Ivanhoe* with great admiration.

Saturday, April 30 Colds, wretched weather, but R. works and finishes the intermezzo ('Hagen's Watch' – Brünnhilde contemplating the ring), which, as he says, is more a sort of cadenza, like a parenthesis, not an intermezzo. Letter from Herr *Simson* in Berlin: in four weeks I must present myself to the priest, and then the proceedings will begin. Hans has returned to Florence.

Wednesday, May 4 At lunch it cuts me to the quick when he says that in

---

[1] Hans Bronsart von Schellendorf, a pupil of Liszt and director of the opera in Hanover.

the excitement of work he has often wanted to come up to me, but, knowing that I was busy teaching the children, he stayed away. He said I should really engage a governess for the children. I have to weep, for I feel I have to make this sacrifice, yet how much I want him always to be contented! Letter to R. from the King in the usual strain – that he could never be unfaithful to him, etc.

Saturday, May 7 We get on the topic of Berlioz's memoirs, which he is now reading. 'In him one can so clearly see the reciprocity between natural inclinations and external conditions and relationships. Everything in Paris is horrible to him, and yet he cannot give it up – this horribleness is for him the whole world. His main grief was opera, which he could never master.' – R. says that Berlioz's memoirs have strengthened his resolve never again to have anything to do with Paris. In the evening began on [Plato's] *Phaedo*.

Sunday, May 8 Nice but pale weather. R. works, I to a rehearsal of the '*Huldigungsmarsch*'[1] at the barracks. God knows how this will turn out, perhaps my star will help me, but I am somewhat nervous.

Tuesday, May 10 Arrival of Prof. Nietzsche's speech in Latin, then of a lovely spring outfit which R. had ordered for me as a surprise! – When I come down to R. in the afternoon, he plays me a piece he has just thought out, 'Blackbird Theme, Scherzo in the Beethoven Manner' – he copied it from our blackbird. 'When I hear something like that, I call it quite simply a Beethoven allegro, meaning that he is the creator of this form, he is the master, without him it would not exist.' 'How I should like now to write poetry!' he says. 'What easy, swift work – what is it compared with writing scores? It is the skeleton, like bare branches, the tree in winter; music is the blossom, the leaves.' Music in the evening. He plays me passages from the first act of *Götterdämmerung*. – He then complains of the difficulty of the scene between Waltraute and Brünnhilde, the one in agitated haste, the other expansively moved that a friend has come to visit her.

Friday, May 13 The Beethoven Committee in Vienna invites R. to conduct the 9th Symphony (Lachner *Fidelio*, my father the *Missa Solemnis*); R. does not want to: 'When I at last have a home of my own, I shall conduct the Symphony for you, but I want nothing to do with all that rabble.'

Sunday, May 15 Very seemly letter from the conductor Levi, who has refused to conduct *Die Walküre*. Gloriously fine day; burning sunshine; to the sounds of Fidi's 'Dadadada' R. sketches part of Waltraute's narration (he 'sends off the ravens'). Family lunch in the best of spirits. – Visit from our lawyer, who does not understand the procedure in Berlin and cannot at all foresee when it will end.

Monday, May 16 If only we could curb passion – if only it could be

---

[1] March written by Wagner in 1864 in honour of King Ludwig II.

banished from our lives! Its approach now grieves me, as if it were the death of love.

Friday, May 20 I prepare Lusch to release the birds given to her on her birthday; it costs her a great struggle, but she decides to keep birds only in winter and to free them in summer. How much I praise the star which has allowed the children to pass their youth in this solitary place and in R.'s proximity! None of life's battles, no anguish will ever be able to affect this felicity. – After lunch, when we are reading *Wallenstein*, Jakob comes in struggling for breath: the King's coachman is here, has brought a horse. The arrival of Grane, the children's joy, Thespis wagon (the little ones jump on to the wagon and dance). Poor Fritz![1] The coachman brings good news of the King. Happy walk with R. in the evening in the finest May weather. Fidi on the horse, earnest, wondering, but secure.

Saturday, May 21 Awake at four o'clock, rise at 4.30 and write a poem for Loulou to speak while freeing her birds tomorrow. Did the children's hair and made further preparations. Letters from R.'s old acquaintance and companion in misery, E. Kietz[2], who wants to visit him. Arrival of the certificates of baptism. I drive to the rehearsal – as far as I can judge, the piece is going well.

Sunday, May 22 During the night decorated the stairs and the vestibule, but I note by my mood that I am no longer up to festive occasions, and now, even before the day begins, here I sit, writing this and weeping. God grant my children joy today; whoever has suffered much loses the capacity to laugh. On festive days in particular one realizes how sad life is! The unremarked passing of days without unspoken fears is surely the best thing for sore hearts. God bless all whom I love, and give me rest soon! – The pleasure R. felt soon swept my melancholy mood away. At eight o'clock I positioned the children with wreaths of roses: Loldi and Eva at the front door; farther down in the bower, beneath a laurel, Boni; at the bottom of the steps, beside the bust loaded down with flowers, myself and Fidi; at the end of the tableau Loulou. The music ('*Huldigungsmarsch*') began at 8.30, the 45 soldiers grouped under the fir tree, at the conclusion R. emerged sobbing from the house and thanked the conductor; he was deeply moved, making me almost regret having arranged this little ceremony. Afterwards the children recited poems to him, we breakfasted in gay spirits and then went off to rest. In the afternoon the birds were to be released and some fireworks lit, but a huge storm came up and we ended the day quietly. Many letters and telegrams (King, Richter, Standhartner[3], etc.), a nice letter from Prof. Nietzsche. A telegram from my father ('Forever with you, on bright as on gloomy days') pleased and moved me greatly.

---

[1] Wagner's aging carriage horse.
[2] The painter Ernst Benedikt Kietz, Wagner's friend in Paris, 1840–42.
[3] Joseph Standhartner (b. 1818), a physician whom Wagner met in Vienna in 1852 and who remained one of his most loyal friends.

Monday, May 23 Long sleep; then the delayed festivities. Arrival of the playpen designed by Hans, I put Fidi in it, the children gather around it, Loulou recites her poem in front of the cage, then we carry the cage into the garden; four of the birds fly away immediately; only a single chaffinch remains behind, unwilling to follow the calls of its brethren; for fear that the cat might get it, I tell Jakob to take it out and give it to Loulou to place on a bush; this is done, but probably the shock numbed it, for it flew, not upwards, but downwards, and Jakob's dog, which we had not even noticed, pounced on it – it was dead. Thus this little festival of joy ended in tragedy, the poor bird had sensed its coming death. What a grim lesson – how wretched the human being's pitiful good intentions in relation to Fate! The finch had to pay with its life for the freedom of its brethren. – I write to Prof. Nietzsche; after lunch, first drive with Grane to Stanz. In the evening our fireworks. Alluding to the morning serenade, R. calls me the conductor of his life.

Wednesday, May 25 Arrival of two pineapples from Paris, we suspect Judith. Richter reports that Wüllner is to conduct *Die Walküre* in Munich!! Arrival of flowers, the King has sent them. In the evening R. remarks that Fidi has literally blossomed in the open air; in the morning he had been so small, in the afternoon in the garden he was strong – 'that is how we see it, anyway.' I: 'If we see it, then it must be so, for what brings about change in us will also affect the child.' 'That is just the problem,' R. replies and, going on from there, explains to me the nature of Schopenhauer's Will (from Brahma to Buddha), 'the urge towards life, then towards knowledge, and finally towards destruction. Remorse – that is to say, the knowledge that inside us something lives which is much more powerful than our idea of evil.' R. spoke for a long time, beautifully and movingly, and I felt as if through him I were penetrating into the secrets of the world, but only through him.

Sunday, May 29 At lunch we spoke of the need to possess Shakespeare in English, Walter Scott, too; regarding the latter, it suddenly occurs to R. that he covered the whole of English history in his novels, except for the period Shakespeare dealt with. – A murder case which is filling the newspapers (the entire family of an inoffensive smith murdered by a thief) reminds us of the terrible fate which governs us all. It is not the murder itself which fills us with horror, but the fearful lot which can be meted out to any one of us. Vreneli tells us she heard in the town that a boat had been sucked into the paddle of the steamer, and the man and child in it killed; our people in Tribschen heard the screams of the passengers on the steamer. With such warnings, such signs, who can call himself fortunate here below? – Conversation at supper brings us to Mozart. Dealing with *Die Zauberflöte*, R. says, 'Mozart is the founder of German declamation – what fine humanity resounds in the Priest's replies to Tamino! Think how stiff such high priests are in Gluck. When you consider this text, which was meant to be a farce, and the theatre for which it was written, and compare what was written before Mozart's time (even Cimarosa's still-famous *Matrimonio Segreto*) – on the one side the wretched German *Singspiel*, on the other the ornate Italian opera – one is amazed by the soul he managed to breathe into such a text. And what a life he led! A bit of tinsel at the time of his popularity, but for that he had then to pay all the more dearly. He did not complete his work, which is why one cannot really compare him with Raphael, for there is still too much convention in him.'

Tuesday, May 31 In the morning R. receives me wearing a tail coat and a stand-up collar – 'since you like formality so much'. The children say he looks like 'a gentleman'. At eleven o'clock arrival of the painter Kietz. – In the evening we are rather tired from so much talking and listening; the May wine helps a little, but we are off our usual track. It has an odd effect on me, I relapse more and more into silence and feel that I am incapable of sustaining any sort of contact with other people; my mood becomes despondent, indefinable fears oppress me, my heart is like a creature in flight.

Wednesday, June 1 When I come down to breakfast, R. greets me in song with the melody from the Ninth Symphony: 'Who has pulled off the great triumph, husband of this wife to be,' etc. 'That is my "Ode to Joy," he says. – While I was contemplating my happiness yesterday before going to sleep, I found myself thinking of the sufferings of others; I was appalled, and, just as I long ago renounced the sensual expression of love, so I now resolved to sacrifice any kind of little joy, even indeed of comfort, in order to pay down to the very last penny for this one single nameless happiness: to behold and to share in R.'s progress! (Arrival of the money order, which I at once send to the steamship company, and thus have put aside 5,500 francs for the children in the past year.)

Thursday, June 2 Yesterday morning I entered his room and he played and sang the sketch he had just made of Siegfried's arrival in disguise at Brünnhilde's rock. Lunch with the children and Herr Kietz, who leaves at four o'clock; his visit has not given R. much pleasure, he finds he has sunk very low in the world.

Friday, June 3 'The words convey only the ghostliness of the apparition, the music sounds just innocently grieving,' R. said yesterday. Before that he exclaimed: 'When I have finished this first act, I shall have unloaded a formidable piece of work. To me the most singular thing of all is that I have managed to do the Norns' scene to my own satisfaction.'

Saturday, June 4 R. shows me in the sketch the theme from the love scene between Br[ünnhilde] and Siegfried, which appears like a mirage as S. overpowers Br. and she subsconsciously recognizes him. R. says, 'When the ring was snatched from her I thought of Alberich; the noblest character suffers the same as the ignoble, in every creature the will is identical.' – At lunch he again complains about music as a profession: 'Every kind of work which is unconnected with reason is a joke compared with it; here nothing can be forced, just as one cannot resume a dream by an effort of will, one has just to wait until it literally flies into one's mind.' – In the evening I suddenly abandon the children and wander to the piano, something I normally never do now; R., returning home from his walk, is quite put out, because he wanted to use the piano himself, or, rather, had to, since the musical treatment of Siegfried's sword-drawing was running through his head; laughing over our identity of thought, I left the room, he started writing, I put the children to bed.

Sunday, June 5 R. today finishes the pencil sketch of the first act of *Götterdämmerung*. But he says the thought of completing it 'in ink' makes him shudder.

Monday, June 6 My child, my son, your birth – my highest happiness – is connected with the greatest affliction of another, this was my life's sin, never forget this, recognize in it a portrait of life, and atone for it as best you can. But my blessings on you as the realization of my most blissful dream! – At 4.30 I am awakened by sweet sounds, R. at the piano proclaiming to me the hour of birth. Flowers and stars (in a little golden frame) are then brought to me by Loldi and Eva; later Fidi, in white on the red blanket, receives the congratulations of his sisters and gives them gifts; at the foot of the 'sacrificial altar', as in a pagoda, he looks like a little Buddha, bestowing favours as he is worshipped. R. exclaims: 'What a beautiful morning! How happy I am!' Lulu pleases us with her affection for Fidi, the dear girl has a warm heart, may life's course not break it.

Friday, June 10 Much joy in Fidi, who is becoming very lively and sturdy. – Yesterday I read in the newspaper that Hans is to play in Nuremberg and Würzburg on behalf of the Hans Sachs monument – for the last time in Germany.

Saturday, June 11 I suddenly feel very unwell and go for a drive with the children to recover a little. Returning home, I find Prof. Nietzsche and his friend Herr Rohde[1], also a philologist, who had announced their coming yesterday. Lively and serious conversation. In the evening Prof. N. reads us a lecture on the Greek music drama, a title for which R. pulls him up, explaining the reason for his disapproval. The lecture is a good one and shows that he has a true feeling for Greek art. (Prof. N. has brought me Dürer's *Melancholie*.)

Sunday, June 12 Breakfast all together, then with our guests to the Lion of Lucerne[2], while R. works. At lunch R. is very lively and good-humoured, he starts talking about musicians, 'who are wild beasts, not educated

---

[1] Erwin Rohde (b. 1845).
[2] Memorial to Swiss Guards who died in Paris in 1792.

creatures, very close in fact to actors. To demand of our present-day musicians, with their quintets, trios, cantatas, etc., that they conduct, is like suddenly demanding from a writer of novels that he play comic roles.' At five o'clock we accompany our guests to the railway station; then home; glorious weather, lovely moonlight; after supper *W[ihelm] Meister.* [1]

Tuesday, June 14 In the evening, contemplation of the print *Die Melancholie,* which Prof. Nietzsche gave me, brings us to a comparison between A. Dürer and [J.] S. Bach. 'Both,' says R., 'should be regarded as the conclusion of the Middle Ages, for it is nonsense to regard Bach as of our own time. Both endowed with this rich and mysterious imagination, dispensing with beauty but achieving sublimity, which is greater than all beauty. The poet one might put beside them is Dante, though he is less congenial because not so human, meaning not a Protestant.' The *A.A.Z.* arrives and contains a nasty piece about *Die Walküre:* 'Previously the interest in W[agner]'s work was great, now nobody talks about it.' R. very upset by this malicious distortion of all known facts. 'It is not the malice itself which constantly amazes one, but the new forms it continually and with downright genius manages to find.' When I tell Vreneli always to hand the newspapers to me first, she informs me that in the spring some vile caricatures, the contents of which she is quite unable to confide to me, had been sent from Munich; she had burned them!

Wednesday, June 15 Arrival of my wedding dress, plans for Fidi's future, R. plays to him, he listens earnestly. – Passing then to our plans for the production of the *Nibelungen:* 'What is gratitude, what is time? Once it is there, it will exist for humanity forever. Even if I know I shall never change the masses, never transform anything permanent, all I ask is that the good things also have their place, their refuge. The common and the bad must occupy and retain the main expanse, but the good can perhaps still find asylum.' 'You'll see,' he exclaimed yesterday, 'you'll see, *Die Walküre* will still turn out to my advantage; it is true I can have nothing to do with it, but something will emerge which will be of more advantage to me, to my plans, than if the present silence persisted unbroken.'

Thursday, June 16 R. suddenly writes to the King, asking him to stage *Die Walküre* for himself alone. Continued reading of *W. Meister* restores his high spirits, then, as he seals his letter, he says, 'One stands between the good spirit and the demon; you belong to the good spirits, the King to the demons.'

Friday, June 17 In the garden the two little ones play with the convicts, who are cutting the grass under supervision, and give them strawberries. Loldi takes one of them some money, which we gave her for this purpose; a touching picture, but the faces terrible. 'What a study!' R. says. 'The whole obstinacy of Nature's immutability is reflected in such faces.'

---

[1] Novel by Goethe.

Saturday, June 18 R. works; letter from Catulle Mendès, who tells R. they will not be able to resist the temptation of seeing *Die Walküre* in Munich; R. replies that in that case he (R.) must resist the temptation of seeing them in Tribschen.

Monday, June 20 Telegram from Catulle Mendès begging pardon, they will not go to Munich.

Tuesday, June 21 Letter from the lawyer in Berlin, who tells me of an order according to which I have once again to declare that I do not intend to return home; following this statement comes the final hearing, in which 'presumably the divorce will be promulgated.' Prof. Nietzsche writes very nicely of the impression Tribschen made on him and his friend, and he dedicates to me his lectures on Socrates and Greek art.

Wednesday, June 22 In the newspaper appear reports of Hans's concerts for the Hans Sachs monument. I give Loulou all these copies to preserve. – R. unfortunately very worn out by his work, but still more by worry about *Die Walküre*. A friendly letter from Marie Muchanoff, the Wagner performances in Weimar have begun with *Der [Fliegende] Holländer*. In the afternoon to Countess Bassenheim's, the Prince died in the morning; saw the corpse, the serenity of death, the agony of life, a profound impression.

Friday, June 24 From town comes a letter from Franz Müller[1] in Munich; he emphatically reports the enthusiasm of *all* for *Die Walküre*! *Die W.* is to be given there on Sunday, then three times in succession *Das Rheingold* and *Die Walküre*. 'It really is wonderful,' R. says bitterly. 'Perfall as manager, Wüllner as conductor, Grandaur[2] as producer, Müller as historian, and only then the King of Bavaria and my work.' It pierces my heart like a dagger, and I ask myself whether this disgraceful act will really go unavenged? Shortly beforehand R. had said to me, 'You are the King of Bavaria's sister, you have joined hands to save my life – he, it is true, as a foolish character, you as a good woman.' I cannot make out the King's feelings – though, as an Indian proverb says, this one can never do with kings anywhere. – The evening shows the melancholy effects of that stupid letter: R. so beside himself and also so physically worn out that I stand there disconsolate, not knowing what to do.

Saturday, June 25 Since the effects of yesterday's letter were so very bad, I gave instructions that all letters from Munich must first be handed to me. I am very glad to have made this rule; a letter from Councillor Düfflipp announces that not only will the King *not* command the production for himself alone, but also he himself will not attend the first performance – only the one to be given in conjunction with *Das Rheingold*! I reply as best I can and say I am keeping all reports from the master's eyes. R. did a lot

---

[1] A writer on music and theatre.
[2] Franz Grandaur, stage director in Munich.

of work yesterday, and today he resumes it. Arrival of the legal document, reply to it. Letter from Frau Dr. Wille inviting R. and me to stay with her. The great friendliness with which this is done touches us very much, R. thanks her and promises her the first visit after our marriage. Visit from Count Bassenheim, he asks me to write to Düfflipp: the Countess would like to have the Prince's estate changed to a female inheritance. I write. – Letter from von Bronsart, the theatre manager in Hanover; *Die Msinger* has not been a success there.

Sunday, June 26 Towards noon Richter arrives, to our great delight; he did not attend the rehearsal of *Die Walküre* in Munich, which was very nice of him. R. is in good spirits, we talk of Bayreuth and forget about Munich! Fidi, our Monsieur Sunbeam.

Wednesday, June 29 Yesterday a money order arrived from Pest, *Tannhäuser* has brought in an unexpected 500 florins, which pleases R. greatly. – Today the outside world brings us only a letter from Herr Schafer[1] in Munich; according to him the success of *Die Walküre* is very great, and the manager of the Berlin Court theatre is said to have applauded unceasingly and to have made notes on the casting in Berlin (!!).

Saturday, July 2 R. works, and completes the sketch of the first act. Simultaneously with my great joy over this outcome, I have to read in the *A.A.Z.* a contemptible review of his *Die Walküre*; I tear the wretched thing up. Pohl has written, too, in *Die Signale*; very weak and insipid.

Monday, July 4 Newspapers of all sorts with stupidities about *Die Walküre*; the King truly did not attend either the dress rehearsal or the first two performances, and for that he spent 40,000 florins and offended R.'s feelings!

Tuesday, July 5 R. talks of the bringing together of several themes in music; the ear perceives only one, but the addition of the others as accompaniment to it tremendously sharpens and heightens the impact of this single melody which one hears. However, one must be capable of arranging the themes in such a way that the main melody can really be heard; Berlioz, for example, was not successful in the '*Scène au Bal*',[2] where the love motive sounds like the bass line.

Friday, July 8 Rumours of war, because of a Prussian prince's[3] ascending the Spanish throne; the French as always ridiculously excited by something happening without their consent.

Sunday, July 10 At four o'clock drive to Hergeschwyl in very fine weather, from there the ascent of Mount Pilatus, a veritable caravan with guides, porters, sedan-chair attendants, Richter, Jakob, and the two *big* girls. A gay ride; with the ascent a gradual alleviation of cares, love alone holds sway

---

[1] Correctly, Reinhard Schaefer, with whom Wagner stayed for a short time in Munich in 1869.

[2] Correctly '*Un Bal*', second movement of the *Symphonie Fantastique*.

[3] Prince Leopold von Hohenzollern-Sigmaringen, whose candidature the French opposed.

and manifests itself in the high, pure ether. Sublime impressions of stillness and solitude; on such impressions he based the life of the gods in the *Ring des Nibelungen*. Lovely moonlight on the Pilatus peak. The children merry.

Monday, July 11 Watched the sunrise by myself, great and peaceful impression. – Otherwise we are very tired, the ride had wearied us, and rest was not possible during the night on account of the many guests. We take a walk across loose stones to a meadow covered with Alpine roses, settle ourselves down there, and the day passes in an attempt to make up our lost sleep.

Wednesday, July 13 I spend the whole day in bed, most unwell. R. in his love and kindness reads to me. – A guide brings news that an ultimatum has been sent from Paris to the King of Prussia, saying he should forbid his relative to accept the crown, otherwise war!! I am quite beside myself over this example of French insolence; this nation deserves a merciless chastisement. –

Thursday, July 14 Rain. I feel somewhat better and get up. R. says to me that it is wrong of us to seek diversions such as other people have need of, we could never make a success of an outing of this sort, in place of it we have our own happiness. In the evening the weather clears up and we are able to climb the Esel.

Friday, July 15 In the morning I hear the '*Morgentraumdeutweise*'[1]; shortly afterwards R. comes to me saying that Karl Klindworth[2] is here, in fact with Richter, who, scarcely arrived below, has come up again. We prepare to take leave of the heights. Klindworth has seen Hans in Berlin. He says Hans is well and very contented with his stay in Florence; he is now planning a journey to America. If I am truly to be given, on top of all else, the consolation of knowing that things are well with Hans, then, dear God, there will never have been a happier woman than I! – K.Kl. saw *Die Walküre* in Munich and says it made an overwhelming impression on him; he also tells me that my father is travelling with a bevy of acquaintances to see *Die Walküre*, and is going on to the Passion play in Oberammergau. How different this life from our own, how turned outward, avid for distraction, how wide the gap between us! – The arrogant and wicked French are not content with the withdrawal of the Prince of Hohenzollern, they are demanding through their envoy Benedetti a promise from the King of Prussia that he will never give his approval to the acceptance of the Spanish crown by any Prussian prince. The King quite rightly refuses to receive the envoy. So now they are arming! This news upsets us greatly.

Saturday, July 16 Not a wink of sleep, the excitement is too great! According to a letter from Catulle Mendès, our friends will probably not

[1] The melody of the first two stanzas of Walther's 'Prize Song' in Act III of *Die Meistersinger*.
[2] Pianist, conductor and composer (b. 1830), friend of Wagner since their meeting in London in 1855.

visit us, and of that we are glad, for to see a Frenchman now would be very unpleasant. Letter from Prof. Nietzsche, who out of consideration for us did not go to see *Die Walküre* in Munich; I reply to him and try as hard as I can to arouse his enthusiasm for Prussia's right to represent Germany. – What lies ahead of us, how will, how can this frightful war end? – The King of Bavaria ill, did not attend any performance of *Die Walküre*.

Sunday, July 17 Frightful thunderstorm; I declare that the gods are angry with the French. War has been declared; in Paris nothing but phrases. The Prussians quietly firm and resolved. – Confidential talk with Herr Klindworth, who is departing for Germany and will see Hans there. I beg him to tell Hans everything I had intended to write to him. I am very moved by our conversation. – Klindworth finds R. rejuvenated and in his state of mind unrecognizable; Hans had told him that, if R. were ever again to write a single note, it would be thanks to me. – Letter from Herr Villiers, who sends his play and with typical French insolence makes fun of the *excellents Prussiens*. R. is against his visit and says all our sympathies are with the Prussians.

Monday, July 18 R. says he is beginning to feel hopeful; war is something noble, it shows the unimportance of the individual; war is, so to speak, a dance performed with the most dreadful of powers, like a Beethoven finale in which he unleashes all the demons in a magnificent dance.

Tuesday, July 19 R., who had almost completed his essay *Beethoven and the German Nation* in his own mind, cannot now capture the mood to begin it. Outward events do not affect the core of the matter, but they are unsettling, and the inner lantern stops glowing, the winds of Fate blow the flame hither and thither. – Mendès, Villiers, etc. arrive. Feelings of great embarrassment, though the dear people are friendly.

Friday, July 22 We walk in the morning in the garden, R. and I, and discuss the war. All at once one can feel where one belongs, there is a connection which in times of peace cannot make itself felt, since only the bad things float to the surface. Inside one feels something which cannot be talked about, yet it is present in everything, and in this emotion one puts all one's hopes and wishes. Thus says R. – Eva suddenly becomes ill, with convulsions. As I am standing beside her bed, Vreneli brings me the news that our dairy farmer, who supplied us with fish, has been drowned, and right in front of our house; what life can bring us, Vreneli says drily and rightly. – In the evening the Mendès couple.

Saturday, July 23 Eva still unwell; a letter from Claire, her son has had to join the navy. Judith with us at lunch, afterwards I translate with her *Damayanti and Nala*[1]. In the evening music from *Die Msinger*. (Letter from my mother.)

---

[1] From the *Mahábhárata* (sacred book of the Hindus).

Sunday, July 24 I continue translating at Eva's bedside; family lunch; we drink a toast to General Moltke[1].

Tuesday, July 26 Eva well again, made progress with the translation. When our French visitors arrive, there comes from R. a long speech on the German character and how difficult it is for us at this moment to consort with French people.

Wednesday, July 27 R. still at his *Beethoven*; I with the children. No war news. Drive in the afternoon with R. to our friends'; on our return Richter hands over a letter, it is from Hallwachs and reports that on July 18 the divorce was made final. There is no happiness on this earth, my children, for at this news I only had tears.

Thursday, July 28 Visit from Prof. Nietzsche, in the evening the French visitors, music, the Norns' scene, and *Tristan*.

Friday, July 29 After lunch Herr N. introduces his sister[2] to me, a nice, modest girl. Later, sudden arrival of our friend R. Pohl, engaged in fleeing from Baden territory. Richard compares our motley company with [Boccaccio's] *Decameron* – as they fled from the plague, so we from the war. The French visitors arrive as usual and the conversation is lively. (Austria, as well as England, Italy, and Switzerland, is behaving abominably – that so-called sage objectivity which accords the same treatment to an honest man – Bismarck – as to a rogue – Napoleon.) –

Saturday, July 30 Our last dinner with the French; at the end of the evening a long conversation between Catulle M. and R. in consequence of a reading by M. Villiers, whose hypocritical trend, bombastic style, and theatrical presentation had made us thoroughly indignant. R. draws their attention to the objectionable nature of their rhetorical poetry. Catulle listens, full of understanding and much affected; we have come really to like him because of his sensitive nature and fine intellect, but his friend is becoming increasingly intolerable. Parting from Catulle and Judith, that good, deeply distressed couple who both possess real beauty of soul.

Sunday, July 31 A day and evening of lovely peace, R. drinks his beer in the garden outside the house, and the passing mention of a line in *Hamlet* brings him to a comparison between Sh[akespeare] and Beethoven; as in Shakespeare the characters, so in Beethoven the melodies – unmistakable, incomparable, an entire, inexplicable world.

Monday, August 1 At eleven, as a storm approaches, R. goes off to see the Protestant parson Tschudi, from whom he returns very content. When the document announcing my divorce is received here, we shall probably have no difficulties at all. R., when I ask him whether all of this is agreeable to him, says he knows of no creature anywhere in the world with whom he

[1] The Prussian Chief of Staff.
[2] Elisabeth Nietzsche (b. 1846), married Bernhard Forster in 1885.

would wish to be united except me! If he had not had me, he says, he would have entered a monastery. – In the afternoon I order our wedding rings, in the traditional Lucerne form. In the evening a letter from Herr Praeger[1] in London, reporting on the performance there of *Der Fl. Holländer* (in Italian) and its success. –

Tuesday, August 2 A wild night for R. and me, he dreams of his wife, who was insolent and malicious towards us and against whom he could defend himself only by crying out, 'But you are dead.' With this cry he woke up; I heard him, too, but, being still in the grip of a dream which robbed me of the German language, called out to him in French, '*J'ai bien dormi,*' although I only wanted to ask, 'What is the matter?' He, already awake: 'Why are you talking French?' I, half-awake: 'You cried out in French.' But his dream keeps on recurring throughout the night. In the morning it made us laugh a lot. And as usual R.'s dream was associated with my thoughts during the day.

Wednesday, August 3 Worked with the children, at one o'clock Frl. v. M[eysenbug] with Frl. Herzen[2]; a pleasant, sympathetic visit. At lunch I receive the document confirming my divorce.

Thursday, August 4 Ever-mounting pleasure in Bismarck, whose revelations show ever more clearly how wisely and at the same time how righteously he has been acting; He says he did in fact have to temporize with the French in order to enjoy at least a few years of peace. The French diplomacy, which could make such proposals to a German minister, he described as the *most obtuse of diplomacies.* A German minister! One hears the words for the first time, and how noble and proud does this minister appear! – How uplifting it must be for Bavaria, Saxony, and Württemberg to be fighting now as a German army! – In the evening we read poems by Byron.

Tuesday, August 9 Letter from Prof. Nietzsche, who has resolved to join the army. I reply to him, saying the time is not yet ripe. We are having trouble with Richter, for he, too, would like to join up. Our one consolation yesterday we found in scenes from Shakespeare's *Henry V.* – Letter from Claire, her son has departed without being able to say goodbye! – In the morning R. read me some splendid passages from his essay on Beethoven.

Saturday, August 13 Pleasure in Loulou and Boni, because they prefer working for the soldiers to playing. R. remarks on the prettiness of Loldi's cheeks, and says: 'Even as a child I always sought for beauty in the cheeks; I did not realize that what I meant by that was a kind smile, spreading across the whole face. I once looked at myself in a mirror to find out whether my appearance was not too repellent. Handsome you are not, I thought to myself, but also not too ugly, for your cheeks are certainly not ugly.' – In the evening now always the newspaper; the heroic, melancholy details of our victories.

---

[1] Ferdinand Praeger (b. 1815), German composer and teacher settled in London; Wagner met him there in 1855; author of *Wagner as I Knew Him.*

[2] Olga Herzen, daughter of the Russian writer Alexander Herzen and M. von Meysenbug's ward.

Monday, August 15 As I prepare lint in the morning with Frl. von Meysenbug, who, along with Olga Herzen, spent the night with us, we talk about Hans; everything she tells me about his position in Florence is highly pleasing. He himself is supposed to have said, 'If I ever become a likeable person, I shall have Florence to thank for it.' Marie Muchanoff wrote yesterday that my father sobbed throughout the whole of *Die Walküre*, and she had been unable to watch the scene between Brünnhilde and Siegmund for a 3rd time, so much was she affected by it. – In the evening the conversation brings us to Minna, R.'s first wife; some things told me by Frl. Meysenbug brought me face to face with a veritable abyss of meanness. With tears in his eyes R. tells me more about it: 'That was the main ingredient of my earlier life and all else linked with it, culminating in a complete fiasco.' I must, he said, have patience with and understanding for him, for I could never imagine the atmosphere in which he had lived. 'The first person ever to give me the impression of nobility was your father.' How must such words affect me, whose only feelings for him are of admiration and respect!

Tuesday, August 16 I receive two letters from Prof. Nietzsche, the first, delayed, from Basel, the other from Erlangen, where he is already tending the wounded. In a few days he will be going to Metz. I feel that Richter should also go, but he lacks the means, and we are in no position to support him adequately, either, which is sad, but must be borne.

Thursday, August 18 Richter, whom I sent to the Sonnenberg, brings me 50 francs for the wounded, I do some collecting myself and am able to give Countess B. 137 francs. R. says the burning of Paris would be a symbol of the world's liberation at last from the pressure of all that is bad. R. would like to write to Bismarck, requesting him to shoot all of Paris down. – When I return home from town, Dr. Pohl is there, and R. is singing the last scene of the first act of *Götterdämmerung* for him. R. is very impatient at receiving no news from Cl[emens] Brockhaus[1], he much desires our marriage to take place on the 25th.

Friday, August 19 Thirteen years ago, in the same wet weather, my wedding day; I did not know what I was then promising, for I never kept to it; if I now know what has assumed control of me, I wish never to forget the sin, but to stare it constantly in the face, in order to learn humility and submissiveness. In the morning R. reads to me from his *Beethoven*, magnificent the description of the C-sharp Minor Quartet and the comparison with Shakespeare. The remainder of the day passes in a discussion of the situation; our troops have been fighting for four days now; the French are constantly reporting victories, but they do not mention any good results arising from their victories.

Saturday, August 20 R. drafts a fine poem for the King and copies it out on the title page of the first act of *Götterdämmerung*, which he is sending the

[1] Theologian, son (b. 1837) of Wagner's sister Ottilie.

King for his birthday. – Late in the evening a letter from Judith M., they want to come here after all, which is certainly rather curious.

Sunday, August 21 Today our banns are called in the church; and on Thursday, the King's birthday, we are to be married. Loldi is lying ill in bed. (Letter from Prof. Nietzsche; he is composing music in the military hospital.)

Monday, August 22 R. writes a splendid letter to my mother; I write to Frau Wesendonck and ask R. if he is satisfied with the letter; he feels it goes too far, and says he had always thrown a poetic veil over this relationship, in order not to admit its triviality, but now he himself has lost his poetic feelings for it, and he does not care to be reminded. He thinks I might receive an unpleasant answer, but I do not believe that, for I believe my attitude is not lacking in delicacy. – The wedding rings arrive. R. says he wants to laugh out loud like a child when he sees my signature: Cosima Wagner; it seems to him like a dream. I beg God, in His grace towards me in my joy, not to forget those who are mourning and suffering.

Wednesday, August 24 To remind me that we should never lose sight of the seriousness of life, my Loldi is so unwell that she will not be able to attend the wedding tomorrow; we shall leave Eva with her for company. And so a veil is cast over the happy ceremony. R. drives to town to make the last preparations, and I explain to the children what is happening tomorrow. They weep with me and then smile with me, too, and finally Boni laughs, almost out loud: 'You are marrying Uncle Richard.'

Thursday, August 25 At eight o'clock we were married; may I be worthy of bearing R.'s name! My prayers were concentrated on two points: R.'s well-being – that I might always promote it; Han's happiness – that it might be granted him, separated from me, to lead a cheerful life. The Mendès couple did not come, also sent no word. We are worried about them. In the afternoon a letter from Judith; Catulle would be considered a deserter if he were now to leave Paris. Then a telegram from Marie Muchanoff, signed also by Tausig and Lenbach, congratulating us. In the afternoon we become very worried about Loldi, who still has a high temperature. We put off the christening, which was to have been next Sunday.

Friday, August 26 Letter from Herr Lenbach, who is presenting me with a portrait, which delights me very much on R.'s account. Congratulatory telegram from the King. We pay our calls (to Frau Am Rhyn, the Bassenheims, the parson, and Frl. Meysenbug). Returning home, we send off the 120 *'faire part'*; a bouquet of edelweiss, sent to me by Frau Wesendonck.

Sunday, August 28 In the morning R. calls out to me, 'Cosima *Helferica* Wagner, that is what you should be named, for you have truly helped.' At ten o'clock we start out, and arrive in Mariafeld towards two o'clock. Very friendly reception from the whole family; Frau Dr. [Wille] says to me, 'I have been watching you with great sympathy; you have taken and borne enormous things on your shoulders, though you are so young.' She tells me my father said, 'Now my daughter has a husband who is worthy of her.' We spend a nice day there. Dr. W[ille] has a great many tales to tell, among them, about Napoleon III: how, when one of his protégés needs money, he takes to his bed, which then causes a slump in which his favourite can make a profit. – A lot of witty things are said, and above all it pleases R. that he can always refer to me as Frau Wagner. I am happy that an old and trusted friend of R.'s is glad to see his destiny placed in my hands.

Monday, August 29 We take leave of the kind family and arrive back here. Loldi is considerably better, and the remaining children lively and healthy.

Thursday, September 1 In town we learn that MacMahon[1] has been beaten at Beaumont. Splendid feeling, damped only by some lines from Prof. Nietzsche (in Hagenau), who describes the terrible state and inadequacy of the medical care on the battlefields.

Friday, September 2 The great event of the Tribschen household is the arrival of a *goose* – we do not know from where; the children very pleased, the dogs very astonished. Lessons with the children; Loldi gets up for a few hours. The doctor comes and is addressed with terrible vehemence by R., because he is of the opinion that it is 'not good' *to take Alsace and Lorraine away from the French!* R. enlightens him as to the disgracefulness of a neutral policy.

Saturday, September 3 We receive from Colonel Am Rhyn in the evening the news that MacMahon has been wounded, the entire army under Wimpffen has capitulated, Napoleon III has surrendered to the King!!! What a christening present for Fidi! Nine battles within a month, all victorious, and now this conclusion!

Sunday, September 4 The news is correct, we have seen the bulletin. God in Heaven, what an outcome! 'I am bad for the Napoleons,' R. says. 'When I was six months old there was the Battle of Leipzig, and now Fidi is hacking up the whole of France.' Letter from his sister Luise, her 18-year-old grandson has died. R. is expecting a *coup d'état* in Paris. Yesterday R. told me he would like to compose funeral music for the fallen, and wished he could be commissioned to do it. Not a victory hymn – that he could not do. I write to Marie Muchanoff about this, so that she might use her influence to get him the commission. At three o'clock arrival of the Wille family, then the Bassenheims, at four o'clock the christening takes place. *Helferich Siegfried Richard Wagner* behaves passably well.

Monday, September 5 The mail brought a letter from the lawyer Simson; in answer to my inquiry about my liabilities, he says that Herr von B[ülow] has decided to bear all the costs of the suit. This distresses me, but there is nothing I can do about it. – My union with R. is like a palingenesis, a reincarnation which brings me nearer to perfection, a deliverance from a previous erring existence; yet I feel, and tell him, that it is only in death

[1] Maurice, Marquis de MacMahon, French field marshal.

that we shall be united completely, freed from the barriers of individuality. When I try to tell him how much I love him, I feel the complete impotence of existence, and know that only in our last living embrace will I be able to tell him! That is why I always start to weep when I try to come close to him and tell him how my soul worships him. Before going to bed he once more asks me not to spend so much time bringing up the children. He says, 'No mother brings up her children alone.' 'Yet I believe my children will be grateful to me for having been so much to them.' 'You were also not brought up by your mother.' 'I might have turned out better if I had had a mother to care for me.' He does not like to hear me say that and becomes angry. We part between tears and smiles.

Wednesday, September 7 Violent fever, I have to stay in bed, the doctor comes and thinks it is smallpox, since I have a bad headache. Under R.'s heavenly care I spend the day in great pain, without seeing the children. R. finishes his *Beethoven.*

Thursday, September 8 I feel better, all that remains is a bad cough. I see the children again. Letter from Marie Muchanoff; she says that at the patriotic demonstration [in Munich] which followed the tremendous news of the capitulation of the French army the King did not make an appearance, so that the Prussian ambassador was the centre of the delirious ovations. How very foolish of the King! – She also says my father has written very sadly, he had wanted to visit the wounded, but worldly considerations had restrained him, something he now deeply regrets. She says he is more isolated than he himself realizes.

Friday, September 9 I am vexed with Countess B.; she asked that my children take part in some *tableaux vivants* for wounded soldiers; I consented. Then I fell ill and discovered that, whereas [her daughter] Marie was to portray a noblewoman and young Elizabeth, my children had to appear as beggar maids. It should not really matter, and, praise God, Boni and Loulou noticed nothing at all; but I understand what is meant by it, and I am sorry that maternal vanity should induce so magnanimous a woman as the Countess to act so inconsiderately. Even at the christening I noticed she was not at all pleased to see my children looking so pretty in their little curls. I resolve to tell her quite calmly what is in my mind.

Saturday, September 10 Today I have completely lost my voice; whatever it is seems to be taking a little walk through my whole body. I nevertheless get up and sit down to lunch with R. and Richter. Soon back in bed, however. In the evening R. reads me the conclusion of *R[ichard] II*; every word a world in itself. The children, whom I sent to watch the *tableaux vivants*, did not return until eleven o'clock, which worries me. But then I take pleasure in the impartiality with which they admire the other children, how prettily they were dressed and made to look prettier still, and never give a thought to themselves. But when they are out of the room, I am foolish enough to weep; I tell R. that this instance shows me once again that I have far more sympathy for the Countess than she has for me; for she knows how anxious and concerned I am that my children should not be treated in a less friendly way than others. Well, may God help my dear good little ones! R. is heavenly, he comforts me, begs me to be calm and gives me a letter from Claire to distract my mind.

Monday, September 12 Letters from C. Mendès, very elegiac, he thinks of dying beneath the walls of Paris. R. revises his *Beethoven* and writes in strong terms to Catulle, always reiterating: You got what you deserved. Visit from Countess B.; owing to R.'s kind persuasions I am now sufficiently calm to receive her, and when we begin to talk of the *tableaux vivants* I say to her, 'I did not send my children to you, firstly because I could not be present, and secondly, because I feared their father would be surprised to hear that on the first little occasion in which they were called on to show themselves they were accorded no more favourable roles than those of beggar maids.' We then slid away from the subject.

Tuesday, September 13 Still indisposed, but able to give the children their lessons. Prof. Nietzsche writes to R., he is back in Erlangen and is ill. I wrote to Rothschild for my money – God knows whether I shall still receive anything. R. works on his *Beethoven* – too much, in fact, for he gets floating specks before his eyes.

Friday, September 16 Letter from Prof. Nietzsche, who seems to be deeply upset; then from my mother, who is rather hurt by my frank opinion of France. Still cold, inhospitable weather, worked with the children. In the evening a letter from poor Claire, who is quite disconsolate. – Paris is now cut off, we shall hear nothing for some while.

Sunday, September 18 In the newspaper we read that Paris will be able to hold out for a long time still, also that Toul and Strassburg are still defending themselves stoutly, and it is said that Bazaine[1] is still well stocked with provisions. When will it end, how many more sacrifices must our men make?

Monday, September 19 Yesterday Richard spoke of making a trip to Berlin this winter, in order to give a lecture at the Academy to promote our performances in Bayreuth. He wants me to go with him, and misunderstands me when I say it would be better for me to remain here. He believes I am being constrained by worldly considerations, my previous relationship with Hans's family, whereas it is just my inner voice, which tells me, 'You have nothing more to seek in this world; because you caused severe suffering, you have resolved to live now only within these four walls for the children and the One and Only.' I do not wish to explain this to R., in order not to upset him, and God will help me to do what is right!

---

[1] François Achille Bazaine, French field marshal and commander of the Rhine Army.

Saturday, September 24 The publisher Fritzsch[1] in Leipzig is very eager to have *Beethoven,* and R. will give it to him.

Sunday, September 25 In the evening we are summoned by the children; on their own initiative they are presenting *tableaux vivants* in the gallery; they have arranged chairs in the dining room and now they summon the whole household, which duly assembles to form a lively demos. Everything is then, to our great surprise, performed under Loulou's direction, outstandingly well, by the children. I am deeply touched, with tears in my eyes. The play acting is forgotten, all I see is the gravity of life hanging over these four heads. Oh, children, my children, if only I could help you! Loulou distinguishes herself through much hard work and dexterity, Boni through her confident manner, Eva with amiability and wit, Loldi, however, through a rare earnestness, which does not desert her even in the curtsy with which she and her three sisters acknowledge our applause at the end. They had dressed themselves up with great dexterity as peasant children and depicted groups from their picture books.

Wednesday, September 28 The day spent in excessive worry about Fidi, who is very weak and run down; he has only four teeth so far, and the coming of the others seems to torment him so. – Strassburg has capitulated.

Saturday, October 1 Visit from Countess Bassenheim; she suggests that I send Loulou and Boni along with her daughter to a new school which is being opened. I find difficulty in agreeing; R. wishes it, to give me more rest: I intend to see the schoolmistress. In the evening to *Knie's Circus* with the four children, R., Richter and Hermine. Great excitement among the children. In the carriage R. embraces me, exclaiming: 'That I am on such a pleasure outing with you and the children! It is a dream.'

Sunday, October 2 R. drafts his *Proclamation*[2] As an exposition of the requirements of the Bayreuth performance it seems to be simple and persuasive, but he fears the obtuseness of the princes.

Tuesday, October 4 I am learning to knit! I find it difficult, but I want to make some leggings for the children. Constantly with Fidi, whose recovery is progressing fast. Walk with R., in the evening [Aeschylus's] *Persae.* Sublime impact, and observation that all the present misery of France could never provide the basis for a tragedy, indeed hardly for a lament!

Wednesday, October 5 Lenbach's fine picture is here! I had learned of its arrival yesterday evening and I awoke in the morning saying, 'Now it is returning home, now you can depart.' When Vreneli told me it was unpacked, she added, 'But the black frame will give you a shock.' It was not I who received the shock, but Richard, who thought he was seeing me dead or my father in monk's clothing – in short, the black frame made a

---

[1] Ernst Wilhelm Fritzsch published Wagner's collected writings, also the periodical *Musikalisches Wochenblatt.*

[2] A declaration of his plans to build a theatre; it was published in April 1871.

violent impression on his imagination. But gradually the picture had its effect, and he has come to love it beyond words. Our mood was deeply serious all day long; we now have no delights except such sublime and solemn ones. – To Countess Bassenheim's, there meet the school-mistress; I find it hard to give up teaching the children; only the thought that the children might perhaps prefer to work with other children could bring me to it. – R. writes to Lenbach.

Thursday, October 6 Always the picture! It is marvellously beautiful. I write to Lenbach and to Marie M. – Stimulated by the arrival of the picture, R. has again taken up the instrumentation of *Siegfried*.

Saturday, October 8 R. decides on an outing to Brunnen, the children are got ready; the sky clouds over, R. is about to tell the children that we are staying at home, but the dismay of the 'regiment in blue' deters him, and we set off after all. Renewed lesson that we should not undertake anything outside; a foehn storm in Brunnen, we take a walk after lunch but are driven back by whirling dust. Since the steamer does not stop in Brunnen (on account of the foehn) we drive to Gersau. There everything is quiet and peaceful, and we spend a happy hour on the terrace. Journey home in the dark, I give R. my hand, 'the only hand' – he exclaims – 'I know what I am holding when I take this hand.' His expression, nobly sad, moves me greatly. The children's games tear us from our contemplative mood; R. has to try on all the children's hats, and thus he romps around until we arrive in Lucerne. When we are about to descend the gangway we miss Rus[1], we call for him, and at last the captain tells us unconcernedly that he fell into the water. Awful moment, R. wants to go after him, we implore the captain not to let the ship sail, he reluctantly and surlily gives in, I have to hold on to the weeping children, I cry out to Richter on no account to let Wagner do anything; whistling, calling for Rus; if the ship moves, our dear dog will be done for. At last he swims ashore, at the place where the boats tie up, led there by his instinct. R. meets him sobbing. I turned to stone with anxiety for R. Thus ended this pleasure outing; always I hear the voice that cries out to me: Stay in the haven to which you have come! However, the children enjoyed themselves greatly.

Sunday, October 9 Cheerful morning with R. and Fidi in spite of the violent storm outside; towards noon, thunder and lightning. Family lunch in almost total darkness, but cheerful and gay. In the afternoon, just as R. completes a page of instrumentation, I see, exactly between the two poplars on the terrace in front of the house, a wonderful rainbow. I call out to R.: a perfect triumphal arch! *Rheingold*, I say; Bayreuth, says R.; and at that very moment Prell, the bookseller, comes in to give us his notes on Bayreuth. A good omen, R. exclaims.

Saturday, October 15 At lunch R. says that Bavarian and Prussian troops are

---

[1] Wagner's Newfoundland dog, usually spelt Russ.

disputing with one another, the latter wanting to plant their black-and-white flag everywhere, the former insisting either that the black, red and gold should be used for all, or the white and blue for Bavaria, the black and white for Prussia, etc. – and they are right. We deplore the Prussians' rigid and narrow-minded approach to this matter. Rainy day, R. goes through the second act of *Siegfried* with Richter. In the evening [Byron's] *Don Juan*; I realize that I do not understand much, indeed hardly any of the satire in it, but on the other hand thoroughly enjoy the sublime lyrical episodes.

Sunday, October 16 Discussion of our artistic plan, R. thinks it might be a good idea, when the war ends, to send Bismarck his pamphlet *Art and Politics*[1] along with a few lines. I agree with him, for so powerful a person must be made to see how important the theatre is. Returning home, I find Loulou unwell and put her to bed; meanwhile the two little ones romp around with R. He is pleased and amazed that all the children always look so clean, he says he does not understand how it is done, and it always makes him feel so aristocratic. In the evening *Don Juan*. Comparing Byron with Goethe and Schiller, R. says: 'Everything in the lord's work is too violent, his work gives off a dry glow, for heat he certainly has. Our poets, just as clearly conscious of the hollowness and wickedness of the world, seek their salvation in other ways. And Goethe handles satire much more powerfully in his Mephisto. Byron is no good at drama, he can describe, but he cannot depict.'

Tuesday, October 18 I am full of grief; our dear old Fritz has now been sacrificed, he had become completely incapacitated and he was ill, now he has been put to death. We do not speak of it in the house, but I feel as if I have committed a sin in recognizing and approving the need for a death. R. goes for a very long walk; the weather is glorious; I remain with Loulou and put the summer things away. In the evening *Don Juan*, which we are now discontinuing.

Thursday, October 20 R. orchestrates the scene between Wotan and Siegfried and says its words are the finest he has ever written, then adds jokingly, 'Wotan is tragic because his life is too long, Siegfried because his is too short.'

Friday, October 21 Richter is quite astounded by the introduction to the third act of *Siegfried*, which he is now copying; he discusses the instrumentation, particularly of the Norns' theme. R. laughs: 'Yes, it sounds like a child shrieking. As well as something holy and sublime there is a demonically childish and shrieking quality in it, like a virgin who has never loved or borne children. One cannot imagine a witch's voice as anything but high and childish; it lacks the vibrating tones of the heart.'

Sunday, October 23 Walk with R. along the highway to Hergeschwyl. Once again we come upon an old acquaintance – a barking dog. R. says, 'I could imagine walking the earth again as a ghost, just to satisfy my thwarted

---

[1] Correctly, *German Art and German Politics*, the essay by Wagner that led to his departure from Munich in 1865.

longing to thrash that dog.' – Then he started to talk of the dramatic art of ancient Greece, of the cothurnus, which represents more or less the same as the doubling of the various wind instruments. In the evening *The Peace* by Aristophanes. I suspect that R. has to skip many things in order to be able to read these plays to me; all the same I get immense enjoyment from observing this incomparable fusing together of people and poet, from the bubbling inventive talent and the reckless mixture of earnestness and humour. –

Monday, October 24 Letter from Prof. Nietzsche, who has returned to Basel; he voices his fears that in the coming days militarism, and above all pietism, will make their pressure felt everywhere. R. very incensed by this thought. 'I will tolerate anything', he exclaims, 'police, soldiers, muzzling of the press, restrictions of Parliament, but on no account obscurantism. The only thing human beings can be proud of is the freedom of the spirit, it is the only thing which raises them above animals; to restrict or take away this freedom is worse even than castrating them.'

Wednesday, October 26 Departure, grand leave-taking by the children. Yesterday *tableaux vivants* in Richter's room; all the children with him, and finally I and R., much noise; Eva presents 'Mother and Child', forgets the mother, however, and just sets down Willy Stocker and then disappears into the wings (Richter's bed the curtain). Cheerful journey with R., balmy foehn atmosphere, the weather is mild. Met in Zurich by Arnold Wille, whose friendly conversation tires us a little. His mother, Frau Wille, delights us once again with her warm heart and her great and deep intelligence. In the evening Richard reads part of his biography (to Frau Wille and her husband alone).

Thursday, October 27 Breakfast with the family, with much feeling I take my leave of the excellent lady, who had some wonderful things to say about R. 's biography. I then go alone to visit Frau Wesendonck. Despite my attempts to persuade him, R. would not accompany me – her poems ('A Call to the German People', etc.) had greatly displeased him; he also maintains that in the end she had behaved badly towards him. So now for the first time in eleven years I again entered the rooms in which I once played the role of a sort of intermediary and confidante[1]. I found that the hospitable lady had now become a brunette, whereas in Munich four years ago she had been blonde; this disconcerted me; I was pleased by her friendly welcome, looked at her pictures, and on the way home reflected on the curious dreamlike quality of life. Eleven years ago, when I tried to make her feel more charitably disposed towards R., if anyone had then told me that I myself should be closely interwoven with his fate, I might indeed have believed it, but I should have been terribly alarmed. From the Wesendonck villa to the Hotel Baur, where Councillor Sulzer and Professor

[1] Cosima's second visit to the Wesendonck home in Zurich in August 1858, when the jealousy between Mathilde and Minna was at its height.

Hagenbuch[1] (also Richter) came to see us. Dr. Sulzer in particular pleased and touched us; his suffering features, his refined, precise, yet never harsh speech, his blindness, his whole reserved yet warmhearted nature, move me inexpressibly. He informs me that his family life (he has lost his wife and has five children) has been wiped out entirely by his participation in state affairs, and from this participation he can expect no satisfaction of any kind. I beg him to let his children visit mine. Our meeting is a gay one; for the first time the two state councillors met again at a friendly table, for in police affairs they are divided. – We also visit Frau Heim[2], a former friend of R.'s, and find her with her hair powdered. This hair colouring makes both her and the brunette Frau Wesendonck seem literally like ghosts to me. But she was very delighted with our visit. Journey home with Richter.

Friday, October 28 Loulou returned from her piano lesson and told us that Bazaine had surrendered! So another 150,000 Frenchmen to be cared for – it sounds like a fairy tale.

Wednesday, November 2 All Souls' Day. Paris is to be bombarded – who has no ears to hear must feel it, to put it vulgarly. – I compose a prayer for the dead for the children. Yesterday R. said, with regard to the hymns our soldiers sing after their battles: 'If someone were to ask me whether there is a God, I should reply: "Can you not hear him? At this moment in which thousands of human beings are singing to him, God is alive, he is there." To imagine him as someone watching and calling things good or bad is foolish; he exists in and for himself, but at certain moments in the life of nations or individuals, he is there, he awakes.' – Letter from my mother, who, banished from the Jura, is seeking a refuge. Discussion with R. as to whether, for her sake, I should offer it to her here, in view of the fact that our seclusion, our German outlook, and our whole way of life would not be congenial to her.

Sunday, November 6 R. brings home a letter from my mother, who encloses a letter addressed to the Crown Prince of Prussia, aimed at retaining Alsace for France!!! – R. says that the French government in balloons would be a subject for an Aristophanic comedy; a government like that, up in the air in both senses, would provide a writer of comedy with some splendid ideas[3]. – In the evening *Othello*, every page an experience in itself.

Monday, November 7 Continual grey skies, which depress R., but he forces himself to work. In the evening the last three acts of *Othello*; unutterably moved; I tell R. that I shall never really get to know these plays, because I am always much too deeply affected by them to take in the precise details. Lost my wedding ring on the way to Hergeschwyl!

Tuesday, November 8 Fidi naughty to his papa! Around noon R. comes and

---

[1] Friends from Wagner's Zurich years: Johann Jakob Sulzer (b. 1821) and Franz Hagenbuch (b. 1819) were both cantonal secretaries.

[2] Emilie Heim, a singer and wife of Ignaz Heim, director of music in Zurich.

[3] During the siege of Paris balloons were frequently used to evacuate refugees.

calls to me that he wishes to read me something: it left him no peace, he had to sketch out a farce in the style of Aristophanes, *Die Kapitulation*[1]; Richter can write the music for it, and then it can be played in the little theatres. His first thought was that I would be offended or worried because he had put aside his orchestration to do it, but I am content with anything that cheers and stimulates him. Anyway, he completed a page of the score in the evening. – We decide at lunch to drink to the venture, and R. says to Jakob, 'The Baroness would like the Marcobrunner.' I laugh at R. for using my old title. 'Well, I still cannot really believe that you are mine, I still feel you have only been lent to me, you are the visitor from the fairy world who will soon vanish.' – The roses are still blooming in our garden; yesterday when I awoke I found three lovely roses with buds lying in my lap; R. had placed them there while I was sleeping.

Wednesday, November 9 R. begins to work out his farce, but his mind is not completely on it, he is unwell. Searched for my ring on the highway, but did not find it.

Friday, November 11 R. is writing – though without much pleasure – *Die Kapitulation*. Bad weather, we do not go out. We discuss many things. For me the passionate side of love has disappeared, for R. it is still alive; when with constant dismay I am made aware of it, R. tells me that it is precisely this which gives him the great and calming assurance that our union is blessed by Nature; from that time onwards a new life began for him, and he looked back on his previous life as into a ghostly pit. –

Saturday, November 12 Yesterday in my bath I thought how I might encourage Lulu to devote her whole life to her father – may Heaven grant me the boon of achieving this! With every sacrifice one makes one throws from one's shoulders a part of the burden of life and walks more freely; self-will and self-love are the heavy ballast which restricts the soul's flight! – Very bad news: the Bavarians have been repulsed by the French at Orléans. Very depressed mood on this account.

Sunday, November 13 My mother writes me a long letter which shows that a mind drilled in French can never shake itself free of its fantasies! – In the afternoon, during their siesta time, Jakob comes in to announce that a woman brought back my wedding ring, which she had found on the parade ground – where I had not even been. What a remarkable stroke of fortune! Must I not gratefully recognize that the gods are kind and favourably disposed towards me? I tell R. that when I was searching for the ring on the road to Hergeschwyl I had mechanically repeated the little prayer of my searching childhood to Saint Antony of Padua. 'Oh, you Age of Reason!' exclaims R.

Tuesday, November 15 At last sunshine again, and with it a conflict between Russia and Turkey! The day is a solemn one for me: two years ago today I

---

[1] The play is printed in vol. 9 of Wagner's collected writings under the title *Eine Kapitulation* (*A Capitulation*).

took leave of Hans forever. R. says my religion dates from this Hegira, I pray with all my heart. In the night Fidi called; half asleep, I thought I was hearing Hans's complaining voice!

Wednesday, November 16 R. finishes his play, I think it is excellent. Richter is now to write the music for it.

Sunday, November 20 A friend of Richter's writes that after the battle at Sedan the military band played the prayer from *Lohengrin* as the King of Prussia appeared! – Also that the King of Bavaria is having an affair with a Frl. Scheffsky (a singer)[1]. R. does not really believe it.

Wednesday, November 23 R. is making sketches for the second act of *Götterdämmerung*, but he does not wish any notice to be taken of it. 'Otherwise I lose the urge.' I notice it from his agitated mood. But towards me he is always unutterably kind. – Richter, with his violin, pretends to the children that he is a water sprite; much jubilation. – In the afternoon a Beethoven sonata (Opus 96) with Richter; R. says that when playing the piano I look too serious, my eyes turn brown, and I become so immersed in it that he feels afraid of me! I almost regret having played, concerned that it might not be what he really wants, though he himself requested it.

Friday, November 25 At lunch R. remembers how once, when he complained (of his physical condition), my father took up the *Nibelungen*, looked at him, and said, 'He complains of abdominal troubles and writes things like this.' R. goes on to say that without a doubt my father is the greatest man of originality and genius he has ever met, and after him Hans, because he has fire. 'Thus does one think and work, contained within a very close circle of friends, and now this circle has been more or less split up. *"For when women come on the scene, they turn things upside down – things which had been going well up till then."* That was Herwegh's[2] comment on my *Nibelungen* poem!'

Saturday, November 26 Arrival of Prof. Nietzsche. Music (Richter and I), in the evening R. reads aloud his *Nicht kapituliert*[3].

Tuesday, November 29 Letter from my mother, who wants me to visit her, but I shudder at the thought of any separation from Tribschen. R., to whom I confide the news, says that he has no intention of undertaking anything without me. Toothache, piano practice, news of two victories, in Amiens and over Garibaldi. In the evening *Nicht kapituliert* sent off to the singer Betz with a letter of recommendation from R.

Sunday, December 4 Fear that I am pregnant. R. has a cold and is despondent; a conversation which touched on the King yesterday has deeply upset him; the thought that 'his work, his highest ideal, should be trampled underfoot to earn him his bread' depresses him. He forces himself

---

[1] Josephine Scheffsky (variously spelt in programmes Schefsky, Scheffzky) was a singer in Munich 1871–79; she sang Sieglinde in Bayreuth in 1876.

[2] The German poet Georg Herwegh was a close friend during Wagner's Zurich years.

[3] *Eine Kapitulation.*

to work. At lunch he exclaims: 'What is the thing written down as compared
with the inspiration? What is notation in comparison with imagination? The
former is governed by the specific laws of convention, the latter is free,
boundless. That is the tremendous thing about Beethoven, that in his last
quartets he was able to remember and record improvisations, which could
only be done through art of the highest, highest order. With me it is always
the drama which flouts convention and opens up new possibilities.' – I
think I understand him, for the relationship of the written to the improvised is the same as speech to emotions. I could never express what is
stirring my emotions at the present time, I feel as if my heart had been
broken into pieces, and love, like a bird used to a cage, is fluttering around,
knocking against everything, wounding itself – I want so much to express
it now, but I just cannot! – Loldi doing a bear's dance, Eva leaping like a
poodle to Richter's fiddling; Loldi amuses us with her affected speech, she
talks as if she really spoke another language and had learned German quite
separately. – The printed *Beethoven* has arrived. Sending copies off.

Monday, December 5 Uncle Liszt[1] sends me 15,000 francs in my father's
name. At R.'s request I return them with the remark that I had asked for
my affairs with Rothschild to be put in order, not for help in a time of
embarrassment. The remittance vexes R. extremely.

Tuesday, December 6 I tell R. of my pregnancy; he smiles and has no worries
on his own behalf; I will willingly bear all the difficulties and face the
problematic future without fear.

Wednesday, December 7 I have to whisper in R.'s ear that I was wrong; this
moves him to tears, for he had been pleased and had thought that Fate
desired me to bring a child into the world without fear and in the full
happiness of love. – I come upon R. in conversation with Richter about
Weber – how before the latter no one had any inkling of the sinister quality
of certain instruments (oboe, clarinet); just as before Beethoven no one
knew anything about *repetition*; what in Rossini is a sensual effect here
becomes a form of melody; and everything combines to make it so, the
instrumentation, the key, everything. – Telegrams from Leipzig about the
great success of *Die Msinger* there.

Friday, December 9 *My Life* has now been bound; I beg R. not to make a
present of it to the King, so that Fidi will not be deprived, on account of
some possible indiscretion, of his only capital (publication after our death).
– The demand from the steamship company – about 500 francs – brings
us to a dismal theme; R. thinks I have a lot in the savings bank, and I have
to explain to him that I have only 2,000 francs. This causes slight concern
and arouses despondent thoughts of the children's future. I promise – as I
had already decided in any case – to give no more presents, to spend

[1] Eduard Liszt (b. 1817), son of Liszt's grandfather and thus Cosima's great uncle.

nothing, and to put my allowance aside regularly. But shall I be receiving this? The state of affairs does not inspire confidence.

Saturday, December 10 Letter from Grandmama[1] in London, reporting the death of Hans's stepbrother Heinz von Bülow, who died at Châteauneuf; I weep a lot, for of course I knew the young man.

Wednesday, December 14 Very nice and intelligent letter from Clemens Brockhaus about *Die Msinger* in Leipzig and *Beethoven*. The cordial, familiar tone of R.'s nephew pleases me very much, I think of Fidi – that he might perhaps find a friendly relationship there. I am also touched by the decidedly friendly attitude towards me. 'Oh, they know what is what,' R. says. 'Anybody who gets to know you can be in no doubt at all about you. It was ordained in the stars that you should dedicate yourself to me.' Laughing, he adds, as he looks at my picture: 'Oh, yes, the proud little lady was quite determined. I'll show you, she is thinking.'

Friday, December 16 We are depressed about the news from France. Paris is reported to have laid in provisions during the recent fighting, and they claim to have 400,000 men mobilized. One cannot predict how long this slaughter will still go on, and I am beset by worry whether it will turn out as it should, in our favour. In the evening Richter plays us his music for *Die Kapitulation* and admits to us that he would find it embarrassing to put his name to it; he declares that the reason Betz does not reply to him is undoubtedly that he thinks Richter needs money and has therefore started to compose! – We laugh, and R. says how heavily one has to pay for such ideas; it had cost him a lot, too, to write the thing; but he had done it in order not to get into the habit of giving things up too easily. (Letter to my mother.)

Saturday, December 17 Betz returns *Die Kapitulation*: the theatres are frightened of the production costs. R. is basically glad, for the situation in Paris has changed, the mood is no longer the same, it is a decree of Fate. 'To stretch out a hand to the outside world is a dead loss, to withdraw it and fold one's arms is wisdom and peace.'

Wednesday, December 21 While we are drinking coffee in the downstairs *salon*, R. looks up at the gallery and says he can recall the surprise he felt on his birthday in '69, when he listened there to the quartet and saw for the first time the painted windowpane. 'You must prepare no more such surprises,' he said, 'for I can imagine how difficult it was for you all the time you were preparing it. In a love like ours it is surely almost unbearable having to conceal things from each other.' I admit to him that when he questioned me about my correspondence with Herr Müller over the quartet and always accepted my answer without question, I did feel deeply ashamed.

Friday, December 23 Nothing to report except Christmas preparations. I

---

[1] Franziska von Bülow, Hans's mother; Heinz was the son of Hans's father Eduard and his second wife Luise.

drive to town in a sleigh and return home half frozen. In the evening I decorate the tree. The children work in secret. Great excitement everywhere.

Saturday, December 24 My day is devoted to laying out the presents, which I do with melancholy; the report concerning our people taken prisoner in Pau, and starving, dominates my feelings, and I also think of Hans. At five o'clock R. returns from town, bringing Prof. Nietzsche with him, at seven o'clock we light the candles. It is the first Christmas on which I am giving R. no present and will receive none from him – so that is all right. A telegram from Dr. Sulzer says he is accepting R.'s invitation and will arrive at midday tomorrow from Bern. Everybody is happy and content, our good Stockers think we have done too much for them. – The children blissful!

Sunday, December 25 About this day, my children, I can tell you nothing – nothing about my feelings, nothing about my mood, nothing, nothing. I shall just tell you, drily and plainly, what happened. When I woke up I heard a sound, it grew ever louder, I could no longer imagine myself in a dream, music was sounding, and what music! After it had died away, R. came in to me with the five children and put into my hands the score of his 'Symphonic Birthday Greeting'. I was in tears, but so, too, was the whole household; R. had set up his orchestra on the stairs and thus consecrated our Tribschen forever! *The Tribschen Idyll* – thus the work is called[1]. – At midday Dr. Sulzer arrived, surely the most important of R.'s friends! After breakfast the orchestra again assembled, and now once again the *Idyll* was heard in the lower apartment, moving us all profoundly (Countess B. was also there, on my invitation); after it the *Lohengrin* wedding procession, Beethoven's Septet, and, to end with, once more the work of which I shall never hear enough! – Now at last I understood all R.'s working in secret, also dear Richter's trumpet (he blazed out the Siegfried theme splendidly and had learned the trumpet especially to do it), which had won him many admonishments from me. 'Now let me die,' I exclaimed to R. 'It would be easier to die for me than to live for me,' he replied. – In the evening R. reads his *Meistersinger* to Dr. Sulzer, who did not know it; and I take as much delight in it as if it were something completely new. This makes R. say, 'I wanted to read Sulzer *Die Ms*, and it turned into a dialogue between us two.'

Monday, December 26 The whole day long I go about as if in a dream, my spirit listens for the vanished sounds and brings them back to birth for itself, my heart, oppressed by its emotions, seeks redemption in music; a twilight dream emerges – seeing nothing more, hearing everything in the depths of silence, love ruling supreme, boundaries melting away, an unawareness of existence – 'the height of bliss'. – In the evening R. reads aloud passages from the manuscript Prof. Nietzsche gave me as a birthday

---

[1] Later to be known as *The Siegfried Idyll*.

gift; it is entitled *The Birth of the Tragic Concept*[1] and is of the greatest value; the depth and excellence of his survey, conveyed with a very concentrated brevity, is quite remarkable; we follow his thoughts with the greatest and liveliest interest. My greatest pleasure is in seeing how R.'s ideas can be extended in this field. – Christmas Eve brought us a letter from Alex. Serov, who made an official journey from St. Petersburg to Vienna for the Beethoven festivities. His highly original description of this shows that it was Judea which celebrated the greatest of our heroes. All of it must have been absurd and ridiculous and, for us, an affront.

Tuesday, December 27 Played with the children in the morning. (Fidi over-excited by the music and other Christmas pleasures – could not sleep all night and kept on laughing and being skittish. During the *Idyll* he pleased and captivated all the musicians with his lively and spirited enjoyment of the music.) – We are concerned to have had no news from the King at Christmas; R. fears that he is angry about not having been sent *Siegfried*.

Friday, December 30 The music publisher [Peters] wants a coronation march and offers R. 1,500 francs for it; the only pity is that R. cannot write to order, and particularly not a coronation march. – The newspapers report the total dissolution of the Loire army. – God grant it is true!

Saturday, December 31 R. and I pay New Year calls to our clergyman Tschudi (whom R. greets not without emotion, since he was so friendly towards us). Then the Bassenheims, who are also in R.'s eyes hallowed and worthy of respect, since they were present at our wedding. In the carriage R. looks back over the past and says: 'How long did I suffer on Hans's account before I recognized that here, as in *Tristan*, a power reigned against which everyone was helpless.' The reading of *Tristan* made me melancholy inasmuch as it reminded me of Richard's situation at that time in Zurich, and I cannot think of such false images, disappointments, and fleeting emanations of madness without tears; R. reproves me for these feelings and says I imagine things as far more significant than they had in fact been, though certainly in becoming aware of them I had matured. – In the afternoon the quartet players from Zurich, R. rehearsed them in the F Major Quartet, Opus 59 (a favourite work of mine, if one may speak thus of such divine things), then the last (also F Major). Towards eleven o'clock the musicians go away, we stay up, Prof. Nietzsche, our good Richter, and we two. Midnight arrives, we wish each other a Happy New Year. May God bring us all peace! –

[1] Later entitled *The Dionysian Outlook*.

1871

Sunday, January 1 The children, all five, come with greetings, Loulou recites her English poem to me in a good accent and proves in this, too, her easy powers of comprehension, just as she yesterday delighted me with her lively attentiveness while listening to music. Boni also listened with devotion. – Family lunch; at about four o'clock Prof. N. takes his departure. – Fidi starts the year with 'Herr-mine', the word which to him expresses everything.

Tuesday, January 3 Letter to Prof. Nietzsche, who has been instrumental in getting *our* nephew Fritz Brockhaus[1] called to Basel.

Thursday, January 5 The bombardment of Paris has now begun in earnest. Family lunch; afterwards a visit from Countess B., who tells us to our great delight that the King has granted their fief[2]. We accompany her home; on the return journey, as we passed the Protestant church in the town, R. saluted it and said: 'What a friendly wedding morn that was! One felt as if all one's cares were being smoothed away. All the people who took part in that ceremony are sacred to me.' – In the evening Richter brings back a letter from a Herr Langer in Pest, on behalf of the management, offering him the conductor's post there. Richter will have to accept it, but for us it will be difficult to let him go – we look on him, after all, as our eldest son! – Talking about Prof. N.'s work, R. says, 'He is the only living person, apart from Constantin Frantz, who has provided me with something, a positive enrichment of my outlook.'

Saturday, January 7 At lunch R. notices that Richter is absent-minded and believes he wishes he were already in Pest. 'I myself,' says R., 'am quite resigned, I am ready to give up everything at once. What do I get from performances except exertion and trouble, and just the satisfaction that nothing has gone wrong? But it leaves no impression. My things give me pleasure only up to the first working out in ink, when the nebulous pencilled ideas suddenly emerge clearly and distinctly before my eyes. Even the instrumentation belongs too much to the outside world.'

Monday, January 9 With the children; R. orchestrates. In the afternoon

[1] Friedrich Arnold (b. 1838), son of Hermann and Ottilie Brockhaus.
[2] Giving her possession as sole heiress of her father's estates in Bavaria.

sleigh ride with the two little ones. Bureau de Musique Peters[1] (thus the signature) writes: 'I am still hoping for the composition of the coronation march.' The day before yesterday R. said to me, 'If the worst comes to the worst, I shall write the march.'

Tuesday, January 10 The news of the bombardment of Paris is good, and it seems the French themselves realize the hopelessness of their position. – Arrival of the Shakespeare which R. is giving me; a beautiful English edition. In the evening read Gibbon with R.: his childish views on the 'barbarian' Germans made us laugh heartily, but also give us cause for thought.

Friday, January 13 Since my eyes are very weak, I consult the eye specialist; I have to take care of my eyesight. – A friendly New Year's greeting from Frau Wille, on the other hand an unpleasant exchange with Colonel Am Rhyn about the sleigh, he objects to our use of it; we give in immediately and hire one from the town. Richard is very much occupied with one passage in his instrumentation; he says he could not endow even the coronation march with more splendour than this scene of recognition between Siegfried and Brünnhilde.

Monday, January 16 My eyes are weak, I am not allowed to read, write or sew. At lunch R. talks again about [Wilhelmine] Schröder-Devrient and her performance as Romeo. 'That really made me feel that everything hangs on the dramatic action; all the classicality (even quartets sound like so much squeaking!) crumbled in my eyes at the sight of this human warmth. In fact the libretto is not at all badly done, and it had its effect on me when I decided to reduce *Tristan* to three love scenes.' His intended work *The Destiny of Opera*[2] is very much occupying R.'s thoughts, and many of his conversations now lead in this direction. The significance of the orchestra, its position as the ancient chorus, its huge advantage over the latter, which talks about the action in words, whereas the orchestra conveys to us the soul of this action – all this he explains to us in detail. – First drive out with Fidi, in the new sleigh.

Wednesday, January 18 Letter from E. Ollivier, who is living in isolation near Turin. R. says, 'He is a good and intelligent person, but shares his country's insolence, which robbed him of his senses and forced him into war.' Our groom, Friedrich, is being taken from us, has to go as a soldier to the border, where fighting has been going on for the past two days. (My eyes are trying me sorely.)

Sunday, January 22 'We are living like gods, and there's nothing more to be said,' R. exclaims to me in the morning, and then sings a melody from [Bellini's] *La Straniera*, which reminds us once more of the effect of such

[1] Original name of the famous Edition Peters.
[2] The promised lecture for the Berlin Academy.

things. 'Vivid portrayal with it – an interesting singer – and goodbye to all classicality. That is where the drama must come in. I am no poet, and I don't care at all if people reproach me for my choice of words, in my works the action is everything. To a certain extent it is a matter of indifference to me whether people understand my verses, since they will certainly understand my dramatic action. Poets are nonentities compared to musicians, painters and sculptors – it is only dramatists who can compete with them.' – Talking about musicians and indiscriminate composing, he said yesterday: 'Everybody should improvise, every good musician can produce something interesting in his improvisation. But writing it down is quite a different process, then it has to be turned into a sonata, a suite, and so on, and it takes a lot to revitalize a familiar, defined form.' 'Beethoven was the first to write music which was listened to purely as music, all previous things were designed to enliven social gatherings or to accompany what was going on in the church or on the stage.' Family lunch and later on the musicians; E-flat Major Quartet under R.'s direction, true bliss. The children happy, even the servants much moved.

Monday, January 23 I am very unwell, my eyes are becoming very weak and are painful, and even the great pleasure of yesterday was too much for me, I am having to pay for it today. R. is also not completely well, but he works all the same. He tells me he will embark soon on *The Destiny of Opera* and begin the second act of *Götterdämmerung* later, promises me (!!), however, to compose the two acts without interruption. Joy over our victories, which appear to be very great; vanished now is the fine European Court which was such a great humiliation for Germany; that is Bismarck's immortal achievement.

Wednesday, January 25 R. was unwell and worked on poems extolling the German troops; when he confided this to me, I encouraged him, but he replied: 'Yes, but how? If I send it to the *N.A.Z.* without my name, it will receive hardly any attention at all. So should I sign it? With a name which any Jewboy can mock at as that of an opera composer one can't put oneself forward as a patriot.' – Next morning his ideas had vanished. – When I go into his room in the morning, I notice that he is disconcerted, and turn to leave; he calls me back and tells me he has just hidden the paper on which he had after all written down his poem to the German people[1]; he had been ashamed to let me see! At noon he reads it to me; I feel that it ought to be more extensive, and he intends to add another verse.

Thursday, January 26 R. has added two verses to his poem, he reads it over family lunch, and, since I advise him not to have it published in a newspaper but, rather, to send it to Count Bismarck, he asks me to arrange

---

[1] Published for the first time in Vol. 9 of the Collected Writings under the title 'To the German Army outside Paris'.

this through Councillor Bucher. This brings the conversation to the people who have accomplished these deeds, and R. says: 'There are individuals who stand above Fate and literally direct it themselves – these are the very rare geniuses like Frederick the Great. Then there are others who, though less talented, possess certain qualities which the Universal Spirit needs in order to achieve great things. Such a one is King Wilhelm, whose decency and trustworthiness are just what were required to bring about the downfall of the French.'

Friday, January 27 'My dear good wife,' R. exclaims to me early in the morning, 'Nature wanted me to bring a son into the world, and you alone could bear me this son; anything else would have been nonsense and absurdity. This gave me the strength to accomplish and bear unimaginable things in order to get us united. That must be our comfort, for Nature's purpose goes far beyond all else.' – I send off his fine poem to L. Bucher for Bismarck – what will the latter think of it??

Saturday, January 28 After lunch I lie down to rest, R. comes into the silent room and, uncertain whether I am asleep or not, says in Saxon dialect, 'I am lighting a peace cigar, Paris has capitulated.' Electrified, I leap to my feet and ask if it is true. It really is true – Jakob brought the news from town, completely phlegmatic in the usual Swiss way. It was not unexpected, yet it comes to me as such a surprise, so breathtakingly sudden. We shall not march into Paris, and that is splendid. In great excitement all evening, but read Gibbon attentively all the same.

Sunday, January 29 The five children at my bedside in their Sunday clothes. 'Such dignity surrounding you,' R. says, laughing, 'and you are only a child yourself. All these beings depend on you – you are the axle on which it all turns.' At midday the musicians, and a bowl of salad over my favourite dress!

Monday, January 30 Yesterday I was not feeling well, today I am better. R. is pleased and says the quartet has cured me. – R. yesterday told the musicians that the difference between the last quartets and the earlier ones lies in their tremendous concision, and this is also where the difficulty of interpreting these works lies; since everything in them is solid core and they no longer contain any frills, each note must be played consciously, otherwise the result is unclear. – After lunch the musicians played us the *Idyll* in an arrangement by Richter; much emotion! R. said how curious it seemed to him: all he had set out to do was to work the theme which had come to him in Starnberg (when we were living there together), and which he had promised me as a quartet, into a morning serenade, and then he had unconsciously woven our whole life into it – Fidi's birth, my recuperation, Fidi's bird, etc. As Schopenhauer said, this is the way a musician works, he expresses life in a language which reason does not understand.

Tuesday, January 31 A tenor (Schleich) asks for an attestation that the role of Lohengrin cannot be sung when one has catarrh; R. gives it to him. – R. has been composing coronation marches during the night; he is thinking a little about it because of the money.

Saturday, February 4 From Councillor Düfflipp a letter to R., saying the King is asking about the score of *Siegfried*!! This puts a great weight on R.'s spirits.

Sunday, February 5 Letter from E.O[llivier], very elegiac; we are both of the opinion that he cannot be exonerated; whatever he did, he should not have allowed himself to be dragged along and advocate war against his original convictions. – R. completes his *Siegfried*[1] today, I am beside him as he writes the last notes! This the day's happening which fills me with rapture.

Monday, February 6 Luise Bülow writes a fine and composed letter to Loulou. Her son fell while crying out, 'Dear Fatherland, you can rest in peace' – everything noble must always be mixed with a grain of absurdity, says R.

Wednesday, February 8 Frau Wesendonck sends me her *Friedrich der Grosse*[2]; R. is utterly opposed to women's venturing into the market in this way, he sees it as a sign of lack of taste. From London he receives an invitation to write a cantata for the opening of the industrial exhibition. Naturally he does not accept, he says he has enough trouble already with the coronation march; he has a tremendous number of themes, but he lacks the concentration to select.

Thursday, February 9 I thank Frau W. for sending her book; I avoid praising the book itself, but speak earnestly and warmly about its subject. R., to whom I read my letter, is utterly against it and says to me, 'What words are left for genuine things if we treat stupidities in this way?' When I reply that I find it impossible not to treat seriously people who have shown friendship towards him and for whom he has felt sympathy, he replies: 'If you did it only out of consideration for me, it makes me feel downright degraded. To guard against any sentimental mistakes, I sent this lady her letters back and had mine burned, for I do not want anything to remain which might suggest it was ever a serious relationship. The fact that I once spoke in tones such as you use in this letter is something for which I have already had to pay dearly enough.' – Family lunch, at which I notice that R. is despondent; in reply to my question he tells me that our friend Serov has died, suddenly and in a manner as gentle as his soul!

Monday, February 13 R. called me to him around midday and said that he now had a clear first draft of the coronation march[3]; he plays some of it to me and I like it very much.

---

[1] The full orchestral score.
[2] A drama (*Frederick the Great*).
[3] Later entitled *Kaiser-Marsch*.

Tuesday, February 14 Letters from Paris, our friend Nuitter wrote immediately (on January 31) after the capitulation. His touching letter has only just arrived. Claire also writes to me, with extraordinary self-control, talking only about small things, ignoring the whole disaster. When we speak of various friends who have no sympathy for present developments in Germany, R. says: 'Who suffered more than I did under the drawbacks of life in Germany? Indeed, I even got to the stage of wishing to see the whole nation dissolved, but always in the hope of building something new, something more in line with the German spirit.' – Great ardour on R.'s part puts me into a despondent mood; best of all I should like to live my life here unnoticed, reaping only beaming glances; I have suffered too much to be susceptible to other pleasures!

Wednesday, February 15 Yesterday he showed great displeasure with his march: 'I can't do things when I can't imagine something behind it. And if I imagine something, it gets out of hand. A march is an absurdity; the most it can be is a popular song, but it is not meant to be sung, which is nonsensical. I must have some great vehicle, on which I can reel off my music; like this I can do nothing.'

Thursday, February 16 Work with the children, then nothing really except travel preparations; great excitement among the children, because Eva's birthday is to be celebrated tomorrow in Zurich.

Friday, February 17 Fine weather, arrival in good spirits. Tidied ourselves up a little in the Hotel Baur, then drove to the Wesendoncks'. After seven years I had brought him back there, and I was glad to have succeeded. Frau W. was to all appearances pleased to see R. again – and to see him looking so happy. Her black hair disturbed him a little, but he grew accustomed to it and found her well disposed and friendly. The children behaved splendidly, endured the long-drawn-out meal with patience and good manners, and afterwards they played with the W. children. At six o'clock listened to quartets (E-flat Major, F Minor, B-flat Major) in our hotel; the Wesendoncks and the Willes also there, the musicians played very well, and a congenial atmosphere prevailed.

Saturday, February 18 Zurich. At eleven o'clock drove to the Willes; a merry day for the children; the Wesendonck house too fine for them, children and toys too splendid, here everything much freer and more amusing. But R. is very worn out. Frau Wesendonck arrives with her daughter, and we invite them to visit us. Dr. Wille very clever and original, as always. Frau Wille very kind, she always speaks to me with such deep sympathy and understanding. We all discuss the German situation, and R. sums up his attitude thus: 'We have Bismarck to thank for keeping Germany from becoming a large Alsace.' Took our departure at six o'clock, the children having again behaved very well. R. dead tired, I glad to be journeying home, we no longer belong among other people, we are only happy when alone in our own home. We welcome the sight of our 'home' hill, our Tribschen, here we are away from the world! – An iron stove in the carriage was so overheated that it almost killed us. R. felt the consequence of it in the evening and looked very ill.

Sunday, February 19 R. tells me that what so wears him down in others is their talking to him – that is why he tends so often to express himself at great length, solely in order to spare himself certain questions which seem to him like an attack on his very existence. What had reconciled him in his re-encounter with Frau Wesendonck was, he says, the fact that she seemed to him to be a good person who was cordially pleased to see him now in a state of happiness.

Monday, February 20 R. works on his march and plays me his sketch, I believe it will be very fine. – With R. to town, where I find a letter from Baron Rothschild, sending me the 2,000 francs, though under the name Baroness von Bülow; this rightly annoys R., and he requests me to demand from my father a rectification. I am reluctant to demand this of my father, but after an inner struggle I decide to do so. R., who had been watching my face, says, 'Your eyes are shining, as if you had decided to do me a favour,' and indeed the thought that I was making a little sacrifice on his behalf had uplifted me. Bitter feelings about my father. R. has given me the score of *Siegfried*, bound, as a present. A new treasure for my room! . . . In the evening began Carlyle's *Frederick the Great*. R. says Carlyle is not a writer, but he has an original mind.

Tuesday, February 21 Foehn and a letter from the King, in his usual style. The King asks R. to tell him his plans and complains about the political situation; we have to smile at the realization that, while everybody is applauding his German outlook, he is probably serving the German cause only very reluctantly, because he is obliged to. – I send the 2,000 francs to the savings bank – I now have 7,000 francs laid aside for the children. – In the evening Carlyle, whose style makes us suffer greatly.

Thursday, February 23 In the morning R. tells me that he has thought out his 'petition' (to the King of Bavaria on the building of our theatre). He asks me to write to Councillor Düfflipp in his name, which I do. He continues with his march; recently he asked me about a turn in it and approved my choice, a matter of the greatest pride for me, and yet I must always and ever say to myself, 'Know not what he finds in me.'[1]

Saturday, February 25 We lack money; Hanover, Vienna, Dresden are making difficulties for us with their royalty payments. When R. yesterday observed Fidi's indisposition[2] he said, 'It causes you such difficulty to bite, and when at last you are able to bite, you may have nothing to bite.' 'Are

---

[1] Gretchen in Goethe's *Faust*.
[2] He was teething.

things so bad?' I ask. 'God knows they are,' he answers with a sigh. – After lunch R. plays us his march, to our delight. From town the children bring back several letters; one really startles us with its gigantic handwriting, R. guesses Bismarck, and truly it is Bismarck, thanking him for the poem. I believe R. would have been happier if he had not written, for he had not been expecting it, but the autograph gives me a childish joy. Third letter from the exhibition committee in London; they have decided to perform the March from *Tannhäuser* and ask R. to conduct it, for which they offer him 20 pounds!

Wednesday, March 1 Fine letter from our friend Nuitter, who takes a stand high above it all; the good Pasdeloup, however, is professing to hate the Germans, and he will not perform any of their works. '*Cela se calmera,*' Nuitter observes. In the Grand Opéra fragments from *Tannhäuser* have been performed, always with great success, in spite of newspaper protests. – R. says how important and fruitful it has been to read Gibbon, since it has shown him that the idea of the Roman Empire still lives on as the wisest form of government, and it is only a matter of who puts it into practice. – Letter from my mother, incorrigible as ever, still abusing the Germans!

Friday, March 3 Thiers[1] has put forward the peace terms, with tears and the usual protestations of helplessness!! The same terms which he has spent so many weeks in negotiating! – Letter from Judith Mendès, suggesting that my letter has hurt her – I don't know why it should. They appear to have suffered very much.

Saturday, March 4 R. is glad the time has come when one no longer needs to read the newspapers so avidly. – Conversation about Bayreuth – that we three, R., Richter and myself, will do *everything*: no producer, no nothing, just a treasurer.

Wednesday, March 8 It saddens us that the soldiers could have had so little pleasure from their entry into Paris. 'The best thing about it,' says R., 'is the effect it had on the Parisians.' We laugh over their silent appearance on the boulevards; they cannot stay in their homes, and there were certainly some mourning clothes to be seen – 'contrition hats, resignation jackets, revenge gloves,' and so on! – Richter has been in Zurich since yesterday, we are again alone at table, so the talk is more intimate. Speaking of his life, R. says: 'If we had not come together, I should have grown very old and apathetic. Your father noticed it when he visited me here (1866). That shook me.'

Monday, March 13 Fidi's nursemaid is leaving us, and we learn that the lower servants are in fact continually plotting against us, 'We do not belong here,' R. says. – My resolve to change to the Protestant faith is growing ever deeper; I shall do it in Bayreuth. But Bayreuth – when? The King keeps silent.

---

[1] Adolphe Thiers, president of the French Assembly.

Tuesday, March 14 R. is working out a folk song for his march, to be sung by the soldiers. He is working hard, but it is a strain on him, for he is no longer cut out for having to complete things by a certain date. Delight in the starlings, who are making a fearful din in the trees.

Wednesday, March 15 R. finishes his '*Kaisermarsch*' and sends it off to Berlin. Letter from Judith Mendès, she is nice and friendly and admits she was unjust. In the evening Gibbon.

Thursday, March 16 The whole countryside covered with snow, the poor starlings will starve! We do not go out. R. drafts his poem; at first he thought of demanding 500 francs from the publisher for it, so as to have 2,000 francs for our journey (1,500 for the March). But he does not want it to be tacked on; his ambition is for it to be taken for a folk song, and for that reason it should sound quite artless[1]. I come upon him at work, he is altering the words to fit the melody, and says: 'Nothing worthwhile will come just from writing a good poem and then putting a melody to it. I can see how the irregularities of the Greek choruses arose; I also knew what I was doing when I constructed my *Nibelungen* metre – I knew it would accommodate itself to the music.' – At lunch he had also considered whether he could not send his march to the London exhibition, replacing '*Ein' feste Burg*' with 'God Save the King'. 'That would mean 50 pounds, but it would spoil the March.'

Saturday, March 18 We discuss Bayreuth and Berlin, I ask him whether it would not be better if he refrained from giving a lecture and just tried to set up his subscription scheme; I shrink from any personal intervention. R. feels that, though it could do harm, it could also do a great deal of good, and defends his idea. I am apprehensive about it, I wish we could get things done without touching Berlin. . . . From the King we hear nothing, Yet his approval is the most important of all. We are now short of money, and I really do not dare discuss this subject with R.

Sunday, March 19 Letter from my mother, she is arriving on Thursday. Quartets again at last; our three people arrive from Zurich and play with Richter the A Minor, which affects us deeply. Then Op. 95 and 74 – somewhat 'cold' music, as R. says, with wonderful passages.

Tuesday, March 21 R. reads me the work he has begun[2]; it is wonderfully fine, and it seems to me to matter not at all whether it makes an impression in Berlin – the main thing is that it should be said. -- If Bayreuth is refused us, we shall think of Strassburg. Peters sent the 1,500 francs.

Thursday, March 23 The day passes in preparations for my mother. I sort out papers and read old letters from my father, which show me once again that I had neither a father nor a mother. R. has been everything to me, he

---

[1] Though Wagner set his '*Kaiserlied*' to music in such a way that it could be tacked on to the *Kaisermarsch*, he did not regard this as really desirable.
[2] *The Destiny of Opera.*

alone has loved me. – I teach the children R.'s '*Kaiserlied*', which they sing very nicely. R. spends a long time considering how to add it to the score, for on no account does he want choral societies and glee clubs to sing it.

Friday, March 24 At one o'clock to the railway station to meet my mother. She does not arrive, which casts a slight shadow over the reception ceremony. But at six o'clock she arrives, and we spend the evening talking. She is well in spite of what she has been through and now faces.

Saturday, March 25 Stormy day, talked over the past and future with my mother. She likes it here. I feel very strange towards her, but she is pleasant company because of her wide education. We talk a lot and about all sorts of things, the conditions in Paris are horrifying.

Sunday, March 26 Family lunch; my mother finds the children very well mannered and well behaved, but they seem to her very pale, for which the cough which afflicted them all is to blame. In the afternoon quartets, but the players are not in such good form as usual. – Richter receives a letter from Munich. There people are talking of an arrangement between Trib-schen, the King and the Emperor to present the *Nibelungen* in Bayreuth. We compare this piece of news with the silence towards us and ask ourselves what it means; is there some mischief brewing? . . . I am fearful. (Rothschild sends the bill of exchange to 'Frau Wagner'.)

Monday, March 27 Sent the 1,000 francs to the savings bank; I now have 8,141 francs laid aside for the children. Visit from Count Bassenheim, who inflicts a dismal afternoon on me, since I did not know how to get rid of him and R. does not like being alone with my mother; he says he can talk only to and with me, it depends on me whether he flies or creeps. My mother gets Richter to play many things from R.'s works and seems overwhelmed by this glimpse into a (for her) totally new world.

Wednesday, March 29 Work with the children, whom my mother likes very much. Walk with my mother in a lovely sunset. In the evening R. reads the first act of *Tristan*, which impresses me with its sublime perfection and moves me indescribably.

Friday, March 31 Lovely weather again, lovely walk to Winkel. In the evening music from *Tannhäuser*, otherwise just repetition of the difficulties with my mother. R.'s love is my only refuge, I know no other!

Sunday, April 2 My mother leaves us; R. thanks her for having come, I am very moved as I embrace her for the last time; all the sadness of life overcomes me! Dismal return home in dismal weather; R. offended by a joke on my part, I somewhat pained by his touchiness; everyone with colds and indisposed.

Monday, April 3 R. comes to my bed in the very early morning, kisses my hands and feet, says that if anything is guilty of casting a shadow between us it is the abundance of our feelings for each other that makes us so sensitive. Deep happiness, a feeling of redemption! – At breakfast

Prof. Nietzsche is suddenly announced, he comes from Lugano and will spend some days here. He appears very run down.

Tuesday, April 4 A letter from Councillor Düffl[ipp] – the same old song! The King wants *Siegfried* and is offended by R.'s writing so truthfully about the performances in Munich. However, he wishes to send D. R. arranges for a meeting in Augsburg, but he is sad, for once again he has not been understood.

Wednesday, April 5 Prof. N. reads to me from a work (*The Origin and Aim of Greek Tragedy*[1]) which he wants to dedicate to R; great delight over that; in it one sees a gifted man imbued with R.'s ideas in his own way. We are spending these days in a lively discussion of our plans. Dr. Gruppe[2] writes from Berlin that R. can give his lecture there on the 28th.

Saturday, April 8 Prof. Nietzsche departs. I write letters; R. drafts some lines to be distributed among the patrons of our undertaking. Great tiredness – why do I so fear this journey?

Monday, April 10 R. announces to me that Richter is to leave us (because he wants to assist his mother[3] in Vienna), and he asks me to lend him a thousand francs from my savings so that he can give Richter a small present. I do it willingly, though with a heavy heart; I feel as if we shall never be able to set anything aside, God help us! My mood regarding our journey is becoming more and more despondent, it seems like blasphemy for me to seek contact with the outside world again.

Thursday, April 13 My eye affliction troubles me so severely that I think seriously of going blind; how to bear this – not only to bear it but to welcome it as an act of atonement – occupies me throughout the night. When I wake, Fidi is brought into my room, his face is as white as a corpse, a terrible shock. Yesterday he had been wrapped in cold cloths (his feet), was left alone by his nurse, woke up, and cried; R. alone heard him, rushed to him, and found him standing up, prey to a chill. R. utterly beside himself, believes his appearance to be the result of this chill. The doctor reassures us. We had already given up our journey, but resume it.

Saturday, April 15 At five o'clock kissed the (sleeping) children, then off, dread in my heart. (Thoughts of R.'s being murdered by a Berlin Jew.) A wait in Zurich, telegraphed and wrote to the children. In the evening neither Düfflipp nor Cornelius at the station, which surprises us. Misunderstandings – we come together in the Drei Mohren hotel. Düfflipp not difficult, tells us the cheerless news that the King has been thinking of performing the two acts of *Siegfried*, since the third is not ready. R. becomes very solemn and says he would burn his *Siegfried* before yielding it up like that, and then go out begging.

[1] The first draft of *The Birth of Tragedy*.
[2] Otto Friedrich Gruppe, permanent secretary of the Royal Academy of Arts, Berlin.
[3] Josephine Csazinsky, a singing teacher.

Sunday, April 16 Continued on to Nuremberg.

Monday, April 17 Left at one o'clock, in Bayreuth at five. Charming impression of the town.

Tuesday, April 18 Terrible night of worry and alarm. R. wakes up suddenly with fits of shivering; I send for the doctor, who is pensive, wants to wait and see how it goes, but cannot help laughing and saying: 'The things that can happen to one! Who could have told me that I should this night be making the acquaintance of R. Wagner?' As he came in, he asked, 'Are you *the* Richard Wagner, I mean the particular R. Wagner?' Whereupon R.: 'If you mean the one who has written such pretty things – yes, I am he.' – R. gets somewhat better, but has to stay in bed, I read [Goethe's] *Italian Journey* to him.

Wednesday, April 19 R. would by now be quite restored if a shocking noise in the hotel had not laid the whole night waste. Some gentlemen were giving a party and behaving like the roughest of coach drivers. We drive to the theatre, a charming monument which tells us much about the productivity of German art in the 18th century[1]. In the florid ornaments, shells, etc., of the eighteenth century one finds the same spirit of fantasy, though of course much distorted, which inspired German work in the 16th century. But the theatre will not do for us at all; so we must build – and all the better. Now to find a house. With the curator of the palace we drive all over the town, nothing is quite suitable, so we must build for ourselves, too. Lovely drive to the Eremitage[2]; the old curator there is delighted to see R. and says that it was only the priests who separated R. from the King, the people love him. In the evening R. is very tired. The Bayreuth population in an uproar over his presence.

Thursday, April 20 Left at one o'clock. At ten o'clock in Leipzig, where Parson Clemens [Brockhaus] is at the station. Entry into the Hôtel de Prusse, laurel wreaths, poems, transparencies, and so on; rooms in the royal apartment. Spent the evening very pleasantly with Hermann Brockhaus and Ottilie.

Friday, April 21 In the morning the conductor Schmidt, the rehearsal [of *Die Meistersinger*] at twelve. Richard greeted with a flourish, everything well and good, but the orchestra! In despair R. takes the baton himself, but nothing sounds right – a terrible decline! Dinner with the Brockhauses.

Saturday, April 22 Morning with the family, at one o'clock on to Dresden, to escape the Leipzig *Meistersinger*, set down for today. At the railway station Councillor Pusinelli[3], who has found us splendid lodgings in the Tower

[1] The Markgräfliches Opernhaus, one of the finest examples of baroque architecture still in existence, completed 1748.
[2] A rococo summer residence just outside Bayreuth, belonging now to King Ludwig.
[3] Anton Pusinelli (b. 1815), physician and friend of Wagner and Minna since 1842, and the one in whom he most closely confided.

(Hotel Weber). Charming impression of Dresden, saw the house in which R. composed *Tannhäuser*. Then to his sister Luise; friendly but melancholy reception, for she has lost a grandson and son-in-law in the war. Spent the evening with the Pusinellis, homely family atmosphere – '*Seid umschlungen Millionen*', for the children are innumerable.

Sunday, April 23 Reunion with Countess Krockow, much to my delight. At two o'clock to Luise's for lunch, she is pleased with her brother, finds he has become gentler, 'fatherly', thanks me for my courage, my courage is my happiness. In the evening to the theatre, the wooden barn does not displease R., it holds a lot of people; he observes everything with an eye towards Bayreuth. The actors beneath all criticism, their vulgarity, stupidity etc., etc., is now common throughout Germany. Sad impression.

Monday, April 24 While my friends are all attending the performance of *Die Meistersinger*, we wander in the evening through the streets of Dresden; when will death at last come to us? When we are with the children we are conscious of our duty to go on living, but when we are with other people, the longing for death comes over us with almost unconquerable force. I see the shop where R. sold Schiller's poems in order to buy cream puffs. We near the theatre, and I wish to hear how far they have got in *Die Meistersinger*; from far away we could hear it, but close to we hear nothing, then suddenly a run on the clarinet comes through to us – it sounds like *Tristan und Isolde*! We return home; it is cold outside and I cannot help weeping.

Tuesday, April 25 Off to Berlin. I feel shut up inside, God knows I no longer belong among people. Arrived at ten o'clock; met with flowers, to the hotel. Marie Schleinitz very friendly and warm, everything Wagner asked for (three rehearsals, so-and-so many violins, etc.) has been granted. Wagner very pleased with the friendly lady.

Thursday, April 27 Tausig so changed that we scarcely recognize him; amazement on my part at the tone in which Bismarck is talked about – 'more luck than judgment, no character'. Saw Lothar Bucher again, much joy. Johanna[1] now the sentimental niece after having at the height of her career behaved very badly indeed. Hotel du Parc, where we are staying, much besieged and noisy.

Friday, April 28 At midday in the hotel a visit from Alwine Frommann[2], which gave us great pleasure. She is utterly *ancien régime*. We go for a walk with her. At six o'clock Dr. Gruppe calls to conduct R. to his lecture in the Academy. He comes home towards nine o'clock; he laughs and says that

---

[1] Johanna Jachmann-Wagner (b. 1826), adopted daughter of Wagner's brother Albert and wife of Alfred Jachmann, a district councillor; Wagner's first Elisabeth in *Tannhäuser*, she had had a brilliant career as an opera singer before losing her voice in 1862.

[2] Alwine Frommann (b. 1800), reader for the Prussian queen, was a friend and supporter of Wagner since seeing *Der Fliegende Holländer* in Berlin in 1844.

the whole enterprise had been mad, he had expected large public sittings such as take place in Paris, but the Academy of Sciences was not even present, and at the green table he read his thing out to musicians, sculptors and painters. He was introduced to each in turn, came to Joachim[1], who said, 'It is a long time since I last saw you.' 'A long time indeed,' R. replied. To Dorn R. said, 'I should not have expected to see you here,' whereupon the insolent man replied, 'I am always interested in anything you do.' And so on.

Saturday, April 29 We keep this morning free in order to visit the aquarium; great impression: it turns one into a philosopher, here one comes to realize that Man is also nothing but an animal with desires, here one understands that only renunciation can provide an ending to this terrible hell of existence; the grabbing plants are a horrible sight! In the evening with Frau von Schleinitz. R. reads *Parzival* to her; indescribable emotion. If no single tone of it, no verse ever gets written, this draft is eternal and perhaps the sublimest vision R. has ever beheld. – Eckert[2] calls to take R. to the banquet, during which Councillor Bucher visits me and tells me many interesting things about his stay in Versailles. The most curious thing about it is certainly, as we recently heard from Alwine, that the leading figures in the war were by no means of one mind.

Sunday, April 30 At twelve o'clock our old friend Weitzmann[3] comes to conduct us to the Singakademie, where R. is to be received; it all takes place in the friendliest way; the orchestra, consisting of various poor musicians, play the *Faust* Overture and the *Tannhäuser* March, not at all badly, so nicely, in fact, that R. feels disposed to say a few words and then to take up the baton and conduct the Overture again, amid great applause. Dohm's prologue (spoken by niece Johanna) was very pretty. R. was genuinely moved, and the whole thing was much better than expected. But afterwards R. is very tired.

Monday, May 1 R. is now writing to Councillor D[üfflipp], from whom we found a very discouraging letter awaiting us here; the King does not really like our project, he wishes to keep everything for himself in Munich. R. answers very earnestly, saying that this is his final plan; if it is not approved, he will give it up and live only for his family. He tells me how blissful he feels to be able to write about his family. He thinks of the children practically all the time with the most touching tenderness, he is happy to know these little creatures are waiting for us back there in Paradise. At nine o'clock with His Excellency [the United States ambassador George B. Bancroft], a mixed company, R. reads aloud his *Destiny of Opera*.

Tuesday, May 2 Bad night for R., but at ten o'clock to the rehearsal. R.

---

[1] The violinist Joseph Joachim (b. 1831), whom Wagner disliked intensely; he was at this time director of the Royal Academy of Music in Berlin.
[2] Karl Eckert (b. 1820), a friend of long standing, now conductor at the Court theatre in Berlin.
[3] Karl Friedrich Weitzmann (b. 1808), chorus master and teacher of composition.

greeted with a flourish; the orchestra seems to us better than previously, and the people exert themselves. In the evening Tausig comes and plays Bach chorales for us. Lothar Bucher came and on Bismarck's behest asked R. to call on the Prince [Bismarck].

Wednesday, May 3 (Day of Repentance) R. very indisposed, had another bad night! At four o'clock dinner with Cäcilie Avenarius, then I go to the Repentance concert with Ernst Dohm. Bancroft sits beside me; bad acoustics, *Eroica* symphony wretched. Everyone in black, since it is an occasion of mourning in honour of the fallen. I return home and R. drives to see the Prince, who had invited him. He returns highly satisfied, a great and simple character having been revealed to him. When R. gives expression to his respect, Bismarck says, 'The only thing that can count as an accomplishment is that now and then I have obtained a signature.' And then, 'All I did was to find the hole in the crown through which the smoke could rise.' R. is utterly enchanted with the genuine charm of his character, not a trace of reticence, an easy tone, the most cordial communicativeness, all of it arousing trust and sympathy. 'But,' says R., 'we can only observe each other, each in his own sphere; to have anything to do with him, to win him over, to ask him to support my cause, would not occur to me. But this meeting remains very precious to me.'

Friday, May 5 At ten o'clock to the final rehearsal in the opera house; listened to it surrounded by friends; it goes very well. I am overcome by tiredness, am put to bed, giddiness, fainting fits, and God knows what else prevent my getting dressed; a quarter of an hour before the concert, when R. is about to cancel it on my account, I pull myself together, throw my dress over my head, and drive with R. to the concert. The auditorium in festive mood, the Court present, it all goes well, the orchestra makes a lovely sound (thanks to the acoustic barrier R. had erected), unanimous, unending applause. My main impression [Beethoven's] C Minor Symphony. R. satisfied, and our dear good minister's wife beaming. – R. reaches home in quite a good mood, feeling touched by the good will of the orchestra.

Saturday, May 6 We spend the day in bed and see only our good [Alwine] Frommann and [Elisabeth] Krockow. We get up in the evening to visit Johanna Jachmann. A large gathering; she sings 'Elisabeth's Prayer', '*Blick ich umher*', and the '*Abendstern*'[1]. We are quite impressed with her husband, the district magistrate.

Sunday, May 7 At twelve o'clock breakfast with Tausig at Marie Schleinitz's house. The minister tells us the Emperor claims never to have heard anything so perfect as this concert, it was *sublime*. After breakfast the selection of the committee members, whereupon I drive to the

[1] All from *Tannhäuser.*

Wesendoncks' to invite him to take part, but obtain little satisfaction there. R. at the same time goes with Tausig to seek out 'the touching Jew' Löser[1], orders cigars for him, and gives him his pamphlets in gratitude. On the journey he tells Tausig how and for what he is living, and speaks of Fidi, whereupon Tausig exclaims, 'He must be a splendid boy.' – In the evening dinner with the Eckerts, very pleasant, then some friends at home.

Monday, May 8 Early in the morning drove (with Elisabeth Krockow) to the cemetery, where I visit Daniel's grave. Sombre mood; he was the victim of my father's and mother's thoughtlessness and the cruel indifference of Princess Wittgenstein; at the time I was too young and inexperienced to oppose them effectively and take firm measures. Much soreness of heart standing at this grave; where are you now, my brother, whither are you wandering, where is your pure spirit suffering or resting? In my soul you live on; have my children, Siegfried perhaps, absorbed your being? – Departed from Berlin as if in a dream, all is vain to those who have looked upon death. At five o'clock arrived in Leipzig and were cordially welcomed by the Brockhaus family, Ottilie and Hermann beings beyond compare.

Tuesday, May 9 Today Daniel would have been 32 years old. ... We wander, R. and I, through the city to make purchases for the children, who write me sweet letters. Councillor Düfflipp has now also written; the King will give 25,000 thalers towards our venture, but otherwise wants nothing to do with it, he is engaged in so much that his budget is completely committed.

Thursday, May 11 To the eye specialist *Ceccius* on account of my eyes, he says the affliction is of nervous origin; then purchases for the children. In the evening a party at the Brockhauses'. I learn this evening from Clemens Br[ockhaus] that Prof. Nietzsche has now dedicated his *Homer*, which he once dedicated to me, to his sister, and with the same poem. I had to laugh at first, but then, after discussing it with R., see it as a dubious streak, an addiction to treachery, as it were – as if he were seeking to avenge himself for some great impression.

Saturday, May 13 Affectionate parting from the dear people with whom we have felt so much at home. I pack once more for R., and he says it is like a dream, the way I scold him for his untidiness, it makes him feel so good, and everyone is amazed how well he looks. Booked tickets for Darmstadt, the joy of being alone together in the carriage. Arrived at the Traube in Darmstadt at ten o'clock, drank some punch and went to bed.

Sunday, May 14 Slept well, awoke in good spirits, at 10 o'clock the machinist Brandt[2], with whom R. discusses the arrangements for our future

[1] Bernhard Löser, a financier, founder of the Wagneriana, a society that aimed at establishing a Wagner festival in Berlin.
[2] Karl Brandt (b. 1828), technical director of the theatre in Darmstadt; he enjoyed a high reputation throughout Germany.

stage. Continued the rail journey to Heidelberg. Lovely evening, saw the ruins in the splendour of a sunset, walked in the garden, had dinner on the terrace, then wandered home along the leafy garden paths in excellent spirits. Reaching our street, we are on the point of going to look at the Neckar bridge again when loud laughter coming from the square reminds me of the Kasperl theatre I had noticed in passing during the day; I ask R. whether we should not visit it, and, since he assented, we had an evening of the most splendid entertainment. We stood there rooted to the spot till past ten o'clock and drew veritable consolation from the various ideas and fancies; the folk wit of the Germans is still alive. Particularly delicious was the rapport between the audience (mainly little boys) and Kasperl, they talked to each other, and the smallest of the children joined in the action. Richard gave the woman with the collection box a florin, and that may well have spurred the man on, for he worked untiringly until at last Kasperl came on in a herald's cloak and said the show was at an end. Why? Because the lights were being 'spat out'. Going to bed, we agree that this evening with our walk and the Kasperl was the nicest moment of our whole journey.

Monday, May 15 At one o'clock took leave of Heidelberg. At eight o'clock in Basel, where we spend a nice evening in the hotel with Prof. Nietzsche and our nephew Friedrich Brockhaus.

Tuesday, May 16 Going home! Great impatience to get there, dull weather, at two o'clock we at last arrived! Loulou and Boni weeping for joy, the little ones quieter, Fidi magnificent, plump and sturdy, all well. Family lunch and then distribution of presents; played the whole afternoon and evening. At bedtime R. says to me, 'Remain kind to me, you dispenser of bounty.' Feeling of utter bliss to be back in his world.

Wednesday, May 17 A rainy day; letter from Judith M[endès]. They are in Orleans. Her husband was condemned to death by the Commune, concealed, and escaped! Early to bed, for we have much sleep to make up.

Friday, May 19 The poem[1] at last arrives, the children learn it in the garden. R. writes to Frau von Schleinitz. Emil Heckel[2] from Mannheim writes introducing himself, after having read the green pamphlet.

Monday, May 22 Up at four o'clock to arrange the *salon*; set up the statuettes around R.'s bust, as if in a grove; later the children in their costumes, Loulou as Senta, Boni Elisabeth, Eva, Isolde, each in front of her 'man'; at about eight o'clock we are ready (I at the foot of the bust as Sieglinde with Fidi in my arms). We do our piece well and R. is happy, indeed moved. All the children do honour to their names, and R. praises

[1] From Peter Cornelius, for Wagner's birthday.
[2] Emil Heckel (b. 1831), a music dealer in Mannheim who suggested the founding of Wagner Societies in various towns to raise funds for the Bayreuth festival, and who from now on played an important part in the whole enterprise. The green pamphlet was 'On the Production of the Stage Festival Play *Der Ring des Nibelungen*', in which Wagner developed his ideas for the theatre in Bayreuth.

the costumes. Amicable breakfast with the children and the loveliest of weather for the loveliest of our days! In the afternoon visit from Countess Bassenheim, drove out to Winkel with her, R., and all the children. On our return we found Prof. Nietzsche in the house. We perform our birthday greeting once again. R. says it touches him all too deeply to see me in the guise of Sieglinde. Prof. N. tells us that he intends to found a periodical, under R.'s auspices, two years hence, till then he will be busy preparing it.

Tuesday, May 23 A letter from Marie Schleinitz: my father is joining the committee and desires a few lines from me and a meeting in a neutral place!

Wednesday, May 24 R. is arranging his writings, which he intends to publish in chronological order, since he does not wish to be regarded as a poet or an author. I teach the children. In the afternoon a visit from Professor Nietzsche.

Thursday, May 25 R. calls out to me that Paris is on fire, the Louvre in flames, whereupon I let out a cry of anguish which, R. observes, hardly 20 people in France would echo. I write to Marie Schleinitz, explaining to her why I do not write to my father and why I wish to see him only *here*.

Friday, May 26 Letter from my mother; in the way the French have of never being able to stop admiring themselves, she finds *'beaucoup de vie dans nos folies et nos ruines'*[1]! Did not allow the children to work much, for they are unwell again; the whooping cough is starting all over again, it is all so hopeless!

Saturday, May 27 Wet weather, for me camphor and pepper for the winter things. At midday arrival of our nephew Fritz Brockhaus, who pleases us very much with his intelligence and his kind heart. Prof. Nietzsche does not come, the events in Paris have upset him too much.

Sunday, May 28 At midday arrival of Prof. Nietzsche (with sister), whom Richard had summoned by telegram. R. speaks sharply to him about the fire and its significance: 'If you are not capable of painting pictures again, you are not worthy of possessing them.' Prof. N. says that for the scholar such events mean the end of all existence.[2]

Monday, May 29 After lunch discussion about Aeschylus and the misunderstood saying that 'he was always drunk,' about actors and also, in passing, about Sophocles; and that tragedy had certainly evolved out of improvisation. All this contributed by Prof. Nietzsche, together with Sophocles's saying about Aeschylus, that 'he does the right thing without knowing it,' which R. compares with Schopenhauer's saying about musicians – that they speak the highest wisdom in a language which their reason does not understand. – Our friends leave; R. is very worn out.

Tuesday, May 30 The Louvre is saved. – R. wraps himself in blankets, in

---

[1] 'Much life among our follies and our ruins.'
[2] The fire started by the Communards in Paris in fact touched only the corner of the Louvre that contained the library.

order to get rid of an obstinate catarrh. It does him good. He remarks cheerfully at breakfast how well I look. He says: 'You are lovelier than you used to be: previously your face looked earnest and severe, now you have in your eyes the gleam of joy I have seen in so few faces. Your father has good will, kindness, cordiality, but he does not have joy, and that is the divinest attribute of a human face.' Letter from Marie Schleinitz, who understands why I want to see my father only here, but she asks me to write to him, since he had authorized her to tell me that he wished for such a letter. I talk to R. about this; we think of Hans – what would his feelings be over a reconciliation of this kind? I fear, very bitter. In the evening read Carlyle's *Frederick the Great* with much enjoyment.

Wednesday, May 31 The King writes from Hochkopf, and in a friendly way. I write to Marie Schleinitz that I am expecting my father to approach me, but I cannot write to him.

Thursday, June 1 R. goes through the essays of his youth for the collected writings. I copy out the first scene of *Tannhäuser*. In the evening had supper in the garden, designed our house. – Will we ever bring all this into being??

Saturday, June 3 Still cold. The cask of wine has arrived from the King. Also letters, one from 'Bureau Peters', he is willing to pay 1,000 thalers for an overture.

Friday, June 9 In the evening a letter from Tausig; the committee is now in Weimar, and T. begs me to write to my father after all! He clearly wants a letter of some kind, never mind what. I cannot write to him, I must wait and see what happens.

Saturday, June 10 R. receives from Fürstner (publisher in Berlin) 500 francs for '*Der Tannenbaum*,'[1] which amuses him greatly. R. presents me with a very pretty new summer hat; he ordered it according to his own taste and it is decorated with a lovely big rose. -- We talk about my father; what kind of reunion would that be, he in his religious robes, I on the verge of becoming a Protestant, so that I can at least rest with R. in a single grave?

Sunday, June 11 'Cosima, I shall still be able to compose,' R. calls to me in the morning. He then goes to the piano and plays something which will, I believe, introduce the scene by moonlight between Alberich and Hagen.

Monday, June 12 It is a lovely afternoon; after reading me his introduction to the first volume, R. suggests an outing to Stanz, and at about 3 o'clock we set off with the four girls. Beyond Winkel a cart with three horses and some drunken peasants runs into us, Grane takes fright, leaps aside on to the meadow, drags us madly across ditches and bogs, until the carriage breaks and he is at last brought to a halt, badly injured, by the coachman. The children in extreme fear, but R. and I calm enough to stop their screaming and make them sit still. No mishaps apart from Grane's injury,

---

[1] A song Wagner wrote in 1838 in Riga.

though that is severe. The cantonal magistrate makes a record of it, we continue the long journey on foot, R. heads for Tribschen while I take the children to the confectioner's. When I return home, R. says, 'I see that I love you more than you love me; I stood a long time looking after you, and you did not turn towards me, you are not so much in need of connections as I am.' (!) – He then tells me of the alarm in the household when the carriage was towed home by a cart, and Friedrich, still in a state of shock, found it impossible to say a word. But then Fidi's look of joy, when his father greeted him – 'I do not know what to do for happiness,' my One and Only tells me! – The fright strikes me dumb and I can only thank God in silence. R. says, 'Throughout my life it has always been the same with the warnings of Fate – within an inch of an accident, but always coming through unscathed.' – In the evening reading, only I am too tired and have to go to bed.

Wednesday, June 14 Grane is still very ill, he is feverish. Meanwhile the Swiss mills begin to grind. Jakob discovers in town that the magistrate in Horw, who wrote down our statement, has not yet made a charge of any sort to the law courts in Lucerne, because he is a Conservative, and the farmer who ran into us is also a Conservative. We have resigned ourselves to the prospect of having to pay the court costs on top of all the damage.

Sunday, June 18 R. arranges his first four volumes and writes the foreword to the third and fourth volumes, which he reads to me in the afternoon.

Monday, June 19 R. in very good spirits after having sent everything off to Fritzsch[1] We go for a walk. During it I tell him how glad I am that through him Fidi will learn the right attitude towards everything – art, philosophy, Jews, religion, politics – so that he will be spared sterile misconceptions. Military music is wafted across to us from Lucerne, and R. says, 'Military music is the most unbearable thing I know – the epitome of the world's vulgarity.'

Tuesday, June 20 R. is girding himself for composition; his first act both pleases and dismays him: 'Shall I continue like this?' The scene between Waltraute and Brünnhilde he finds 'utterly incomprehensible', so completely did he forget it. He says: 'I shall be uneasy if I did not know that everything I do passes through a very narrow door; I write nothing which is not entirely clear to me. The most difficult thing in this respect was the last act of *Tristan*, and I made no mistakes there.'

Wednesday, June 21 Today, as I read the description of the entry of the troops into Berlin, I had to weep for joy and pride. R. is sorry that the memorial ceremony was not entrusted to him. I work on my copy [of the autobiography *My Life*] for the King and tell R. we really must complete this work. 'Yes,' says R., 'up to your arrival here. Then Fidi can carry on.'

---

[1] Ernst Wilhelm Fritzsch, Leipzig, published the collected writings.

'Just when I should like to be composing something comfortable I come on all this emotional stuff! I have landed myself in a nice pickle.' – While I am playing ball with Lusch, a letter from Marie M[uchanoff] is brought to me; she beseeches me to write to my father; his dignity does not allow him to take the first step! Feelings of bitterness. I write at once – not emotionally, as my friend desires, but simply and soberly. R. says with a laugh, 'I am all right, I can afford to be conciliatory, I have you!' Carlyle's *Frederick the Great* still.

Friday, June 23 Richter writes from Vienna that the funeral music[1] has been brought out by Meser in Dresden; R. was just about to sell it to Fritzsch; without a single word the Dresden publisher has cheated him out of it. But he settles down to work after all, and as we go to lunch he says: 'I am now sketching out a big aria for Hagen, but only for the orchestra. It is incredible what a bungler I am – I can't transcribe at all. With me, composing is a curious affair; while thinking it up, I have it all in my mind, endless, but then comes the job of writing it down, and the mere physical actions get in the way. It becomes "How did it go?" instead of "How is it?"; not "How is it to be?" but "How was it?" – and then having to search about till one finds it again. Mendelssohn would raise his hands in horror if he ever saw me composing.' We eat in the garden, for I want to enjoy Tribschen to the full as long as we still live here; this dream life – shall we ever be able to capture it again?

Saturday, June 24 We are expecting bad experiences with our Bayreuth venture, but at least it will show us where we stand. 'Previously,' says R., 'after we had given each other up, we were dependent on great artistic successes; we had to submerge the sacrifice we had made in some great outward activity. That is why, when we did not achieve our aim, I was in fact inwardly glad – I felt it would bring us together. But things are different now. If this venture does not succeed, well, we still have each other, and we have the work of art, too. But it would certainly be bad if I had to yield up the last two parts of the work as well to the King in order to keep going; I could not do that.'

Tuesday, June 27 R. has composed Hagen's aria. He says, 'While doing it I was thinking of you asleep; I was uncertain whether to let him express himself in silence or not; then I remembered how you talk in your dreams, and I saw I could let Hagen voice his emotions, which is much better.'

Wednesday, June 28 R. works; at lunch he talks of the curious process of collecting one's thoughts, which looks like absent-mindedness; now he adjusts a cushion, now thinks of politics, but all the time he is collecting his thoughts, and suddenly it comes. But nothing from outside must

---

[1] Written by Wagner in 1844 to accompany the reburial in Dresden of Weber's ashes, in the transfer of which from London he had played an active part.

intrude. 'The difficulties I had in getting down the finale to the second act of *Die Meistersinger* were due to the fact that you had gone away. You will not believe me, will tell me I managed to work in my earlier days, but then I was drawing on my capital – now I am dependent.' – In the afternoon a letter from Marie Muchanoff; she returns my letter, did not give it to my father, since he has changed his mind, thinks it is still too early!! We smile.

Thursday, June 29 Letter from Claire, my mother has become deranged again. 'Your father and mother do not bring you much joy,' R. observes.

Sunday, July 2 We spend all day in the garden. Fidi's mission in life? R. says he often thinks that, were he to die suddenly, his work would be uncompleted – who would finish it for him? It would not be too inconceivable that Fidi might have the same gifts as himself and might continue his life. I have my doubts, not believing in so swift a recurrence of genius, since there is no instance of it anywhere in history; I shall be happy if our son has a steadfast character and enlightened intelligence. 'Yes,' R. says, 'for he would possess no individuality of his own if he were simply to follow in my footsteps. God knows what lies ahead for him.' – I said that at the end of June we had celebrated the 7th year of our love. 'Not that,' R. said, 'and also not its explosion, but the knowledge that we could no longer live apart from each other. And if Hans had been only a shade different, more trivial or more profound, we should not have been completely united, for what did we not attempt on his account?' We wander through the Tribschen grounds and settle down on the hill beside the hermitage, watching the curious cloud formations, in which a thunderstorm lurks. 'We newer races are very restricted in our imaginings, not knowing the tropical regions – India, for example. How can I think of the god Thor behind Mount Pilatus? These myths all originated in the Himalayas.' We come to the subject of the Egyptians, the veneration of the Nile and of the cow, and that leads us to Io and the curious dialogue between her and Prometheus. 'The reason why the Greek legends have made such an impression on you is that they were seized on by such tremendous poets.' We see a cow in the meadow, and R. points out to me how it moves just like a snake, the same stretching and elongating. A lovely moment in time, Richard! Life is beautiful after all!

Wednesday, July 5 C. Mendès sends us his book about the Commune. In Paris madness and baseness; R. is alarmed by the thought that Prussia might not have crushed the people sufficiently and might soon have to begin all over again! – Letters from E. Ollivier, asking me for papers, on the assumption that my father had arranged a dowry for me as for Blandine; I reply that I was given nothing, and remind him of the jewellery which my mother's father had given me and Blandine, which I had signed over to Blandine and which he had illegally withheld from me; probably this will be met with silence! Letter from Claire; things look bad with my mother.

Thursday, July 6 R. slept well, 'the devil of composition' is tormenting him, for he finds that he expended too much on the first oath (Hagen Gunther Siegfried), intends to transfer the orchestral interludes to the oath in the second act and compose something new – an experience quite new to him.

Friday, July 7 Fine weather again. When I tell R. of my mother's condition (she hits out and raves, then becomes quiet and gentle again), R. says: 'How dreadfully human beings behave! No animal in a fury can behave like that; it is closer to Nature, which protects it; but what happens to a human being when his intelligence begins to waver, we can now see in your mother, whose intelligence made her so lovable and estimable. That is why we always look to the common people, in the hope that they have remained closer to Nature.' – While I am working with the children in the garden, he calls out to me, 'I have a wonderful idea, but I can't tell it to you.' I run up to his room, and there he informs me that the theme I had already heard and liked, which comes on Siegfried's sudden appearance from the bushes, is the same one which the vassals will sing when they laugh at Hagen; a sort of Gibichung song which expresses the curious and genial mood of Hagen. How blissful I feel when he tells me things like this! It is as if there has never been sorrow and can never be sorrow.

Tuesday, July 11 Jakob has taken the 1,000 francs to the savings bank, where I now have 5,641 francs; 3,500 in the steamship company, which so far has brought me in nothing; 2,000 francs with R., who is very angry if I do not assume that he will pay me back and in the meantime pay interest on them; and 1,000 in the Paris insurance company. – R. works.

Thursday, July 13 R. had a very bad night; he has been reading Mendès's *Commune* and says: 'What play actors these Frenchmen are! As long as they were playing to the world, it worked, but now the world is no longer looking, they become Charenton[1] inmates, imagining themselves to be this person or that.' – In the evening R. wonders whether or not to inform Bismarck of his plans; I observe that it would be better to wait until the finances are secured and then to send him a report which makes no demands on him.

Monday, July 17 *Siegfried* has arrived, R. corrects the proofs [of the piano version] in the afternoon.

Tuesday, July 18 After lunch he plays the third act of *Siegfried* to me – wonderful beyond all words; he shows me the harp sounds he has added in Brünnhilde's greeting to Siegfried, like the harps of the skalds when they welcome a hero in Valhalla. These sounds are to be heard again at Siegfried's death. A profound, indescribable impression; a wooing of the utmost beauty; Siegfried's fear, the fear of guilt through love, Brünnhilde's fear a premonition of the approaching doom; her virginal and pure love for

---

[1] A French lunatic asylum.

Siegfried truly German. – I try to imagine which people would be able to appreciate such things; my father, and also Tausig, come to mind. Friedrich returns from the post office and brings me a letter from Countess Krockow: she is in the Leipzig hospital with Tausig, who is dying of typhus! A great shock.

Thursday, July 20 Terrible, stormy night; I do not sleep a wink. In the morning a letter from Elisabeth [Krockow] brings news that Tausig is dead. Complete stupefaction, then reminiscence – how many friends already gone, Uhlig, Schnorr, Serov, how many! In T. we have certainly lost a great pillar of our enterprise, but that leaves us indifferent. R. says: 'I look upon it as upon a cloud; the vapours rise – will they be dispersed or will they form themselves into a life-bringing cloud? God knows. I just look on, my life seems to me godlike, for even its worries are now beautiful; they are about the children.' – Contemplation of Tausig's sad life; so precocious, Schopenhauer already worked through at the age of 16; conscious of the curse of his Jewishness; no pleasure in his tremendous virtuosity, my father's even greater, and he too remarkable to see himself just as a pupil; the marriage with a Jewess, ended almost at once; completely finished at 29, yet still not a man. 'What must the sleepless nights of such a person be like? What occupied his thoughts?' asks R., who shrugs his shoulders over the stupidity of Fate, snatching Tausig away at the moment when a great new activity would have brought him inner joy and satisfaction. – This was to be a sad day, in every respect; at midday Vreneli came in and declared that Kos could no longer be saved, and Jakob would take him today to the apothecary. I said he should be shown to me before he was taken away, so that I could say goodbye to him, but they did not do so, and it pained me very much. The poor little creature shared with me the worst days of my life; Hans brought him to Zurich in '66 to give me 'at least a little joy' in difficult, oppressive days. He was ill for the past three years; now he is gone and is buried here in Tribschen.

Friday, July 21 When I go to lie down after lunch, R. comes to my room, having just heard from Loldi that Kos is dead and buried. He weeps. When I come downstairs, he is still much affected. – The American[1] and his wife visit us; very nice people. We then talk much, R. and I, about the English language, which I enjoy speaking, but against which R. has an insuperable antipathy; he says a German can only regard it as a dialect, not a serious language.

Saturday, July 22 R. tells me: 'I dreamed the two little girls (Eva and Loldi) went on a tiny, unsteady boat, and my shock gave me enough strength to wake up and break the dream. Then of Schröder-Devrient, I had a

---

[1] Benjamin Johnson Lang (b.1837), pianist and conductor, a pupil of Liszt; he and Cosima had first met 14 years previously and had renewed their acquaintance during the recent visit to Berlin.

relationship with her.' 'Of what sort?' I ask. 'As always, not of any sentimental kind. No, she could never have aroused love longings in me, there was no longer enough modesty in her, no mystery in which to probe.'

Sunday, July 23 Letter from E. Krockow; in his final days Tausig had called us (Wagner and me) 'two great natural forces'! – In the afternoon visit from Countess Bassenheim; just returned from Munich, she tells us the most horrible things about the King, what ill-mannered jealousy he showed towards the Crown Prince (during the ceremonial entry of the troops), how the peasants scoff at him for having his hunting lodges gilded and furnishing them in Louis XIV style, etc., etc. R. very despondent about it – alas, this dependence on him!

Monday, July 24 R. in despondent spirits: the King, the King! Also, in order to deter people of note in Bayreuth, word is being spread that the King does not approve of our venture! – R. finishes the second scene of his act, but feels not at all well.

Tuesday, July 25 R. does not work today, he is too worn out, he plays the two scenes for me, then lies down and reads. He says he would like to take a few days' break and write an obituary of Auber[1].

Thursday, July 27 R. says to me around noon: 'Do you know what I have done today? Thrown out everything I did yesterday. Hagen's call sounded *too composed*, I did not like it, it had to be altered.' Walk with R. We are talking about all sorts of things when R. suddenly breaks off to say: 'I have heavy thoughts that I shall never be happy and well again. The humiliation of being dependent on this King – it is scandalous and insupportable! If he would only take up a stand, if he had only supported my cause, one could justify both oneself and him. But like this –!' – (The King has replied to Prince Albert[2], who asked him to come without fail to the banquet the town is giving in honour of the Crown Prince, 'He can fetch his vivats by himself'!!)

Friday, July 28 Friend Nuitter sends R.'s articles from the *Gazette Musicale*, I look forward to translating them back into German[3].

Sunday, July 30 Herr von Gersdorff visits us, he is a friend of Prof. Nietzsche's who went right through the war and has all the noble and earnest characteristics of the North German.

Tuesday, August 1 R. feels so unwell that he has taken refuge in cold packs. It indeed does him good, and at lunch he is lively and talkative. We have the same companionable guests[4], with whom I go out in a boat while R. settles some things in town.

---

[1] The French composer died on 12 May 1871.

[2] Crown Prince of Saxony, King from 1873.

[3] Articles : stories written in Paris in 1840–41; though originally written in German, they had been transl. ed into French and had now to be retranslated.

[4] Ger... had now been joined by Nietzsche and Friedrich Brockhaus (Fritz).

Thursday, August 3 At five o'clock Herr von G. and Prof. Nietzsche leave us. The latter is certainly the most gifted of our young friends, but a not quite natural reserve makes his behaviour in many respects most displeasing. It is as if he were trying to resist the overwhelming effect of Wagner's personality.

Saturday, August 5 Fritz, our excellent nephew, who has been very pleasant company, makes his departure.

Sunday, August 6 In the morning the machinist Brandt arrives from Darmstadt, and in the afternoon the Neumanns also arrive, and a little conference about Bayreuth takes place[1].

Monday, August 7 Conference all day, in which our good Neumann conducts himself like 'a bull in a china shop'; the excellent Brandt, however, efficient, intelligent, earnest and inventive; he is utterly inspired by his task. The Neumanns depart after we also discussed our house, Brandt stays till evening.

Thursday, August 17 R. has completed his articles; he now has as much material as is required for the first volume; he has tidied up his youthful pieces and much enjoyed this curious task; he says he enjoys being an author, it is so easy. In the evening he reads me the essays, and I remark, in connection with a simile, that the moon does not get its light from the earth, but from the sun, which he is unwilling to believe; we look it up in the encyclopedia, and laugh when we discover that I am right!

Monday, August 21 Visit from Marie Schleinitz along with Baron Loën; discussion about entrusting everything to small committees, nothing to my father or Marie Muchanoff; the Willes and Wesendoncks also entirely uninvolved.

Friday, August 25 Our wedding day! R. comes to me early in the morning and congratulates – himself! – Letter from Councillor Düfflipp saying that he has been seriously considering asking for his dismissal, once again he can do nothing right for the King.

Monday, August 28 Fine day, with a touch of autumn already in the air. Work with the children. R. composes, and tells me that he does not intend to assemble a large chorus at 'Hagen's Call', but individual vassals who appear from the farmsteads nearby. – Prof. Nohl[2] sends another book about Beethoven and touches us by telling us that he had been in Lucerne, had looked at Tribschen from the outside, but had been reminded by the sign outside it, 'Entry Prohibited' that everybody must be careful not to disturb.

Tuesday, August 29 Richter writes from Pest; but he annoys R. because he has not been working for him and has not yet prepared the score of *Das*

---

[1] Wilhelm Neumann, inspector of the royal buildings in Berlin, and his wife Hedwig; Neumann had been invited to work out plans for the Bayreuth festival theatre.

[2] Ludwig Nohl, writer on music and Beethoven authority.

Rheingold for Schott. At eleven o'clock Baron Loën comes for a conference, he is taking Tausig's place, and R. is very pleased with him and his enthusiasm. We are glad to have found him and believe that things will now go more smoothly. Just as we are settling down to a siesta, Jakob announces Herr Bucher, and it really is our old friend, whom we welcome with joy to Tribschen.

Friday, September 1 At table R. says to me: 'I have been thinking again about actors, poets, and so on, and have even made some notes on the subject in my sketchbook. An improviser such as an actor must belong entirely to the present moment, never think of what is to come, indeed not even know it, as it were. The peculiar thing about me as an artist, for instance, is that I look on each detail as an entirety and never say to myself, "Since this or that will follow, you must do such and such, modulate like this or like that." I think, "Something will turn up." Otherwise I should be lost; and yet I know I am unconsciously obeying a plan. The so-called genius of form, on the other hand, reflects, "This or that follows, so I must do such and such," and he does it with ease.' – Visit from Count Bassenheim, who gives us another shock with the news that the King has ordered a coronation carriage with six pictures from the Bible and six allegories about Louis XIV, for 20,000 florins. R. says we shall certainly soon receive news from that quarter of sudden insanity or death; deep concern, we will be without house or home. – R. goes to town and returns home with a Herr Hey[1], who wants to force his singing method on him at all costs; he is very agitated by this foolish interruption.

Saturday, September 2 Lovely moonlit night, R. gives L. B[ucher] *Art and Politics* to take to Bismarck. – In the night we are awakened by Rus's barking – a 'crazy woman', as Jakob says, was prowling around Tribschen; R. thinks she was crazy enough to want to steal something.

Sunday, September 3 Our friend has left. – It turns out (through the vet) that Rus has been poisoned and that the woman from yesterday knew about it and, assuming his death, had planned a robbery attempt. I had heard footsteps and, during our evening walk, noticed that someone was hiding in the bushes, though R. laughed off my fears; Rus, however, who had at first growled, ran at once to the open *salon* door and lay across it, the loyal watchdog.

Monday, September 4 Towards noon R. calls me and plays me his 'inspiration' – Brünnhilde's reception by the vassals; her appearance will be characterized by the motive we heard when she becomes frightened of Siegfried, 'when the *other thing* overcomes her,' as R. says. – R. brings me a letter from my mother, the first for several months; she complains of great

---

[1] Julius Hey (b. 1831), a singing teacher destined to play a significant part in the Bayreuth venture, despite this inauspicious beginning.

weakness in the brain, but is thrilled by developments in France – the republic is assured, she says!! – In the evening Carlyle.

Tuesday, September 5 R. works 'in ink'; after lunch I reply to my mother; letter from Marie Muchanoff with all sorts of objections from my father: not Bayreuth, but a national theatre, etc.; R. laughs and says, 'Ah, yes, I know, the Goethe Foundation[1].' Then he becomes more vexed and says, 'That is arrogance – not to accept another person's idea just as it is, being too unsettled himself even to be able to grasp it!' – Many disagreeable feelings, which are then swept away by an indescribable shock I experienced; I can distinctly hear the fluttering of a bird on the terrace, R. does not hear it, also does not hear the chirping of the cicadas; this impression starts a worry in me which no joy can dispel; all keenness of hearing is now accursed for me. Curiously enough, however, R. can hear quite distinctly the trickling of the fountain and the very distant sound of the breaking waves. A merciful God will help!

Wednesday, September 6 We talk of the love between Siegfried and Brünnhilde, which achieves no universal deed of redemption, produces no Fidi; *Götterdämmerung* is the most tragic work of all, but before that one sees the great happiness arising from the union of two complete beings. Siegfried does not know what he is guilty of; as a man, committed entirely to deeds, he knows nothing, he must fall in order that Brünnhilde may rise to the heights of perception.

Thursday, September 7 Family lunch with Fidi, who as a man is already demonstrating his superiority over his sisters. Drive after lunch; with the children. E.Ollivier has sent us his defence[2], he shows that it was France and not the government which wanted war. – I am alarmed by the fact that R. leaves his window open during the night, I ask him to shut it, but do not dare tell him this is on account of his hearing. He does not shut it.

Tuesday, September 12 Visit from Countess B. – Prince Georg[3] wants to meet us this evening at her house. R. feels too unwell and ill-humoured, and asks me to go alone, which I do reluctantly. – The evening with Countess B. passes tolerably well; it must be very wounding for R. the way all his admirers, among whom Prince Georg can also be counted, carefully avoid talking about our venture!

Thursday, September 14 At four in the morning R. comes to inquire how I am, for I was indisposed yesterday evening and still am. Then he could no longer sleep, and went downstairs to write Herr Brandt a letter, asking him for a first estimate of the cost of putting in the foundations of the theatre;

---

[1] Liszt made proposals in 1849 (the centenary of Goethe's birth) for an olympiad of all the arts under the patronage of the Grand Duke of Weimar; lack of funds prevented its realization, but Liszt never abandoned his plan.

[2] *Le Procès historique*, 1871.

[3] Son of Prince Friedrich of Prussia; wrote plays under the pseudonym G. Conrad.

he would then lay the foundation stone in the middle of October, if Baron Loën makes a favourable report, and would make a speech. 'Then,' R. says, 'the whole thing, as far as I am concerned, can hang fire for years. My speech, which will afterwards be published as an appeal, ought to make some sort of impact.' It fills me with sorrow to see R. so worried and agitated that he cannot possibly continue his creative work cheerfully and remain in good health. He said yesterday, 'I am so churned up inside that even something like Tausig's death goes in one ear and out the other, and that is not good.' – I do not wish to look even a day into the future, so dizzy does it all make me feel. – He is worried because Fritzsch, his publisher, sends him no word. I have another worry, namely, that Baron Loën will be restrained by his master, the Grand Duke of Weimar, from taking part in our venture; the Grand Duke has in fact flatly rejected Marie M.'s request to become a patron! But I do not tell R. this.

Friday, September 15 A letter from Frau Wesendonck; she says she is going to Munich to see *Rheingold* or *Walküre*, but does not mention our Bayreuth venture in even a single word. R. is extremely annoyed about it, asks me not to reply, and complains of having spent his whole life consorting with pitiful creatures. 'For,' he says, 'she knew all about it; our whole intercourse revolved around this production of the *Nibelungen* – and now just to ignore it all! The worst of it is that one cannot wipe out experiences; one can remove them from one's heart, but they remain in one's life.' The bare mention of the production in Munich is like a dagger in his heart – 'and now I am supposed to continue with my work, but how can I?' – His grief makes me miserable. He knows that all his friends will go running off to Munich again and none will give a thought to him! – [Carlyle's] *Frederick the Great* provides some slight distraction.

Saturday, September 16 Hermine has had to go home, so the entire quintet is left in my hands; Loldi, the only one who misses Hermine, becomes ill; great woes. R. works. He tells me to ignore Frau W. entirely; but I find it impossible to offend someone who once played a role in his life, and I tell her in a few words what these Munich performances mean to us. . . . At lunch – for what reason I do not know – R. told me that in his youth the worst thing he could imagine was to take leave of somebody for ever, and he knew now that he could never have had Fritz and Kos put to death if he had had to say goodbye to them. I understand that; I once had to take leave of somebody, and from that hour, which also brought me my first grey hairs, I realized the true meaning of life; up till then everything I had read in the poets about the dreadfulness and blameworthiness of life I could feel only intuitively; but when I gave Hans my hand in farewell, I felt it all inside myself, and the veil of illusion was torn forever. From then on I understood life and death, and from then on I have wished for nothing more. – I put Loldi to bed and go for a drive with the other children; Fidi is also not quite well. The day is rather tiring, but I love such emergencies, and it does me good to know that the children enjoy being alone with me!

Sunday, September 17 Loldi had a terrible night, I stayed up with her throughout; in the morning, however, she is a bit better; but the doctor fears diphtheria. Richter's National Theatre in Pest has been burned down.

Tuesday, September 19 As I am giving the two 'big' girls their lessons, a carriage arrives, and there is our nephew Clemens, who is very welcome. Amiable lunch, I beset on all sides. In the afternoon drove to Marie Schl.'s[1]; she, alarmed to the highest degree by R.'s intention to lay the foundation stone next month, says that most of the people intend to give their money only when 100,000 thalers have been subscribed, etc. I return home in melancholy spirits! – A visit from Prince Georg.

Wednesday, September 20 In the morning I have to inform R. of Frau v. Schl.'s misgivings about the laying of the foundation stone; R. very put out: 'From these circles I can expect nothing more; I must turn to others and show them that I am in earnest.' I find nothing more terrible than when I have to speak a discouraging word to him; between him and the world no understanding is possible, it is just a battle, in which he must either conquer or be defeated.

Tuesday, September 26 Letter from Tausig's father; he does not have the score of *Tristan und Isolde* for which I asked – it seems to have been stolen!

Thursday, September 28 Today I learn the reason for R.'s nervous absorption; the passage in which Brünnhilde tells Siegfried how the sword had hung sweetly between them was going through his mind, and today he established it to his satisfaction: 'The important thing was concision, and that there should be no modulation.' The trumpet had pleased him. He says to me: 'If you only knew all the things I say to you when you are not there!' – Surprised by a letter from my father in Rome! ... R. can never remember Saint Cosmas; now my father writes to congratulate me, and he says, 'It is Catholic, you see – that divides us.' Which makes us laugh.

Friday, September 29 'I have composed a Greek chorus,' R. exclaims to me in the morning, 'but a chorus which will be sung, so to speak, by the orchestra; after Siegfried's death, while the scene is being changed, the Siegmund theme will be played, as if the chorus were saying: "This was his father"; then the sword motive; and finally his own theme; then the curtain goes up, Gutrune enters, thinking she has heard his horn. How could words ever make the impression that these solemn themes, in their new form, will evoke? Music always expresses the direct present.' – I write my reply to my father while R. is working. At lunch I show it to him, he feels it could be misinterpreted, and I tear the letter up. Letter from Baron Loën, who is full

---

[1] She was spending some days in Lucerne.

of confidence about Bayreuth affairs, but nevertheless has not understood R. and says nothing about the laying of the foundation stone.

Saturday, September 30 Letter from Dr. Kafka[1]: the Society in Vienna is making great strides, contains 50 members from all walks of life, and now wishes very much for R. to conduct several concerts. I write to my father and send the letter off after showing it to R.

Tuesday, October 3 R. works and then plays me the splendidly daemonic 'Helle Wehr' of poor Brünnhilde. Often, he says, he shudders to think that he might suddenly grow tired of writing this work – 'but,' he consoles me, 'now that I have got so far, I shall finish it.' Wrote to Rothschild, who has again not sent me my money!

Saturday, October 7 Letter from Herr Rothschild; he ignores the fact that he made me no payments at all during the siege of Paris and sends me nothing for this October, reckoning that from January onwards he has paid me for the whole year 1871. On top of this unpleasantness comes R.'s talk of the need to receive and entertain the people who come to the laying of the foundation stone in Bayreuth, though we do not really have the means for it, and R. still has several debts to pay. Deep concern over this; I realize with sorrow that in this matter I cannot share R.'s cheerful spirits, I would rather do without even the most important things than be in debt; also, I have no confidence about the earnings R. expects to make. I overcome all my worries and keep silent; but how hard life is, how dismal! Who would want more of it?

Sunday, October 8 Very dismal experience with Blandine; I am told that recently she read aloud from a book, 'There was once a nasty mama, she left the papa and married someone else; that was very nasty, I shall never do it.' And that in front of two maidservants, who are telling others about it. All that is left for me to do is to look after this child as I have so far done and do without her love – God will aid me. At first I wanted to ignore the whole thing, but my mother's heart cannot bear to regard the situation as hopeless, and so I chose the end of family lunch to tell the children and R. what Boni had done. Great consternation; I hope it will not be forgotten. In the course of the day I am persuaded by various reports that Hermine has been a bad influence on the children, and, in spite of the difficulties in which I find myself at present, I write her not to return.

Tuesday, October 10 We receive two issues of the *Süddeutsche Presse*, full of invective against *Rheingold* and *Walküre*, R. beside himself over the scorn and abuse he has to put up with. – Rothschild informs me that he cannot pay me!

Wednesday, October 11 I write to Eduard Liszt about the Rothschild matter; to Marie Schleinitz – who had written to us – and to Councillor D[üfflipp], sending him the abusive articles, with a humble request to the King now at last to withdraw *Rheingold* and *Walküre*.

---

[1] Theodor Kafka, active in the Wagner Society in Vienna.

Thursday, October 12 I write to Herr von Gersdorff, entrusting the *Tristan* affair to him. Hermine's sister writes me a letter full of invective; R. takes this matter into his own hands and sends her 100 florins.

Friday, October 13 Mannheim sends money for *Rienzi*, which is used to pay Hermine. Letter from my father, who seems to have got pleasure from mine. In the evening sang songs with the children, and Fidi joined in roaring, which made us all laugh loudly.

Tuesday, October 17 The children come along suddenly with a little dog, which refuses to leave our yard; Loldi first discovered him, and he bears a remarkable resemblance to our poor Kos. The children are hugely pleased about it. I send my father a birthday greeting.

Wednesday, October 18 R. is very worn out, does not work, but is thinking of it all the time; he has the theme for the Rhinemaidens in the third act, but he says he will have to make an alteration to the text, which he does not like doing. – Jakob took the little dog to the market, thinking it would then find its way back to its master, but the dog followed him everywhere and returned home with him. We are increasingly struck with his resemblance to Kos and think he may have been his son, since there are no others of this breed in Lucerne. This thought moves and pleases us all very much, we are calling the little stray *Vito* and hope to keep him.

Thursday, October 19 Marie M. writes to me from Heidelberg that Tausig probably gave the *Tristan* score to Countess Dönhoff[1]! Inquiry to El. Krockow in this connection; still no answer from Cousin Eduard! – In the evening Carlyle.

Monday, October 23 Letter from Karl v. Gersdorff; Papa Tausig will do nothing more in the matter of the manuscript, and it seems no legal steps can be taken, which means that this affair has come to a bad end!

Tuesday, October 24 Letter from Clemens with enclosures from Herr Feustel and Herr Kolb[2] in Bayreuth, which testify to the excellent sentiments of the people there. Letter from Baron Loën; he now has about 25,000 thalers and has no doubts about success.

Wednesday, October 25 The collected writings give R. great pleasure, he is so glad to have managed them, and so successfully, too. He is pleased that his writings should bring him some money: '*Siegfried* – what use is that? As soon as it appears, then the troubles will really begin, whereas the writings are quite complete in themselves – and there will be a second edition, you will see. I must just stay alive.' – Today R. has completed the pencilled sketch of his second act; may each and every god and benevolent spirit be blessed and thanked!

---

[1] Marie Dönhoff (b.1848), wife of Count Karl Dönhoff, first secretary in the German Embassy in Vienna.

[2] Friedrich, Feustel (b.1824), a banker who was to play a leading part in festival affairs; there were two Kolbs in Bayreuth: Johann and Karl, both leading businessmen there.

Thursday, October 26 Letter from my uncle Eduard, who now, realizing that I am right, is writing to Rothschild; whether it will do any good we shall see. – R. reads me an alteration he has made in Brünnhilde's last words; I beg him to leave it as it was, and he agrees, saying that the new version comes too close to literary drama. – News that the theatre in Darmstadt has been burned down; a satanic stroke – it means our Brandt will now have no time to work for us. 'It is a calamity, such as always strikes me when I find somebody.'

Friday, October 27 Letter to me from Hans about what he intends to do for the children! – Telegram from Bratfisch[1], saying he has the manuscript of *Tristan* and is returning it to us. – Wonderful day! – In the afternoon surprise visit by Prof. Nietzsche from Basel. He tells us the title of his book, which will be called *The Emergence of Tragedy from Music*[2]. In the evening R. reads us his essay on Auber, begun today.

Saturday, October 28 Letter from Rothschild, who now at last has sent me my 1,000 francs. Visited Marie M[uchanoff] with Prof. N.; great admiration for this good friend, who spends the evening with us, along with Countess B. Marie M. relates that the Empress of Germany does not like the '*Kaisermarsch*'!!

Sunday, October 29 I write a long and detailed letter to Hans and ask him for permission to have the children converted to Protestantism.

Tuesday, October 31 Took our friend to the station, where we parted from this unique woman with feelings of sadness. – In the evening R. reads me his magnificent essay on Auber. – He took it amiss that in my letter to Hans I spoke only of 10,000 francs which I had set aside, taking that to mean I was assuming that the 3,000 francs I had lent him were now lost!!

Wednesday, November 1 Arrival of the score of *Tristan und Isolde*! Overwhelming joy!

Friday, November 3 Very nice letter from Marie M. – I send 10,000 francs off to the banker J[oachim] and beg L. Bucher to see he takes great care of them.

Sunday, November 5 Letter from Hans! He consents to my wishes, although – as he says – he hates everything German. Melancholy. From Bayreuth a very heartening reply from Herr Feustel – they are starting a Wagner Society there, too!

Monday, November 6 Marie Schleinitz writes and reports that Herr Löser is taking up 60 certificates of patronage for the Wagneriana and responsibility for the engagement of the orchestra for Bayreuth. – R. is now laughing about his own present productivity.

Thursday, November 16 While working with the children I receive from the banker the dismal news that he has not received the money order. How to

[1] Probably Georg Bratfisch, music publisher, Frankfurt an der Oder.
[2] Final English title: *The Birth of Tragedy out of the Spirit of Music*.

bear it? First resolve: not to tell R. while he is working; second: to keep the children as much as possible from noticing anything. All my little savings now probably lost – I have to weep bitterly, though I know that many others suffer similar misfortunes. – At lunch R. notices that Jakob is not serving, I have to inform him that I have sent him to the post office concerning the lost money order. It gives R. a great shock. Jakob returns home bringing the receipt. Has it been misappropriated by the Prussian mail, or even perhaps by the banker himself? The name Joachim was ominous! – On top of this misfortune, Grane took fright in town and knocked down a child, badly injuring it.

Friday, November 17 Letter from my father: he is leaving Rome. After lunch we receive the news that the banker in Frankfurt has not paid out on the money order, so in consequence my money is safe. This is a happy outcome; but the matter with the horse is looking bad; the child is dying, and its people are turning the tragedy to their own advantage, regarding it as 'a stroke of luck'.

Saturday, November 18 The city councillors of Baden[-Baden] intend to invite R. to build his theatre in Baden; that, at any rate, is what R. Pohl writes us.

Sunday, November 19 At midday Richard brings me his completed second act and says, 'Now I have written you one act every year.' Great joy! – In the evening R. suddenly says to me, half joking: 'I should still like to meet a magician, I understand magic making, I often have the feeling I could do it myself, like, for example, in certain conditions jumping over a huge distance. And my music making is in fact magic making, for I just cannot produce music coolly and mechanically. Even the soprano clef of a five-voice piece by Bach upsets me, I feel like transcribing it, but in a mood of ecstasy I can lead my voices through the most hair-raising contortions without a moment's hesitation; it all pours out so steadily, as if from a machine; but I can do nothing coolly.'

Friday, November 24 R. receives a very nice letter from his publisher Lucca[1], who declares himself to be *'felice e superbo'* on account of *Lohengrin*; letters from Richter and Boito[2]. Arrival of Herr Spiegel[3] to copy the sketch for the King; no very pleasant addition to our household.

Thursday, November 30 In the evening a remark by Herr Spiegel brings R. to the subject of the Germans; he becomes very lively, indeed emphatic, and to our great astonishment our copyist is much affected by his outburst and says he can now see how much W. loves Germany when he can grow

[1] Francesco Lucca, whose wife Giovanna was also active in their publishing business.
[2] Arrigo Boito, Verdi's librettist and a great admirer of Wagner's works (he translated *Rienzi* and *Tristan* into Italian).
[3] A music teacher from Zurich, engaged to copy the orchestral sketch of Act II of *Götterdämmerung* for King Ludwig.

so violently heated about the shortcomings and the wretched social conditions of the nation. With ice-cold fingers he presses the hands of R., who feels quite moved.

Friday, December 1 R. works on his pamphlet about the history of his *Ring des Nibelungen*[1].

Saturday, December 2 R. works on his essay. Report from Italy, Verdi at a performance of *Lohengrin*, applauded by the public on that account, but he stayed at the back of his box so as not to distract from the solemnity of the performance.

Sunday, December 3 Spoke very seriously with the children, wept and prayed with them, brought them to the point of asking me for punishment[2]. (Incidentally, heard very unpleasant things about Herr Spiegel.) As I am talking to them, a letter comes from Hans; he asks me to make the children practise the greatest reserve towards their grandmother and aunt; the family is tormenting him (to take the children away from me), but he is turning a deaf ear. Then he tells me that my father agrees with my decision to convert with the children to Protestantism. Important matters! That the family, annoyed by seeing me treated with respect, wishes to affront me under the pretext of furthering the children's interests, while in fact not considering them at all – that does not surprise me; but I am despondent about it, and am guilty of the great injustice of letting R. see that I am.

Monday, December 4 Great joy over the arrival of Anna Stadelmann for the children. Hope that better order will result.

Friday, December 8 Preparations for R.'s departure[3]. Disturbed, sad day; on top of it a dismal letter from Math. Maier; they seem to have lost all they possess.

Saturday, December 9 At five o'clock took R. to the station; the cold cruel; final sorrow. Home alone, to bed. It must all be borne in God's name! At ten o'clock telegram from R. in Zurich, announcing a letter. Lunch with the children. Wrote to Hans, afterwards fetched my letter; it had arrived. – R. had a cold journey, very cold, but 'his heart kept him warm.'

Sunday, December 10 Dreary day, longing and depression! My heart is heavy, heavy, heavy. I write to R., but do not know where the letter will find him!

Wednesday, December 13 Rather unwell, but still strong enough to work with the children. Towards noon a telegram from R. that everything has been approved and he is leaving in great satisfaction for Bayreuth this evening.

Friday, December 15 From R. a telegram from Bayreuth that all arrangements are in excellent shape. Also receive a pheasant and a bashlyk, sent

---

[1] 'Report on the Fates and Circumstances that Attended the Execution of the Stage Festival Play *Der Ring des Nibelungen*.'

[2] There had been complaints of lying and untidiness.

[3] On a visit to Munich and Bayreuth, then to a conducting engagement in Mannheim.

by him. Worked with the children and then walked into town. Letter from poor Mathilde Maier, who now in her dire need is learning photography! Great sorrow not to be taking Lulu with me, God grant that by this means untruthfulness will be driven from her heart forever![1] My one consolation is that the cold is so intense that the punishment might turn out to have been prudent.

Saturday, December 16 In Basel at nine o'clock; evening with Fritz Br. and Prof. Nietzsche.

Sunday, December 17 Coffee with the two Basel professors at three o'clock; after steadfastly reading Schlegel's lectures on history, arrived in Mannheim. Three gentlemen who were sitting in my compartment get out before me, so that R. does not see me; I wait on the platform, and at last he finds me! Lengthy joking about the occurrence, R. says I was standing there like a saga, so earnest and long! – Good reports on everything: 'I have managed my affairs well'; many good things about Feustel and all the Bayreuth people, good, too, of the King. In the evening visit the Wagner Society; excellent people (Heckel, Koch, Zeroni[2]).

Monday, December 18 Rehearsal, *Zauberflöte* Overture and [Beethoven's] A Major Symphony – indescribable impression. Arrival of Prof. Nietzsche, who has literally run away from Basel.

Tuesday, December 19 Wander through the dreary city while R. is resting. Arrival of the Ritters[3].

Wednesday, December 20 Rehearsal, the *Idyll*, great sorrow on my part to see it performed in front of so many strangers, but it sounds lovely. Returned to the hotel. Dinner with Ritters, Pohl, Nietzsche; R. animated, talks about the *Idyll*, and in the process hurts me very much. At six o'clock in the evening the concert; Grand Duke and Grand Duchess, also many Jews. R. already vexed at rehearsals by the universal success of the *Lohengrin* Prelude! – In the evening a banquet. After the concert R. tells me about his conversation with the Grand Duke and the Grand Duchess, which took place in public during the intermission; horribly superficial, the Grand Duke turning as red as a beet when R. mentioned the King of B. and said he owed the completion of his *Nibelungen* to him.

Thursday, December 21 Departure at twelve o'clock, escorted by all our friends. – Travelled with Levi, the conductor, and Pohl. Evening in Basel with nephew and friend. R. relates much about Bayreuth; foundation-stone laying fixed for May 22; the Stuckberg site[4] presented to R. by the town.

---

[1] Cosima had decided not to take Daniela to Mannheim as a punishment for her lying.

[2] Friedrich Koch; Dr. Zeroni, a physician, was chairman of the Mannheim Wagner Society.

[3] Alexander Ritter (Sascha, b.1833) was the son of Wagner's former benefactress, Julie Ritter; his wife Franziska (b.1829) was the daughter of Wagner's brother Albert.

[4] A site in Bayreuth earmarked for the festival theatre, but eventually superseded.

Friday, December 22 Return to Tribschen! Day spent with the children, R. touched, happy, many blissful tears, high spirits, melancholy, joy, hope!

Sunday, December 24 Letter from Hans with photographs and remittance for the children. Prepared the presents, in the evening jubilation around the Christmas tree, but R. is sad because the picture by Lenbach, meant for me, has not arrived; this deeply distresses him; he also feels that the Mannheim treat – his real birthday present for me – had been spoiled.

Monday, December 25 The children wish me many happy returns, but R. declares I must remain aged 33 until New Year's Eve. – I write to Hans to thank him, he is sad about leaving Italy. Children's games, family lunch, all happy and merry. I contemplative, as always on my birthday. Fine letter from Prof. Nietzsche, who has sent me a musical composition.

Sunday, December 31 New Year's Eve; the children and we ourselves very merry. The King sends photographs of *Tristan*! In the afternoon we light the tree again and dance around it; R. plays for us. Stayed up until midnight, looked back on our year and found it good; affectionate good wishes. Between one and two we go off to bed.

1872

Monday, January 1 Children's voices wake me, they are singing 'All hail to the mother' and come garlanded to my bedside; very touched by the singing, the faces, and the goodness of R., who rehearsed them. I am made to go downstairs while things are set up, then I am summoned, the garlanded children sing once more, bring me their gifts on cushions, and I see R.'s picture by Lenbach and a portrait of my father (also by Lenbach). Joy beyond words over the masterpieces and the whole presentation ceremony! But immediately afterwards I become aware that Lulu is unwell; I put her to bed, the doctor discovers that she has a high temperature; sorrow and concern.

Tuesday, January 2 R. prepares himself to start on his third act; this makes me boundlessly happy, indeed lighthearted, in spite of my concern over Lusch; and, since the very splendid weather gives us a view of the gleaming mountains which we have long been without, we go for a walk, I almost overpowered by my high spirits. We return home and drink tea with Lulu.

Wednesday, January 3 Lenbach's portrait pleases me more and more, although I know that R. can also look quite different, as, for example, when I saw him at the railway station in Mannheim, beaming, transfigured, and with such a sweet expression on his face that his features looked small and delicate; here everything is sharp and energetic, unyielding; R. is humorously vexed that he is so ugly. – R. has today begun his third act; thrice-blessed day! – On the subject of my father's *Christus*, which he is having performed in Vienna[1] and about which Marie Much. is concerned on account of the bad conductor (Rubinstein), R. says: 'How curious your father is! He allows the most horrible performances to take place, smiling when I talk of model performances, yet he wants his things to be performed in front of an audience for which he thinks anything is good enough. It is all just a matter of appearances, that is how the world judges things, and people like us are regarded as peasants when they prefer to produce nothing, rather than something false.' – In the evening we read Nietzsche's book[2], which is

---

[1] The first part of Liszt's oratorio *Christus* was performed in Vienna on 31 December 1871 with Anton Rubinstein as conductor and Anton Bruckner as organist.
[2] *The Birth of Tragedy out of the Spirit of Music.*

really splendid; R. thinks of the people who at the moment set the tone in Germany and wonders what the fate of this book will be; he hopes in Bayreuth to start a periodical, which Prof. Nietzsche would edit.

Friday, January 5 R. works and laughs at my being so happy about it: he says, 'Yes, I know, I am just a composing machine.' He goes into town and returns with the news that his sister Luise is dead! We had not even heard that she was ill.

Saturday, January 6 Lulu somewhat better; I constantly with her. Thaw and foehn. – Finished Prof. Nietzsche's book in the evening. 'This is the book I have been longing for,' says R.

Monday, January 8 From Bayreuth the banker Feustel and the mayor[1] suddenly announce a visit! They actually come, spend the day with us, and please us very much. They offer another site for the theatre, better than the one previously chosen[2], and we settle on moving there in the summer.

Wednesday, January 10 Yesterday R. disclosed to me his decision to combine a musical performance with the laying of the foundation stone, and I had to dance for joy, for I had had this very thought myself, but had been scared of expressing it, fearing to cause him yet further excitement and to appear (as it were) to be saying that the laying of the foundation stone was not enough for me. I ask for the Ninth Symphony. And R. intends to put an appeal in the newspapers, saying that he is going to perform the Symphony in Bayreuth, is prepared to pay travel and living expenses, and now invites musicians to come along; he needs 300 singers and 100 orchestral players, and his only condition is that they have to have taken part in a performance of the Symphony before. He says he will then see how far his power extends confronted with conductors, managers, choral institutions, etc. 'Hardly has the cur got over his blows than he is back again nibbling!' The dear man is working! He shows me Brünnhilde's last words again and says he wants to use some of the new verse. R. goes into town and takes care of my affairs; I now have 12,000 francs for the children with the banker and 182 francs laid aside in the savings bank, and, since R. insists that I reckon the other 3,000 francs with that, the total would be 15,000.

Monday, January 15 Letter from Richter, saying that Hans was in Pest, looked very well, was very pleasant, his playing perhaps even more outstanding than before. – Arrival of the manuscript of the Ninth Symphony[3]; infinite joy; this manuscript, well preserved by Schotts', is now more than 40 years old, and now it has come into my hands! R. says

---

[1] Theodor Muncker (b. 1823), mayor since 1863, became a staunch friend and member of the management committee of the festival.
[2] The 'green hill' of Bürgerreuth, on which the theatre still stands.
[3] In 1830 Wagner made a piano arrangement of Beethoven's Ninth Symphony; Schott had kept the MS., which he had not published.

jokingly, 'You have stored up my whole life around me – without you I should know nothing of my life.' – R. works; he says he again has to write fateful episodes, which he cannot bear; things like the *Lohengrin* Prelude, the 'Bridal March', etc., he enjoys doing. – R. says: 'With my so-called love affairs it was just as with my marriage; Minna married me when I was in a very wretched position, attacked even as a conductor, utterly without glory, and she was pretty and much sought after, but all the same I was quite without influence over her. And thus it was, too, with the other relationships, they all belonged in another sphere, and the only unaccountable thing about them is the power I exercized in passing, making Minna marry me, for example.' He then adds, 'Incidentally, no one else would have suited or fitted me better; you were the only one who complemented me; with all the others I spoke in monologues.'

Wednesday, January 17 We discuss the performance of the Ninth in Bayreuth, how to organize it. When we talk of the Symphony itself, R. says, 'When the theme in fifths recurs in the middle of the first movement, it always strikes me as a sort of Macbethian witches' cauldron, in which disasters are being brewed – it does literally seethe.' Richard works.

Saturday, January 20 In the afternoon, as I am working with the children, and R. on his proofs, Prof. Nietzsche pays us a surprise visit, which pleases us very much. Many things discussed: plans for the future, school reform, etc.; he plays us his composition[1] very beautifully.

Monday, January 22 Feustel reports that Cohn[2] has not yet sent anything, and that the credit for the whole building operation must be secured before work can begin. At the same time R. receives a letter from Baron Cohn, showing a subscription of 20,000 thalers! Baron Loën had spoken of 50,000 and reported that he himself had signatures for 28,000 thalers in his portfolio, yet for Baron Cohn he lists only 12,000! R. very alarmed at this news; we walk to town in silence and return home; R. has the idea of making a journey in order to come to an understanding with the Wagneriana.

Tuesday, January 23 R. feels he will have to make the journey – so goodbye now to the working mood – oh, how sad, how sad! I feel crushed. So dive down deep, Rhinemaidens – alas, for how long?

Wednesday, January 24 Departure today. At one o'clock to the railway station. 'I remain in your protection,' he says to me. 'I am happy – just look at me: an old man like me, and what a beautiful wife I have been given!' Embracing and waving, and then gone! I have no urge to go home, do some shopping.

---

[1] Nietzsche wrote two pieces of music in November 1871: presumably it was one of these.
[2] Baron Cohn, a banker in Dessau, in charge with Loën of the patrons' fund, i.e., subscriptions to fund the festival.

Saturday, January 27 Letter from my father, with reports on Hans's great successes in Vienna and Pest. He sends the libretto of his *Christus*.

Sunday, January 28 Drove to town with Fidi; bought cakes for the evening party, having invited my four daughters to tea! Much delight among the little ones, who dress themselves with the utmost elegance. But we soon have to put an end to our pleasure, since Loldi is unwell. Towards half past ten I hear a loud knocking, and Fitzo [Vito] barks; I call Käthchen [her personal maid], who had already heard the noise (knocking) and was up; we look around, but see or find nothing; great fear. I have my mattress put on the floor in Käthchen's room and sleep (or, rather, lie awake) thus.

Monday, January 29 Telegram from R. in Berlin, he is just (8 a.m.) leaving for Weimar. 'Business settled' – so the warning was not on his account! – Loldi seriously unwell; I put her to bed and stay beside her. In the evening a letter from R., everything seems satisfactory, if not exactly brilliant; our conquest is Feustel, who is being helpful in everything.

Tuesday, January 30 Loldi somewhat better; with her the whole day. – In the night a curious knocking again.

Thursday, February 1 Telegram from R., saying he has arrived safely in Bayreuth. He has acquired the site for our house.

Friday, February 2 Terrible day! My children walk into town with Anna, take Fitzo with them, return home weeping, and tell me that Fitzo has been run over by the locomotive. I run to the spot and bury our poor little dog. It is a holiday, people come and go, the sun shines, and I feel as if I were to blame for his death. Today, when the bell rang and I did not hear his barking, I felt so desolate; I cannot help thinking that recently Kos was calling Fitzo; Fitzo heard the knocking and wanted to fly to me for protection. I feel as if I had lost Kos twice, and the terrible sight of that poor, mangled body will never leave me.

Monday, February 5 Day of return! I expect R. at twelve, and he really comes! Happiness, joy, delight, bliss; all, all of this for us in this hour of reunion. R. says that my letters always seemed to him like a voice from the Ganges, and now he is back again on the Ganges! Much to be related; The Wagneriana vanished into thin air, much Jewishness to put up with; but, on the other hand, Bayreuth, 'my greatest practical stroke of genius'.

Thursday, February 8 R. works, and at midday is able to play me his sketch for the Prelude.

Friday, February 9 A Herr Voltz[1], wine merchant in Mainz, claims to have found a way of enabling R. to receive earnings from his works and from performances of them.

Monday, February 12 R. has now done the 'Song of the Rhinemaidens' in ink; the children sing it in the garden; and R. says, 'If I had an audience of

[1] Karl Voltz, a theatre agent in Mainz who, with Karl Batz of Wiesbaden, was given the task of collecting royalties on Wagner's behalf.

Italians and French people for that, all hell would be let loose in this first scene – it's just as well that I can reckon on German stick-in-the-muds to preserve the unity of the impact.' Pleasure in Bismarck, who is starting his battle with the Catholic party: 'He is doing enough already, he doesn't need to think of the art of the future.'

Shrove Tuesday, February 13 In Berlin Herr Löser, that most useless and pathetic of Jews, wants to organize a lottery along the lines of the one for Cologne Cathedral; R. is protesting.

Monday, February 19 R., who had a good night, after breakfast plays the first scene to our friend[1], and that upsets him so much that the whole day through he can eat nothing and is very run down. – The dean of Bayreuth[2] sends his book *Pax Vobis* (on the reconciliation of Protestants and Catholics) with some very friendly words for me.

Wednesday, February 21 R. works and completes Siegfried's reply to the Rhinemaidens, cutting two verses, which are too reflective: 'Siegfried is all action – though he does recognize the fate which he has taken on himself.' He plays me what he has just completed – sublime and tragic impression! – In the evening we read *State and Religion*[3], but at ten o'clock we are interrupted: Jakob announces that Vreneli's time has come; I stay with her until three o'clock, when she gives birth to a girl: suffering and fellow suffering!

Friday, February 23 R. is well and works; at lunch we talk about the Rhinemaidens' scene; he shows me how the maidens come very close to Siegfried, then dive down again, consigning him amid laughter and rejoicing to his downfall with all the childlike cruelty of Nature, which only indicates motives and indifferently sacrifices the individual – thus, in fact, demonstrating a supreme wisdom which is only transcended by the wisdom of the saint. – We go for a drive, R. returns home on foot, I visit the parson, Herr Tschudi, who is very friendly; returning home late, I hear that Voltz, our former wine merchant, who wants to help R. receive royalties from his operas, has announced his coming. He arrives with a lawyer also, and business is discussed.

Saturday, February 24 The discussion affected R. badly; he had a wretched night, and now he has to devote this morning as well to giving these two people authority to act on his behalf! I am disconsolate and ask myself what will come of it.

Sunday, February 25 R. had a good night and is able to work; he has now completed the first scene in ink. 'I have given Siegfried a cry! The fellow cries out like a wild goose.' – In the evening we read Schopenhauer, and when I ask R. for some explanations, he gives them in so lively a manner

---

[1] Nietzsche, who had arrived the previous day.
[2] Dr. Dittmar, who was to become a very close friend.
[3] Wagner's essay, written in 1864.

that I tell him he reminds me of the professor of philosophy in Molière's play, who in the end lashes out with his fists. This amuses him greatly. – 'The way the will sometimes takes matters into its own hands can be seen in me,' R. says. 'It had its ideas for me, and since I should otherwise have stopped cooperating, it brought us together in real life – independent of the fact that outside of time and space we belong to each other anyway – with the result that I started cooperating again. It's just like an employer raising the wages when he sees his employees leaving him.'

Monday, February 26 Over coffee after lunch R. says: 'It is strange how certain things are linked in my memory with the themes which came to me then. With *"Ich flehe um sein Heil"* in *Tannhäuser*, for instance, I always see a fence just in front of the big garden in Dresden, where this theme occurred to me.' – I: 'You also once told me that a theme in *Die Walküre* was connected with a certain walk in Zurich.' 'Yes – curiously enough, for these external things really have nothing to do with it; living impressions, as far as creation is concerned, are somewhat like the box on the ear which was given in earlier times to the youngest member of the community when the boundary stone was set, so that he should remember it.'

Saturday, March 2 Letter from our good Feustel. Much confusion with the Ninth Symphony; instead of 200 singers Herr Stern[1] allocates 38; then people from Schwerin want seats for the performance of the *Nibelungen*, and the mayor of Schweinfurt offers to beat a drum; on top of that, people asking R. to find them lodgings – much foolishness. R. works. In the afternoon our nephew Fritz arrives, an always welcome guest. We spend a cosy evening conversing.

Sunday, March 3 Letter from Hans Richter, who is sending 1,000 florins to Bayreuth, the proceeds of a concert which he conducted. A Wagner Society is also being formed in Pest.

Monday, March 4 Letter from a Herr Dannreuther[2] (very good), who reports the setting up of the Society in London.

Tuesday, March 5 Letter from my father, short and unexpansive. – The Crown Prince of Prussia has suddenly become anti-Wagnerian through his wife and belongs to the Joachim clique.

Thursday, March 7 Outside the foehn is raging, we do not go out. Letters arrive, among others a very remarkable one from Josef Rubinstein[3], beginning 'I am a Jew' and demanding salvation through participation in the production of the *Nibelungen*. R. sends him a very friendly reply. Also a telegram from Herr Hellmesberger[4] in Vienna; he is successfully recruiting singers there.

[1] Julius Stern, conductor of a choral society in Berlin.
[2] Edward Dannreuther, author of *Wagner and the Reform of the Opera*.
[3] Josef Rubinstein (no relation to Anton), born 1847 into a wealthy Russian family, was a pianist, a pupil of Liszt; his appeal to Wagner followed his reading *Judaism in Music*.
[4] Joseph Hellmesberger, Austrian conductor and director of the Gesellschaft der Musikfreunde in Vienna.

Saturday, March 9 The *Rivista Europea* prints a nice article about the Bayreuth venture, and in Italy a Wagner subscription fund is now being opened; the periodical itself has started it off with 150 francs. R. works. In the afternoon letters arrive, all very unsatisfactory. Betz agrees to sing in the Ninth, but says Niemann[1] is feeling offended by R.

Tuesday, March 12 Somewhat indisposed; R. claims it is the dancing exercises I give the children which so wear me out, he says I am making him hate the idea of duty! He works, and towards noon plays me the splendid death symphony[2]. 'That is his heroic ode, thus will he and his ancestors be sung in later times.' 'Siegfried lives entirely in the present, he is the hero, the finest gift of the will.' When we come down, we find the plans of our house, to our great joy. – In the evening we read *Romeo and Juliet*. Pitiful letter from Herr Lauterbach[3]: no musician from Dresden will take part! 'That's how it is everywhere I lived and worked – that's how people behave.'

Friday, March 15 Letter from Hans in Zurich, saying he will not be able to see the children. He tells me of his journey to America, and I feel apprehensive, because he is travelling at the same time as Rubinstein, who has an insanely high contract, and whose sponsors must therefore do all they can to ruin his competitors. Should I write to him about this? – After lunch R. receives – from a member of the Dresden orchestra – the most extraordinary revelations concerning Herr Lauterbach, who has, it seems, just been thwarting our attempts!

Saturday, March 16 Herr Riedel[4] from Leipzig wants to supply more than 300 singers and says people are begging on their knees to take part.

Sunday, March 17 R. says he is very tired of composing, he has already done so much, and on the arrival of Siegfried's corpse he could in fact just write in the score, 'See *Tristan*, Act III.' – We read in the newspaper that Baron von Lerchenfeld[5] has had an audience with the King, and this makes an unpleasant impression on us, since we know the King will certainly not give people confidence in our venture! – R.'s indisposition casts a shadow over our whole life, he is spitting up a little blood and his digestion is so bad. He thinks work is a great strain on him. Alas, happy – who is ever happy? Herr Betz writes that Niemann would like to sing the solo part in the Ninth.

Wednesday, March 20 Boni's tenth birthday; celebrations, holiday, snow and sunshine outside. – I informed R. yesterday that Herr Hüffer[6] was opposed

---

[1] Albert Niemann (b. 1831), tenor in Hanover, then in Berlin; despite Wagner's vexations with him (e.g., as Tannhäuser in Paris in 1861), Wagner respected his talents as actor and singer, and constantly returned to him.

[2] 'Siegfried's Funeral March' in Act III of *Götterdämmerung*.

[3] Johann Lauterbach, concertmaster of the Dresden opera orchestra.

[4] Karl Riedel, chorus master and president of the Leipzig Wagner Society.

[5] District President of Upper Franconia, with his seat in Bayreuth.

[6] Franz Hüffer had sent an article on Wagner that had appeared in an English review.

to Ortrud's appearance and the transformation of the swan in the third act. 'These people have no idea of theatre,' he answers. 'How would Lohengrin ever have got away otherwise without everyone's running after him? The point here was to create a diversion and to make Lohengrin's departure an unexpected surprise. But that's the way of people, to talk without thinking; he should just tell me how he visualizes it on the stage.' – R. is able to work, and he calls me to show me how he has effected Brünnhilde's entry after the raising of Siegfried's hand.

Tuesday, March 26 In gay spirits R. walks into town and returns home with a changed expression: he found a letter from Councillor Düfflipp at the post office! We were not wrong to have been alarmed by Baron Lerchenfeld's audience; the King now wishes it brought to our notice, firstly, that he has learned that the cost of our theatre undertaking would far exceed 900,000 thalers, and the many festival performances would cause the Bayreuth people much expense; secondly, that the Bayreuth newspapers were talking of the luxury of our house, which was very unpleasant for the King; thirdly, that the King requires *Siegfried,* since he acquired it by purchase. I at once beg R. to return the house to the King, that is to say, to ask Düfflipp to cancel the purchase of the site; to say that the score of *Siegfried* is not yet completed; and finally to say that he knows where these statements, of which he had heard nothing, came from. – And so we are once more exposed to the old misery! Long conference with R.; he will ask the people in Bayreuth for a statement; should this be subdued in tone, we will abandon the whole project, for we cannot succeed if the King himself is against us. R. would probably also have to give up his allowance, and we to manage as best we could.

Wednesday, March 27 R. awakes early; he is thinking of giving everything up, making a contract with Schott, assigning the *Nibelungen* to them for a lot of money, and travelling with me to Italy. 'This proud Bayreuth edifice was based on my personal independence, and this root is defective.' We intend to await the outcome of the two letters to Munich and Bayreuth! – With all this he is expected to compose! Yet he showed me a theme which he had worked out in his notebook early this morning. Naturally enough our conversations keep coming back to this latest trial. – The only musician in Dresden to volunteer for the performance in Bayreuth is the cellist Grützmacher[1], and there is also a cellist from Italy – while we ourselves are wondering whether we shall now remain in Germany!

Thursday, March 28 R. calls to me that he is thinking of requesting an audience with Bismarck. Only a few days ago he had been voicing his sorrow over Bismarck's lack of interest, and I had resolved to write to Lothar Bucher. – Towards noon arrival of Professor Nietzsche, who brings

[1] Friedrich Grützmacher, who was to become concertmaster of the Bayreuth Festival orchestra in 1876.

Lulu 100 francs in coins from her father. He saw a lot of Hans in Basel and found him contented and in good spirits.

Monday, April 1 A slight sore throat forces me to remain in bed. R. is also depressed. Prof. Nietzsche takes his leave. Yesterday we tried without success to make a table move; we had spoken about it at lunchtime. R. explains it as a matter of will power, I as fraud.

Wednesday, April 3 Everyone indisposed, the children hoarse and stuffed up; the climate here does not suit R., and then his thoughts – always 'disgust, sorrow, worry, and with it the fear of not keeping up with my work.' Italy, perhaps one day our place of refuge, but very alien to R. And we can also expect nothing in the future, since the next German Emperor, egged on by his mother and his wife, is proving unfriendly, though he was once enraptured by R.'s art! It is all melancholy! We hear from Munich that *Rheingold* and *Walküre* are being performed there as a matter of course.

Thursday, April 4 Rich. just goes on with his work, but he cannot achieve much in this evil atmosphere. At lunch he says: 'I have cut several things, for example, "*Glücklich in Leid und Lust*"[1], etc. I shall retain it in the reading text, but what is this maxim doing in the drama? One knows it anyway, having just gone through it all. It would seem almost childish if she were yet again to turn to the people to proclaim her wisdom.'

Friday, April 5 In the post office we find very splendid letters from Herr Feustel and the mayor, which R. immediately sends to Councillor Düfflipp. They say that in the Bayreuth newspapers not a word has been said about our house, which so bothered the King! The old story. –

Sunday, April 7 Feustel sends 900 certificates of patronage for signature; R. had already signed 200 in Bayreuth. R. writes Feustel a letter which both moves and perturbs me, so truthful is it with regard to our position and the King.

Monday, April 8 Letter from Feustel: Neumann has done no work on the plans all winter, so must be dismissed. R. sends a telegram to Brandt, the machinist, who is also keeping silent; R. thinks he has been lured away by Munich, a view confirmed by a telegram from his son: 'Father away from home.' Letter from Councillor D. saying 'everything will remain as it was before' – the only pity being that we no longer want that!

Tuesday, April 9 R. gets up in good spirits in spite of all and everything; he comes down early and has completed the pencil sketch of the third act! Yesterday he improvised on it for the children, and they danced furiously to it!

Tuesday, April 16 Letter from the landlord of the Fantaisie[2], R. cannot

---

[1] Correctly, '*selig in Lust and Leid*'; the passage in which these words occur was cut entirely.
[2] A hotel in the grounds of the Fantaisie palace, just outside Bayreuth, owned by the dukes of Württemberg; Feustel had rented a floor there for Wagner.

easily get out of his commitment there, and since the climate here does not agree with him and he is also required in Bayreuth for a conference, he decides that we shall spend the summer at the Fantaisie. Feelings of melancholy. Letter from Herr Feustel: The Bavarian Ministry of the Interior has forbidden the governmental architect to concern himself with the erection of our theatre! Herr Neumann impossible, because of his unreliability and negligence.

Thursday, April 18 R. looks through his pencil sketches, those splendid things! When will he find peace to complete the work? ... In the afternoon he goes to see Herr Am Rhyn and is glad to find him in a gentlemanly mood, so that our departure will take place without unpleasant disputes.

Sunday, April 21 R. sketches out his speech for the foundation ceremony, which moves me to tears. Herr Am Rhyn comes to say goodbye and is visibly moved. – R. is greatly vexed because the royalties from Berlin do not come. – In the evening Herr Josef Rubinstein suddenly arrives from Kharkov – a curious spectacle and experience; with him a Dr. Cohen, his companion, who, concealed in the boathouse without the young man's knowledge, wants to tell us that he needs to be treated with great consideration! – R. is infinitely kind to the young man and advises him to take things easy, offers him access to Bayreuth.

Monday, April 22 Last morning together in Tribschen; melancholy activity! – The mail brings the letter from Berlin, and R. has to laugh, since this quarter has brought in so much (1,000 thalers); the performances must always have been full to bursting. Departure! R. left at one o'clock. I had a nervous night. God help poor us! Returned home with Vreneli, had a heartfelt conversation with her; then busied myself with the papers, sorted them, R.'s letters to Minna!!

Wednesday, April 24 Still sorting papers, from morning to evening. In the evening telegram from R. in Bayreuth, he has arrived safely! – Splendid sunset, alpenglow, trees in blossom, the cuckoo calls, the cowbells tinkle, a blackbird calls, melancholy farewell! Glorious moonlight across the water, shining stillness all around me – how different things will be now!

Thursday, April 25 Up early, continued sorting; Countess B. comes to say goodbye. Towards six o'clock sudden arrival of Prof. Nietzsche from Montreux.

Friday, April 26 Walked to town, last boat ride. Packing. In the evening some music. Prof. N. plays for me.

Saturday, April 27 Nice telegram from R., then letter, he is content with everything. – Purchases. Walk to Winkel. Prof. Nietzsche gone. Great weariness!

Sunday, April 28 (These are the first words written at the Fantaisie.) – Telegram from R., he is worried that I have not yet signalled our departure; so I resolve to set off tomorrow. Much work in consequence. In the evening prolonged ramble through the whole of Tribschen, full of gratitude to the gods for granting me such happiness here; it was always lovely, even the difficult times.

Monday, April 29 Packed, cabled R., said goodbye to Vreneli, who is very grieved, telegram from R., departure at 1.20; my five children with Anna, Käthchen with baby, Jakob with Rus. First stop in Zurich; concern for Lulu, who has a cough. Terrible storm, crossing in the night steamer, Loldi fell into a puddle, darkness, endless hand luggage, streaming rain, customs examination, at last boarded the train at Lindau, said goodbye to Jakob, I to look after Rus, all goes well as far as Augsburg, then the luggage car is too full, the dog car impossible, so take him in the compartment with us, astonishment when I lead him out and give him a drink. At long, long last arrival in Bayreuth on *Tuesday the 30th* at 4.30, the children lively, Rus well, and R. to greet us! In the evening went immediately for a walk around the Fantaisie, splendid park, even more remote from the world than Tribschen. R. happy that we are here, calls me his vital force. Conversed with R. until ten o'clock, then to bed.

Wednesday, May 1 R. unfortunately did not sleep well; Rus barked loudly. But he gets up early in order to show the children the splendid park immediately; peacocks fill the air with their wild call, which we so love; R. says, 'I always feel as if I were hearing Sanskrit words.' A turkey, 'almost certainly the prototype of the sailing ship,' gives us great delight, swans, guinea fowls, etc. The day before R. paid his visit to the Duke of Württemberg, whom he found very kind and gracious. We have complete freedom here. R. then holds a conference with the new architect of the theatre, Brückwald[1]; our Herr Neumann had got a carpenter to draw up the plan of the theatre! Brandt is beside himself with relief at not having to have anything more to do with that man! The agents Voltz and Batz are conducting themselves splendidly – from Leipzig, for instance, they got 1,500 thalers; R. hopes to win a fortune through the new copyright law[2]. Fine weather; a magic dream world here, as in Tribschen! – A letter from Councillor D. – they seem to want everything to be resolved in a friendly spirit.

Thursday, May 2 With the children to Bayreuth, visit to Frau Feustel and Frau Muncker, inspection of our site, then of the house we are to rent. Went into the opera house, splendid impression, the proscenium taken out by R., the building revealed in all its original glory; very moved by the knowledge that all these preparations and provisions are being made for the sake of Beethoven's splendid work – its creator could certainly never have dreamed of it! – R. told me that on my arrival the melody from the first

---

[1] Otto Brückwald (b. 1841), court architect in Leipzig, built the municipal theatre there.

[2] Before the copyright law of 1870 Wagner had no legal claim to royalties on performances of his works.

movement had come into his mind and he had said to himself, 'You have never done anything like that.' He reminds me that, when we visited the opera house last year, I had said to him: 'Impossible for the *Nibelungen*, but how fine for concerts!' – 'You see, I do everything you say,' he adds! – Home around seven o'clock; there had been music at the Fantaisie; they had played the *Tannhäuser* March, and since she much regretted not having heard it, Lusch went down with our permission and asked for it again; they played it, but unfortunately like a march of 'hollow priests', as R. puts it. Conversation with R. in the evening. The patrons have not yet all been identified; very bad behaviour from Baron Loën, who does not reply – spite or negligence?? ... My father? ... R. says the Wesendoncks are also not to be found on any list, and he remarks, 'It is really humiliating when one assumes that people will behave well and are on one's side, and then suddenly receives proof of the contrary.'

Friday, May 3 Business letters; R. still working on his orchestra, he needs second oboists. I write letters, we talked a lot about the Ninth Symphony, which is so awkward in many technical details, yet throughout so intoxicating in the power of its thought. R. feels it would be very much to the advantage of the work if much of it were to be reorchestrated.

Saturday, May 4 This morning R. woke me with a passage from the *Idyll*. Eternal times now past! We drive into town, R. holds his conference, and I make purchases, my first in Bayreuth! The agents Voltz and Batz send 535 florins. The first beginnings. Home rather late and then to bed.

Sunday, May 5 Packed; Käthchen is coming [to Vienna] with us; the children's goodbyes are cool, which worries R., though I had indeed forbidden them to cry too much. Left at five o'clock; the mayor with his wife at the station.

Monday, May 6 Arrival at ten o'clock, many Wagner Societyites, reassurance concerning Kafka, nice accommodation with the Standhartners. Unfortunately, after lunch Herbeck[1] expecting us to attend a performance of one of the Wagner works. *Rienzi* is finally approved, since so unfamiliar to R.

Tuesday, May 7 R. slept well; went shopping with him, we are glad to be in Vienna *together* – which of us would ever have dreamed it? After lunch, visit from Countess Dönhoff, pretty and charming, a unique personality among the best Wagnerians. In the evening the excellent Dr. Kafka, also an enthusiast of a peerless kind.

Wednesday, May 8 Drove to the rehearsal; nice reception, the players glowing with pleasure at playing under R. (music from *Tannhäuser* and *Tristan*). R. allows the students from the Conservatoire in, much cheering. After the rehearsal he lies down and I return Countess D.'s visit, heard nice

[1] Johann Herbeck, conductor in Vienna.

things about Hans, am told he speaks of me with respect, says how happy he is that his children have the best of mothers, while he is the worst of fathers. – At seven o'clock *Rienzi*, execrably played to a brilliant audience.

Thursday, May 9 Countess D. says there is much in the newspaper about me and my life with R. – and also asserting that she had paraded with R. in the foyer – this miserable press! Thank God that it will stay away from Bayreuth – the *Nationalzeitung* has already written to R. offering to send Herr Gumprecht[1], but he is being firmly repulsed. – In the evening a party at Dr. Nettke's[2]; patrons, members of the Wagner Society, Lenbach, and Makart[3]. Herbeck proposes a toast to Bayreuth, R. replies that he puts his trust in the German spirit. Unfortunately too much to eat and drink.

Friday, May 10 Headache. Letter from the children. In the Belvedere with Lenbach; splendid Titians. At nine o'clock rehearsal, R. dissatisfied, the orchestra has got ten per cent worse in ten years. – R. says the orchestral players clapped too much, out of idleness, to produce an easy-going atmosphere.

Sunday, May 12 Drove to the concert at twelve. I, in the director's box, can follow every movement of R.'s face. Fine, packed hall, an indescribable reception, mounds of laurel leaves; at the conclusion, since the calls do not cease, R. speaks a few words. During the 'Magic Fire Music' a thunderstorm broke, which added a lot more still to the effect; R. said that the Greeks regarded this as a good sign and he would do the same, and he expressed his hope of receiving true sympathy and support in Vienna for his German venture. – (With Gluck's overture dropped, the programme is: *Eroica*, music from *Tannhäuser*, *Tristan und Isolde* Prelude, 'Magic Fire Music'.) – At lunch arrival of Richter, just as usual, splendid and excellent, he makes his singers pay fines when they alter something in the operas!

Monday, May 13 Affectionate parting from our excellent hosts and friends; at five o'clock departure with Richter. Sleepless night.

Tuesday, May 14 Arrival at eight o'clock; nice reception by the mayor, who arranges everything quietly and prudently.

Thursday, May 16 Paper hangers at five in the morning, much work; our landlords muddled and unmethodical. But the children always lively and enjoying themselves. The location here pleases us more and more, the close proximity is worth so much to R., that and the cultural atmosphere. Our rooms have now been furnished, pictures hung, etc., and R. is content. It is almost quieter and more peaceful than Tribschen!

Friday, May 17 R. is trying to concentrate on his speeches, 'to memorize them like Beckmesser!' – But then he decides to write the speech down and read it, since he does not wish to prepare himself like an actor, but is also

[1] Otto Gumprecht, a journalist working for the Berlin *Nationalzeitung*.
[2] Rudolph Nettke, one of the founders of the Wagner Society in Vienna.
[3] Hans Makart (b. 1840), Austrian painter.

unwilling to improvise, since the speech is to be preserved as a document. I call on Frau von Lerchenfeld; the district president himself is out of town during these days!

Saturday, May 18 Arrival of Prof. Nietzsche, Herr v. Gersdorff and the Ritters. Herr Heckel of Mannheim is also here, is spending the night at the Fantaisie with Richter. Cheerful, companionable atmosphere, we all belong together. Many of the musicians already here. (R. writes to my father and in splendid words invites him here.)

Sunday, May 19 Whitsunday and many visits; Cornelius, Porges, Schäfer, not very pleasant, later Ritter, Nietzsche, Gersdorff, then Countess Krockow; finally, and most charming, Frau v. Schleinitz and Countess Dönhoff. R. in town greeting the singers, much coming and going, but gay spirits. Rain, shortage of carriages.

Monday, May 20 First rehearsal, fine and touching welcome to the musicians from R., all in solemn mood, the only ones out of place the critics Gumprecht and Engel[1], who, in spite of R.'s veto, have taken up certificates of patronage in order to be here. Much to be learned; the musicians as yet have no idea of the interpretation. Another rehearsal in the afternoon, this time with the singers. Frl. Lehmann[2] very good. – Malwida Meysenbug also here, to our great delight. R. to bed immediately after the rehearsal; tired, but very exhilerated by his success.

Tuesday, May 21 Morning rehearsal, many Bayreuth people in my box, but friends, too, among them Dr. Standhartner, who has come all the way from Vienna. Johanna Jachmann gives no pleasure and does the occasion no honour, since she does not even know her part. Lusch and Boni at the rehearsal. It goes well, indeed splendidly, R. very affected, but the musicians and all of us even more so, greatest triumph of genius! – At a moment of foreboding Schiller wrote his words to joy, which nobody perhaps understood until Beethoven came along and understood them and made us in moments of foreboding understand them, too, but misunderstood they remained until, in a sublime and foreboding moment, Richard made them resound in words and music. – All of us, so various in ourselves, were assembled here in a single faith and hope! Niemann kisses R.'s hand; Betz has not yet quite achieved the accents R. wants for '*Freunde, nicht diese Töne*' (trembling indignation) – but he is trying. In the evening, driving home, we see columns of people making a pilgrimage to the Fantaisie; singers of both sexes in open farm wagons, since there is nothing else to be had. The choral society sings a serenade to R. We go down to join the people, which pleases them greatly, and, although he is hoarse, R. speaks a few words to them in his uniquely affecting way.

[1] Gustav Engel, music critic of the *Vossische Zeitung*, Berlin.
[2] Marie Lehmann (b. 1851), sister of Lilli Lehmann; Marie was the soprano soloist, the other soloists being Johanna Jachmann-Wagner, Albert Niemann and Franz Betz.

Wednesday, May 22 Birthday! I wish R. many happy returns very simply this time, for he is preparing the great treat himself. Daniella recites to him a little poem written by *Clemens* [Brockhaus], the children present him with a Bible; Fidi very pretty in the blouse embroidered by Countess Bassenheim. Everything in good order, but rain and rain, not a single ray of sunshine in the offing! – R. relates that in a dream he saw Fidi with his face full of wounds. What can this mean? – We drive to the meeting place, Feustel's house, rain, rain, but despite it all in good spirits. Arrival of the King's telegram, which is to be enclosed in the capsule with other things. R. then goes to the festival site, where, in spite of the rain, countless people – including women – had gathered, and lays the foundation stone. The speeches, however, are made in the opera house. In Feustel's house I give Herr Julius Lang[1] (who in a letter from Vienna had told me that he had sent Prince Bismarck a telegram about the concert in Vienna) a piece of my mind concerning his compromising activities with regard to our affairs during the past ten years. I did it in fear and trembling, but I did it, so as from now on to be rid of such an individual. – In the opera house R. fetches me from my box to sit with the five children on the stage beside him. Very fine impression, even the gravest among the men have tears in their eyes. Dinner at the Fantaisie with Standhartner, who, like everybody else, praised the behaviour of the children, particularly of Fidi, at the ceremony. At five o'clock the performance, beginning with the '*Kaisermarsch*'. The Ninth Symphony quite magnificent, everyone feeling himself freed from the burden of mortal existence; at the conclusion sublime words from R. on what this celebration means to him! – Then to the banquet. Before the concert a Frau von Meyendorff, just arrived from Weimar, handed over a letter from my father[2] – the letter very nice, but the woman, unfortunately, very unpleasant. Her manner is cold and disapproving. – At the banquet R. proposes the first toast to the King, then to Bayreuth; we leave at about half past nine. Niemann and Betz had left earlier out of wounded vanity. I sit with Frau von Schl. and attempt to converse with Frau von Meyendorff; because of her obstinacy the conversation takes place in French. R. enters during it and is vexed with the ugly note here introduced; an angry mood on his part, sorrow on mine. In the end he returns to the banquet, I stay behind with Marie Schl., Marie Dönhoff and Count Hohenthal. Home at twelve o'clock. (Count Krockow gives R. a leopard which he shot in Africa.)

Thursday, May 23 R. dreams of a room which he is obliged to enter and on which is written '*Ici on parle français*,' then of Betz and Niemann, with

---

[1] Julius Lang, editor of a fine arts journal (*Blätter für die bildenden Künste*); though mentioned several times disapprovingly in the Diaries, Cosima never gives a reason for her aversion to him.

[2] Olga von Meyendorff (b. 1838), wife of the Russian envoy in Weimar and Liszt's close companion.

whom he had quarrelled. Up early and into town, R. to the patrons' meeting, which decides unanimously to build the theatre; I with Frl. von Schorn[1] from Weimar and Elisabeth Krockow (beforehand tried to appease Frau Niemann). To Frl. von Sch[orn], who invites me to go to Weimar, I say that I shall do this only along with Wagner – either a complete reunion or none at all. Breakfast with Marie Schl.; visit to the festival site, then farewell to many friends; in the evening, however, still a great many of them with us, among them the splendid Mme Lucca from Milan, of whom R. says Nature originally intended to make a man, until it realized that in Italy the men were not much use, and quickly corrected itself. R. very tired in the evening, but cheerful. The weather fine today; we persuade ourselves that with yesterday's wretched weather we had paid our debt to Fate and, because of that, worse things had been spared us. But the nicest thing was that this misfortune had not been able to spoil our mood.

Friday, May 24 Touching letter from a working man, who asks us to be godfather and godmother to his child, born on the 22nd. We consent with pleasure. – In the morning a conference took place with Brandt, who is quite an outstanding person, fully aware of the difficulties involved but always ready to help with imaginative ideas.

Saturday, May 25 Brückwald, the architect, comes in the morning, many things are discussed, I advise letting the stage tower rise boldly above the whole building as its main feature and not concealing it, but keeping the auditorium as low as possible as a sort of low entry hall to the stage. – R. rests a bit, we once more discuss the Jewish question, since the Israelite participation in the Berlin Wagner Society leaves us with a very bad taste. R. says he still hopes that this whole phenomenon is a sickness which will disappear; an amalgamation is impossible, and we cannot believe that the Germans will be subjugated by the Jews, our military exploits have shown us to be too strong for that. – Our friend Gersdorff takes his leave with tears in his eyes. And so it has all gone past like a dream – who was not there? what did not happen? – all vanished now, a lovely dream!

Sunday, May 26 R. slept somewhat better. Telegram from Betz, he is also appeased. Frl. von M. tells us she has heard that Bismarck is very concerned for our undertaking and is following it with interest as a matter of national importance, which pleases us very much. – Letter from Vreneli, foxes are stealing the chickens at Tribschen, so quiet is it there!

Monday, May 27 A nasty letter from Hans, reproaching me for having gone on the stage with the children.

Tuesday, May 28 Since yesterday working again with the children; wrote to Hans. Visit from *Diener*[2], the tenor, who has a good voice but also all the

[1] Adelheid von Schorn (b. 1841) had been enjoined by Princess Wittgenstein (now living in Rome) to keep an eye on Liszt in Weimar.
[2] The tenor Franz Diener (b. 1849) sang in Cologne, Berlin and Dresden.

bad habits of present-day singers, who can only produce bursts, no sustained notes; R. will try to save him from the 'theatre lark'.

Wednesday, May 29 Around noon the architect Wölffel[1], discussion about our house; walk with M. Meysenbug, but without R., who is too run down. Very fine letters from Prof. N. to R. and to me. Certainly few people have so much feeling for our sufferings and joys as he.

Sunday, June 2 Left home at ten o'clock, christening day, first R. and myself alone, then M. Meysenbug with my three girls. I have to leave Daniella at home, because yesterday she again caused me great sorrow with her obstinate lying, with her joy in bearing tales and her roughness towards her sisters. – Before the christening visited Frau Kolb, Frau Landgraf (the wife of the doctor), and finally the excellent Dean Dittmar, a magnificent old gentleman who receives us with the most lively friendliness; he talks with much fire about the performance, but admits that the '*Kaisermarsch*' made more impression on him than the Ninth Symphony. Following this visit, dinner in the Sonne (in the room we first sat in a year ago), then fetched the baby and drove to the church. I am moved to tears by the ceremony and the words 'Now through the spirit and the water shalt thou be part of the redemption.' We take the little girl, Richardis Cosima, home, her father impressed and earnest, her mother very modest – good and worthy working people with whom one cannot take liberties. They press us to wine and coffee and provide a large cake with it; their apartment, two rooms, with five children in it, looks clean, many people at the windows and doors of the workingmen's houses, but the windows look out on gardens and hills. We are very moved.

Monday, June 3 In the afternoon went to the Schweizerei[2]; talked with Malwida about R.'s life, she is utterly dismayed at all she finds in the biography, the calumnies quite horrify her. R. meets us in the Schweizerei, the sky is overcast, but we put our trust in a ray of sunshine which suddenly breaks through and follow R. on a roundabout route. When we are far away from anywhere a terrible thunderstorm breaks; no umbrellas, no cover, the five children and three not very robust women. The situation is such that we laugh aloud. But Fidi cries; R. lifts him up and is both touched and pleased when the little boy throws his arms around his neck and calms down. We arrive home in an indescribable state, the children put to bed at once; R. has a chill after all, our friends also go to lie down, they are scarcely able to take off their clothes and their shoes. R. talks about the incident in the evening: 'That is my fate – what demon drives me to seek out devious paths when the sky is overcast? On top of that I took a wrong turning, and you follow behind, unhesitating; we are a nice pair of fools!' We go to bed in good spirits.

[1] Carl Wölffel (b. 1833), architect in Bayreuth.
[2] A restaurant on the outskirts of Bayreuth.

Tuesday, June 4 Drove to town in the afternoon, marked out our building site, R.'s plan is now ready. Visited Herr Kraussold[1], the consistorial councillor; touching simplicity of their living habits, his wife receives us in the vegetable garden. He talks excellently about the position of school and church. How helpless and powerless Protestantism is! It has to atone for the guilt of the Catholic church, and thus Catholicism is protected. A philologist, Herr von Wilamowitz[2], hurls at us his polemic against Nietzsche's book, under the title *Zukunftsphilosophie*. It is said to be contemptible.

Thursday, June 6 Birthday greetings to Fidi, who is three today. R. cuddles and kisses him. Letter from Dr. Kafka, who announces 20 certificates of patronage. In contrast, one of the workers declared yesterday that, if the wages are not raised, they will stop work on the building. – Around six o'clock R. drives off to the Thursday gathering[3], where he meets the always refreshing Feustel and the magnificent dean.

Friday, June 7 Before lunch I hear him playing passages from my father's *Christus*; what I have so far heard of this work makes no great impression on me: 'That one can so use the resources of a great and noble art to imitate the blubbering of priests,' says R., 'that is a sign of intellectual poverty.' – We deplore this development in my father, for which Princess W[ittgenstein] is certainly mainly to blame. – At lunch, speaking of yesterday's meeting, R. says: 'And so I have come back to the point from which I started; my childhood surroundings were like these people and these houses; plain middle class, with, if you will, a limited outlook, and yet vital and with a sound core.' The conversation flowed on, and R.: 'One can only understand one's life when one is older; when I think what it was that impelled me to sketch *Tristan*, just at the time of your first visit with Hans to Zurich, while up till then I had been calmly completing the two acts of *Siegfried*, and when I now look back at the whole chain of events up to the production of *Tristan* in Munich! In this one can see how everything is metaphysical, and how deceptive the things of which one is conscious can be. How different it will look to someone who can see the whole from the way it looked as it was happening! As with Romeo, the seed of a tremendous passion was being sown, and it appeared in the consciousness as a tenderness towards Rosaline. What is consciousness? The day following an often wretched night, and daylight ghosts! And it literally seems as if one can assume that Fate does take care of one, for, looking at my whole life, my marriage with Minna, does not everything look hopeless? And yet the miracle happened, though indeed in a different and more painful way than through annunciations and so on. And I know that, however pleasant I

---

[1] Dr Lorenz Kraussold, Bayreuth.

[2] The classical philologist Ulrich von Wilamowitz-Moellendorff published his polemic against Nietzsche's *The Birth of Tragedy* in May.

[3] The so called *Kränzchen*, a private club of prominent Bayreuth citizens who met in each other's homes.

found this kind and sympathetic friendship – someone who would and could care for me – I was always close to running away.'

Sunday, June 9 In the afternoon R. plays and sings passages from *Götterdämmerung*, but he is melancholy because it has become so alien to him, he sees the necessity of getting down to music again. Letter from Prof. N., who sends us Herr von Wilamowitz's pamphlet attacking him.

Monday, June 10 Our friends leave us, to our great regret. They are to see *Tristan* in Munich. R. reads Herr von Wilamowitz's pamphlet and is provoked by it into writing an open letter to Prof. Nietzsche, which he reads to me in the evening[1]. Walk with the composer Svendsen[2] and his wife.

Thursday, June 13 To town with R. First to our architect, R. very satisfied with the execution of his plan for our house. Then to the Feustels', from there to the festival site; the working men make a fantastic impression on us.

Monday, June 17 R. has a buzzing and stabbing sensation in his ears, something he also had severely 8 years ago in Starnberg. It both worries and alarms me, and I am also worried by the very great expense of our life here – alas, the poor dear man has much to bear! – He is not at all well, can do little work, and does not go for a walk. In the evening the good Svendsens come and he has to leave, for he can talk to nobody.

Monday, June 24 Midsummer's Day! R. works, but has trouble with his paper, which has become damp and smudges the notes. He has written to H. Porges, because he is pleased with his article on the performance of the 9th, and, as he says: 'I can never forget it when someone has behaved well towards me. In the evil days in Vienna he was the only one to whom I could turn, so he can go on sinning for quite a while before I strike him off my good books.' – We spoke of his first marriage. 'My God,' says R., 'it was no extravagant urge which drove me to it, but a truly respectable one, and it is true that this marriage kept me from all unsettling relation-ships and helped to develop my artistic side. I reached the age of 40 without even believing in a more serious relationship with a woman, as for example mine with Jessie Laussot. While the powers of your father's soul were stirred from his earliest days by such relationships, mine stayed firmly fixed on my artistic development!' 'Certainly,' he says, laughing, 'I had to pay rather dearly for this conservation.' R. plays me what he wrote today, the beginning of Siegfried's narration.

Thursday, June 27 Visit from the conductor Herbeck. Proposals for Vienna, inquiry whether R. would perhaps do *Die Walküre* there, before Bayreuth – all of it nonsense. R. has done some work, despite the interruption of Herr H.

---

[1] Published in the *Augsburger Allgemeine Zeitung* on June 12.
[2] Johan Svendsen (b. 1840), Norwegian composer.

Sunday, June 30 Letters, from M. Muchanoff in Kassel: she invites me to visit her in Weimar and to visit my father, then my father would come to Bayreuth! – M.M[eysenbug] writes from Munich, where *Tristan* was performed; I am always beset by bitter feelings when I think about these performances, which delight our friends, taking place in our absence. (Prof. Nietzsche and Herr v.G. were also there.)

Monday, July 1 R., Fidi and I to the Schweizerei, where the other children then joined us. On the way home Fidi is wilful; in order to punish him I make him walk by himself (he only wanted to give me his hand), and that puts R. out of humour – which distresses me. In the evening R. says I must forgive him his moody manner; either he is not in a working mood, and then he is despondent, or he is in it, and then he could complete his work to the end without interruption, and everything – eating, drinking, sleeping, speaking – becomes an obstacle which causes him suffering and vexes him. – Alas, what distresses me is simply not having the power to smooth his path completely.

Thursday, July 4 At three o'clock arrival of Herr v. Gersdorff, much about *Tristan*, tremendous impression on everybody. At 9.15 our friend [Marie Muchanoff]; R. buys sausages, and I accompany our friend to the Fantaisie. The great joy of seeing her is soon clouded over by reports of *this* world. She relates among other things that Frau von Meyendorff complained of the poor reception she was accorded here!

Friday, July 5 Herr v. Gersdorff informs me of a plan by which Prof. Nietzsche will issue an appeal for a collection in which all who cannot buy certificates of patronage, or do not wish by means of single contributions to join a Wagner Society, can take part.

Sunday, July 7 Departure of Herr von Gersdorff.

Monday, July 8 I accompany our friend to the railway station; she seems content with her stay here, the children behaved very well. – Though we ourselves got great pleasure from her visit, it has nevertheless left behind a melancholy impression; the restless and joyless life of this outstanding woman, and particularly what she relates of the outside world, is so gloomy and sad (tragedy without dignity, as Schopenhauer says), that we always avert our eyes in disgust. Emotional parting from her. – R. was unable to work today, there has been too much distraction around him. It is very hot. In the evening we take the children to look for glowworms in the park. Meeting with the Duke, a fight between our dogs, but the Duke extremely friendly.

Saturday, July 13 In the afternoon and evening the Feustels, also J. Rubinstein, arriving from Munich. The latter's piano playing pleases us greatly, in particular a fugue by Bach (from the 48 Preludes and Fugues, D-flat Major[1]) puts us into ecstasies: 'It is as if music were really being

---

[1] Presumably the C-sharp Major.

heard for the first time,' says R. When I tell R. that this scherzando has filled me, curiously, with tremendous melancholy, R. says: 'I can understand that; it is like a restless forward striding, as if he were saying: "Here you have everything with which you will later work, where you will lie down and rest; I know it all already, I must go on." A sphinx – but that is German. How shallow and conventional does the sonata form – that product of Italy – seem in comparison! It was only by breathing such tremendous life into the accessories of this form that Beethoven brought music back close to Bach.'

Monday, July 15 In the evening went through the third act of *Siegfried* with Herr R. It is curious how *Siegfried* seems to be so completely unknown and misunderstood, even among devoted Wagnerians; I should have expected it to be seen as a thoroughly popular work.

Thursday, July 18 R. receives the contract for our house for signature; he recently dreamed of his burial beneath the chestnut trees on our terrace, which were already very large, so that he felt he would live for a long time, since we have only just planted the chestnut trees.

Friday, July 19 To the festival site (before that to our house). Terrifying excavation works; R. says to me, 'The people must be wondering if I am not mad, "making us work down here so deep under the earth, just so he can perform his plays up there above." ' – Homeward drive by night; the moon glows red-gold through the shadows of the woods, in which fireflies are swarming; we are reminded of *Faust*: 'Couldst thou but see, full moonlight!' – 'How splendid,' says R., 'that Goethe completed *Faust* in his youth and old age he felt himself to be a poet, his life between was a sort of distraction. "Once more you hover near me, forms and faces, seen long ago with troubled youthful gaze" – how splendid that is! One sees him greeting the friendly essence of his youth. I have no forms and faces, I know of no being whom I could name in connection with any of my works – but instead I found you, I now have Cosima.' – Deep emotion on our journey, lovely homecoming.

Saturday, July 20 R. says he must now compose his verses for the end of the world, and he does indeed work without stopping. Letter from my mother, who is now sufficiently recovered to be able to write to me. In the evening Herr R. and Svendsens; R. sings the first scene of the third act of *Tristan*, but forbids anything more of his own, since he is too much occupied with working out his last scene.

Sunday, July 21 R. is unfortunately disturbed in the morning by our architect, Herr Wölffel, then he settles down again to work and reaches the end of the act, but he is in a very excitable state about the task still ahead. I tell him how in earlier times I had considered how I should celebrate the completion of the *Nibelungen*, but now I could do nothing. 'So it is not enough for you,' says R., 'that you alone gave me the strength to complete it, you alone made it possible for me? There must also be some outward sign – how vain women are!'

Monday, July 22 I do not have the strength to describe the emotion that gripped me when R. called me to say that he had completed his sketch. He plays the ending to me, and I do not know which stirred me more deeply, the noble sounds or the noble deed. I feel as if *my* goal has been reached and I can now close my eyes.

Tuesday, July 23 Unfortunately R. did not have a good night, but he works out his 'figurations', so that only today is he really finished. 'Music has no ending,' he says. 'It is like the genesis of things, it can always start again from the beginning, go over to the opposite, but it is never really complete. Do you remember how undecided I was about the ending of the first act of *Die Meistersinger?* I am glad that I kept back Sieglinde's theme of praise for Brünnhilde, to become as it were a hymn to heroes.'

Wednesday, July 24 Fidi with us as usual at breakfast. 'Turn out humorous and kind, then I shall be satisfied,' R. says. 'Whether you will turn out a great genius straightaway, we shan't inquire.' 'So now after all I have set this whole poem to music from beginning to end; previously I never believed it, not only on account of the impossibility of performing it, but also my inability to remain so persistently in the right mood; but I did remain in it – right up to the last verse I was as moved by it as at the very first word.' 'I have been thinking whether I should not become choirmaster here, learn the organ and play it, in order to be of some use to the people. For it is here, from the friends I have gained here, that I now expect everything, not from what is perhaps being arranged for me outside.' I go into the garden, the girls before me, Fidi beside me carrying his large book. From the balcony R. calls, 'Pythia with the acolyte, who is bearing the prophecy'. – R. said to me at lunch, 'If things go well with me, I do believe it won't be long before I start on *Parzival.*'

Monday, July 29 Letter from R.'s excellent publisher Fritzsch, who reports that the collected works are selling very well, which pleases R. all the more in view of the fact that the other publishers always claimed that there was no demand for any of these things. R. is still correcting the biography; in the afternoon he takes Herr Diener[1] in hand, gets him to sing Wolfram's song slowly and softly, and is very happy with the way he manages it; less so with Herr Rubinstein, whose playing is still very undisciplined. They take up *Die Walküre*; tremendous impression on me, as if I did not know it at all. In the morning R. prepared the text of the *Ring* for Herr Fritzsch and wrote in the final verses. – In the evening he is a little vexed over always having only immature people to deal with, and having to begin with them right from the start.

[1] He came to Bayreuth on July 27.

Tuesday, July 30 R. writes to a scene designer in Vienna, Herr Hoffmann[1], who, it seems, would like to take on the work for Bayreuth. – He completes the corrections to his third volume and laughs over the fact that he begins it with the reunion with Minna in Zurich and ends it with their reunion in Paris. 'All this squandering of my life's and my soul's energies!' he exclaims. 'The nonsense of all these relationships; I really believe that I must live only for my mission in life, for in Paris, for instance, nothing of a positive value emerged, I gained nothing from it; I just became harsher and harsher. Today I was correcting proofs of the time of the third act of *Tristan* and thought: If only the Grand Duke of Baden had offered me asylum then! But I was destined for other things, it all had to come about other than by a direct route.'

Friday, August 2 We work on the biography and reach the point of Minna's arrival in Paris, where R. now wishes to break off. – Visit from the dean, truly risen from the dead[2]; he is a man who through his kindness and lively intelligence really delights us; the only sad thing is that we got to know him so late in life. He is reading Nietzsche's book and is much captivated by it, says there are things in it which belong to the best our literature has produced. He makes the question of my conversion very much easier for me, says that his first glance into my eyes had told him many things, and he intends to take good care of the honour and peace of my family. We are very moved as we bid goodbye to this splendid man whom, scarcely discovered, we nearly lost and whom, now, won anew, we shall probably not be permitted to enjoy for very long.

Saturday, August 3 R. sings a cantilena from *I Puritani* and remarks that Bellini wrote melodies lovelier than one's dreams.

Monday, August 5 I correct some pages in R.s biography while he works on his essay[3]. My mother sends the first volume of her history of the Netherlands[4].

Saturday, August 10 R. continues work on his essay and remarks with a laugh that he never has anything to tell me, since he is always just writing up his conversations with me. – In the evening read Gibbon again, after a long break. (Finished knitting my first legging for R.; I tell him laughingly that not even a god would previously have induced me to take up such work.)

Monday, August 12 With the children in the garden; much joking about the end of the world, proclaimed for today. Drove into town; *Götterdämmerung*, very finely copied out (third act) by Herr Rubinstein and appropriately completed on the day the world will end, is taken to the bookbinders to be

---

[1] Josef Haffmann (b.1831), an academic painter in Vienna.
[2] He had been seriously ill recently.
[3] *Actors and Singers.*
[4] *Histoire des commencements de la republique aux Pays-Bas* 1581–1625 by Daniel Stern (1872).

bound (in orange velvet) for the King. Then visit our upward-growing house, which will be very pretty. After that to the Feustels'; fresh trouble with the theatre – Herr Brückwald also appears to be unreliable.

Tuesday, August 13 Yesterday we read in a newspaper that Hans intended to conduct a concert in Munich on behalf of Bayreuth, and this is confirmed by Marie Muchanoff.

Friday, August 16 Final evening with the Svendsens; cordial parting from these dear, excellent and very well educated people.

Saturday, August 17 In the afternoon Herr Niemann and Herr Levi, the conductor; the former goes through part of Siegmund with R.

Sunday, August 18 Family lunch. Afterwards the musicians – five in number. R. plays them the third act of *Götterdämmerung*, which absolutely stuns them. Herr Niemann says that no one will ever be able to perform it like R. himself. At parting, Herr L. tells me he is downright glad to be leaving, for he feels such a complete nonentity here, and will have to try and find himself again; a curious attitude – I should have thought one would only find oneself properly when one was confronted with a great man and could forget oneself.

Monday, August 19 A collection of costume sketches for the *Ring* from a gentleman in Nuremberg, which are so frightful that they are really funny. While I am working in the garden with the children I am called in: Frl. Lehmann[1] has arrived. R. gets her to sing something from *Lohengrin*; her voice is good and she is musical, but the faults in delivery are incredible. She and her mother, whom R. has known for more than 40 years, stay for lunch, though we are shocked by the conversation during it: the German Emperor's behaviour with Mme Lucca[2], who addresses him familiarly on the stage and allows him to fasten her costume – all this makes us sad. Such things do no honour either to the crown or to art. Late in the evening Herr Niemann. The crudeness of these creatures is truly frightening – yet there is a solid core in N. – But we shall never find another Schnorr!

Thursday, August 22 Around midday Niemann comes to say goodbye, he kisses R.'s hand, which obliges R. to offer him his cheek. As we were driving into town yesterday, R. recalled his experiences with this singer, how he betrayed him in Paris, how, when R. was once singing to some friends this same *Walküre* which Niemann now sings so enthusiastically, the tenor giggled and could not wait for it to finish. 'Well,' R. says, 'that was all so long ago that he now seems like a different person to me, it is all as good as forgotten, but I shall never get emotional about him, he can say what he likes.' – The elder children please me by giving lessons to the little ones.

---

[1] Lilli Lehmann (b.1848) was still on the threshold of her brilliant career, now engaged in Berlin. She and her sister Marie were both trained by their mother, Marie Loew, a former opera singer in Kassel, whom Wagner knew well.

[2] Pauline Lucca, soprano in Berlin.

Friday, August 23 In the evening the tenor Diener, who pleases R. greatly with his diligence – he gets him to sing me something from *Lohengrin*. This young man could now be earning himself 600 thalers a month in Cologne, but prefers working with R.

Saturday, August 24 I write to Marie M., who is again opening the subject of a visit to my father; she advises me strongly to tell him I am coming – but as my father has kept silent towards me since Frau v. M[eyendorff]'s visit here, I do not consider this advisable. R. shows me a telegram which he is sending to Pastor Tschudi, announcing a contribution to the church: 'That is the only thing I can give you for tomorrow as a present.'

Sunday, August 25 Lovely, bright day. R. comes to me in the morning with his good wishes. We celebrate our [wedding] day by spending it together, R. and I; he reads me what he has written in his essay and then we walk with the children to the bench by the playground and dream together. R. leaves me at about 6.30 in case somebody is waiting in the house; I remain behind, and, as the sun goes down and the fir trees flow in its rays, I think gratefully of my good fortune. What might have become of me? Despised, robbed of my children, not married to R., I should have had to hide away – now I am permitted to stay at his side as his wife and to live for my children. Indescribable feelings of gratitude – and blessings on Hans, who made it all possible.

Monday, August 26 R. has to go to town early today: Brückwald and Brandt are there, and there are many things to be discussed. More letters from Marie M., she worries me with the report that Hans would dearly like to remain in Munich. His concert for Bayreuth (sonatas) is said to have been brilliant. R. returns home at about seven in the evening; completely hoarse! He also brings some money. I am sad that so much is spent, alas, and I worry over our moving to a new house, worry because our expenditure is always increasing and our income not, worry because R. is becoming so involved in his enterprise before the certificates are signed. – My only help is the grateful belief that God, who has protected us so far, will continue to protect us! R. is very pleased with his machinist. But he is very tired!

Wednesday, August 28 Once more Marie M. asks me to visit my father! Unsatisfactory discussion with R.; great misgivings, this journey seems to us foolhardy – God knows what we shall decide; whichever way, we shall feel apprehensive.

Thursday, August 29 Letter from Herr Schäfer: [Hans's] concert in Munich has brought in 1,400 florins! Renewed discussion with R. about the Weimar visit; he becomes angry, and I ask him not to talk of it again. At noon he tells me he felt the urge to come to me, take me in his arms, and tell me that I should go to Weimar and that he would come to fetch me. This seems to me a good solution, but since at family lunch R. remarks ironically, regarding this journey, 'Yes, one must play at diplomacy,' etc., I again beg him to think no more of the matter, we shall simply let it rest. He resolves then to write to my father himself, which he does at once, declaring our readiness to visit him, but demanding a word from him, then touching on the episode of the visit of his friend [Frau v. Meyendorff]. The letter is wonderful and clears up the situation at once.

Sunday, September 1 In the afternoon with the children in the park; they play. R. joins us at the playground, brings a nice letter from my father, and we resolve to make the journey. Hasty packing during the evening.

Monday, September 2 We leave at eleven o'clock amid the fluttering of Sedan flags. Bonfires and illuminations – arrived in Weimar at nine o'clock! My father well and pleased, pleasant time together in the Russischer Hof.

Tuesday, September 3 Visited my father during the morning in the pretty Hofgärtnerei, lunched with him and R. at one o'clock, then unfortunately many people (before lunch visited Frau v. Meyendorff with him). We part just before five o'clock, to meet at his house again in the evening, with the Loëns (whom we visited in the morning) and Frau v. M. That is a lot for such recluses as ourselves – the best of it was that my father played me '*Am stillen Herd*' and the '*Liebestod*'[1]. I am terribly upset by my father's weariness of soul. In the evening, when he scarcely spoke and I related all sorts of things, and R., in order to do his bit towards sustaining a cheerful atmosphere, jokingly disputed with Baron Loën about his (R.'s) supposed popularity, I saw the tragedy of my father's life as in a vision – during the night I shed many tears!

Wednesday, September 4 I send a note to my father asking whether he has had some rest – my melancholy regarding him remains with me to such an extent that, when Frau von Meyend. returns my visit and asks me how I find him, I cannot help bursting into tears, which gives her a shock. Other visits are returned, then to the Erholung[2] with my father and Dr. Gille[3] in the burning heat. Very pleasant, merry and earnest atmosphere! In the evening at Baroness Meyend.'s house, where my father plays us the andante from Beethoven's G Major [Piano Concerto], the Preludes of Chopin and his own *Mephisto-Walzer* at my request. He talks a lot about old times, when together we bought fruit in the market in Berlin – and the old feelings of familiarity are recaptured. R. is in very good spirits, asks Dr. Gille whether he is any relation to the Spanish Gil with the green hose, which, since the unhappy man casts a fleeting glance at his nether garments, makes us all laugh very much, laughter which I in my naïveté only increase by explaining to my father, 'The Spanish play is a very decorous play, since it is a woman who was wearing the trousers.'

Thursday, September 5 R. complaining humorously of his lack of popularity

---

[1] From *Die Meistersinger* and *Tristan* respectively.
[2] A restaurant in Weimar.
[3] Carl Gille (b.1813), concert director in Jena.

in Weimar; nobody recognizes him. We visit our dear old Alwine From-mann, in whose little apartment, with its portrait of La Roche Jacquelein (!)[1] we feel very much at home. Home at about eleven, my father comes to fetch us. I notice at once that his mood has changed – he has had to pay for having shown his great affection for me yesterday! We went to his house to make music, *Götterdämmerung* – but the music making would not work. He came to Baroness Loën's, where we were all invited for lunch (with the Bojanowskis[2] and Baroness Meyendorff), and was silent and fatigued; Frau v. M. also silent, but content. After lunch we returned to Fräulein Frommann's and stayed there some time before going on to my father's. The same mood – R. very charming, helping out with witticisms: 'I wish I had your eyebrows,' he says to my father, which makes us laugh a lot. My father plays us the adagio from [Beethoven's sonata, Opus] 106 – but everything with reserve, he hardly looked at me at table, spoke only to Frau v. M. – and of his idea, put forward explicitly yesterday, of accompanying us as far as Eisenach, nothing more has been said.

Friday, September 6 Up at half past three, off about five, my father has breakfast with us and takes us to the railway station; quiet farewell. I depart in sorrow – it is not the separation which pains me, but the fear of entirely losing touch. In the train R. has an outburst of jealousy towards my father, but he is soon pacified.

Monday, September 16 While putting the new house[3] in order I take up my diary again. Every day since Monday the 9th I have been driving into town at eight o'clock, returning to the Fantaisie in the evening at six, even seven o'clock; many furnishing difficulties, but in good spirits. R. always comes to fetch me.

Wednesday, September 18 (still at the Fantaisie) A word R. let fall yesterday cast a complete mantle of grief over my spirits: he said he believed there was something wrong with his heart! I go into the park with the children and we take a walk of almost four hours with Fidi, the children very merry, I taking leave in my heart of the trees I have come so much to love. We return to find R. looking unwell, and after lunch he becomes ill-humoured. We drive into town in deep silence, and as we are passing the cemetery, R. points a finger towards it. – The house still very behindhand; the Stockers have packed things immensely unskilfully – half of them, the most necessary, still missing. On top of that, R. has a very unpleasant encounter with a Herr Kastner[4], who had been recommended to him as a copyist by Herr Lassen in Weimar, the conductor with whom we once had a bad

---

[1] A French royalist general.
[2] Relatives of Hans von Bülow, whose sister Isa married Viktor von Bojanowski.
[3] Dammallee 7, Bayreuth, a villa rented pending completion of Wahnfried.
[4] Emmerich Kastner (b.1847), a member of Wagner's group of copyists, the so-called Nibelungen Chancery, up to January 1873.

experience (though we have forgotten the details). This Herr Kastner makes a very unpleasant impression on R., though he affects very great enthusiasm (would rather be a copyist here than a conductor anywhere else, etc.).

Thursday, September 19 A letter from Marie Schleinitz, reporting that the Sultan [of Turkey, Abdul-Aziz] is taking ten certificates of patronage, a piece of news which gives R. little pleasure, since it wounds the pride of our *German* enterprise.

Tuesday, September 24 (in the new house in town). Moved out and in on Saturday: lunch in the Sonne, much misery; no cook, not even a housemaid! *Sunday:* difficulties with breakfast, the refined temporary cook makes us no coffee, uses up all the water; coffee is at last made around ten, and our watchman pours it away, which at any rate turns our ill humour into loud laughter. In the afternoon arrival of our nephew Fritz Brockhaus – not exactly convenient, since everything still in a state of disorder and R. unfortunately not at all well. *Monday:* the day goes by better; shopping, accompanied Fritz to the railway station with the five children; lunched haphazardly at home, R. still unwell; in the evening played through some Beethoven sonatas. (Visit from Herr Feustel, who tells us many things about the discord between Prussia and Bavaria; the King upset the Crown Prince by failing to offer him any of his empty palaces to live in when the Crown Prince announced his intention of visiting Bavaria; the Crown Prince thereupon offends the King by simply announcing that he will inspect the army, which by the terms of the Treaty of Versailles can only be done with the consent of the Bavarian government; so the King then commands Herr v. Gasser[1] to set up an administration to safeguard his rights; this comes to nothing, since the King refuses to receive Herr v. Gasser! God knows how it will all end.) – Herr Hoffmann, the scene designer, has at last written to us, and there is to be a conference. (R. tells the Feustels about the Sultan's certificates of patronage and says, 'Now we shall have to look after a harem as well.')

Wednesday, September 25 Today the remainder of R.'s library at last arrived, so we are now able to set to work on his room; R. very restless and disgruntled: he can do nothing, is still not well, and what arrives from outside is not exactly heartening – but towards me he is all love and kindness and says amid tears that he is sorry for me!

Friday, September 27 We now have a temporary cook, so are able to eat very comfortably at home again with the children. In the evening our good J. Rubinstein to bid us farewell – R. reproaches me for having dismissed him too coldly, which I very much regret.

Saturday, September 28 In the evening the senior copyist from Pest, recommended by Richter; yesterday the excitable Israelite, today the

---

[1] Rudolf, Baron von Gasser, councillor of state and Bavarian envoy.

taciturn Magyar[1]! – But R. is satisfied with my domestic arrangements, which makes me happy.

Tuesday, October 1 Catastrophic lunch – our cook just cannot cook. R., however, very kind and patient about it! Towards evening friend Feustel, who tells us about all sorts of things, among others the King's illness: he rode off to his highest hunting lodge during the cold weather, had to walk on foot an hour and a half through the snow, spent three days alone there, and then returned home with severe catarrh. Feustel has more or less been offered the Finance Ministry, but he does not want it at any price.

Wednesday, October 2 R. had a very bad night, has congestion and something much like hallucinations (he cannot remember the name of our governess, mentioned by Fidi). The soft air, the new house, the smelly stoves, perhaps too-strong coffee after his bad night – all this has caused it. Great sorrow for me! – After lunch the doctor comes to examine R. and prescribes a new diet: no coffee, no sausage, etc., a roast dish in the evening, long walks. We start on it at once, and, after signing the papers regarding the conversion of the children to Protestantism at the lawyer's, we go for a long walk in the meadows beside the river Main. Mild air, too mild, even – it does not agree with R.

Thursday, October 3 In the evening to to bed with a temperature. After a wretched night the doctor is called, and it turns out that I have an inflammation of the throat which keeps me in bed for four days.

Sunday, October 13 from my bed. Had a relapse, my tonsils are inflamed, but I do not have a temperature. R. had his conference with the machinist Brandt and the scene designer Hoffmann from Vienna, the latter somewhat verbose and 'cultured', but apparently sensible. – Schott is causing R. much trouble, and the agents do not seem to be of much use; Schott does not wish to pay what he owes on the first three parts of the *Ring* before he has received *Götterdämmerung*, which R. does not wish to give him. I feel very pleased at being able to get up today in order to join in the family lunch. R., who is also pleased, says to me, 'You are the hook on which I hang above the abyss.'

Tuesday, October 15 R. attends to business affairs, lunch at one o'clock, when suddenly Käthchen reports, 'The Herr Doktor is just coming up the steps' – and, indeed, it is my father, arriving from Schillingsfürst, where he has been spending a few days with Cardinal Hohenlohe[2]. He has survived an appalling journey, having had to change carriages five times during the night, etc. – a typical Bayreuth arrival. He comes to the house on foot with his servant Mischka and a porter, but he is cheerful and in good health, lively conversation.

---

[1] Anton Seidl (b. 1850), who later became one of the finest of Wagner conductors.
[2] Prince Hohenlohe-Schillingsfürst, brother of Princes Chlodwig and Constantin Hohenlohe and a friend of Princess Wittgenstein.

Wednesday, October 16 In the afternoon drive to the building site, inspection of the opera house and of our house. In the evening the mayor and Feustel; my father plays passages from his *Christus*, which certainly sounds different beneath his fingers.

Thursday, October 17 Long talk with my father; Princess Wittgenstein is tormenting him on our account – he should flee from Wagner's influence, artistic as well as moral, should not see me again, his self-respect demands this, we murdered Hans from a moral point of view, etc. I am very upset that my father should be tormented like this – he is so tired and is always being so torn about! Particularly this wretched woman in Rome has never done anything but goad him – but he does not intend to give me and us up. This conversation keeps me long at my father's side, and unfortunately R. is offended by my leaving him alone so long; I do not find it easy to ask his pardon, and a slight shadow of discord persists between us all day. Herr Feustel calls to fetch us for a drive; I had promised Frau v. Schleinitz to inspect an estate for her, we drive along wretched highways, get out, and hardly are we out when the carriage slides into the ditch and turns over. We are an hour's walk from the town, my father in no state to walk. R. sets off to order a carriage while we take shelter in a farmhouse, but at last Feustel's coach is sufficiently restored to enable us to start our journey home, amid laughter.

Friday, October 18 My father prepares a programme for the evening, when we shall have about 20 gentlemen from Bayreuth with us! Herr and Frau Kastner (the man is proving to be a capable and modest copyist) are to appear with him. In the afternoon I make my little preparations, and in the evening my father really does play for the people and captivates them all.

Saturday, October 19 A remark of the Grand Duke of Weimar to my father (*'Je ne donnerai pas le sou pour Bayreuth'*) after he had enacted a complete comedy of enthusiasm to R. last winter, and another remark by Princess M. Hohenlohe[1], who told my father she had so far collected 18,000 florins for W. (of which not a word is true) annoy R. extremely. He cannot get over the mendacity of these people. In the evening R. reads *Parzival* to us, everyone extremely moved – it really is R.'s finest conception, 'and all this time you are still romping about with singers and actors,' my father says to him (the pamphlet on *Actors and Singers* has just appeared).

Sunday, October 20 In the evening music – my father plays fugues by Bach, the 'A-flat Major' from *Tristan* and several of his own compositions. A great, relaxed feeling that he belongs with us, that we should not let him part from us. Plans of a permanent residence here. But alas, I hardly believe in common sense any more. My father in all matters remarkably liberal, admires Bismarck, recognizes the power of Protestant hymns, thinks the Clerical party finished – but he is tired, tired!

---

[1] Marie (b. 1837), the daughter of Princess Wittgenstein and wife of Prince Constantin Hohenlohe.

Monday, October 21 Melancholy morning, farewells. My father is going to Regensburg to spend his birthday there, quiet and undisturbed. Nobody, and particularly not Princess W., knows where he will be spending tomorrow. – At eleven o'clock he departs, he likes Bayreuth. We are left with sad thoughts. Everything he tells us about the outside world, to which he after all belongs, is horrible. – At lunch R. observes that my soul is divided, he says he finds himself in a position which is new to him: previously I had taken notice only of him, had hung entirely on him and his words, and that had borne him up, made him happy; now, he feels, it is different. He is profoundly wrong, but I cannot prove it to him and can only keep silent.

Saturday, October 26 In the evening the 'copyistery'[1], consisting of four men and Mme Kastner as well. When they are gone, R. speaks in melancholy of his lot, always having to begin anew, getting nothing from his works but trouble and torment (he had been through a scene from *Das Rheingold* with these people); he says the whole of the *Nibelungen* seems to him so remote, so outlived, and now having constantly to teach beginners the ABC's of its interpretation – the only thing which gives him pleasure is his abstract traffic with the world through his writings. (He is writing an essay on the term 'music drama' for Fritzsch.)

Monday, October 28 Visit from our good dean – everything is in readiness for Thursday; if I understand my inner duty correctly, it is to keep my guilt and transgression constantly before my eyes and at the same time to retain all the serenity of love, to fulfil my joyful duties solely towards R.! –

Wednesday, October 30 Long discussion about the children with R., who in the course of it reveals all his infinite love and kindness towards me. As the three little ones were romping yesterday, singing and shouting beside us (as always in the evenings!), R. said, 'We do not realize how happy we are!' – After lunch R. recalled my communings with my father, and he becomes so heated that I am reduced to silence. I must doubtless have been remiss in some way during this time, that R. can remain so jealous, but it is not right of him, I feel, to reproach me so repeatedly. – Now, for the sake of peace, I ought to wish that my father would stop coming. – This I do not do, because I hope next time to be happier and more skilful. – Hans's letter to Daniella also gives us a great deal to think about. – In the evening I am faced with the awful problem of whether it is better to soil one's soul with a lie or, by being truthful, to ignite in the soul of the other person an agony which cannot be extinguished. Deep reflection; where to find help? In prayer and meditation.

Thursday, October 31 Up early, R. did not have a good night, but he is in a

---

[1] An invented word (in German '*Kopisterei*'): beside Kastner and Seidl were now Franz Fischer (b. 1849) and Hermann Zumpe (b. 1850), both to become prominent conductors.

gentler, meditative mood; we set out at ten o'clock for the dean's house, where my conversion is recorded in front of the witnesses, Herr Feustel and the mayor; then to the vestry, where I receive the sacrament with R.; a deeply moving occasion, my whole soul trembles, our dean speaks from the depths of his heart, R. is profoundly touched. What a lovely thing religion is! What other power could produce such feelings? We are all in a state of sublime and solemn devoutness. 'God is love,' the dean says once again. Oh, could I but die in such a spirit, could one remain in it to the end of one's life! As we embraced, R. and I, I felt as if our bond had only now been truly sealed, that now we were united in Jesus Christ. Oh, may this most solemn of acts have turned me into a new person, may I learn to love suffering, to seek it out for myself, to dispense joy! I am happy, for I have the need to belong to a Christian community, to feel myself a Christian, and to act in that spirit. This has now been vouchsafed me, and I accept my gift with a grateful and remorseful heart. For me it has seemed more significant almost to have gone with R. to Communion than to the marriage altar – oh, how kind Fate has been to me! How could I ever have deserved it? Everything is grace; the grace of love, the grace of Heaven –

Friday, November 1 Marie Muchanoff comes from Munich, very tired and agitated; she says *Tristan* had much affected her; it had gone very well under Bülow's direction. She tells us all sorts of curious things about Hans, which do not surprise me. On one occasion, she says, he would be extremely cordial, on the next downright rude, so that one never knew quite how to approach him.

Saturday, November 2 To our friend early, accompanied her at eleven o'clock to the railway station. When shall we see our poor friend again? We are concerned about her. – At supper we discuss the news which Marie M. brought us concerning the King, which is very alarming; among the people there is already talk of insanity, and on top of that the King's hatred of Prussia, his only protection! . . . I beg R. to put all worries on this score out of his mind, since predictions of a catastrophe can neither improve nor alter the situation. – Later R. comes to the subject of our holy event: 'How beautiful it was in that little vestry, how powerful the voice of our dean sounded – like the voice of a lion emerging from a cave! What substitute could there be for the feelings aroused in one when the indescribably moving words "This is my body" are spoken?' The monotonous sound of the Liturgy also touched his heart. 'I could almost say – if I did not shrink from the word in this connection – that it all made an artistic impression, even the little acts of pouring wine, etc.'

Monday, November 4 In the afternoon we go for a walk; first we walk, then inspect our house, and R. takes me up on the scaffolding; while descending, I behave very stupidly, become dizzy and scream! R. says it is a lack of confidence in him – Good Heavens!

Saturday, November 9 A letter to R. from Prof. Nietzsche, who reports that this semester every one of his students has stayed away! And so he has been excommunicated on account of his book; the news affects us very deeply, for it is a serious matter and puts our friend in an impossible situation. – We start thinking up extravagant ideas and plans for sending students to Basel; of forcing from Bismarck an appointment in Berlin – all kinds of impossibilities. – We are literally being outlawed; yesterday the dean told us that one of the precepts of the Catholic party is that its members must speak against Wagner and Bayreuth.

Sunday, November 10 Saying goodbye to the children, very sad – may God take good care of them! Good and peaceful journey with R.[1]. We arrive in Würzburg in good spirits. The excellent Ritters[2] come to meet us; accommodation in the Kronprinz hotel, at seven o'clock to *Don Giovanni*, but the worthy time-beater spoils it all, leaving R. with a melancholy impression; the singers (particularly the women) are tolerably gifted, but disgracefully led.

Tuesday, November 12 A great shock in the morning, 500 florins missing – our only hope that R. left them in his wallet in Bayreuth. Cabled there at once. Departure from Würzburg and the Ritters. In Frankfurt at nine o'clock; the luxury of our hotel and our rooms (we are occupying the *salon* in which Bismarck and Favre signed the peace treaty) makes me feel sad – even more a walk through the opulent city, and two acts of [Meyerbeer's] *Le Prophète* do the rest: I weep, but am obliged to conceal it.

Wednesday, November 13 A day completely lost! Caught a chill. At last (around midday) a telegram from Käthchen – the children are well and the 500 florins *were* left behind.

Thursday, November 14 At six o'clock in Darmstadt, straight to the theatre, Auber's *Le Maçon*. This pretty opera is completely ruined and once again by the time-beater and the producer. The voices are for the most part good, and something could be done with them. But R. has to weep, there in the theatre, over the decline in standards. – While still in Frankfurt we had a telegram from Mme Lucca, that a great *vittoria* had been achieved in Bologna with *Tannhäuser*.

Friday, November 15 A too-opulent meal, particularly for R.'s run-down state; but Brandt excellent, tactful, intelligent and good. Departure at eight o'clock, arrival in Mannheim at 9.50 p.m., where we stay with the excellent Heckels.

Saturday, November 16 We are awakened by the '*Wach' auf*' chorale and the 'Prize Song' from *Die Meistersinger*, played quite splendidly by the brass section of the orchestra. Wonderful impression! 'That's what I once did for

---

[1] On a tour of Germany in search of singers for the festival.
[2] Sascha and Franziska.

you,' says R. – Talked a lot with Heckel about the present state of our undertaking, also with Brandt; it seems that innumerable disgraceful attacks are being made against it – everyone agrees that nobody has ever been so much attacked as R., which is why his supporters tend to feel somewhat like religious fanatics.

Sunday, November 17 The orchestral players (the strings) serenade us again, this time with *Tannhäuser.* In the evening *Holländer,* cuts all over the place by the conductor, Vincenz Lachner[1], wherever he scented the chance of making an effect. The audience calls thunderously for R., but we leave after the second act, because the cut at the end – useless and insolent – has angered R.

Tuesday, November 19 A member of the orchestra presents R. with an autograph by Beethoven. We leave Mannheim around five o'clock, after R. received remarkable proofs of the sympathy and enthusiasm of the populace, who literally formed lanes wherever he went. We arrive in Darmstadt around nine o'clock.

Wednesday, November 20 R. confers with Brandt, also has Frau Jaide[2] (whom we heard in *Le Maçon*) brought to see him, and she sings him something from Ortrud; wonderful voice and an intelligent woman. Perhaps a Brünnhilde?.... In the evening Wagner Society banquet, very lively; the military band of the Regiment of Guards, 54 strong, played a serenade in pouring rain – the Overture to *Tannhäuser,* the 'Bridal Chorus' from *Lohengrin;* great enthusiasm, R. went down and presented the conductor with the laurel wreath he himself had received upstairs.

Thursday, November 21 Left at eleven o'clock, at five o'clock in Stuttgart, surprise meeting with Marie Muchanoff, much mutual delight. We eat together in the Hotel Marquardt with a Dr. Hemsen, librarian to the King [of Württemberg]; he tells me that he and the King are busy reading the collected writings, and he has acquired Nietzsche's book for the library. However, the Queen is under the thumb of Herr Lübke[3] – so nothing for us here, either, since the King is shy and is considered stupid. To *Les Huguenots;* terrible stuff, almost worse than *Le Prophète.*

Friday, November 22 At six o'clock to Strassburg. Our nephew Major Kessinger[4] puts in an appearance, and immediately afterwards friend Nietzsche. He looks robust and well and is cheerful and in good heart (in spite of his experiences).

Saturday, November 23 R. has received a letter from Feustel, urgently begging him to do what he can, for he is reluctant to proceed further with the finances in their present state. R. writes to Hamburg and says if he can

[1] Brother of the conductor Franz Lachner in Munich.
[2] Louise Jaide (b. 1842) sang Erda and Waltraute in the first Bayreuth festival.
[3] Wilhelm Lübke, an art historian hostile to Wagner.
[4] Kurt von Kessinger was married to Klara, daughter of Luise Brockhaus.

be promised a colossal fee he is willing to conduct a symphony for them. In the evening to the Kessingers'; talked a lot about the war, for the major had taken part in all the great events.

Monday, November 25 Karlsruhe in sunshine. I sleep away almost the entire afternoon, since I am very tired. In the evening *Tannhäuser*, the tempi either dragged or hurried by good Herr Kalliwoda, the conductor; the production dating from Herr Devrient[1], ridiculous and impossible (the guests in the second act perform a veritable *chasse* [?] *anglaise*, then in the third act Elisabeth disappears into the forest, since Herr Devrient did not consider it plausible that she could climb the hill and return as a corpse in such a short time; she is discovered in the forest, and so all Wolfram's gazing after her and the idea of the evening star also disappear; this among other things). One good singer (Venus). In the evening R. reproaches me for not making things easier for myself – he says that it pains him, for instance, to see me packing and unpacking by myself. etc.; and that he would rather I remain at home than do that. I never know what to reply to such statements.

Tuesday, November 26 'Some people are never aware of their good fortune in having you, and that is why they torment you,' R. exclaims to me today, and so everything is all right again. He was received in the most cordial manner ('in the old style') in the Grand Duke's study, and there he put forward his request, which is that the Grand Duke support the Bayreuth undertaking, now that it is so far advanced. When he told the Grand Duke that he was the first German prince whom he had approached, the Duke thanked him and said he could well understand how difficult R. must find it to apply for help, and he was very grateful to him. R. left with a very favourable impression of the Duke's cordiality and integrity, as also of his friendly modesty. In Mainz we are met by Mathilde Maier. In place of the advertised *Fidelio*, the opera house is doing [Flotow's] *Stradella*. We stay in our hotel and in the evening merely accompany our friend home, through the narrow and confusing little lanes.

Wednesday, November 27 Not a very good night, the trains pass close to our hotel, the walls of the fortress rise forbiddingly outside our window; we decide to move to Wiesbaden.

Thursday, November 28 At midday the military band of the 85th Regiment comes and plays for us; after the first two pieces (*Tannhäuser* and *Oberon*) R. gets up, sends the conductor off for a meal, and himself conducts the Prayer and Finale from *Lohengrin*. Then he drinks with all the people out of a large tankard. In the afternoon we take a little rest, then to the theatre in Mainz. *Fidelio* much better than we expected.

---

[1] Eduard Devrient (b. 1801), stage director in Karlsruhe with whom Wagner fell out when the projected production of *Tristan* was abandoned in 1859.

Saturday, November 30 Departure from Wiesbaden. Poor Mathilde, cut off
from us through her deafness, touches us very much. Lovely journey along
the Rhine, lovely colours, a deep impression. In Cologne around six o'clock.
We are met by Herr Lesimple and Herr Ahn, the heads of the Wagner
Society, and the tenor Diener. Letters of all kinds. Good news of the
children; and from New York the news that they have already collected
5,000 dollars. The W. Society here has a difficult territory – not only
because Herr Hiller[1] is powerful (says Herr Ahn), but also because he is an
intriguer and, by undermining us, forestalls us in places where we might
have been able to gain a little ground. We go to bed really tired.

Sunday, December 1 In the evening *Die Zauberflöte* – appalling. Not a singer
of talent, a stupid conductor, and the stamp of vulgarity on everything –
here it is the opulent broker who sets the tone. When R. talks to people
about this, they say the audience is such and such. 'Don't talk to me about
audiences,' R. replies. 'That is a world one does not criticize, but accepts
just as it is; the fault lies entirely with the artists – they can seize an audience
out purely for entertainment and raise it up. An audience does at least show
a lively interest in everything; if a few people turn head over heels, it does
at any rate laugh, which means it is better than these pygmies of conductors
and producers, who don't know that, when the Queen of the Night appears,
it must be night on the stage – one must put out the lights. Just as in church
– when things are done properly, as they seldom are – a soul finds refuge
from the petty pressures of its own miseries, so in the theatre the audience
is raised up by means of its desire to enjoy itself!'

Tuesday, December 3 R. is not sleeping well and is very restless, he longs to
return home in order to work on his score. We go at five to Bonn, to see
[Auber's] *La Muette de Portici* there; great disappointment with Herr Diener,
whose voice is plummy and who now seems to us, among all the tenors we
have so far heard, to be vocally the least gifted. How to tell this to the
worthy man, who is nevertheless in great demand with all theatre managers
and directors?

Thursday, December 5 To Düsseldorf, where we are told that Handel's
Solomon is being performed with visiting artists. Unfortunately Diener, who
is appearing in it, had talked about R.'s arrival, and so there is a reception,
invitation to a banquet, etc., which drives R. to despair. We listen to the
first part of the stiff and boring oratorio and then hurry away (Diener again
singing 'from his stomach to his palate'). Night train, arriving at two o'clock
in Hanover. Rheinischer Hof.

Friday, December 6 Not a very good night, since we could hear the
whistling of the trains, but we are glad to see nobody here and spend the

[1] Ferdinand Hiller (b. 1811), composer and conductor in Cologne since 1850; Hiller was a converted
Jew, and his hostility dated from the publication of *Judaism in Music*.

morning peacefully writing letters. – The news that Herr Reinecke[1], here from Leipzig to give a piano recital, lost all his music during the journey (which did not upset the audience, since it meant he had to play Beethoven instead of his own things) causes us great concern with regard to *Götterdämmerung*, which we have brought with us; R. says, 'What a laugh for Hiller and his consorts if I were to advertise the fact that this manuscript is irreplaceable – what jeering there would be!' – At seven o'clock to the theatre, where *Oberon* is being performed. Very fine auditorium; and a fine orchestra, but conducting and producing very bad; in this short score they cut an aria and a march, and the stage setting is worse than in the smallest of theatres. Orchestra arranged as it was 40 years ago, brass here, strings there, so that one can hardly hear the latter! And yet the manager, von Bronsart, was the man we ourselves wanted in Berlin, since we saw him as a very sensitive artist – he was a pupil of my father's.

Saturday, December 7 Constant wet weather! Towards midday we go for a little walk in the city and leave at four o'clock for Bremen, after having been bothered by the curiosity of the public, who had got wind of R.'s presence after all.

Sunday, December 8 Went for a little walk in the town [Bremen], which pleases us immensely, lovely parks with a mill in the centre, which delights R. greatly. At six o'clock performance of *Die Msinger*, R. is received with a flourish by the orchestra and great acclamation by the audience. The work, it seems, has made a tremendous impression here, and indeed the conductor [Karl Martin Reinthaler] really has done all that is possible with his orchestra, which, though small, consists of very respectable players. But the production is again very pitiful, and the most annoying thing is that Herr Schott has thought fit to send here the parts from Mannheim, which were prepared by Herr Lachner, who makes cuts even in *Der Freischütz*. In consequence the whole third act unrecognizable and boring. We discover a very good David, an intelligent Sachs and a promising Eva. – Home very tired, the nonsense of the third act, in which Herr Lachner has inserted passages of his own, has exhausted us.

Tuesday, December 10 At seven o'clock in Magdeburg; after supper we go for a little walk. – From the outside the theatre is still as R. knew it; he tells me how, when he was conducting there, he felt himself in Heaven – in his sky-blue coat with its huge cuffs[2]. He shows me the street in which Minna lived, with whom he 'spent the whole day'; also the Stadt Braunschweig, where he had to pacify (settle with) his creditors!

Wednesday, December 11 At three o'clock arrival in Dessau; met by the conductor [Eduard] Thiele, who was R.'s predecessor in Magdeburg. At six o'clock to the theatre, a very handsome and elegant auditorium. The

---

[1] Carl Reinecke, pianist and composer.
[2] Wagner was conductor of the opera there in 1834–36.

manager, Herr von Normann[1], receives us very charmingly; the performance begins with the Prelude to *Die Msinger*, at the end of which the curtain rises to disclose a *tableau vivant*, 'The Crowning of Hans Sachs' – it touches us deeply. Since part of his company is absent through illness, the ingenious manager seized on this expedient, and with it achieved the finest of effects. However, it was the performance of [Gluck's] *Orfeo* which revealed to us all the worth of this remarkable man; splendid the first act with the chorus, the second no less so, and, if there were a few mistakes in the Elysian fields, they did not prove at all disturbing. The first really artistic impression from our whole journey! We return home deeply affected by this unexpected discovery, amazed that more is not known about the intelligent management of this theatre.

Thursday, December 12 R. had a very bad night and feels so unwell that he asks the Duke[2] for a postponement of his audience. He goes there at twelve o'clock. He had been invited to a meal, but refused the invitation, saying he was not seeking marks of honour, but wanted simply to lay his proposition in front of the Duke. He returns very charmed by the Duchess as well as the Duke, both earnest, sympathetic, encouraging. – We leave at two o'clock, after Herr von Normann showed me around the palace. In the evening in Leipzig, the whole family, Clemens with his young wife, Hermann, the rector of the university, Ottilie and Anna. Very pleasant, but R. is tired.

Saturday, December 14 Spent the evening with our publisher Fritzsch; Scaria[3] and Gura[4], neither of whom R. had wished to see, either in the Gewandhaus or in the '*Margarethe*' theatre[5]; R. is satisfied with both of them, particularly with Scaria, who is to do the giant Fafner, Hunding and Hagen. – We leave Fritzsch's house at about ten, R. telling me he could get in a fury and hit out whenever he sees the usual rows of bottles, the rolls and the folded table napkins laid out for dinner.

Sunday, December 15 Left at 6.30 in the morning, we cannot wait to be home; fears of bad discoveries. Arrive at last, around noon, the children at least on their feet, but looking peaky, especially Boni and Eva; Fidi has been indisposed and was extraordinarily affected by our arrival; a touching sight, and R. says he looks exactly like the child in Raphael's *Sistine Madonna*. – Delight in being home again. But by the evening there are already worries: Eva's appearance grieves us, Boni's as well, and besides that unpleasantnesses among the copyists.

---

[1] Rudolf von Normann (b. 1806), director of the Court theatre in Dessau.

[2] Friedrich Leopold von Anhalt-Dessau, duke since May 1871.

[3] Emil Scaria (b. 1840), bass, Vienna.

[4] Eugen Gura (b. 1842), baritone, Leipzig.

[5] Leipzig concert hall and opera house respectively, the nickname given to the latter presumably a sarcastic reference to the fact that Gounod's *Faust* (known in Germany as *Margarethe*) was being played there.

Monday, December 16 Spent the morning with the children; wretched weather; R. goes to Angermann's[1] again to drink his beer, accompanied by Rus, who was almost mad with joy. But in the afternoon great vexations arise; Herr Am Rhyn thinks it nice, after R. put 20,000 francs into his house, to send him a bill for 3,000 francs! R. answers briefly and to the point; besides that, bills from Lucerne of the most bare-faced kind. I am very despondent whenever I think of our constant financial state; every purchase becomes a torment.

Wednesday, December 18 R. is not well, consults the doctor; rest is ordered. Herr Gross[2] comes, tells us that the Grand Duke of Baden has taken up two certificates of patronage!!

Friday, December 20 There are now only 50,000 florins in the bank, and Feustel declares he cannot complete the contracts with the workers on the strength of this sum, not knowing what might still come in. We agree that complete honesty must be shown all around, and if by April there is not as much in hand as is necessary, the whole undertaking must be put off for a year. – At supper F. tells us the remarkable story of his life, which touches us very much – he, too, is a love child.

Saturday, December 21 We resolve to leave Berlin out and to concentrate the (unfortunately necessary) concert activity in Cologne, Hamburg and Prague, assuming that R. can bear it. – Today he writes to the King – a task which is becoming increasingly difficult – then to the people in Bremen and to Herr v. Normann, urgently pleading our cause. – The management committee here has decided after all to complete the contracts, relying on the miracles R. is to perform.... May God be with us!

Monday, December 23 R. works on his article about our journey for Fritzsch's newspaper[3]; I am busy more or less from morning till evening on the Christmas tree, gilding, decorating, spurring on.

Tuesday, December 24 With the children at the fair, while R. finishes his article. When I timidly ask him whether he ought to call everybody by name at this point, when he is hoping for help from the German Reich, he flares up. This is the only thing he cares about, he says – to express candidly his indignation about all the things that are bad – and the only people he will have anything to do with are those who share his indignation. I have to admit that he is right. R. goes to the theatre site, returns very affected. It looks so noble, he says; now he is committed, no longer free, but fettered; his imagination and the faith of a few others have brought it into being and he cannot now turn back. He is very solemn. We light the tree at half past five.

The copyists are also there, somewhat trying, for the good people speak

---

[1] An inn in Bayreuth.

[2] Adolf von Gross (b. 1845), a banker in Bayreuth and Feustel's son-in-law.

[3] 'A Glance at the German Operatic Stage of Today', published in January 1873 in the *Musikalisches Wochenblatt*.

so little, but R. gives the ⌐ a regular course in execution, with examples. He begins with Beethoven's *Vittoria*[1], stressing the popular character of the theme: 'To what shallow conversational levels did Mendelssohn then lead music back, after Beethoven had made it so splendidly popular in flavour!' Following that *Egmont*, then *Zauberflöte*, *Euryanthe* – the *Egmont* music moves me unutterably. The people leave, the children thank us for the pleasure they have had, and then we are left alone, R. and I. He plays, I weep! – My birth. Oh, could I but wipe it out and thereby end all the suffering it has caused! Midnight arrives, and with it my birthday; tearful embrace – how gladly would we die! . . . The melancholy turns into cheerfulness as R. gets up and mysteriously presents me with a fan, which had pleased me in Strassburg, and a case for storing the manuscripts. We laugh a lot, and my tears begin again only after I am in bed.

Wednesday, December 25 Birthday greetings from the children, then wreaths and singing. – In the evening R., regretting that he has no present for me, tells me he had thought of having the *Idyll* published and thus earning for me 100 imperials. How sad that would have made me – my 'sweet secret' thus betrayed! – A children's party, at which I show our magic lantern.

Friday, December 27 Visit from Feustel in the evening – and we discuss Bismarck's resignation from the Prussian government[2]. It is said that he could not persuade the Emperor to take the measures he considered necessary, and he will now devote himself exclusively to Reich affairs.

Monday, December 30 R. works on his report of our journey, Herr Feustel brings a letter from Baron Loën, who reports that the princes have written, putting off payment (in connection with the Bayreuth project). Much weakness and wretched behaviour everywhere, the hardest to understand being the Grand Duke of Weimar. Baron Loën is doubtless well intentioned towards us, but he does not dare to show it, and the disposition of his superiors encourages all his bad qualities, such as indolence, weakness, etc.

Tuesday, December 31 R. very unwell, goes to bed early; I stay up to look through the housekeeping books, deplore the heavy expenditure. Sorted and prepared children's clothing. – It is nearly twelve o'clock as I write this; this year is ending gloomily, and the new lies gloomily in front of us; R. is weary of life, and I can only follow behind him, suffer with him, not help him! Faith is all I have, hope hardly any – the world is not ours, it belongs to other powers. But I would gladly suffer until my dying day, and I prefer being sad to being happy – if I could be that only for myself. But we cannot choose, and we should not wish for things, just take what comes. So at the midnight hour let me humbly accept as deserved whatever the coming year may bring, however hard, and may God give me the grace to do good!

---

[1] The so-called *Battle* Symphony of 1813, Opus 91.
[2] As Prime Minister, but he still remained Reich Chancellor.

1873

Wednesday – Saturday, January 1–4 Various things by mail, among them a folder of manuscripts from Prof. Nietzsche containing forewords to unwritten books. Otherwise nothing to give us pleasure; the people in Vienna more and more incomprehensible, nobody knows how much there is in the bank. We work out a plan for a concert in Berlin and a reading in Frau von Schleinitz's house before the assembled might of intellect and breeding. It is such a gloomy phase which we are now entering, as if everything were against us; one is literally set upon by ugly things, a newspaper is sent to us which reports that someone has asked for an album leaf, whereupon R. sent him two certificates of patronage, which he dutifully signed! No wonder that R. is utterly dispirited and ill. He has written to London asking if it would be possible to earn a large sum there – God knows! – Prof. Nietzsche's manuscript also does not restore our spirits, there are now and again signs of a clumsy abruptness, however deep the underlying feelings. Today (the 4th) Richter arrives, bringing good news of my father.

Sunday, January 5 Very fine weather – still no winter. The copyists come in the evening (without Herr Kastner, who has fulfilled all our worst misgivings), and Richter, who tells us all sorts of unpleasant things about Hans: his unbounded rudeness, etc.; that makes me very sad. Thank goodness, R. goes through parts of Act III of *Götterdämmerung*, then *Tristan*, and finally the *Idyll*, which charms us all. 'Yes,' says, R., 'that was our poetic period, the dawn of our life, now we are in the full glare of the midday sun, my dear wife, and climbing the mountain.' The memory moves me to tears, but much more the work itself. Alas, what gifts have here been deposited in an earthly frame, how well I understand what he must suffer when life eternally keeps him from pouring out these gifts! He must be in a continual state of convulsion, like a poor bird kept from flying!

Thursday, January 9 Paid calls, among others to Herr Grossmann, the headmaster, to make some comments on the girls' school[1]. When I return home R. shows me a telegram from Strassburg which states that the things for me which R. has been expecting since Christmas have still not arrived.

---

[1] Which Daniela, Blandine and Isolde were now attending.

I go into the *salon* and find a huge array of things to wear, each lovelier than the next! . . . My delight makes R. laugh.

Friday, January 10 R. has a letter from England which gives him little joy, like all news from outside at the moment. Proposal for a concert in the Crystal Palace with half of the proceeds going to the C.P. company!

Sunday, January 12 In Chemnitz at eight o'clock, much pleasure in seeing R.'s sister Klara [Wolfram] again, at ten o'clock in Dresden[1]. Put up at the Hotel Bellevue. – In the train, thinking of Fidi, R. spoke of his own impressions of *Der Freischütz* in his fifth year, how he tried to imitate Samiel lurking in the bushes and to sing the theme – these early impressions had surely done him no harm, on the contrary. He continues: 'If only Weber had set all the dialogue to music – from the drinking song to the end of the act – what a splendid scene it would have made! That is my real innovation: that I have incorporated dialogue into opera, and not just as recitative.'

Monday, January 13 Welcomed by Elis. Krockow. *Rienzi*, better here than in Vienna, again keeps me very interested, but the absurd cuts in the fourth act drive us out. In the evening the Wesendoncks visited us.

Wednesday, January 15 In the morning the military band of the Regiment of Grenadier Guards came and played the Overture to *Rienzi*, the 'Bridal Procession' from *Lohengrin* and the '*Kaisermarsch*', all very beautifully; R. goes downstairs to thank them, and since there is no door to the yard and he did not feel able to go into the street in his morning suit with beret and jacket, he had a ground-floor apartment unlocked and climbed through the window. Let us hope the poor people are not made to pay for their friendliness! The conductor did not have his commandant's permission. – Left at 2.50 p.m. in splendid weather. – At nine o'clock in Berlin. Put up again in the Tiergarten Hotel, Marie Schleinitz comes and delights us once more with her friendliness and lively interest.

Friday, January 17 In the morning to Marie Schl.'s to make some final arrangements with regard to the evening; she requests the removal from the introductory remarks[2] of certain details (the mating, the pregnancy) out of consideration for prudes! – The reading starts at nine o'clock before a mixed but very select audience (Lepsius, Helmholtz, Delbrück, Moltke, the Crown Prince of Württemberg, Prince Georg of Prussia, virtually all the ambassadors). I cannot judge the impression the reading made, but I believe it was considerable. It is 20 years since I first heard this work, in Paris, read by R.!

Saturday, January 18 At eight o'clock in Hamburg, met by a considerable number of cheering people. Great weariness, making us irritable.

---

[1] They were setting out on a second tour in search of singers, combined with some conducting engagements and other money-making enterprises.

[2] To a reading of *Götterdämmerung*; Wagner's introductory remarks would refer to the incestuous relationship between Siegmund and Sieglinde that led to the conception of Siegfried.

Sunday, January 19 Military band serenade: Overture to *Rienzi*, *Tannhäuser*, Act II, *Rienzi* recitative. Rehearsal from nine till twelve, nice welcome, R. in some difficulty since we are dealing with a municipal orchestra – there is no Court here to ensure even a modicum of refinement! 'The public spirit has become so vulgar,' R. remarks, 'that we must be glad we still have Courts.' '*Kaisermarsch*', *Lohengrin* and *Tristan* Prelude are rehearsed. R. is not too severely taxed by it, thank goodness.

Monday, January 20 A good night, rehearsal at ten o'clock, C Minor Symphony; the good people do their best and it goes really well, they understand R. at once. – At 9.15 in the evening we are fetched by Dr. Baumeister[1] and taken to the Sagebiel restaurant; a lavish banquet, in the best of styles and the best of company; the speaker, Dr. Baumeister, reveals himself to be a thorough connoisseur of R.'s writings and welcomes him as a patriot, author, poet, etc., in words full of significance. R. replied, very moved. The banquet ends at two o'clock – it was the finest ever given for us. (Good news from the children.)

Tuesday, January 21 At seven o'clock the concert; the C Minor Symphony does not go as R. wishes it, the orchestra having been assembled from all over the place, and R. decides at once not to include any Beethoven in the second concert, since it vexes him far too much when these works are not played properly. 'Siegmund's Love Song' is encored, and the success seems to have been very great. R. very tired, goes to bed at once. When I, too, lay myself down to rest, I am assailed by terrible melancholy – over the thought that R. is obliged to do this!

Wednesday, January 22 Unfortunately a very bad performance of *Die Meistersinger* and after it a gala dinner given by the performers, who had not been admitted to the patricians' first banquet! Great weariness and some vexation over the awkwardness of the arrangements.

Thursday, January 23 At seven o'clock the concert, smaller attendance than the first. It goes tolerably well, particularly the *Tristan* Prelude – which fascinates the players most of all – and the '*Kaisermarsch*'.

Friday, January 24 An additional day here, in order to rest – but no rest possible; first of all the visit from Herr *Zacharias*[2], an enthusiastic business-man who intends to sell 20 certificates of patronage in Hamburg and speaks of the founding of a Northwest German Wagner Society. Following him, the committee which arranged the concerts; they report receipts of 5,000 thalers and expenditure of 1,500 thalers. In the evening we have dinner with Herr and Frau Zacharias, whose fine and intelligently chosen library gives us great pleasure and arouses our confidence in the participation of this man, who possesses all of R.'s works from their first editions onwards.

[1] Hermann Baumeister, President of the City Parliament.
[2] A banker, friend of Feustel.

Saturday, January 25 I pack again, and around eleven o'clock we leave Hamburg, accompanied by a hearty cheer, for which the excellent Baumeister gives the lead with great emotion. – We arrive in Schwerin very tired, but we visit the Italian opera and see the last act of [Rossini's] *Barbiere*. We watch the performance from the box of Herr von Wolzogen[1], a former enemy who now behaves in a very friendly manner. Back at the hotel we hear a murmuring in the street, R. laughs and from the window shows me the familiar lanterns, the ring of people, and right away the *Tannhäuser* March begins, then the '*Kaisermarsch*' and the *Rienzi* Overture, played by the military band – and indeed very nicely and in front of virtually the whole population of Schwerin. – This surprise makes us laugh a lot.

Sunday, January 26 R. is summoned to the Grand Duke at twelve o'clock; he returns from the audience well satisfied, the Prince has pleasant memories of Bayreuth. The Duke takes up six certificates of patronage. At six o'clock performance of *Der Fl. Holländer*, after the Overture the conductor, Herr [Aloys] Schmitt, calls for a cheer and flourish for the 'writer and composer, who is present.' In the first act the singer Hill[2] at once makes a tremendous impression on us, and R. sees in him the kind of singer he needs. We are deeply moved by his performance. Between the second and third acts we are both summoned to the Grand Duke's box, the two royal ladies converse with R., the Grand Duke with me; very friendly and good. – After the performance a banquet with about 160 people.

Monday, January 27 Invitation from the wife of the Master of the Household, [Bernhard] von Bülow – Hill is to sing songs to us there at twelve. At the moment of leaving, R. annoyed by this presumption, and he offends me – I admit it, to my shame – with the way in which he tells me he will not accompany me. – Frau von Bülow I discover to be a charming and gracious woman; Hill sings his songs very well, it seems to me – but my thoughts are elsewhere. Silent journey to Berlin, we are both of us sad!

Wednesday, January 29 At last everything resolved between R. and me! He says nothing can affect him except not being in utter harmony with me – that cuts at his very roots!

Sunday, February 2 In the evening Bucher visits us, we are sincerely pleased to see him. Talked a lot about the German Reich, our worries concerning it – the Crown Prince very ill, some say poisoned, and they may very well be right. The Empress and the Crown Princess[3] hostile to Germans – the former has made it a condition that her servants wear black beards and be Catholics. – Bucher relates how worried Bismarck is about the future of the German Reich, how he is strengthening the trade connections.

[1] Alfred, Baron von Wolzogen, director of the Court theatre in Schwerin, father of Hans von Wolzogen, who will figure frequently in the Diaries later.
[2] Karl Hill (b. 1831), bass, sang Alberich in the first Bayreuth festival.
[3] Queen Victoria's eldest daughter, Victoria, the Princess Royal.

Monday, February 3 At ten o'clock rehearsal – the orchestra players coming from all over the place – but very attentive and full of fire. Listening to the *Tannhäuser* Overture, I had to think of its first performance in Berlin, in the year '56, under Hans's direction; it was severely hissed, Hans fainted; I returned to his mother's house and stayed up late until he arrived, so that he should realize that there was one human soul who would thank him for his efforts. This gratitude was the seed from which our union sprang. – Returning home, I pay my respects to Frau von Meyendorff, who has come from Weimar to attend the concert, and I am touched by her question as to whether I can forgive her 'for having been so malicious,' and altogether by her feelings for my father.

Tuesday, February 4 The concert at 7.30 in the evening, the Emperor and Empress present; the aristocratic audience which only Berlin can supply, hardly any Jews. Laurel wreaths, flowers, and a flourish on R.'s entry; called back repeatedly at the end. R. is very exhausted; the only thing he enjoyed performing, he says, was the '*Kaisermarsch*' in front of the Emperor – this had really inspired him (unfortunately the Emperor left before the March, he had thought the chorus was to be sung, and it embarrasses him to hear himself praised).

Wednesday, February 5 Notification of the proceeds of the concert – 5,400 thalers, which pleases R. very much. – After the concert yesterday he tells me that during 'Wotan's Farewell' he turned to look at me, saw me sitting in Frau v. Schl.'s box completely absorbed, his eyes filled with tears, and he suddenly noticed from the violins that his beat had gone astray – 'I nearly upset everything.'

Thursday, February 6 Amiable arrival in Dresden (R. wishes to get to know the tenor Herr Jäger[1] there). Putting up at the Hotel Bellevue, we learn that *Lohengrin* is being performed today; pleasantly surprised, we go in; in the first act R. is very gripped and moved, Elsa had some good expressions, and, as R. said, 'one is so willing to become intoxicated.' But in the second act so many stupidities occur that we leave before the end.

Saturday, February 8 In Bayreuth by one o'clock. Rapturous welcome from the children – all well and in good spirits.

Monday, February 10 R. is very worn out and tired; but he goes to visit our house and is pleased with the fine proportions of the whole and the good use of the available space. – In the evening we begin Darwin's *Origin of Species*, and R. observes that between Schopenhauer and Darwin the same thing has happened as between Kant and Laplace: the *idea* came from Schopenhauer and Darwin developed it, perhaps even without having known Schopenhauer, just as Laplace certainly did not know Kant.

Monday, February 17 Letters arrive, one from Lucerne – Herr Am Rhyn

---

[1] Ferdinand Jäger (b. 1838) sang Parsifal at Bayreuth in 1882.

stands revealed as a complete rogue: after R., out of consideration for him, paid the rent in advance and gave him the key, he refuses to allow the assessment on our behalf to be made, and allows nobody into the house, which belongs to us until April, because he himself has caused damage in it, for which he now wants to sue us . . . . . Hardly is this chapter completed when R. notices that three 20-mark gold coins are missing from his writing desk (always unlocked)! House search, in the cook's room several things are discovered which belong to us, horrible appearance of the culprit! I avoid all scenes, everything is done in apparent calmness. On top of that Boni very unwell!

Tuesday, February 18 Our cook has disappeared; the servants think she has thrown herself into the river! A violent ring on the doorbell, caused by no visible hand, gives the servants the idea that we are being told of her death! Blandine is in much pain (rheumatism).

Wednesday, February 19 After scarcely sleeping all night, we learn that the woman presumed to be dead is staying with a friend; in the afternoon she comes along herself, says she is 'a Catholic Christian', begins by insolently denying everything, then at last admits to me that she has stolen other things from me besides the three gold coins. This scene of persuasion – appealing to her conscience, speaking as woman to woman, and the glimpse it affords me of depravity and wretchedness – puts a terrible strain on me! – Afterwards I go for a walk with Fidi, to the new house, which – since the staircase is completed – I can now look over thoroughly, admiring R.'s powers of invention.

Thursday, February 20 In the afternoon went with the children to the stretch of ice to watch Lusch; R. tries it, too, Rus rushes at his skates to pull them off and snaps when one tries to restrain him; the man says, 'The dog is too faithful; you can't go skating.' Much laughter from the children. – Letter from Marie Muchanoff; she says the Emperor did not give R. an audience because he could not do such a thing to the King of Saxony, who goes wild every time he even hears Wagner's name!

Saturday, February 22 From Munich a man writes to say that he has been driven mad by R.'s music, and what should he do about it?!

Wednesday, February 26 The Feustels visit us, he comes from Vienna and brings shattering news: instead of 50,000 florins, as they claimed, they have only 20,000 *subscribed*, not yet paid! – Grave consideration whether it would harm or help the undertaking to announce the postponement publicly. – In the afternoon R. goes to see Feustel again; while he is there, Zacharias applies for 90 certificates of patronage – along with these, our journey will have brought in 19,200 thalers.

Thursday, February 27 A third of the money, 100,000 thalers, has now arrived – will the other 200,000 materialize?

Saturday, March 1 R. is now working on his essay on the Ninth Symphony and correcting the *Rheingold* proofs. – In the evening one of the copyists, Herr Zumpe, comes to visit, R. talks about the Italian company in Dresden and comes to the subject of Rossini and the *Gazza Ladra* Overture in particular. When our copyist admits with a smile that he does not know it, R. gets heated and says, 'My dear man, only Beethoven stands above Rossini,' and he describes how Rossini's music expresses the whole of elegant society with its beautiful Italian women and their chatter. 'Beethoven did not write music for any assembly, except perhaps for an assembly of gods.' He plays the *Gazza Ladra* Overture and then the A Major Symphony, which Herr Z. is to conduct for the amateur society. Of all [Beethoven's] works R. considers the Seventh and the Eighth incomparably the boldest and most original; but, he says, if he himself were ever to conduct them again, he would not hesitate to change some things in the orchestration, which Beeth. had written thus only because he could no longer hear it.

Wednesday, March 5 A complete hospital: Lusch, Loldi, Boni, Eva ill or indisposed, Käthchen unwell, and no cook! No choice but to throw back my shoulders and carry on.

Saturday, March 8 R. has to leave home early: Herr Brandt and Herr Brückwald are here, and a conference is held, the important outcome of which is that the performance is put off for a year. – I write to Marie M., in order to explain to her that W.'s true friends must stop urging him to conduct concerts.

Sunday, March 9 In the evening we work on the biography. I remark jokingly to R. what capital we are bequeathing to Fidi: he will receive the house (the decorations of which are keeping us much occupied at the moment), then until 30 years after our death our royalties, and at the end of these 30 years he can publish the biography. 'And then,' says R., 'he can compose *Parzival*.' I shake my head, and R. continues: 'Yes, who can lay such things down? He must cut himself off from us entirely – if not to the same degree, nevertheless in the same way that I cut myself off from my family. He must develop in his own way, which we cannot foresee, and then he may amount to something.'

Tuesday, March 11 R. gives me the conclusion of his wonderful essay[1] to read; talking to me about it, he says, 'I have the right to suggest certain alterations in places where even the best of performances cannot adequately bring out the melodic content, for in all else I insist throughout on correctness of execution and tell people that, if they understand and play only the nuances as indicated by Beethoven, they will find themselves on the right path.' –

Friday, March 14 We go out together, first to the antiquarian's, then to our

---

[1] 'On Performing Beethoven's Ninth Symphony'.

house, and there he shows me the place where he wants our grave to be, where we shall rest side by side all by ourselves. Solemn and serene feelings, 'undivided, eternally united!'

Saturday, March 15 R. sorts out his books in complete absorption and delights in his riches. In the evening we are much alarmed by convulsive attacks which beset Fidi; I take him into my bed and spend the night comforting and soothing him.

Sunday, March 16 This morning R. was much amused to see his pamphlet *Judaism in Music* advertised as a rare antiquarian object at six times its original price. – As I was singing a theme today, R. asked me who had written it; when I say Chopin, he regrets that he himself plays the piano so little, for in consequence all these things have remained virtually unknown to him. 'By merely being heard,' he says, 'they have not impressed themselves on my mind.' – R. is pleased with his books, particularly with the newly arrived mystics. 'The mystic is the man for me, even if he is mistaken – the man who feels the urge to ignite for himself the inner light in contrast to the outer brightness which shows him nothing.'

Monday, March 17 After lunch we visit our house, and in the evening go to the rehearsal of [Beethoven's] Sixth Symphony which the amateur orchestra is playing here under the direction of Herr Zumpe, our copyist. Again I have to admire R., who cannot let things be and gives words of advice to the poor people and their autocratic conductor. The tempi!

Tuesday, March 18 R. discusses with the mayor the question of our tomb in the garden; the mayor is horrified, but R. explains to him that we look forward to our eternal rest with cheerful serenity. R. says one really ought to conform with the community, for what remains of us we have in common with everybody – but it is nice to imagine ourselves remaining united here below as well, in our earthly guise. – In the evening R. dictates five pages [of the biography] to me; he says it costs him a great effort to transport himself back to those trivial times, when he had no faith in anything and his best years were wasted in vain enterprises.

Wednesday, March 19 The spring weather has changed – east wind and cold! – At lunch discussion of the difficulties of our undertaking, in six months the copyists have not yet finished *Die Walküre*, and how do things look with the machinery, etc.? 'He could talk,' says R. with a laugh, pointing at Beethoven's picture. 'He wrote his symphonies, couldn't hear them, and then ran around half-naked in the woods striking terror into everybody, and now I must pay for his having got his cart stuck in the mud with his ideas!'

Friday, March 21 The Lucerne Am Rhyn affair not too upsetting, after all. During lunch a telegram comes from Mme Lucca, saying that *Lohengrin* has triumphed against great opposition in Milan, and the second performance will take place tomorrow. – R. goes to Herr Feustel's, and learns that many certificates of patronage have been ordered from Mainz, where a large movement is beginning to emerge!... – In the evening chance puts some essays by Carlyle about Goethe and Schiller into our hands, and we are edified to read his fine words of praise for Goethe, uttered on the very eve of his death. Carlyle's words on how little one really knows about great men and in what a shadowy guise they appear to posterity make me think of these diaries, in which I want to convey the essence of R. to my children with all possible clarity, and in consequence try to set down every word he speaks, even about myself, forgetting all modesty, so that the picture is kept intact for them – yet I feel the attempt is failing: how can I convey the sound of his voice, the intonations, his movements and the expression in his eyes? But perhaps it is better than nothing, and so I shall continue with my bungling efforts. I am much moved by the praise for Goethe, which also fits R. like a glove – the genuineness, the truth, the courage, the kindness, the prophetic powers. R. likes Carlyle, he says that despite his many banalities and completely unphilosophic mind one recognizes in him a man of original ideas with a feeling for the genuine and the great. (He thinks for a moment of sending Carlyle his *Beethoven*.)

Saturday, March 22 I reflect how R.'s nature consists, like his works, of a mixture of great strength and delicacy; his mouth, ears, skin are as fine and delicate as a woman's, his bone structure sturdy, even gnarled. – We greet each other very cheerfully at breakfast; I ask him whether he does not feel inclined to work on his score, but he is fearful of being interrupted.

Sunday, March 23 Today we are celebrating Boni's birthday. Hans has sent her a book; Frau Ritter wrote that he had stayed a while in Würzburg, tired from his many journeys; he is going to Karlsruhe to give three concerts for Bayreuth under the sponsorship of the Grand Duke, then to London. – All sorts of letters – from London one which makes us decide not to go there, despite the theatrical organization which wants to arrange everything according to R.'s ideas! – Splendid spring weather, I go for a walk with R.; up to the theatre, slow work, strange thoughts! 'Not a plank in it,' says R., 'which national feeling has brought me, only personal sympathy, and a kind of blackmail arising from this.' – In the evening, dictation – this time happily, in cheerful spirits.

Wednesday, March 26 At lunch he reads me his essay on Bayreuth[1], which moves me to tears. – Feustel has reported that the performance in Munich brought in 550 florins and one certificate of patronage!!

Friday, March 28 R. learns from the mayor that there is nothing to prevent our building our grave on our own land. Great joy about this. At our evening meal I am given the last drop out of the bottle, which means the recipient will be married before the year is out. 'Then I shall have to die,' says R. 'I know to whom I shall then be wedded,' I say, thinking of death

[1] 'The Festival Theatre in Bayreuth', written for the ninth volume of the collected writings.

as I put my glass down; it gently touches the other glass and soundlessly breaks in two!

Saturday, March 29 We go, R. and I, to the new house, and R. is vexed that it is progressing so slowly. We recently spoke of the many moves R. has undertaken, the innumerable houses in which he has lived. 'Now for the first time,' he says, 'the foundation has been laid for a sensible life; I always had too few means, too irregular an income – I have always been living like a beggar, in fact.' The Philharmonic Society in New York has made R. an honorary member. Yet New York regularly sends us a newspaper which contains nothing but abuse of R.! – In the evening dictation.

Sunday, April 6 Family lunch and afterwards, quite unexpectedly, Herr Gedon[1], a sculptor from Munich and friend of Lenbach's, to whom we wished to entrust the decoration of our house, but whom we did not expect so soon. After him Professors Nietzsche and Rohde then arrive, and we visit the house, which Gedon cannot praise too highly.

Monday, April 7 Sore foot; R. goes with our friends to the theatre, which Gedon thinks very fine, too. At lunch the two professors, the mayor and the dean, who makes a fine speech to the three 'men of the future,' as he calls R. and his two young friends – what awaits them in joy and sorrow. Very affecting. Dispute between him and R. over the Jews; the dean feels that intermarriage is the solution to the problem, but R. maintains that the Germans would then cease to exist, since the fair German blood is not strong enough to withstand this 'alkali'. We can see, he says, how the Franks and the Normans were turned into Frenchmen, and Jewish blood is far more corrosive than Latin blood. R. goes on to say that his only hope is that 'these fellows' will become so arrogant that they will no longer form misalliances with us; they might even give up speaking German – we should then learn Hebrew, in order to keep things running smoothly, but we should still remain Germans. With this joke the conversation is concluded.

Saturday, April 12 Last day with our friends. In the afternoon R. plays passages from *Götterdämmerung*.

Tuesday, April 15 Constant fine weather; we (the whole family) make an outing. Today to Berneck; much pleasure in the sunshine, the woods, birds, castles, and also the people there. And particularly in Fidi, who walks well and talks charmingly with us. R. recalls that it was on a journey from Berneck, when he was 23, that he first saw Bayreuth lying before him in the evening sun; he is looking forward to seeing it again like that; but the sun treacherously hides; still, the missing rays are replaced by the rays within our hearts: 'To think I am now treading this same path again – and this time with you and Fidi!'

Sunday, April 20 Took leave of the children[2], who are well, thank

---

[1] Lorenz Gedon (b. 1843) was also an architect.
[2] As they set out on their third tour of Germany.

goodness! Also of the mayor, and R. tells him not to expect too much. R. tells me how embarrassing he finds this play acting for the sake of keeping up people's spirits, etc. He feels happy only in an atmosphere of complete truth. In Würzburg at five o'clock, once again at the Kronprinz.

Monday, April 21 Birds twittering in the early hours, then military music and artillery, less enjoyable. Very cordial parting from the Ritters; I hope they will come to Bayreuth; I feel the need to preserve R.'s relationship with all the people to whom he was once close, so that he can find compensation for the sad instability of his previous outward life in the continuity of his inner relationships. At seven in the evening in Cologne.

Tuesday, April 22 Around six o'clock rehearsal. The orchestra tolerable, but inexperienced in interpretation. They do not greet R. at the start, but when he raises his baton to conduct the '*Kaisermarsch*' they play a prolonged flourish. R. thought at first how badly they were playing, and the misunderstanding led to much laughter. I stay for only part of the rehearsal, since I go to meet Marie Schleinitz who, good and friendly as always, arrived today from Berlin.

Wednesday, April 23 The most curious night. R. yesterday sent a message up to Frau v.Schl. and me, saying that we would not inconvenience him if we were to come downstairs. Since the servant delivered this message clumsily, I told R. when I came down that he should not in future give him any more such messages to convey; the fact that, after a separation, I had nothing but that to say to him put him into a rage. It was late at night, there was a rehearsal early this morning, so I crept away silent and concerned; in an agony of remorse such as I have seldom known, I prayed to God to grant him a good night in spite of my imprudence; in bitter tears of concern for his health, I felt myself near to the godhead which is love, and that will help me – it recognizes my need. When I perceived that R. was asleep, my agony dissolved, and I spent the rest of the night in grateful prayer. I had eaten nothing since one o'clock the previous day, and, though feeling somewhat indisposed on account of it, I vowed not to have any breakfast and only to take refreshment after the rehearsal, if R. was not feeling too miserable. How much the remorseful heart feels the need for atonement! . . .

Thursday, April 24 Rehearsal and concert; the latter, nicely full, brings in 3,400 thalers, and the Wagner Society is happy over 'the hole that has been drilled'. Diener sang the 'Prize Song' well; R. rehearsed it with him. – After the concert R. tells me he would like to burn the parts, so as never again to have to conduct a concert!

Sunday, April 27 We visit the splendid gallery [in Kassel] before leaving at twelve noon for Leipzig. – At ten o'clock in the Hôtel de Prusse, chosen as a meeting place with my father.

Monday, April 28 My father arrives with the early train at five o'clock, he looks well, and the first few moments are spent in a sort of rueful cheerfulness. But in the afternoon he touches on matters which pain me – whether I intend to continue bringing up the children myself, Hans had spoken bitterly about them, etc. Then about Princess Wittgenstein, who maintains that we were married a second time in Bayreuth, our first wedding (in a chapel at Tribschen) had not been valid, and it was for this reason that we had decided on conversion – and similar absurdities! . . .

Tuesday, April 29 Departed at six o'clock in the morning in severe cold; in melancholy mood. Once more we are appalled by people's malice, as shown in the rumours we heard from my father. Arrive at the Dammallee at one o'clock, the children well and good. I come across a letter to Daniella from Hans which completely belies all the foolish rumours; he is now in London and was happy with the proceeds of his concert tour.

Friday, May 2 The fine weather has returned, R. works on his score, which at first he finds difficult. One page is completed today. In the afternoon with the children to the new house. The mayor is having a fine plane tree planted, the children watch eagerly, blackbirds are singing, on a high chimney a stork on its nest – 'This is happiness,' I think.

Saturday, May 3 R. speaks of my father, who does not have to do a thing, has just to be present to have all the women falling over him – 'whereas people like me always have to be noble.' He hurts me very much by saying that I am in my element when I am with my father. Noticing this, he says: 'All the things one says are foolish, a great deal of life has to remain unexpressed, like muddled dreams. I am content if you glance into my heart and understand that my complaints come from the tenderness of love, and I suffer only when I think you are not sharing my feelings.' – In the evening our copyists; they play the *Meistersinger* Prelude and horrify R. with their broad, funeral-march tempo.

Monday, May 5 Much, much trouble and sorrow over my little surprise for R.'s birthday; no one is really helping me! R. works on his orchestration, but has vexations as well – for the people in Cologne, instead of sending 3,000 thalers, send only 1,000 'for the time being'. – In the afternoon to the house; from our architect we hear curious things! Count Castell[1] has made an offer to the King to buy up all the free entrances to the palace gardens for 90,000 florins – just so that entry can be denied us! Poor Bayreuth, otherwise completely forgotten, has suddenly become an object of governmental intrigue. The King has not consented to the proposal, the good people can keep their entrances, which they have held since the time of the margraves, and we shall perhaps be allowed ours. – Nice letter from my father, who says he is completely on our side; R., however, is annoyed

---

[1]　Master of the Household to King Ludwing II.

by the thought that I might go to the performance of *Christus* in Weimar without him, and scolds me!

Thursday, May 8 R. to the Thursday gathering. – Claire writes that my mother has received a prize from the Academy[1]. – When R. returns late, he tells me more about the proposed purchase of the plots with entrances to the palace gardens: the gentlemen were saying that the King might come and use it to consort in private with Wagner; to facilitate this, all palace gardens – not only here, but throughout Bavaria – were to be closed to the public. This is a worthy addition to our previous experiences of Munich.

Friday, May 9 Gloomy weather and gloomy thoughts: the children – the two elder ones – do not conform to my efforts and my wishes, they do not make my difficult task easy, and I have the feeling that, people being so malicious, ugly accusations will be made about my methods of bringing them up, or I shall be reproached with neglect. A great struggle within me – whether I should approach the children's father and ask him to send them to a school, for I am not strict enough, I quite see that. Or is this perhaps just vanity on my part, an attempt to rid myself of a responsibility from which I now feel I can gain little praise? Resolve to continue to do what I can and accept all trials – both present and future – as an atonement! . . . The King sends to ask what R. would like for his birthday (still without saying whether he wishes to see him). R. intends to ask for a gate into the palace gardens.

Saturday, May 10 In the afternoon, along with Prof. Ott[2] selected the players for the *tableaux vivants* – wretched impression of the whole pack, depravity and stupidity on every face! My good professor leaves the whole examination to me, but afterwards admires my ability to deal with people! – I am feeling apprehensive about the whole thing; the vanity of the principal figures must now be taken into account – the sensitivity of my nephew [Sascha], to whom I was obliged to write that the amateurs would have difficulty in getting used to him, after having studied with Zumpe! God knows – and on top of all this trouble, a heavy heart!

Monday, May 12 Lost my voice, but journeys necessary all the same in connection with the celebrations. R. orchestrates, but is constantly distracted by thoughts concerning his undertaking. – Unfortunately he is not well, suddenly spits blood – he frequently forgets names, and that embarrasses him; he looks worn out, and his speech, though still full of feeling, is flat. The doctor says it is nothing – but the worry – who can dispel that?

Wednesday, May 14 I am having many difficulties with my secrecy, have to call the Thursday gathering for today, so that I can secretly go to the rehearsal. R. suspects nothing so far – how dearly I wish to give him a little pleasure! Sascha Ritter arrived today – he also here in secret.

[1] From the Académie Française for her history of the Netherlands.
[2] An art teacher in Bayreuth.

Thursday, May 15 R. tells me in the morning that he dreamed he had received 600 francs in gold; when he got up he discovered that Fritzsch had actually sent him nearly this sum. – R. goes out and returns in high spirits – the palace gardener has been ordered to construct our gate! Happy enjoyment of this victory! – Unfortunately our high spirits are much damped by a letter from Herr Fürstner in Berlin. He intends to publish *Tannhäuser* in French and German, and what is the point of this affront, except to bypass R. by buying the new scenes from Flaxland[1]? So from one Jew to another! Yet he feels no shame in telling R. of it!

Friday, May 16 The wretchedness of Herr Fürstner gives R. no rest, he writes to him early in the morning.

Sunday, May 18 Choir rehearsal. Returning home, I find R. working. In the evening [Shakespeare's] *A Winter's Tale*, great admiration for its artistic structure.

Tuesday, May 20 I am considerably indisposed, did not sleep a wink all night. Arrival of young Brandt[2]; discussions at the Ritters' – trouble over the arrangement of the orchestra; not enough room – the boldness of my suggestions horrifies the amateur management. Difficulties of all kinds.

Wednesday, May 21 I am so unwell that I have to stay in bed and cannot attend the rehearsal of the *tableaux vivants*. Friends arrive, 'the three Moors'[3] (sent by Fritzsch from Leipzig), Cornelius, concertmaster Abel[4], Buonamici[5] from Munich, also little Karl Ritter[6], besides the 20 people from Würzburg. – R. is invited by Feustel to a preliminary celebration, and I am able to attend the rehearsal. – Some things unsatisfactory, the final *tableau vivant* in particular causes many problems, and I decide to set it up anew; it turns out a bit better.

Thursday, May 22 At five in the morning the Dammallee is already besieged, but it is 7.45 a.m. before the music begins – coming from the Hofmanns' garden opposite, so that R. shall not see the people. It is mixed with the ringing of church bells. R. has a headache from the previous evening, so my noble good intentions are a little spoiled. At twelve o'clock rehearsal, took the children with me – including Fidi; it goes quite well. R. receives visitors, is still unsuspecting. At lunch the toasts. I ask, 'Long live who, Daniella?' 'Our most loyal guardian' – rising to her feet with glass in hand. 'Long live who, Blandine?' 'Our dearest friend.' 'Long live who, Isolde?' 'Our kindest father.' 'Long live who, Fidi?' 'My papa' – whereupon the military band plays the introduction to the third act of *Lohengrin*. We

---

[1] Fürstner had acquired publishing rights in the Dresden *Tannhäuser* from Meser; the rights in the new scenes for the Paris version had been acquired by the French music publisher Flaxland.

[2] Fritz Brandt (b. 1854), pupil of his father Karl and later theatre machinist in his own right.

[3] The Ximenez brothers from Cuba.

[4] Ludwig Abel, violinist, Munich.

[5] Giuseppe Buonamici, Italian pianist, teacher at the music school in Munich.

[6] Son of Alexander and Franziska.

are all in copious tears. – In the morning the children recited a 16th-century poem, then Daniella carried in the Laurana Gallery etchings of Raphael drawings, which R. had once seen and admired at the home of the painter Hübner; Blandine, *L'Introduction à l'histoire du Buddhisme* by Burnouf; and the two little girls *Le Roman des douze pairs* from R.'s former library. Fidi brings in a poodle, chosen for me by the Krockows, almost too fragile (we had wanted a strong and solid poodle), but a nice and affectionate little creature, whom we christened *Putz*. Towards evening I tell R., who still thinks the Thursday gathering is to be held in our house, that the amateur society wants to put on a little celebration of half an hour at the most, and we cannot spoil it for them. We walk to the opera house, which is full to bursting and looks very elegant. R. thinks at first that Zumpe has composed a festival overture for his birthday, but the programme sets him straight. And now one surprise follows another, until finally he sees Franziska on the stage. He says he feels stunned, he had had no inkling of any of it – our surprise succeeded completely. – After the performance a party in the Anker. R. expresses his thanks, as 'a musician in need of help' he needs love! – Home quite late. (A nice telegram from the King.)[1]

Friday, May 23 R. had a sad dream that I sent him away, because he sold my jewellery in order to gamble, and I told him I could no longer live with such a wicked person!... If one wants to feel the full melancholy of life profoundly, one should celebrate festive occasions – I always have the feeling that it is not proper for me to do so, that I should not make my personal presence felt through a wish or a deed, but simply be on hand with friendly advice; when my enthusiasm carries me away, I feel guilty – it is a feeling difficult to describe – and an insuperable melancholy takes possession of me, a longing to be free of an existence in which even joy is suffering. – The Ritters to lunch. In the evening a party – all the people who took part, including 'the three Moors'; they play nicely, and Kummer plays '*Träume*' and '*Der Engel*'. During these, R.'s whole life is revealed to my soul, like layers of fog dispersing. – R. also plays the *Idyll* and says to

[1] The 60th birthday celebrations: The artist Julius Hübner lived from 1839 in Dresden, where Wagner met him. Eugène Burnouf, French Orientalist. R.'s former library: In *My Life* Wagner describes how in the 1840s he set up a library in his Dresden apartment; this included much old German and medieval literature, including the 'valuable and rare' old *Roman des douze pairs*; on his flight from Dresden in 1849 the library was claimed by Heinrich Brockhaus as a recompense for 500 thalers that Wagner owed him. The programme in the Markgräfliches Opernhaus: The works performed were a Concert Overture composed by Wagner in 1831; Ludwig Geyer's two-act play, *Der bethlehemitische Kindermord*; Wagner's song '*Träume*' (from the *Wesendonck-Lieder*) in his own arrangement for violin and orchestra (soloist: Alexander Kummer); and finally a stage presentation put together by Peter Cornelius, using music Wagner had composed in 1835 in Magdeburg for a New Year's cantata, in which a series of *tableaux vivants* based on the pictures of Genelli was enacted; Cornelius's text was spoken by Franziska Ritter, and Alexander Ritter was the conductor of an orchestra made up of amateur players from Bayreuth and Würzburg; Geyer's play was performed by a professional company then giving a season in Bayreuth, and the stage manager was Fritz Brandt.

me jokingly when we are alone, 'I suppose it would have pleased you better if things had not progressed beyond my first poem to you, if there had never been an idyll – you would certainly have found it more interesting!' What I want and what I should have wished for I do not know – but certainly that he should be happy, calm and contented, and that I should no longer be conscious of my miserable ego in any shape or form.

Sunday, May 25 The town, it is said, is of one opinion – how lovely the celebrations were; and indeed the nice thing about it was that the whole town took part and fêted R. Visit of the sculptor Kietz[1] from Dresden, who wants to make a bust of R. He visits our house and admires the way in which no thought was given to the façade, it was built from the inside, with the result that from the outside something acceptable has also been achieved.

Tuesday, May 27 The big question now is whether we shall go to Weimar for the performance of *Christus,* neither of us wants to say a definite yes or no. R. writes a page of his score and sends a telegram to say we are not going.

Wednesday, May 28 The journey is decreed, and Daniella is to come, too. Somewhat lengthy and tiring journey, arrival at nine o'clock in Weimar, my father is at rehearsals, we are met by Frau v. Meyendorff. Great laments from everyone (except my father) about the rehearsal. Late in the night, arrival of Marie Schleinitz.

Thursday, May 29 Lunch with my father; afterwards many Hungarians, who have come to hear *Christus.* At six o'clock to the church, the performance goes on until nine. Remarkable, peculiar impression, best summed up in the words R. said to me in the evening: 'He is the last great victim of this Latin-Roman world.' During the very first bars R. said to me, 'He conducts splendidly, it will be magnificent.' It is a formulation of faith in the new church order, which dispenses with faith; the naïve feeling of this highly unnaïve creation; popular tendency towards pomp, although in the church this pomp is only a cruel net in which such feelings are trapped. The whole work thoroughly un-German, and only made possible by appealing to German sensibilities at their best; it could only be performed by Germans. R.'s reaction covers all extremes, from ravishment to immense indignation, in his attempt to do it both profound and loving justice.

Friday, May 30 Numerous farewells! R. addresses fine words to my father as we leave, and I thank him from my very soul for having undertaken this journey, which he did purely for my sake. – Nice journey home. A deep and fervent love of Germany stirs within me – it is the only country in which one can live! Arrival in Bayreuth at ten o'clock. Everybody asleep, but well; we are home again!

---

[1] Gustav Adolf Kietz (b. 1824), brother of Wagner's former friend Ernst Benedikt Kietz.

Sunday, June 1 Wrote to Herr v. Gersdorff, who has told me about a serious eye complaint affecting our friend Nietzsche, and to Richter, who was accused by my father's young Hungarian friends of allowing himself to be used against my father.

Tuesday, June 3 Strikes all over Germany; two workers from Berlin were here and made speeches which are now filling the heads of the local people, with the result that one can no longer do anything with them. – At lunch an amusing scene with a weaver, who had heard that we wanted to teach our dog tricks. He provided us with a delicious picture of a character from Shakespeare. With the help of blows he had taught two sheepdogs to hold a pipe in their mouths, and now he intended to subject our delicate Putz to the same treatment!

Wednesday, June 4 R. works on his score, I write to Frau v. Schl., chiefly to sort out the confusion in Vienna, since Marie Dönhoff, the only one to have been active there, is with her. Instead of the 21,000 florins which Feustel saw entered in their books, they send 4,000 thalers – the task now is to find out at all costs which of the people recruited by Marie D. have not yet paid, and not to send tickets to these unreliable people. – Our nephew Ritter finds us a dog trainer in Weidenberg, and Putz is sent off.

Friday, June 6 'A son is born, a darling son,' R. sings to the melody of the shepherd boy greeting the month of May in *Tannhäuser.* I think of the orange room in Tribschen, in which the sun will today have shone on emptiness as it celebrates Fidi's birth. Today I am and remain in a serious mood, weighed down with sorrow; how strangely I am being punished, how true does Nature remain to itself! It punishes me through the eldest child of my marriage with Hans, thus showing me how unblessed this marriage was, and it also punishes me by completely destroying my cherished wish to raise a noble being to serve as Hans's only consolation. Should I send the girl to a boarding school? R. is in favour of it and he is certainly right, but I find it so hard! ... I feel more full of worries than I have ever been before, and only the thought of atonement sustains me; for I have to acknowledge that my child has a base outlook.

Saturday, June 14 Reconciliation at last with my child, and the hope that she has learned her lesson. – A cloudburst, Bayreuth flooded. Letter from Marie Schl.: the Khedive[1] has taken eleven certificates of patronage. Departure of Sascha R. and young Kummer.

Monday, June 16 Violent downpours, Fidi has caught cold, is coughing; besides that, bad news of our poor little Putz – with every new creature arises a new wellspring of torment. We send the veterinary surgeon to Weidenberg and hope for an improvement. – Herr Kietz is here again, to make a bust of R.

---

[1] Ismael Pasha, Khedive of Egypt.

Tuesday, June 17 At last fine weather again. I go for a walk with the children; as I return home, R. calls to me through the window, 'Putz is here, his delight knows no bounds!' Arriving indoors, I discover that the little creature has learned nothing and was ill with homesickness. The children are overjoyed, and so now everything is back as it was after an abortive experiment.

Thursday, June 19 In the afternoon in our garden, which is already giving us much joy; R. is sitting for Herr Kietz, but I fear the bust will not be good.

Tuesday, June 24 R. is putting his *Kapitulation* in the 9th volume, with a foreword which he reads to me. He had no manuscripts of it, and that is why he decided to publish this work, which he has so far preferred to keep for ourselves. He says he must always be doing things of which I cannot entirely approve, yet, when it has happened, I never reproach him, which shows that I am better than he is – he reminds me in this connection of the publication of the Jewish pamphlet.

Friday, June 27 Vexation with our local newspaper; the news concerning our building in the foreign papers is to the effect that the material resources for our undertaking are assured, and only the care needed to find the performing artists is delaying the performances – a report which our man here questions! R. discovers that the editor has been changed, and a man from Berlin – probably a Jew! – has been engaged.

Sunday, June 29 R. works. Family lunch with our good Kietz, whose work makes me more and more melancholy!

Tuesday, July 1 To the new house, sitting; the bust is beginning to look better, and the good sculptor touches me with his remark that Wagner now looks completely different and that he has never before seen him so cheerful and so well, and that one would previously never have been able to visualize him at the centre of such a family life.

Wednesday, July 2 Bismarck is said to have proposed to King Wilhelm that he take over the government again, and the latter is said to have refused. R. considers the situation of Bismarck, who is now in solitary retirement in Varzin, a tragic one – he is breaking up the Prussian monarchy and he is right to do so, but where is he heading, what has happened to the German idea? – The weather is cold, but we go to the new house, where Fidi has a conversation with the mason; he is now quite different since his hair has been cut short, more conscious of his maleness; he will not go with the other children to the mayor's in spite of cake and strawberries, or with me either, insists on being called Helferich and hits Eva, telling her, 'My name is now Helferich!'

Saturday, July 5 Richard is not at all well and had a bad night; but he works a little. In the afternoon to the sitting, from there via the theatre to the Bürgerreuth[1]. A feeling of fear, which I cannot describe, overcomes me

---

[1] An inn on the hill above the festival theatre.

when I see the giant scaffolding and the wide auditorium! As long as it was all just an idea inside us, I was not alarmed by its remoteness from reality, but now, taking shape in front of our eyes, it frightens me with its boldness, and it all looks to me like a grave (the Pyramids!). I keep my feelings to myself, and we eat our supper gaily in the Bürgerreuth before returning home to bed.

Tuesday, July 8 Charming letter from Marie Dönhoff with three new certificates of patronage. R. works, but is dissatisfied, having to write one page again. To the new house, the bust is finished and is really quite good.

Wednesday, July 9 Herr Brandt is here to inspect the theatre building, we admit to one another our mutual *anxiety!* Lunch with Herr Br. and the Kietzes; his wife has also arrived, and R. says it is remarkable to see what sort of wives artists always choose in Germany. But the bust has finally turned out very well, and I am really grateful to the good man for the way he accepted all my remarks so patiently and willingly and responded to them. R. has much vexation with the new house, Herr Wölffel is behaving rudely and deceitfully. – Royalties from Berlin, the works were performed only three times in the whole quarter, and a performance of *Lohengrin* on R.'s birthday brought in 5,000 thalers.

Thursday, July 10 In the afternoon we drive to the Eremitage, set the fountains[1] going, great enjoyment for the children, a bit tiring for us; thoughts of Frederick the Great[2] with us throughout. R. is delighted with Fidi and says: 'All this happiness gained through you! And the people who imagine that something of the past must still remain in me, my relations with Minna or the various M-Ms' (thus he dubs his relationships with women!). 'It is all unreal, I remember nothing of it.' We catch sight of the theatre in the distance, standing imposingly in the beautiful sunshine. It makes a great and fine impression.

Tuesday, July 22 Wrote to my father, inviting him to the roof-raising ceremony.

Wednesday, July 23 The people are now working on our burial vault. R. goes to the Riedelsberg[3] to discuss the roof-raising ceremony, I accompany him part of the way and return home through the meadows in a lovely sunset. Deep reflection as I walk – I believe no monk could be more detached from things than I am, I even thought of a heavy lot for the children in the future and accepted it – for thus it is (and we cannot take away the cup, either for ourselves or those near us). Curious how cheerful one remains in spite of it all, at least to outward appearances; but the struggle to retain this cheerfulness is often very violent, one's wings droop and one longs for rest.

[1] Ingenious and intricate fountains are a feature of this rococo palace.
[2] Wilhelmine, Margravine of Bayreuth, who was responsible for both the Markgräfliches Opernhaus and the Eremitage, was Frederick the Great's sister.
[3] Feustel's residence.

Friday, July 25 (Interruption of 14 days – I take up my diary again on Friday, August 8, and write from memory.) – Captain von Steinitz and wife[1] arrive and spend the evening with us. The good lady has the best intentions, but also all the bad theatrical habits, and R. hardly thinks he will be able to use her.

Saturday, July 26 Friend Klindworth arrived suddenly and unexpectedly to fetch *Götterdämmerung* for arranging [for the pianoforte]. At three o'clock my father, very tired and worn out. In the evening music; with Frau v. St[einitz] R. sings the scene from *Der Fl. Holländer*, making a profound and moving impression; he himself much affected to be singing this particular scene, in which he sees our whole situation, in front of my father. After they have all gone, we remain for a long time under the influence of our emotions – never again will the Dutchman's words sound quite like that.

Monday, July 28 My father talks to me about Hans, says that he is well, that he has brilliant prospects in England, that he has already put aside 30,000 thalers for the children. In the afternoon music, the third act of *Siegfried*, Herr Klindworth accompanies it with his difficult piano arrangement, R. sings with indescribably moving effect. My father remarked that in 25 years even the best of musicians will scarcely appreciate all the riches in these things.

Tuesday, July 29 Quiet and uneventful life with my father, who has regained his health and seems to enjoy sharing with us a life to which he is not accustomed. In the evening first movement and scherzo from [Beethoven's Opus] 106, the A-flat Minor Prelude from Bach's 48 Preludes and Fugues, conjured up by my father's magic.

Thursday, July 31 Invitation from my father, all the children at table, much fun, but unfortunately an ugly quarrel breaks out among the children when they get home, directed as always against Eva, and I have to call on R. for help, to punish the older girls; I tell him about the incidents which have piled up, and ask him to exercise the strict office of a father; for the first time he gives Daniella and Blandine each a blow, they are profoundly shocked. – In the evening the dean, the mayor, Dr. Landgraf; my father plays the adagio from [Opus] 106 unforgettably, and from time to time R. contributes an explanatory word; our guests, completely unprepared, appear to be utterly overwhelmed. – When they have all gone, R. sinks into profound melancholy, he weeps and sobs for having inflicted punishment on the children, says he had no right to do it, and seems to be suffering terrible pangs of remorse.

Friday, August 1 Little preparations for the roof-raising ceremony tomorrow, we want the dean to write the verse for the *foreman*.

---

[1] An Austrian army officer, met in Bremen, where his wife was a ballet dancer with (apparently) ambitions as a singer.

Saturday, August 2 In the morning the dean brings his pretty verses, but R. cuts the first stanza, since he does not wish to be celebrated as the owner of a building, and instead writes about the German spirit; he also quickly drafts a poem, 'On the Roof-raising Ceremony'. We set out at about five o'clock, strange ascent right up onto the scaffolding, the most wonderful thoughts, for the first time a theatre has been built for an idea and for a particular work, says my father. As the *Tannhäuser* March is played, and in place of the noble knights (or rather, ignoble actors dressed up as noble knights) genuine working people appear with a simple greeting, and the last hammer blows are heard, I feel as if this March has received its true consecration. The hymn *'Nun danket alle Gott'* ['Now thank we all our God'] lifts up my heart as it is sung in the open air against a smiling landscape beneath a splendid blue sky, sung after this victory; as my nervousness of the scaffolding disappeared, so, too, my timorousness in face of this bold undertaking, faith raises our wings and fills us with bliss! – Our visit to the workers at the conclusion warms my heart – they know nothing, but they can feel it. – What memories will it all bring back to the children?

Sunday, August 3 My father gives us another two days, R. thanks him warmly for having come, he alone of all our friends was present on this festive occasion, he represented them all; however separated, however divided, all were united on this simple, serene day!

Tuesday, August 5 The plan I thought up yesterday to accompany my father as far as Bamberg with all the children is cordially accepted by R., we hastily get ready, and at eleven o'clock, in great haste, all nine of us (the nursemaid is with us) depart. In Bamberg we say goodbye to my father; I am overcome by a great melancholy, which vexes R., and he gives way to those passionate outbursts with which I am confronted after every reunion with my father. – When my father has gone, we go to the hotel Bamberger Hof; in the afternoon a visit to the cathedral.

Wednesday, August 6 Visited the library, great delight in the old manuscripts, but even more in the Dürer drawings, the portrait of Emperor Maximilian and a Christ arouse our admiration in particular; if the 14th-century crucifix in the cathedral and the tomb of Heinrich II had moved us profoundly, the sight of this drawing brings tears to our eyes. The ugliness of the German women makes us laugh. Left the Bamberger Hof at about two o'clock and drove to Forchheim. From there a carriage to Muggendorf; lovely evening, idyllic sojourn, splendid moonrise – but R. unfortunately still in an ill humour, an unhappy parallel I drew between my father's playing and the art of [Wilhelmine] Schröder-Devrient makes him angry and indignant. Half-asleep, I believe I hear him saying unpleasant things; when I tell him this, he loses his temper, but it all resolves itself in passionate and loving explanations, and then the night passes peacefully.

Thursday, August 7 Arrived home around nine in the evening.

Friday, August 15 The theatre has made more good progress; the sight of it arouses weighty and noble thoughts in us; R. says he explains his frequently recurring dreams of financial fraud by the nightmare that the sight of the theatre gives him – is he himself not perhaps a swindler, as it were?

Saturday, August 16 Fine weather, I in the garden with the children, while R. works diligently on his score. Over dessert he says to me: 'The worst thing about old age is not that one loses one's fire, but that one's sum total of bad experiences literally forces one not to think about the world. In youth ambition plays such a big role – you write your *Holländer* and your *Tannhäuser*, fine, but you don't yet know whether and in what way you are a somebody; but in old age ambition has nothing more to say, and to keep the will to work you have, like Goethe, to follow a rigorous discipline. One's conception of the world and of life become more and more dismal, and need begins to look like a protection against sorrow!' – At the theatre yesterday we spoke about *Parcival*, whose abode is being built; will he be permitted to write it? This is my constant question, this my prayer!

Sunday, August 17 Received some visitors (R. working), then a letter from my father, and finally Malwida von Meysenbug, who because of us is coming to live here permanently[1]; talked about many things, showed her the house. I am glad that this outstanding woman has come to join us – may she find some pleasure living here!

Tuesday, August 19 News from Feustel that, if 10,000 florins cannot be found by October, the building work will have to be broken off. Should I hand over my savings? If I were sure of my children's feelings, how gladly and easily I should do it, but now it is a decision I must debate within myself. R. knows nothing of it – may I do the right thing! R. goes to see friend Feustel to discuss the matter. If the King were to promise a guarantee, everything would be all right, and a loan would be made.

Thursday, August 21 We had disturbing news of our King – Malwida had heard it from a Court official sympathetic to the King; he is said, among other things, recently to have ordered a dinner for twelve persons in Partenkirchen, to have come alone, greeted the empty places, and sat down. Also that he never goes out through the doors of his palaces, but through the windows. What is impending here – and how soon? – The ninth volume of the collected writings has arrived, so that task is now completed.

Sunday, August 24 Alone with R. in the evening and read him Renan's *L'Antéchrist*[2] – we laughed a lot over his refined and distinguished Jesus and his obtuse Saint Paul – everything always cut to suit Parisian tastes. – For some days now the Moorish serenade from Mozart's *Entführung* has been

[1] In an apartment in the town which Cosima had found and arranged for her.
[2] Vol. 4 of Ernest Renan's *History of the Origins of Christianity*; the Antichrist is Nero.

our favourite piece, I sing it to Fidi, R. plays it and delights in the tremendous genius of this little invention.

Monday, August 25 The King's birthday and our wedding day, which we celebrate quietly, as always. Malwida brings us flowers, we drink to the King's birthday – all good wishes for him! . . . In the afternoon in the garden, the architect Brückwald has come here from Leipzig to inspect the theatre and finds everything in order. We christen the little summer-house with an improvised supper. Lovely evening, blissful feeling of being at one with R.!

Thursday, August 28 Night of thunderstorms; early in the morning the news that President von Lerchenfeld has died suddenly. The shock is a severe one – who can shut his eyes to the possibilities which lie ahead? . . . The great closeness of the weather also has a numbing effect on our nerves; but R. works.

Friday, August 29 R. follows the president's funeral cortège; I hope that we shall not be faced here with a worse! R. has difficulty in rescuing something of the morning for his work. – After lunch in the garden, the weather cold; R. arrives, followed by three people from Vienna, and I recognize in them the ominous figures from the Wagner Society – unpleasant, Jewish impression. – Voltz and Batz have also written, saying that they are still unable to make any payments – all difficult and trying matters. – Our sole pleasure is Fidi; his sparkling eyes lead us to talk of eyes in general and those of my father in particular, which are so peculiar. 'They have a brightness,' says R., 'like those of a saint in his grave – something ascetically, fanatically friendly!'

Thursday, September 4 Dispatching the circulars[1]. In the course of it, R. breaks the gold pen with which he wrote *Tristan, Die Meistersinger* and in fact everything since '68. It grieves me all the more since it happened while he was just pointing with the pen to the place on which I was to put a stack of the circulars. R. is not well, the business of dispatching is a strain on him. After lunch in the garden, where very unexpectedly Schuré[2] comes rushing towards us! A hearty welcome in spite of everything! At supper, when he asks for Bordeaux wine 'out of patriotism', and I reprove him for trying to provoke us, R. explains to him earnestly and at length what it means to be and to wish to be German, that is to say, to feel a longing which cannot be fulfilled in Latin countries; here in Germany, he says, the question can at least still be asked; our armies have shown that strength is still there, and now we are anxiously waiting to see whether this strength can extend to other fields. 'My dear friend,' he concludes, 'I am not to be counted among the ranks of the present-day patriots, for what a person can

---

[1] A report to his patrons.
[2] Edouard Schuré (b. 1841), a French writer and champion of Wagner's cause in France; the friendship cooled at the time of the Franco-Prussian War.

suffer under present conditions I am already suffering – I am, as it were, nailed on the cross of the German ideal.'

Saturday, September 6 I go to the garden to listen to a reading by our friend Schuré on the history of music and poetry. In the garden I meet our friend Kietz, who has come here really and truly at R.'s behest to make a bust of me, which gives me little pleasure. The German Crown Prince will be coming to Bayreuth within a week. A real blow for us, however the visit turns out – whether he shows any interest in the theatre or not, in either case it is awkward. The evening arrives, the dean, Feustel (who reports that Bismarck is again in disgrace), Kietz, Schuré and Malwida. R. very agitated (before the arrival of the guests I had conversed with Schuré in French, as was our habit in the past, and that also annoyed him), and he hardly departs from the topic of France and Germany all evening; this makes me feel embarrassed, particularly for Schuré, who strikes me as defenceless here. When the guests leave early, I unfortunately remark to R. that the evening was uncomfortable, and he gets very angry!

Monday, September 8 First sitting with friend Kietz. R. kept from his work – what I call his real work! – by the corrections to [the proofs of] *Die Walküre*. A grief to me.

Thursday, September 11 Arrival of the box containing the original scores of *Lohengrin* and *Fl. Holländer*, the unpleasant feeling that my father has sent it without love; we had asked him for a copy of the parts not yet published; now he sends us the whole thing, and I know what comments others will make about this. – In the afternoon a sitting – in the house, which is also an object more of vexation than joy. – Our last evening with friend Schuré, whom we now with a quiet conscience yield to France.

Friday, September 12 R. writes to the Grand Duke of Oldenburg and the King of W[ürttemberg] on behalf of his undertaking. My heart is so heavy – how many days is it now that he has been unable to work on his score? I have a real fear that, if things go on like this, he will never get his score finished. We are thinking again about concerts. – And the King of B. has just bought himself a castle for 200,000 florins! Herr Krausse[1], the painter, comes to carry out the *sgraffito* panel on our house. I constantly feel that R. is again becoming much too much involved in commissions, but I do not dare to speak, for fear of exacerbating his great worries with my worries.

Saturday, September 13 Although he has not got down to his work for weeks and is having nothing but unpleasant experiences, R. is today full of good and amusing ideas for the sculptors! . . . He says the good progress of my bust is giving him pleasure. Sitting twice daily robs me of much time, but if it brings him the least little bit of satisfaction, that is reward enough! – My mother writes for the first time since February. My father also writes,

[1] Robert Krausse from Leipzig; *the sgraffito*: a decorative panel above the front door of Wahnfried.

only to say the original scores of *Lohengrin* and *Holländer* are a gift, but alas, alas, I cannot accept this, for it is being done without feeling! – At 7.30 arrival of the Crown Prince; the question of whether our theatre should be illuminated is answered by the mayor in the affirmative, and like an apparition, like Wotan's castle, it rises twice into view, bathed in a red light. The people give the Crown Prince a nice, spontaneous welcome; thoughts of the King – how everything takes its course. Very moved by the sight of the theatre, we embrace each other, and R. says, 'It is coloured red with our blood!' ...

Sunday, September 14 Friend Feustel, arriving from Munich in the early morning, has hopes that the King will take over the guarantee! Splendid weather; the sun of the Hohenzollerns shone today as yesterday: 'I must be sure to order it for my festival,' says R. The Prince visits church, opera house, palaces, but not our theatre, which stands there by itself, solitary and remote, the cross to which we are nailed, the temple in which we pray. – Sitting in the morning; at lunch Malwida.

Monday, September 15 At last R. gets down again to his score, though he still has no pen which he likes. I write to my father (sending back the scores), my mother, the Englishman who sent a fine translation of *Die Walküre*[1], etc. – In the evening R. plays the third act of *Tristan*, the bliss of melancholy, the desolation of the sea, profound calm, Nature's sorrow, Nature's consolation – all, all here in this most wonderful of poems! When I speak of it to R., he says, 'In my other works the motives serve the action; in this, one might say that the action arises out of the motives.' When I tell him I should like to die to these strains, he says, 'But better to the strains with which Siegfried dies.'

Tuesday, September 16 Friend Feustel tells us that the Crown Prince made the King's jealousy his excuse for not viewing more things here.

Saturday, September 20 R. is able to orchestrate again; I again have a sitting. A difference with R. with regard to the children; in view of their great carelessness I have had tin mugs made for them to drink from; R. will not tolerate this punishment; I give way, but am inwardly sad about it. Letter to R. from Prof. Nietzsche, after a long silence; but his eye trouble is not yet cured.

Wednesday, September 24 Long discussion with R.; resolve on my part to use no more strictness towards the children, and even to stifle all thoughts of what I hold to be good in this matter. Visited the theatre in lovely weather; splendid decoration supplied by the supporting beams, which are simply to be painted over – thus a downright primitive art form results: no deliberate ornamentation – the bricks provide the red background, the beams provide the lines which, painted yellow, gleam in the sunshine like gold. The whole

[1] Alfred Forman: his translation of the complete *Ring* was published in 1877.

thing stands there like a fairy tale in the midst of clumsy reality. God knows what will come of it. R. said the building supervisor was so pleased by the success of his work: 'Everyone will laugh when we weep.' – And yet how one's energies droop! It is only one's little bit of intelligence which still flutters and takes pleasure, now as before, in the great and the beautiful.

Friday-Saturday, September 26–27 Arrival of my sister-in-law Ottilie with her son Fritz; the two days are devoted to them and pass very pleasantly. – R. receives a letter from Councillor D., saying the King will *not* give the guarantee; he has taken on too much himself! . . .

Sunday, September 28 In the garden with children and relations; an all-but-angry interchange with Ottilie concerning Prof. Nietzsche; she is so bound up in university ways that she talks about the book *The Birth of Tragedy* without stopping to consider that N. has jeopardized his whole career for the sake of her brother, and that it is therefore insensitive of her to pass on to us the contemptuous and libellous opinions of the top academics; I see from the sentiments of W.'s sister towards her brother's most loyal supporter how even the warmest heart can cool when it is constantly confronted with power!

Monday, September 29 Will work on the theatre have to be stopped? That is the question which alarms and occupies us. R. writes to Councillor Düffl. and to Herr Zacharias, instructing the latter to form a consortium of patrons. I write to Emil Heckel. As we have just completed these letters, Loldi comes to tell us that a worker has fallen to his death from the top scaffolding of the theatre. A sad shock – I had felt it to be a blessing that no such accident had yet accompanied the building work.

Tuesday, September 30 Departure of our relations, which leaves me in a mood of great melancholy; I see clearly that the way in which R. and his undertaking are spoken of in my sister-in-law's circles has had an influence on her, and her heart is not big enough to follow him. – R. writes letters, clearing things up so that from tomorrow on he can get to work on the score. My bust is packed away; departure of the excellent Kietz.

Wednesday, October 1 R. goes back to his score – a great joy, for then things are easier to bear. Schott pays for *Götterdämmerung* (10,000 francs) and is thus behaving agreeably. But this is probably our last large piece of income, and our growing expenses fill me with worry. R. has an unquenchable confidence in himself, and I an all-absorbing mistrust in Fate.

Saturday, October 4 R. dreamed that he was in his theatre, surveying from the princes' gallery the whole lovely, completed auditorium. 'How will we feel when we come to the performances?' he asks. 'After all that has gone before, one is so tired that one has no feelings at all – one is in a complete dream state, as I was when I sat in the King's box at the first performance of *Die Meistersinger*.' While we are talking about the old Nordic sagas, R. says he knows what Odin whispered in Baldur's ear, that insoluble riddle:

resignation, the breaking of the will – the ethical theme of *Der Ring des Nibelungen*. R. works, and during his work comes to the following conclusion: 'There are two ways of looking at the orchestra: as a homophonous body in which one instrument stands in for another; or my way, where every instrument is regarded as an individual standing by itself; that is why I am so annoyed when an instrument does not possess a particular note.' – R. visits the theatre and returns home in silence – the workmen are making no progress with the shell of the building! The worker who fell from the scaffolding did not die, but he is much mutilated.

Sunday, October 5 My mother writes; she encloses newspaper clippings which report on the theatre in Bayreuth; she also tells me that E. Ollivier bears a grudge against me for my German feelings!

Tuesday, October 7 There comes from the Liszt Committee in Pest an invitation to me and R. to attend the ceremony marking my father's 50 years of professional activity[1]. R. very vexed about it, I still undecided whether I shall *have* to go. Best of all is that R. is remaining true to his vow of working every day on his score.

Wednesday, October 8 R. is very unwell, he forces himself to work, which worries me, what with his headache, his sore foot, his abdominal troubles, and on top of all those his depression arising from our situation. The single purest joy is our Siegfried, a ray of cheerfulness. – A visit from the dean, who first of all reports that the Crown Prince spoke at length and significantly about R. with the mayor, calling him the first 'to have represented the German ideal in art.' Then he announces the arrival of a Herr von Thon (with wife), who is suggesting a banker who wishes to put money into our undertaking! ... This couple does in fact arrive during the afternoon. Baron von Thon is a delegate to the synod and a district magistrate as well as a member of the Wagner Society in Regensburg; both make an excellent impression on us. – Can we really count on help?

Sunday, October 12 In the afternoon we go to the railway station to meet Marie Schleinitz, who in her charming way is paying us a visit. She has just seen and heard Hans in Munich and tells us wonderful things about his playing, but he is still capricious in his moods; he boasts, however, of having put aside a fortune for his children! – Letter from my father in Rome, with the programme of the festivities. My father apparently expects me to go.

Monday, October 13 Fine morning, I drive with our friend to the Eremitage, which looks very delightful, and after that lunch at home with the mayor and friend Feustel, who is not downhearted in spite of the bad state of things; he urges R. to go with him to Munich and to present himself to the

---

[1] His first appearances as pianist (at the age of 11) were in Vienna, Pest and Pressburg in 1822–23.

King – he says the last word has not yet been spoken in this affair. God knows! ...

Tuesday, October 14 Drove with our friend to Neumarkt and there said goodbye to her; in the meantime R. completed his page of orchestration.

Thursday, October 16 R.'s bad foot worries me greatly. We discuss my possible journey to Pest, a great disruption in our lives. But R. is working regularly. Visit to the new house, the conservatory has been stocked and the fine green plants give me much pleasure, though as with all property the sight makes me melancholy. A word from Baron Thon, mentioning by name the banker Haymann in Regensburg, who is willing to make a loan against security. I do not much trust Israelite aid.

Monday, October 20 Attempt to design a hat for myself from the dreadful fashions, which really seem to have been created just for disreputable women. No reading in the evening, but a Haydn symphony (in D) played as a piano duet with R., great delight in it.

Friday, October 24 Letter from Herr Haymann – he much regrets! ... R. promises Herr Feustel to go to Munich with him around November 15 – Berlin surprises us with a royalty payment of 234 thalers for two performances in the off season, and Batz reports that a settlement is being worked out with the management with regard to Wiesbaden, Kassel and Hanover.

Sunday, October 26 My father relieves me of the necessity of travelling to Pest; R. both glad and sorry about it, says that I have to give up so much on his account! So a heavy sacrifice on my part is over and done with. R. still not well and cannot work – in the morning we go for a walk together; in the afternoon first long rest in the conservatory!

Monday, October 27 In the evening started Meurer's life of Luther[1] – great pleasure in the true German character, in which we recognize Goethe, Beethoven and all that we venerate among the Germans; and here it is not a game, it concerns the very nerve centre of life.

Tuesday, October 28 Talked with R. about Buddhism and Christianity. Perception of the world much greater in Buddhism, which, however, has no monument like the Gospels, in which divinity is conveyed to our consciousness in a truly historic form. The advantage of Buddhism is that it derives from Brahmanism, whose dogmas can be put to use where science reveals gaps, so far-reaching are its symbols. The Christian teaching is, however, derived from the Jewish religion, and that is its dilemma. Christ's suffering moves us more than Buddha's fellow suffering, we suffer with him and become Buddhas, through contemplation. Christ wishes to suffer, suffers, and redeems us; Buddha looks on, commiserates, and

---

[1] *Luthers Leben*, a three-vol. biography by Moritz Meurer.

teaches us how to achieve redemption. – Professor Nietzsche sends us his 'Appeal to the Germans',[1] but who will be prepared to sign it?

Thursday, October 30 Arrival of our good friend Heckel, who tells us all sorts of curious things, for instance, of a travelling salesman who told him he would not give a cent for Bayreuth, even if he were a millionaire. 'Why not?' He liked the *first* works – *Tannhäuser, Lohengrin, Die Meistersinger* – but to build a theatre especially for *Rienzi* – no!! – In the afternoon a meeting in the street with Prof. Nietzsche[2]. He, completely outlawed, tells us unbelievable things: that the International is reckoning him as one of their own, encouraged in that direction by a writer in *Die Grenzboten*, whose article, entitled 'Herr Nietzsche and German Culture', exceeds all bounds and actually denounces our friend!

Friday, October 31 Went through Prof. Nietzsche's very fine 'Appeal' with him. Is it wise to issue this – but what use is wisdom to us? Only faith and truth can help. All too few people have come to the meeting, and God knows whether anything advantageous will come of it, but what else can we do? ... In the evening a little banquet at the Sonne with the delegates and management committee. The meeting resolved not to proceed with the 'Appeal'; the Societies feel they have no right to use such bold language, and who apart from them would sign it? All the proposals of the excellent Heckel are adopted. Herr Wesendonck creates real indignation by sending proposals and demands (cost estimates, etc.) which amount to a vote of no confidence in the management committee, whereas this committee has achieved wonders with the little money it has. The evening ends merrily.

Saturday, November 1 Today the sun is shining, and yesterday the poor patrons had to view the theatre in the worst weather! We shall have to get used to these edicts of Fate. Today there is another meeting of delegates, and they adopt a proposal by Dr. Stern[3] for a simple appeal for subscriptions.

Sunday, November 2 All Souls' Day! I go to confession and Holy Communion – the dean administers it. – Departure of friend Nietzsche, who is causing us profound concern. – I am very tired all day and cannot go out in spite of the splendid weather. Boni also indisposed, she keeps me company; agreeable impression of the settled nature of this child, whose strength and harmony lie in her reserve. Read *Luther*.

Monday, November 3 R. writes to the King, once again appealing to him for a guarantee and announcing his visit on the 15th. – At the house, which is now making progress; I in the conservatory until moonlight falls on the leaves.

[1] An appeal for aid for the festival theatre.
[2] Both Heckel and Nietzsche were in Bayreuth to attend a meeting of patrons to discuss the financial problems regarding the festival theatre.
[3] Adolf Stern (b.1835), professor of literature, wrote the 'simple appeal' referred to here.

Sunday, November 16 R. is trying to clarify the origin of the name Parzival. He was looking for it in Greece, since the Celts (Germans) came first of all into contact with the Greeks. – Lusch asks me questions about Hell, Heaven, the soul; I answer as best I can, directing her to the Gospels; R. says I can describe the soul as the Immutable by contrasting it with the mutability of appearances. Regarding the way babies come into the world (does God mould them? – but the girls in school were saying the mothers are always ill at the time), she asks Malwida, and I tell her to say to Lusch: From their mothers, as with animals.

Tuesday, November 18 R. makes plans for a journey to Munich to speak with Councillor Düfflipp, since he does not reply. R. is finding work very difficult because of his constant preoccupations. – In the evening Luther's marriage, very fine; R. returns again and again to his idea of a comedy on the subject. 'One must have seen Dürer's women (in Bamberg) to understand these marriages. Certainly there is nothing in them of the searing love which devours the man, as in *Tristan* or in *Antony and Cleopatra*, where we have the additional knowledge that the woman is bad. It is this love which Brünnhilde exalts, and it was very remarkable that in the middle of my work on the *Nibelungen* I felt the need to deal exhaustively with this one aspect, which could not be dealt with fully in my huge poem, and so I worked out *Tristan*. All of it subconscious, just always driven on. Among the Rhine-maidens love is just a phenomenon of Nature, to which it returns in the end, after, however, having been turned through Brünnhilde into a world-destroying, world-redeeming force.'

Thursday, November 20 R. off at eleven in the morning with Herr Feustel and wife – God's blessing on him! The house seems empty and dreary. At one o'clock wrote to R. Spent the evening with Malwida, started on Köppen's history of Buddhism[1]. Deeply impressed, definition of Brahma!

Friday, November 21 Malwida to lunch, talked a lot with her about the children. Will my desire for one of them to devote herself unselfishly to her father be realized? I doubt it. They will not believe my teachings, will make their own mistakes, and not seek the bliss of bearing the cross rapturously on their shoulders – will not *choose* that. How sad it makes me to know that my experience can spare them nothing!

Saturday, November 22 R. home at three o'clock, I meet him with Fidi. He is glad to be back. – He was given hope of a favourable decision from the King by Councillor Düfflipp, who received him very affectionately. But of the King himself alarming news: every day he has some inspiration, and has hardly been persuaded out of it when he returns to it again. He no longer goes out of doors, takes his midday meal at seven o'clock, has 60 candles lit in one small room, in which he remains, eating again at eleven o'clock

[1] A two-vol. work by Fr. Köppen, 1857–59.

and going to bed at 2 a.m., then, since he cannot sleep, taking pills! He would see nobody except his equerry, who conveyed a reprimand to the adjutant, Count Hohenstein – whereupon the latter resigned his post! . . . Worry upon worry. I cannot sleep a wink.

Sunday, November 23 Melancholy morning, I try to persuade R. not to hasten the furnishing of our house by taking out loans. – He does not receive this well, finding me timid. This makes me weep, for I have absolutely no more wishes of my own, and am only haunted by cata-strophes which I see looming on all sides. I try hard to get a grip on myself and hope to give no further impression of melancholy. Malwida's indispo-sition is also worrying us. The children (Daniella and Blandine) present a puppet play, Boni surprising us with her wit and calm, Daniella excitedly directing it all. R. plays the overture and entr'acte music.

Tuesday, November 25 Arrival of my bust, which delights R.; he places it above his writing desk and sings, 'Nothing is so dear to me as the room in which I bide, for now I have my fair neighbour standing by my side.' In the evening we go to the amateur concert – *Egmont* Overture and R.'s overture (the one from his birthday).

Wednesday, November 26 R. was very dismayed yesterday by the conductor Zumpe; he had been through both the *Egmont* Overture and the Mozart Symphony with him, and the good man had taken in nothing, or he overdid it all. 'I will talk to them again about tempi,' R. says and wonders whether he was perhaps like that himself in his youth, so dense and inattentive. – He works, I go to see Malwida, and since she feels wretched in her apartment, I beg her urgently to move in with us, which (since she finally accepts) means for me some rearrangements in the house.

Friday, November 28 At three o'clock arrival of the machinist and the painter – the latter has left his sketches (the main thing!) in Passau. Annoying accident, on top of the wretched weather. Our evening conver-sation: the possibility of keeping to our opening date in '75! Herr Hoffmann's peculiar obstinacy; we ask ourselves: Is he a very significant artist, or simply a blatherer? . . . The sketches will provide the answer.

Saturday, November 29 The sketches do not arrive until three o'clock, and so two days have been wasted through carelessness. Brandt and Hoffmann inspect the theatre and find it all in good order. – In the afternoon looked through the sketches – a fine and powerful impression, the only question-able aspect being the downgrading of the dramatic intentions in favour of an elaboration of the scenery. This is particularly disturbing in Hunding's hut, and above all in Gunther's Court, which is designed very sensibly, but is much too ostentatious. A difficult situation for R. – However, Herr Hoffmann is an earnest man, and he will, I believe, adapt himself to R.'s ideas despite his great obstinacy. Spent the evening together with Brandt and Hoffmann. Gunther's hall leads to violent debates; R. is against all pomp, and explains how he turned his back on subjects such as Lohengrin and Tannhäuser in order to do away entirely with outward pomp and present human beings without any conventional frills. – R. is very tired in the evening. *Die Meistersinger* has been staged anew in Berlin and received, so it seems, with tremendous acclaim.

Sunday, November 30 Looked through the sketches again by daylight. A truly beautiful impression; Valhalla depicted with consummate beauty, the sketch of the awakening of the Wala [Erda] quite wonderful. Lunch with the mayor and the painter, the latter turning out to be a cultured man who has, it seems, adopted a stiff and pedantic manner as an antidote to Viennese shallowness. But he seems to have a very great respect for R., and I think an understanding will be possible. The big question, though, is how to find the means? . . .

Monday, December 1 R. works. At lunch the painter Hoffmann, to whom I wrote a few friendly words and who is now less stubbornly insisting on everything. – We part very cordially, and he goes off to Coburg to talk to the scene painters there. He leaves us with the impression of a very decent, open-minded man.

Thursday, December 4 R. works, he has reached the Waltraute scene – and is himself shocked by his harmonic sequences. He talks about his work and says that Siegfried leaves Brünnhilde to go in search of plunder, 'for they have got to live, and so he must get tributes from a few kings.' Of Waltraute he says that she speaks to Brünnhilde not as a mere messenger, but as a person ravaged by sorrow.

Saturday, December 6 Letter to me from Councillor Düfflipp: the chapter of the Order of Maximilian has elected R. a member, and the King wants to know whether R. considers this a favour. They already elected R. 9 years ago, but he, deliberately misinformed (by Pfistermeister[1]), and not knowing that Max. Knights are elected by a chapter, refused the decoration. It caused much bad blood at the time, for the Knights of the Order, unable to assume that R. knew nothing about them, felt themselves to have been deliberately slighted. It is curious that they have come again now, and they cannot very well be refused, although this is very repugnant to R., or, rather, very unimportant.

Monday, December 8 R. is still pleased with my bust. – Yesterday I thought: If only my picture could represent me and I remain invisible, just protecting, watching, serving! The house and the building on the outskirts lie like a nightmare on my soul. I fear the house will lead us into expenditure beyond our means – and the theatre? . . . We hear nothing about the subscriptions.

---

[1] Franz Seraph von Pfistermeister, Cabinet secretary in Munich and the man King Ludwig sent in 1864 to find Wagner and bring him to Munich; Wagner came eventually to see him as an enemy.

Tuesday-Saturday, December 9–13 I have again to dismiss a thief among the servants and do it this time without inner agitation. But the servant problem is a worrisome one – what will come of it? The church has no more influence, through its own fault. – Fidi very handsome now with his 'tousled' hair; R. worried about him, because he seems so sensitive, he feels he should soon have other boys to play with. – The two elder girls, having been taken on the ice several times, are now beginning to conduct themselves more expertly on it. Camellias in the conservatory. The little ones play very nicely at acting, Loldi thinks up and sings a dirge for a deceased sister, very solemn – then immediately starts playing the clown.

Tuesday, December 16 Letter from Herr Hoffmann, he is demanding 1,500 thalers for the work so far done, and later 300 thalers a month. Herr Feustel will see whether Baron Erlanger[1] will at least pay the 1,500 thalers, having subscribed 3,000.

Thursday, December 18 R. works. In the evening a letter arrives from the district president, telling R. that he has been asked to hand over the decoration to him. With some lack of tact, it seems to me, he invites R. to visit him tomorrow morning. R. finds this very repugnant, he says he does not know how he should come to be given instructions by anyone. I beg him not to let any vexations arise from this useless affair, but to suffer it in silence. Our evening is somewhat soured by this interlude.

Friday, December 19 Visit from our friend Gersdorff, returning home from Italy via Basel; I enjoy the presence of this excellent man, who is utterly lacking in vanity, always open, truthful and serious. R., too, thinks a lot of him. He spends the whole day with us. In the evening R. reads out passages from *Henry IV*, since these eternal things always affect one like springtime, the flowers, the sunny blue sky, as if one had never enjoyed them before. R. remarks on the rare dignity and loftiness of Shakespeare's kings, then the way in which he suddenly describes a subsidiary scene, such as that between Hotspur and his wife, in loving detail, as if it were the main theme.

Saturday, December 20 R. works, he wishes to complete the instrumentation of the first act by Christmas. In spite of much indisposition, vexation, worry and exhausting work, he remains, thank goodness, in gay spirits and is utterly good and kind. 'With your picture (the bust),' he says, 'I worship idols while I am orchestrating – if you only knew all the things I say to you!' – Yesterday he went to fetch his decoration, today he is congratulated on it; the president – very courteous, but a very dry official – did not make a graceful ceremony out of it.

Sunday, December 21 Friend Lenbach writes expressing great satisfaction with Hoffmann's sketches. Departure of our good friend Gersdorff, who is now beginning a new career as a farmer, to some extent at our urging.

---

[1] Baron Viktor von Erlanger, a banker in Vienna.

Tuesday, December 23 Slept until nearly midday, yet despite that very tired.
R. works. In the evening I decorate the big fir tree.

Wednesday, December 24 At 5.30 p.m. distribution of presents; to me, too,
R. gives lovely gifts, some splendid Chaillou things to wear indoors, and he
is pleased that they suit me and please me. The tree, tall and wide, stays
long alight, and everyone is gay and happy.

Thursday, December 25 Richard gives me the first act of *Götterdämmerung*,
orchestrated!!! Early in the morning I hear the children in the adjoining
room, singing the '*Kose- und Rosenlied*'[1] – so touching, so affecting! Then they
come to my bedside, and Siegfried recites the poem to me! Deepest feelings
of happiness, all outward things disappear, everything inside me speaks, a
thousand voices rejoice in my soul, singing the song of love, like a thousand
birds in spring, the one and only song! – The sun is shining, I ask R. to
take me to the theatre, and he does so; planks bar the entrance to the stage,
no watchman is on hand, I clamber over them – in spite of satin and velvet
finery – and succeed amid great laughter in reaching the main stage.
Grandiose impression, the whole rising up unrestrained like an Assyrian
edifice, the pillars ranged like sphinxes below, the side wings spread out like
secret passages; the whole thing seems more past than future, yet today it
has a magnificently exhilarating effect on me. From the stage we then go
down into the auditorium, the entrance to it makes a sublime effect such
as no education can bring the onlooker; at once he will feel as if he is being
inaugurated into the mysteries. – Before lunch, after the visit to the theatre,
we went to the new house and wandered, R. and I, in the conservatory; joy
in the lovely plants, dreamlike gaiety; but it is for the children that we enjoy
it – for ourselves the burial vault would be enough, possessions do not
become us; to find each other, to be all in all to each other, and to remain
together in life or in death, that was our wish – but then came His Lordship
Siegfried! . . . In the evening I ask him to play me the *Idyll*, we think of that
morning in Tribschen, then of the *Tristan* time in Munich, all the bliss and
all the sorrow. We go to our beds, I restraining by force my overwhelming
emotion, laying the *Idyll* and the '*Koselied*' beneath my pillow before giving
myself up to gentle slumbers. A happy day.

Friday, December 26 Reality demands its rights! We reflect that there is a
debt of 9,000 florins on the theatre building, and that R. promised Feustel
to give a concert in Vienna in order to raise them – then he would no
longer bother himself about the matter. An idea comes into his mind of
applying to the Emperor, requesting him to command the festival of 1875
as a German celebration of peace with France, and to allocate 100,000
thalers for it; we consider who might sign this petition. A letter comes from

[1] Cosima's name for Wagner's '*Kinderkatechismus*' ('A Children's Catechism') for four girls' voices and
piano, composed for her birthday.

Herr Hoffmann, whom Herr Feustel had referred to Herr Erlanger for his 1,500 thalers (to pay for the sketches); Herr Erlanger, like all his tribe, seeks and finds excuses; deep shame and annoyance; Judea is always the same. – Today R. writes his official letter of thanks for the decoration to the King, from whom we get nothing but silence. – Daniella has received a letter from her father in Meiningen; he sends a Christmas gift and writes contentedly of his stay in England. – At lunch, when I declared that R. now looks younger and better than he did years ago, he says, 'I once looked so blooming that I sat for a painter for a still life of fruit,' which reduces us to a state of uncontrollable laughter.

Saturday, December 27 In the morning R. plays the scene between Alberich and Hagen and looks forward to the impression it will make when Hill and Scaria sing it. 'It will have the effect of two strange animals conversing together – one understands nothing of it, but it is all interesting.' – In the afternoon arrival of our good Richter, whom we are overjoyed to see again.

Sunday, December 28 At midday Richter brings the newly discovered tenor, Dr. (of law) Glatz[1], a tall and imposing young man with a powerful voice, withal independent and determined not to adopt the usual stage career – our Siegfried, perhaps? – In the evening all our musicians together; the *Idyll* is played; Richter distinguishes himself with his rapid grasp of *Götterdämmerung*. Discussion about the fact that of all the instruments the harp is the only one of which R. does not know the technique; but I beg him not to have a single note of his harp passages altered, since I find the virtuosic entrance of a harp very repugnant. Only for the rainbow in *Das Rheingold* does he wish it to be altered: 'The harp should give the effect of a cloud of incense.'

Wednesday, December 31 In the evening the children dance around the tree, while R. plays waltzes from *Die Meistersinger* and by Strauss and Lanner. – Great annoyance from the report in the newspaper that J. Brahms received the Order of Maximilian at the same time as R.; R. realizes that the chapter nominated him only so that they could make the award to 'that silly boy'. He wishes to send it back, but calms down eventually.

[1] Franz Glatz, discovered in Budapest by Richter, had no previous stage experience.

1874

Thursday, January 1 The bells summon in the New Year; we go for a drive. Family lunch; thoughts of past years: 'We have endured difficulties enough for each other's sake.' Thoughts of R.'s father Geyer and how he loved giving them presents. Thoughts of our undertaking, the silence in which we shall wrap ourselves if, as seems likely, the King does not help us. At coffee after lunch I see a raven, which settles with outspread wings on the tree before my window and then soon flies away. R. says it is a good sign, the raven was the chief bird of the Germans. Nevertheless, the sign alarms me. In the evening R. is seized by a shivering fit, I put him to bed, the doctor comes and hopes it will lead to nothing worse.

Friday, January 2 The night passed tolerably, but in the morning R. is very weak and in need of the utmost care. I take over the supervision of the house and settle myself in the conservatory both morning and afternoon. The plants have a very calming effect on me, but at home I find R. still weak and depressed. The uncertainty in which the King has left him absolutely oppresses him. In the evening we at last take up our *Luther* again.

Sunday, January 4 In the morning I said goodbye to Malwida, who, constantly indisposed, wants to consult a doctor in Munich, to find out whether she should move to the south. Shall we see her again? The parting fills me with great melancholy. I give her a few lines for Councillor D. With indescribable feelings I see the days of this first week pass by without a favourable decision, which means that the orders cannot be placed and in consequence the year '75 not adhered to. R. wants to announce the cancellation of the performances.

Monday, January 5 R. again had a bad night, and I am literally afraid of being together with him; talking about the affair oppresses him as much as not talking about it; I see him literally succumbing, and there is nothing I can do! The 'cloak of misery' has been donned again, God help us; and in addition there are material worries about my little bit of capital, which my mother still withholds from me, the interest on it has not yet been paid to me.

Tuesday, January 6 At four in the morning R. comes to me, saying he cannot sleep; since I am also awake, we discuss a circular to the patrons, relating all our experiences, then the decision to abandon the performances entirely, since 1875 cannot be adhered to. R. cables Dücflipp, saying he must be told yes or no. A difficult decision! But at breakfast R. seems downright relieved, he says at five o'clock he even wrote a verse: Since Germany won't give us the means, I can't let Hoffmann paint the scenes. Malwida writes, Dücflipp cables – the King refuses to give the guarantee! . . . In the afternoon to the conservatory again, supervising from there. Returning home, I find R. in consultation with friend Feustel: 25,000 florins are still outstanding on the theatre. The problem: how to procure them, how to get money and at the same time not deceive the people. R. first sends a telegram to Heckel – he must be told the truth.

Wednesday, January 7 At breakfast R. says, 'You'll be hearing *Der Ring des Nibelungen* after all.' He has the idea of not setting any deadline, but simply saying that if 200,000 are available, well and good – but do not imagine it will come along of its own accord. In the evening, impelled by I know not what, I say to R., 'But how lovely it is, to be deserted by everybody!' R. grasps this exclamation eagerly and says, 'Oh, yes, it is the only worthy state to be in.' Yesterday and today I put my whole being into a prayer: to die at the same time as Richard! To wander this earth only so long as my gaze can meet his, my hand hold his, my poor spirit look upon and grasp his spirit! R., to whom I state this quite simply, replies, 'We shall go on living together for a long time yet.' – Letter from Bucher, saying that the Prince has indeed read the pamphlet and given it to his minister Delbrück for an appraisal. It seems not entirely impossible that he will take over the guarantee, as I had requested, overcoming my great repugnance against making any appeal to my friends.

Thursday, January 8 In the afternoon Heckel, joined in the evening by Feustel; we learn only now what Councillor D. told Feustel back in December – that the King was incensed with R. because he had not set Herr Dahn's hymn to the King to music; Herr Dahn had sent R.'s letter to him to the King, and the latter was very incensed by it and had in consequence refused the guarantee!!![1] R. is requested by our friends not to make any public statement, but to try to wipe out the debts by means of concerts (!!). Heckel should approach the Grand Duke of Baden, asking him to form a consortium of princes, which should then issue an appeal to the Reich.

Friday, January 9 R. writes to the King about the F. Dahn affair. He writes that, if his royal benefactor requires music from him, he hopes he will allow R. to write his own verses for it; also that he did not pay any particular attention to Herr Dahn's poem, since he gets scores of such requests, and anyway he could have found no melody suitable for such an archaic verse

---

[1] A poet, Felix Dahn, had sent Wagner an ode addressed to the King, suggesting Wagner set it to music; Wagner wrote him a letter of refusal.

metre. At the same time he told the King of his decision to abandon the performances. – Everything ridiculously unpleasant we now call *Felix Dahn*. When one considers that the granting of a guarantee hangs from a thread such as this, what an insight one gets into the ridiculousness of this world!

Saturday, January 10 Wrote in the conservatory, in brilliant sunshine, an indescribably comforting spot – no book in the world could, I think, have such a good effect as these green leaves stretching out soothingly and caressingly towards me. – Today R. cut Loldi's toenails! And says: 'I so much enjoy doing such things for a child.'

Wednesday, January 14 R. tells me he has been thinking of doing the *Idyll* for a large orchestra, but it would not come out so well; I tell him I should be appalled to see this work handed over to the general public. In the evening read the Upanishads[1]; I feel that no one who has not worked through the philosophy of Schopenhauer would be able to understand their secrets, and I see why our brother-in-law Brockhaus spoke of 'some insane Brahman who wrote this thing.' Salvation and pleasure as opposites – this strikes one like lightning. We talk about the divine wisdom of these people who, in order to express something which cannot really be expressed in words (like, for example, that reason stands above the heart – yet without a turbulent heart genuine reason is not attained, though a turbulent heart by itself is evil) invented all these gradations – Atma, Purusha, the endless subdivisions. Through this wisdom they really have succeeded in building a religion on abstract conceptions which an ordinary person can never hope to understand. We cannot read much of it at a time. – And after a short pause, led there by the winter of our discontent, we pick up *R[ichard] III* and cannot get away from it – not even in our conversation! Among other things that interjection – 'Margaret.' 'Richard!' 'Ha!' – is one of those lightning flashes which sharply emphasize the truthfulness of a scene, while making the poet himself even more invisibly elusive. What was he like, this incredible man before whose might all must vanish?

Thursday, January 15 R. writes Heckel a letter for the Grand Duke of Baden and says, 'One does this, but one has no faith, no belief in it all – one does it just so as to have left nothing untried.'

Saturday, January 17 R. had a bad night with wild dreams, among others that Frau Wesendonck showed him a newborn child, remarking that in her case this does not cease; then, with the utmost naïveté, she gave the child the breast; it had a curious decoration on its head and looked precocious, making R. think it had white hair. 'How naïve people are here!' R. said. Then a great, powerful hawk attacked the mother and child, R. drove it off, but it kept swooping down on them again. – Then he woke up. – After that he met me in the street in Paris, dressed in black and looking very pale and

---

[1] System of Brahminic philosophy.

sad, and he wanted to take me home. 'But, my God, Minna is still alive – she'll again say she has nothing in the oven. A stop must be put to this nonsense.' – In silence we had then started on our way, losing ourselves in the streets, which became more and more confusing. – In the evening played Beethoven quartets with R.; the composure of the heart spoken of in the Upanishads is thus miraculously attained, and on this composure a ringing delight floats as on clear, still water. Here is *Brahman*, devoutness achieved, this is non-existence and one is close to the All-Seeing.

Tuesday, January 20 R. is orchestrating the second act – this the best news of the day! Utterly springlike today, starlings twittering in the palace gardens.

Friday, January 23 In America a second edition of *Beethoven* is being published, and it is described there as one of the most significant books of our time – a very remarkable sign! The people in New York also send 2,000 thalers, the people in Vienna 600, Lenbach 300, and Antonie Petersen[1] five pounds – in all about 3,000 thalers. – All the same, next to nothing when one thinks what is needed.

Saturday, January 24 The long-awaited royalties from Berlin arrive at last – it seems Herr von Hülsen always sends them with chagrin, and R. must always cable for them. For this quarter they amount to 1,400 thalers, and show that R.'s works produce the biggest receipts. Today he hit upon the idea of suggesting to Schott six overtures, which he intends to start writing next year, against an advance of 10,000 florins. Once before he promised me to write these overtures – 'Lohengrin's Ocean Voyage,' 'Tristan the Hero', and 'Dirge for Romeo and Juliet'. The others he does not yet know.

Sunday, January 25 Prof. Hoffmann writes that people are jamming his studio to see the sketches. He also asks about the commission for them. How and what is one to reply? I have to admire R. for remaining so cheerful amid all the depressing worry and uncertainty.

Tuesday, January 27 Went to the house early; when I return home, R. shows me a letter from the King which he did not wish to read – I should tell him what it contains. I see at once that it is very friendly. The King promises never to give up his mission in life, and says the delay was forced on him only by the state of his purse. He treats Prof. Dahn's poem as sycophancy and knows that R. has better things to do than to embellish such verses. But still we are left in uncertainty – will he grant the guarantee or will he not? . . .

Wednesday, January 28 The question which was this morning tormenting R. is whether he should write to Prof. Hoffmann in Vienna that the whole undertaking has been indefinitely postponed, or whether, relying on the

[1] Daughter of Karl Petersen, chief of police in Hamburg, met during the conducting tour in January 1873.

King's letter of yesterday, he should count on the guarantee. While I am paying some calls he makes up his mind, but I do not dare ask him in what direction; I am just glad to distract him a little, if it lies in my power.

Thursday, January 29 R. works on his second act. After lunch he goes to see Herr Feustel, who cannot understand the King's remarks about the Dahn poem, since in Councillor Düfflipp's office he had seen telegrams reporting that the King was feeling extremely ungracious towards R.! – The bank in Coburg is prepared to advance 50,000 florins on the spot, once the guarantee is given! Well, at least the men have now been paid 10,000 florins. – Today it was also my lot to be put to a fearful test. When the two elder children came upstairs to say good night, I joked with Blandinchen about coming times. As the children leave, I notice that Daniella is saying something and call Blandinchen back to ask about it. 'How boring,' is what she had said about my joke! . . . R. horrified, I preserving silence, bidding my soul to be calm, and in this calmness stammering a prayer of submission. All I can do here is accept. With distress I now realize that blame lies not in my divorce from Hans, but in my marriage to him. Profound effort to control my soul, to raise it to the level of thanking God for my punishment, resolve not to let the cheerfulness fade which is so vital to R.; holding back my tears, praying!

Friday, January 30 I find it difficult to speak to R. about anything except what happened yesterday! . . . But I do not let my sorrow show. Daniella, returning from school, wants to beg my pardon for having so offended me, but I reply that she does not have to beg my pardon, since she had not offended me; I told her that when she misbehaved, lied or was impertinent, I should continue as before to punish her; but when, after a day spent in harmony, she makes such a remark about an affectionate little joke addressed to her sister, I could make no punishment, no reproach – for me it had been a revelation, and on this level I could only commune with God, who bestows both blessings and curses. I allow her to work beside me, treat her as usual, and bear no bitter feelings against my lot, no grudge against my child, and believe I have thus achieved understanding. R. wants her to be sent away, but I fight against this, for I believe that despite everything she is happier here than anywhere else and that the good aspects of her character will be brought out better. If in my heart I am sorrowful and if I humbly bear this pain, perhaps I shall not be denied the blessing of seeing my child become a good person; and the fact that my way of doing things remains a mystery to her is of course of no importance to her.

Monday, February 2 Our new servants arrive – a man, his wife and three children, from Berlin. In the evening picked up our old Gibbon again after a long break, with great enjoyment.

Tuesday, February 3 To the new house in the morning, to see how the newly arrived family (complete with canary and Bible) is getting along. In the evening the copyists' group enriched by a Macedonian, Herr Lalas[1], sent by Richter (who has now become director of the opera in Pest).

Wednesday, February 4 R. is in a state of torment just now, wondering whether the date can be adhered to if the King now gives the guarantee, and he is worried about the turmoil which will result. A gloomy evening in consequence. -- My sick eyes condemn me to idleness, and I am becoming more and more turned in on myself -- at times I feel that I shall never be able to speak again.

Thursday, February 5 A letter from friend Heckel, saying the Grand Duke of Baden regrets not being able to do what R. asks, since he is convinced the step would prove unsuccessful! And Herr Wesendonck is prepared, 'with reservations', to subscribe 700 thalers to the guarantee fund. We, R. and I, cannot help laughing. 'One has done one's best,' R. says. 'I didn't expect much, but one acts as if one expects something and leaves nothing untried.'

Saturday, February 7 The sight of the theatre now actually offends me. 'Perhaps something still unforeseen will come along,' R. says, 'since the known factors on which we built have so completely deserted us.'

Sunday, February 8 The building supervisor tells us about the harshness of the foremen, who have been declaring in all the taverns that they intend to sue the management committee unless they are paid. The sum involved is now only 5,000 florins, and R. and I decide to pay them from my small savings if the King deserts us again.

Monday, February 9 Letters from Herr Schott, R. and he conclude the contract, which, in R.'s words, 'is equally honourable for both sides.' In the afternoon comes a letter from friend Feustel, saying the King has asked for a formulation of the guarantee and at the same time for an expert opinion from the management committee.

Tuesday-Monday, February 10–16 Did not write in my diary all week, my eyes being bad. Herr Schott sends the 10,000 florins, and R. reflects on the overtures: 'Lohengrin's Journey', 'Tristan', 'Epilogue to Romeo and Juliet', 'Brünnhilde', 'Wieland the Smith'. – Brandt writes that it will probably not be possible to put on the performances before '76, which is probably a good thing. – The mayor recently touched R. greatly by the way he said, 'An undertaking like this must be brought to completion; a deed so selfless as this of R.'s must receive recognition; for R. has no need of fame and does not need his name and his works spread around, etc.'

Friday, February 20 Went on the ice with the children, R. in the afternoon to Feustel's, for the conference. The King does not wish to give a guarantee, but will advance money up to a limit of 100,000 thalers; until this money is refunded, the stage decorations, etc., etc., will belong to him. . . .

---

[1] Demetrius Lalas, who later became director of the conservatoire in Athens.

R. returned from the conference in an ill humour; the committee was downhearted, because of the impossibility of keeping to the original year, and Feustel once more talked of concerts. – In short, nothing good, and especially no joy.

Thursday, February 26 R. works. From Hamburg he has received 60 thalers as the result of a concert given for the benefit of Bayreuth by the military band in Hamburg. Still very touching proofs of interest.

Thursday, March 5 Herr Gross comes in the morning to tell us that the King has signed the agreement. I write to Malwida. In the afternoon at the house. R. very worn out, he writes to Richter to find out if in three months' time he can be at his disposal (from May). In the evening the Thursday gathering; the question of hotels during performance season debated with Karl Kolb.

Saturday, March 7 R. writes to Niemann and Betz; then also to other singers (Hill, etc.); the state of the male ensemble is good, but with the women the situation is bad. In the evening R. is upset by an official letter from the management committee, asking him to keep to the year 1875 and to give concerts to this end! R. answers in great detail and also raises the question of accommodation for the patrons coming here. In the evening read Gibbon. (Sad letter from Frau v. Meyendorff, my father seems to have deserted her; R. feels no sympathy for her, he says that only genuine relationships arouse his concern.)

Monday, March 9 Today, after an interruption of several days, R. wanted to get down to his score again, but then Herr Feustel arrives with Herr Riederer[1], the latter showing not the slightest trace of any willingness to help in providing new hotels. Quite by chance a hotel owner, Herr Albert from Mannheim, arrives in the afternoon and puts forward some plans; R. takes him to see Feustel, but brings home little that is encouraging or edifying: friend Feustel declares that no corporation could be formed here to promote such things – the town is too poor. – Gloomy evening; R. did in fact manage by sheer will power to complete a page of his score, but he is thoroughly depressed by the great difficulties of his task.

Tuesday, March 10 R. at a conference with the management committee, the subjects to be discussed being the contracts with Hoffmann and Brandt, the preservation of '75 as the opening date, and, finally, accommodation for the guests. In the end Herr Albert is brought in, and he makes such a good impression that the mood improves and agreement is reached.

Friday, March 13 Two very nice letters from the singers Betz and Niemann, who agree unconditionally to work for R. and are demanding no fee.

Saturday, March 14 We receive from the bookseller Giessel[2] the news that

---

[1] Carl Riederer, hotelkeeper at the Fantaisie.
[2] Carl Giessel, bookseller in Bayreuth and publisher of the local newspaper *Bayreuther Tagblatt*.

19 letters written by Richard and his wife between the years 1860 and 1867[1] are being advertised for sale in the *Reichsanzeiger* – with the comment that they are highly interesting! What can this mean? – I suspect Malwina Schnorr[2], who, probably egged on by Munich, has chosen precisely this time to publicize these things – she was an intimate friend of ours. This, God knows, will certainly put an end to our being granted credit! R. turns to the lawyers for help, but there seems little hope of taking any effective steps, and there is nothing for it but to put up with this new piece of malice. – In the evening R. reads me a long letter from him to his first wife; dismal to see how he strove in vain to bring this low-minded woman into a nobler frame of mind; in the margin of his letter, which from this point of view is truly sublime, she has written in her distress: Schopenhauer lies. Shabby and crude!! – In the evening a melancholy prayer – who would not grow weary on this hard path?

Monday, March 16 Early this morning a visit from friend Feustel, who has at last received friend Brandt's calculations and again plunges us in gloom. – I feel it as a true liberation when R. reads me some scenes from *The Tempest* in the evening. (Mimi Schl. writes about an approaching auction of works of art in aid of Bayreuth.)

Sunday, March 22 The bookseller is offering the letters for 100 thalers, which we do not have at present! But there is no other protection against such indiscretions. We consider the question from all angles and finally decide to buy the letters.

Tuesday, March 24 Perfect spring weather, but R. unfortunately not well, he cannot work. The dean said today that, whenever R. is spoken of, it is only the Jews here who react bitterly. I read some quotations from a novel by [Benjamin] Disraeli – how he claims for Israel all the great men in art, science, even religion (the first Jesuists, he says, were Jews). A very curious phenomenon.

Thursday, March 26 The letters arrive from Strassburg, completely harmless; now we can be prepared for constant black-mail, but all the same I am happy to have these letters from the earliest times.

Friday, March 27 R. is feeling better, he has slept well and is in consequence cheerful; he notes with amazement the hairless whiteness of his skin (Fidi has the same), and says that Goethe and Byron were said to have been similar.

Saturday, March 28 The young trees I asked to have sent from Tribschen have arrived – a spruce, to be planted on the grave, a fruit tree, two lindens – I receive them with great emotion; happy the person who has a place that

[1] The dates are clearly wrong, since Minna died in 1866, and later Cosima refers to them as 'letters from the earliest times'.

[2] The first Isolde and widow of Ludwig Schnorr von Carolsfeld (the first Tristan); Wagner had since quarrelled with her, after she attempted to stir up trouble with the King over his relations with Cosima.

is sacred to him, a nirvana, a land free of delusions! – 'That will be the day,'
says R. 'Everything will be all right, and the simple fact of your existence
is my guarantee, it keeps me alive.'

Wednesday, April 1 We talk of Bismarck and the present situation, hoping
for a dissolution of the Reichstag. 'We might at a pinch have a German
Reich, but we have no German nation. In France, on the other hand,
everyone is a Frenchman, held fast in the vice.' R. wishes Germany to have
a completely different form of representation. – God knows how we came
to speak of Minna. He says what drove him to marriage was in part the fact
that he had approached her very thoughtlessly and had then perceived that
she was a respectable person and that relationships with others which he
had believed to be dishonourable had in fact been quite honourable ones.
'The difference in intelligence is the worst of it,' he says. 'Persons of
different character attract and complement one another, but when the
intelligence cannot keep pace, then the character, too, becomes demor-
alized. Also, I lacked a maternal home to which I would have been glad to
return; my marriage was a sort of emancipation.'

Thursday, April 2 We are both very concerned about the illness of our old
Rus; the poor huge dog is groaning pitifully, and the veterinary surgeon says
it is rheumatism. – A schoolteacher, a cantor in Soest, sends us 80 thalers,
the proceeds of a concert in support of Bayreuth – very touching. – In the
evening R. goes to the Thursday gathering, but only, as he says, to give
himself the walk home, since he feels too indisposed, downright suffocated.
– He told me that when he went out in the garden today he forced himself
to walk slowly, and suddenly his cramp vanished, and he realized how much
good it would do him if only he could take everything more calmly.

Saturday, April 4 Some letters; governess affairs, and a very melancholy
one from our friend Nietzsche, who is tormenting himself. R. exclaims, 'He
should either marry or write an opera, though doubtless the latter would be
such that it would never get produced, and so would not bring him into
contact with life.' – R. takes his first bath in the house and feels so good
in it and so well after it that he comes home a different man. A cheerful
lunch in consequence.

Tuesday, April 7 Everybody ill, even I plagued by a headache and
hoarseness. R. divinely good, takes over all commissions for the house and
remains in a good, cheerful mood.

Friday, April 10 Herr Peters-Friedländer[1] writes of the continued success
of the '*Kaisermarsch*' and offers 5,000 marks for an overture! And yesterday
Herr Eckert wrote to say that this quarter had brought in 1,750 thalers in
Berlin, houses continually sold out and prices raised.

Thursday, April 16 Still under house arrest, and the house looking like a

---

[1] Julius Friedländer, proprietor of the publishing firm C.F.Peters.

desert, since curtains and furniture have already been removed. R. does not work, but writes to the King's secretary, 'amiably' complaining that though a great favour has been granted him, he has received no word about it. – The well in the house at last made to function with a pump, a lot of chickens in the yard; besides this a barometer purchased and an excellent gardener acquired: Konrad Rausch, who himself looks just like an old root.

Saturday, April 18 I am again confined to my bed and am now a completely useless member of the family! – I ask R. to bring me *Woodstock*, and he is glad that I wish to read it, saying, 'I was thinking only recently that history is only enjoyable in the hands of an artist such as W[alter]Scott; otherwise it is the dreariest, most forbidding thing possible.' – R. has been much distracted from his work today and has decided to write the last page tomorrow. And so it is: the last thing written in the old house is '*bei des Speeres Spitze*'.[1] From the 19th to the 28th all the exertions of moving, during which I receive a terrible blow with the news of Marie Muchanoff's mortal illness and awful pain...

Many treasure from the rich contents of mind and heart are now lost to this book for ever, since, numbed by the shock and in any case overworked, I only take up my pen again in the new house on 29th. But isolated details I can still note down. R. packs his books away, and we keep out only Shakespeare, the Indian proverbs and Schopenhauer. The last of these was the only one to which I could listen on the day I received the news that my friend was dying. Then we read *Julius Caesar*, which always impresses me as the most tragic of all tragedies. – The last letters I receive in the old house are from my mother and E.O[llivier]; the former cannot send me my 40,000 francs, and the latter will not return my jewellery (left with my sister Blandine)! – At last –

Tuesday, April 28 – move into the new house! It is not yet finished, far from it, but we shall conquer. Nice lunch at the Feustels'; at four o'clock consecration of the dining room with a conference among Herr Hoffmann, Brandt, Brückwald, the management committee, and the Brückner brothers[2], scene painters from Coburg. At Prof. Hoffmann's suggestion, the task of preparing the scenery according to his sketches is entrusted to these two. R. tells me about the fine mood which prevailed throughout, and how everyone was filled with a spirit of complete dedication to the cause. The house could have been accorded no finer consecration. Cosy supper; the three little ones, Eva as leader, thank us for having given them such nice rooms. Fidi has a room of his own. Moonlight; going out on the balcony, R. and I see the grave, and he christens the house '*Zum letzten Glück*' ['The Final Happiness'].

[1] 'On the point of this spear': sung by both Siegfried and Brünnhilde in the oath-taking scene (*Götterdämmerung*, Act II, Scene 4).
[2] Max (b.1836) and Gotthold (b.1844).

Wednesday, April 29 Disturbed night. In the morning another conference, contracts signed, cordial leave-taking from all participants. Our first lunch, very happy and gay, all in good health. I pick up this book again after a break of ten days. Heavy on my heart lie the mortal sickness of my distant friend and the report in a newspaper that Hans has fallen ill in Moscow! Early to bed.

Monday, May 4 R. wanted to work today, but he had given his last page to the copyists, who are now living in the theatre, and he takes a walk there. The young people are freezing, but are proud of consecrating the building! – In the afternoon R. reminded me that I had always wished him to christen the house, and now he had a name for it – 'Wahnfriedheim.' There was a place called Wahnfried[1] in Hesse, he said, and this juxtaposition of the two words had always touched him, it was so mystical[2]. – We drink our afternoon coffee in the hall, which is very resonant. Yesterday the children sang the *Kose- und Rosenlied* and '*Freude schöner Götterfunken*' down to us from the gallery as we sat below, with very moving effect. – Early this morning R. said to me: 'I regret very much not being able to show you my symphony[3]. Mendelssohn probably destroyed it – it's possible that it revealed to him certain things which he found unpleasant.' In the evening *J.Caesar* again. The children's first bath; much laughter.

Tuesday, May 5 Today, when I voice my concern about the very enlarged household we are now running, R. says: 'Wait and see, it will all be right – for Fidi, too. I would have to be ousted by a new opera composer, meaning that my things were no longer performed, but I do not think it will come to that.' Again R. did not manage to work today.

Friday, May 8 As we are drinking our after-lunch coffee in the hall and he is looking at the pictures, R. says: 'What a strange night that must have been when Wotan subjugated Erda! That is my own invention entirely – I know nothing about Zeus and Gaea, for instance, and nothing struck me in another poet, the way we are sometimes much struck by some feature which escapes other people. The night when Brünnhilde was begotten – it can only be seen as something divine; the urge to subjugate this prophetic woman, to learn all from her! Such outbreaks of natural force I have witnessed in the animal world – our only analogue for the divine is in the animal world.' – Soon afterwards he exclaims: 'Well, who would ever have thought that I would one day be sitting here with you in such comfort! And so whatever it was that put an end to our endeavours in Munich was for the best; it was the working of some awesome Will, which did not wish to see our love spoiled and destroyed, as would have happened in favourable

---

[1] In fact, Wanfried.

[2] '*Wahn*' has many shades of meaning in German: 'madness', 'illusion', 'delusion'; '*Friede*' means 'peace'.

[3] His Symphony in C Major: after its performance in Leipzig in 1833 Wagner sent the score to Mendelssohn, who never returned it.

circumstances, because it knew that such a love would not occur again and must therefore be put to use. It led us towards our union along cruel paths, telling itself, 'Never mind, they will bear it.' And that's why I believe I shall live with you for many, many years.' 'Nobody knows how much I love you – not even you yourself,' he cries out to me as we part.

Monday, May 11 Now Herr Schott has died in Milan[1].

Wednesday, May 13 Still arranging rooms! – R. receives some more proofs from Basel, which he finds very opportune, since he still – alas! – cannot get down to his score. – As the evening ends I say to R., 'I should like to be with you on a lonely island.' 'And so we really are,' says R. 'I am now living after my death – that's something one must achieve. It happened to our good Haydn, who really died when Mozart arrived on the scene but after Mozart's death wrote his best things and also enjoyed his life. For me, too, how dead the world is! Heavens, when I think of my Uncle Adolph[2]! I should have been proud to introduce you to him, to say to you: This is the race from which I stem. The fine and gentle tone of his speech, the noble and free form of his mind; he was a genuine product of the school of Goethe.' He glanced through his biography and, astonished at all the detail in it, observed that he had only remembered it all in order to tell me about it.

Thursday, May 14 Visit from our good mayor, who is clearly pleased to see such a handsome house in Bayreuth. R. says that never before has he been on such good terms with the police. – In the evening read the first act of [Shakespeare's] *Titus Andronicus* with some distaste.

Friday, May 15 We talked at breakfast about *T. Andronicus* and wondered whether it is genuine. Then about our particular favourites among the plays. R. says that when we last read *Lear* the tremendous mounting tension, the coming and going, the scene division, the tremendous rapidity combined with an overall leisureliness had made quite a unique impression on him; otherwise *Othello* lay closest to his heart. For me *J. Caesar* – I myself do not know why – remains, not my favourite (how can one speak in that way?), but at any rate quite peculiarly affecting. – I receive a letter from Herr Muchanoff, asking me in his wife's name not to come to Warsaw; at the same time he tells me about her terrible agony. This oppresses me deeply. – In the afternoon a telegram arrives from my friend, and I literally creep away to weep!

Friday, May 22 The children, all by themselves, stick 61 candles on R.'s bathtub and surround it with wreaths and bunches of flowers, merry laughter about it all. Doves fly out of the loft for the first time and flutter around our house. I make no celebrations for R. this year. Marie Dönhoff

---

[1] Franz Schott died on May 8.

[2] Cosima spelled the name wrong: Adolf Wagner (1774–1835), younger brother of R.'s father, was a writer and translator, a scholar who had known Schiller and in whom Wagner always took much pride.

arrives at nine o'clock in the morning, as charming as ever, and friend Gersdorff joins us for lunch. The children recite their poem[1], and only Eva gets stuck. After lunch an excursion to the theatre. – Return home in dull weather, at 8 o'clock serenade by the choral society and military band (at midday they had played the '*Kaisermarsch*' and the 'Pilgrims' Chorus' [from *Tannhäuser*] very prettily.) R. drinks with them from a silver horn and conducts them. In the middle of the most frantic rejoicings I receive a telegram – Marie is dead, she passed away peacefully. The people go off to the strains of the vulgarest of marches – thus is our sobbing accompanied here below. I keep the news from R. I had thought of her at lunchtime.

Saturday, May 23 All day with Marie Dönhoff, listening to her outpourings, my pain stays unexpressed. The painter Hoffmann arrives with his sketches, but unfortunately he has altered nothing.

Sunday, May 24, Whitsunday In the afternoon the lovely lady departs, in the evening a confidential talk with the painter Hoffmann, who is very self-willed.

Monday, May 25 Departure of friend Gersdorff and Herr Hoffmann. Dull weather, Parson Tschudi, the good man who married us, has now also died.

Wednesday, May 27 Today I have to sign a paper permitting R. to make what use he pleases of the money I have saved, for payments on the house. I am deep in worries, for R.'s condition is also causing me great concern, and I fear we might overstep our material resources. R. reproaches me for not having given him a birthday present.

Thursday, May 28 I have to prepare Lulu for her confirmation, and I address myself earnestly to her heart; my theme is the splendid and simple myth of the Fall, the misery that came from it for the world, a misery whose cure can be found only in salvation; our urges are more powerful than we ourselves, but more powerful than these urges is grace, which can change us – this miracle happens every day. The child much moved. I give her a crucifix.

Sunday, May 31 At eight o'clock to church and there until almost twelve; R. also comes, and all the children, including Fidi, deep emotion and awareness of the solemnity of religion and communal feeling. – R. did some work, but he tells me he would need a second full orchestra to express his thoughts exactly as he wished. He speaks of the theme depicting Brünnhilde's feelings as Siegfried hurries away amid boisterous rejoicing in the second act. 'With me it is not the urge to produce effects, but always to bring in different instruments to provide an interchange with the others – not just virtuoso tricks. And on top of that I am a pedant who wants to write a good score for the printers.'

Monday, June 1 In the evening the mayor and his wife and the musicians,

[1] Written by Cosima.

including Josef Rubinstein, newly arrived from Kharkov; his piano playing has made great strides.

Wednesday, June 3 My night was gloomy, I kept thinking of the term R. said to me to describe the expression which he declares is habitual to me – melancholy rapture, and I know that inside me ecstasy always turns into tears. – The manuscript of the sketch of *Tristan und Isolde*, which R. had presented to Marie Muchanoff, arrives here from Warsaw in the afternoon. A sad acquisition! . . . Children's party. R. orchestrates.

Monday, June 8 The children playing a lot with Richter[1]. Sketches from Hoffmann, who has at last made the alterations! R. works. The musicians come in the evening, and the third act of *Siegfried* is gone through.

Tuesday, June 9 In the evening the 'Nibelungen Kanzlei', as they are everywhere called here, being recognized even by the post office[2]. R. makes music with them, the great scene between Wotan and Fricka [in Act II of *Die Walküre*] 'in which the joy in living is vanquished' and the following one. During the night a raging thunderstorm, lightning flashes advance on us like fiery dragons.

Wednesday, June 10 The theatre grounds are discussed; two plans have been put forward, neither of which R. particularly likes, and he is also not happy that the restaurant is to be placed directly on the site. However, with the lack of money it is not of much moment what he likes or does not like.

Thursday, June 11 R. goes through *Götterdämmerung* with Richter in the afternoon, various parts of *Die Walküre* with the other musicians in the evening.

Tuesday, June 16 A lot of bills are coming in; I remark to R. how curious it is that I, who have never known real financial need, should be in a constant state of worry, whereas he, who has suffered so much from it, never feels any alarm. – Richter goes to see *Don Giovanni* and thinks he has discovered a Valkyrie in the Elvira[3].

Wednesday, June 17 Marvellous clear weather, yesterday R. pointed out to me the crescent moon with the evening star, that lovely celestial emblem. The marble slabs bearing the motto[4] are affixed to our house, people in the street watching curiously.

Thursday, June 18 First visitor in the morning: friend Lenbach; great joy at seeing him again. At one o'clock the little Countess [Dönhoff], friendly meeting. Lenbach delights us with his pleasure in Bayreuth, which he finds interesting.

Saturday, June 20 In dull weather accompanied the charming little Countess

---

[1] He had arrived the previous day.
[2] The copyists.
[3] Friederike Sadler-Grün, who sang Fricka and the Third Norn in the 1876 festival.
[4] '*Hier, wo mein Wähnen Frieden fand, "Wahnfried" sei dieses Haus von mir benannt*' (in Ernest Newman's translation: 'Here where my illusion found peace, be this house named by me "Peace from Illusion" ').

to the railway station. Is anyone happy? Spent the rest of the day with Lenbach. My father writes that Hans has 150,000 francs set aside for the children.

Sunday, June 21 Spoke a lot with Lenbach about a lot of things, discovered in him a noble, selfless, unusually talented person; R. is also coming to like him, about which I am glad. Departure at four o'clock, which does not come easily to any of the three of us.

Thursday, June 25 A Rhinemaiden presents herself (Frau Pauli[1] from Hanover), good voice, but no conception of enunciation. Celebrations in Nuremberg for Hans Sachs, but nobody has the idea of inviting R. to them! . . . Speeches, music, all sorts of things, but not a note of *Die Meistersinger*.

Friday, June 26 Today it is a Mime who introduces himself; R. is shocked by the unclear speech of these people, who all possess no consonants, particularly no S's.

Saturday, June 27 Arrival of the singer Scaria (Hagen). He sings some of Hagen's music straightaway, but since he knows nothing of the text, R. reads it to him (*Götterdämmerung*).

Sunday, June 28 The hall finally furnished and looking lovely. R. very pleased with it, I haunted by the constant fear that we are heading for disaster. – Scaria works in the morning with Richter, in the evening he shows us some of the results of his studying. In the afternoon visited the theatre. He admits that only now does he understand why R. wanted to build it.

Monday, June 29 An American soprano with an aria by Donizetti – she has come all the way from New York to find out from R. whether she has a voice!

Wednesday, July 1 Today Fidi made his first big outing – he walked all by himself to Herr Feustel's house, delivered a message in excellent style, and returned home with the greatest assurance.

Monday, July 6 R. wanted to start today on the 3rd act of *Götterdämmerung*, but all sorts of things cropped up, and it is not so easy to get back to the thread. – The harpist from the theatre in Pest[2] is here on a visit, and R. discusses many things with him -- what needs to be altered in *Rheingold*, *Walküre*, etc. – since R. is not familiar with the technique of this instrument. This very mannerly person is full of praise for Richter's direction of the theatre and the way it is flourishing under him.

Thursday, July 9 R. receives a letter and a photograph from Frau Materna[3], highly recommended by Herr Scaria; attractive, if you like, but so ungainly! A Hamlet-like mood overcomes him, he almost loses all inclination to

---

[1] She had sung Orfeo in the performance in Dessau that so impressed Wagner, but did not sing in the 1876 festival.
[2] Peter Dubez: Wagner took his advice and made changes in his scores.
[3] Amalie Materna (b.1844), Austrian soprano, sang Brünnhilde in the 1876 festival.

concern himself with these people! But shortly after writing the last lines, I am shown that one should never give way to vexation through making the acquaintance of three singers. In Frau [Sadler-] Grün from Coburg we have made a real discovery: the voice is lovely and her whole character reveals a good musician and a fine woman. Besides her, a good bass and a good baritone (Fasolt and Donner). The fragments from *Tannhäuser* sung by Frau Grün move me profoundly – I do not know why *Tannhäuser*, of all R.'s works, affects me most deeply. – The many things we heard before this encouraging experience had not been very pleasant; Richter tells me of an article in the *Börsencourier* which deals maliciously with the singers and the sacrifices they are making on our behalf, and which adds that I (Frau Cosima Wagner) will now no longer have any cause to doubt the keenness and self-sacrifice of these people. The last words are printed in quotation marks, so as to give the impression that I had said some such thing, thereby offending the singers and possibly stopping them from coming here. Very pitiful stuff – and the way they always drag me in, in God's name!

Friday, July 10 R. receives a letter from Councillor Düfflipp: the King sends friendly greetings to him and me. He orchestrates a page of *Götterdämmerung*. In the evening the musicians again; we learn that the article, which has been reproduced in all newspapers, has alarmed some singers, who, however much they would like to appear here, do not have the means to do so without payment. In such ways can this unholy press cause damage and difficulties!

Saturday, July 11 A prolonged and good spell of work with Lusch – literature, English, French. In the afternoon arrival of Herr Betz, who came together with Herr Brandt.

A tenor, Herr Unger[1], is introduced to us today – perhaps for Loge.

Friday, July 17 I feel quite indisposed and can hold myself erect only with an effort. Glorious weather, an incomparably fine summer, the heat not oppressive. R. works on his third act, but has many vexations, among other things the loss of the arrangement of the second act of *Götterdämmerung*, which would now be very necessary to him[2].

Thursday, July 23 The whole day and evening devoted to Herr Hill; R. reminds me that I had remarked, after the first few bars he sang in Schwerin, 'This is the most remarkable of them all.' An unusually powerful personality with great fire – in short, all the qualities R. needs. He sings to us from *Lohengrin* and *Holländer* – tells us that the Court in Schwerin is very well disposed towards both R. and me.

Friday, July 24 R. tells me how once, on an outing with Dr. Wille and Herwegh to [*place name left blank*], he became so tired that he asked the two

---

[1] Georg Unger (b. 1837), tenor in Mannheim recommended by Heckel; Siegfried in the 1876 festival.
[2] Klindworth's piano arrangement was lost on the journey from Moscow.

men to leave him at a certain point and to go on without him; Dr. Wille, believing in his insensitivity that it was simply idleness, had then given him a shove in the back and told him to get moving; R.'s rage had vented itself in a vulgar expletive, and during this scene the whole of Loge's address to the Rhinemaidens (words and music), which he had not originally had in mind, came to him. 'The way it just flies into one's mind – impossible to say how it happens! When I sit down at the piano, it is just to refresh my memory, nothing new comes to me there, I am just trying to find the things which occurred to me now and then during the most exasperating situations. This used to upset Minna, my first wife – the way I would keep calm during the terrible scenes she was making, because something had occurred to me for *Tristan* or *Walküre*.' He feels that, because in anger a person's powers are stretched, his true nature is also goaded into activity in spite of all the incongruities; only for working out one's ideas are tranquillity and a certain bodily well-being necessary, artistic work demands these things, but inspiration laughs at all difficulties as well as all comfort. Composition is a search for things which come into one's mind God knows how, where or when.

Saturday, July 25 Departure of Richter, the children in mourning rags, tears and wailing, Rus as the funeral horse!

Tuesday, July 28 Telegram from our friend Standhartner, saying he is arriving today with his daughter, preparations and reception. Great joy at seeing this dear, loyal and understanding friend again. Made music in the evening; third act of *Siegfried*. To my delight Dr. Standhartner finds that R. is looking very well.

Friday, July 31 Sudden arrival of Frau Materna, who pleases us enormously. In the evening there are 60 people gathered together, and she surprises us with the fullness and freshness of her voice and her command of her material.

Saturday, August 1 R. works, but we stay quietly at home. In the afternoon music, the divine *Meistersinger*, with memories of the times in which it was composed, and the ending of *Götterdämmerung*. In the evening alone with our friends; conversation about Herr Brahms and his damaging and bigotted influence on the educated middle classes.

Sunday, August 2 R. very unwell, he seems to have caught cold yesterday, and singing is always a great strain on him. I alone accompany our friends to the railway station; I am glad of Standhartner's love for Richard and his delight in what he calls R.'s good fortune. Comfortingly he finds him more cheerful than previously.

Monday, August 3 R. somewhat better, but still very run down. Family lunch after work with the children. R. is able to do some orchestrating. In the evening visit from Frau Materna and her husband; she is hoarse, but she is given the part of Brünnhilde – may God grant His blessing!

Tuesday, August 4 Friend Klindworth arrives to do another arrangement of the second act of *Götterdämmerung*, the first version having got lost between

Moscow and Bayreuth. He tells us many things about Hans, his moods, his present passion for England, etc. Hans is said to have the intention, on returning from his American tour, of looking around for a conductor's post in Germany – yet he is constantly abusing Germany!

Wednesday, August 5 In the afternoon a note tells us that Prof. Nietzsche is here, but lying ill in his hotel, the Sonne. R. goes there and brings him back to our house at once. He soon recovers, and we spend a cheerful evening together.

Thursday, August 6 Prof. Nietzsche tells us about a publisher in Schloss-Chemnitz [Ernst Schmeitzner] who has offered his services; he is said to be connected with the Social Democratic party, but all the same, both N. and Prof. Overbeck are accepting his offer, since they could not hope to find any other publisher in the whole of Germany; indeed, if they were to give up their professorships, they would probably be without bread, for not even a position as private tutor would be open to them. Our friend N. brings along the *Triumphlied* by Brahms[1], and R. laughs loudly at the idea of setting such a word as *Gerechtigkeit* ['justice'] to music.

Friday, August 7 Breakfast with our friends in the summer-house, conversation about Berlioz: according to R., his works could be played in open-air concerts, to which the whole cultured world would flock, but they are not easy to fit into concerts at which Mozart and Beethoven are played.

Saturday, August 8 Fine weather, a walk with R. in the palace gardens, after breakfast everybody to work – I with Lusch, R. to his score, friend Klindworth to his arrangement. In the afternoon we play Brahms's *Triumphlied*, much dismay over the meagre character of this composition which even friend Nietzsche has praised to us: Handel, Mendelssohn and Schumann wrapped in leather. R. very angry, he talks about his longing one day to find in music something that expresses Christ's transcendence, something in which creative impulse, an emotion which speaks to the emotions, can be seen.

Sunday-Tuesday, August 9–18 A succession of visits keeps me from writing in my diary. Friend Klindworth completed the piano arrangement and left on *Friday the 14th*; on the following day Prof. N. departed, having caused R. many difficult hours. Among other things, he maintains that the German language gives him no pleasure, and he would rather talk Latin, etc. During this Klindworth-Nietzsche week, Frl. Lilli Lehmann arrived with her mother and took over the organization of the Rhinemaidens. . . . *Saturday the 15th*. Frl. Brandt[2] of the Berlin Court theatre arrives and begins to study the part of Waltraute. *Sunday the 16th*. Had to receive many visitors; in the afternoon shaken to my very core by a letter from my father, enclosing one from Hans; Hans complains of the over-excited state of his nerves, he lost

[1] A choral work (Opus 55) written in 1872 to celebrate victory in the Franco-Prussisn War.
[2] Marianne Brandt (b. 1842), Austrian mezzo-soprano.

both his memory and his strength, his cure in Salzungen was a failure, dismal symptoms of over-exertion!...I struggle against low spirits and stifle my tears as best I can. In the evening Frl. Brandt, musically very good and accomplished, but very unattractive, a Viennese child of the people, without any culture. *Monday, the 17th.* R. works with Frl. Brandt and the singer [Ludwig] Kneiss. In the evening the former delighted us with her Waltraute, whose narration moves us all deeply. But the good lady does not seem best pleased at having to sing what she calls a 'small' role. *Tuesday the 18th.* At last able to work a little with the children. Invited to a coffee party, and having gone there, I am fetched away because Herr Niemann has arrived. His admiration for our house gives R. great pleasure.

Wednesday, August 19 R. unfortunately not well, he cannot stand this constant disturbance; at lunch, to which we had invited Herr Niemann, he felt so indisposed that he had to leave the table. Frl. Brandt takes her leave, and our tenor cheers R. up by telling him some Berlin jokes.

Thursday, August 20. In the afternoon Herr Voltz, whom R. had to take severely to task, for he has had the impertinence to demand a Prussian decoration for a possible consent to do *Tristan und Isolde!* Also they (Batz and Voltz) have made certain deductions to which they are not entitled. After him, Herr Schmeitzner, the publisher of the future, to whom R. suggests the purchase of Fritzsch's business (he being in great difficulties and having shown himself to be a very poor businessman).

Saturday, August 22 Yesterday I was able to make R. laugh heartily when I said that every time Voltz and Batz came to see him I thought of the murderers who come to the kings in Shakespeare's plays: 'Enter two murderers.' – In the afternoon R. does some studying with Herr Niemann and is satisfied. During the evening we have to laugh tremendously at the curious remarks of this man, by no means untalented but completely uncultured, who, not understanding that we have settled in Bayreuth, prophesies that we shall not remain here; he rashly declares that the inscription on our grave will one day read, 'Here lies Meyer Cohn' – for we would sell the house and move to Berlin! Curious mixture of profound fellow feeling and utter lack of understanding, of talent and obtuseness, wisdom and foolishness – people without roots, says R.

Monday, August 24 R. receives Herr Brandt, great annoyance caused by Herr Hoffmann, who, having finished his model three weeks ago, goes off on a trip to the Rhine without leaving his address. Lengthy consideration of whether to open the packing cases.

Tuesday, August 25 R. is warned by Herr Feustel not to open the cases, but nevertheless he does it in the evening with the help of Herr Brandt and Herr Brückner from Coburg, and he comes to the conclusion that much will have to be rejected entirely.

Saturday, August 29 R. is feeling well and is able to work a bit. But unfortunately he has many interruptions. Today the singer Schlosser[1] has come here from Munich to study Mime with R. This is the man whom R. took from a bakery to play his David [in *Die Meistersinger*]. He makes, it seems, an intelligent start, but the task of coaching him proves such a strain on R. that I feel great concern.

Saturday, September 5 R. works, finds it difficult to concentrate, however, and has to orchestrate one page twice. Last night, since he was not sleeping, R. thought about his will, worked out some details. 'I don't believe it would have hurt me to have been brought up to such a property,' R. says. I observe that he would have sold it to put his ideas into effect!

Sunday, September 6 At eleven o'clock I go to the railway station to meet Marie Schleinitz. With her until around mid-night. Affairs of the world and the emotions! –

Monday, September 7 We take our friend, who is extraordinarily pretty and interesting in her appearance, to see the theatre – it is very doubtful whether the Crown Prince will come to the performances when they materialize! – Surprised at midday by the painter Krausse, who brings with him the whole completed cartoon for the *sgraffito* on the front of our house. A matter of great alarm for me – only the day before I had discussed with R. how fortunate it was that Herr Krausse, from whom we had heard nothing for a whole year, seemed to have forgotten us! –

Wednesday, September 9 Farewell visit from our friendly sponsors[2], who were extremely kind to the children. Erection of the scaffolding [for the *sgraffito*].

Tuesday, September 22 Worked with the children, began W. Scott's *Quentin Durward* with Lusch. R. worked on his score despite a bad night, he is plagued by eczema on three fingers. At noon Herr Hoffmann and wife, R. has at last persuaded him to make a new sketch! – Regarding his score, R. tells me that during Siegfried's narration in the forest [in Act III of *Götterdämmerung*], the 'Forest Murmurs' from *Siegfried* would only be hinted at in the orchestra, for here it is Siegfried's fate which must make an impact, and a natural phenomenon must not be allowed to obscure it; there was a difference, he said, between then, when he wanted the rustling of the forest itself to make an impression, and now; and anyway he could never just repeat anything, in such cases he could not even find the right notes for the transcription.

Thursday, September 24 Still bad nights for R., so bad, in fact, that he cannot work much. I work with the children. At lunch the painter Krausse, who is working diligently on the *sgraffito*. R. is upset by our present financial situation; the theatre in Pest has still not paid the 1,000 florins (long overdue) for *Rienzi*, and there are so many bills to pay.

Monday, September 28 R. has been writing to the King for several days, his

[1] Karl (sometimes called Max) Schlosser (b.1835) sang Mime in Munich in 1869 and again in Bayreuth in 1876.
[2] Herr von Schleinitz had joined his wife the previous day.

letter grows and grows, at the King's wish he is writing a complete report on our undertaking, also on our life here. In the evening we begin on Xenophon's *Anabasis*.

Tuesday, September 29 Friend Feustel has seen Councillor Düfflipp in Munich and found him in an extremely bad mood. If another demand were made regarding the theatre, he would strenuously resist it! Feustel told us in the morning that money is very short. Great unpleasantnesses with the painters Brückner and Hoffmann, God knows how they will be settled.

Thursday, October 1 R. finishes his letter of seven full sheets to the King[1]; then starts again on his work.

Wednesday, October 7 The embarrassing meeting [of the management committee to discuss the Hoffmann-Brückner dispute] goes on until after seven o'clock; in the course of it Herr Hoffmann is confronted by R. and Herr Brandt with all his sins of presumptuousness, obstinacy and financial greed, and the whole pitiful character of the man comes to light. Although neither Herr Brandt nor the Brückner brothers are prepared to have anything more to do with him, he cannot be persuaded to terminate his contract, and he insists on being paid for a supervisory function which cannot be implemented, though he is the only person who has so far earned substantial rewards from the undertaking (5,000 thalers and copyright in the sketches). As R. says, 'He is a quibbler, both mentally and emotionally.'

Thursday, October 8 I have to be at the mayor's at nine o'clock to ask him to exert what pressure he can on the troublesome painter in order to induce him at least to beat an honourable retreat. The mayor tells me that at the conference R. had shown admirable moderation and integrity. – R. is very tired, he had a bad night, and on top of that he is much tormented by eczema on two fingers, which makes him very irritable. In the evening *Anabasis*, to help us recover from all life's muddles.

Sunday, October 11 The good professor has now got his brother-in-law to come from Vienna. The mayor told me in the afternoon of the horrible quarrels which had taken place, when the claim of honour had been utilized to improve the deal!! – Besides the Hoffmann capers, the question of Wotan's hat is causing a lot of bother: we ruled out the mythological helmet and asked our *sgraffito* artist to change it into Wotan's hat – but the task is now to find the right shape for that! Holbein and our own imaginations have helped us to a certain extent, after long vacillations and reflections. R. is now working on the 'funeral music', as he calls it.

Monday, October 12 Hoffmann has been persuaded to renounce his participation, and the management committee is to pay him 600 thalers in compensation for his inactivity during the past months! – In the afternoon Frau Hoffmann and her brother visit me, and we part in a friendly manner,

[1] The letter is nearly 6,000 words long.

she telling me that my husband's letter had worked like balm on her husband[1]. News that Hans in recovering.

Thursday, October 15 Yesterday a telegram arrived from friend Richter, announcing his engagement; we congratulate him all the more joyfully since he is said to have chosen a good and pretty girl from a good family, with means of her own. The painters Brückner arrive and say how happy they are to be rid of Herr Hoffmann. They make no demands of any kind and are now going joyfully to work. – In the evening finished *Anabasis*. R. complains to me that he still has 50 pages of his score to write!

Friday, October 16 Making provisions for my departure tomorrow[2], R. is complaining about it and making more difficult what is already difficult enough for me! But I cannot give it up.

Friday, October 23 Yesterday I returned home from Dresden; I have kept no diary of my stay there, since R. was unable to accompany me. I went to see a dentist, and also to visit the Luisenstift. It made a good impression on me, and I think I shall do well to send the girls there for a few years. On Thursday the 22nd, I left Leipzig at six o'clock with the two girls, having spent the evening there in the company of Frau v. Meyendorff; at twelve R. met me at Neumarkt with the three children. He had written to me every day, yet how much we still had to say to each other on our reunion! He was unwilling to receive anyone during my absence: 'They should know what it means when you are at home.' – Today R. is well and cheerful; he says, 'When you are away, the hook is missing on which I hang, and then I fall down in a heap.' The many interruptions make it difficult for R. to work; I write to Hans, informing him of my plan to send the children to the boarding school.

Monday, October 26 Our *sgraffito* is now all but finished. In the evening R. works on his score and strikes Gunther dead, as he puts it.

Tuesday, October 27 Our *sgraffito* is costing us more than 400 thalers; I would rather have left our house unadorned, but I say nothing about this to R., who is pleased with the ornament.

Wednesday, October 28 Yesterday evening Fidi entertained us with his account of the twelve boys ('I've had enough of girls') with whom he would one day live, and how he would examine his sisters' nails before allowing them to touch his books, etc. – Herr Runckwitz[3] came in the afternoon – trouble with the orchestra pit in the theatre, there has been some miscalculation. – News of the death of Peter Cornelius[4]; another being swept away whose fate was in many ways linked with our own! –

[1] In his letter to Hoffmann Wagner wrote: 'My one genuine wish is that you and I, two honourable men, should – for now – part in peace...As soon as the share of Messrs. Brückner in the final preparation of the scenery can be established, I promise faithfully to consider in connection with the further use of the author's rights how you are to be compensated for your share up till now.'
[2] To inspect a boarding school in Dresden, the Luisenstift.
[3] Karl Runckwitz, building supervisor on the theatre site.
[4] Cornelius died in Mainz on October 26 in his 50th year.

Thursday, October 29 R. again has a restless night; he dreamed at first that his first wife mocked him, that he then struck her and she poisoned herself, and that some drops of the poison fell on him; then that he was jealous of Lenbach on my account, and Mimi Schl. tried to console him! – I write to Peter Cornelius's poor widow.

Friday, October 30 R. sings something from the conclusion of *Götterdämmerung* and says he noticed yesterday in the way things come together in this conclusion that he can do anything when he wants to; when I reply with a laugh that I can well believe it, he says, 'No, as a rule I am very much lacking in routine – I have to want something.' – Letter from Hans, agreeing very kindly with my boarding-school idea and wishing for only one thing – the preservation of my maternal authority and the avoidance of any discordant impressions for the children. I am now asking myself whether I am doing right to send the children away from their home. Deep concern – oh, if only a God would enlighten us! . . .

Tuesday, November 3 Discussion over our finances, decide to pay for the children's board out of my allowance and to leave Hans's fund untouched. Herr Feustel has warned me that we shall have to tread very carefully before we get things in order, and my small savings have all been used up! Our evening is much enlivened by the return of our Macedonian, who brings with him a hookah for R., a Turkish rug for me, and Turkish delight for the children. – Late in the evening R. tells me the news, which he has just received, of his brother's death[1]; thoughts on the triviality of certain family relationships; his last meeting with his brother so meaningless.

Wednesday, November 4 A letter from Constantin Frantz, after many years – he reproaches R. with disloyalty, says the '*Kaisermarsch*' had stabbed him to the heart! . . . At the same time he sends two pamphlets, *The Prussian Intelligence and Its Limitations* and *Jews and the Reich Constitution*.

Friday, November 6 In the morning a discussion with R., who is quite unwilling to admit the need for caution in regard to our finances. – We are little edified by C. Frantz's pamphlet; he has no feeling for the magnificence of Bismarck's personality, and that is bad. – (Loldi yesterday rescued a hen which had fallen into the water, and Fidi sang to it a song of his own making: 'It is not so easy to die.')

Tuesday, November 10 I read yesterday in a newspaper that Hans gave a very well attended matinée recital in London; I thank Fate for shaping his career as a virtuoso so favourably; how different it might all have been, and how dismal! The month of November is always the most eventful in my life – if *Götterdämmerung* is really completed this month, then in silence and humility I shall understand you, O sublime power who guides me!

Friday, November 13 R. at his work, I at mine; at eleven he calls me down to show me how the sun is falling on my Lenbach portrait and transfiguring

---

[1] Albert Wagner died in Berlin on October 31.

it! He does not go out today. In the evening I discover him utterly depressed – as long as the children are present he does not speak, but when they have left he bursts out: 'What is the point of all this hard work with which I have burdened myself and which will only be abused? Who cares about it? Even the best of them, Liszt and Bülow, seek only to get on top of it as quickly as possible. What encouragement have I for working it all out so laboriously except the thought that it might be enjoyed? It is madness – where am I supposed to get the strength?' I try to cheer him up as far as my poor abilities allow.

Saturday, November 14 Yesterday Brünnhilde leaped into the flames, today he had some alterations to make and spent so long reflecting on them that he did not finish his page.

Wednesday, November 18 I find R. reading *Oedipus* in the evening, after his work, comparing the translation with the text. 'It is like a Persian carpet,' he says, 'a torrent of beauty – now vanished forever; we are barbarians.' We then come to the *Oresteia*, the scene of Cassandra with the chorus, and R. declares it to be the most perfect thing mortal art has ever produced.

Saturday, November 21 Thrice sacred, memorable day! Towards the hour of noon R. calls to me upstairs, asking me to bring him the newspapers; since he had yesterday complained how worn out he felt and had also assured me that he would not finish before Sunday, I thought that tiredness had prevented his working any longer, but I was too shy to ask him; to distract him, I put down my father's letter, which had just arrived, thinking – since my father was friendly towards our projected journey to Pest – thus to distract him. The noon hour strikes, I find him reading the letter, he asks me for explanations, I tell him what I intend to reply to it, and purposely refrain from looking at the page of the score, in order not to offend him. Offended, he shows me that it is finished and then says bitterly to me that, when a letter arrives from my father, all thought for him is entirely swept away. I repress my pain at lunchtime, but when R. afterwards repeats his complaint, I cannot help breaking into tears, and I am still weeping now as I write this. Thus have I been robbed of this my greatest joy, and certainly not because of the slightest bad intention on my part! '*Dass wissend würde ein Weib*' ['That a woman should learn to know'][1]. The fact that I dedicated my life in suffering to this work has not earned me the right to celebrate its completion in joy. Thus I celebrate it in suffering, bless the fair and wonderful work with my tears, and thank the malicious God who ordained that I must first atone in suffering for its completion. To whom impart, to whom complain of this suffering? With R. I can only be silent; so I confide it to these pages, to my Siegfried – that it may teach

---

[1] Brünnhilde in the final scene of *Götterdämmerung* ('The purest of men had to betray me, so that a woman should learn to know.')

him to feel no rancour, no hatred towards the miserable creature that a human being is, but only boundless pity. And thus I am glad of my suffering and fold my hands in grateful prayer. – What imposed it on me was nothing evil, let my consolation be to accept it with my whole soul, without bitterness for my lot, without reproach for anyone. – May other suffering be atoned for by this, the most unutterable of all! The children see me weeping and weep with me, but are soon consoled. R. goes to his rest with a final bitter word, I search the piano for *Tristan* sounds; every theme is, however, too harsh for my mood, I can only sink down inside myself, pray, worship! How could I spend this day more piously? How could I express my gratitude other than through the destruction of all urges towards a personal existence? Greetings, eventful day, greetings, day of fulfilment! If a genius completes his flight at so lofty a level, what is left for a poor woman to do? To suffer in love and rapture.

Thursday, December 3 Since that day I have been unable to write in my diary, I was too upset. In the evening, after I had written down those lines, R. came to me, embraced me, and said we loved each other too intensely, this was the cause of our suffering. We had to go to a party at Herr Gross's, and my face was completely tear-stained. On Sunday, the 22nd, we celebrated the completion of the work, but then R. had many business letters to attend to. On Tuesday the 24th, R. writes letters to Voltz and Batz, etc., and I receive one from my father, who says he is quite willing to take part in the concert in Pest. On Wednesday the 25th, preparations for a very large party, which we more or less owe to our Bayreuth acquaintances. – An experience with Fidi which affects his father very much: he was naughty towards his father and was for that reason sent upstairs without his supper; he wanted to beg pardon through his nurse and at the same time ask for some food, but the girl stupidly went straight to the manservant, who said he had received no orders; without saying a word or making any sort of murmur the little fellow went off to sleep, which caused his father a very restless and worried night. Next morning the boy seemed to have forgotten all about it, but one could see in his behaviour towards his father remorse and resolve. The party takes place in our house on Friday the 27th – some 50 people of all classes in Bayreuth enjoy Wahnfried. Frau Grün, coming from Coburg, sings, and everybody seems happy. – At ten o'clock departure for Coburg. Saw the backdrop of the mountain ridge at the Brückners'[1], gigantic proportions, R. says it really made him aware of his foolhardiness. On Wednesday the 2nd, home.

Friday, December 4 From Berlin R. receives a letter, signed by Emperor Wilhelm, according to which he will from now on receive royalties on *Der Fl. Holländer* as well, which is pleasant news for him.

---

[1] Scenery for the *Ring* in the Brückners' workshop.

Wednesday, December 9 In the evening we get J. Rubinstein to play [Beethoven's] 33 Variations [*on a Waltz by Diabelli*] after R. has worked out with Herr Feustel and the lawyer Skutsch a final agreement with Voltz and Batz. It is becoming increasingly clear that the two gentlemen have abused R.'s trust in a most shameless manner, and Herr Feustel, whose prudence and loyalty R. again has reason to appreciate very clearly, advises R. no longer to correspond with them directly.

Sunday, December 13 Letter from Marie Schl.: the sale in Berlin has brought in 10,000 thalers. – I at once write to thank this peerless woman.

Tuesday, December 15 R. dreamed that he had another son, a little lad one year old with fair, curly hair, and R. was delighted with the way he was flourishing and how he could already look him straight in the eye. 'This comes from the jumping,' R. says, for yesterday the children were jumping over the Persian pouffe in the middle of the *salon* and R. had shown them how to do it, himself jumping higher and better than any of them.

Friday, December 18 Good news for the undertaking from the outside world; the people in Vienna send 900 thalers, Frau Schott 300, a concert to take place under Richter's direction also promises well. Much money will be needed, too, if R. is to announce his rehearsals for next summer.

Tuesday, December 22 We talk about *Der Ring des Nibelungen*, and R. remarks how curious it was that he designed it as he did without knowing the philosophy of Schopenhauer: 'If I had known it, I should have been less uninhibited in my choice of expressive means.' He says, 'When I first read Schopenhauer, I did not understand him at all, because I was no longer armed with the strength with which I wrote my poem.' – Conference between Herr Feustel and the lawyer Skutsch, through which the fraudulent nature of Herr Batz stands fully revealed. Friend Feustel will now see how he can extricate R. from this connection.

Wednesday, December 23 From noon on occupied with the tree, I tell R. that the motto for this Christmas is; 'Nonsense, thou hast won!'[1] Our four musicians come in the evening, and, while I stand on the highest rung of the ladder, the 'Nibelungen Chancellors' hand me the various shining objects; at the same time R. is talking about the primitive Christians in Gfrörer's book[2], which he is reading with the greatest interest. Towards eleven o'clock we are finished.

Thursday, December 24 Working uninterruptedly on setting things up, which lasts from morning until five o'clock in the evening. The whole household along with the Nibelung Chancellery, 25 people in all, come through the *salon* into the hall, and all seem pleased and in good spirits. On my table lies the *Götterdämmerung* sketch! – On the previous evening I came upon R.

---

[1] Quotation from Schiller's *Die Jungfrau von Orleans*: continues, 'and I must perish.'
[2] *Geschichte des Urchristentums* by August Friedrich Gfrörer.

in tears – the 50 francs, which he can no longer send to poor Parson Tschudi, he had just sent to Vreneli, and he was recalling in deep emotion our life together in Tribschen, and thanking me for having borne so much for his sake.

Friday, December 25 In the morning I hear the *Idyll,* and after it the '*Kose- und Rosenlied*' – R. and I in tears! Afterwards I learn how R. arranged the whole secret. The orchestra from Hof was engaged, and he conducted the rehearsal yesterday in the Hotel Sonne. He tells me how well the children behaved at the rehearsal, modest and without giving themselves airs. We breakfast in the *salon,* while the musicians play pieces from *Lohengrin, Tannhäuser* and *Die Meistersinger.* Blessed day! In fair sounds and sweet words R. is telling me that I may count my birthday blessed, since he thus celebrates it. What right do I have to this crown?! . . . Lovely evening with the children, a sacred occasion. – We are transported to solemn reflections by the fact that R. met Prof. Nägelsbach, our neighbour, and, asking him how the holidays had begun, received the answer: 'Not well, for our youngest child died at ten o'clock! Just as if the little one had not wished to spoil our pleasure – we were still able to give the others their presents; when we then went up to the bedroom, the child was dying.' – Today a mason fell from the theatre building and was killed. It reminds one of Eduard and Ottilie [in Goethe's novel *Elective Affinities*], when at such times one always wishes to be and is happy, yet what can dim the happiness of love, this star that gleams through all tempests? . . . When I told R. in the evening that this had been my happiest birthday, he asked me why, and I replied, 'Because *Götterdämmerung* has been completed and thus the real worry of our life removed!'

Monday, December 28 Visit from friend Feustel concerning the affair of the mason and especially the clause in the contract whereby from the 410th certificate of patronage onwards all money coming in must be paid to the royal treasury; the concerts are also included; and money can only be requested for use on decorations and machinery! . . . Fine winter weather, though very cold. The children on the ice.

Thursday, December 31 I go to church with Fidi and Eva; '*Nun danket alle Gott*' by candlelight. All kinds of music up to midnight, a Haydn symphony, pieces from [Marschner's] *Templer und Jüdin* (in which R. points out the great talent and the complete lack of taste and style of the Germans, also that for the musician the *situation* is everything, never the words). The bells ring in the New Year, our servants come to exchange greetings, I go up to the children, who are asleep; Loldi is the only one to wake up, and we wish each other happiness.

1875

Friday, January 1 I begin my new year with a headache, I write in this book and attend to business matters, some letters and also room tidying, in order to start the year well. – I find it very strange that R. should try to recall the theme of the scherzo of his symphony at the very time I am trying to put my hands on this lost symphony for his birthday[1].

Tuesday, January 5 Spent the whole day in bed with a severe headache; great amusement over the fact that I am the first casualty of Schopenhauer as an educator; he recommends spending two hours each day out of doors, which I did on a cold day, and as a result I am now suffering!

Wednesday, January 6 R. tells me a lot more about what he is reading in Gfrörer's book, which he finds of endless interest; among other things, for example, the definition of the Trinity made shortly before Christ's birth – God the Father, masculine; the Holy Ghost, feminine; the Redeemer as the world stemming from them; will, idea and world, the world emerging from the division of the sexes.

Friday, January 8 Lohengrin has had a tremendous success in Boston, I write across the seas to see whether the Elsa there (Frl. Albany) might be won for Sieglinde[2].

Saturday, January 9 Nice letter from Baron Augusz, containing a few words from my father, who relates that Rubini, when asked in St. Petersburg whether he would sing in a concert given by my father, replied that for Liszt he would even dance, if that is what he wanted; in the same way, says my father, he would be ready to do anything for Wagner. R. has a wide variety of things to attend to (accounts, concert, orchestra, circular for the singers, etc.), while I attend to outfitting my two eldest girls, whom I shall now send to the boarding school when I go away. This is the outcome of long reflection, painful recognition. . . .

Wednesday, January 13 Arrival of the picture of Schopenhauer, in which Lenbach has wrought a real miracle! He saw Sch. once in Frankfurt, without knowing who he was; when he was later shown a photograph of the great man, he recognized the face, which had made an impression on him, and

---

[1] The Symphony in C Major, first performed in Leipzig in 1833; in 1836 Wagner sent the score to Mendelssohn, who did not return it; but see Cosima's entry for November 27, 1877.
[2] Emma Albani, Canadian-born soprano, London's first Elsa in *Lohengrin*; she did not sing in Bayreuth.

now he has reproduced its character in a unique way. Resemblance to R.: chin, the relationship of the head to the face, one eye half closed, the other wide open, the sorrowfully acute gaze which is peculiar to all geniuses. But one also finds Sch.'s whole character in it: his energy, purity, even the methodical business sense of the merchant's son. – The gift downright oppresses me – how to repay it? . . . – Spent the morning looking through bills, dismal look at our tremendous spending. – R. has a conference with Feustel and the lawyer Skutsch. Feustel says he understands that Voltz has sold everything to Batz.

Thursday, January 14 A statistical account of the incredibly small number of schools in London (compared with this country) rouses R. to a long discourse on the wickedness and heartlessness of conditions in England. In London he had seen how the police chased the poor people from one courtyard to another, never directing them to a place where they might find shelter. Among these people a woman with beautiful features.

Monday, January 18 R. tormented by his cold, an abscess in his gums about to burst. Decision to take Schopenhauer down from the wall, 'because he does not belong with Goethe, Schiller, Beethoven; the philosopher must stand alone – translating into wisdom everything the others express emotionally.' R. gets very indignant about Beethoven's being pushed into a corner: 'Who can be compared to him? What is the equal of a melody, that direct gift from Heaven?'

Friday, January 22 At noon Herr Glatz, our future Siegfried. He brings news of Richter, whose fiancée is of Jewish origin[1].

Saturday, January 23 In the evening Herr Glatz, a very well educated, pleasant and good-looking man, his voice is powerful, but the consequences of the training he has undergone[2] are dire!

Tuesday, January 26 R. had a better night and starts to study with Herr Glatz; there is everything still to be done, but he is not without hope. It turns out that nothing can be done about the contract with Voltz and Batz! . . .

Thursday, January 28 R. not very well, nor is Herr Glatz, no study, but instead of that arguments, and not very pleasant ones; the object is to prove to the good man that he has learned nothing from Frau Richter and will learn nothing. Arrival of my father's *Die Glocken von Strassburg*[3], a curious work; done with great effect, but so alien to us . . .

Friday, January 29 R. despondent on account of the hopelessness of Glatz. 'I need savages,' R. says, 'not cultivated barbarians.' Conference regarding a restaurant to be built – one difficulty after another, but R. is still satisfied with the people on his management committee.

---

[1] Marie von Szitányi (b. 1855), daughter of a Hungarian land-owner, who was a converted Christian.
[2] With Richter's mother.
[3] Correctly, *Die Glocken des Strassburger Münsters* (*The Bells of Strassburg Cathedral*) for solo voices, chorus and orchestra to a text by Longfellow, to whom it is dedicated.)

Saturday, January 30 R. works on his '*Albumblatt*' for Frau Schott[1]. But the rash on his three fingers is a great torment to him. In the evening Gfrörer's *Primitive Christianity*, in which a saying of the Jews makes a deep imprint on my mind: 'One should pray for a good eye, a humble spirit and a soul free from desire.'

Thursday, February 4 Much correspondence between Richard and singers, who are all behaving well in every respect; less well, on the other hand, the members of the Karlsruhe orchestra.

Friday, February 5 At two o'clock Richter with his wife[2], he still the magnificent creature of old, she to my mind strange, a decidedly Jewish type; the children help us over our awkwardness. – There are business decisions to be made, the news generally unfavourable; my father's composition will involve great expense and attract nobody to the concert; the proceeds in Pest will be less than once hoped; in Vienna the intrigues are starting; a new opera being prepared for production will make rehearsals difficult; and various other things of this sort! When I reflect that the concerts are only a dismal sign of the way things are going, and when I now see that even they are beset with difficulties, I feel my heart will break; on top of all this the abortive Siegfried, the troubles which only increase the nearer we come to our goal, and R.'s age – it is as much as I can do to bear the burden on my heart.

Sunday, February 7 I dreamed I had a mouthful of pins. – Departure of the Richters. What does not belong together soon falls apart, however close the relationship has been; I have the very definite feeling that Richter will now be pursuing other paths; he did not understand R. at all with regard to Herr Glatz.

Monday, February 8 In the evening Herr Glatz tells us that he is returning to Pest on account of a legacy; the dead ride swiftly, says R. – We go through the symphony of the poor Viennese organist Bruckner, who has been brushed aside by Herr Herbeck and others because he came to Bayreuth to ask R. to accept the dedication of a symphony[3]! It is terrible what goes on in this musical world. – Andante from Schumann's E-flat Symphony; some fine accents, but such hollowness; Schumann spoiled by not recognizing his limitations; an overextended talent.

Wednesday, February 10 R. occupied with business affairs: 'I wish all this nonsense were over, so that I could get down to *Parzival*,' he says. – Our friend the Macedonian pleases R. more and more; since he does the copying here without any pay, R. offered him an honorarium so that he could go with us to Vienna, but he refused in some embarrassment, saying he would

---

[1] Piano piece in E-flat, in gratitude for a lottery in Mainz, which brought in 6,000 marks for Bayreuth.
[2] They were married on January 27.
[3] On September 13–14, 1873; Cosima did not mention the visit in her diary at the time; presumably the symphony R. and she were going through now was the third, which Bruckner dedicated to him.

be able to accompany us without it. – R. very reluctant to go to Pest, he is very hurt by my father's non-participation in Vienna.

Saturday, February 13 In the morning R. talks about the possibility that the German Empire might one day rule over the entire West: 'Although world history teaches us that good never prevails, one never ceases to hope.' The wretched situation nowadays after these victories – everywhere financial crises and misery; also emigration. No understanding of prosperity. Also a dismal lack of idealism among the rulers. 'We shall see,' says R., 'whether there will be an end to obtuseness after the tremendous exertions of our performances here, and whether people will then begin to think of providing an endowment.' I fear not.

Monday, February 15 Arrival of Frl. Nietzsche; pretty, friendly, cheerful, she is to stay here during our absence.

Wednesday, February 17 R. wishes to break with Schott and make an agreement with Peters, who is offering him three times as much for an overture. Proof that Messrs. Voltz and Batz have been stealing (Frankfurt theatre). R. is afraid of breaking off with them, since there is nobody else to look after his affairs. Feustel very concerned about our situation. A new loan. R. deeply upset.

Thursday, February 18 A further ground for worry is that I have suddenly been advised very strongly against the Luisenstift; its pietism is said to be quite frightening!! Frl. Brandt sends the part of Waltraute back. Nowhere a Sieglinde. Or a Siegfried. – Karl Kolb in the evening, we explain the position to him; at first he gives us the same over-confident answers as the mayor – the people here have their parlours, the guests are coming on R.'s account and are not interested in comfort, etc. To this R. reacts very violently, I calmly but insistently, and in the end Kolb declares himself convinced and promises to help.

Friday, February 19 The children, thank God, well and very happy with Elisabeth.

Saturday, February 20 Waved to the children from the train. R. and I 'the first time alone'[1] for a long time, which means momentarily relieved of our cares. We feel our spirits rise; can trust, too, that the children are being well looked after. A lot of fun, a lot of sausages, a lot of Marcobrunner – moonlight, a cold but good night. In Vienna at ten o'clock on Sunday; Standhartner, the *Academic* W. Society, 80 young people, and all sorts of others. Taken to Standhartner's house, cordial welcome.

Monday, February 22 In the evening to *Fidelio*, not too atrocious a performance. R. not with me.

Tuesday, February 23 Drove in the afternoon to Princess Hohenlohe's, our first meeting in 15 years, curious impression. Then with charming Marie

---

[1] Quotation from *Lohengrin* (bridal chamber scene in Act III).

D[önhoff], saw Prince Liechtenstein[1] again. R. holds a rehearsal with Frau Materna and Glatz; the latter makes no very good impression, but Materna glorious.

Wednesday, February 24 First rehearsal – much trouble caused by Richter's incredible neglectfulness (he has not sent the tubas, and the tuba players, promised us quite definitely, will not come!). Nevertheless, since the orchestra is good at sight-reading, the effect is overwhelming.

Thursday, February 25 Second rehearsal; though the tubas are now there, Richter has forgotten to have the harp parts copied. The orchestra rebellious; since these people always have bad conductors, who can only get through by giving in, discipline has now completely vanished; they also have so much to do – concerts, in the theatre every evening (playing to empty houses on account of the general bankruptcy) – that their irritability can be excused. But much that is splendid is already emerging.

Monday, March 1 The concert at seven in the evening[2]. Unprecedented reception, unending applause for R., whole heaps of laurels with fine inscriptions: 'To the saviour of German art', 'to the master of humour', 'to the creator of *Die Meistersinger,*' 'to the connoisseur and renovator of the ancient saga', 'to the reformer', 'to the sublime master', 'to the dramatic poet', 'to the greatest of masters', etc. R. has to address some words to the audience, he thanks the splendid Viennese public. Called back again, he brought Materna with him and said he was leaving Vienna a pledge in the person of this outstanding artist. The worthy Glatz, on the other hand, was a complete failure.

Wednesday, March 3 Received calls, in the evening a *soirée* in Makart's studio in R.'s honour – Count and Countess Andrássy, Count and Countess Széchenyi, Countess Festetics, lady in waiting to the Empress, who told me in the morning that for her R.'s art is like the creation of the world ... Prince Liechtenstein, the Standhartner family, the [Eduard] Liszt family, Prince Metternich, the Hellmesberger Quartet, Semper (whom R., seeing him for the first time in eight years, does not at first recognize), Countess Dönhoff and many others – perhaps 60 people in all.

Thursday, March 4 Went to the Belvedere with Rich., then to poor Semper, whose plans we looked at. Very sad impression. Despite his commissions and the Emperor's protection he remains poor, so poor that he does not venture to take a carriage, and he looks so worn out that I do not believe he will live long. Yet, in spite of it, all these colossal plans for a crumbling state!

Saturday, March 6 Departure at 3.58 p.m.; my father and Frau von

---

[1] Rudolph Liechtenstein (b. 1838), a friend since 1861, when he was studying musical theory with Cornelius.

[2] The programme consisted of the '*Kaisermarsch*' and excerpts from *Götterdämmerung*.

Meyendorff to meet us at Neuenkirchen. My father well, cheerful and decidedly glad to see us. Put up at the Hungaria.

Sunday, March 7 We decide to accept Richter's hospitality for this short time. We are living at Waiznerstrasse 1, in the home of his mother-in-law, who is away. In the afternoon a rehearsal of *Die Glocken von Strassburg* in the theatre, very unsatisfactory.

Monday, March 8 Dinner in the evening at the Casino. Afterwards music in Richter's home, my father plays the '*Schlummerlied im Grabe*' for Marie Muchanoff[1]. Deep emotion in remembrance.

Tuesday, March 9 Dress rehearsal; an ugly hall, bad acoustics, insufficient preliminary rehearsals; my father absolutely overwhelms us with the way he plays the Beethoven Concerto – a tremendous impression! Magic without parallel – this is not playing, it is pure sound. R. says it annihilates everything else. In the evening *Der Fl. Holländer* conducted by Richter; sung in Hungarian and Italian. Great disappointment! Nowhere else has so much been cut in the *Holländer*, and Richter has also introduced cymbals, etc. Astonishment over this Wagnerian *par excellence*!

Wednesday, March 10 On the whole a very dismal impression of Hungary as a country, it seems to be heading for complete dissolution. Within the administration robbery is a matter of course, and then the delusions of grandeur – it is not permitted to speak a word of German. Life is appallingly expensive; no middle class, only an inflated, uncultivated aristocracy. The musical situation just as dismal, my father is barred from everything, from any activity – he is in fact a complete stranger here. But Richter seems to be doing well. Concert at seven o'clock[2]. A very full hall, very brilliant, and great enthusiasm as well.

Thursday, March 11 Left at eight o'clock; my father accompanies us to the station. Sad parting! . . . At two o'clock welcomed by the good Standhartners in Vienna.

Friday, March 12 In the morning Rubinstein arrives from Pest and informs us that the proceeds there amounted to 5,300 florins net; the first concert here brought in 9,600 florins net, so our people in Bayreuth can be satisfied.

Saturday, March 13 In the evening a nice *soirée* at the Dönhoffs', at which R. met Marie Hohenlohe again for the first time in 19 years. After great intimacy a complete estrangement, but R. recognizes her again and finds her not uninteresting, despite the gaps and the coldness of her nature.

Sunday, March 14 At three o'clock the concert[3]; R. conducts with tense

[1] Published in 1875 as '*Elégie*'.
[2] The programme consisted of Liszt's *Die Glocken des Strassburger Münsters*, Beethoven's Fifth Piano Concerto (the *Emperor*), with Liszt as soloist, and various extracts from the *Ring* with Glatz and Lang (a baritone from the Pest opera).
[3] The programme was the same as on March 1, but with the Swedish tenor Leonard Labatt replacing Glatz.

alertness, and the performance is splendid, the enthusiasm just as great as, if not even greater than on the first occasion, but R. somewhat tired.

Monday, March 15 Left around 7 o'clock. Reach Bayreuth at 4 p.m. on the 16th, splendid, loving welcome from our children, all looking well.

Wednesday, March 17 I now have to take my badly disordered household in hand, and start right away, busying myself all day long with the linen. In the evening R. laughs and says, 'I'm glad to see that I also married a housekeeper.' – Letter from Hans, who offers me 2,500 francs towards the extra expenses for the children; I hope I shall not need to spend them, so that they can be added to the children's savings.

Friday-Wednesday, March 19–24 The days pass in unremitting efforts to retain the services of our manservant, for whose wife and children we also provide, asking only in return the proper respect. On Sunday he so far forgets himself towards R. that he has to be dismissed at once. One of our saddest experiences of the wickedness of human nature: we have provided for, made gifts to, and paid high wages to seven people, and in reward have reaped scorn and insolence! – In the midst of all the sad servant troubles we receive news of the death of R.'s sister Klara[1]; just at that moment I am so busy checking the linen that I scarcely take it in, and R. is also so busy that he does not give way to grief. It is not until the evening, when we are in bed, that he says how talented she was, how miserable her life – of all his relations she had been his favourite.

Maundy Thursday, March 25 Departure of Elisabeth Nietzsche, who has done me such a great favour.

Good Friday, March 26 Received a letter from Ritter, who is now working as a shop assistant! We swiftly resolve to take his son into our house and to pay a small pension to his wife (400 marks annually). How dreadful, the way in which whole families can come down so in the world! . . . And through no fault of their own. – R. wants to take me with him to Munich, where he has to see *Tristan und Isolde* on account of the Vogl couple: 'If you are not there, I shall certainly go to sleep.' He tells me how he told my father in all soberness, 'She is perfect'!! Yesterday he wrote a wonderful letter to my father.

Tuesday, March 30 R. has reached a difficult state of deadlock – he can complete neither his company of singers nor his orchestra. In the afternoon an excursion to the theatre, R. much concerned about the delay in the ground clearance; while R. was away exerting himself, nothing was done here! . . . Hans writes to me and sends one hundred pounds for the children. – Recently R. sang the entrance of the Commendatore from *Don Giovanni* and said: 'Nothing in our romantic era could be more romantic than isolated passages in this scene. God, what fellows they were, Mozart and Beethoven – music literally raged inside them like a fever!'

[1] Klara Wolfram died in Leipzig on March 17.

Saturday, April 3 R. expresses his longing to be able to get down to work again. *Parcival!* He also wants to write *Die Sieger*. I, too, wish we were rid of the whole business! . . . Visit from Feustel, the cost of gas equipment, etc., is enormous. R. very concerned about it.

Sunday, April 4 Lovely spring weather; R. receives a nice letter from Sascha Ritter, who is prepared to entrust his son to us. – Our household expenses are downright alarming.

Monday, April 5 Splendid spring weather, of which I take advantage to drive with the children to the Fantaisie. Memories of our lovely days there. Telegram that Betty Schott is dead! Another living thread snapped forever.

Tuesday, April 6 R. complains of the obtuseness of his fellow citizens – it looks, he says, as if he will have to give concerts in order to provide the necessary guesthouses as well! . . . R. walks to the theatre and makes another painful discovery there: they have built the orchestra pit too small!

Wednesday, April 7 Luckily the alterations to the orchestra pit will not cause too much trouble, it seems. I am still busy putting my whole household in order, and R. laughs when he sees me doing accounts with my cook. R. returns with the mayor to the unhappy subject of restaurants. – Too many worries of various kinds are clashing in heart and mind.

Thursday, April 8 Departure at one o'clock; the little ones weep bitterly as they take leave of their older sisters; Fidi literally screams. I arrive in Dresden with the two older girls at ten o'clock. . . . Gloomy mood, how hard the path!

Friday, April 9 Breakfast with the Pusinellis, the good people! Cordial atmosphere. At two we drive to the school, the children make a good impression; but how strange this world – will they feel at home in it? . . . Left at 5.15. It was necessary – but necessity is hard. Around seven to Frau Wesendonck, with whom I spend a friendly evening, she finds me worn out and aged.

Saturday, April 10 Left at 9.30. R. meets me at the station [in Leipzig], is fortunately looking very well, but says that whenever I go away he falls ill. Went to the theatre in the evening: Schumann's *Genoveva*. Utter dismay over the vulgarity and crudeness of this work.

Sunday, April 11 At four o'clock in Hanover, where I am writing this. At seven in the evening a performance of *Lohengrin*, unfortunately not good, the tenor William Müller making a pleasant impression with his voice at the start, but in the course of the work becoming sugary and absurd; costumes, scenery, tempi terrible.

Tuesday, April 13 First letter from the children in the Luisenstift, they seem content! . . . At two o'clock departure from Brunswick; R. uncertain about Frl. Weckerlin (Sieglinde or Gutrune)[1]. In the hotel properly fleeced, as is now customary in Germany. R. calls on the theatre manager Herr v. Rudolphi, who makes a good impression on him.

---

[1] Mathilde Weckerlin (b. 1848), Gutrune at Bayreuth in 1876.

Wednesday, April 14 In the evening *Tannhäuser*, very dismal impression of the singer [Hermann] Schroetter.

Thursday, April 15 Departure at three o'clock amid a large crowd. At 8.30 arrival in Berlin. Reunion with Mimi.

Friday, April 16 Letters from the children, good. Saw Lenbach's portrait of R. in Frau v. Schl.'s house – by far the best that has been done of R.; feelings of sadness not to possess it, though without envy.

Saturday, April 17 In the evening with Prof. Doepler[1], our costume designer, to see [Kleist's play] *Die Hermannsschlacht*, performed by the Meiningen company[2]; the play very gripping in spite of many peculiarities, and the acting very remarkable; the work (very much of its own time) outstanding, modern, but the historic realism of the costumes distorted it into a farce; all the same, very interesting to watch, and much of it even moving.

Sunday, April 18 Very tired, I feel at times I can no longer get through the day!... R. was with Herr von Hülsen yesterday and thus brought to an end a prolonged situation stupidly fostered by the theatre director – to the latter's great surprise.

Thursday, April 22 Rehearsal at ten o'clock; the orchestra is becoming ever better and more fiery, as always after a certain amount of contact with R....

Friday, April 23 Dress rehearsal, R. not well, however. He is longing to be back with the children. In the evening a *soirée* at the Office of the Royal Household in honour of Frau Materna. (R. decides on Schroetter for Siegfried.)

Saturday, April 24 At half past seven the concert[3]. Great enthusiasm by Berlin thermometers, though the performance was not good and R. greatly exhausted and in consequence out of humour. Bucher affected by music for the first time, in the concert hall he literally cries out, which, coming from this taciturn man, sounds very strange.

Sunday, April 25 A long sleep, after which we immediately got dressed for the second concert, at twelve o'clock. Atmosphere very nice and cordial, a better performance, audience friendly, Materna and Niemann in tears, R. very cheerful afterwards. Worked out a plan with Herr v. Radowitz[4] to force the state to intervene in Bayreuth affairs!

Monday, April 26 At five o'clock dinner in the Office of the Royal Household. There I talk to the editor of *Kladderadatsch* and demand the support of his periodical for Bayreuth. – Departure at seven o'clock; the

---

[1] Carl Emil Doepler, Berlin, designed the costumes for the *Ring* in 1876.

[2] This company, formed by Duke Georg II of Saxe-Meiningen (b. 1826), had a powerful influence on stagecraft throughout Europe, based on ensemble acting and historical accuracy of costumes and settings.

[3] The programme of both Berlin concerts was the same as those in Vienna in March, with Materna and Niemann as soloists.

[4] Joseph Maria von Radowitz of the Foreign Office in Berlin.

two concerts have brought in about 6,000 thalers – a lot in view of the unfavourable circumstances. Journeyed through the night, glad and happy to be back on Bavarian soil.

Tuesday, April 27 In Bayreuth at eight o'clock, the children at the station, well and full of glee. We both very sleepy.

Wednesday, April 28 A day of correspondence and accounts, on top of that the house in disorder. – We hear that Hans has been swindled out of fifteen hundred pounds in England; grievous news.

Friday, April 30 R. definitely wants me with him in Vienna, I should like to stay at home to keep an eye on the house. He composes the concert ending to 'Hagen's Watch', which puts him in good spirits. In the afternoon a drive to the theatre; terrible impression again – nothing done about the ground clearance, all the rubble still lying around, no plantings possible this year!

Saturday, May 1 R. resolves to return a part of the site to the town, since it is so mean about doing anything. I am always comparing R. to the poor hare in the fairy tale, wearing himself out while the two hedgehogs look calmly on! . . . In the afternoon drove to the theatre in fine weather, Rus following behind, barking and leaping; there inspected the orchestra pit once again; firm decision made.

Sunday, May 2 A sad day – we are told of Rus's death from a ruptured lung, caused, it seems, by our drive yesterday. With him we certainly lose one of our best friends. I noticed again yesterday how anxious and concerned for R. he was as R. climbed down into the orchestra pit. If one of us were to have died, the dog would doubtless have known it in advance, but we are taken by surprise – this on top of everything else.

Monday, May 3 At twelve o'clock burial of Rus[1]; when I told Fidi of his death, he said: 'Oh, good heavens, what will his wife say when she comes?!' Fidi knew that we had ordered a mate for Rus. At five o'clock left for Vienna, tolerable night journey; arrival at the Standhartners' at nine.

Tuesday, May 4 Not good news of the concert at all, the proceeds will be small. At lunch we are visited by the opera director Jauner[2]; Richter, now a conductor there on R.'s recommendation, also presents himself, but does not make a pleasant impression.

Wednesday, May 5 Rehearsal, 'Hagen's Watch' very beautifully sung by Scaria. Voice of the very darkest colouring.

Thursday, May 6 Concert at twelve o'clock – fine impression, 'Hagen's Watch' repeated. – In the evening Semper, very interesting – he literally comes to life in conversation with R.

Friday, May 7 R. encountered a group of poor blind musicians in a courtyard; they were playing the Andante from [Beethoven's] Second Symphony so wonderfully that he could not tear himself away from them,

[1] Beside the grave in the garden of Wahnfried; a stone still marks the spot.
[2] Franz Jauner (b. 1832), newly appointed director of the Court opera in Vienna.

and he told me about it with tears in his eyes. – In such ways does one really feel the power of music! The violinist's playing, he says, was as pure as gold! . . . Departure at ten in the evening (sleeping car).

Saturday, May 8 Arrival home at one o'clock in the afternoon; sorrowful letters from Lusch at the boarding school. What shall I do?

Sunday, May 9 In the evening some acquaintances, among them Feustel, once more bringing us nasty news; whereas, by giving up the ground clearance, R. thought he had made sure of the rehearsals, it turns out now that the building has swallowed up all the money!

Tuesday, May 11 Arrival of Marco and Blanca, whom R. renames Marke and Brange[1], nice dogs, both of them, who bring new life to the garden.

Friday, May 14 In the evening read [Plato's] *Timaeus*, the first book I have had in my hands for a long time! – A prayer that good may triumph leads us to the *Oresteia*, and a glance into that work strikes absolute terror into our hearts! . . . In the evening Marke and Brange stationed in front of the door to the *salon* in the moonlight; a very lovely sight!

Saturday, May 15 Very fine letter from friend Nietzsche about *Götterdämmerung*. R. said to me, 'That must make you glad, you know that I created such a work under your protection.' I reply that he would have gone on creating anyway, even without me. 'Yes, but I should never have written that, it was you who coaxed those sounds out of me.' He is thinking a lot about *Parzival*, intends to guide his reading in that direction. May God bless him! In the evening tea in the garden, a registered letter from Brunswick, R. at once had a premonition, and, true enough, Schroetter, the newly won Siegfried, now declines the part. . . . With the customary calm he always shows when things go wrong, R. says, 'And I thought I now only had the accommodation problem to worry about!'

Sunday, May 16 R. drafts a circular to the orchestra players; starts on his treatment of medicinal waters, breakfast in the garden; modest meal with young Brandt, the two Lalas brothers and Herr Zimmer[2]. Herr Rubinstein, back from Brunswick, confirms the news about Schroetter, adding that the director was offended because R. did not write to him.

Friday, May 21 R. occupied with many letters, I with the birthday and lessons to the children as well. Surprised by the Ritters, Franziska and Alexander, evening of cheerful conversation.

Saturday, May 22 Very early in the morning the children wishing many happy returns, Venetian glass (if the glass breaks, good fortune will persist); at eleven o'clock a second round of greetings, Faith, Love, Hope (Fidi, Loldi, Eva), 62 illuminated balloons set alight in the hall, with it the '*Huldigungsmarsch*'. R. tells me I have given him everything, taken care of him like a mother – the children very earnest and solemn, they speak their

---

[1] Newfoundland dogs.
[2] Hermann Zimmer, Karlsruhe, joined the copyists on 11 May.

verses nicely; Eva very moved. – In the evening Wahnfried illuminated, fireworks, accompanied by Strauss waltzes and children's torchlight procession; everything turns out well, the weather favourable, R. cheerful and touched. I invariably melancholy, as always on festive occasions – may Heaven bless him! (Many telegrams, among others from the King.)

Thursday, May 27 Departure of the Ritters, made arrangements for their son to come to us in August. Arrival of Brückwald, conference in the theatre, at which R. wants me to be present – with me there he finds it a pleasure, otherwise everything is an agony to him. Lighting problems, the mystic chasm[1], curtain, ceilings are discussed, Brandt the most resourceful and decisive. – In the afternoon a letter from the director in Vienna, Herr Jauner, he has managed to secure royalty payments for us (seven percent) from next August on.

Tuesday, June 1 In the evening Herr Unger with Herr Rubinstein; the former hoarse, sings extracts from Loge in a nice voice, but....

Wednesday, June 9 Great heat, R. not very well, gives up his treatment of medicinal waters. No encouraging news from anywhere, the number of patrons does not increase, but demands are growing higher, as, for example, Frau Materna asking for 30 florins a day. We decide on a drive to Alexandersbad.

Thursday, June 10 Since the barometer has fallen, we do not set out, despite a fine sunrise and the urgings of the household. A triumph for science: the weather turns awful, causing great amusement.

Sunday, June 13 In honour of the barometer, drive to Alexandersbad in a very rough wind. Much amusement about the 'triumph for science', the swallows are flying very low, and the wind is awful; all the same, the journey from Berneck to Bischofsgrün is very lovely, the fir trees nodding. Fine trout in Bischofsgrün, very good spirits; R. consults the barometer in the cashier's office, knocks over potted plants, but sees that it has risen. Splendid weather in Alexandersbad, climbed the Luisenburg, not so well suited to us. In the hotel Fidi decides to make fireworks for himself and sets fire to the curtain! Great alarm. He speechless, draws attention to the fire by rattling the door, and disappears through the back door; R., changing his clothes, puts out the fire in a state of complete nudity; as he is doing so, something happens which he has so often experienced in dreams: the entire Kurhaus sees the fire from outside and storms in to put it out; R. has trouble withdrawing in his ridiculous state. In good spirits afterwards, Fidi surely cured forever of playing with matches, I almost ill with shock. Fidi does not want to sleep in his room any more, thinks it is still burning!

Monday, June 14 Home at seven o'clock; pleasure in the house.

Tuesday, June 15 A good night for R., but still a mountain of worries. At lunch, thank goodness, *King Lear* – how full of genius the first scene, how

[1] Wagner's and Cosima's name for the covered orchestra pit.

wise *artistically!* Looking back, one feels that the recklessness with which Gloster speaks of the birth of Edmund, like any cavalier, is the cause of his downfall. Did Shakespeare plan it exactly like that? Or did he make many corrections, like Beethoven? *He* had his sketches in front of him, made corrections in them.

Wednesday, June 16 Departure at eleven o'clock[1]. Much reflection during the journey. In Weimar at seven o'clock, my father and Mimi Schleinitz at the station. My father apparently well. Spent the evening with him.

Thursday, June 17 The service at three o'clock, very moving.

Friday, June 18 A letter from R. in French! . . . My father unfortunately very unwell, a shock for me! With torn feelings to the performance of *Tristan und Isolde* – much absurdity and shoddiness, but I beg the Vogls to come to Bayreuth[2].

Saturday, June 19 R. sent me a very curious letter from Herr Brahms, as artificial and unedifying as his compositions[3]. – At nine o'clock took leave of my father, heartbreaking, he is very, very wretched! . . . At 11 in the evening met by R. in Neumarkt – much to tell him, among other things, about my two-hour conversation with the Grand Duke of Weimar.

Sunday, June 20 Good awakening, R. tells me that he does not really live at all when I am not there, nothing has any meaning, he did not even have the gas lit. – I write the better part of 10 letters during the day; R. has many inquiries from Americans and is reckoning on these to fill his hall in the end – nothing for the Germans to be proud of!

Monday, June 21 In the afternoon arrival of the dressing case which the King of the Netherlands presented to my father and he now to me, along with the manuscripts (*Lohengrin, Tannhäuser*), melancholy feelings. – R. continues to study with the singer Unger, some hope after much exertion!

Wednesday, June 23 In the evening Prof. Doepler with sketches of the costumes; much in them very fine.

Thursday, June 24 In the evening Prof. Doepler and friend Feustel. Again the accommodation problem, it seems definite that a hotel cannot be built, and now it is a matter of making the necessary arrangements. The question of the cost of the costumes is also discussed. 'My undertaking looks to me like a will-o'-the-wisp over a marsh,' R. says to me.

Sunday, June 27 Prof. Hey from Munich to take part in Herr Unger's studies. The latter sings the 'Forging Songs' before our quite numerous Sunday gathering in a way that gives grounds for hope. –

Monday, June 28 In the afternoon to Turkish coffee with friend Lalas; what he has to tell us about Albanians and Turks is highly interesting; the

[1] To attend a memorial service for Marie Muchanoff.

[2] This was the first staging outside Munich; Heinrich and Therese Vogl in the main roles.

[3] The score of the revised *Tannhäuser* had come into Brahms's hands via Cornelius and Tausig; Wagner had asked Brahms to return it, but Brahms claimed it was his by right.

Albanians possess no state, but in their customs there is more culture than among ourselves. – In the evening the musicians, R. says that he has sent Herr Brahms the score of *Das Rheingold* as a well-preserved substitute for a badly kept manuscript, and once more, with amazement, we read through the letter with all its embroideries[1].

Wednesday, June 30 In the morning a letter from Hans in Hall in the Tirol; he informs me of his great (too great) loss and at the same time that he has had a slight stroke, the consequences of which he cannot foresee. Once more a sword twisted in my heart and all my wounds torn open again – how often will this continue to occur? I reply at once with details of the property I shall be able to leave to my children, and at the same time I implore him to give up his plan of going to America, to which he is still holding firm with the object of procuring a certain sum of money for the children. In this painful state I have to welcome the first of our singers (Hill, the Lehmanns).

Friday, July 2 Rehearsals morning and afternoon; visited the theatre; guests at lunch, guests in the evening, always managing between times to do a little work with the children. The Brückner brothers are also here, much activity, R. visibly pleased.

Saturday, July 3 Still more arrivals, everyone in the best of spirits, each singer as if born for his role, the correct deployment of forces has already achieved an amazing result in *Das Rheingold*. Indescribable impression.

Monday, July 5 Worked with the children; at eleven o'clock correspondence, among other things a note from Hans, thanking me for mine. I say nothing to R., neither about the letter nor my reply, and weep silently by myself – as far as that is possible, for instructing the new chambermaid, attending to the feeding of our guests allow little leisure, and I perform my daily tasks as if weighed down with lead, unrelieved.

Tuesday, July 6 R. luckily still in good health, holds rehearsals morning and afternoon, in the evening the guests stay on. We hardly manage to exchange a word between ourselves, and I go around with my never-to-be-removed burden of pain, during the day as if in a hot, dry fever, during the night in tears. –

Wednesday, July 7 Continuation of this life; the Vogl couple arrive from Munich – Herr Unger causing many difficulties. – Still more, however, the construction work at the theatre – it turns out that the building supervisor was not up to his duties, neglected everything, so that Brandt is in utter despair; nothing is ready. Wrote many letters in the morning, among others to the bird-maker man in London[2].

Thursday, July 8 A time of cloudbursts, the Heavens empty themselves

---

[1] Wagner sent Brahms a copy of the limited de luxe edition in order to induce him to surrender the *Tannhäuser* score, which Brahms duly did.

[2] Richard Keene, a well-known maker of pantomime stage properties; orders sent him included 'a car with a yoke of rams', a bear and a dragon.

upon us. – In the evening, rehearsal; when a violent thundershower threatens, the whole company disappears, we lightheartedly astonished, surprised to find ourselves once again alone in the *salon*. R. reads me the strangely sagacious letter which Herr Brahms has written him, thanking him for sending *Das Rheingold*.

Sunday, July 11 Up very early, to church with the two big girls[1]. The whole of *Das Rheingold* is being rehearsed, it is going very well.

Tuesday, July 13 Letter from Hans, informing me of his last wishes! . . . I am now spending my hours in almost ceaseless prayer, and searching for opportunities to sacrifice anything that might afford me pleasure. Is there happiness?? . . .

Monday-Thursday, July 19–22 Constant rehearsing. R. very worn out by it. Herr Jauner departs in great excitement after talking to me about his plan to produce the *Ring* cycle in the Prater as an Austrian folk festivity. I write to my father about it. Jauner full of astonished admiration for R. at rehearsals. Unfortunately his feet are hurting him, he can hardly set them on the ground! – He talks of the sacrifices I am making for him in opening my house every day to company which is not mine, and he says that with me he can do anything, without me nothing! Arrival and erection of the huge bust of the King[2].

Friday-Wednesday, July 23–28 First rehearsal with scenery, splendid sight, magnificent sound; R. greatly moved. A curiosity: Herr von Hülsen, the long-standing foe; he spends the evening with us. – Herr Niemann, a disturbing influence, conceited and demanding, contributing nothing, he joins up with Richter to visit taverns, scoffs at the rest of the deserving company. I make amends and bear it as best I can; on Wednesday and Sunday the Bayreuth people. Prof. Doepler with his costume sketches – Herr Fricke, the ballet master from Dessau[3], dancing lessons for the children, sad discovery that Lusch has become somewhat crooked in posture. – On the 28th splendid rehearsal of the first act of *Götterdämmerung*.

Thursday, July 29 Arrival of my father, he is looking well and is glad to be with us. Herr Niemann comes to the rehearsal in the evening; behaves in such a dismally conceited way during it and is so arrogant that R. can hardly contain himself and angrily gives vent to his feelings in front of the others. On top of that Herr Unger lamentable in the second act of *Götterdämmerung*.

Friday, July 30 R. had a very bad night, in indignation and agitation – how things repeat themselves in life: Niemann returns his script for Siegmund! . . . We think of Paris and the shrug of the shoulders with which the wretched man appeared before the curtain, exonerating himself! . . .

---

[1] They had come home from school the previous day.

[2] By Caspar Zumbusch, a birthday gift from Ludwig II; it was set up in front of the entrance to Wahnfried.

[3] Richard Fricke (b. 1818), met at the performance of Gluck's *Orfeo* in November 1872; assisted Wagner with movement and grouping.

Saturday-Monday, July 31-August 23 Wrote nothing during these days, how much now lies between! – On Saturday the 31st, large banquet for our singers. This assembly can be looked upon as really successful. On the afternoon of Sunday the 1st, rehearsal to test the orchestra tone quality; R. received by the orchestra with cheers, Betz sings '*Vollendet der Bau*'[1], heavenly sound, overwhelming impression, R. very moved. – Monday, August 2, *Rheingold* rehearsal in the morning with orchestra only, in the afternoon with the singers, my father there throughout; friend Mimi arrives and also attends everything, in the evening always a party, every day some guests at table. On Tuesday, second part of *Rheingold* and the same life, from Wednesday on one act each day; everyone, musicians and singers, taking part with unstinted enthusiasm and joy, indescribable impression on the very large audience of our friends, the Schleinitzes (the minister having come, too), the Eckerts, Rohde, Overbeck, Gersdorff, the Heckels, the Schirmers (America)[2], the painter [Adolph] Menzel and many others. At the end there is so much emotion that all the participants declare they do not know how they will be able to bear ordinary life again, particularly ordinary theatrical life. – Alwine Frommann dead!

On the 13th R. gives a garden party for the orchestra and the singers who are still present, and he makes a speech in which he mentions gratefully that such times arouse feelings which usually remain slumbering within him. He invites my father to play for the orchestra members, who have not all heard him, my father does so and plays his 'Saint Francis Legend' – so well chosen for the occasion – splendidly. On the following day all depart, with great emotion. My father, whom Frau v. Meyendorff had visited here, leaves on Tuesday the 17th. In the final days of his presence here he received the peculiar reward which the public always holds ready for him. Since there is nothing more one can say about him, his attitude towards everything and his miraculous achievements being well known, it is now I on whom abuse is loaded; it is said that I offend everybody, denounce to my husband all his friends, Prof. Hoffmann, Betz, Niemann, Richter, etc. – I have offended everyone, in fact, down to the costumier of the Munich theatre. R. declares publicly that these are all lies and then writes to Richter, telling him that his attitude towards our house (never to appear when he is invited) is providing a pretext for such slanders; he demands from him an apology and a promise that things will be different in the future. Long silence from Richter, in the meantime letters to me, a complete madhouse activity, for which Niemann's return of his script provided the main incentive. At last – on

Tuesday, August 24th – a letter from Richter, so foolish and crude that one wonders how it is possible; R. receives it, tells me nothing about it, but in the night he gets up and writes; on my inquiry, he tells me what Richter's letter contained and that he is answering it. I reflect and then – on

[1] Correctly, '*Vollendet das ewige Werk*', Wotan's greeting to Valhalla in Scene 2 of *Das Rheingold*.
[2] Gustav Schirmer, the music publisher, and his wife.

Wednesday, August 25th – I write with a full heart to Richter early in the morning, pointing out to him that it does not matter at all what his feelings are towards me, but if he does not sincerely repent having allowed himself to be turned against R. through gossip, it will be impossible for him ever again to have anything to do with R. R. had indeed already indicated this to him, without himself holding out any such hope. R. takes me by surprise as I am writing and, after he had read me the two letters (Richter's and his), I read him mine, which touches him, and he says he will demand it back if R[ichter] does not respond in the manner it requests.

Thursday, August 26 The children working with their new governess, granddaughter of the headmaster Baumgarten-Crusius, whom R. knew at the Kreuzschule[1]; her character pleases me greatly. Repentant telegram from Richter.

Sunday, August 29 Fine autumnal weather after a violent thunderstorm. R. busy with correspondence and I with friendship. On Monday the 30th, our friends have another meal with us, and on Tuesday the 31st they leave us, to our great sorrow. – In the afternoon we go for a walk with the children in dull weather; the sky clears, and we walk as far as the vaults of the Angermann concern, a complete Teniers picture; we sit down near the huge gate, '*Quasimodo*'[2] brings us filled glasses from the deepest depths, up above a sort of window is opened sideways, we see barrels standing on top of one another, coopers walking to and fro; the children run into the cave, from the end of which a distant light is shining, outside in the meadows cows are grazing, beside us the three dogs. Very cheerful homeward journey.

Thursday, September 2 Sedan celebrations, very wet! The children illuminate their room in the annex and constantly delight us with their merriment. In the evening San-Marte[3] on Parcival, R. comes to the conclusion that the Holy Grail evolved entirely outside the church as a peaceful disengagement from it.

Friday, September 10 R. resolves on a short outing to Bohemia; invitation from Baroness Staff[4], which we intend to accept.

Sunday, September 12 Great excitement among the children, departure at one o'clock, arrival at Münchberg at three, nice welcome from the Staffs, pleasant country life, illuminations in the evening.

Monday, September 13 At Konradsreuth in the morning; at two o'clock to Hof, spent the evening in Karlsbad in splendid moonlight. Put up at the Goldener Schild, where R. stayed 42 years ago!

---

[1] As a schoolboy, 1821–27.

[2] The hunchback in Hugo's novel *Notre Dame de Paris*.

[3] Pseudonym of Albert Schultz, author of a life on Wolfram von Eschenbach and 3 volumes of Parzival studies (*Parzival-Studien*).

[4] Baron Staff and his wife, Klara Staff-Reitzenstein were neighbours and friends in Bayreuth.

Tuesday, September 14 Karlsbad soon exhausted, though very nice, many Israelites. Departure at three, in Teplitz at seven in the evening, put up at the König von Preussen.

Wednesday, September 15 A bad night, nasty smells, the lack of cleanliness in Germany, we leave the hotel. Breakfast in the Kurhaus, climbed up to the Schlackenburg. R. shows me the pheasant reserve in which he read the text of *Tannhäuser* to his mother. Also the house Zum Paradies, where he paid a surprise visit to his family as a young man, having walked from Leipzig to Teplitz. Walk in the lovely palace gardens, full of memories, then to Schönau, saw the Eiche, where R. had lived when he was a conductor, was shown the path where he met Baumgarten, the headmaster whose granddaughter is now our children's governess; the farmhouse in which he ate. Bathed in the Kaisersbad (splendid) and stayed there overnight.

Thursday, September 16 Off early to Aussig, at the station I am approached by Emilie Sierzputowska, who had closed Marie Muchanoff's eyes – profound impression! . . . At two o'clock left for Prague; arrival there at eight; I receive the friend of my friend, she tells me how Marie had loved me, a very moving conversation, my impressions of which remain throughout the night: 'No one has ever seen greatness who did not see Marie die.'

Friday, September 17 Said goodbye again to my new friend – and then wandered through the city with clouded thoughts. Pleasant impression, not much Israel. My friend gave me a medallion which Marie had worn, and so I am now adorned with the Immaculata! . . .

Sunday, September 19 Home in Wahnfried, somewhat tired but very content.

Wednesday, September 22 R. unwell, has to stay in bed! It seems to be a chill. Spent much of the day with the children (wrote to the two eldest), in the evening alone in my little grey room. It is very stormy, autumnal equinox; people say it is not good to be at sea at such a time, I wonder whether Hans is not now on his way to America, and feel alarmed! I am very tranquil and, I think, cheerful, though my wounds are still open, incurable. A favourite memory for me now is Mabuse's *Saint Luke* in Prague – his air of remoteness and his composure, the meditativeness of a saint and the circumspection of a genius, and besides that the magnificent surroundings, which for such a man do not even exist.

Thursday, September 23 R. is convinced that his indisposition comes from the annoyance Niemann is causing him. I tell him one must just decide to regard him as a meteor, then put up with the meteorites which fall on one's head.

Friday, September 24 R., going in the afternoon to try out Herr Unger, returns with the firm conviction that he *will be able to sing* Siegfried – I hardly dare trust my unconditional faith in R.'s judgement – so great a happiness would this be! Happy atmosphere in consequence, a good night!

Sunday, September 26 R. entirely recovered; reads *Parzival*. In the afternoon to the theatre, Herr Unger sings parts of *Siegfried* (final scene); the voice pliant and full, the enunciation very good, some flaws still remain, but I quite definitely share R.'s belief that he is capable of improvement.

Tuesday, September 28 The resolve to go to Vienna grows ever more difficult to mention; the decorations for the second act [of *Tannhäuser*] have arrived, looking as if they had been concocted by a bookbinder and a confectioner combined! On top of that Herr Jauner offers us Frau [Maria] Wilt (known for her colossal figure) as Elisabeth. In the evening read *Parzival*, joy in the great poet; R. believes that the 'fisher king' comes from a misunderstanding of the word *pêcheur*, and that it should really be the 'sinner king', that is to say, Amfortas.

Friday, October 1 Letters at last from Munich; the royal treasury lays claim to three-fifths of the incoming certificates of patronage, two-fifths can be retained.

Saturday, October 2 While R. is in conference, I go through my books, write down what was spent during the last quarter, and am alarmed by the sum of 8,200-odd florins. – Truly the worries are piling up. The agreement with the royal treasury, Voltz and Batz, the household expenses, the opera director Scherbarth, who is not willing to release Herr Unger, in the background Herr Fürstner, before us Vienna (with the 'one-eyed Swedish Jew' [Labatt] as Tannhäuser, as R. says); on top of that our dogs sent back to us by the director in Zahna with mange; everywhere fraud, when it is not stupidity. R. says when people come and congratulate him on his energy, his genius, he feels like flying into a rage! . . .

Monday, October 4 Letter from friend Feustel, telling R. that the treasury stipulations make the aid provided downright illusory; in consequence of this, R. decides to approach the Emperor, but first I am to inquire of Mimi.

Wednesday, October 6 In the evening our musicians, we go through the *Symphonie fantastique*; the first movement, lamenting, melancholy, pleases us most. R. says, 'That was Berlioz's best feature.' '*Scène aux champs*' reminds us too much of the *Pastoral*, and the finale is stiff and disagreeable. What particularly strikes me is Berlioz's inability to develop his themes, which are often very fine, something he shares with Schubert; he does not perceive, as Beethoven, Bach, R. so profoundly perceive, all that a theme contains, that it is the seed from which the whole plant must emerge!

Wednesday, October 20 We decide to travel to Vienna via Munich, in order to discuss several things with Councillor Düfflipp – particularly, R. feels, the use of the palaces here for the various princes.

Friday, October 22 Frau W[esendonck] with us all day; the three Br.'s from the theatre too – Brandt, Brückwald, Brückner; selected patterns for the curtain, very lovely! . . . Brandt, however, still complaining that the building shows signs of neglect, he says the rain comes in.

Saturday, October 30 Departure; friendly farewells from friends at the station, we are told a touching thing: a cantor, Fischer, from Zittau inquired some time ago whether he might be given a free seat if he canvassed on behalf of our undertaking, he said he was very poor, but he wished to try to do something for the cause – now he has sent 6,000 marks! . . . In Munich at 8 in the evening; reunion with Lenbach, Unger and Prof. Hey.

Sunday, October 31 Sorrowful thoughts lacerate me – my first time here in seven years; thoughts of Hans! – At Lenbach's studio, later showed the children around while R. was receiving Councillor Düfflipp. We have a meal with Lenbach and are at the station at eight in the evening, the same one from which I departed seven years ago!

Monday, November 1 Battered arrival at six o'clock in the morning; friend Standhartner at the station – terrible conditions in the Grand Hotel, muddle everywhere.

Tuesday, November 2 We decide to move, great commotion. Paid some calls; Ellen, now the wife of the Duke of Meiningen[1], seen for the first time in 14 years; she had news of Hans, it all sounds so sad that I feel my heart will break. . . . In the evening Verdi's *Requiem*, about which it would certainly be best to say nothing.

Wednesday, November 3 Moving! We are now staying in the Hotel Imperial. R. has a rehearsal at twelve o'clock and finds it a great strain, since he has to explain *everything* to these principal singers. Good relations with the Richters. In the evening [Bizet's] *Carmen*, a new French work, interesting for the glaringness of the modern French manner.

Saturday, November 6 Rehearsals[2] all the time, I myself occupied with the costumes, unrewarding insofar as there is not enough time to produce anything really beautiful.

Monday, November 8 R. holds a rehearsal of the first scene, he is more satisfied with Herr Labatt than he expected to be, but the Wolfram (Herr Bignio) causes him tremendous trouble. In the evening we go together to see *Andrea*, an excessively bad play by Sardou, though acted very nicely by Frau Niemann[3]. Together with her in the evening at Herr Jauner's, discussed her husband's absurd behaviour in Bayreuth, I think that this stupidity is now safely past!

Wednesday, November 10 R. at rehearsal all the time from eleven to two, afterwards very exhausted, he takes a rest and then goes for a little walk with the children; I pay calls. In the evening with R. to *Die Königin von Saba* by Goldmark and Mosenthal – no gold, no marks, but plenty of Mosenthal! . . .

Thursday, November 11 Complete hoarseness keeps me at home, part of the time in bed – R. has two rehearsals of *Tannhäuser* during the day, the scenery

---

[1] Helene, Baroness von Heldburg (b. 1839), had been an actress in Berlin (under the name Ellen Franz), a pupil of Hans von Bülow and a friend of Cosima; she married the Duke of Meiningen morganatically in 1873.

[2] Of *Tannhäuser* (Paris version).

[3] Hedwig Niemann-Raabe (b. 1844).

for *Lohengrin* in the evening; he tells me curious things about the helplessness in all matters of scenery; for the church bells in the first act of *T[annhäuser]* a peal of alarm bells, the flock of sheep represented by two hand bells, etc. – The greatest pleasure is when we can forget all this nonsense and occupy ourselves with the children ('the finest gift you could ever have given me, the only means of restoring my links with life!') or talk about our reading. R. is reading with interest [Reinhart] Dozy's *The Moors in Spain*. I the letters and diary of Dürer, recognizing with dismay how wickedly and wretchedly the world has always behaved towards men of genius; again and again it is just a matter of a few hundred florins.

Friday, November 12 R. at rehearsal, returns particularly dissatisfied with Lucile Grahn[1]. In the evening he goes to hear an act of [Meyerbeer's] *L'Africaine* and says that, if he were to live in Vienna and be connected with the theatre, he would never again raise a pen to write music, so profaned did it all appear to him. The present times reminded him of *Tannhäuser* in Paris, he said, where, after nine years of seclusion in Switzerland, he had also been obliged to sit through the most worthless of works in order to assess singers, and he had felt then, as he does now, in a state of sin.

Sunday, November 14 R. says that Herr Fürstner has lodged a protest against the performance of *Tannhäuser*[2] and Herr Batz is demanding recompense for his alleged efforts!!

Monday, November 15 R. had a wretched night! He wrote his protest against Herr Fürstner – this the reward for all his trouble! . . . Saw *Die Zauberflöte* with the children.

Tuesday, November 16 Orchestra rehearsal (second act), shattering impression! – But it cost R. a lot of trouble. Only in Bayreuth will he ever achieve a really good performance of *Tannhäuser*. – Dinner with the Duke of Meiningen; R. discovers in him something completely typical of the old house of Wettin, something firm, reserved, powerful about the features, which one could easily trace back to Widukind – in earlier times it would have served very well, but in the restricted circumstances of today it could degenerate into viciousness. R. finds the Prince very interesting on this account.

Thursday, November 18 R. is holding individual rehearsals and returns home more discontented each time. – In the evening a *soirée* with the Hellmesberger Quartet, I make the acquaintance of Herr Brahms, who plays a piano quartet of his own making[3], a red, crude-looking man, his opus very dry and stilted.

Saturday, November 20 Much fuss about the dress rehearsal, which takes place at six in the evening, though unfortunately only to R.'s sorrow! The

---

[1] Former ballet dancer, now ballet mistress at the Court opera, Munich; she had choreographed the Venusberg scene in the Munich production.
[2] He claimed to be entitled to payment for the use of the Paris Venusberg scene.
[3] In C Minor, Opus 60, completed in this year.

orchestra lifeless, the ballet quite out of keeping with the music, the singers inadequate, the decorations deficient, the stage mechanics bungled. – All the same, R. remains admirably calm and makes a very cordial speech to the orchestra at the end, begging their pardon for taking up their time with such an old 'war horse'.

Monday, November 22 At half past six the performance of *Tannhäuser*,[1] good beyond all expectations; nothing quite as R. really intended it, but very full of life throughout. R. often has to take a bow from his box, and at the end he appears on stage with the singers, something which always arouses feelings of embarrassment in me.

Tuesday, November 23 A day of rest for everybody. In the evening Semper and Prince Liechtenstein to dinner with us. R. very cheerful, the Prince highly congenial, Semper rather tired.

Wednesday, November 24 All kinds of absurdities, the aristocracy vexed at R.'s taking a bow from his box, the singers hurt by his speech[2]!

Thursday, November 25 R. makes a speech to his singers, whom the newspapers have aroused to rebellion, peace is restored and the second performance takes place in the evening; my vexation over the foolish situation in which we have been obliged to place ourselves is so great that the first two acts leave me unaffected, but in the third I am again brought to a mood of utter devoutness and feel released from the pressures of life's ballast!

Tuesday, November 30 Hear that Herr Labatt has reported sick – whether this is incompetence, ill will or genuine indisposition is hard to decide. Gounod's *Roméo et Juliette* is given in place of *Tannhäuser*, the true nausea produced by this performance, the impressions R. is receiving from the *Lohengrin* rehearsals, make him think of leaving Vienna tomorrow. I give him my full support. What all the news amounts to is that nothing but rabble has been in evidence here.

Wednesday, December 1 R. asks Herr Jauner to call on him, to make known his intentions; the director is so alarmed at the thought of R.'s leaving that R. then promises him to go on trying with *Lohengrin*! Much upset by this....

Thursday, December 2 Arose late in despondent mood. R. has to write yet again to Herr Fürstner, who is not budging from his demands, and R. will probably have to withdraw the new scene in *Tannhäuser*! On top of that, very dismal impressions from the *Lohengrin* rehearsals.

Monday-Friday, December 6–17 Vicissitudes of the *Lohengrin* production, R. utterly exhausted by the rehearsals, during which the newspapers continue to publish their nasty reports and Herr Fürstner starts legal proceedings! R.

---

[1] Conducted by Hans Richter.
[2] According to a newspaper clipping attached to the diaries, Wagner made a speech from the stage in which he said that the applause given to his artists would encourage him to continue with the production of his works, as far as the means allowed; the singers were said to have taken these last six words as a reflection on their abilities.

wants to leave after the dress rehearsal (13th), but Herr Jauner beseeches him to stay, whereupon the decision is altered. On the 14th christening at the Richters', the little girl is named Richardis Cosima Eva. On the 15th a wonderful performance of *Lohengrin*[1] – R. watches it from the second circle with the children, I from a parterre box with the Dönhoffs. A storm of applause from the audience after the first act; at the end, after the entire company has taken several curtain calls, R. goes down to thank them, the curtain rises while he is doing so, and audience and singers cheer him endlessly! . . . Cheerful spirits in the evening, we stay up until two o'clock. – After the newspapers have constantly reported that R. was at loggerheads with the management and the singers, it makes us all laugh heartily to see the entire company giving him this public ovation, followed by a speech of thanks. On the 16th departure; farewell calls, in the evening many friends at the station. A wretched night, but soon behind us. At eleven o'clock back here in Bayreuth, Brange, Marke, Putz, Ross, Rausch, Viktor – dogs and people in a real act of rejoicing[2]!

Saturday, December 18 Very good night in our own home! The children out in the garden early; I write some letters, put business matters in order; friend Feustel comes to discuss Batz, Fürstner; he and I know, but R. not yet, that Prince Bismarck has cancelled the 30,000 thalers which the Emperor would have been willing to lend from Reich funds!!! In the evening 'the two big girls' arrive from the boarding school, Blandine affectionate and gentle, Daniella's behaviour down-right alarming. –

Sunday, December 19 The children have brought back very bad reports, my reproaches about this get a very dismal reception from Daniella; Boni also relapses into invective, but then feels real remorse; Daniella, poor child, seems to have decided that she will achieve something by defiance! . . . What remains for me to do? . . . Is this to become the great trial of my life? In the evening music, Handel's 'Saint Cecilia', pleasure in its magnificent individual features.

Tuesday-Wednesday, December 21–22 A request has come from America for a composition for the opening of the exhibition[3] – perhaps he will accept the commission. – The main difficulty at the moment is paying the bills, since the 30,000 thalers from the Reich funds are not available. R. has declared his willingness to conduct concerts all over the place following the performances, but this is insufficient security for borrowing money. It is pointed out that R. might die! – R. remarks that it is now once more four years since he last wrote a note of music; how this pains me! . . . In the evening Herr Gross brings a letter from Herr Scaria: he is demanding 2,700

---

[1] Conducted by Richter.
[2] The first three dogs, the second three servants in Wahnfried.
[3] The Centennial Exposition in Philadelphia, celebrating the American Declaration of Independence.

thalers for the month of August and 250 marks for each evening rehearsal – R. dispenses with the services of this gentleman. Now he has to look around for a new Hagen! . . . R. in cheerful mood in spite of everything and everybody.

Friday, December 24 Preparations from morning till evening, in the evening R. gives me a lovely dress, but loveliest of all are his words to me: 'The only god I possess is my love for you.' After the distribution of presents in the evening, R. reads *Don Quixote* aloud, and we laugh as heartily as if there were no such things as sorrow and concern.

Saturday, December 25 I thank Heaven and earth for my existence, since I was given a mission and permitted to perform it, remorsefully I beg forgiveness for the suffering caused by me, and I will courageously bear what my courage refuses to put into words! Breakfast with the children; birthday cake with candles, singing! R. unfortunately not well.

Tuesday, December 28 Although I have a firm arrangement with R. not to discuss unpleasant things, but to fight against them or bear them, and only to talk about the beautiful things, I manage to inform him of Mimi's letter; thereupon he drafts a letter to Prince Bismarck, a copy of which I sent to Bucher. Everything gloomy and harsh can be borne in love! – But in the evening I am plagued by a violent headache.

Friday, December 31 New Year's Eve begins for R. with a letter from Herr Fürstner's lawyer, the insolence of which transcends everything – Herr Fürstner should receive 1% on *Tannhäuser*, not only with the new scenes, but also without them! . . . R. starts legal proceedings, alleging deliberate fraud. – On this last day of the year we are not exactly cheerful; but in the evening, around the lighted Christmas tree, the mood becomes merrier, fortunes are told with lead: for Fidi helmet and shield, for Isolde a bird's nest, an idyll, for Boni a young man, for Lulu a dragon, for Eva the goddess Fortuna! After that, shoe throwing. We go to bed intending to enter the New Year sleeping, but it finds me still awake! From the bottom of my heart I wish peace to the evil, fulfilment to the good. I have no bad feelings for anybody, certainly not even for those who wish me and us evil. – A great longing for peace! Resolution to fulfil all my duties!

Tribschen and Mount Pilatus

Isolde and Blandine standing behind Eva,
Siegfried and Daniela, 1872/3

Haus Wahnfried. Drawing, 1874/5

The Wagner Theatre, 1876. Wood engraving; some details invented

The Rhinemaidens, 1876: Lilli Lehmann, Marie Lehmann, Minna Lammert

Swimming machine for the Rhinemaidens, who rode on bunks elevated on poles

Richard Wagner, 1877

Cosima Wagner, 1877

Garden of the Palazzo Rufalo, Ravello

'Richard Wagner with wife and children.
Klingsor's Magic Garden has been found!'

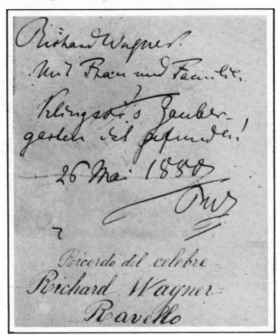

Family picture in Wahnfried, August 23, 1881. Richard and Cosima Wagner,
Heinrich von Stein, Paul von Joukowsky, Daniela and Blandine

Reception at Wahnfried, 1882. Front, from left: Siegfried, Cosima,
Amalie Materna, Richard Wagner; back, from left: Franz von Lenbach,
Emil Scaria, Franz Fischer, Fritz Brandt, Hermann Levi; at the piano:
Franz Liszt, Franz Betz, Hans Richter, Albert Niemann;
right front seated: Countess Schleinitz

Richard Wagner while
playing the piano,
Palazzo Vendramin,
February 12, 1883.
Pencil drawing by
Paul von Joukowsky

Palazzo Vendramin, Venice. The Wagners' quarters were in the rear wing

1876

Saturday, January 1 R. discovers that the newspapers are saying that Herr Scaria demanded 2,000 florins for his entire stay in Bayreuth and had been turned down by the management committee! R. is requesting a correction through Standhartner. – R. is despondent: 'The meanness one is confronted with,' he says, 'gets worse and worse; I never before experienced what I am going through now.' Herr Gross told him that, when they tried here to counter the lies about the sale of our house, no newspaper would accept the item!

Sunday, January 2 Today we have our Bayreuth friends to lunch (the Feustels, the Grosses, the mayor and his wife). R. drinks to them, says that his good experiences of the past year have been due to them alone.

Tuesday, January 4 In the afternoon Herr Feustel comes to speak to me, he is in low spirits: the advance has not arrived from the treasury, and he has been unable to pay Herr Brandt! A letter from Frau v. Schl. shows me that R.'s letter to the Prince has had no effect at all. She and Bucher are thinking about approaching the Reichstag! In the evening read *As You Like It*, after discussing all the bad news with R.; the lowest of spirits must yield to this divine humour.

Wednesday, January 5 I tried to persuade R. to return to the biography, but he asks me to wait until these bad times have been decided one way or another. Today I suggested to Herr Feustel that my property be pledged and that he approach my father in this connection; he promises to do that 'if all else fails.'

Thursday, January 6 R. dreamed that he had to conduct the Ninth Symphony, in Dresden or Munich, and passed beforehand through a railway station restaurant which had frankfurters; being very hungry, he ordered some; coming back to fetch them, he sees two men eating his portion, the assistant at the buffet maliciously insolent, also the manageress, who refuses him not only the sausages, but beer as well; he is angry, then tries friendly words, all to no avail. In the end he leaves the restaurant, cursing, arrives at the concert hall, walks through the orchestra, is greeted with applause, but has to climb, relies on his agility, but comes to a place which is too steep; when he cannot jump over it, he wakes up! . . . He says, 'All one needs is bad experiences to stop the brain from carrying out the task it is there to do, for demons of all kinds to take control and produce nothing but horrible images!'... Decisions regarding my Daniella; I shall keep Blandine at home.

Friday, January 7 Departure of Daniella, I clearly feel that in her the severest trial of my life has been inflicted on me.

Saturday, January 8 In the evening, selecting the curtain for the Gibichung's hall. This work on artistic things the only means of cheering myself up. . . .

Sunday, January 9 R. has good news of Herr Unger, God grant that no disappointments will arise here! Mimi Schl. writes advising a petition from the management committee to the Reichstag, Bucher believes the mood to be favourable. In such a difficult situation, anyway, it is impossible to do more damage, since nothing helps!... R. in despondent mood, I try to persuade him to start again on the biography tomorrow, and he promises. God forbid any obstacles!

Monday, January 10 Lessons for the children very early in the morning, then *dictation*! In the afternoon to the ice with the children and worked with them in the evening before supper. R. was with the mayor, who is very much against a petition to the Reichstag. R. writes to Councillor Düfflipp to inquire whether H.M. would take this ill!

Wednesday, January 12 No dictation today! R. is thinking of business matters; he is deeply annoyed at being referred to the Reichstag, when he had appealed to the Emperor's grace.

Friday, January 14 Letters, a very good one from Standhartner with an account of the royalties, then a nice one (as always) from the King, a sad one from Councillor Düfflipp, complaining of the difficulties of the royal treasury; R. sends a telegram saying he has decided not to approach the Reichstag, and to give concerts in Brussels. A conference yesterday with Feustel and the mayor did in fact reveal that the emergency is not such a dire one, and that a rebuff from the Reichstag would discredit our whole undertaking – Bismarck probably only too anxious for this rebuff, in order to justify his own behaviour.

Monday, January 17 R. wrote down a theme which came to him during the evening, and discovers that the countertheme can be found in a simple reversal of it; he says there are melody spectra for the ear just as there are light spectra for the eyes. Dictation. – Herr Gross brings us a note from Feustel; the latter has received a letter from Berlin which makes it seem advisable after all to approach the Reichstag and the Prince personally with a request. R. very much against it. Bismarck's secretary writes somewhat confusedly, but also seems of the opinion that the difficulties would be less if one were to approach the Reichstag!

Tuesday, January 18 The King sends us a life-size photograph of himself; Dr. Strecker[1] (successor of the 'Sons' in the firm of *B. Schott's Sons*) visits

---

[1] Ludwig Strecker (b. 1853) was at this time manager of the publishing firm, of which he subsequently became owner.

us, bringing the score of *Siegfried*. He pleases us with his very good manners. More dictation, and work with Boni.

Wednesday, January 19 Dictation and work. Herr Jauner reports that as a condition of his engagement Herr Scaria is demanding 2,500 thalers from July 15 onwards, to be paid now *in advance*. This makes R. so indignant that he feels like dispensing with Scaria right away, but he cables Betz first, inviting his and Niemann's opinion.

Thursday, January 20 Further dictation and lessons; R. receives Herr Betz's opinion that Scaria will have to be dispensed with. R. writes to Herr Jauner accordingly. How will Frau Materna now react?

Friday, January 21 Lessons and dictation. More and more we are considering, R. and I, the question of education; thoughts of establishing a model school, with Nietzsche, Rohde, Overbeck, Lagarde. Could the King be induced to sponsor it? . . .

Saturday, January 29 Dictation and lessons. Lothar Bucher writes, telling us on no account to undertake anything just now, the Prince is the only person on whom one can rely, and he is ill. – In the evening *Don Quixote*.

Monday, January 31 R. has a conference in the afternoon, from which he returns very depressed. To contemplate going on with the performances looks like foolhardiness! Only 488 patrons so far! And the expenditure is mounting, the press closed to us even for announcements!

Friday, February 4 R. wanders up to the theatre, it is like a desert up there! The preparations for accommodations are having to be pursued very casually, since nobody has the slightest idea who will come!

Saturday, February 5 R. says if our journey to Berlin were not impending he would start work on *Parzival*. But unfortunately we shall have to make this excursion.

Sunday, February 6 It is being said in Meiningen that Hans has bought a house there and intends to marry a beaatiful Russian woman; how gladly I would believe this, but I have no hopes in this regard. I am having to struggle against an increasing melancholy!

Monday, February 7 A bailiff arrives, and we rack our brains wondering what he wants, all sorts of possible and impossible things occur to R.; then to our great amusement it turns out that a woman in Vienna is laying claim to Scaria's earnings here; we are told he owes her 25,800 thalers and is under an obligation to her. At least we are glad to have an explanation for Scaria's unbelievable behaviour!

Wednesday, February 9 No dictation today, R. works on his composition for the Americans (opening of the World's Fair, Centennial of Independence); he has asked for 5,000 dollars for it – we wonder whether the promoters will agree to this. When I go to lunch, he is playing a gentle, rocking theme – he says nothing occurs to him to represent American pomp.

Monday, February 14 R. still working, complains of being unable to visualize anything to himself in this composition; it had been different with the '*Kaisermarsch*', he says, even with 'Rule Britannia'[1], where he had thought of a great ship, but here he can think of nothing but the 5,000 dollars he has demanded and perhaps will not get. A conference in the evening. The situation is tolerable on the whole, though Feustel informs us that Bismarck has declared to Jachmann that, since we had not followed his advice to go to the Reichstag, where he would have exerted all his power on behalf of our cause, he wished to hear nothing more about the matter! . . .

Wednesday, February 16 After lunch R. shows me his latest album leaf, 'an attempt to be American', and says it is the chorus the women will sing to Parzival: '*Komm, schöner Knabe!* '[2] . . . He is thinking a lot about *Parzival* and is grieved that so many things intervene.

Friday, February 18 Springtime, the starlings are here; but R. is unwell, he thinks because he has too many things on his mind – *Tristan* in Berlin, court cases, accommodation matters, *Lohengrin* in Vienna, on top of that the American composition is supposed to be finished by March 15!

Saturday, February 19 R. works, I give lessons. Recently Herr Niemann cabled for the parts of the so-called love song for a Court concert in Meiningen – the first direct sign of life from him since he returned the part of Siegmund; when I ask R. whether he intends to send them, he replies, 'You don't look a gift Siegmund in the mouth!'

Sunday, February 20 R. has completed his draft, plays it for me, it is splendid, much good cheer about this.

Tuesday, February 22 R. writes to Herr Jauner, asking whether the performance [of *Lohengrin*][3] could not be put off to another time, since conditions are now so bad. – Brandt complained yesterday that one can get nothing in Germany; he needed pink glass for a sunrise, and had to order it from France. 'Bismarck,' says R., 'has handled the country's welfare like a student.'

Friday, February 25 R. works on the score, but since he has had no reply from America, he decides not to hurry himself. A telegram from Herr Jauner settles our journey to Vienna.

Sunday, February 27 I write Hans a report on the state of our artistic affairs; this almost exhausts me. The only emotion to which my heart clings for support is that, even if I wish more happiness for all those I love than is vouchsafed them, I do not wish better things for myself; the more deeply I suffer, the stronger grows this strange ecstasy of suffering within me. I should like to be able to assume that, just as earthly vapours turn into fertilizing rain, so too might the sighs and tears which come from me rain

[1] An overture that Wagner composed in 1837.

[2] Correctly, '*Komm', komm', holder Knabe*' ('come, fair youth'), sung by the Flower Maidens in Act II of *Parsifal*.

[3] Wagner had promised to conduct a performance of *Lohengrin* in Vienna for the benefit of the chorus.

down as blessings on my children; however, if that were so, suffering would be a mirage, and it must be extreme reality!

Monday, February 28 Poor Brange is ill, yesterday she had three puppies, which are already dead! A silently suffering animal – how noble compared with the dissatisfied, complaining human being! . . . [*Added by R. W.; 'Enough of that!!'*] This joke of R.'s makes us laugh, but otherwise there is not much to cheer us; preparations for our departure.

Wednesday, March 1 Arrival in Vienna at 8 in the evening, met by our friends and the chorus.

Thursday, March 2 At half past six *Lohengrin*, R.'s magical conducting works miracles, the orchestra plays the Prelude as I have never heard it played before, the chorus is magnificent, the individual singers unfortunately worse than mediocre, incorrect, voiceless, without style.

Friday, March 3 To Marie Dönhoff and Marie Hohenlohe. After that a very nice dinner at Herr Jauner's; departure at eight o'clock, the chorus again at the station; the '*Wach' auf*' chorus [from *Die Meistersinger*], wonderfully sung by them in the waiting room, leaves a very deep impression. The high room, dimly lit, this crowd of poor people suddenly bursting into sublime song, this leaves behind a deep impression and a transfigured image!

Saturday, March 4 Good night in the sleeping car, in Berlin at two o'clock; Mimi the first to greet us; the impossibility of understanding the Reich Chancellor's attitude towards our undertaking . . .

Sunday, March 5 Dinner at the Schleinitzes', in the evening to [Gluck's] *Armide* to hear Frau Voggenhuber, who seems to us better than she has been made out to be[1].

Monday, March 6 R. had his first rehearsal [of *Tristan und Isolde*] today and was not exactly dissatisfied; it was just that the main singer [Niemann] completely lacks the necessary nobility and dark glow. We then drive to Doepler's house and look at his lovely costumes for the *Ring*; they really are very lovely, of great variety, and simple, suggesting to one an entire civilization; I myself should have preferred a more mystical impression, everything too clearly defined visually is to my mind detrimental to the effect of the music and the tragic action, but if the visual aspect must be emphasized, it could not be done more beautifully or artistically.

Tuesday, March 7 Another bass singer, a Herr [Josef] Kögel, with whom R. is very pleased. He returns fairly contented from the rehearsal. At noon, just as I am about to set out on calls, Mimi brings me a newspaper report of my mother's death[2]. At first I am unable to believe it – I cable to Paris,

---

[1] Vilma von Voggenhuber (b. 1845) was to sing Isolde in the production of *Tristan* that Wagner had come to Berlin to supervise.

[2] She died in Paris on March 5.

receive no answer. R. tells me all the newspapers are reporting the same! – Claire does not know my present address.

Wednesday, March 8 A letter of the 2nd, held up in Bayreuth, reaches me today, telling me about an illness which was not considered serious. A telegram from Schuré in response to an inquiry from R. informs us that my mother was buried yesterday!... All inquiries addressed to Claire remain unanswered. – I drive to the cemetery with R., making the same journey I made 16 years ago behind the coffin of my brother. The grave is well looked after. I intend to have it fenced in.

Thursday, March 9 Days of silence. This evening an express letter came, I thought it was news from Paris, but it was only a notification from Philadelphia that R.'s terms had been accepted. – I wrote to the children.

Friday, March 10 Letter from Schuré about the funeral. Also from Claire, but still without an address, so that I am not yet released from my state of complete isolation!

Sunday, March 12 Today R. writes five pages of his score, since he has no rehearsal. Took a drive with R., who likes Berlin better than Vienna.

Thursday-Monday, March 16–20 Did not write in all this time. On the 17th R. finishes the American march and is receiving 5,000 dollars (25,000 francs) for it. Dinner with Herr von Hülsen and several dignitaries! On Monday the 20th, utter turmoil with the tickets, up to 150 marks being offered for the better seats; the performance begins at six o'clock, the Emperor and all his Court plus many minor Courts, present on account of the Emperor's birthday; a tremendous crush in the corridors, and much activity; R. with the Emperor and Empress during the first intermission; otherwise with me in von Hülsen's box. Curtain calls, flowers, wreaths and the usual, on top of it attempts by the opposition, loud laughter from three or four people following the shepherd's tune. Betz splendid as Marke; Niemann bad, [Marianne] Brandt good as Brangäne, Frau Voggenhuber (Isolde) surprising in many ways, though inadequate as a whole.

Wednesday, March 22 Emperor's birthday with terrible snow flurries; it brings me in addition a number of business letters to write, for the lawyer informs me that the 40,000 francs due to or inherited by me are greatly endangered by the other clauses! A dismal situation, from any point of view! ... I do what is in my power to avert the loss, while protecting all that is holy to me. – R. is receiving large offers for the American march (Herr Peters 9,000 marks, which Messrs. Bote & Bock want to outbid).

Thursday, March 23 Farewell dinner with Mimi. The Emperor, she says, declares that *Tristan* is a '*magnifique*' work, the Crown Princess earnestly occupying herself with it. At eight in the evening took leave of the excellent woman. Spent the night in Leipzig.

Friday, March 24 Home at one o'clock, the children well and cheerful. Great weariness. Early to bed.

Wednesday, March 29 Conference, in which the machinist Brandt once again shows his utter superiority; he alone has ideas; the ceiling, which can no longer be made here, is to be done on canvas by the Brückner brothers.

Sunday, April 2 Wrote to E. O[llivier], who is trying to make me suspicious of Claire Charnacé!

Friday, April 7 R. receives a letter from Herr Vogl, saying his wife is expecting a baby; now a new Sieglinde has to be found, R. sends a telegram to Frau v. Voggenhuber. – Herr. v. Hülsen informs us that the proceeds from the 1st performance of *Tristan* will yield 13,000-odd marks.

Wednesday, April 12 R. receives a letter from Dr. Standhartner, saying Herr Jauner is making the release of Frau Materna conditional on the performances of *Tristan* and *Walküre* in Vienna next winter. So, before the work has even been done here, the seeds of its dissolution are being sown! R. complains about having to earn his living through the humiliation of his work; he says already he must admit to himself that the performances here will do nothing towards altering the wretched artistic situation. Nothing noble can last long in this world of ours.

Wednesday, April 19 Letter from Herr Jauner, delighted to get *Die Walküre* for Vienna (condition for Frau Materna!!!), intends to start on scenery right away. – R. beside himself; and on top of that the contracts for the chorus singers we need have not yet been sent; everyone there rotten, treacherous. And so crude – despite indescribable efforts R. not yet at his goal here, and he is to desecrate his work in advance for the sake of Vienna! Telegram from Herr Unger, he does not wish to come before Saturday – is in Kassel with his fiancée! R. now knows nothing about the progress he has made. And at three o'clock a telegram from Frau Voggenhuber, she has been unable to free herself from her commitments and so will not be able to sing Sieglinde! ... All this in a single afternoon; R. observes that the easiest to bear is what Fate brings, but the treachery of human beings! ... Their crude enthusiasm.

Thursday, April 20 Departure of Richter[1]; he says plainly that nobody in Vienna cares at all whether Bayreuth comes to anything or not, and that the breach with Scaria was provoked deliberately. In the afternoon R. receives news from the conductor Levi that, since the Munich opera is re-opening on August 15, it will be impossible to provide some of our requirements here! ... In the evening *Don Quixote*.

Friday, April 21 For R. nothing but ill tidings – Herr Unger arrives, but with a throat ailment! No word from [Marianne] Brandt, who should now be taking over Sieglinde, and – worst of all – Lilli Lehmann and [Minna] Lammert[2] are being refused leave; Herr v. Hülsen is keeping the theatre

---

[1] He had arrived from Vienna two days before.
[2] Singer in Berlin (b. 1852), sang Flosshilde (Rhinemaiden) in the first festival.

open until July 1! Frau Grün informs us that Eilers (Fasolt)[1] has heart trouble and is dangerously ill!! And on top of all this the state of the theatre! ...But requests for accommodation are said to be arriving in great numbers.

Monday, April 24 In the evening a letter from Lilli Lehmann – Frau v. Voggenhuber is in the same condition as Frau Vogl!... Everybody declares Frl. Brandt, R.'s choice, to be impossible, which is in very poor taste, since it is only because she is not pretty to look at. [Mathilde] Mallinger is said to have declared that she would like to sing Sieglinde, so R. sent her a telegram yesterday. – R. is magnificent in the way he bears all these adversities.

Tuesday, April 25 Nothing from Hülsen, nothing from Mallinger, nothing from [Josephine] Scheffsky[2], nothing from Jauner or from Materna! Great anxiety!

Wednesday, April 26 Frau Mallinger cables a refusal; still no Sieglinde. – R. goes to the theatre with Herr Brückwald, who has at last been awakened by an angry letter from Feustel – everything still behindhand; and the ceiling promised by the brothers Brückner has not arrived, the canvas was wrong, they say!

Thursday, April 27 First rehearsal with Herr Unger, R. seems not dissatisfied, but also not entirely satisfied. In the morning Herr Gross visited me and said that R. had recently made a mistake – the sale of certificates of patronage had so far only reached the halfway stage. Feelings of discouragement. I go for a walk in the palace gardens with R., the hawthorn in bloom, lovely fragrance. – In the evening a man from Markneukirchen with an instrument which is said to replace a whole orchestra – it turns out to be an accordion! On the other hand, he has made a violin with a very lovely tone; the man himself a serious person.

Friday, April 28 A real devil of a day, the peppering of the winter things reveals all the great deficiencies of the household!... On top of that, a conference in the evening with gloomy news, friend Feustel believes war to be imminent.

Saturday, April 29 R. holds his third rehearsal with Herr Unger and is satisfied with him. A comical letter from Herr Krolop[3], remarking that if only the role of Sieglinde had been assigned three months earlier – !... – I cry to you, dear God, from the abyss! I am answered by the sad tune, and the whole of life stretches emptily before me, like the sea before poor Tristan.

Sunday, April 30 With the little ones quietly in the garden, playing croquet,

---

[1] Albert Eilers (b. 1830), Coburg, did in fact sing Fasolt.
[2] She had also been offered the role of Sieglinde.
[3] The singer Franz Krolop was Vilma von Voggenhuber's husband.

The Arabian Nights; suddenly friend Doepler with his sketches for the 'Ride of the Valkyries', very fine. Pleasant evening discussing all sorts of things.

Monday, May 1 Spoke a lot with Prof. Doepler about the Nibelung hoard, also about reducing ornamentation as much as possible; I beg, for example, that Brünnhilde not be given a wedding dress, and Wotan no braided cloak in the great scene with Brünnhilde.

Wednesday, May 3 Better news; Herr v. Hülsen reports with amiable brevity that everything has now been arranged; Herr Jauner puts off *Die Walküre* at least until January; Frl. Scheffsky will be arriving next Monday. – R. rehearses the last scene of the third act and is satisfied; he relates that the theme '*Sangst du mir nicht dein Wissen*', etc.,[1] occurred to him on the road from Hergeschwyl one time while he was driving home with me. Connection of motives with localities, the American march, for instance, with the old gate here.

Thursday, May 4 Mimi writes that Herr von Bronsart is arranging a concert on behalf of Bayreuth, and that my father has agreed to play the E-flat Concerto in it. Herr v. Bronsart seems now to have regained the courage to voice his old convictions, since Herr v. Hülsen is well disposed. Pitiful creatures!

Friday, May 5 All now settled in Vienna and Berlin; in their place we have typhoid fever, which, making a harmless appearance among the soldiers, has been built up in the most malicious way by the newspapers; inquiries for certificates are ceasing to arrive, all people want to know is the state of the epidemic!

Sunday, May 7 Violent toothache, on top of that insufferable squabbling among the servants, whereby we note that one can never get the better of women. – Telegram that *Tannhäuser* has been performed in London, in Italian, with great success; in Berlin an extra, seventh performance of *Tristan* with very great success.

Monday, May 8 Bad night and very wretched day with a toothache; leeches applied, some relief; R. has to receive Frl. Scheffsky, particularly recommended to him by Councillor Düfflipp as a modest and diligent girl. The voice and personality good, he accepts her for Sieglinde; she complains about her position in Munich, says the King is the only one who shows her favour, that in order that she might see who her friends were, he had sent her the conductors' and managers' reports – to the effect that 'nothing would come of her.'

Tuesday, May 9 Very listless, but less pain, I keep to my room; read W. Scott's *Count Robert of Paris* with unalloyed enjoyment. – Bad rations are said to have made the soldiers ill – the suppliers are all Jews and they deliver bad bread, bad meat, etc.

---

[1] Sung by Siegfried in Act III of *Siegfried* to the motive known variously as 'Love of Siegfried' and 'World Inheritance'.

Friday, May 12 Telegram from America that the march was a great success. R. is worried that he may have been foolish in choosing Frl. Scheffsky for Sieglinde.

Tuesday, May 16 Some guests at lunch and in the evening, but practically all of it has vanished from my memory. The scaffolding, still in place inside the theatre, plunges R. into utter despair; when he informs the architect Brückwald, the latter begs pardon humbly and nicely, the building supervisor Runckwitz, on the other hand, is very spiteful and rude.

Wednesday, May 17 Bad, rough weather and little to bring us pleasure. Among other things, Herr Rubinstein complaining of not being admitted to the rehearsals to accompany, though he has quarrelled with all the other musicians here. R. very indignant about it. The singers are also becoming more demanding.

Monday, May 22 R.'s birthday: my little gifts – majolica bowls with flowers, a lovely polar bear – give him pleasure; several calls, many telegrams of good wishes, among them a nice one from the King. In the evening we open the artists' restaurant; R. presiding in merriest mood (he brings things to an end with '*Hört, ihr Leute*'[1].

Wednesday-Monday, May 24–29 Drove with R. on one of these days up to the theatre, the scaffolding has been taken down, sublime impression from the auditorium as well as from the stage, like a dream; it makes one feel noble and melancholy! How little true sympathy has accompanied the spirit now made manifest here, how remote it seems! – The building shines down on me like a setting sun; not a dawn! One could take much pleasure in the approaching work, were one not so weighed down by worry.

Wednesday, May 31 Rehearsal of *Siegfried*; splendid! Unger good beyond all expectations, reminds one somewhat of Schnorr! – In the theatre in the evening, most of the orchestra players already here, also Frau Jaide. Thunderstorm, the rain comes in through the pasteboard roof! Despite everything a most powerful impression. R. very tired.

Thursday, June 1 Still machine rehearsals. R. demonstrates everything himself, climbs, acts, to the amazement of all. Herr Hill has arrived, his keenness very gratifying.

Friday, June 2 Rehearsal between Alberich and Mime! It goes very well; in the theatre in the evening Hill wants to climb up and fall into the abyss himself, in spite of giddiness and other difficulties – great triumph for R.

Saturday, June 3 First orchestra rehearsal, it sounds wonderful, R. says. – In the evening he returns home very happy, the experiment has succeeded, the Rhinemaiden singers mount the machines in person, Hill does his own climbing, the magic of genius has truly achieved the impossible! – I am overcome by an unutterable melancholy, my thoughts range far, return like

---

[1] The night watchman's song in *Die Meistersinger*.

heavy clouds, unburden themselves in tears, and rise up again in prayer. Listened to the birds, the Bülow bird is singing, the oriole! . . .

Sunday, June 4 Whitsunday – still more arrivals – in the evening heard the orchestra again, then watched the Rhine-maidens swimming!

Monday, June 5 Second dinner for the artists in our house, Betz, Wilhelmj,[1] etc., cheerful atmosphere. Inspection of the horse Grane. Then *Rheingold* rehearsal, first scene with orchestra and singers. The children with us – incredible that such things are possible!

Tuesday, June 6 Fidi 7 years old; R. surprises me with the *Idyll*, brings Fidi to my bed while I am still asleep, and then I hear it being played. At the conclusion Fidi is introduced to the players in the gallery, they cheer him, he thanks them! A stork is flying around the house – good omen. In the evening R. has a rehearsal (positioning, second scene of *Rheingold*); the ballet master Fricke is said to have achieved wonders, with local athletes as Nibelung dwarfs. But R. is terribly worn out and annoyed by how behindhand many things are, above all the decorations of the Brückner brothers, who in the meantime have painted 14 decorations for the Duke of Meiningen.

Friday, June 9 Positioning rehearsal of conclusion of *Das Rheingold*, it already makes a very powerful impression! Richter tells me on Saturday the 10th that after the final rehearsal of the orchestra alone, the entire orchestra broke out in cheers. All with sparkling eyes, cheerful faces, say they are different people here, are literally coming to life.

Sunday, June 11 Final rehearsal of *Rheingold*.

Monday, June 12 R. indisposed – headache, gumboil, he applies leeches and insists afterwards on driving to rehearsal. (He also, in the middle of a raging toothache, writes to the King.) After rehearsal very unwell. First act of *Walküre*; Niemann, Scheffsky, Eilers – R. again drilled them in everything, every movement, every single word.

Tuesday, June 13 R. had a terrible night, an abscess is forming on his gums. He has to stay away from rehearsal, which is run by Niemann, Fricke and Richter. – Herr Feustel sends us the following report. [*Attached is part of a letter, stating among other things:* 'Present level of admission tickets: for the first performance, 702; for the second, 642; and for the third, 570.'] A warning! *Memento mori*[2] – and that divine things do not produce divinities.

Wednesday, June 14 R. quite indisposed, had a bad night; there can be no question of his running the rehearsal; I pay a visit to the theatre and am able to bring him good news of it. Despite his pain, he jokes and says it seems to be his fate that *Die Walküre* should be performed behind his back!

Thursday, June 15 R.'s condition ever worse! Again no possibility of

[1] The famed violinist August Wilhelmj (b.1845) helped recruit the orchestras (which he also led) for both the laying of the foundation stone of the theatre and the first festival.
[2] Remember you must die.

running the rehearsal . . . Today the second act – but when he is not there, nothing can be done; good will, application, etc., are no help. As I was driving up, Herr Feustel called me into his office to ask me if I am still prepared to come to the aid of the undertaking with my expected inheritance, since things are in a bad way. I say yes and write at once to Claire, inquiring when I might expect to receive my 40,000 francs. Feustel does not seem to believe that all the certificates will be sold.

Friday, June 16 With the help of chloral R. has a tolerable night, 'swollen up like a hippopotamus', as he says. But he cannot attend the rehearsal, which then becomes 'a groping in the dark', to use Richter's words. In the evening I inform R. of Feustel's worries; he says the main thing is to get the thing done; if there is a deficit afterwards he can turn to the Reichstag and also to the princes.

Saturday, June 17 Since R. slept well (again with the help of chloral), he decides to run the rehearsal; orchestra and singers then completely different people! R. decides to leave out the horse in the scene between Brünnhilde and Siegmund, since it is distracting. Tremendous effect of the whole. – Feustel says the Crown Prince and Princess have refused invitations to attend the performances.

Sunday, June 18 Day of rest for everybody, for me much to-ing and fro-ing.

Tuesday, June 20 In the afternoon the second rehearsal of the third act (*Walküre*). Yesterday was the first, a shattering experience for all participants and onlookers. When R. demonstrated to Frl. Scheffsky the gesture with which she passes from frozen despair to startled joy and enraptured exultation, tears were running down all our faces. Prof. Doepler told me very prettily how every evening the artists raved about Wagner and pitied the poor patrons, who would see only a few performances and really know nothing about it at all. 'We should pay the 300 thalers,' he observes, 'since we are having an enjoyable time.' The grouping of the Valkyries splendid – the rock looks like a Valkyries' nest.

Wednesday, June 21 Third *Walküre* rehearsal, much vexation. Incorrect tempi in the orchestra, and Frl. Scheffsky all but impossible!

Thursday, June 22 First *Siegfried* rehearsal with piano – Herr Unger pleases R. greatly, he says he is the only one who has learned something from him.

Saturday, June 24 R. very run down, the abscess still there, but he drives to the orchestra rehearsal. Prof. Doepler offended by R.'s vehemence (everything still lacking, stage properties, etc.). In the evening R. effects a reconciliation in his own nice way.

Sunday, June 25 Today Herr Kögel[1] is at last to sing Hagen in front of R. – The children liked the first act of *Siegfried* best of all – which pleases R.,

---

[1] Joseph Kögel, Hamburg, engaged to replace Scaria.

for it supplies proof of its folk character, whereas all the artists have up to now treated this first act as if it were quite incomprehensible.

Monday, June 26 First rehearsal of *Siegfried* second act, Herr Unger hoarse, which is really distressing, not to say serious. All the same, the act makes a wonderful impression. The scenery is outstandingly beautiful, and Herr Brandt has once again worked wonders. R. returned home at noon very sad, the scenery was not at all what he had wished for – our masterly Brandt put it all in order in the space of only a few hours. On that account a very cheerful mood in the evening.

Wednesday, June 28 Still no governess, which makes us – since the children are being very good – laugh and call them our Pestalozzis, since they are teaching one another. R. has a rehearsal with Herr Kögel in the morning, a great strain for him; in the evening 2nd act of *Siegfried* with orchestra – but Herr Unger still hoarse!!

Thursday, June 29 Third act of *Siegfried*, R. setting things up, very tiring for him; Herr Brandt in despair, because the Brückner brothers are leaving him in the lurch, the mechanics in London have *nothing* finished, on top of it news of war!!!

Friday, June 30 Letter from Councillor Düfflipp, promising postponement up to the 800th certificate of patronage. R. beside himself. – Arrival of the English governess[1]. Very welcome to me, since the German characters so far very disagreeable. In the evening *Siegfried*, Herr Unger still hoarse, nevertheless a magnificent impression! Unparalleled.

Saturday–Tuesday, July 1–11 The whole of *Götterdämmerung*!!! Unger well again; instead, trouble with Hagen – Herr Kögel, losing his nerve, departs; negotiations with Scaria, who remains true to his meanness. Great financial difficulties, every day costs 2,000 marks, little coming in, Herr Feustel reports that in 3 weeks we shall have nothing left. I try to get my capital sent from Paris, without success! At last, on the 10th, the news that 6,600 marks have been paid into the account, and the political situation calmer. Arrival of Malwida Meysenbug, and a splendid piece by Nietzsche, *R. Wagner in Bayreuth*[2]. – *Götterdämmerung* uniquely moving, inspiring. Shattering news of the sudden death of one of our orchestra players – a Herr Richter from Berlin!

Wednesday, July 12 R. holds a rehearsal in the morning with Frau Materna, in the afternoon third act of *Götterdämmerung* with orchestra, indescribable impression! In the evening in the restaurant, where R. gets very angry with the Brückners, who express themselves very clumsily (they say they could not neglect their oldest '*customer*', the Duke of Meiningen!). The word 'customer' upsets R. terribly. He regrets this, however, and cordially begs

---

[1] Presumably Mrs Cooper.

[2] The fourth book of *Thoughts out of Season*, published in 1876 by Schmeitzner.

pardon of the B.'s. But then he decides not to visit the restaurant any more, deeply grieved by his excessive reaction.

Thursday, July 13 No rehearsal; we drive up to the theatre, however, since R. wants to discuss the last scene (the appearance of Wotan) with Brandt and to see the Doepler figurines. I am much grieved by them, revealing as they do an archaeologist's fantasy, to the detriment of the tragic and mythical elements. I should like everything to be much simpler, more primitive. As it is, it is all mere pretence. – The piano rehearsals ended with the wholesale dismissal of Herr Rubinstein, who here once more displayed all the dismal characteristics of his race.

Friday, July 14 In the afternoon rehearsal of *Rheingold*. – Herr Niemann 'graciously' present, as I say to him in fun. We remain in the restaurant after all, since R. wishes to 'invent' something with Brandt so that the glare from the orchestra will not spoil the effects in *Rheingold*.

Saturday, July 15 Herr Siehr[1] at rehearsal; R., satisfied with him, engages him for Hagen! In the evening final rehearsal of *Das Rheingold*; many vexations for R. in the course of it, the rainbow bridge wrong (so far), the steam fails to work, because Herr Brandt, warned by the management committee about the need for economy, could not produce the proper vapours! The Brückner brothers have painted in haste, so there are ineradicable mistakes in the decorations! . . .

Sunday, July 16 Letter from the King, signifying his intention to come, forbids any sort of ovation, wants to see nobody. Mimi's arrival, great joy over this, we spend the day together. It is doubtful whether the German Emperor will come.

Monday, July 17 First act of *Walküre*, Frl. Scheffsky terrible! Herr Niemann *does* it well. Got Mimi installed, also spent the day with her. R. very tired, little demand for seats.

Tuesday, July 18 Second act of *Walküre*, Frl. Scheffsky even more horrible; she previously at lunch, an excess of ungainliness and gracelessness! Conference over whether to get rid of her at all costs. Fears that another singer would no longer have time to learn it.

Wednesday, July 19 Most of my time spent with Mimi. In the evening third act of *Walküre*, splendid impression. Herr Brandt's 'Magic Fire' magnificent, Herr Doepler's representations of the Valkyries not good yet.

Thursday, July 20 First act of *Siegfried*, Herr Unger quite good, in spite of the players' not giving him enough support. Unfortunately Herr Schlosser has forgotten a lot of Mime through having had to sing all sorts of different things in Munich.

Friday, July 21 A good day for the box office today – 5,200 marks come in – enough to keep us for two days. The final scene of *Götterdämmerung* is

---

[1] Gustav Siehr (b.1837), Wiesbaden, sang Hagen in 1876 and Gurnemanz (*Parsifal*) in 1882.

given shape – with human forms, not transparencies. Nice telegram from the King, thanking us for the Nietzsche pamphlet. Second act of *Siegfried*, Herr Unger in very good voice! R. very tired. He sleeps now only until three or four in the morning!

Saturday, July 22 Rehearsal of third act of *Siegfried* to the jubilation of all. R. tired. At 11.20 in the evening I go to fetch Lusch. She has grown and looks nice, strikingly like her father! R. wakes up as I come home, goes to the window, greets the constellation of the Great Bear, which is shining most beautifully. 'Good star, protect my wife and my children, do with me what you will!' He tells me he has been thinking of his death. He embraces me tenderly, saying that nobody knows all the things he owes to me.

Sunday, July 23 Pleasure in Lusch, who has become quite grown-up. Paid some calls with her. Several guests in the evening. In the meantime great vexation. Without telling R. anything about it, the management committee has advertised a public rehearsal with seats at three marks. R. beside himself.

Monday, July 24 All seats are said to have been sold within half an hour, which delights friend Feustel! Prof. Nietzsche has also arrived, and the Dannreuthers and several others. First act of *Götterdämmerung*, Princess Barjatinsky[1], Mimi and I in the princes' gallery[2], the children with us.

Tuesday, July 25 Dinner with Princess B., Mimi, Wilhelmj. Afterwards the second act in public; Herr Siehr very good as Hagen. After the audience has left, second rehearsal. Afterwards Herr Brandt offended, declares his intention of leaving, because he is described in a programme merely as a machinist!! I try to calm him down and to prove to him that R. knew nothing about the whole thing. With difficulty I half succeed!

Wednesday, July 26 R. opens a letter written yesterday by Herr Feustel, who announces his resignation from the management committee – because R. had admitted the fire brigade to the rehearsal free of charge! R. writes back jokingly, and Heckel mediates! In the evening third act. – Increasing awareness of the imperfections in the representation!! The performance will lag as far behind the work as the work is removed from our own times!

Thursday, July 27 News today that Herr von Baligand[3] has quarrelled with the management committee and departed!! Who will now prepare the palace for the princely guests? Absurdities like this a daily occurrence now! In the afternoon costume rehearsal, little pleasure in it, much conventionalism, lack of beauty, little inventiveness and too much ornateness. R. again splendid in his patience and kindness!

Friday, July 28 In the evening costume rehearsal; on my request to

---

[1] Presumably the wife of the Russian Prince Viktor Barjatinsky, who held a certificate of patronage.
[2] A row of boxes at the back of the auditorium.
[3] President of the Munich Wagner Society.

Professor Doepler to make Siegfried's clothes a little less close-fitting and to dress Gutrune's ladies less brightly, the poor man becomes so angry and rude that I realize for the first time what a hack one is having to deal with! The costumes are reminiscent throughout of Red Indian chiefs and still bear, along with their ethnographic absurdity, all the marks of provincial tastelessness. I am much dismayed by them and also rather shocked by the professor's manner. R. is having great trouble with Wotan's hat; it is a veritable musketeer's hat!

Saturday, July 29 R. goes to the theatre; rehearsal with Prof. Doepler, who behaves like a 'schoolboy'. In the evening first *Rheingold* rehearsal in costume, R. very sad afterwards, because Herr Brandt himself is in error. The singers very good, particularly Herr Vogl as Loge. After the rehearsal R. and I at home by ourselves, R. deeply worried.

Monday, July 31 Get a fleeting idea of what floods of ugly talk and opinion are always flowing about here. What most shocks me is the falseness and mendacity behind it, and I feel very much like wishing, with our good Falstaff, that it were bedtime and all past. In the evening *Walküre*, rehearsal of the entr'actes.

Tuesday, August 1 Visitors of all kinds, and finally fetched my father from the railway station. He is very well and R. decidedly refreshed by his arrival.

Wednesday, August 2 Family lunch with my father; Olga Meyendorff also here. Lulu considered very well mannered. In the evening *Siegfried*, Unger quite good. Much that is unsatisfactory. The costumes, particularly Alberich's, almost ludicrous – Alberich with coat and epaulettes.

Thursday, August 3 Deep inner despondency! Hans in Godesberg is said to be so very, very unwell! . . . The tidings oppress my soul like an overwhelming shadow, joy is unthinkable, only patience and work!

Friday, August 4 Slept little, submerged in thought, thoughts, sighs and entreaties; a return of the inexorable powers! I take up writing again on September 8 – will my memory serve me sufficiently? . . .

Saturday, August 5 R. goes at midnight to fetch the King, I accompany him as far as the railway station near the Eremitage, then R. drives away with the King and returns home late, but in raptures about his kindliness[1].

Sunday, August 6 In the evening dress rehearsal without an audience, the King sends for me as well and tells me I should never have doubted that he would remain loyal to us. The rehearsal goes very well. Great illuminations and cheers for the King.

Monday, August 7 Rehearsal of *Die Walküre* in front of an audience, since it improves the acoustics. Much abuse with the tickets. Public rehearsals also on 8th and 9th, R. with the King throughout; R. professes to have

---

[1] The King, who was accompanied only by his head equerry and an aide-de-camp, stayed at the Eremitage.

detected a certain ill feeling as he takes his departure – the King has forbidden any sort of ovation, yet he seems astonished when none takes place. – On the 12th arrival of the Emperor, the Grand Duke of Schwerin with wife and daughter, the Grand Duchess of Baden, Anhalt-Dessau, Schwarzburg-Sondershausen, etc., etc.; R. goes to meet the Emperor, who, in very friendly mood, talks about a national festival. At last, on

Sunday, August 13, first performance of *Rheingold,* under a completely unlucky star: Betz loses the ring, runs into the wings twice during the curse, a stagehand raises the backdrop too soon during the first scene change and one sees people standing around in shirt sleeves and the back wall of the theatre, all the singers embarrassed, etc., etc. – Each of us returns home separately, R. at first very upset, but gradually regains his spirits, and the sudden visit of the Emperor of Brazil[1] restores the mood of ebullience. We go to bed in very good spirits.

Monday, August 14 Walküre, this time without trouble – except for an incident which alarms R. greatly: he is summoned to the Emperor, who praises everything highly, says jokingly that, if he were an orchestra player, R. would never have got him down (into the orchestra pit), regrets not being able to remain for more than the two performances, whereupon R. replies, 'Favour is not dependent on time and place.' The Grand Duchess, however, says she is staying on. R.: 'Then you extend the favour.' The Emperor, jokingly: 'That was a dig.' He says goodbye, takes a step backwards, does not notice the doorstep, stumbles so awkwardly that it takes all of R.'s strength to hold him; he is convinced that this backward fall would have meant the death of the Emperor!

Tuesday, August 15 Herr Betz has *Siegfried* postponed! He says he is hoarse. Much ill feeling; the newspapers, already extremely malicious, will draw inferences from it.

Wednesday, August 16 Siegfried goes off well, people are saying that Herr Betz was never hoarse at all! Let others attempt to explain such characters, we do not understand them.

Thursday, August 17 Götterdämmerung also goes well.

Friday, August 18 Calls, dinners, a tremendous amount of coming and going, in the evening a banquet; R., quite without preparation, makes a wonderful speech, paraphrasing the final chorus from *Faust* – 'All things transitory are sent but as symbols.' The idea: 'The eternally feminine leads us on.' The Reichstag deputy chooses very unfortunate words: one could not know what posterity would think of it all, but the *striving* was worthy of recognition! Following that, Count Apponyi splendidly compares R. with Siegfried; he has brought tragedy back to life, because he never learned the

---

[1] Dom Pedro II arrived in Bayreuth without any ceremony and put up in a hotel, where on the registration form he gave his occupation as 'Emperor'.

meaning of fear. Quite splendid. Then R. proposes a wonderful toast to my father, without whom, he says, no one would have known anything about him, R. – A very, very lovely evening! All the singers absent except for Hill, Frau Grün, Reichenberg, Herr Siehr (outstanding as Hagen)! After working for three months with R., they do not consider it necessary on such an occasion to gather around him; they are said to be angry because we do not allow curtain calls in our theatre.

Saturday, August 19 Day of rest, that is to say, day of farewells and welcomings; the audience for the first series is now leaving, that for the second is now arriving. In the evening more than 200 people at our house.

Sunday, August 20 The King writes quite wonderfully about the impression the performances made on him, and he announces his visit for the third cycle. – Visit of the Duke of Meiningen and his wife. In the evening *Rheingold*, this time very good, except that Herr Betz is extraordinarily lifeless.

Monday-Wednesday, August 21–23 Walküre, Siegfried, Götterdämmerung proceeded undisturbed; I miss the first act of *Die Walküre*, being over-tired; but for the second R. comes himself to fetch me, saying he cannot bear my not being there.

Thursday, August 24 The Duke of Meiningen dines with us, he has given Frau Materna a decoration; in the evening a large reception here, Saint-Saëns[1] plays the piano, Marie Dönhoff and her mother, Mme Minghetti[2], the latter very gifted.

Friday, August 25 The King's birthday, dinner with the district president, in the evening departure of Lusch, who is returning to the boarding school, very painful in many ways, the girl's character worries me.

Sunday, August 27 R. again went to fetch the King during the night. Visit from Prince Georg in the morning. In the evening *Rheingold*. Demand for the third cycle great, the bad rumours have had time to prove false. Herr Betz increasingly negligent.

Monday, August 28 Walküre goes very well, except that Herr Betz is quite openly rebelling against his role, he laughs out loud when there is applause and the majority of the audience calls for quiet, so that it can listen. R. requests from the King the Order of Saint Michael for him and Herr Niemann, which is granted.

Tuesday-Wednesday, August 29–30 Siegfried and *Götterdämmerung*, and thus, most astonishingly, the programme which nobody thought possible has been adhered to. At the end of it R. addresses some fine words to the audience and introduces his artists, saying that it was they who had given

---

[1] Wagner had met the French composer in Paris in 1860, while preparing *Tannhäuser* there.
[2] Formerly Princess Camporeale, whom Saint-Saëns accompanied at the piano when in Paris in 1861 she sang Isolde's '*Liebestod*' in Wagner's presence and much impressed him.

him courage, by believing in him. R. takes his leave of the King. I alone with my father. Nice evening.

Friday, September 1 Departures, dinner with the Schleinitzes, Malwida and other friends. In the evening my father plays [Beethoven's] Opus 106 (Adagio and first movement) to a very small circle of us – so wonderfully.

Saturday, September 2 Departure of my father.

Sunday, September 3 Only R. Liechtenstein, Malwida, Gersdorff left, lunch and evening with them. In the morning R. has a conference with the management committee, the finances do not seem to be as bad as expected, and a repetition next year is practically certain.

Monday, September 4 Last departure; family lunch for the first time, I very tired, go to lie down. Fine autumn day. The days following the last cycle were terrible, whereas the weather was very kind to the performances themselves.

Friday, September 8 Our copyists to lunch, last meal together; very melancholy! Harsh things said about Herr Brandt, his rudeness, not justified by his achievements, his nasty attitude towards R., etc. R. is very hurt and does all he can to defend his colleague, but it is hard to defend all his actions. This makes him very sad.

Saturday, September 9 Departure of Math. Maier – the last visitor. After that preparations for the journey. In the evening a long discussion about the performances and the experiences gained during them. R. no longer wants the matadors Betz and Niemann; the former, in his rage at not being called before the curtain, made a downright mockery of his role! Brandt's achievements far short of what one might have expected! Richter not sure of a single tempo – dismal experiences indeed! I mention the scene between Waltraute and Brünnhilde and observe that – wonderful as it is – it does prove tiring, because already too much music has been heard before it; R. agrees with me and decides to divide up the 1st act, to make a long pause after the introduction and begin the act with the orchestral 'Siegfried's Journey'. In this way *Götterdämmerung* would be a repetition of the whole, an introduction and three parts. – Costumes, scenery, everything must be done anew for the repeat performances. R. is very sad, says he wishes he could die! – He very comically calls Betz and N. theatre parasites!

Sunday-Thursday, September 10–14 Preparations for the journey; departure at one o'clock; children weeping over the dogs! In Munich at eight o'clock, Hotel Vier Jahreszeiten, rude waiter, rain; my neckerchief catches fire, hair begins to burn, the barber, Schnappauf[1], who is with us, extinguishes it.

Friday, September 15 At eleven o'clock arrival in Verona, hotel muddles, much laughter, at one o'clock at last to bed.

---

[1] Bernhard Schnappauf, a Bayreuth barber, was also the Wagner family factotum.

Saturday, September 16 Up early with Richard and children. Much merriment. In the evening to the Teatro Ristori, [Rossini's] *Otello*, very bad.

Tuesday, September 19 At 11.30 departure for Venice, arrival at 3.30! Very fine impression from the start. Put up at the Hôtel de l'Europe.

Wednesday, September 20 Divine air. No desire to think, dream! . . . Meeting with Tesarini, the *corbo bianco*[1], the earliest Wagnerian in Italy, a true Venetian. Spent the evening on the Piazza San Marco.

Saturday, September 23 Fine letter from the King, he has truly grasped the idea of Bayreuth – this our greatest triumph! Less pleasing letter from friend Feustel, who reports debts amounting to about 120,000 marks. Discussion with R., plans, projects, much effort in store, a whole baggage train of activities.

Tuesday, September 26 To the Accadèmia di belli Arti, R. giving me pleasure by accompanying me there, as difficult to part from these divine things as from Venice itself, which we leave at one o'clock. From few human beings have I found it harder to part than from this city, which went straight to my heart as I know no other will ever do. – Arrival in Bologna at five o'clock.

Wednesday, September 27 Made the acquaintance of the syndic (Count Tacconi), who greets R. as an honorary citizen.

Thursday, September 28 Reached Naples at ten in the evening, Hôtel Vittoria; during this long and very tiring journey in immense heat the children remained good-natured, Siegfried in particular is indefatigably cheerful and good.

Saturday, September 30 A long rest, after that a little walk; in the afternoon siesta and reading (Sismondi[2]). In the evening a trip on the sea.

Thursday, October 5 Departure for Sorrento; as the ship leaves, beggars swim around in the water, among them a boy who stands out on account of his brown skin, his beauty and liveliness and agility – 'like something direct from Nature's workshop,' says R. – he gathers the coins thrown into the sea in his mouth. On the ship singers and guitarists and fiddlers, cheerful and mournful popular songs, at the same time wickerwork and oysters being bartered, all languages being spoken; while a dark-blue sea sings its eternal lullaby, and the blue line of hills encloses it all – a curious dream! Is it its strangeness or its familiarity which makes us feel so melancholy – a gentle yearning, I might call it, but for what? Not for living! – A gentleman from Magdeburg speaks to R., he was at our performances and speaks very nicely about them. Sorrento, the Hôtel Vittoria, we have taken the little cottage beside the hotel, wonderful peace.

---

[1] Luigi Tesarini, a piano teacher whom Wagner met in 1858, when he himself was living in Venice; '*corbo bianco*' ('white raven') was his own name for himself as an Italian with a taste for German music.
[2] A French-Swiss historian whose 16-volume *History of the Italian Republics During the Middle Ages* was published 1807–24.

Friday, October 6 Picked up lessons with the children again; they have forgotten quite a bit!

Monday, October 9 At eight o'clock set sail for Capri, breakfast in the Hôtel du Louvre, whose ridiculous name amuses us greatly; ride to the Villa Tiberio; stop at the Leap; our donkey girls dance the tarantella for us. Journey home amid shooting stars and phosphorescent waves! Unforgettable impression; the white houses in all that green, the splendid flowers, later the calm sea, a perfect summer night. Unfortunately, however, the shadow of gloomy thoughts at home. R. is wondering whether he should repeat the performances! Not a single one of the princes, having distributed decorations to all the participants, has asked R. what can be done for him, how he might be helped or supported!

Wednesday, October 11 Lessons, bathing, reading, a resumption of our Tribschen life, unfortunately with many reflections for and against; for R., how to get the performances started again?

Saturday, October 14 R. writes to Herr v. Radowitz, asking him for his opinion about what should be done. I give the children lessons; in the afternoon a walk; this spot here is becoming increasingly dear to me.

Monday, October 16 Moving; we leave the pretty cottage, which is slightly damp, and move to the third floor of the big hotel.

Friday, October 20 I take out a boat and float for a while on the sea, constantly changing, in eternal motion, neither wave nor cloud pays heed to my woe, and the motionless mountain throws it back; movement and rigidity, deaf and unreceptive; will a mortal being hear the sound? Perhaps a mother's heart! – We talk to R. about the beauty of this spot. 'Yes,' he observes, 'if one did not always bring one's thoughts with one.'

Thursday, October 26 Yesterday R. woke me up with a lovely improvisation; I should like to persuade him to forget all the *Nibelungen* troubles and to start on a new work. He was thinking again recently about a symphony of mourning for those who fell in the war, in which he would use his *Romeo and Juliet* theme. He saw the coffins being brought into a hall, more and more of them, so that individual grief was gradually submerged in general suffering. Only after that the song of triumph. But who shares his feelings? A wonderful drive in the afternoon, splendid sky, the island lying blissfully before us in a golden light, Vesuvius with the villages on its slopes, reddish-grey and brownish-gold, sombrely threatening. From Meta home on foot, a long walk in the moonlight; everything looking wonderful. I feel as if life has granted me a respite here!

Friday, October 27 Visit from Malwida, Dr. Rée[1] and our friend Nietzsche, the latter very run down and much concerned with his health. They are staying in Sorrento.

---

[1] Paul Rée (b. 1849), a philosopher, friend of Nietzsche since 1873.

Monday, October 30 Visit to Malwida with the children, in splendid weather. R. constantly reading Sismondi, with much enjoyment. We go for a walk in the afternoon. He is, as he tells me, grateful for everything which distracts him from the round of thoughts so oppressing him. We admit to each other that we frequently keep silent just in order not to have to impart to each other our gloomy thoughts concerning the present situation and all our past experiences. – R. has been looking through San-Marte's *Parzival* in a search for names, but he says it is very abstruse and of no use at all.

Wednesday, November 1 In the evening we are visited by Dr. Rée, whose cold and precise character does not appeal to us; on closer inspection we come to the conclusion that he must be an Israelite.

Friday, November 3 Letter from my father, also from Herr V. Schleinitz, very friendly, but nothing from Herr v. Radowitz; only friend Heckel writes and says that it is not R.'s task to approach the patrons about paying off the deficit, that the patrons themselves should take this over, settle it among themselves. He is the only one so far to show any feeling in the matter. Otherwise all we perceive is scorn and sneering.

Sunday, November 5 Winter has come; the sea is driving along its white horses and the wind blows cold; we think of leaving. In the evening, conversation with R., during which I try to talk about all sorts of strange things, but we always come back to the one dismal subject. R. says that his main feeling during the performances was, 'Never again, never again!' He winced so much, he says, that the King asked him what was the matter, and then he had to restrain himself forcibly.

Tuesday, November 7 Packed and left at eleven o'clock.

Thursday, November 9 Arrived in Rome.

Saturday, November 11 Saw Princess Wittgenstein again for the first time in about 16 years; met the Helbigs[1], etc.-

Thursday, November 16 The Sistine Chapel!!! ... Spent the evening at home. How happy we might be here if we were not besieged by gloomy thoughts! R. has received no answer of any kind from Herr v. Radowitz, everyone is silent except Feustel, who reminds us of the deficit, as if we had forgotten it!

Sunday, November 19 In the evening quite a large reception at the German ambassador's; Herr Sgambati[2] plays a quintet of his own which genuinely interests R. and is very remarkable; this accomplished musician is entirely lost and neglected here.

Tuesday, November 21 In the morning we visited the Vatican again; entering the Sistine Chapel R. said, 'This is like my theatre, one feels it is no place for jokes.' Returning home late, R. discovers that the post office was not prepared to hand over the long-awaited letter from Herr v. R. to the

---

[1] Wolfgang Helbig, a German archaeologist, and his wife Nadine, a pupil of Liszt.

[2] Giovanni Sgambati (b. 1841), Italian composer and pianist.

servant. Finally, one minute before closing time, he is given the letter, which says that nothing can be done for him.

Thursday, November 23 R. writes to Herr Feustel stating his opinion that he can do nothing until the deficit is paid off; for he cannot engage Herr Niemann and Herr Betz again without offering them a substantial fee.

Wednesday, November 29 Yesterday evening I read Herr Feustel's letter to R., which makes me think that the only course worthy of us would be to pay the deficit out of our own resources and then live in poverty, preserving silence towards all and everything. R., who did not read the letter until this afternoon, does not feel the necessity as strongly as I do, but nevertheless he writes to Herr Feustel in this sense. I know that for me real satisfaction would begin with this new phase of our life.

Thursday, November 30 R. has interested his own publisher in Mainz in the composer Sgambati, which gives him great delight. On the evening of the 30th a *soirée* by Italian artists, fine songs by Sgambati, a mandolin band. – Made the pleasant acquaintance of Count Gobineau[1], the French ambassador in Sweden.

Sunday, December 3 Departure at eleven o'clock, in Florence at nine in the evening – Hôtel du Nord.

Wednesday, December 6 We pay some calls, first of all to Frau Laussot[2].

Sunday, December 10 We drive with Prof. Hillebrand and Mme Laussot to Bello Sguardo. Talked much with R. about the possibility of settling down here; R. feels himself to be a German and concludes, 'In Germany I can earn my living, well or badly, and I can make every effort to do so in an honourable manner; but here I should have to live as a pensioner, which would make me feel very odd.'

Sunday, December 17 Departure at seven o'clock. On the evening of the 18th, the children still in splendid spirits, in the Marienbad Hotel in Munich!

Tuesday, December 19 Councillor Düfflipp; the King is inclined to lay our case before the Reichstag! Düfflipp wants to come to us between Christmas and New Year's to discuss business matters with Feustel. Great – and pleasant – surprise for us!

Wednesday, December 20 Departure at three o'clock. The children become increasingly lively the nearer we get, Siegfried improvises a scene in English, and the jubilation when we arrive knows no bounds. There at eleven o'clock in the evening. Welcome with torches, etc.!!

Thursday, December 21 To start with, great trouble in the house, everything to be restored to order! Pleasure for me in the work, which prevents all looking ahead or behind. The children blissful with the dogs.

---

[1] Joseph Arthur Gobineau (b. 1816) had just retired from his diplomatic career; he had already won much attention in Germany with his book extolling the Nordic races (*Essai sur l'inégalité des races humaines*); he was to become a close friend.

[2] Wagner's former friend, Jessie Laussot, was now living in Florence, as was the historian Karl Hillebrand, whom she married in 1879.

Friday, December 22 Herr Betz has written a very curious letter, in which he says that he cannot and will not take on the role of Wotan again, since he had not been equal to his task before.

Sunday, December 24 Just the Christmas tree, morning and evening; for R., Sismondi, which wholly absorbs him. Nice letter from Prof. Nietzsche, though informing us that he now rejects Schopenhauer's teachings!

Monday, December 25 My 39 years! . . . R. proposes my health very movingly. I feel how much of me has already died, and how little I must bother myself about myself.

Wednesday-Sunday, December 27–31 On Saturday the 30th sudden arrival of Richter, who could no longer bear Vienna and took advantage of three free evenings to spend a day with us. Great joy! On the 31st let the whole of our Tribschen life pass literally before our eyes, those distant, unforgettable times!

1877

Thursday, January 4 The children are flourishing, the four of them, and I also have good hopes for Daniella. In the evening read *Childe Harold*. Since the print is too small for my eyes, R. takes over the reading in German, and we greatly enjoy this final canto; I remark that Byron had the same sort of impressions as R.

Friday, January 5 After lunch R. talks about Fidi's education and his future – he would already have enough to occupy him if he were to take over his father's intellectual heritage, win and create new ground for his ideas. R. also says he would write *Parzival* for him, making the condition that it be produced 30 years after our death (R.'s and my death).

Monday, January 8 R. reads me his appeal for the foundation of a Society of Patrons[1]. In the evening friend Feustel visits us, and this is also read to him; he does not seem to approve of it, he wants the festival to be announced right away, on account of the deficit. Daniella today taken back to school by Mrs. Cooper.

Tuesday, January 9 In the evening the mayor and friend Feustel, they agree that Richard's idea of establishing a school (so that he can first train his singers here) is a very good one, but they ask permission to take steps towards announcing the festival. R. very agitated – 'I don't want to be obliged to stage a festival on account of the deficit.' – But he gives way in the end.

Wednesday, January 10 Today R. took part for the first time in an election, to elect Herr Feustel to the Reichstag. Dr. Strecker (B. Schott's Söhne) comes to inquire about *Parzival*! . . . Alas, Parzival, when will thy star shine forth?

Friday, January 19 R. speaks of handing it [the *Ring*] over to an entrepreneur; I have to weep, for I would wish it otherwise, would rather we pledged all our resources for years ahead but kept a hold on the work; R. does not want this, he also feels it would not be possible, the debt is too great for us to pay off. God protect us!

Saturday, January 20 Friend Feustel, now a Reichstag deputy, informs us on

---

[1] An appeal that the Wagner Societies join together to form an association that would take over responsibility for the funding of future festivals.

his return from Munich that Councillor Dükflipp wishes to come here tomorrow, and that the opinion in Munich is very favourable!

Monday, January 22 R. not well, gives me instructions to represent him at the conference between Herr Feustel and Herr Dükflipp, who meet downstairs at 10.30. I join the gentlemen and note with astonishment that the councillor has no intention of making proposals of any sort, he says he has no idea whether the King still wants the performances, etc. Herr Feustel proposes that the cost of the deficit should be divided up between various patrons, who would then be approached. Lunch with the gentlemen, along with the mayor and Herr Gross. Our good councillor does not emerge from his shell, and the purpose and point of his journey remain unclear to us.

Tuesday, January 23 Departure of the councillor, who thanks me very much for our friendly reception! – R. has the idea of going to England and giving concerts there to cover the deficit. I cause him displeasure by reminding him that England is the only place in which Hans (still ill in Hanover) seems to have been able to establish himself, and I fear our undertaking might damage him there. In the evening R. is very indisposed. We do not read together, he continues with Nohl's *Beethoven* and I attend to my accounts.

Thursday, January 25 We talked a lot about Beethoven. Then he calls out to me: 'There is something I won't tell you.' 'Oh, please tell me!' 'I am going to begin *Parzival* and shan't let it out of my sight until it is finished' – whereupon I laugh aloud for joy.

Saturday, January 27 R. talks about the names in *Parzival* – what to call his old man? Gurnemanz is not right, Arabic, something Gothic must be found.

Monday, January 29 Letter to Judith, to thank her for the children's *Nibelungen* theatre, which she made herself, providing it with the characters, scenery and stage properties for all four evenings.

Tuesday, January 30 At lunch R. told me that he had got over the worst in *Parzival*; what is important is not the question, but the recovery of the spear. The scene between Kundry and the old man (Gurnemanz in the sketch) would describe the myth; the difficulty, R. says, is that one is now dealing with a world which has so little feeling for myth.

Wednesday, January 31 Our good Dean Dittmar died this morning – my first and my best friend here!... I do not tell R. the news at once. He is fairly well and in good spirits. He recalls that it is 15 years since he last wrote a new text, *Die Meistersinger* in Paris. He tells me he is trying to turn the morning into the productive continuation of the dream; and that is why I do not tell him the dismal news until later. – Siegfried touching in his sympathy for me.

Thursday, February 1 When I have completed my work with the children, I go to the home of our old friend and see him lying there in peace and simplicity; in him I feel I have lost the soul of our little town. Friend Feustel has sent me the attached letter [*from a fellow freemason of Feustel's in Hanover, reporting that Hans von Bülow is on the road to recovery but does not intend to return to England for some time*] – so according to this we should be able to go to England!!

Friday, February 2 Wretched night, filled with heavy thoughts. Work with the children, Siegfried carries wreaths and palm leaves to the mortuary; thinking of our friend, Daniella's confirmation, my conversion, sacred memories, yet at the same time Hans constantly in my mind; overcome with grief, I collapse and fall into a heavy sleep (the sleep of Kundry, says R.). R. goes into the garden, hears the bell tolling for the funeral. I wake up at about four o'clock, wander in the garden, watch the setting sun, and in tears beg it to greet our old friend. – Herr Rubinstein writes a curious letter, asking forgiveness for his behaviour last autumn!

Saturday-Wednesday, February 3–7 R. very depressed over the fact that his first report to the patrons concerning the deficit brought no reply, except from old Fräulein Plüddemann in Kolberg, who has sent 100 marks. But he works on the sketch for *Parzival* and reports that he has completed the dialogue of the first act.

Thursday, February 8 Still weather of the most inhospitable kind, the sky grey, the air damp, the ground muddy. In the evening our friend Feustel, it is more or less decided that we must go to England, many of the singers cannot come, it has become quite evident that no performances will be possible this year.

Monday, February 12 Rehearsals of *Rheingold* with the children for the toy theatre made by Judith, great exertions, morning, afternoon, and evening rehearsals with music. As a reward I am able to hear many things from *Die Meistersinger* in the evening. – As he works on *Parzival* R. seems to me now like Walther [von Stolzing] in the song we have just heard about the wonderful bird who spread his wings despite all the crows and jackdaws! He tells me today that he will treat the women in Klingsor's castle like saplings – this has been suggested to him by the melody of his chorus, and he says he wants to present them as languishing figures, not as demons.

Wednesday, February 14 I hear from Herr Feustel that Councillor Düfflipp told him (in Munich) that he had played a very stupid role in Bayreuth, but he had known that the King had not intended to do anything more, and he had only been able to hope that the King might perhaps change his mind after R. had written to him; however, this had not been the case.

Monday, February 19 We are informed of a letter to Feustel from an impresario, Mr. Hodge[1], who promises R. huge success and unparalleled renown if he comes to England for a month. It is indeed strange how

---

[1] Messrs. Hodge and Essex, a new firm of concert agents in London, were promoting the series of concerts Wagner was preparing for the Albert Hall.

everything encouraging from the outside world now arouses the deepest melancholy within me. I reflect how Hans lost all the fruits of his laborious work in the very same land which now promises us profit and glory!

Saturday, February 24 Telegram from Wilhelmj, Mr. Hodge is proposing *20 concerts* in England in May! Asks what fee requested for these. We reply that he should state it himself. Negotiations with Frau Materna, Unger, etc. . . .

Monday, February 26 Continual storm and grey skies. R. says how sad it is that he has now reached the stage of wishing to hear nothing more about the *Ring des Nibelungen* and wishing the theatre would go up in flames. Dr. Förster[1] writes, very willing to engage Herr Unger and at the same time asking for the *Ring*.

Wednesday, February 28 R. wrote busily yesterday evening and this morning as well, in order (as he told me) to give me a surprise. And at lunch he does indeed give me *Parzival*, completed in prose dialogue; we drink its health at table, and in the afternoon I read it by myself. This is bliss, this is solace, this is sublimity and devotion!! – The redeemer unchained! . . .

Friday, March 2 R. not exactly encouraged by the response of the singers who are wanted in London with him. He compares actors with a stag, which does nothing as long as it is shy and frightened but, if one is kind to it, butts one with its horns!

Sunday, March 4 In the evening read Lassen's Indians[2]; R. is reading my mother's history of Holland by himself, is very conscious of the woman's approach, but he likes that, apart from the French phrases about God.

Wednesday, March 7 Many telegrams arrived yesterday from Vienna about the 'success' of *Die Walküre*, which has been employed from the very start to denigrate the festival performances. Feelings of bitterness: the work, gained by perfidious means, is being used to make fun of its author!

Friday, March 9 Departure for Meiningen; arrival at four o'clock, the Duke and his wife receive us on the steps of the palace, in which we are given very fine rooms. To the theatre in the evening [Grillparzer's] *Esther* and [Molière's] *Le Melade Imaginaire* with the promotion scene, the latter much too long drawn out, but the comedy excellently done. In the evening the Duke and his wife have tea in our rooms, cordial and cheerful conversation.

Saturday, March 10 All kinds of marks of attention, quartet from *Rheingold*, military band, rehearsal in the palace of the *Idyll*, [Liszt's] *Festklänge* and the *Faust* Overture. Banquet at two o'clock, very pleasant.

Sunday, March 11 In the evening *Julius Caesar*! Since Brutus, Cassius, Casca,

---

[1] August Förster (b.1828), co-director of the Leipzig theatre with Angelo Neumann (b.1838); Neumann, newly appointed, was a former singer with a great love for Wagner's music, hence Leipzig's sudden interest in him.

[2] Christian Lassen was the founder of Indian studies in Germany, teaching in Bonn; his principal work was a study of ancient Indian civilizations, published in four vols., 1844–61.

Caesar were only mediocre, I was very worried at the beginning for R., who was sitting with me at the Duke's side in the central box; but the assassination of Caesar, the Marcus Antonius (Herr Dettmer from Dresden) and the great street scene were so splendid that allowances were willingly made, and the impression produced by this incomparable work again triumphed over all shortcomings in the presentation.

Monday, March 12 Took our leave of the friendly, serious-minded gentleman, to whom R. could say in all honesty that he would like to give proof of his gratitude. Departure at ten o'clock, decorated with flowers, arrival at four o'clock.

Wednesday, March 14 R. writing his stage *dedication* play[1]; at lunch he tells me: 'She will be called Gundrigia, the weaver of war,' but then he decides to keep to '*Kundry*'. And he will be called Parsifal.

Thursday, March 15 We receive the contract from London, which is very reasonable and is signed at once.

Friday, March 16 R. talks about his verses, he has not yet used a rhyme; the more natural the music, he says, the less appropriate an end rhyme.

Monday, March 19 In spite of London and everything else, R. still finds the will power to continue writing *Parsifal* in the morning. – The afternoon does indeed pass in a fever of reckoning, as he says, since his thoughts and deeds are now fixed on London. – In Vienna the fourth performance of *Die Walküre* with increasing success; the Emperor saw it for the third time, which is considered very remarkable. It seems to me that a tried and tested prince might well be able to understand Wotan.

Saturday, March 24 Arrival of Lusch at nine o'clock, at eleven o'clock my father; much pleasurable chat, mostly concerning Vienna, where my father played for the Beethoven memorial. *Die Walküre* seems to be enjoying an enormous success. My father received instructions to offer 20,000 marks and a cross, perhaps even a grand ribbon, if R. would consent to have the other three works done! . . . R. requests that the Emperor should announce this wish to him through his minister Hofmann.

Sunday, March 25 Dr. Förster from Leipzig here, R. tries to persuade him to take over the festival, and then he would also allow him to do the work in Leipzig. Dr. Förster seemed *not* entirely unwilling.

Monday, March 26 Work with the children, R. on *Parsifal*, my father correcting proofs of his *Chopin*[2].

Wednesday, March 28 God be praised! R. is continuing to work on *Parsifal*, even though it means we sometimes have to deal with repugnant business matters till late in the night. Herr Hodge asks for a postponement of the guaranteed payment, we grant it to him through the lawyer. – Arrival of

[1] *Bühnenweihspiel*, a word invented by Wagner to describe *Parsifal*: Cosima underlined '*Weih*' ('dedication').
[2] Liszt was working on the revision of his biography *Frederic Chopin*, first published in 1852; the revised version appeared in 1879.

Richter, very vulgarly bringing the 20,000 marks, with the request that R. should sign a declaration of consent to the performance of the other three works. R. is standing by what my father had written to Standhartner. R[ichter] praises *Die Walküre* in Vienna – from my father's account, I gather that it lacks all dedication and nobility.

Thursday, March 29 Today R. concludes the first act of *Parsifal*[1]!

Saturday, March 31 For R. all too many London problems, which I actively share to the extent that I have to write the letters; Herr Unger sluggish, alarmed by having to learn Tristan! Problems with orchestra parts, nobody yet sure where to obtain them all. And Messrs. Hodge and Essex are getting nervous about the costs.

Monday, April 2 My father's name day; R. gives him his *Life* with a dedication which deeply pleases and touches my father; in the afternoon R. reads his wonderful first act to us, and in the evening my father plays his sonata. A lovely, cherished day, on which I can thank Heaven for the comforting feeling that nothing – no deeply tragic parting of the ways, no malice on the part of others, no differences in character – could ever separate us three. – Oh, if only it were possible to add a fourth to our numbers here! But that an inexorable Fate forbids, and for me every joy and every exaltation ends with an anxious cry to my inner being! . . .

Tuesday, April 3 Departure of my father. In the evening a letter from Mr. Hodge, complaints regarding the high cost of the singers; also, upsettingly enough, a telegram from Richter[2]! He had refused to come to London to conduct the rehearsals; finally persuaded by R. while he was here, he was supposed to apply for leave, and my father wrote in that connection to Prince and Princess Hohenlohe; now they would dearly like to repeat the game they played last year with *Die Walküre*! . . . R. wanted to send Richter an indignant telegram, I beg him not to.

Thursday, April 5 We are surprised by a visit from Herr Essex, who requests another postponement of the guaranteed payment. We consent, since personally Herr Essex makes a good impression and Wilhelmj pleads on his behalf.

Saturday, April 7 A gloomy, very gloomy day! – Herr Gross visits me, to report that Düfflipp has told his father-in-law that, according to the contract made in 1865[3], R. has no right to sell the *Nibelungen* work to Vienna or anywhere else. R. much agitated and vexed about this, he writes to Councillor Düfflipp, requesting that the contract be annulled, since in view of the failure of his Bayreuth plans he has no alternative but to release the work. He adds that he no longer has any objection to its performance in Munich. – At one o'clock arrival of Frau Dr. Herz from Altenburg; at

---

[1] The text only.
[2] He had returned to Vienna on March 29.
[3] This stipulated that the *Ring* would become the property of Ludwig II.

my request she examines the children. I am thunderstruck when it turns out that Isolde is very round-shouldered and should be sent to the institute in Altenburg. Silent tears!

Wednesday, April 11 Telegram from Richter, saying he will be given leave only if the three works are granted! . . . R. writes to him, saying that nothing can be got from him this way.

Friday, April 13 Today R. completes the second act of *Parsifal* and is cheerful and happy, despite the fact that there is again no lack of 'rats and mice', as R. calls them. For example, Herr Mazière[1] writes to say that Messrs. Brandt, Brückner, Hoffmann and Doepler are demanding royalties for all performances of the *Nibelungen* everywhere (though they have already been overgenerously paid for their work), and that they have appointed Herr Batz their representative! R. says he cannot imagine how he will ever be able to compose *Parsifal* with all these bogeys constantly in his mind.

Sunday, April 15 A not-at-all-nice letter from Richter, in which he says that Jauner is waiting for R.'s consent before approving Richter's leave of absence, since R. is the one who is making demands. R. sends a telegram saying that his consent depends on negotiations with Munich and various other things; but if Richter's leave is not approved, *a complete break*. A letter from Herr Schlesinger[2] and a telegram from London, also not encouraging. The £1,500 have still not yet been paid.

Monday, April 16 Departure! I take Isolde to Altenburg. A most painful moment as she says goodbye to her sisters and brother, she remains silent throughout the journey.

Tuesday, April 17 First gymnastic exercises for Loldchen, then introduced her to the head of the school, then paid calls with her. Rough weather. The little girl accepts her lot uncomplainingly; a very nice parson's daughter and another child help her to do this.

Thursday, April 19 My little girl examined. She does not emerge from it well. Weeping, but no complaining. Left at half past one. Apathy! Memories of another parting. In Neumarkt at eight in the evening, R. there to meet me. A cheerful evening, in spite of pain and worry, due to reunion! *Parsifal* is finished!

Friday, April 20 Work again with the children, one fewer, it does not make things easier, quite the contrary. In London the business side is still unclear, but the rehearsals are said to be progressing better than expected[3]. In the evening R. reads me the third act of *Parsifal* and then gives me the poem, which I regard as my greatest solace in life's misery.

---

[1] Adam Ludwig Mazière, manager of the firm of Schott.
[2] Maximilian Schlesinger, a Hungarian emigrant working in London for German newspapers; he looked after the financial side of the London concerts.
[3] The specially assembled orchestra of 169 players was led by Wilhelmj, and Seidl and Fischer were the rehearsal conductors.

Saturday, April 21 A letter from Councillor Düfflipp informs us that the King would like consideration to be given to the repayment of the money borrowed (for our theatre).

Sunday, April 22 R. writes to Councillor Düfflipp, offering the decorations, costumes and machinery in repayment of the advance; or he might sell all these things to the theatre director in Leipzig and then pay the money to the King.

Thursday, April 26 R. settles his business affairs, Dr. Förster is engaging Herr Unger, paying ten percent and an advance of 2,000 thalers, is receiving in exchange the rights in the work in North Germany.

Sunday, April 29 Apprehensive departure; after saying goodbye to the children, left on Monday the 30th at 6 a.m. with the mail train.

Tuesday, May 1 In Brussels in the early morning, in Ostend at ten o'clock after receiving a nice, pleasant impression of the scenery. In Dover at one o'clock after a disagreeable crossing for R.: he is utterly seasick, so that I feel almost ashamed at feeling nothing of this wretched condition but, rather, taking a kind of pleasure in this unusual journey. Dover makes a powerful impression on us, and the first drive through London not only a powerful, but also a pleasing impression. Almost the entire orchestra is gathered on the platform at Charing Cross, with Wilhelmj, Dannreuther, Seidl, Fischer, etc. We are living very pleasantly and comfortably with the Dannreuthers; the night passes very quietly. Visit to the Albert Hall, which we like very much, in spite of its enormous dimensions. Our singers have already arrived[1]. Then I drive with R. in a hansom cab; the fog gives everything a ghostly appearance and it is precisely here, in this centre of the utmost activity, that I feel most closely aware of the ideality of things and the dreamlike quality of life. The huge buildings cannot be ignored, are there, and then vanish. The low houses and large gardens give a feeling of freedom and comfort. If I had to choose a large city, it would be London.

Thursday, May 3 I have to give R. bad news regarding the state of our business here; H. and Essex seem to be very good people, but they are very inexperienced, and the whole of Israel is once more working against us.

Friday, May 4 Rehearsal, to R.'s great satisfaction; he is very cheered by the sound of the orchestra and by the very good orchestra – he says as long as that gives him pleasure he can put up with everything else. Dinner in the evening at Herr Schlesinger's with the poet Browning, the painter R. Lehmann, Wilhelmj, Richter[2], etc.

Saturday, May 5 Fine day in spite of great cold; I visit the National Gallery,

[1] Dannreuther, who lived at 12 Orme Square, Bayswater, had helped assemble the orchestra and conduct some of the preliminary rehearsals; the singers were: Materna, Sadler-Grün, Hill, Schlosser and Unger, with Frl. Exter, Frl. Waibel, and Chaudon for minor roles.

[2] Though Cosima does not specifically state it, Richter's presence was due to Wagner's consenting to release the *Ring* to Vienna; Richter shared the conducting of the London concerts with Wagner.

make the acquaintance of Reynolds with great pleasure, gain a fairer impression of Hogarth and receive light and warmth again from the Italians. In the afternoon rehearsal at home with the singers, in the evening we have some guests, all of whom were in Bayreuth at the performances.

Sunday, May 6 Wrote letters, visited the Zoological Gardens, made the acquaintance of George Eliot, the famous woman writer, who makes a noble and pleasant impression. In the evening dinner at Herr Sainton's with Lüders, R.'s two old friends[1].

Monday, May 7 Full rehearsal; R. tired, not by the event itself, but by the signs of negligence, for example, in the parts, etc. And what confronts us here is not, alas, calculated to restore his spirits! The concert at eight in the evening; I sit with the two Leweses[2] in the *grand tier* and am horrified by the sound, a double echo, no impression possible! On top of that, our singers very feeble. Sad feelings, despite the brilliant reception for R.

Tuesday, May 8 Rehearsal, after which a nice lunch with Wilhelmj and the D[annreuther]s in Kensington Museum. Cheerful spirits in spite of everything.

Wednesday, May 9 Rehearsal, in the evening the concert, an even greater success; afterwards I go to a reception given by Lady Lindsay[3] in the Grosvenor Gallery, 400 people, very magnificent.

Thursday, May 10 It turns out that things are even worse than we had supposed; Messrs. H. and E. are on the verge of bankruptcy! The last concert brought in £600 – in such circumstances there is no question of even covering the costs! Great despondency. In the evening went with R. to *R[ichard] III*; the company not good, but some things in it gripping and well done.

Friday, May 11 Rehearsal, very moving. After this obliged to discuss our position with R. America? Then never again a return to Germany! ... Visit to the British Museum. On the homeward journey saw R. in a cab in Regent Street, after him, caught up with him finally in the sea of vehicles, laughter.

Saturday, May 12 Crystal Palace, flower show, and then our 3rd concert in the afternoon; Materna magnificent in *Walküre*; the 'Ride of the Valkyries' repeated. R. is received by the Prince of Wales, who says he was present at the Philharmonic concert 20 years ago, R. repeats something the Queen said to him then – that all the Italians here were Germans and in consequence R.'s works could very well be performed here. – But R. very depressed, we spend the evening quietly at home.

Sunday, May 13 I go to the High Church to hear a famous preacher (Rowssell)[4], did not understand much, and the preceding service soul-de-

---

[1] Prosper Sainton and his companion, Charles Lüders, both musicians, were friends from the time of Wagner's visit to London in 1855.
[2] George Henry Lewes and George Eliot.
[3] Her husband was president of the Wagner Society in London.
[4] Correctly, Thomas James Rowsell, vicar of St. Stephen's, Westbourne Park.

stroying, much worse than ours – I can see why the Roman Catholics are making so much propaganda here, as I have been told. While I am there, R. writes to Herr Feustel, asking him to start a subscription to help clear up the deficit. In the afternoon I have some calls to pay, in the evening a German dinner at Herr v. Ernst's; Dr. Schliemann, the archaeologist, a guest, not very impressive; on the other hand, Dr. Siemens very impressive, to all appearances[1]. R. very cheerful and friendly.

Monday, May 14 Rehearsal till one o'clock, after which I to Mr. and Mrs. Lewes' for lunch and then with them to the studio of the Pre-Raphaelite painter Burne-Jones. Pretty, delicate pictures, he himself very pleasant. At eight in the evening the concert, a substantial number of the royal family and a fairly full house. Herr Unger already shows signs of hoarseness in the *Lohengrin* duet, and he declares he will be unable to sing the 'Forging Songs'; it is decided to repeat 'Wotan's Farewell', but Herr Hill has already gone home – persisting confusion, finally Mr. Hodge tells the audience that the 'Ride of the Valkyries' will be played instead of the forging scene, but the concert ends, after all, with the farewell scene between Siegfried and Brünnhilde, though indeed only Frau Materna can be heard. This is the last straw – that now the programme cannot even be adhered to!

Tuesday, May 15 Rehearsal; great concern, the Court complains about the alterations in the programme, but there is absolutely no chance of keeping to it, since Herr Unger will certainly not recover in time; the public, already intimidated by the press and by Herr Joachim and consorts, will doubtless become even more timid, despite the brilliant reception given every time to both R. himself and all the pieces played. Requests are being made from all sides not to alter the programme, but how can it be adhered to? – I attend a session of Parliament with Miss Cartwright[2]. At ten in the evening Herr Hill sends word that he is hoarse. R. has to go over to see Richter, in order to discuss the programme once again!

Wednesday, May 16 Rehearsal from ten until one o'clock, in the evening concert, great impact of *Götterdämmerung* with Materna, the 'Ride of the Valkyries', *Meistersinger* Prelude as well. Between rehearsal and concert drove through the City with R.

Thursday, May 17 To the British Museum to see the drawings, then rendezvous with R. at the railway station to visit Windsor. There he is received by the Queen and Prince Leopold, who talks to him about Rus, whom he once saw in Lucerne. Windsor makes a powerful impression, though its interior furnishings are much out of keeping with its exterior; and even the lovely van Dycks, the splendid Holbein and the miraculous Rembrandt do not match it. How different the palaces in Italy! In the evening Lewes for dinner, then some others, to whom R. reads *Parsifal*.

---

[1] Schliemann, the excavator of Troy; William Siemens, the electrical engineer; Ernst not identified.
[2] Wanda Cartwright, described as 'active in London political life'.

Friday, May 18 Rehearsal. Afterwards R. has a long conference with Messrs. Schl[esinger], Hodge and E., the secretary of the Albert Hall, etc., about giving three more concerts. He thinks he has convinced them, and is very upset when he learns from Herr Schl. that only two instead of three concerts will be possible, and that only in ten days' time.

Saturday, May 19 Today I am indisposed and have to force myself to attend the concert. It turns out brilliantly; proceeds of £1,600 and a very animated audience – very un-English, we are told. R. crowned with a laurel wreath, speech from the orchestra and unending cheers.

Sunday, May 20 Went twice to Westminster Abbey to hear the dean[1]. Fine impression. – R. unfortunately not well. I have to go by myself to dine with the painter Millais.

Monday, May 21 I have to speak to the singers, asking them (Hill, Frau Grün) to reduce their exorbitant demands somewhat, since R. will now have to pay them himself! R. is not well. I go out alone to breakfast and dine, visit the studio of the painter Watts, in which there hangs a quite amazing picture of Joachim; I can read the whole biography of this thoroughly bad person in this picture; that is not what the painter intended, but it is the very thing which reveals his talent – that he had depicted the truth without realizing it!

Tuesday, May 22 R.'s birthday! Very nice letters from all the children and all sorts of greetings besides. In the evening a banquet, at which R. distributes the medallions which I gave him: probably the last work of Semper, the great master! Materna, Richter, Wilhelmj receive them.

Wednesday, May 23 R. is very tired and today goes only to the Athenaeum, where Dr. Siemens has arranged a small dinner for him; I visit Westminster Abbey, Canon Hartford[2] shows me all the features of this remarkable house of God; I found it very moving that 'Elisabeth's Prayer'[3] was played on the organ at the conclusion of the service; the crowds dispersed in silence, and above their heads this pure soul spread her wings; they return to their lives, silent and unheeding, while she yields herself singing to Death!

Thursday, May 24 Session with the photographer, not to be avoided! In the evening we hold a reception.

Friday, May 25 Good letter from Councillor Düfflipp, according to which they seem willing in Munich to buy the machinery. R. replies by return. I visit the British Museum again and take pleasure in the splendid drawings. Afterwards rendezvous with R. at Charing Cross and fish dinner in Greenwich. Return home by steamer, very successful, mild, grey weather, tremendous impression, R. says, 'This is Alberich's dream come true – Nibelheim, world dominion, activity, work, everywhere the oppressive

---

[1] Arthur Penrhyn Stanley.
[2] Correctly, Frederick Kill Harford.
[3] From Act III of *Tannhäuser*.

feeling of steam and fog.' – In the evening *Tannhäuser* in Italian! Oh! . . . All of it terrible, only the orchestra wonderful, but unfortunately directed by a conductor who is not at all good[1]. Our friend Wilhelmj ill.

Sunday, May 27 Sitting for the painter Herkomer[2], then lunch at the Schlesingers' and visit to the Leweses', where it was decided that I should sit for the painter Burne-Jones[3]. At home in the evening.

Monday, May 28 Rehearsal for the concert; it ends at twelve o'clock and the concert begins at three; it goes quite well; Wilhelmj absent owing to illness.

Tuesday, May 29 Rehearsal from 10 to 1, Herr Unger sings the 'Forging Songs' and 'Brünnhilde's Awakening' very well; after the rehearsal a sitting for Burne-Jones, then a nice walk in fine weather through Holland Park and Kensington Gardens. In the evening the concert; Herr Unger produces not a single note, does not ask to be excused, but stands there utterly unperturbed, with poor Materna exerting herself in the awakening scene, Richter cursing, R. sending him looks to turn him to stone, not making the slightest effort; R. tells him afterwards that he was not hoarse, but had lain down tired after eating too much and had clogged his palate. This tops everything. The audience very good-natured.

Wednesday, May 30 Another sitting for Burne-Jones. After that, accounts; it turns out that, after R. has paid everything off, £700 will remain for Bayreuth; it is some relief to me, for I was expecting the worst; but R. is very depressed.

Thursday, May 31 Farewell visits, sitting for Burne-Jones, in Kensington in the evening, party of engineers.

Friday, June 1 Stormy weather! All the same, we plan to leave tomorrow. In the evening dinner with Herr Ionides, brother of Charicleas Dannreuther[4]. Made the acquaintance of the writer Mr. Morris[5]. – D.'s child ill.

Saturday, June 2 Departure impossible on account of the storm; attended the Caxton celebrations in Westminster Abbey; very curious impression; Mendelssohn's '*Lobgesang*' ['Hymn of Praise'] as much out of place there as all the monuments. – In the evening dinner with Herr Schlesinger.

Monday, June 4 Left London! Very mixed feelings. Calm sea, R. in good spirits, I melancholy as always with any change in my circumstances! Cramped cabin and bunk: 'The latitude here must be very narrow,' R. says with a laugh.

Tuesday, June 5 Arrival at six o'clock in Ems, where R. is supposed to take

---

[1] This, the first production of *Tannhäuser* in London, had opened at Covent Garden on May 6 with Fernando Carpi, Emma Albani and Victor Maurel in the main roles and Auguste Vianesi conducting.
[2] Herkomer's gouache of Wagner vanished in 1945.
[3] This portrait of Cosima has not been discovered.
[4] Correctly, Chariclea, wife of Edward Dannreuther.
[5] William Morris.

the cure. The children (except for Loldi) at the station; Fidi's gaze fixed in tender sympathy on his father. The *Bayreuther Tagblatt* is said to have published some really disgraceful articles about the London concerts; the boy seems to have heard about them, and that is why he now looks at his father thus!

Wednesday, June 6 Siegfried's birthday! My darling child! Distribution of gifts all round. A construction set for Fidi, acquired in London by R. personally. Bad weather, consequently no outing. Letters from Feustel! Rebellion among the people who had been put off with promises till after the London concerts. I beg R. to make use of my 40,000 francs – along with the London proceeds that makes about 50,000 marks. I firmly believe that my children will not hold this against me, and I know that God will bless them for it. – The negotiations have been broken off with Leipzig and taken up with Hanover; Herr Unger, I hope, after his behaviour in London, done with. – God bless you, my child!

Friday, June 8 I start copying out *Parsifal* and resume lessons with the children.

Thursday, June 14 Letter from the King, beside himself over the news that R. intends to emigrate to America. R. had written to Feustel saying he would perhaps have to go to America, in which case he would not return home again! –

Saturday, June 16 Arrival of the Emperor. Very little enthusiasm, but considerable heat. – R. decides to take the Marienbad instead of the Ems waters.

Monday, June 18 My father sends us a letter from Herr v. Bronsart to him, from which it transpires that Herr von Hülsen is utterly hostile to the idea of having the *Nibelungen* performed in Hanover. 'Are you quite blind to the fiasco in Bayreuth and the fiasco in London, where the people streamed out of the hall during the *Ring* pieces?' Hülsen writes to Bronsart. So this is what comes from the lying newspaper reports!

Thursday, June 21 In the evening Herr Heckel arrives.

Friday-Saturday, June 22–23 I go for a walk with our friend, and the good man tells me, among many other disagreeable things, that the *Neue Freie Presse* is now advertising that it has bought up some letters from R. to a milliner and intends to publish and annotate them[1]. When R. now talks about emigrating to America, I no longer have the courage to speak against it.

Wednesday, July 4 Letter from Herr Gross: Count Magnis Ullersdorff has sent 5,000 marks towards the deficit. Besides that, news from Herr Simson that R. has won his case against Herr Fürstner in the court of appeal as well. Both very pleasing.

---

[1] These letters to Bertha Goldwag concerning some fabrics he wished to order while living in Vienna in 1862–64 were published in the *Neue Freie Presse*, Vienna, on July 16–17.

Thursday, July 5 Farewells of all kinds. I send Fidi to the Kurhaus to give a bunch of cornflowers to the Emperor. Fidi sees and also speaks to the very friendly old gentleman. Probably for the first and last time. Departure at 10 o'clock, great merriness and high spirits from R. and the children, only Fidi with a slight sore throat – it gets worse, and when we arrive in Heidelberg, we decide to stay, since the Schlosshotel is very pleasant. In the evening Herr Heckel, Dr. Zeroni, Herr Lang, a serenade by the choral society; 6,000 people present. (R. conducts *Gaudeamus igitur* from the balcony.)

Wednesday, July 18 At ten o'clock left the cosy spot where we have spent such lovely, quiet days. – Yesterday we talked about the tragedy of life, about Hans! The nearer I come to the places I know in Switzerland, the more I feel as if someone were talking about my past life, with gentle melancholy; it has ceased to exist for me, yet the melancholy remains. Arrived here (Lucerne) in the evening, to our great surprise Richter on the platform, then Countess Bassenheim, the Stocker family, in short, our whole past.

Thursday, July 19 It is raining; in the morning conversation with Countess Bassenheim; in the afternoon a drive to Tribschen in spite of the rain; it is neglected and overgrown, some French Jews are living there: 'Too much for one time,' says R. – Visit from the Stockers. The sky remains gloomy, as if we were being told not to grieve that the Tribschen days are past.

Friday, July 20 Early departure. In Munich around eight o'clock in the evening. Friend Lenbach at the station.

Saturday, July 21 Munich. At eight o'clock Councillor Düfflipp, I go out, so that R. can speak to him more unrestrainedly, and show the children the city. When I come home, R. declares to my surprise that we will leave tomorrow, since we have nothing more to do here. The King has given no instructions of any sort with regard to our affair, and since he himself is in financial difficulties, he is just afraid of being obliged to pay further advances, indeed also of not getting his advances back. Councillor Düfflipp suggests that R. talk to Herr von Perfall; R. consents, and at eleven goes to Düfflipp's office. It is proposed that the Munich theatre management present the festival next year in Bayreuth, and then in Munich. This proposal is now to be worked out between Herr v. P. and Düffl. R. says to me, 'I must be glad that, when the master sends me away, the servants give me something to eat!'

Monday, July 23 Arrival [in Weimar] at seven o'clock, found my father very well, thank God.

Tuesday, July 24 Frau v. Schleinitz and friend Dohm come here to greet us, very friendly meeting. In the evening met the Grand Duke in my father's house; R. in scintillating mood. *Arrival of Loldi!* . . .

Wednesday, July 25 Joyful reunion with our child, who seems to us transfigured by joy and sorrow. – R. had sent to Altenburg for her so that we could visit my father with the whole family. – Frau v. Schl. tells us all sorts of curious things about Berlin; Bismarck, who literally hates both her and her husband, gets the newspapers to declare that Bayreuth is only a subterfuge for her Catholic party intrigues, etc. Absurd, angry rubbish.

Thursday, July 26 Lunch in the Erbprinz, with us my father and Frau v. Meyendorff with her son. The Grand Duke pays us a call and sits down at our table to say many friendly things to R. about *Die Msinger.*

Saturday, July 28 R. and the children to Bayreuth, I with Loldchen.

Monday, July 30 Packing and departure, taking leave of my father. In Altenburg at midnight.

Tuesday, July 31 A talk with Frau Herz, great blow for my Loldchen, she must stay another six weeks!

Wednesday, August 1 Departure at five o'clock, no farewells, so as not to upset her too much. Arrive in Bayreuth at one o'clock. R. at the station with Fidi, a dear, kind and tender welcome. Once again in Wahnfried. Friend Standhartner.

Thursday, August 2 R. has arranged his studio for *Parsifal*, and today I heard a few of the first notes!

Friday, August 3 R. unwell; friend Standhartner departs. Many household duties for me, the fight with the dragon, as R. calls it – that is to say, against the excessive spending.

Sunday, August 5 Still fighting with the dragon, difficult to get into the heads of the servants that we are methodical people with no wish to squander.

Saturday, August 11 Expecting the arrival of my father, he cables that he will not come till tomorrow, melancholy return home. Then many affectionate outpourings and finally the revelation of '*Nehmt hin mein Blut*' ['Take ye my blood']¹ – R. tells me he wrote it down shortly before my return, with his hat and coat on, just as he was about to go out to meet me. He has had to alter the words to fit it, he says; this scene of Holy Communion will be the main scene, the core of the whole work; with the 'Prize Song' in *Die Meistersinger* too the melody came first, and he had adapted the words to it. He had already told me yesterday that one must beware of having to extend a melody for the sake of the words – now today the chief passage is there complete, in all its mildness, suffering, simplicity and exaltation. 'Amfortas's sufferings are contained in it,' R. says to me. – Its impression on me is overwhelming, and I am incapable of putting my mind to anything.

Sunday, August 12 Went to fetch my father, he arrives at the same time as friend Dannreuther. R. says it is a happy day and presents the children with the 4 thalers he still has left from our travelling expenses. Cheerful, indeed exuberant mood!

---

¹ Sung by boys' voices offstage during the scene in the temple in Act I of *Parsifal*.

Wednesday, August 15 Departure [of my father]. In the evening a sculptor[1] from Leipzig who has been commissioned to make a large bust of R. for the theatre; a private citizen is donating it. R. is reluctant to sit for it.

Thursday, August 16 R. begs me most movingly to forgive his bad mood, he is so unwell, physically, that it takes nothing at all to bring on black thoughts. – Friend Dannreuther brought with him £500 from our English friends, decision to return the money with thanks[2].

Wednesday, August 22 Last day with our friend Dannreuther, to whom we give the task of returning the money to our friends in England. In addition to that, I discuss with him the possibility of Daniella's return to her father if he were to settle in London. But what of his health? Oh, if only God in his mercy would grant this destiny a conciliatory ending through our child!

Thursday, August 23 Alone together again; R. says I am all he wants for company. I have quite a lot to attend to with the children, worry about Siegfried, who seems to me much too soft! . . .

Saturday, August 25 Our wedding day. In the morning R. tells me he is now fashioning the musical garb for his hero Parsifal. Lucian in the evening; strangely enough, I am not offended by the very brazen things contained in it, though in a modern writer even a hint in this direction would be repugnant. R. feels it is on account of the openness with which everything is treated, it is secretiveness which makes things look improper. R. says that dialogue is without doubt the best, indeed the only form in which one can be objective.

Tuesday, September 4 Letter from my father, saying that Hans has accepted a position as conductor in Hanover, and also the direction of the concerts in Glasgow[3].

Saturday-Wednesday, September 8–19 All sorts of things prevented my writing in my diary, among others the presence on the 14th and 15th of the various Wagner Society delegates to discuss measures to be adopted. On the morning of Saturday the 15th, R. made his speech in the theatre, in wonderful weather; there seem to be great hopes of founding a school here. Friend Heckel proposes the establishment of a reserve fund, and 6,000 marks are subscribed. Once certain difficulties have been overcome, friend Pohl is to take over the *Tagblatt* here. Hans v. Wolzogen[4] intends to take up residence here. Herr Hey is to be responsible for training singers. Herr Porges brings news from Councillor Düfflipp that the first proposal

---

[1] Professor zur Strassen; Wagner finally agreed to sit for the bust.

[2] The money (actually £561) had been raised by the Wagner Society in London in gratitude for the London concerts, and it was intended for Wagner personally; but, when returning it with warm thanks, he maintained (untruthfully) that other methods to cover the deficit on the Bayreuth festival had been found.

[3] A festival given by the Glasgow Choral Union orchestra in 1878.

[4] Hans von Wolzogen (b. 1848, son of Baron Alfred von Wolzogen, q.v.) had been invited by Wagner to edit the festival magazine, *Bayreuther Blätter.*

concerning the Munich theatre's takeover of the Bayreuth festivals has not received the King's approval, and now a second proposal has been put forward. On Sunday the 16th, R. reads *Parsifal* to all our friends, who stayed on for that purpose, and it appears to have affected them all greatly. – In me all this planning arouses the sad feeling that R. is being diverted from his true creative work. On Monday the 17th, R. returns to his work; he seems really to be making sketches now. The Heavens bless him and his work! The Wolzogens are still here, he pleases us with his deep and earnest character. R. works and writes to the King, telling him of the plans for the school.

Friday, September 21 The American dentist Mr. Jenkins[1] arrives from Dresden at my request, to attend to R., and the very agreeable man starts his operation immediately during the afternoon.

Saturday, September 22 Another operation, R. bears it patiently, says that yesterday, while it was going on, he was composing! Departure of Mr. Jenkins, who utterly declines to accept any money from R.

Sunday, September 23 After lunch went with R. for a walk in the palace gardens, he tells me that these gardens have a connection with his work, as localities always do – there is a modulation, for instance, in the girls' school on the corner. – An embarrassing altercation with the governess, who has given vent to her bad temper. In the evening R. plays a splendid theme and says he would be able to play me the whole prelude if he had yet written it in ink.

Monday, September 24 Resumption of usual routine. R. works, telling me that when he writes music he feels as if he were always beginning again from the start. In the afternoon he writes his appeal for the school.

Wednesday, September 26 In the afternoon, towards evening, I see R. busily writing. And in the evening he says (with fatigued eyes), 'It has to be finished in time for Saint Cosmas!' He plays me the Prelude, from the orchestral sketch! My emotion lasts long – then he speaks to me about this feature, in the mystery of the Grail, of blood turning into wine, which permits us to turn our gaze refreshed back to earth, whereas the conversion of wine into blood draws us away from the earth. Wonderful mingling in the Prelude of mysticism and chivalry. The D Major modulation is for him like the spreading of the tender revelation across the whole world. But in order to impart the spiritual quality of Christ's words, their detachment from all material things, he intends to use a mixture of voices: 'A baritone voice, for example, would make it all sound material; it must be neither man nor woman, but neuter in the highest sense of the word.' We continue for a long time to talk about Christ, the Gospel account of the day before his death, the sublimest thing ever produced by Man, incomparable, divine! He

[1] Newell Sill Jenkins, later to become a friend as well as the family dentist.

plays me once more the passage in which, as he says, 'the transfigured gaze breaks.'

Thursday, September 27 'Greetings from Saint Cosmas!' I ink in the page in the nursery. An old and enjoyable occupation, of which I have been deprived for many years. – My patron saint brings me a splendid day, we go for a walk, R., Lusch and I, and enjoy the sun and the sky. In the evening Euripides's *Phoenissae*, whose influence on Goethe and Schiller was immeasurable, R. observes. Then R. plays me the Prelude once again. 'I also have some accents for Mademoiselle Condrie, I already have her laughter, for instance.' A long time lost in our memories, gladdened by our earlier times together, saddened by the intermingling of fellow suffering. I beg my good patron saint to lay his healing hand on all wounds, for my greatest feelings of happiness always remind me of the sufferings of another. – R. recalls how much we have already achieved together – and in what circumstances! Had our feelings been less genuine, those circumstances would certainly have brought us to ruin! – 'You and I will go on living in human memory,' he exclaims. 'You for sure,' I exclaim with a laugh. Farewell, lovely, cherished day, let me remember thee in humility!

Saturday, September 29 Fine weather, which I use to go for a long walk; meeting Herr Feustel on the way, I have in R. 's name to yield to his urgings to release parts for the *Ring* for use in concerts in support of the school, something R. is reluctant to do. R. works, and is satisfied with his work.

Thursday, October 4 In the evening Dr. Strecker. A great battle; he wants the *Idyll* and the text of *Parsifal* in order to pay off our debt, I offer him youthful works by R.! . . .

Friday, October 5 Morning negotiations with Dr. Strecker! Oh, if only this debt did not exist! I shall probably have to surrender the *Idyll* to extricate us! Deep melancholy. However, R. is working, and so our life is bathed in sunshine.

Sunday, October 7 R. works, he says to me: 'Oh, these key signatures! One must take very good care not to become untidy!' – At midday arrival of Isolde!

Monday, October 8 News about the school not at all good; Herr Hey is making very high demands! The leaflets go out into the world, but so far there has been no response; R. laughs and says, 'If my school comes to nothing, what a slap in the face for me!' – In the evening he plays me a splendid theme for a symphony and says he has so many themes of this kind, they are always occurring to him, but he cannot use such merry things in *Parsifal*.

Wednesday, October 10 At breakfast R. says to me: 'When you receive the next page, you will see that I have had a lot of trouble with it; I wanted a somewhat drawn-out triple time for Amfortas's procession, so as to make the words of Gurnemanz fit. No artificial idea is of any help at such times, for it should all sound as if it must be like this and nothing else. But I have found it now.'

Friday, October 19 R.'s foot is causing him much suffering! A walk of any kind is a great exertion, and especially today, when the three dogs were busy chasing everything, cats, children, ducks, sheep, chickens.

Sunday, October 21 R. receives a letter from a theatre director in Melbourne, according to which *Lohengrin* last month made its ceremonious entry there too[1]. – Splendid autumn weather, R. unfortunately unable to enjoy it. In the evening friend Gross, discussion about the periodical; there have been no applications yet for the school.

Tuesday, October 23 R. again had a wretched night; abdominal troubles – he reads Darwin (*The Descent of Man*), feels cold. I cannot say how sad it makes me to see him, at the start of his great work, so hindered by bodily ailments. However, he works in the morning.

Wednesday, October 24 R. had a bad night, I come up on him reading Darwin! . . . Work in the house; in the afternoon I go for a drive with R. Back home, I am soon summoned by R., who does not feel well and wants me near him. 'I only hope it is not heart trouble,' he says. We walk up and down in the *salon*, the foliage on the trees is faded, the sun sinks palely to rest, my heart is heavy, but I leave R. with spirits restored, he settles down to work by lamplight.

Thursday, October 25 At last a good night for R. and work. I ink in another page which he gave me; he works, tells me afterwards that he is seizing every opportunity to conjure up a little musical paradise, as, for example, when Amfortas is carried to the lake. Letter from Herr Pollini[2] in Hamburg, he wants *Die Walküre*. R. replies that he will give *Die Walküre* only to directors and managers who intend to perform the whole of the *Ring des Nibelungen*.

Saturday, October 27 Around midday R. played me what he had so far worked out 'in ink', unimagined currents of sublimity flow through my soul and soothe away all sorrow and suffering!

Monday, October 29 On account of my eyes, I unfortunately have to interrupt my inking in of the pencilled sketches, but I begin instead on the translation of *Parsifal* into French, and R. and I have to laugh a lot over the difficulties arising for me from this unyielding and prosaic language. – Herr Gross brings me some news; Baron Perfall writes that the King desires the performance of the *Ring* as soon as possible, and in order to meet this request, Herr Seitz[3] and others from the Munich Court theatre will be coming to Bayreuth to make an inventory and take away the things which will be needed in Munich. Friend Feustel writes saying we should stop and consider before handing over any articles in the theatre, since that would

---

[1] Presented by the impresario William Saurin Lyster.
[2] Bernhard Pollini, originally named Baruch Pohl, director of the Hamburg opera.
[3] Franz von Seitz, costume designer and technical director at the Munich opera.

at once lead to legal action by the creditors, whose claims have been kept at bay only with the greatest difficulty.

Tuesday, October 30 Herr Pollini writes to R., accepting R. 's conditions, but he wants to begin with *Die Walküre*; he will give an advance of 16,000 marks, which will be earned by the year '80; up till then four percent royalties, and after that eight percent.

Wednesday, October 31 R. settles with Herr Pollini. And so the splendid work has now been given away!

Friday, November 2 R. works, in the afternoon some inspiration which he had thought good in the morning sounds garish to him – he closes the lid of the piano to damp it down, finds his way again, and, in order to give me, as I work above with the children, a signal that he is satisfied, plays the charming theme from the coda of the first movement of Mozart's C Major [Jupiter] Symphony.

Monday, November 5 Yesterday R. received a letter from Councillor D. with the news of his resignation: his successor is said to be a devotee of W.'s works[1]. The King has ordered a performance of *Siegfried*, but does not want the Bayreuth decorations, which he says did not please him. – R. writes a very friendly reply, Düfflipp is someone with whom he has had a lot to do over the past eleven years.

Tuesday, November 6 My weak eyes keep me from continuing the translation, as they did the inking of the pages. – In the evening went through the first act of *Tannhäuser* with Herr Seidl; R. says he has in mind shortening the new first scene considerably, it weighs the rest down too much, there is a lack of balance, this scene goes beyond the style of *Tannhäuser* as a whole. – I argue in its defence, saying that it casts over the audience the magic spell which causes Tannhäuser's downfall, and thus it makes the second act more understandable; it is also fitting that the magic underworld is different from the simple world above. 'That is what I told myself,' R. observes, 'but it is not right.' – The problem occupies him greatly.

Saturday, November 10 R. talks about his attitude towards the world and how utterly isolated he feels in it, having been so forsaken in connection with his undertaking and now so ignored with regard to his school. He has me and the children, he says, but otherwise nothing. – Terrible news of the sudden death of our nephew Clemens[2].

Monday, November 12 R. in good and cheerful mood, talks of our tomb, how he designed it and how mice and rats have got in: 'He who digs a pit sees others fall into it.' Much laughter about this.

Monday, November 19 The *Idyll* is sent off today; the secret treasure is to become public property – may the pleasure others take in it match the

---

[1] Ludwig von Bürkel, who had formerly served in the police department.
[2] Clemens Brockhaus died on November 8.

sacrifice I am making! – R. works, we then go for a walk, quite a long one, unfortunately it brings back the pain in his foot.

Tuesday, November 20 R. did not have a very good night, but he works. In the evening he plays me Gurnemanz's narration about the coming of the angels to Titurel. Then we go through the first act of *Parsifal* (in French).

Friday, November 23 R. again had a very bad night; I should dearly like to ascribe it to the foehn weather, but my concern makes me call the doctor. He does not seem at all alarmed. – R. finishes Gurnemanz's narration; however, at my request he does no more work. In the evening the first act of *Henry VI Part I*. Dannreuther writes to say that Hans has once again made an unaccountable attack on English musicians; but my worry about R.'s health makes me impervious to everything else. Thus is one saved by one worry from another!

Monday, November 26 R. slept well! He told me recently that I cured him of worry; I thank thee, God, for that! Great joy in the gift of the manuscript of the Sonata in A Major, which Gebrüder Hug[1] have suddenly sent of their own free will. R. plays it, I like it, but R. suddenly has doubts about publishing his youthful works and this A Major Sonata. – We read a scene from *Henry VI Part II*. A really good, fine day, for R. worked as well; continued with his work for more than an hour past his usual time, we lunched happily at 2.15.

Tuesday, November 27 Letter from Herr Tappert[2] – he thinks he has discovered R.'s symphony!

Sunday, December 2 R. works, and after lunch he says, 'I am writing *Parsifal* only for my wife – if I had to depend on the German spirit, I should have nothing more to say.' After the fourth act of *Henry VI* he says to me, 'I still intend to write my music of mourning for the fallen, but there won't be any apotheosis at the end, you can be sure of that.' – Worry about Fidi: we have tried to find boys for him to play with, but it has brought us nothing but coarseness, vulgarity, mean idleness, quite horrifying. In the evening the children play *Cinderella* for us, and Fidi plays one of the ugly sisters very amusingly. After this very funny comedy we conclude the tragedy, our admiration and emotion increasing all the time. We continue for a long time to talk about the poet, who sees, feels and describes absolutely everything, without ever giving a sign of his own feelings. We think of friend Nietzsche, who rebelled against Sh[akespeare]: 'He always demands a certain kind of form,' says R., 'and this is a malformation of sublimity and revelation.' And so we take leave of the work which has provided us with a complete picture of the dreadfulness of life. If only I

[1] Music dealers in Zurich; the A Major Sonata, written in 1832, was not published until 1920.
[2] Wilhelm Tappert, lecturer at the Neue Akademie der Tonkunst in Berlin and an old friend; orchestral parts of Wagner's Symphony in C Major had been discovered in an old trunk Wagner had left behind in Dresden.

could describe how fine, great, sublime in expression, sound and gesture R. appeared as he was reading it! How much I enjoy the privilege of perceiving and watching him like this all by myself, yet I would still like to let the whole world share it! I now feel as if we were once more living our Tribschen life – once more we have turned our backs on everything, R. is working, the children flourishing, and I forget everything in contemplating his kindness and his love!

Tuesday, December 4 R. had a tolerable night and he works. But school and periodical are causing him difficulties; he would most prefer not to start anything new outside, and the enrolments are so few that it seems almost absurd not to turn down the half-dozen people concerned. However, the presence here of H. v. W[olzogen], who is otherwise of much value to us, obliges R. to find some activity for him. – And so the periodical! – The idea of addressing any more words to the public is distasteful to R., and my only desire is that he have tranquillity in order to create. A curious situation. In the evening R. and I laugh heartily about it, in spite of the worry it causes us.

Wednesday, December 5 R. works. Visit from our friend Pohl, to whom we announce the abandonment of the school. Main activity of our friends is now to be the organization of the Patrons' Society and, through this and on behalf of this, the publication of the periodical; the ultimate aim of the Society the performance of *Parsifal*. I settle all this with Herr v. W. and report on it to R., who is very satisfied and says he will give me a power of attorney, so I can do just as I wish! Merriment.

Thursday, December 6 Work, I am able to do some translation. In the afternoon I visit Herr Feustel, and have then, unfortunately, to inform R. that he is very surprised by the latest decisions. R. very upset by this, and in consequence unwell!

Friday, December 7 Yesterday I felt I had to tell him about my visit to Herr Feustel, but now I think I should have kept silent, let come what may, rather than torment him. – To Herr Feustel in the evening to meet the mayor. Herr Feustel and the mayor comply with R.'s wishes, though it is decided only that the school will not open *for the time being*. – We return home in cheerful spirits, and R. thanks me! Oh, God! – When he said to me today, 'I am hard to put up with – one has to unload one's vexation and worry on the person one loves best,' I did not know what to say: the only thing I find hard is to see him suffering!

Sunday, December 9 R. tells me that the *Idyll* has already been performed in Mainz, and he reads me the stupid words which accompanied the performance (that in it Fidi's joys are depicted!). – I knew when I made the sacrifice just what a sacrifice it really was, yet curiously enough this review affects me as if I had never foreseen it! – I could not be more estranged from the world than I am, never less involved in its joys, less sympathetic towards its doings, yet at this very time I am obliged to yield to it my most cherished possession! I have the feeling, since I was obliged to yield it up, that I have proved unworthy of it – and I hasten to my room, there to weep and lament and once again accept within myself that my hard lot is just, that what I cherish must be yielded up as too sublime for me. Why should I alone be made happy, I alone be blissful? . . .

Tuesday, December 11 R. works; during the night we laughed heartily because yesterday, in his agitation, he went downstairs instead of going to bed; becoming worried after a while, I left my bed and crept downstairs after him; he was sitting in the *salon*, asleep, the lamp alight, Schlegel's *Greeks and Romans* at his side. Much relieved, I waited until he woke up, which soon happened, and the situation caused us much laughter.

Thursday, December 13 R., dissatisfied with his morning's work, intends to discard it. Ill humour in consequence.

Friday, December 14 R. says he has now 'put right' yesterday's errors – one must be careful, he observes, not to let oneself be led astray by the melodies – that happened to him yesterday, and it had put him right out of the mood.

Sunday, December 16 Church and snow! R. works, he has at last brought Kundry into the bushes, he tells me at lunch. Before supper he shows me what he has already worked on in ink, the shining men of *Parsifal*! . . . At table his whole countenance radiates genius and goodness! He told me recently that his vehemence had been given him to compensate for his softness. He shrank away, to the point of cowardice, from saying harsh things to anybody. And it is true, people might consider him to be completely ungenuine, for he does not like telling people what he thinks of them, and for that reason his only defence lies in seclusion.

Wednesday, December 19 Arrival of a large Gloucester cheese from Herr Schlesinger, which gives R. great pleasure. In the evening we hear from London of the dispatch of another cheese – Stilton – which makes us laugh.

Thursday, December 20 R. does not feel very well, he tries to work but is not satisfied with what he does. He does not go out, but he has a good appetite in the evening; he laughs over it and says: 'If you knew what is bothering me! It is a rhythmical battle. This morning I suddenly understood none of my things.'

Friday, December 21 R. has survived his rhythmical battle and tells me when he comes from his work, 'Today I have set a philosophical precept to music: "Here space becomes time".'

Monday, December 24 R. does some work; I occupied all day long by the *Christkind*. At last, at about 6 o'clock, I come into the *salon* and am greeted with a song, 'Welcome, dear Christ!' When he came home and saw the house and 'all its joys', it had occurred to R. that Christ was not only a 'bringer of salvation', but a 'bringer of joy' as well! Under Lulu's supervision the children learned the words at once and sang them very nicely. R. had built up a splendid pile for me, including the 'manuscript', inscribed 'from the one who loves you.' And a thousand other things, all sought out with kindness and loving care. [*Attached to this page a water-colour drawing with the inscription:* 'Japanese négligé given to me by Richard, Christmas 1877.'] All this had led to a long correspondence between him and Judith, during which it had unfortunately become clear to him that even the best of French people cannot overcome certain limitations! For instance, Judith cannot believe that it is impossible to translate *Parsifal* into French! But of course they do not know *the other thing*!

Tuesday, December 25 Real brilliant sunshine, the first time for two months! R. says to me, 'Your birthday is my Sunday!' He decides on a walk with the children before lunch, we go into the palace gardens, Siegfried's new suit, in old Germanic style, gives us much pleasure. A merry meal, R. solemnly proposes my health. In the evening [Dozy's] history of the Arabs again, after which R. reads the first 3 cantos of the *Divina commedia*, to our great delight; then I ask him for something from *Parsifal*, and he plays Gurnemanz's narration, the entry of Parsifal – divine blessings for my birthday!

Thursday, December 27 Herr [Joseph] R[ubinstein] sends his piano arrangement of the *Idyll* – R. is pleased with the wonderful, cherished work! – R. works on the 'Holy Grail March' and says he must go to Marienbad or Ems next year to hear it – it is the proper march for a spa!

Monday, December 31 A merry New Year's Eve, telling fortunes with molten lead and lighting the tree, *Divina commedia* and the strains of *Parsifal*. – How inwardly content and inwardly inspired are we as we come to the end of this so difficult year! 'Now thank we all our God' – oh, how I thank him!

1878

Saturday, January 5 R. works and, around noon, calls me in order to play me the conclusion of the entrance [of the Knights of the Grail] and Titurel's wonderfully melancholic appeal. 'I have spoiled things for the spa orchestras,' he says with a laugh; 'my entrance ends without suffering!'

Sunday, January 6 Today he works on his essay for the [*Bayreuther*] *Blätter*[1], which will soon be published. He told me that, if he had not invited Herr v. W. to settle here, nothing would have induced him to say a single word more.

Monday, January 7 R. works on his essay. When I told R. yesterday that, if he was not in the mood to write it, he should drop it, he replied, 'Oh, I can't be such a weakling.' I: 'The weakness which is creating *Parsifal*.' He: 'What comes pouring out of one's soul can't be described as work.'

Sunday, January 13 Thinking about various dates in his life, R. felt he had made a mistake in his biography, and that it was only the stillness of the Asyl garden which felt in his memory like a Good Friday, it had not been Good Friday in fact[2]. – In the evening R. says he will have to rewrite everything he wrote during the morning. He was looking for a certain key, and mechanical modulation is something he finds impossible! 'I'm a fine musician,' he says with a laugh, adding that it is only when he is working without reflection that he finds what he wants – if he starts to consider how to transpose a theme into another key, he gets confused! – He sings us Titurel and the beginning of Amfortas.

Tuesday, January 15 Our friend Wolzogen works out the membership statistics of the Society of Patrons, according to which we possess about 11,000 marks! In the evening R. seems to me to be in a somewhat bad mood; I fear it is due to financial worries.

Wednesday, January 16 Without his knowledge I write to the King, begging him to give orders that royalties be paid on R.'s works to help wipe out the deficit.

Sunday, January 20 Everything evenly balanced: love and the blessings of

---

[1] The introductory article for the first issue of his own periodical.
[2] Wagner's assertion in *My Life* that the idea for *Parsifal* came to him on Good Friday 1857 in the garden of the Asyl has always been disputed, since he did not move into the Asyl until 18 days after Good Friday of that year.

work. In the evening R. improvises the Communion service in the way he has now designed it: 'The percussion will accompany the singing, like a faint earth tremor.' – R. looked through Berlioz's scores of the *Requiem* and *Te Deum* and laughed over the many instructions they contain for the percussion players, etc., etc.; he said it reminded him of a theatre director setting straight the wigs of his actors; the uproar on the '*rex tremendae majestatis*' made him laugh heartily. He goes for a short walk in the palace gardens. I am delighted with his appearance in the evening: 'I feel so well,' he tells me with shining eyes. I am filled with both bliss and apprehension – oh, this mortal life! R. says, 'Fidi looks at me the way Parsifal looks on the Grail, in a wonder of amazement.'

Monday, January 21 A curious interruption in our sublime life is provided by the visit of the opera director Angelo Neumann from Leipzig and Israel. He has come for the *Ring* but would also like to have *Parsifal*! Coaxes R. out of half the royalties for the subscription quota – in short, is just what such gentlemen always are. R. says he has nothing against his coming, insofar as it shows they still need him – and we need money, so agreement is reached!

Tuesday, January 22 Around lunchtime R. calls me and says he has something to show me; he plays and sings to me the heavenly scene of the uncovering of the Grail! As tender and exalted as Salvation itself! The words '*Wein und Brot des letzten Mahles*' ['wine and bread of the Last Supper'] sound like an ancient saga told by angels. . . . 'But I won't let the old man [Titurel] appear again,' R. says; 'he would remind me too much of that old gondolier in Venice who always butted in when others were singing.'

Wednesday, January 23 In the evening he says to me, 'You will laugh!,' and he shows me the part of Titurel, whom he has brought in again after all. In the morning we discussed the scenery for the Temple of the Grail, and I suggest a basilica, two naves leading through pillars to doors hidden behind them. In the evening R. plays and sings to us the most glorious scenes ever to have been written and set to music!

Thursday, January 24 Our final words yesterday had to do with the Godhead; I: 'I must believe in it – my unworthiness and my happiness lead me to believe.' He: 'The first part, your unworthiness, you can cross out; Godhead is Nature, the will which seeks salvation and, to quote Darwin, selects the strongest to bring this salvation about.' – We start W. Scott's *The Heart of Midlothian* and find much enjoyment in it.

Tuesday, January 29 On the pencilled sketches is written 'January 29, '78' – they are finished. R. shows me the voice which breathes the words '*selig im Glauben*' once again after Parsifal has been repulsed by Gurnemanz. I said to R. that, just like the imperceptible change and the unfelt development within Parsifal himself, this music develops, changes, hovers – one is wrapped up and borne along by it as if by magic; light gives way to dark as in the colours of clouds at sunset, and all one feels is a constant, unchanging sense of spiritual well-being as one is borne along by it.

Saturday, February 2 Splendid letter to me from the King, he is approving royalties as a means of wiping out the deficit. And this news I am able to bring R.! – The King's letter is very beautiful. R. jokes and calls me his *Jeanie*[1], who looks after him; we are really delighted, particularly since the solution comes from R.'s earnings (royalties on his works).

Sunday, February 3 I write to the King to thank him. In the evening we finish *The Heart of Midlothian* with great satisfaction. 'A great writer, the crown of a civilized period, a great master,' says R.

Tuesday-Wednesday, February 5–6 The contract with Munich has arrived. R. has had sent to him the symphony by Brahms[2] which has been performed with tremendous success in Vienna and Leipzig. After reading it through, he says: 'One can't really wonder that such things get written; there is nothing in it, but the public cheers! As far as they are concerned, Beethoven and the great poets have lived in vain.' The symphony, with all its triviality blown up by orchestral effects, its tremolando theme which might have come from the introduction to a Strauss waltz, we find utterly shocking.

Thursday, February 7 R. tells me he has started work again, I helped him to it! A little gift (a tablecloth with roses), which I presented to him to celebrate the conclusion of the first act, has given him pleasure. Better than anyone else he can take delight in the smallest of things. Klingsor will be very brutal, he says – 'brooding, as you can imagine.' – He has also got Kundry's cry. – Arrival of the *Bayreuther Blätter*.

Friday, February 8 R. works, I have all kinds of things to arrange and put away, much fighting with the dragon. R. sketches out a canon for a domestic symphony, then he writes to the King, describing our life in Tribschen at the time of the *Idyll*, which he sends to the King as a gift, saying that he is now enjoying the happiest days of his life. His words move me deeply, and I pray we may be granted a prolongation of them.

Tuesday, February 12 The grief I was fearing has not passed me by; it has come upon me from outside[3]. May God help me! . . . Oh, sorrow, my old companion, come back and dwell within me; we know each other well – how long wilt thou stay with me this time, most loyal and dependable of friends? Purify me, make me worthy of thee, I shall not flee from thee – but when wilt thou bring me thy brother? . . . Splendid weather, R. is able

[1] In Scott's *The Heart of Midlothian* Jeanie Deans walks from Scotland to London to plead with the Queen for her condemned sister's life.

[2] The Second Symphony, first performed (under Hans Richter) in Vienna on December 30, 1877.

[3] This suggests that Cosima had discovered the secret correspondence between Wagner and Judith Gautier that had been going on since the previous autumn with Schnappauf as go-between, or that Wagner had admitted it to her; on February 10 Wagner wrote to Judith asking her in future to correspond only with Cosima.

to go out for a while, but not much, on account of his foot. W. Scott in the evening. The scenes in the castle of Tillietudlem[1] rather too prolonged.

Saturday, February 16 R. asks me whether I am cheerful, for only then does his ideal world exist for him, only then can he work. This helps to dispel all the clouds, I see my sad thoughts dispersing like patches of fog, and though weariness remains, it is of a gentle nature. R. is working! He is delighted with the F he has given Klingsor at the start, and he also shows me the surging movement he has placed beneath Klingsor's sombre and mysterious melody. – Before we begin our reading we hear issuing from the *salon* the beginning of the 'Holy Grail March' – Loldi is playing it and adding a kind of upper voice to it; this pleases R. very much, and it is truly very moving – 'the best testimony to my work,' says R.

Tuesday, February 19 I am not well, and we lunch together upstairs. 'Who is Titurel?' he asks me. I reflect. 'Wotan,' he says. 'After his renunciation of the world he is granted salvation, the greatest of possessions is entrusted to his care, and now he is guarding it like a mortal god' – a lovely thought!

Friday, February 22 R. talks of a symphony he intends to dedicate to Fidi, another theme for it occurred to him today, and he says it would be as merry and friendly as the boy himself! – To have discovered and declared that a generous and pure heart is greater than all genius – this is something for which R. praises Schopenhauer particularly.

Saturday, February 23 After lunch R. comes back to Mozart, and particularly *Die Zauberflöte*; he says that certain things in it marked a turning point in the history of art; Sarastro introduced dignity of spirit in place of conventional dignity. – Certain things in Mozart will and can never be excelled, he says.

Tuesday, February 26 R. works; in a very nice letter he has written to my father he says, 'I am composing now all day long, like Raff or Brahms.' He is in a splendid mood, his eyes radiate joy, kindness and cheerfulness. – In the evening [Scott's] *Waverley*, after walking secretly to the theatre with the children[2]. Much enjoyment from this beautiful and serene book.

Saturday, March 2 Herr Kipke[3] in Leipzig informs us that bankruptcy proceedings have been started against poor Herr Fritzsch. Of R.'s collected writings 1,500 copies have been sold, 700 still remain; Herr K. wants R. Schott's Söhne to buy them for 12,000 marks, and R. suggests it to Herr Strecker. – *Waverley* in the evening. – Comparison between Alberich and Klingsor; R. tells me that he once felt every sympathy for Alberich, who represents the ugly person's longing for beauty. In Alberich the naïveté of the non-Christian world, in Klingsor the peculiar quality which Christianity brought into the world; just like the Jesuits, he does not believe in

[1] In *Old Mortality*.
[2] In connection with costumes for Wagner's birthday.
[3] Karl Kipke, a writer on music.

goodness, and this is his strength but at the same time his downfall, for through the ages *one* good man does occasionally emerge.

Sunday, March 3 Arrival of our amiable friend Frau v. Schleinitz, who intends to spend a few days near us. Much chatting about a world which seems ever stranger to us.

Monday, March 4 R. well, working cheerfully, although he wishes the 'duet'[1] were already behind him – he is looking forward to the third act.

Wednesday, March 6 R. is very interested in his symphony, which Seidl is copying out from the orchestral parts[2]; R. says it could have been written by a young composer between the first and second symphonies of Beethoven. But in the evening he is dismayed by the second theme. Letter from Schwerin, they agree to R.'s terms for *Der Ring des Nibelungen*, which makes R. remark that Berlin will now be surrounded on all sides: Hamburg, Schwerin, Brunswick, Leipzig, Vienna, Munich are all doing the *Ring*.

Thursday, March 7 In the evening conversation with our friend, then some music. R. played various Italian themes, from Bellini's *I Capuleti ed i Montecchi, La Straniera* and *Norma*, and said: 'For all the poverty of invention, there is real passion and feeling there, and the right singer has only to get up and sing it for it to win all hearts. I have learned things from them which Messrs. Brahms & Co. have never learned, and they can be seen in my melodies.' Second issue of the *Bayreuther Blätter*, very good.

Friday, March 8 Snow squalls, R. somewhat worn out, but he works all the same. Affectionate parting from our friend.

Monday, March 11 R. remarks that I again have my 'melancholy, eager look,' which means that I am completely restored, and indeed the sweet habit of existence has me in its grip again! My work with the children and nothing to disturb my close life with R. – Yesterday evening the children were reading aloud, and R. was captivated by the sight of Fidi's fair head as he listened: 'We must be glad that we lived to hear these children's voices,' he says. He feels he must write something for the *Blätter*. 'My pencillings have just reached a point where I can break off. After these furious affairs it will be strange for me to have to compose nothing but pleasantnesses. Maybe I won't succeed.' Regarding his article ['*Modern*'], he says he enjoys writing it, but one always has too much to say.

Wednesday, March 13 In the evening our friend Count Du Moulin[3], announcing 27 members – our little Society is growing. – 'It is as impossible to write music without melody,' R. says in the course of the conversation, 'as to speak without thoughts: melody is musical thought.' In the evening

[1] Between Klingsor and Kundry in Act II.
[2] The original score was still missing, but from the orchestral parts discovered in Dresden Seidl was now reconstructing the score.
[3] Count Eduard Du Moulin of the Society of Patrons in Regensburg, father of Cosima's biographer, Count Richard Du Moulin-Eckart.

we went through the Prelude to *Parsifal,* friend Seidl played it and R. had to spend much time talking about the tempo, which S. took too slowly, or rather, incorrectly. R. says that tempo cannot be written down, every piece has its own way of being played; of course there are pieces, he says, in which the tempo must be taken with tremendous sharpness and precision, but one must know which they are, and that must be learned from the composer. That is why he had wanted to found a school, 'where I should have vexed myself to death every day,' he added.

Thursday, March 14 With friend Gross; the contract from Munich here, a few points unacceptable. Returning home, I find R. in the *salon* between the first movement of his symphony and the sketches; he greets me with the words 'I have just composed a trio for the Scherzo of my symphony,' and he plays it to me. I: 'It's a veritable composing factory here!' Laughter! He inquires about the contract, insists on the repayment of my 32,000 marks from the proceeds of *Parsifal,* which hurts me very much, but I let it pass, so as not to spoil R.'s splendidly cheerful spirits.

Sunday, March 17 Friend Heckel would like very much to have *Die Walküre.* R. writes to him saying he would gladly give him personally the whole of the *Ring* for nothing, but he would not make the Mannheim theatre a present of a single cent. At lunch R. laughs over their imagining they could cast *Die Walküre* properly. 'I ought to advise them to do *Tristan und Isolde,* for at least they've got a good flute player.'

Tuesday, March 19 Friend Feustel arrives with extremely unpleasant accounts of the King's position, it is being said that a trustee will have to be appointed to control his affairs, but nobody dares take the responsibility for such an act. – R. brought me the first pencil sketches of the second act. – R. told me recently that he owes the 'yes' in Parsifal and Kundry's dialogue (Act I) to the children's conversations here – that importantly eager 'yes'!

Wednesday, March 20 In the evening I read aloud from Schop.'s biography,[1] everything about him from his earliest youth is profound and significant. We decide to let Fidi read *only* Schop. as his introduction to philosophy, then after him Plato and Kant. – The painters Böcklin and Seitz Junior[2] decline to make me scenery and costume sketches for *Parsifal.* The architect [Camillo] Sitte demands to hear the music first. Oh, Germany!

Saturday, March 23 Yesterday evening R said, 'I had looked forward to my Flower Maidens, now they are proving difficult too.' He asked me what they should wear on their first appearance: 'Perhaps something suggesting flower stems, and then they might decorate themselves with petals.' – Snowfall. R. is very exasperated by the weather. But in the afternoon he goes through the second act of *Parsifal* with friend S. Oh, what does one

---

[1] Wilhelm von Gwinner's biography of Schopenhauer had just been published.
[2] The Swiss painter Arnold Böcklin had also declined to design the scenery for the *Ring* in 1876; Rudolf Seitz was the son of Franz von Seitz, the costume designer at the Munich opera.

care then about the lack of sunshine, about difficulties and cares – how unimportant and petty they all seem! – I can scarcely express my emotion with an embrace – how, then, for you, my children, in words? The whole world of sin writhes and laments, sighs and laughs in these sounds, how frail Kundry's existence, her initial 'I will not,' how frail even her rebellion, how overpowering her laugh of desire! And Parsifal's appearance, childlike, heroic, victorious, radiantly pure and strong as steel as he resists all their pressure! 'They could not catch him, unlike Siegfried,' says R., 'the fly was too large.' R. rests for a while, but he cannot sleep. He is also pleased with his work, which is unparalleled – even compared with Erda's awakening, Alberich's curse!

Monday, March 25 R. had to get up during the night; I am alarmed because he is now drinking more cognac than he used to, and I tell him so. – Dear God, everything alarms me now; recently he complained of pressure above his left eye. But he works and is cheerful at lunch. Over coffee he tells me he is now writing words for his maidens.

Tuesday, March 26 R. goes off to his 'street girls'; he says, 'They're giving me a lot of trouble,' but yesterday he was pleased that he had now written over a half of his work, I tell him to me it seems like magic. R. continues working on his text and says he will have 18 maidens, no more. No one in the audience will take any notice of the text, he says, but the singers sing differently and feel like individuals if they do not just have to sing senseless repetitions in chorus, and this adds to the general effect, as, for instance, with the song of the Valkyries. – Yesterday I asked him whether he was contented. 'Infinitely,' he replied. This answer, and the emphatic way he spoke it, flooded me with a feeling of well-being, and with the memory of it I passed blissfully in the evening from waking to sleeping; he was resting quietly beside me, his 'infinitely' stirred in my heart; all my sorrows seemed like departed spirits which would never return, and I enjoyed my moment of exaltation!

Wednesday, March 27 I found it an oppressive day, in reply to my inquiry about the condition of our friend Pusinelli I learned from his daughter that his life is despaired of! I do not tell R. this.

Thursday, March 28 In the morning R. suddenly asks me about Pusinelli; as so often before, he puts my thoughts into words; I have to tell him the truth.

Friday, March 29 Arrival of the 6,000 marks from Schwerin, we take them to the banker Gross, who receives us with the words, 'My joy knows no ending,' meaning the constant flow of subscriptions to the Society of Patrons. – Walking in our garden, we catch sight of the first crocuses, a touching moment. As we return home through the palace gardens, he says: 'It does not say much for Schopenhauer that he did not pay more attention to my *Ring des Nibelungen*[1]. I know no other work in which the breaking of a will (and what a will, which delighted in the creation of a world!) is shown

[1] Wagner sent Schopenhauer a copy of the *Ring* text as soon as it was completed; Schopenhauer did not acknowledge it, but Wagner later heard through friends that he had 'spoken favourably' of it.

as being accomplished through the individual strength of a proud nature *without the intervention of a higher grace*, as it is in Wotan. Almost obliterated by the separation from Brünnhilde, this will rears up once again, bursts into flame in the meeting with Siegfried, flickers in the dispatching of Waltraute, until we see it entirely extinguished at the end in Valhalla.' At supper he returns to this and says: 'I am convinced Sch. would have been annoyed that I discovered this before I knew about his philosophy – I, a political refugee, the indefensibility of whose theories had been proved by his disciple [Ernst] Kossak on the basis of his philosophy, since my music is supposed to have no melody. But it was not very nice. It's the way Goethe treated Kleist, whom he should have acclaimed, as Schumann acclaimed Brahms – but that only seems to happen among donkeys.'

Sunday, March 31 R. fetches me for lunch and says, 'Do you know how Kundry calls to Parsifal?' He sings me the phrase, so piercingly tender, with which she names him: 'It is the first time his name is spoken, and thus his mother had called him! Only music can do that.' 'And only your music,' I add.

Tuesday, April 2 At noon I receive from Marie Pusinelli the news of the death of our dear friend. I decide not to give R. the news until the end of the evening; I order wreaths and conceal my feelings from R., who is enjoying the springlike weather. We go for a walk together. At supper an unkind fate decrees that Herr Stern[1] send me a reply, which I was not expecting. R. opens the telegram. Silence. He gets up and goes out, comes back after a little while; I at once start to read a further instalment of Herr Porges's article; earnest discussion. Our friends leave: 'Let's go straight to bed,' says R. on the stairs I ask, 'You understood the telegram?' He: 'Oh!' We prepare for sleep; in bed he says, 'He was a small man but a great heart, an unflinchingly great heart, which helped him to understand everything, and that was the reason for his happy career.'

Wednesday, April 3 R. slept tolerably. 'You poor little woman,' he says to me, 'what a lot of worries you have, problems you conceal from me!' He relates how pleasant and congenial the Pusinelli home in Dresden had been to him, he had often been there with Minna. He does not work; writes to Frau P. – At midday he receives the Munich theatre representative whom he had asked to come to discuss the serpent question. They have in fact constructed [for *Siegfried*] a winged dragon, which makes R. ask why, if it could fly, it has laboriously to crawl up, and anyway it is nowhere called a dragon, but a *serpent*.

Friday, April 5 Around lunchtime R. calls me and plays me '*Komm', holder Knabe*' from his sketches, that most enchanting of scenes[2]. Yesterday he

---

[1] Adolf Stern, a writer: Cosima had asked him to order wreathes for Pusinelli's funeral.
[2] The Flower Maidens' scene in Act II.

said, 'In the first act I was very sparing of sensuous intervals, but now I am going back to my old paintpot.'

Saturday, April 6 At seven o'clock to the amateur concert to hear Frl. Olden[1] – great disappointment, not to say dismay over the present state of theatrical art. Indescribable tempi. – The programme included the *Danse macabre* by Saint-Saëns, which is at present all the rage in Germany, and R. is amused when I say this work is like a Berlioz *Panaritium*. Home in merry mood.

Monday, April 8 A telegram announcing my father's arrival; at eleven o'clock he is here, much to our joy. – R. takes the contract with Munich to the mayor for signature.

Tuesday, April 9 R. works. Towards evening he receives a wonderfully touching letter from Frau Pusinelli, which profoundly moves him. – Of Saint-Saëns and the *Danse macabre* R. says, 'The donkey doesn't even know how a cock crows; on the dominant: he makes it yodel.'

Friday, April 12 In the evening *Parsifal* for my father, from the entrance into the Temple onwards. A most remarkable, unforgettable sight, R. and my father, the greatness of life, the greatness of withdrawal from it!

Sunday, April 14 Fine spring day, I walk slowly with my father in the palace gardens, and suddenly we meet R., striding along with the two dogs as he returns from the Students' Wood; merry greetings; R., as he goes, cries out to my father, 'I can't be cross with you, since you gave birth to your daughter for me.' In the evening my father again plays us several of his compositions. Some of it does not appeal to R., and this arouses feelings of embarrassment in him, but he takes great pains to show my father only his love and admiration. – It is wonderful and touching to see how these two such fundamentally different natures, who have taken such divergent paths, respect, understand and protect each other, and that is one more jewel in the crown of my happiness. 'Have you still got a body?' R. says to me today, embracing me.

Tuesday, April 16 R. works and is pleased with his '*Du – Tor*'[2], which he sings to me frequently. – Friend Feustel approaches my father regarding capital for the deficit, which, it seems, is not easy to raise at five percent; I beg my father, who is reluctant to touch his investments, only to do so if we are unable to raise the necessary loan elsewhere.

Wednesday, April 17 Departure of my father, whom I accompany as far as Neuenmarkt. R. goes for a walk and works; complains humorously about his problem with the *choreography*, says it will turn out like the so-called street-brawl in *Die Meistersinger*. – Then he tells us how ridiculous it is that, having just composed his *Parsifal*, he should find such things as the cadenza

[1] Fanny Bertram (b. 1855), then a soprano in Frankfurt; she later found international fame as Fanny Moran-Olden.
[2] 'Thou – Fool', the Flower Maidens' final words to Parsifal.

of Princess Elvira's first aria in *La Muette de Portici* coming into his mind as he was 'putting on his trousers and shoes'!

Thursday, April 25 At noon arrival of a new book by friend Nietzsche[1] – feelings of apprehension after a short glance through it. It seems to me to contain much inner rage and sullenness, and R. laughs heartily when I say that Voltaire, here so acclaimed, would less than any other man have understood *The Birth of Tragedy*.

Saturday, April 27 R. was already awake at 5 o'clock, at lunchtime he shows me the [Flower Maidens'] scene, almost completed *in ink*, and he plays the theme, the enchanting theme, to the children. – R. not entirely well, but still working and enjoying his work; only he says he dare not think of the performance: 'When I hear, for instance, that Vogl is already saying he will sing Parsifal, my blood boils.' Firm resolve not to read friend Nietzsche's book, which seems at first glance to be strangely perverse. – In the evening *Ivanhoe*, then amused ourselves with some things from Marschner's *Templer*[2].

Monday, April 29 We find it hard not to speak now and again about friend N.'s sad book, although both of us can only surmise its contents from a few passages, rather than really know it! – At breakfast R. says that, if he were to present anything here after *Parsifal*, it would be *Tristan* and *Die Msinger*, but he doubts whether he could find a singer for Tristan; he says he wants to make some alterations in the third act, also in the second: 'I don't know what devil it was that drove me to produce such stuff – it was the music, which came welling like that out of the subject.' – I study the Flower Maidens' scene, this splendid, incomparable scene, about which R. said to me, 'Yes, I am rather proud of it.'

Tuesday, April 30 I visit friend Gross, to find out how things stand with the capital loan. He tells me it had almost been settled when a jurist (the fourth J.![3]) frightened off the bank. He says the King insists that R. no longer has to worry about it; Herr Bürkel has done as much as he can, but he cannot very well show his face in a bank, for then it would be spread around that the King was getting into debt. – In the evening R. feels severe pain in his leg, the physician discovers a furuncle and orders complete rest. To see him flat on his back robs me of all my strength.

Wednesday, May 1 R. slept well but still has his ailment and has to stay in bed. A sore trial! All the same, he works and writes the conclusion of his 'Public and Popularity' article. In the evening, *Ivanhoe*.

Wednesday, May 8 Now Königsberg also wants to do *Rheingold* and *Walküre*. – R. writes to Herr von Loën, suggesting that instead of royalties the Grand Duke might grant him a small pension until 30 years after his death. In this way he could circumvent Messrs. Voltz and Batz. 'This would be for one

---

[1] This was *Human, All Too Human*.
[2] Marschner's opera *Der Templer und die Jüdin* (1829) is based on Scott's *Ivanhoe*.
[3] To add to Wagner's other three 'abominations': Jews, Jesuits and journalists.

of my 130 daughters,' R. says with a laugh. At supper much merriment over the way I get entangled in my own lies[1]; R. declares that I must have been ordering a trumpet serenade for him from the military band!

Thursday, May 9 R.'s leg still very painful, but the core seems to be loosening. He works. In the evening the curious Herr Schmeitzner[2], I feel we would do better to print our little periodical here!

Friday, May 10 R.'s carbuncle bursting at last, but he still cannot walk; however, he remains in good spirits and is working. But Vienna is causing him great vexation; he had written saying that it was precisely for Siegfried at the Imperial Opera that he wished to coach Herr Jäger, who is proving to be a sterling character. Herr Jauner writes that Herr Glatz has already been engaged for this role. We remember our experiences with Glatz, and R. is hurt by Richter's having 'treacherously' made the engagement without saying anything to him about it.

Sunday, May 19 Much coughing, not a good night. But R. slept well, and though awaiting my recovery with considerable impatience, he is nevertheless well! He works. Yesterday he told me he feared he was tiring, the rewriting was a torment to him, and he was still not satisfied; he would take it as far as the kiss, then break off. As I am wandering up and down in my room (around lunchtime), he gently parts the curtains and says to me, 'It will be all right.' He had interrupted his work to bring me this consolation.

Wednesday, May 22 The day of days! We wake up at the same time, R. and I, to the sound of bells: 'I congratulate myself for having you,' says R. I can say nothing at all, for not even the tenderest of embraces can express what death alone would enable me to say to him. Letter from the King, delivered by a messenger; R. goes off to thank him for it, and during this time we set up our little festival in the hall[3]. We begin it at eleven o'clock, the good children, in a mood of utter dedication, perform their tasks exactly as I instructed them, the pantomime makes a sublime impression, and not for a moment does their earnestness waver. Many, many tears. 'It is the loveliest experience of my life!' R. exclaims. 'What is all care compared with such a moment? Oh, what a lovely death it would have been if I had fallen asleep at the end of this celebration!' He asks to be left alone for a while. A lovely, blissful day! 'Children, I saw you today in a completely different light!' R. says to the little ones, and to me, 'They all came from your womb – that one sees at times like this.' – Then much joking, tales of the winter rehearsals, not a day passing by since the New Year without my doing something for this dear day, my winter blessings. During a pause following

[1] In connection with her arrangements for R.'s birthday.
[2] The *Bayreuther Blätter* was being published by Schmeitzner (Nietzsche's publisher) in Schloss-Chemnitz.
[3] For Wagner's 65th birthday Cosima had devised a 'May Festival.' Written by Wolzogen with the help of Gross and Seidl, it made use of characters and music from Wagner's works, and it was performed by the five children, each taking several roles, on a specially erected stage in the hall of Wahnfried.

the performance R. went into the garden and saw the new carriage[1], he got in, sent for me, and then we were pulled all over the Wahnfried grounds in it, by the Wolzogens, Seidl, the children, Mrs. Cooper and the servants! – Many telegrams, among them one from Herr von Hülsen which causes some surprise; many touching signs of devotion. Walk with R. in the palace gardens, we wander around like blessed spirits, then go off to drink beer with the children and the Wolzogens. Some friends in the evening. *Parsifal* (the first act, from the entrance into the Temple to the end) puts the last sublime crown on a blissful day.

Thursday, May 23 R. wishes to keep the little theatre standing and to have a repeat performance today, for he says his emotion had made him miss much, and he now wants to enjoy it artistically. Siegfried, still somewhat hoarse, is put to bed, so as to be ready for the great moment. The second performance is also successful, and in place of yesterday's tears and sobs we have cheers and merriment at the end. R. even takes pleasure in my little stage, says he loves such conventions; he says he had frequently wondered from where the children made their entrances, and he would now appoint me his stage director! – Herr Loën has written in connection with the suggested pension, saying that over 30 years R.'s works have brought in only 30,000 thalers! Curious indeed.

Monday, May 27 R. does some work. 'I am so well that I feel like composing,' he says. Christening of the carriage with the children, 'Uncle' Seidl and both of us; to the Waldhütte. Splendid mood of gaiety, the new carriage (a birthday gift) fills R. with utter delight. Even my new English hat, bought to celebrate R.'s birthday, pleases him: 'You look like a Roman patrician's lady from the first centuries who has just embraced Christianity but still retains her old habits.' – The children recite their May Festival in the carriage. 'Keep that fast in your memory,' R. exclaims to them, 'and may life never strip this act of dedication from you.' As we are preparing for bed we go once more through the whole splendid day. 'It's a never-ending joy, this carriage,' says R., and 'You are to thank for every day I remain alive.'

Tuesday, May 28 R. is once more filling in his sketches in ink, and when I go downstairs to greet him, around lunchtime, he plays me Parsifal's sorrowful outburst on hearing of his mother's death, so sorrowful and so tender that Herzeleide's whole nature is revealed before one's eyes. In the afternoon R. does some more work and plays to me Kundry's words of consolation.

Wednesday, May 29 In the afternoon I meet R. at the Wolzogens' and am able to tell him the news, just received from Feustel, that the bank in Gera has advanced the sum needed to cover the deficit. He works until supper

---

[1] A light family carriage to replace their hired landau.

and afterwards reads to me, Lusch and friend Seidl two acts of *Macbeth*, with indescribable effect. R. is also of my opinion that in *Macbeth* the English language is particularly true to itself, that the word 'Hail', for instance, sounds completely different from '*Heil*', hoarse and daemonic. 'Yes, that's also something for a fan-waving audience!' he exclaims.

Thursday, May 30 Over coffee he comes back to Prof. Nietzsche and his book, which seems to him so insignificant, whereas the feelings which gave rise to it are so evil. Afterwards music – the heavenly Flower Maidens' scene, in which R. has conjured up for all time spring and its longing, its sweet complaint. And in the middle of it Kundry's cry, like a mortal soul suddenly giving voice to its suffering and its loving amid the innocence of Nature. Recently R. said to me, 'Herzeleide dies very simply; she dies like a twig on a tree.' He feels that in certain places he would like to hear the orchestra at once, to write a few things in orchestral score from the start. This would help him, just as he had written the Prelude to *Das Rheingold* straight out in full score; the sound of the horns – in certain places, he says, he absolutely needs to hear it.

Saturday, June 1 R. works and, as he tells me, produces seven or eight bars. 'What I have let myself in for!' he frequently exclaims, 'It goes far beyond *Tristan*, though I showed enough of the sufferings of love in the third act of that.' – We take the children to the agricultural show; the cocks in particular fascinate R., he remembers how at the livestock exhibition in Paris (during the sixties) he had dearly wanted to buy a cock priced at 800 francs, though he had barely a cent to his name: 'I thought if I owned that bird I should really feel like somebody.' A cock with a splendid wig reminds him of Berlioz, with its violent nervous movements; the dishevelled wig of another reminds him of Beethoven's tousled hair; the din of the crowing amuses him vastly, and he wishes he had a poultry yard like that.

Sunday, June 2 Our gay and peaceful day ends horribly with the news that another attempt has been made on the Emperor's life[1]! These assassination attempts seem to me so un-German, as if the whole German nation has become a stranger to itself.

Tuesday, June 4 R. sends for me: 'I'm about to start.' The scene between Parsifal and Kundry, up to the cry of the former: 'Amfortas!' Indescribably moving! 'A moment of daemonic absorption,' R. calls the bars which accompany Kundry's kiss and in which the fatal motive of love's longing, creeping like poison through the blood, makes a shattering effect. This, along with the tenderly sorrowful sounds of Herzeleide, the majestic way in which Kundry proclaims her liberation from the pressure of remorse – all these things, so richly and variously laid out, so ravishing and so painful, form a whole of unfathomable beauty and nobility. Oh, the wonderful man!

---

[1] He had been shot and wounded while taking a drive in Berlin; there had been a previous attempt on May 12.

– R. sees a resemblance between Wotan and Kundry: both long for salvation and both rebel against it, Kundry in the scene with P., Wotan with Siegfried.

Friday, June 7 Thoughts of a letter to the King of Bavaria, to get him to intervene in the political situation. We listen to a black-bird which is sitting and singing on the branch above the roof of the newly-built Wolzogen house. Seeing Fidi approach in his best suit reminds me of Daniel in his first communion clothes, I can still see his beautiful glistening eyes, and I have to weep. R. notices it as my tears are drying and asks me why; I tell him. 'You had nobler figures around you in your childhood than I did – your father, your mother, your brother, your sister.' We embrace, and then R. asks, 'Which of the W.'s will live in the upper story of the house?' I: 'You mean, who will see our kisses?' He laughs. 'Yes, our friends or their family.' – We part in laughter.

Sunday, June 9 R. works and says at lunch that one passage caused him much trouble until he decided to transpose it – 'Stupid fellow, not D minor, it must be C minor!' – and then everything was all right. – At lunch, when talking about this transposition, R. comes to the subject of Bach's fugues, in most of which there is hardly ever a modulation: 'It is like a cosmic system, which moves according to eternal laws, without feeling; the sorrows of the world are indeed reflected in it, but not in the same way as in other music.' Similarly, he says, he has used only one strong modulation in the *Parsifal* Prelude. The Renz Circus is preparing a Rhinemaidens' scene and a 'Ride of the Valkyries'!

Tuesday, June 11 R. reads me the fine pages in Renan's [*The Life of Christ*] about the unification of Jesus with God. R. develops this subject further in his mind, calling this God which dwells within us 'the inborn antidote to the will.'

Wednesday, June 12 R. begins his cure (Marienbad waters) and intends to interrupt his work, he has got as far as '*O Qual der Liebe*' ['Oh, pang of love']. He talks about the subject which is now occupying him and remarks how through this God, characters such as the Maid of Orleans and Parsifal were deprived for ever of sensual urges by a great impression made on them in their adolescent years. He believes that in this way Christianity could be preached to the world with renewed purity and truth; all the material for its elucidation can be found in Schop. R. says goodbye to Loulou: 'She looked at me exactly as her father used to.' Tender and melancholy parting from my child, who is going to her relations in England.

Thursday, June 13 The little ones rather naughty, R. very solemn, not to say strict, gives Fidi his first box on the ear, Loldi quite beside herself. Tender reconciliation! . . .

Saturday, June 15 R. tells us of a brewery assistant who, having fallen into the brew, now lies dying; his master was not prepared to keep him nor the hospital to take him in, and his father did not want him. I beg R. to bring him to our house; R. sends someone to the surgeon Schnappauf, who informs him that the poor young man has been taken forcibly to his father's house, where he cannot be nursed; R. arranges that, if he can still be moved, he is to be taken to the hospital at his expense.

Sunday, June 16 Blandine's Communion! R. embraces me. 'You have a lot to do, but the blessing is with you.' – It comes from him, and, when I see my good, earnest girl walk around the altar, I think to myself that no preliminary training could have prepared her so well, ploughed her soul so thoroughly for the seed, as living in the sight of *his* image! I ask R. not to come to church, but he appears in time for the sacred act. 'There is a lot to be learned from it,' he says when we return home, 'and it is always the human beings who dismay one at such times, the brutal human beings for whom nevertheless Jesus came to earth.' R. is pleased that in *Parsifal* he has not depicted the action of the service in the Temple, but has concentrated everything into the blessing of the Grail. – During the service the sounds of *Parsifal* echoed within me and accompanied my child.

Monday, June 17 Friend Seidl tells us about the performance of *Siegfried* in Munich, which, to judge by his report, must have been thoroughly bad – they have gone out of their way, it seems, to do everything differently from Bayreuth. 'I don't want to hear a word about it,' R. exclaims, and 'What a curious fate these works have had!'

Tuesday, June 18 In the morning R. finishes Renan's *Life of Jesus* and is in complete agreement with his interpretation, also with his description of the Roman Empire and the mediocrity to which we are now irretrievably devoted.

Wednesday, June 19 The poor brewery assistant has died: an incident of shocking heartlessness. R. has read Renan's *Caliban* and thinks it very childish, about which he is really sorry.

Friday, June 21 In the afternoon R. reads to me the beginning of the *Bhagavad-Gita*[1]. 'How advanced they were!' he exclaims. 'The Greeks in their philosophy were always bound by the law of cause and effect, they always saw things materialistically. Here, in the law of reason, one finds all those things which guide a great general, often without his knowledge. And what a conception it is!'

Sunday, June 23 We talk about the fact that no rich man could be found to promote the festival performances; R. observes that they are all Jews, or, if they are not, they keep their distance, frightened off by the press. At lunch R. says, 'To my sorrow I must state that the *Bhagavad-Gita* is becoming very childish; a downright grotesque hocus-pocus when, as Vishnu, he reveals himself as an *être suprême* [supreme being].' In the evening

[1] 'The Song of the Holy One', Sanskrit philosophical poem.

R. talks about the time of the awakening of sensual feelings in a youth, and how important it is then to guide him towards an ideal.

Monday, June 24 A good letter from Lulu in England. An Israelite in Cologne, Herr Seligmann, is providing the necessary funds for the production of the *Ring* there. – R. reads some of Nietzsche's latest book and is astonished by its pretentious ordinariness. 'I can understand why Rée's company is more congenial to him than mine.' And when I remark that to judge by this book N.'s earlier ones were just reflections of something else, they did not come from within, he says, 'And now they are Rée-flections!'

Tuesday, June 25 R. tells me of the insolent tone in which Disraeli is speaking in Berlin, and Germany has to put up with it! (Over coffee in the summer-house R. quotes '*Nimm den Eid*'[1] and recalls the feeling of satisfaction which then imbues Fricka with dignity; no one, he says, has ever said a word to him about Wotan's inner resolve, and how this is brought about by his having to acknowledge that everything is his own work, all are his creatures, and he can no longer deceive himself about it.)

Thursday, June 27 N.'s book provokes R. into saying playfully, 'Oh, art and religion are just what is left in human beings of the monkey's tail, the remains of an ancient culture!' He also talks about the patience of a genius, which others notice only when now and again it turns into impatience; and about teasing, which R. explains as a kindhearted wish to conceal one's superiority and thus to teach. 'Actually,' R. adds with a laugh, 'genius is simply envy.'

Friday, June 28 In the morning he brings me some pretty material for a negligée which he has had sent for me. He rests, reads N., while I am giving the children their lessons.

Saturday, June 29 R. is having a jacket made for himself out of the same material as my negligée, and I am very pleased about it; he asks me 'whether it would be proper.'

Sunday, June 30 R. has sent for a hairdresser for me and wants my blonde hair to be brought out; I would prefer to keep my grey hairs, but if he wants it thus, I shall also be happy; he wants me to have it done in an Apollo knot and intends to study etchings of the ancient Greeks! He says to me: 'You will have a bit of peace and quiet when the children are all grown up. That is what you lack – *a morning philosophy.*' Much laughter about that.

Monday, July 1 The two children leave with the Wolzogens[2]. In the afternoon, while I am walking in the garden with R., the conductor Levi (who was expected) comes to join us; he has realized that no good production of the *Ring* is possible outside Bayreuth. R. complains about the trend of wanting to do it differently from the way he did it here.

Tuesday, July 2 R. misses Fidi and Loldi. For me still no 'morning

---

[1] 'Take my oath', Wotan to Fricka in *Die Walküre*, Act II.
[2] Isolde and Siegfried were going to Dresden for dental treatment.

philosophy' – a new governess to settle in, lessons, visit from Herr Levi (who touches R. by saying that, as a Jew, he is *a walking anachronism*). R. tells him that, if the Catholics consider themselves superior to the Protestants, the Jews are the most superior of all, being the eldest. R. says he can understand the ecstasy of martyrs, and he believes in their visions. 'Farewell, you strange man,' he says to L. as the latter leaves us. – Concern about W., whose family circumstances in his run-down state of health alarm us (his mother-in-law and two sisters-in-law have arrived here).

Wednesday, July 3 R. reads his 'Public and Popularity' articles, because he wants now to get down to the final instalment, so as to be able to resume *Parsifal* on August 1: 'I shall then finish composing in time for your birthday.' In the evening our friends the Gl[asenapp]s[1]; he brings me a little book containing a puppet play, *Delila*, by L. Geyer, and R. remembers having seen it produced in his home! – Friend Gross also comes, and tells us among other things that the King of B[avaria] is now allowed to go out only with a police escort; the instructions have come from Berlin, and the King finds it very unpleasant, he says.

Thursday, July 4 In the early morning there comes from R.'s room a wondrous fair melody. 'A theme for a quartet for you': with these words R. comes into my room, and after breakfast we part with an embrace, 'the day's blessing', as R. calls it; for me it is blessed indeed! – At noon return of the children. Many things for me to arrange, which earns me R.'s sweet and affectionate chiding. The news that Hans is well came to me like an echo of the theme, as if all my blessings stem from this morning greeting. – As I part from R. in the evening, I tell him that his melody will not leave my mind. 'Yes, such things occur to one during sleepless nights: the early bird gets the first canons.'

Sunday, July 7 Some anonymous person, signing himself in a postscript as 'warning Erda', complains of R.'s misuse of his genius to campaign against the Jews – he should leave state and empire to politicians such as Bismarck! – In the summerhouse R. talks very movingly about a theft in Riga; some articles of clothing belonging to Minna were stolen, and the maid (Lieschen), horror-stricken, at once accused her lover, who was arrested. The police told R. that, if the stolen articles were worth more than one hundred roubles, the accused man would be sent to Siberia. R. put the value as low as possible, but he could not save the man, since he was a recidivist, and he had to look on as the man was brought in with shaved head and dressed in prison garb, already condemned to Siberia. A terrible sight, and he had then and there sworn never to prosecute anyone again; he could not bear to think of it even now. – Returning home from the summerhouse, he spits

---

[1] Carl Friedrich Glasenapp (b. 1847) wrote the first full biography of Wagner, of which the first 2 vols. had already appeared; he was a tireless researcher and was of great help to Cosima in collecting her memorabilia.

up a little blood, talking has tired him; I suppress my concern but go to him in his room: 'The world does bad things to me, but in return I have you – be glad that it is so, for otherwise you would not mean so much.' I: 'Then I would sooner mean nothing.' – The blood has only come from his throat, but he looks worn out.

Wednesday, July 10 I catalogue the manuscripts with friend Glasenapp, a beloved and refreshing occupation for me. When I tell R. about it, he says, 'You foolish girl!' When I tell him I have been reading some of his letters to the King, he says, 'Oh, those don't sound very good, but it wasn't I who set the tone.' R. also begins to feel better.

Friday, July 12 Discussing at lunch the performance in Leipzig and the division of *Götterdäm.* into an introduction and three acts, he decides after all to leave it as it is and just to make some cuts – almost the whole of the Norns' scene and a large part of the scene between Waltraute and Brünnhilde. He does this because he knows that, when badly performed, they are bound to be incomprehensible, and he would rather not sacrifice the transition to the 'Journey to the Rhine', which he knows to be effective; he would have to do this if the introduction were to be separated from the first act. Even here [in Bayreuth] the Norns' scene and the Br.-Walt. scene proved unsuccessful, he says, so how much more likely are they to fail in an ordinary theatre. Indescribable melancholy about this scene! This work also now cast aside and disfigured – and he himself has to take a hand in it!

Saturday, July 13 After lunch R. again enjoins friend Seidl to study tempi, not to drag the adagios, not to rush the allegros. He cites the Andante in the A Major Symphony, for which Beethoven stipulated a very quick tempo; when the second theme is introduced, the tempo must be broadened, but at the end the march rhythm must be retained, and it is quite a different thing whether one is playing a theme for the first time or repeating it. To the Jägers'[1] in the evening; Herr Jäger sings a passage from *Siegfried*, from '*Mein Vöglein schwebte mir fort*'[2] to the end, much of it to R.'s great satisfaction, R. as the Wanderer wonderfully gripping. – Once more to have heard *Siegfried*! . . .

Sunday, July 14 The rare instance of going out in the evening did R. much good, he slept well. At 3 o'clock we gave our farewell banquet for Herr Jäger and Herr Seidl, who are going to Leipzig[3]; a gay little celebration, R. proposes a toast to friend Glasenapp, 'who brings the dead to life and kills off the living by writing biographies!'

Monday, July 15 Today another letter from Secretary Bürkel, saying that the King prefers the Munich decorations to ours here, and he also wishes the

---

[1] Ferdinand Jäger had now come to live in Bayreuth.
[2] 'My wood bird flew from my sight,' *Siegfried*, Act III, Scene 2.
[3] Where *Siegfried* and *Götterdämmerung* were in rehearsal.

Ring not to be given anywhere in its entirety before Munich. R. writes at length to the King about the present German Reich.

Thursday, July 18 He is glad that we are having lunch alone together upstairs, says it is like on our travels. When he came in he was complaining of pains in his chest, but then he grew increasingly cheerful. As he left me, he said, 'Do you know that sometimes, when I have a musical thought, I catch myself with my mouth set just like Beethoven's in his death mask?' – We have supper on the balcony, just the two of us. He returns to the set mouth and says: 'I demonstrated it to you quite wrong, the lower lip should not be thrust forward, it is a grimace of clenched teeth, of keeping silent.' I: 'Probably peculiar to musicians.' He: 'Yes, very often, when I am in the grip of some musical idea, I fall asleep like this; it is a sort of enforced silence, from which the sound then emerges.'

Sunday, July 21 After the lively Frau Jäger and the W.'s have dined with us, we go to Frau J.'s apartment (in the old palace) with the children to watch a company of tightrope walkers. The spacious square, the people in their Sunday best in the sunset glow, the characteristic houses, and on top of that the great skill of the performers, make a merry scene. 'How boring we would find a show like this in Berlin or any other great city!' says R. 'In the Prater in Vienna, for instance.' I did not watch when the younger son walked up the rope right to the roof, boldly and easily, as I was told. It is not the danger that makes me afraid, but a curious feeling of watching my brother fight for his miserable existence with just such an inner application of courage and presence of mind. All the pity of it overcomes me, and I cannot watch. R. is highly delighted with the skill and assurance of one of the men, and, responding to my persuasions, he goes up to him at the end with the children, to make a substantial extra contribution to the collection; I am told the young man behaved with uncommon courtesy when he did so. R. looked at him for a long while and said, 'You have great talent.' 'How much more pleasure,' I said to R., 'does one get from giving a little bit more than one intended to such people, than from paying for a box in some theatre or other!' A lot of talk, too, about the plucky boy who calmly allowed himself to be carried by the tightrope walker along the rope. I cannot remember when a show gave us so much pleasure as a whole, it has no place at all in our present times. In the morning R. worked without interruption on his article and found enjoyment in it; he says that he is taking on Nietzsche in it, but in such a way that a reader who is not fully in the know will not notice.

Monday, July 22 Great but welcome heat, R. busy, as he says, with theology. At lunch a dismal occurrence; Fidi behaves badly towards his father; the dreadful thought that he might prove unworthy of him takes possession of me, and this thought, instead of being turned against myself ir resigned acknowledgement of original sin, turns inside me against my child, and I hit him, so violently that it causes bruises. No words, not even my sobs, can express the horror I feel about myself – oh, fortunate people who lived in times when one could atone! In this instance, as always, R. heavenly towards me. But, alas, no kindness could help me here, and with dread I ask myself what demon constantly lurks in one to cause a normally calm person thus to lose all sense of proportion. It was the first time – will it be the last? I am afraid, and in my desperation I struggle to regain the self-control which is habitual to me. It is not life I now fear, I think, and it is also not death or other people, but *myself*! ... We drive out to the Waldhütte, returning via the Fantaisie, all the children well and very good. Oh, God, R. said to me that I am noble in all things, yet I must hate myself so!

Tuesday, July 23 We drive with the children to the Bürgerreuth; first of all we visit the theatre and take great delight in it. R. regards the furniture with amusement. 'My God, these chairs, these mirrors! And nobody actually owns them.' I: 'Yes, it is probably the only property without an owner.' Then, however, a sad look back on the performances; very emphatically he exclaims: 'I should not like to go through all that again! It was all wrong! ... All the activity kept me going and allowed me to overlook the bad things at the time, but I should not like to go through it again.' All the same, we are glad that the theatre is there, beneath the trees it looks like an eternal sunset, and it pleases us in its simple polychromy.

Thursday, July 25 R. reads to us (myself and the W.'s) his article ['Public and Popularity'], which is no more an article than the '*Kaisermarsch*' is a march! 'Salvation to the saviour,' I say to R., 'that is the motto for this concluding article.' 'You are bold, my little woman,' he replies. He intends to make some alterations in the proofs – regarding Christ's return to earth, for instance, he says his words are somewhat colourless, for he had wanted to avoid being emotional or ironic (with regard to what the theologians have made of Christ, and his assertion that the second coming of Christ can be hoped for only when they have put an end to their confusions). R. thinks he will do no more writing.

Friday, July 26 R. had a good night, and in the morning I again hear sounds of *Parsifal*. Oh, how blissful I feel! ... But we have been deprived entirely of our summer, today it is again continually wet and cold. – In the afternoon he reads Balzac and admires his gift for identifying himself in such detail with some apparently insignificant character; in this respect, he says, Balz. was superior to W. Scott. – He attempts to play some of *Parsifal* but has forgotten almost all of it: 'As a musician I'm not worth the price of a mongrel!' he says with a laugh.

Saturday, July 27 R. slept well. In the morning he gives me the single hairs from his eyebrows which had grown too long above his left eye, and I am carrying them around with me. The fact that he has hardly any eyebrows seems to me to show the complete absence of animality in his nature. – R.

is working! He tells me he must give up reading the Balzac novel in the afternoon, it absorbs him too much and disturbs his necessary morning tranquillity.

Sunday, July 28 Loldi unwell, worry; worry, too, about Boni, but of a different kind. Continual rain.

Monday, July 29 Worry kept me awake, R.'s quiet rest consoled me. He works; I to my sick little daughter, the lower bones of her spine are too prominent; I read her stories from *The Arabian Nights.* In the afternoon Eva also ill, heart palpitations and stitches. Both girls very individual, each in her own way. Coming up to Loldi, R. exclaims, 'Ah, the little Cosima!' – R. takes Fidi to the baths, enjoys what he calls his first paternal act, dries the boy off and takes care that he does not catch cold. – Over coffee I saw him suddenly contemplative, with tears in his eyes, preoccupied; when he then resumed conversation, I asked him what he had been thinking of previously; he told me he had been thinking of a musical passage, whether he should keep it going so long. That was inspiration – and I saw it!

Tuesday, July 30 The girls somewhat better. R. writes to his lawyer in Dresden; he says that, by refusing to allow a note of his to be played there, he wants to find out who can hold out longer, he or the Court theatre. They are maintaining in Dresden that, when he was a conductor there, he was under obligation to write operas for the theatre!

Wednesday, July 31 The doctor calls Loldi's condition a slight attack of rheumatic fever.

Thursday, August 1 Loldi is very much better; R. works, but he does not seem fully satisfied, says a violin passage – 'I am working for Wilhelmj' – is bothering him, he has already written so many of them! – A visit from the conductor Levi, by no means unpleasant, and, as R. says, in his Jewish way he is very touching.

Friday, August 2 I say goodbye to Herr Levi, whose feelings towards us arouse complete sympathy. Speaking of the *B. Bl.,* R. said to Herr Levi, 'I am interested only in complete truthfulness, I seek no quarrel with anybody, but I shall state my opinion of everything that comes into my mind, sparing nobody.' – In the afternoon Herr Kellermann[1], sent by my father at R.'s request to act as piano teacher and copier of scores. A pleasant person with refined features, already bearing the traces of life's hardships. 'We must fatten him up,' says R. – A walk with R., an east wind brings us a clear sky. We speak about my last conversation with Herr Levi. He does not seem fully to understand *Parsifal,* and I tell him that R.'s article theoretically bears almost the same relationship to the poem as his words on music (the *loving* woman) and on drama (the man) in *Opera and Drama* bear to Brünnhilde and Siegfried. Through this R. comes to Nietzsche, of whom he says: 'That

---

[1] Berthold Kellermann (b.1853), pupil of Liszt and teacher at the Stern Conservatoire in Berlin.

bad person has taken everything from me, even the weapons with which he now attacks me. How sad that he should be so perverse – so clever, yet at the same time so shallow!'

Sunday, August 4 In the evening we talk about *Opera and Drama*, I tell R. of the tremendous impression this book makes on me. R. says these three books, *Opera and Drama, Art and Revolution* and *The Artwork of the Future* are his most significant works.

Monday, August 5 Friend Klindworth pays us a visit, he brings with him the good news that Hans is looking and feeling very much better. . . .

Tuesday, August 6 R. has a slight cold, but he settles down to work and announces joyfully that he has overcome the main difficulty. – In the afternoon I go through the first act of *Parsifal* with friend Kl., after which R. plays to me what he wrote today (and has already filled out in ink): it is *terribly* beautiful! A visit from our six friends in the evening; Kl. plays some Chopin, which R. enjoys. Then at last alone together again. – When our friend was reluctant to fold his hands for grace at lunch today, R. reproached him with self-consciousness and spoke splendidly and at length about religion, saying how this trivial cult of atheism is to blame for the loss of reverence and the fact that in religion people now see nothing more than just the Jewish God.

Thursday, August 8 In the evening R. says to me regarding *Parsifal:* 'I sometimes have my doubts about the whole thing, whether it is not nonsense, a complete failure; but I can see the coming and going (during Gurnemanz's narration) and know how it ought to be.' 'Whatever you do, don't think of the production' is then his constant exhortation.

Friday, August 9 R. somewhat run down, he has pains in his chest and a slight haemorrhage. I implore him not to work, and try to ensure that he talk as little as possible.

Saturday, August 10 Departure of friend Kl. –

Monday, August 12 R. had a good night, but he still feels weak and complains of stabbing pains in his heart, he says it is like a clock in which something is blocked up, but the doctors will not allow that there is anything wrong with his heart. Nice, original letter from the King. Although he is so run down, R. goes to his work and begins to feel better as the day proceeds. We go for a walk together in the garden, he inspects the new aviary (I tell him that, like Faust, he is in his element creating external things); then we have our 'beer session' in the garden, feeling happy and content. 'This is what we always wanted,' he says. 'From now on I shall only invite people along when we stop appreciating how happy we are.' – The children with us off and on, climbing (Loldi in particular) fearlessly on the beams of the aviary. – I talk a lot with R. about *Opera and Drama*, he opens the book and, reading a point in it, recognizes with pleasure the unity of his whole life and work.

Wednesday, August 14 R. dreamed that he introduced a ballet into the Kundry scene, including a bolero; that he wanted to play something to his wife Minna, who, on hearing the accompaniment, opened her eyes wide in astonishment and said it was from *La Muette*, whereupon he: 'That is just the accompaniment, stupid, now listen to the melody!' He works, and I have my hands full with housekeeping books, children, etc. – Still wretched weather, rain and wind, draughts everywhere; *Kindschy* is behaving badly, says R., who frequently tells the story of the pastry cook in Leipzig who on Sundays, when the weather would not clear, used to throw his doughnuts towards the sky with the words 'Eat them yourself!'

Thursday, August 15 The presence of Herr Sucher, the conductor in Leipzig, and his wife[1] obliges R. to make conversation, and about things he now finds disagreeable; then the change of diet for our meal – in short, it all has a bad effect on him, and after his afternoon rest he comes to me looking worn out. 'Everything one hears about the outside world only upsets one,' he says. Of the conductor Sucher: 'He is a typical *Musikant*, a brand of persons who do not really belong to me.' Letter from our dear Frau Materna, R. praises her as the only one who is warm and natural. Recently he said that, if all else failed, he would engage her for Kundry after all. In the evening Boni reads to us from *Opera and Drama*, which I find more and more absorbing. R. shares my pleasure. 'It is all an idea,' he says, 'and I can remember with what passion I wrote it. It is a protracted duologue, with Sulzer, for example, to whom I wanted to clarify all the things which had become clear and definite to me in the course of our conversation.'

Friday, August 16 We feel peculiarly sad about the news brought to us by the children that the graceful and daring young tightrope walker to whom R. recently spoke a few friendly words here fell from a rope in Regensburg and is now dead. – R. thinks the authorities should forbid these performances.

Saturday, August 17 I am glad to see how well R. looks, 'Yes,' he says, 'it's sorrow that drags one down,' and with that sudden change from seriousness to humour which is so characteristic of him, he adds with a laugh, 'A peach does less damage than deep sorrow' – for the day before yesterday he had eaten a peach. The play of his eyes when this sudden change of mood takes place is wonderful – humour breaks through the melancholy of his expression like a flash of lightning through thundery clouds. He works; when he tells me that he is making slow progress, I observe that his happiness is responsible, and he agrees.

Sunday, August 18 'The pressure is vanishing,' R. says of his chest, and he

---

[1] Joseph Sucher (b.1843), Austrian conductor currently in Leipzig, where he conducted the *Ring*, his wife Rosa (b.1849) sang Sieglinde in that production.

is looking splendid. He talks about Christianity and Buddhism, how Christ could not have approached his people with visions of eternity, which the Indians grasped so easily; he chose *the kingdom of Heaven*, which is yours if you are good, and no expression could be better than that, so vague and at the same time so certain. Again it is Renan to whom R. owes this view of his. – In the evening R. reads to me the passage in *Opera and Drama* about Antigone; when I express to him my admiration for this work, R. says, 'I was completely obsessed with it at the time, I could not have composed a single note of music, so absorbed was I in it.' Our poor friend Nietzsche seems to have got quite a lot of his ideas on humanity from it.

Monday, August 19 A week has passed since I last wrote in my diary – I must try to remember. In the afternoon of Tuesday the 20th my father arrived, looking better than I have seen him for years; cheerful and talkative, a delight both for R. and for me. Much intimate chat.

Wednesday, August 21 In the morning R. enlarges on my father's unique aristocratic personality, everything about him refined, princely, grand, yet at the same time full of artistic genius. The children given a holiday, but R. works.

Thursday, August 22 For me somewhat distracted life, R., however, works on undisturbed, he tells me I shall see in what a completely different way the Parsifal theme emerges.

Friday, August 23 R. spends the morning writing to the King for his birthday. In the afternoon he plays '*Komm', holder Knabe*' from *Parsifal*, this captivates my father at once, R. fetches the manuscript, and then the whole second act up to the kiss is gone through, R. thrilled by the fascination the divine work exerts on my father and radiating genius, greatness, kindness!

Saturday, August 24 R. somewhat run down, his chest hurts him when he sings; my father is also ill, even has to take to his bed.

Monday, August 26 R. works: [Kundry's] '*Ich sah ihn und lachte.*' – In the afternoon we go through the second act again, to my father's utmost admiration. R. says to me, 'I am content, I have been successful with you again.' My rapture is the tear which flows in bliss at this revelation. After supper a game of whist between Father, Richard and me!

Tuesday, August 27 R. had a good night and he works; I go to the station to meet our dear friend Malwida, and her visit is a great joy to us. In the gayest fashion R. teases her about her socialism. In the evening we go through my father's *Dante* Symphony[1], that is to say, he plays it to us and, after he has left, R. talks about this highly poetic conception, how beautifully he has avoided all suspicion of mere musical scene-painting, a trap into which Berlioz would certainly have fallen. My father's indescribable modesty about his works touches R. very much – he says with splendid

---

[1] Liszt's *Dante* Symphony was dedicated to Wagner.

high spirits that he has himself 'stolen' so much from the symphonic poems. . . .

Wednesday, August 28 At lunch with friend Feustel R. has a discussion about the law on the socialists, which our friend thinks a good one[1]. After lunch R. tells me he has found a melody which pleases him very much, but it was too broad for Kundry's words; he was considering writing new words for it when suddenly a counter-melody occurred to him, and thus he now has what he wanted: the orchestra would get the broad melody, which here expresses the emotions, while she has the theme for her hurried words. – An alarming letter from K. Klindworth, who tells me Hans is again in danger of losing all his savings! – Difficulty in controlling my fears. – Wrote very seriously to Lulu. Arrival of the chickens, peacocks, pheasants, etc., the surprise R. had prepared for me, as he says; since the aviary is not yet finished, they cannot yet be seen, but I hear one of them giving the trombone call from the second act of *Lohengrin*!

Thursday, August 29 R. still well and working in the best of spirits; at lunch he sings the theme which he jokingly mentioned a few days ago, after hearing the *Dante*, when he said he had stolen much from my father; R. calls his symphonic poems *un repaire des voleurs* [a thieves' den], which makes us laugh heartily. All sorts of things are being told us about the chickens, the children declare that one of the cocks sang something from the *Siegfried Idyll*! . . . In the afternoon went through some of *Parsifal* (first act), and in the evening certainly the most original whist game imaginable – my father, Richard and I, and Malwida as onlooker; R. bubbling over with wit, high spirits and friendliness, the very epitome of Nature's serenity, indomitable strength and creative urge; my father mild and amiable, like a reflection of its melancholy! –

Friday, August 30 R. decrees breakfast in front of the chicken house! The birds are enthroned, children, guests and we spend a happy morning of celebration in mild weather. When the 'two geniuses' have left us, I stroll through the garden with Malwida, and she goes into raptures about R., saying she has at last seen an example of an incomparable old age.

Saturday, August 31 Departure of my father.

Wednesday, September 4 Nice morning, R., after a good night's sleep, orders the horses, and in splendid weather, after he has done some work in the morning, we drive out to the Waldhütte. I had the feeling that I had never seen R. looking so radiantly well; with him in indescribable high spirits and the children in constant fits of laughter, we reach the woods in the most glorious sunshine; we leave the carriage for a while outside the Waldhütte and, at R.'s instigation, take a path which is delightful but which necessitates

---

[1] An emergency law directed against the 'dangerous aims' of the Social Democrats was passed in the Reichstag in October.

some climbing; soon R. is no longer looking so well, he becomes silent, I am beset by feelings of gloom, and in a mood as melancholy as it had earlier been carefree we return home as night begins to fall. R. is monosyllabic, but back home he tells me that he suddenly felt the stabbing pains in his chest again and spat up a little blood. Then he remembered that the doctor had advised him against walking uphill.

Saturday, September 7 R. complains a little still about pressure in his chest, but seems somewhat better. At lunch he tells us that in fact he began the morning with a nap, after which he felt terribly heavy, but gradually the weight lifted and he was able to work. But earlier he told me that never again would he compose such passionate scenes as the one he now has in front of him, he had already sworn that while working on *Tristan*. R. goes off for his afternoon rest; when he comes down again, another consignment of birds has arrived; even if he is aware that his grand way of ordering things is almost always abused, nevertheless these new arrivals cause much merriment, 'Berlioz' and 'the doctor' very unusual and comic, the pigeons with their hoods very pretty to look at.

Sunday, September 8 After lunch, as we are walking out to the summer-house, R. goes to the piano and plays a theme, which I guess to belong to the words '*in Ewigkeit wärst du verdammt mit mir*'. 'I am already past that,' says R., 'but the motive is used there too. It is "*die Labung, die dein Leiden endet*", etc., then comes "*ein andres*", and then I call on my waistcoat pocket for aid.' He takes from it and shows me the piece of paper in which he wrote down the theme yesterday. – The topic of conversation – that for a good marriage (indeed for any relationship) equality of intelligence is the main requirement, much more important than identity of character, which is indeed not a good thing – leads him to Minna, the gradual emergence of whose bad qualities was certainly due to her limited intelligence; by nature she had been goodhearted, energetic and helpful, but then she became mistrustful because of her inability to follow R. He does not admit that she was pretty, as is generally maintained, but says that he told the wise, elderly actress Frl. Hacker, who tried to warn him off Minna, 'Nothing means more to me than my poodle, my watch (he had just bought himself a silver watch) and Minna Planer.'

Thursday, September 19 Parsifal again: 'The way he immediately wants to start converting people,' he says with a laugh, 'when he has only just seen the light himself!' Yesterday evening he was pleased with Parsifal as a character, said he had correctly indicated the things which a noble impression in adolescent years produces, overturning the natural instincts; this is the pattern in all the saints: 'With the Saviour himself it was predestined, so to speak, in his mother's womb.' In the afternoon he goes to work, he shows me the *laughter*, then I go away, return through the room again, he complains of his bad luck, that just when he wants to wipe his pen he loses it, but he is cheerful and looks so well and splendid that it is a comfort and a pleasure to see; in the evening, when, as today, he lays his hand on the sofa, that dear, splendid hand, and his eyes shine and his dear voice rings out, my heart rejoices! – To Malwida, dressed in blue, he says, 'You look like your pencil.'

Friday, September 20 R. is rubbed down with olive oil and alcohol liniment; I tell him they represent the two sides of this nature, gentleness and fire. When I did this for him yesterday evening he said, '*Cosa stravagante* – but Rossini could never have composed you.' – At four o'clock Daniella arrives home; much emotion, but also much gaiety, the dear child has experienced a great deal.

Saturday, September 21 The attached telegram gives him pleasure. [Headed 'Leipzig, September 21,' it reads: 'Holy Ghost descends on Unger, first act just completed, tremendous applause, five curtain calls, everyone amazed – Seidl.' The reference is to a performance of *Siegfried*.] When no telegram comes about the second act, R. pretends he has received bad news and goes 'weeping' to Malwida's door to lament, thus bringing the evening to an end in great merriment. R. and I still find time to express our surprise and pleasure at the popularity of this gigantic work: in Munich *Götterdämmerung* is reported to have aroused frenetic applause.

Sunday, September 22 I return to our final topic of last night and tell R. how splendid it is that the *Ring* in particular should make such an impact, for it was to create this work that he had been sent into the world. 'Not at all; it was to marry you,' and, turning things around in his humorous way, he adds: 'That's why you had to go and marry Bülow! The Lord did to you what Lüttichau did to me over the decorations for *Tannhäuser* – started off with a refusal, to enhance the value of the thing.'[1] – In the evening he complains with indescribable humour that now, when he has to compose Kundry, nothing comes into his head but cheerful themes for symphonies. Then he tells us about the lean Brahms who had corrected instrumental parts for him in Vienna[2], and whom he then rediscovered 'fattened up' by fame. He says he has often sung to himself themes from Mendelssohn but found it impossible to do the same with Schumann, whereas with Brahms he had really begun to doubt his musical receptivity till his pleasure in Sgambati showed him he was still capable of taking things in. R. goes through Handel's *Alexander's Feast*; the skip in particular pleases him, and he says Handel was the Rossini of his time.

Monday, September 23 R. looks so well, he is also full of joy, spreading good cheer around. It is my great triumph and inner rejoicing that this splendid

---

[1] In 1845 Baron Lüttichau, director of the Dresden opera, decided in the interests of economy to use a set previously used in Weber's *Oberon* for Act II of *Tannhäuser*, but he was finally persuaded to sanction a new set.

[2] Brahms helped Wagner in this way in connection with concerts in Vienna in 1862–63.

spirit feels so unconstrained, pouring its blessings over us without stint! When we are eating Karlsbad wafers at lunch, R. says, 'This is the sort of thing my Knights of the Grail will get. I can't give them bread and butter, or they will start digging in and not want to leave.' Yesterday, complaining of the difficulties Kundry is causing him, he exclaims humorously, 'And there are still the others to come, with their lances – oh, it's horrible!' In the afternoon he goes for a walk in beautiful sunshine. 'Where have I been?' he says on his return. 'At Mime's place.' By this he means in Angermann's vaults, looked after by his brother. He says that before his beer he asked for some bread and sat down under the trees, a kitten came up to him and held its tail high up in the air for joy when he gave it some bread; he had enjoyed a few moments of great contentment and could see me sitting there with the children. – After telling me this, he comes to his *Parsifal* and says: 'Oh, I hate the thought of all those costumes and grease paint! When I think that characters like Kundry will now have to be dressed up, those dreadful artists' balls immediately spring into my mind. Having created the invisible orchestra, I now feel like inventing the invisible theatre! And the inaudible orchestra,' he adds, concluding his dismal reflections in humorous vein. He would like to put things off for one more year, he said this morning after his work, for there is no escaping a production.

Friday, September 27 R. had a restless night. He dreamed of a clarinet which played by itself. But he goes to his work and becomes so cheerful that he sings the 'What delight does travel bring' aria from [Boieldieu's] *Jean de Paris*, then says this is really what Kundry ought to sing, mockingly, when she sets Parsifal out on the wrong path. Saying farewell to Malwida after coffee, he says, 'God preserve you, Malwida, you are now – emancipated!' But in the afternoon, when I return from a lengthy walk with M., I find him in a bad mood, he is not feeling well and has pains in his chest, and I regret having left the house. He feels disgusted with the world and is particularly vexed with Seidl, who has not written to him; all the same, he writes to Herr Neumann, asking him to engage Seidl.

Saturday, September 28 Arrival of Herr Kellermann, 'l'homme du caveau,'[1] as R. calls him, typical of the wretched times of today. At the conservatory he was paid 1,200 marks by Herr Stern; when he said he was leaving, the latter offered him 5,000! Before that he had delivered newspapers in order to be able to complete his studies, and was glad when he was ill, for then he did not need to eat! A very decent and lively person who, let us hope, will find salvation here. In the evening R. plays the third act of *Tristan*. When I voice my wonder that he could have completed this miracle in a hotel room, with not a soul to look after or care for him, he says, 'Yes,

---

[1] 'Cellar man', French translation of his name; for his work in Wahnfried he received 60 marks monthly and free board; the 1,200 marks paid by Stern were yearly.

people have no idea how divorced from experience and reality these things happen, and how long one is nourished by one's youth! It is true I sometimes felt inclined in my disgust to throw everything into the gutter, and in fact I eventually did so, unwilling as I was to do any more work; but when the German Emperor exclaims, "How deeply Wagner must have been in love at that time," it is really quite ridiculous. – If that were so, I should now be writing *Parsifal* on account of my connections with the Christian church, and you would be Kundry!'

Sunday, September 29 In the evening the children sing (folk songs), R. accompanying them, and then young Brandt, with whom we go through our experiences, pleasant as well as painful. R. says he allows no outsider the right to condemn the [*Ring*] production, which as a whole was so beautiful and beyond compare: 'But among ourselves we must acknowledge that much was not as it should have been; for example, the meadow of the gods before Valhalla not free enough, too restricted by the steps; Erda's cave reminiscent of a door in the usual sort of fantastic comedy show; the steam transformation to Nibelheim – there should have been *shafts* in it, a backcloth which could have been drawn up lengthways, showing these shafts and now and again a fiery glow; then the mountain top was too high – I shall alter that one day, when I produce *Die Walküre* in Heaven at the right hand of God, and the old fellow and I are watching it – the acting area too narrow, so that the fight was spoiled and Wotan's storming in a failure; in *Siegfried* steps again, and not enough room for the fight; and steps also hindering Brünnhilde's struggles, too little room for the Rhinemaidens, and the water sweeping over the funeral pyre, and the hall of the Gibichungs not impressive enough. Then the costumes bad, almost all of them. And so it turned out that this production, as far as the conception was concerned, was on the whole extraordinary, wrong in only a few details.' R. talks of his suffering at the time, the patience with which he kept silent about it all!

Tuesday, October 1 After lunch letters from Leipzig, excellent account of the performances from friend Seidl. I strolled with R. through the palace gardens, first talking about Lecky's book[1], then I tell him about Plutarch's life of Lycurgus, which I am reading to the children. Then *Tristan*, and R. talks again of his need at that time to push himself to the limit musically, since in the *Nibelungen* the requirements of the drama frequently forced him to restrict the musical expression. Over our beer we continue talking, and R. tells me he does not feel like working, he wants to come to grips with the book about religious sects, and, as if making excuses to himself, he says, 'I shall have completed the first two acts within a year; to compose three acts one after another like that –' I interrupt him: '– is not possible.'

[1] Wagner's later remark about religious sects suggests that the book by William Lecky they were reading was *History of European Morals from Augustus to Charlemagne*, which had just been translated into German.

Saturday, October 5 We drive in the most wonderful weather to the Eremitage, the children in front with the four dogs, a proper procession. Merry homecoming; R. goes to his work (completion in ink) and when I go to him in the evening, he says I have come just in time for the kiss (*'war es mein Kuss, der dich hellsichtig machte'*).[1]

Sunday, October 6 Over coffee R. speaks about the curiousness of the musical profession and how he has been reproached for the eternal 4/4 time in *Lohengrin:* 'I have in fact used 3/4 time in both *Tannhäuser* and *L.,* but only where it is needed, in the "Pilgrims' Chorus", in the prayer before the duel; but otherwise the art lies in one's ability to stick to *oratio directa* and not to tell oneself: Now I must make a change, just for change's sake.' Musicians are in fact very petty people who don't know what is important, he says, but then, on the other hand, someone like Mozart comes along, who was like a child but never did anything silly. After lunch, after he had rested, R. and I walk with the children and dogs to Angermann's cellars outside the town, a very merry procession over fields and meadows. We sit beneath the trees in the same place he sat some time ago telling himself, 'You must come back here with your little woman.' Walk home by moonlight past the churchyard in the same animated procession, with the children calling, the dogs barking (Brange kills a cat), delight in Bayreuth, the trees in the palace gardens, R. feels at home, and so do I; a splendid day, and evening too, I am filled with unutterable gratitude for R.'s bubbling spirits. When the children gather around R. at the piano in the evening and he plays them the tarantella from *La Muette,* I think of the time when we shall no longer be here and these memories will live on inside them, and thus I enjoy the experience directly and at the same time in a transfigured way. R. relates many things from his childhood, how he brought home some rabbits and put them in a drawer. Then he talks about *Der Freischütz,* which he had watched Weber conduct from the actor's box: 'I should like to have seen myself!' It was Samiel above all who gripped him, and he was constantly whistling or trying to whistle the devil's whistle. Then yet more music – from [Spohr's] *Jessonda!* R. remarks on its peculiar silliness, in spite of many fine passages. He says this kind of silliness so disgusted him in Marschner, at the time he was orchestrating *Tannhäuser,* that he asked Reissinger to take over *Templer und Jüdin* ('in which the whole orchestra plays throughout'), which he was supposed to conduct – though he was well aware of its finer features. A lovely end to a lovely day!

Monday, October 7 R. goes through passages in the early Beethoven sonatas with Herr Kellermann; astonishment over his ignorance and incapability; great compassion for the poor man, whom the world seems already to have

---

[1] Kundry's kiss ('So it was my kiss that opened thine eyes to the world?').

broken. After he has left the room, R. goes out into the garden and watches him, unperceived, through the window: he is writing a letter, stops, wipes his brow, sadly shakes his head. R. is moved and goes in to him. 'I am not good enough for you, maestro', the poor man says. 'You are not good enough for yourself, my friend, forget all the runs and leaps, take out one piano score after another and get to know them all.' – R. tells us this touching story illustrating his kindness and an unkind fate. 'Your father's personality has caused a lot of trouble: these young people want to imitate something that cannot be imitated, and because of it they miss all the music.'

Wednesday, October 9 In the afternoon R. goes for a walk, then works on *Parsifal* by lamplight ('*Lachte, lachte*'). He is satisfied with his work, and we are rewarded by a merry supper and a nice evening. At my request R. plays the two finales of *Le Nozze di Figaro*, and this abundance of spirit, inventiveness and wit in the musical flow delights and astounds us. 'That is true mastery,' says R., and he points out how even the imperfect cadences, which have an unpleasant effect in the symphonies, are so right here, since they are part of the action, as it were, expressing the tumult and general disorder, until somebody is at last allowed to speak. Before that R. sang to us '*Les Deux Grenadiers*',[1] which we have just received and which I like very much. – Regarding Frau Vogl's leap into the funeral pyre[2], R. observes that he has in fact included it in his stage directions, and it is a part of the action, but if the audience's attention is going to be drawn to it, he would prefer to cut it out.

Thursday, October 10 Twenty-five years ago today I saw R. for the first time! I put on his table the 'litanies' I wrote in memory of that day[3]. At lunchtime he comes to me and says, to my bliss, that when he read my litany he felt quite intoxicated, quite unable either to work or to read, he fell into a sound and gentle sleep from which he rose as if born anew. We eat alone together in the children's *salon* and lose ourselves in memories – all of it so melancholy and all so sweetly transfigured by our happiness! When Malwida comes up with the children, R. cries out to her, 'We are celebrating our 25th anniversary, our silver wedding!' Then he goes off for his rest, and I also lie down. He goes for a walk, and when I awake, I see a reflection of the most golden of sunsets! R.'s spirit shines down on me, pouring blessings! He himself comes to greet me before settling down to work, and, to crown this blissful day, Vreneli sends me photographs of Tribschen and the Schweizerhof, and friend Cyriax writes to say he has discovered the Horseshoe Tavern! A 70-year-old house, the only one still standing, in the

---

[1] Wagner's own setting (in French) of Heine's poem (1839–40).

[2] In the Munich production of *Götterdämmerung*; Therese Vogl prided herself on her horsemanship.

[3] Cosima's first sight of Wagner was when Liszt brought him to dine with his three children in Paris; her poem is in the form of a litany, with the refrain 'Richard, hold me dear.'

City [of London]![1] ... R. is satisfied with his work (Kundry's curse); he eats downstairs with the children and comes up to me with two slices of bread and butter, which he has prepared for me. He wants to talk about the 'litany', asks me whether Malw. knows anything about it; I shake my head. He: 'If I had done something like that, I should have told everyone.'

Friday, October 11 R. tells me he will soon be finished with the second act. Then he talks about his treatment of the orchestra in *Parsifal*, saying that in the *Nibelungen* the singers had not been able to dominate the orchestra; the singer should be like a single instrument, like a clarinet – Materna, for example, in the scene with Waltraute. When I say that it was precisely in this scene that the balance seemed to me so wonderful, he says, 'I am talking about the passionate scenes – I just did not have singers who could dominate.' – He comes to fetch me before lunch and reads me his article ['The Public in Time and Space'], which he calls a proper school essay, 'such an effusion'; it is splendid.

Sunday, October 13 R. promises to tell me when the second act is finished, and at twelve o'clock he does so.... How to find words for this happiness? In the evening R. says that if anybody had come in and seen us, he would have taken us for a couple of lunatics, I 'gobbling up the notes, sometimes helping, guessing', he 'playing furiously'. But it is my pride and joy that I was really able to follow him, and it was all revealed to me! ... 'So I can still compose?' he says to me, when I go on feeling the urge to speak to him about the second act but am unable to say a word!

Monday, October 14 Departure of Malwida, who is going south!

Wednesday, October 16 A bad night! R. frequently out of bed. In the morning we wonder whether it was a tough partridge he ate in the evening which so upset him, or the reading of *Opera and Drama*, or a very evil-smelling ointment he put on his sore thumb. We both had breakfast in bed and, as always, this first morning hour is cheerful in spite of the bad night. R. is gathering strength for the third act; around lunchtime he comes in, bringing me several 'curious bits of paper', some of them from *Tristan*. I ask him to keep them all and give them to me at Christmas, and now I have the joy of already knowing about these precious papers, though I have not yet looked through them.

Thursday, October 17 R. slept well, and after our morning conversation, which concerns Lecky, Mozart and the German Reich, he leaves me with the words, echoing Frederick the Great, 'Now I am going to collect *fuyards* [refugees].' He means all the musical ideas which he has hastily written down; he told me yesterday that most of all he would like to write some

[1] The Schweizerhof was the hotel in Lucerne in which Wagner completed *Tristan* (and first met Vreneli, a chambermaid there); the tavern in London (correctly the Hoop and Horseshoe) was the one in which he and Minna stayed in 1839; Julius Cyriax was a businessman and treasurer of the Wagner Society in London.

symphonies, gay and cheerful works in which he would not venture at all far, but he feels a real need to give vent to this side of himself. He is also thinking of revising Senta's ballade, the beginning of which he finds is quite properly like a folk song, but not characteristic of *Der Holländer*.

Friday, October 18 R. goes to his work, and when he calls me to lunch he now knows exactly how things should be, he must not introduce anything isolatedly, it must all be in context; and so his prelude to the third act will introduce the theme of Titurel's funeral, just as in the prelude to the first act he brought in the song of the Knights of the Grail. There is no place, he says, for a big 'independent affair' depicting Parsifal's wanderings.

Sunday, October 20 In the afternoon R. and I go out, calling on Wolzogen, whose article, 'The Stage Dedication Play', pleases R. very much, though he remarks to me that W. goes too far in calling Parsifal a reflection of the Redeemer: 'I didn't give the Redeemer a thought when I wrote it.' – In the evening he reads the first act of *Die Meistersinger* to me and the girls. Shared memories! Impossible to believe it was ten years ago! – Before reading he played Auber's summons to the meeting in the market place [in *La Muette de Portici*] and found great enjoyment in it; altogether he thinks frequently of Auber, particularly his genius in writing for the trumpet. Towards the end of the evening he plays the finale of *Die Zauberflöte*, 'where the sun went the other way', and exclaims: 'Oh, how beautiful that sounds! How beautiful these sopranos can be!' . . .

Monday, October 21 In the morning R. sang quite an assortment of melodies, my father's 'Loreley', '*Am stillen Herd*'[1], then jokingly challenged me to sing him *one single* melody by Schumann . . . Then he exclaims: 'A melody! What a heavenly thing that is, wrapping everything in purity, ennobling it! When one hears something like that, one has the feeling that nothing ever existed before, as if everything is now beginning to breathe for the first time.' He then sings the melody of the Countess's second aria in *Figaro*: 'There is nothing there to see, nothing to grasp hold of, yet it goes beyond everything, even the graceful gestures of the most exalted moments, which are what come nearest to melody.' – We go to our work, I hear the sounds of music again! When R. fetches me for lunch, he says, 'Now I am writing something which should sound like nothing, nothing at all, Robert Schumann, but there must be method in it – the theme of the march would have been much too definite.' Over coffee, while I am saying something or other, he exclaims, 'That's it – it must be shifted half a bar, held back half a bar.' All the time he is noting things down, a musical or some other idea, but if he were to carry a notebook around with him, he says, and think to himself, 'Today you must write something down,' without a doubt nothing would occur to him. He tells me that again today

---

[1] Sung by Walther von Stolzing in Act I of *Die Meistersinger*.

a theme came to him with which he can do nothing – his room is full of such scraps.

Thursday, October 24 We have our afternoon coffee in my room, R. talks about the sad strains he will now have to compose; they must not contain a single ray of light, he says, for that could lead one far astray. Parsifal's sad wanderings, which must lead up to the situation on Monsalvat. – Telegram saying that Herr Jäger has been engaged for Siegfried in Vienna, which pleases R. – In the afternoon (towards evening) he presents me with the manuscript of *Opera and Drama!* And also seven letters to Uhlig, sent to him by Elsa Uhlig[1] with a very nice accompanying note. We read the letters in the evening, talk about many past events, and then he plays to me some of the gloomy strains, and we end the day happy and uplifted.

Monday, October 28 R. goes out for a little while, I have some things to attend to; when we meet again, he asks me to come up, since he wishes to play something to me and wants my advice. He then plays the prelude to me and shows me the many pages of his preliminary sketches, among them the song for Titurel's funeral. 'To improvise like that, get inspirations – that is not difficult – my difficulty always lies in restraining myself.' Here he has succeeded wonderfully in making his theme stand out against a background of elemental sorrow, and one feels completely at home. Noticing my emotion, R. says, 'So it is good – I am glad.'

Tuesday, October 29 R. says he has composed two bars, but they are very important ones, an addition in the middle of the prelude: they had occupied his mind the minute he awoke in the morning.

Wednesday, October 30 After lunch he goes out, I do some shopping, and we meet on our way home; he says, 'I'm saying nothing, but there's something I want to change, though not at once.' I beg him not to do it, to remember the quintet in *Die Ms.*, which he thought bad until he played it to me, I was moved to tears, and he then kept it. – Then he tells me (somewhat later, when we part after our meeting) that the [Good Friday] meadow will be in D major, in 3/4 time.

Thursday, October 31 We spend the evening alone. He plays the prelude to me; it is very much altered, even more gloomy! It begins like the lament of an extinguished star, after which one discerns, like gestures, Parsifal's arduous wanderings and Kundry's pleas for salvation. 'My preludes must all be elemental, not dramatic like the *Leonore* Overtures, for that makes the drama superfluous.' It seems as if none of this could be sung – only the 'elemental' quality can be felt here, as R. does indeed emphasize. – Lengthy discussion about this new miracle.

Friday, November 1 I tell him about one of our cocks, whose melancholy call today reminded me of the beginning of his prelude. R. says he knows

[1] Daughter of Wagner's friend in Dresden, the violinist Theodor Uhlig, who died in 1853; the letters were published in 1888.

what I mean and it is true: it is the diminished fifth which sounds so peculiar, he would call this his cock theme. Then he tells me of a green material with which he has turned his chair into an 'arbour'. 'But then I am obliged to compose such dismal things,' he says with a laugh. 'People will think I must have written such stuff in an attic, starving and freezing!' We go our separate ways laughing. In the evening R. and I go with the three little ones to welcome the Wolzogens with champagne in their new house; the idea came from R., and he laughs at my readiness to comply, which reminds him of that wheelbarrow in Frankfurt[1]: 'That's how one should be!' he exclaims. The wheelbarrow has become for me the celestial Wain[2], in which he bears me on and on towards our spiritual home.

Monday, November 4 R. tells me that he regards one of our guests, Councillor Kraussold, as a good omen, the councillor is over 70 and still very sturdy. It seems odd to me when R. says such things, for he gives the impression of having nothing to do with age! Very gloomy November day, plenty of rain. Our conversation leads us to the King of Bavaria, his defection from our ideal – how sad, how terrible that was: 'I had found my monarch, and this is what came of it! Now I have to ask the King of Prussia and the Crown Prince for what *he* failed to do for me.' Penultimate conversation in the evening about perfumes, R. speaks of the melancholy in essence of roses, even if it does not reproduce the scent of roses; he is pleased that Plato places fragrance among the aesthetic pleasures which do not arise from necessity, but which come to us as a pure gift.

Thursday, November 7 At lunch R. told us several legends from Lecky about the saints. There had been only one saint who included animals in his compassion and who felt what he, R., had always felt – that for an animal there is no element of reconciliation in suffering, whereas a human being can always overcome it through cognition. He is very impressed by Renan's statement about our present times: that human functions could persist for a while without faith, just as an animal could still continue to live after its brain was removed, but the situation could not last long.

Friday, November 8 At breakfast, when he returns to the subject of Renan and I tell him I cannot imagine any of the present famous German writers being able to formulate such thoughts, he says, 'They are too difficult, too much concerned with "progress".' But then he adds, 'Nietzsche could have done it.' I tell him that Nietzsche had requested that the *Blätter* not be sent to him. 'I'm glad he has taken it to heart,' R. says.

Saturday, November 9 R. is a bit vexed over the visit of the Munich painters[3], fixed for today, since, as he tells me, he has just got everything

[1] In which, in August 1862, Wagner offered to wheel Cosima to her hotel; she was willing to comply, but Bülow's disapproval stopped her.
[2] The Plough or Big Dipper.
[3] Heinrich Döll (b.1824), scene painter at the Munich opera since 1854, responsible for several Wagner productions, and Christian Jank (b.1833), landscape painter and theatre designer.

nicely prepared and would have been able to do some composing. At 12 noon we receive the two gentlemen, discussion about the scenery for *Parsifal!* Both with their heads full of frills and vistas, R. alone putting his finger on what would be right here; he says the cupola should not be visible, only the architrave supporting it. When they have gone, R. asks me: 'Did you look at Döll? There's complete dissipation for you.' When I say I did not think much of Herr Jank either: 'Oh, the utter viciousness, disloyalty, wickedness of them all!' It was both curious and sad to see these creatures who once treated R. so badly, now standing embarrassed and humble before him!

Sunday, November 10 Telegrams from Vienna; and so *Siegfried* has now conquered this stage! – The meeting with Count Du Moulin at Anger-mann's leads R. to the subject of his relations with Munich and the Society of Patrons: 'Only a large legacy could rescue me from their clutches.' Then he adds: 'And then I should be really miserable, for I have nobody, no singers, no conductors, no producers – I tremble at the thought that my little Fricke might not live to a ripe old age. It really is miserable! A legacy would also spoil Italy for me. The best thing would be for me to give these people their money back, but I am scared of the King and of Wolzogen.'

Tuesday, November 12 'How many generations have I outlived!' he says. 'When I think of Tausig and Cornelius, who entered my life so late, and Mendelssohn, already 30 years dead, and it seems only five years ago.' He describes how Schumann was introduced and played his 'ABEGG Vari-ations' – 'full of ornaments, something I hated at that time.' – He comes upstairs to fetch me, sits down beside me, and suddenly laughs about Gurnemanz's herbs and roots: 'He sounds so cross, so disgruntled.' Then he became a bit impatient and said, 'If you only knew!' And soon I do know, for when I enter the *salon*, I see a magnificent Persian carpet for my room lying there!... He had been in correspondence with Standhartner about it, and now he sends off a telegram of thanks, signed 'He and she.' – At lunch he sings a number of Viennese songs to the children, and over coffee we enjoy the carpet, which R. compares to a panther, saying it has the velvet sheen of a panther. Before our evening meal I discover him at his desk, beginning the third act in ink!

Thursday, November 14 We talk about our position (in a business sense), and R. decides on 1880 as the year for performance: 'Either I stick to that year and am then completely free after the performance – for if anything crops up it will be behind my back – or I put off the performance, pay off the deficit to the King out of my income, and give the patrons their money back. What I want now is to complete the composition, without thinking of either performance or nonperformance.' Snow flurries prevent R.'s going out of doors, he works during the afternoon as well and plays to us (the W.'s are present) the prelude to the third act, now written out in ink. Friend

W. calls it seeking the Grail, protecting the spear; I am astonished how R. found it possible to present with such concision a motive which is clearly designed for expansion; just the core of the idea, but this done with such intensity that one has the feeling of being able to develop it oneself. Then he tells us that during the afternoon he re-read Shakespeare in English and felt an utter repugnance for the English language – he would never succeed in learning it. In vindication I point out the advantages of Shakespeare in English, vividness and precision, whereas in German it is all nobler, more elegant, even more poetic; I give the witches' scene as an example. R. agrees with me, and we go through *Macbeth*, in English and German; but how swiftly is all linguistic curiosity dispersed by the strength of its impact! R. says one must always be able to *see* what is going on, how facial expressions change, the person becoming different through his impressions. We also speak of the great artistry in letting the witches start the play and then reappear; R. says, 'One then wonders, not who they are, but what they will say.' Later we come again to speak of the fact that the greatest of poets was obliged to write in such a language. Lecky also leads R. to the subject of the peculiar bigotry of the English, the way in which certain evils cannot be cured because no one is permitted to talk about them by name. Much, much more about cultural matters, always returning to the conclusion that the only true art these days is music. We also talk about the Jews. R. assumes that the present financial calamity in England is also the work of the Israelites (Beaconsfield). It should not be presumed, he says, that these people, who are so separated from us by their religion, have any right to make our laws: 'But why blame the Jews? It is we who lack all feeling for our own identity, all sense of honour.'

Saturday, November 16 Ten years ago today I came to join R. We celebrate the day in our thoughts. 'How quickly these years have passed!' R. says. He recalls that I was very solemn when I first arrived – like Kundry, I had had only one wish, to serve, to serve!...A lovely day, wonderful sunset, rose-coloured clouds, a lovely feeling of being at home here; Tribschen a dream, this the reality, but also ideal, sheltered from the world. – In the evening utter absorption in old times, so many sufferings. How good it was of Fate to have removed him from Munich in '65, R. says, for it precipitated a decision; how fortunate that Hans was just as he was, R. also observes, for otherwise we should either have been destroyed by his nobleness, or made by his baseness to look despicable in each other's eyes. He sends for half a bottle of champagne, we drink to our life together, which has become happier and happier. 'Except that I am too old,' R. observes. 'I should be 15 years younger.' I: 'Why?' 'So that it could last longer.' I tell him that this was the only thing I have contributed, my little bit of youth, and that is already somewhat old! – Alone after this wallowing in reminiscences, I see in my mind once more my parting from Hans, my stay in Augsburg with the two girls, embarking on the ship, the stars, which Loldi noticed, the single light illuminating the dense black night in my heart as I watched over the children in the ship and gazed rigidly and numbly into the unveiled countenance of my destiny. That night was the womb of all my blessings, annihilating all pretence – a holy night, awesome in its acknowledgement of original sin, the silent prophet of love's redeeming power!

Wednesday, November 20 R. says he will draw up lists of themes for the *Blätter* and give a rough outline of his ideas on them, and the other contributors can then fill them out; for example, on the uselessness of the music schools, demonstrated by the poor published editions, poor arrangements, the decline of military bands. 'But the whole trouble is,' R. observes, 'to whom is one speaking?' 'A school ought to be founded here for the preservation of my works, for I have created a new style.' But the next thought is always: Who will teach in it? ... Much about my mother and father; all the noble stature of R.'s noble outlook is conveyed in his opinion of my father's attitude towards Lola Montez[1] and his own repugnance towards it. 'The girl likes you,' my father said to him at the time, 'you are the only man who doesn't pay court to her.' 'I didn't even notice her,' R. said, and he exclaims, 'To wound another heart for the sake of so cold a relationship!'

Friday, November 22 R. says he had wanted to call me in order to play something to me, but in the end had decided against it; he says I could never imagine the state he is in when he is working, how he enjoys fiddling about with a ribbon, a curtain, a coverlet – it is impossible for him to have a book nearby.

Saturday, November 23 Frau Jäger, returning from Vienna, can tell us nothing either new or pleasurable, though it is also not the reverse. But how happy we are when once again all is still around us! R. brings out his cherished, sacred pages and plays and sings to me – never again will these words and this music be sung in such a manner! 'I love Gurnemanz,' he says, and how can one help loving him? ... How utterly is all sorrow, all worry, all tiredness dispelled! Parsifal's approach, his noble, mournful serenity when he realizes where he is, Gurnemanz's fervent greeting to the spear, so filled with wonder – how unearthly and yet how human it all is! My beloved son, let me make you a gift of this evening – may you relive it as you read these poor pages! And may I tell you its crowning glory – and will it make you think your mother vain? ... It happened like this. When, discussing with your father some arrangements for the greenhouse, I said that we had no sunshine for our camellias and the buds were falling off, he replied, 'It is true we have no sunshine,' then, embracing me, 'but I have

---

[1] The Spanish dancer whose liaison with King Ludwig I of Bavaria led to his abdication in 1848; Liszt had known her before that in Dresden.

my sunshine at all times of the day, however grey it is outside!' Oh, my Siegfried, could you but know what miracles occur in my heart when such sunlit words shine on it! Over them my eyes close, slumber enfolds the wondrous blossom of love!

Monday, November 25 In the evening we take up Disraeli's *Tancred;* the beginning strikes us as quite vapid, and R. tells me to skip wherever possible; but the scene between Montacute and his father interests us, and R. says he is looking forward to seeing how the author develops this.

Tuesday, November 26 R. says: 'I am really curious to see what Israelchen [Disraeli] will do, how he will reveal his positive side. It is always difficult to reconcile oneself with the world after criticizing it. What sophistries will he use to show us that revelation is only possible if we all recognize the God on Mount Sinai? But I can understand why such a man appealed to the Queen and the dissatisfied Tories.' 'The poison he gave them must have been very refined,' he said yesterday.

Wednesday, November 27 We have to laugh over Disraeli's glorification of the Jews: 'I have an idea what he is getting at,' says R., 'racial purity and great men; that ruling genius I dreamed about – only the Jews could produce him.'

Thursday, November 28 Smiling meadows![1] . . . The 'smiling meadow' I have spread across his piano pleases him, and at lunchtime he calls me and shows me his room, saying my portrait now rises up like a lotus flower from a pond. 'I have also written something good,' he says, 'not much, but good.' – What delight there is in decorating the home of his ideals a little in accordance with his inclinations! He must be able to immerse himself completely in his dreams there; recently he said he must not be able to see the garden paths, which lead outwards – that is too definite, it disturbs concentration. In Tribschen his windows overlooked the mountains, and that was not quite the same thing. A lovely, mild, glorious day, the sun shining. I go for a long walk, R. comes with the dogs to meet me and conduct me home. He does some work. After supper Disraeli, we skip all the fictional parts in order to confine ourselves to the message. ('For that can't be taken lightly, he is the Prime Minister of England and has the whole Eastern world in his pocket.' During our walk R. said, 'I find it embarrassing to keep coming back to the subject of the Jews, but one can't avoid it when one is thinking of the future.')

Friday, November 29 Over coffee he tells me about his work: 'Sometimes it is just a few bars which hold one up terribly, till one can introduce the key one needs in such a way that it is not noticeable. For more and more I shy away from anything with a startling or blatant effect; then at least four

---

[1] *'Lachende Aue'*: a reference to the Good Friday music in *Parsifal;* the 'smiling meadow' spread across Wagner's piano is presumably a patterned coverlet.

or five possibilities occur to me before I find the one which makes the transition smoothly; I set traps for myself, commit all sorts of stupidities before I discover it.' – R. goes out for a walk, then does some work. In the evening, before supper, he calls me to look at the 'meadow', now laid out nicely in folds! Then a merry supper. Afterwards we finish Disraeli's novel: we had expected more talent, it peters out in trivialities, and even its message is significant only because it is spoken by England's subsequent Premier.

Saturday, November 30 R. is pleased by the sublime and mysterious fact that he has not had to rearrange or alter a single word in *P[arsifal]*, melody and words fit throughout – what he wrote down in the prelude contains all he needs, and it all unfolds like a flower from its bud.

Wednesday, December 4 I have the feeling that his work is wearing him out, he says variants occur to him during the night, 'though they are usually not much use,' but also thoughts of the Society of Patrons and 'Shall We Hope?' 'What fifths I have been writing today – they are tremendous!' But gaiety is utterly beyond me, all my efforts are devoted to concealing my concern from him. When I beg him to take good care of himself, he says, 'Oh, we shall live to a ripe old age: Fate did not bring us together without some purpose in mind.' – He is pleased by the news that our friend Sulzer is taking over the leadership of the socialists: 'We could do with a man like that in Germany,' he says. 'The effort will surely be, not against possessions, but in favour of possessions for everybody.'

Saturday, December 7 R. slept well and gently at first, but then he woke up, got out of bed, read something, lay down again, fell asleep but had spasms in his arms and legs; I took his hand in both of mine and with my pressure fought against his cramp! And truly it subsided, and I had the joy of watching over his sleep, for a few hours at least.

Sunday, December 8 A still worse night, practically no sleep, three hours of reading, then some walking and, as soon as he gets back into bed, spasms! ...I rack my brains over what we should do – perhaps travel?... Wonderful how fresh he remains in spite of it all; before lunch he goes for a walk, and he has a good appetite. Dr. Landgraf refuses to see anything alarming in R.'s condition.

Tuesday, December 10 R. goes for a walk and says, 'When I whistle for the dogs, they just say "Fiddlesticks".' He recommends Turgenev's *Virgin Soil* quite strongly to me, says it aroused very peculiar feelings in him because he himself had been through these revolutionary experiences, the lack of contact with the people. – R. gives me great pleasure by playing the funeral music for Weber's reburial. He loses himself in memories of this ceremony, 'the most successful of my whole life'. After that we play the *Idyll* as a piano duet. We go upstairs in happy, indeed very cheerful, spirits, and when I tell R. I intend to send Glasenapp the stuffed pheasant, he says hardly does a *malheur* occur in Wahnfried but Glasenapp must be made a present of it, stuffed!

Wednesday, December 11 R. begins his 'Retrospect' of the Bayreuth festival[1]. In the evening he once again plays the Weber funeral music and speaks of the effect Weber had on him: 'He was my begetter, it was he who aroused my passion for music. He revealed to me what wind instruments can do – for instance, the entry of a clarinet, what an effect that can make. I wish someone could have seen me as a child when I watched *Der Freischütz* being performed in the small old theatre under Weber's direction. It is a true blessing to have received in childhood such an impression of one of God's chosen spirits.' – From here to *Tristan*; I had asked for the Prelude to *Parsifal*, but R. said he would prefer to play *Tr.* He goes through the love scene and, when this is concluded, exclaims: 'What extraordinary stuff it is! To imagine that as a repertory opera – it's too absurd! It can never become popular.' I dispute this, saying that it was above all *T. und I.* which won him his true supporters, and that it is precisely this spun-out musical evocation of love which provides people with the magic they unconsciously seek in the theatre. 'Yes,' says R., 'in a first-rate performance of it.' Then he says: 'This shows a pair of lovers aglow at the height of sin; they do not confess it to each other, but they feel there is only one escape – through death; first they ask each other, "How did it come about, when we loved each other from the start, that we parted?" Then she does not wish to contemplate the death he has resolved on for them, until he persuades her, and both then find their highest happiness in this decision. Who can follow all that?' I maintain that everyone who has ever been in love, even if it was a false or foolish love, must have felt the tragedy of love and of life, and will respond to the magic; he will feel increasingly liberated from his burdens, transformed by inner impressions which, slumbering inside him, now awake to enlighten him. R. laughs and says, 'I must tell you what Meyerbeer replied to me when I expressed to him my feeling that the staging of the bathing girls' scene (in *Les Huguenots*) did not match the music: "Maybe, Herr Wagner, but not everyone has as much imagination as you."' I say that Wotan's sufferings are much less easily understandable, his farewell to Brünnhilde undoubtedly only made so for most people through the music. R. says I am quite right, and that is what he himself thought at first; also the music, even if he did take it to the utmost limits, always remains melodious.

Friday, December 13 In the evening R. asks me to read the book [*Virgin Soil*] aloud from the point I have reached. Concerning the revolutionary matters in it, he says: 'I was almost at the point of hawking pamphlets myself![2] And when I think of all the things I told Minna, such as that the

---

[1] Published in the *Bayreuther Blätter*, December 1878 and in Vol. 10 of the collected writings.
[2] In 1849 during the uprising in Dresden, in which he was active.

movement was being built up somewhere else, and that it was bound to happen that people like me would be needed, and that I should be appointed secretary of the provisional government. I had to put it to her in the form of a *permanent appointment*, and at the same time humbug myself. But all the same I could not agree with your father when he said to me curtly in Weimar, "Admit you've been foolish." '

Saturday, December 14 Towards noon he complains of tightness in his chest ('I have a mouse scurrying about in my heart, lungs and liver,' he says at lunch; though he means it as a joke, it gnaws at my heart). He told me that by the end of the year he would have reached Parsifal's anointment, and then the rest would follow. When I tell him I am looking forward to Titurel's funeral, he says, 'That is already finished – as good as finished.' To conclude the evening he takes out Bach's 48 Preludes and Fugues and plays several of them. – R. considers the 48 Preludes and Fugues to be the quintessence of Bach.

Monday, December 16 In the evening a dance at Wahnfried! Ten young officers and ten girls. R. orders the polonaise to be danced from the hall into his *salon*, where he plays for it, while Herr Kellermann, not noticing, continues playing in my room. The rest of the music is played by 'Memel and Schwemel', as R. calls our two fiddlers.

Wednesday, December 18 We return to the subject of Bach, and R. says that in his youth he was prompted by the works of E. T. A. Hoffmann to look into these compositions, searching for mysticism, but all he had really felt was boredom. He introduced this remark by exclaiming, 'How necessary education is in all things!' He works on his 'Retrospect', then he goes for a walk before lunch in intense cold. He tells me he would like to make music again, and since we are talking about Fidi, who is uncommonly bright, R. says, 'Wait and see, when I have completed the score of *Parsifal* with much *amore*, I shall occupy myself with the education of my boy.'

Friday, December 20 Sounds of music in Wahnfried again, and when R. parts from me around noon, he says: 'I have been playing the last pages of *Parsifal*. I've never heard any music like it. But I need an awful lot of time!' He adds, 'It moved me very much.'

Saturday, December 21 At lunch I notice that he is very absorbed. He tells me he has been going through his manuscript: I did not yet know Gurnemanz's joy when he recognizes the spear. 'He howls for joy, and the fifths I've got there, you'll be amazed!' – R. puts off the Bach evening, saying he wants to be alone. Things are again brewing inside him, arousing my fears: may this terrible inner process not prove a strain on him! He says: 'All I want now is to finish *Parsifal*, then everything will be all right. Let's hope it won't be a success and people won't insist on founding my school for me, for then I should be lost.'

Monday, December 23 At lunch R. is cheerful, though talking tires him; he laughs a great deal over the story of the death of the conductor Proch, who, shortly before his demise, read in a newspaper that he was dying: 'Now I don't know whether I should drink my coffee or not,' he said, and a few hours later he was dead!

Tuesday, December 24 Christmas activities. R. does not look too worn out at lunch, and in the evening, after the distribution of presents, he is in very high spirits; he tells me that in the palace gardens Jäger fell down in the snow; he was taken to Stützer's tavern and Schnappauf was sent for, but it was nothing, and afterwards Wolz., Seidl, Jäger, Rubinstein and he formed a Serapion Pact[1]. We go to bed early. The Christmas tree is pushed to one side and the children clear away their things, for there is to be a party in Wahnfried tomorrow evening.

Wednesday, December 25 Oh, that one has nothing but words, words! This threadbare language for such joys, such bliss! I feel reluctant to write about it, there is no one to whom I wish to tell what happened today . . . The pen slipped from my fingers, I now take it up again [*noted at foot of page*: 'Friday the 27th'] to preserve for my children what has perhaps not stamped itself sharply enough on their memories. Early in the morning I hear some rustling and think to myself that preparations are being made for the evening, since R. has promised me a party this evening, and last night they had to clear the presents away. Then Siegfried comes skipping into the room and says softly, 'Mama, Papa wants you to know that the Robber is playing something from *Parsifal*,' and then – the Prelude begins, really begins, and is played to the end, while my heart reels in bliss! . . .

And then R. comes to my bed, asks me not to weep or expire, jokes gaily, undresses and gets into bed, breakfasts again with me (he had already breakfasted with Lusch at 7 o'clock), and talks and talks. The orchestra from Meiningen is here, he says, there is to be a house concert this evening, the Fugal Overture, the F Major Symphony[2]; yesterday there were two rehearsals, morning and afternoon, and all those things – Jäger's fall, the Serapion Pact – were fibs! But the rehearsals cured him, he greatly enjoyed them. He went to the first feeling languid after his bad night, but with the Fugal Overture it was all forgotten. He crept home very slowly (he did not want to order a carriage, lest he attract my attention with the sound of its wheels), and when Brange saw him wrapped up in furs, she almost tore him to bits, wanting to get the fur off him, as if she thought something must have happened to him. What can I say to all this? I hold in my hands the baton with which he has just been conducting, and the fan which he gave me along with other lovely things, and do not know whether to utter cries of joy or to expire. Death alone could express my feelings, life can scarcely contain them, and so I remain silent, silent, hearing as if from the farthest

[1] A 'brotherhood' taking its name from E.T.A.Hoffmann's collection of stories *Die Serapionsbrüder.*
[2] Beethoven's Overture *'Zur Weihe des Hauses,'* Opus 124, and his Eighth Symphony.

reaches of Heaven things no mortal being – not even you, my Siegfried – can be allowed to hear from my lips ...

At eleven o'clock rehearsal in Wahnfried! After the [Fugal] Overture, the *Idyll* and *Egmont* and the Andante and Presto from the A Major[1] – this for the children, since Siegfried so loves the Andante. After the rehearsal some construction work in Wahnfried, so that the musicians can have an entrance of their own (work was already started on this yesterday, but secretly, during the evening, and done as if by magic!). Incredible the effect R. has on this by no means very significant orchestra! At lunch, when I express my emotion at his having orchestrated the Prelude, he says, 'Yes, I was always thinking, "Surely she must some time notice that I am not progressing beyond those first few bars of Act III?"' Nothing but revelations at lunchtime! Also much about music, about Beethoven's orchestration, but in him the ideas are so powerful that he triumphs over everything. The evening begins at seven o'clock. – Programme: first part: *'Zur Weihe des Hauses'* Overture (Beethoven), F Major Symphony. Intermission. – second part: *Idyll*, Andante and Presto from the A Major Symphony, *Egmont* Overture. Long intermission, supper, Prelude to *Parsifal*! – With each bar of each work I feel like exclaiming, 'Oh, stay a while, you are so fair!'[2]. From no performance ever have I received such an impression, never! The players, as if transformed by magic, scatter sparks of divinity all around them; it is as if all the themes are being turned to flesh and blood, they approach us like individual people, and even the auditorium looks transfigured. At each intermission R. retires alone, but I am permitted to make sure that he is well; only after the *Egmont* Overture does he have a little headache, but a bit of nourishment restores him. To me it seems that these glorious works have been cleansed of all profanation, of the disparagement inflicted on them by poor, everyday performances; they appear to me like Kundry redeemed by Parsifal; and, as if the ideas themselves were conscious of this, each theme seems to greet the master by displaying all its radiance, gentle or powerful. He and Beethoven! ... But the evening performance of the Prelude is not like the morning one, when I was all prayer and ecstasy; this time I hear the Redeemer's call to salvation, addressed to an unheeding world, a call so sad, so sorrowful, so fervent, I see his countenance and the gaze which fell on Kundry – I recognize the wilderness across which this call resounds, and the awful recognition fills me with bliss! There stands he who has called forth these wonders, and he loves me. He loves me! –

Richard was by no means displeased when Councillor Kraussold, overwhelmed by his impression of *Parsifal*, spoke a few words and called for a

---

[1] Beethoven's Seventh Symphony.
[2] Quotation from Goethe's *Faust*.

cheer; in his speech he touched me with his reference to me: 'she who has no desire to live for an instant without her Richard.' – All took their leave silently, solemn in their exaltation. R. stays up with me and Seidl, and we talk – if talking is the right word for a series of exclamations followed by silence! – We part when R. becomes really tired, only to find, upstairs, that we cannot part! – He is pleased with the white dress he gave me, about which he was involved in a lengthy correspondence. . . .

Thursday, December 26 R. had a very good night – this blessing to crown my happiness! Discussed the glorious performance in detail. Then R. says that Fidi, to whom he had each time thrown his cap for safekeeping, had looked magnificent, resembling his father Geyer. I: 'Father Geyer must surely have been your father.' R.: 'I don't believe that.' 'Then why the resemblance?' R.: 'My mother loved him at the time – elective affinities.' – We eat out today at Lieutenant Colonel Schäffer's[1], but R. is very tired there; on his behalf I beg that he may be allowed to leave, but he stays seated and by the end of the meal looks somewhat better. As we are riding home, he says, 'Yes, we must not leave Wahnfried too often.' We then look at the room which has now really become his music room; the magic still pervades it. Everything – the relationship of the orchestra to the room, the acoustics, the choice of works and order of their playing, the number of people present – it was all just right, successful in all respects; and even the present disorder is not disturbing – it reminds us of what has been! In the evening I put on the 'Marajah', as R. calls another dress he gave me after giving all the measurements to Steckner in Leipzig and bringing into being a very rich, fantastic and extremely becoming article of clothing. We talk away the evening in the lilac *salon*. R. says my dress is like the one Alexander wore after defeating Darius.

Friday, December 27 Merry breakfast with R., he tells me once again how the rehearsal cured him, he had had some trouble with the Prelude to *Parsifal* (they had played it at twice the proper speed in Meiningen, because the conductor had not known how to indicate the rhythm of one passage). – Lunch with the children, R. asks them what they liked best: *Parsifal* and the Beethoven Andante. R. said yesterday again that he would perhaps amuse himself by orchestrating some things afresh.

[1] Correctly, Scheffer, commanding officer of the Bayreuth garrison.

1879

Wednesday, January 1 Who could describe the feelings with which I wish R. good fortune today, at the conclusion of a year we were permitted to spend entirely at Wahnfried, unseparated, in which *Parsifal* came nearer to completion and a significant part of R.'s burden was lifted from his shoulders? – Springlike weather, sunshine; I go out of doors with indescribable emotions, look at the birds in the poultry yard which give R. so much pleasure (particularly the peacock); R. rests for a while, then goes to call on Councillor Kraussold. Returning home, R. settles down to work – on *Parsifal*! I have told him that I no longer wish to hear any music except *Parsifal*, played by him. . . . Before that, returning from his walk, he says to me, 'I have been performing rose miracles in your room.' In the morning he placed on my bureau a little bottle of 'Extract Richard Wagner', which he brewed himself, and in the afternoon he pours a few drops of rose essence on my bouquet.

Thursday, January 2 Before we go to lunch, R. plays me what he has done today in ink: '*Wirkte dies der heilige Tag*', the suggestion of the meadow, so heavenly in its twilight! 'It must be nothing definite, just a slight haze – oh, how beautiful syncopes are, what lightness of movement they impart!'

Wednesday, January 8 'Exactly ten bars today,' he tells me when he fetches me for lunch. He has received news of the death of the stout-hearted Herr Müller[1], and he recalls his friendly judgment on me back in 1857 – 'She is a real thoroughbred' – he (R.) had been so pleased by this, and also by his delight when he saw us come together. 'That must have been a real weight off the minds of all my friends who knew about my disgraceful life. What they all had to put up with from me! Something like an avalanche lies between my former life and my present life.' – We celebrate the '*quinzaine*' of my birthday, I in *white*, as on every Wednesday now, and we remain alone together. Hans's birthday brings our thoughts back to the past; it is all so sad; in the morning R. had thought of my father's visit to him at Tribschen, during which my father was filled with deep pity for his loneliness, but could do no more than point as consolation to the portrait of the King! –

[1] Hermann Müller, a Dresden friend who, like Wagner himself, fled to Switzerland in 1849 and had seen Cosima, first in Zurich in 1857, then in Lucerne in 1870.

R. says: 'Nobody believes in real love – even Hans thought I was just amusing myself.' A letter from E. Nietzsche brings back to us our experiences with her brother. The news that he, N., wants *Parsifal* to be staged makes R. smile bitterly – 'Now they think I have no other wish but to stage another such performance' – whereas all that concerns him is how he can avoid it. I: 'It is only necessary not to wish it.' – R., with a sigh: 'Oh, one would like it to happen, and yet one doesn't want to do it' – that is our sadly conflicting position.

Thursday, January 9 R. works and tells me at lunch that he has completed six bars, but they are very significant ones. In the evening he drinks his grog in my room, after bringing me a belated Christmas gift! – He talks about his composition after we have spent some time, prompted by the parcel from London, talking about extract of roses, whose perfume (a particular favourite of his) he describes as 'rapturous'. He says: 'During the morning I was thinking something I could not tell a soul – that in a scene like this the words and music are concentrated, more or less like this extract, to make a frivolous comparison; I could talk about all kinds of subjects, say things only I could say, there is so much concentrated inside me. Yet one walks the earth in silence and is then forgotten.' I: 'Forgotten!' He: 'Oh, what is posthumous fame? I always think of Schopenhauer's likening it to oyster shells. What does the world know of Goethe and Schiller except the shells? Till someone comes along to whom they mean something.'

Monday, January 13 Visit from Herr Levi, very pleasant. R. plays us his third act, up to the worship of the spear.... He declares that Gurnemanz (whom he wishes he had described as an armourer) is his favourite character – he and similar figures such as H[ans] Sachs, Kurwenal. Later he tells me it would have been better if we had done this when we were by ourselves – all the same, it was indescribable!... Friend Levi stays behind after our other friends have gone, and when he tells us that his father is a rabbi, our conversation comes back to the Israelites – the feeling that they intervened too early in our cultural condition, that the human qualities the German character might have developed from within itself and then passed on to the Jewish character have been stunted by their premature inter-ference in our affairs, before we have become fully aware of ourselves. The conductor speaks of a great movement against the Jews in all spheres of life; in Munich there are attempts to remove them from the town council. He hopes that in 20 years they will be extirpated root and branch, and the audience for the *Ring* will be another kind of public – we 'know differently'! – Alone together again, R. and I discuss the curious attachment individual Jews have for him; he says Wahnfried will soon turn into a synagogue!...

Tuesday, January 14 In the evening, when I come down to supper, he shows me the alteration he has made to '*er starb, ein Mensch wie alle.*' 'It was too much like Cherubini,' he said.

Wednesday, January 15 R. had a good night, but he complains of congestion in the chest and wishes me already to book the villa in Naples for next year. Yesterday afternoon he came to tell me that the royalties from Vienna have been good – all his works, even *Rienzi*, had earned something. I: 'So they are good children, after all.' R.: 'Yes, they have to go begging for me.' – He fetches me for lunch and says, 'I have got Parsifal to the point of fainting – I'm always glad when I've got my people where they ought to be.'

Thursday, January 16 R. slept well, he laughingly tells me of his dream 'while turning over in bed': 'I was between Minna and Mme Wesendonck. She was making horrible advances to me, to annoy Minna, at whom she kept looking. "All right, neither of them," I thought, and tried to get away, went around looking for a purse, in which there were some gold coins. "Is this devilry starting again?" I said to myself on waking, but I was not driven from my bed.' He works and says at lunch that he has reached the point where Kundry arouses Parsifal again and he proposes marriage to her.

Friday, January 17 Around noon, as I am dressing, I hear the cherished voice calling from upstairs, 'Cosi – I want to play something to you.' I fly into his room, he sings to me Gurnemanz's words '*Nicht so*' and all the rest up to '*so weiche jeder Schuld Bekümmernis von dir*'. – After lunch we talk of Naples, whether to go at all – 'it is so lovely here,' he says. But in the afternoon he feels pain in his chest and decides after all on Naples for next winter.

Tuesday, January 20 R. says he now has only nine more pages of his text to set to music, and all the epic scenes are finished.

Thursday, January 23 At lunch he tells me he has been 'composing well'. I read 'The Nibelung Myth' and *Siegfrieds Tod*[1] and talk to R. about them. Later he tells me that he originally designed this more in the mode of antiquity; then, during his secluded life in Zurich, he became interested in Wotan's downfall; in this work he was more a kind of Flying Dutchman. I am surprised by the increased *inspiration* in the revised treatment of the subject and its ever-growing feeling and intensity. When I tell R. of my great pleasure in the Valkyries' scene (up to Brünnhilde), he says, 'It gave me my Valkyries' theme.'

Friday, January 24 R.'s night was a good one, and he works. At two o'clock we receive Dr. Jenkins, who has come to examine R.'s teeth, and he starts work immediately after lunch; R. wonderfully patient and cheerful throughout. He takes a rest, and in the evening a curious conversation develops. The excellent American is certainly surprised by present conditions in Germany, but he has no doubt that the Germans will rise splendidly to the occasion. R. says, 'Yes, because we have had men like Goethe and Beethoven – but ask *them* what they feel about it!' He then enlarges upon

---

[1] The first prose sketch of the *Ring* drama and the first version of *Götterdämmerung*, both in Vol. 2 of the collected writings.

the shortsightedness which has prevented efforts to bring the neighbouring countries which are related to us (Holland, Sweden, Denmark, Switzerland) into an alliance with us! No ideas even of colonization! Dr. Jenkins also talks about the admirable qualities of the Germans in America, and R. says, 'Yes, the emigrants – those are the good ones, just as the earlier wanderers were the heroes; the ones who stayed at home were the Philistines.'

Saturday, January 25 R. does no work, and after we have had a light lunch at twelve o'clock, he undergoes the operation proper, which is painful and exhausting.

Sunday, January 26 R. says goodbye to Dr. Jenkins, after having yesterday given him the *Ring des Nibelungen* with a humorous dedication: Dr. J. had spoken about an art-loving Welshman, King Jen, and said his people were the 'kin' of Jen, this in connection with R.'s joke that he learned his English in Wales and consequently spoke a bad dialect!

Tuesday, January 28 A nice letter from E. Nietzsche brings the conversation round to her brother's dismal book, and R. remarks that, when respect vanishes, everything else vanishes too: 'That is the true definition of religion; unlike Jesus Christ, I cannot be without sin, but I can respect the sinless state, can beg pardon of my ideal when I am disloyal to it. But our times have no feeling for greatness, they cannot recognize a great character. There can be no bond with it.'

Wednesday, January 29 R. tells me that he has sketched Kundry's baptism, and he hopes I shall be satisfied with it. We go for a walk together in the palace gardens but soon return home, since I feel the air is too keen. R. does some more work, and I get the impression that he has had a slight rush of blood to his head. When Herr R. comes, I go through *Parsifal* (Act II) with him, while R. watches us and listens. Apart from a few deficiencies of tempo and execution, we are astounded by the way Herr R. plays from the sketches. But after he has played Parsifal's cry following the kiss, R. springs to his feet and sings this passage, in a way the world will never hear again! . . .

Friday, January 31 Before our reading Herr R. played to us the Overture to *Das Liebesverbot*[1], in which the banning theme seems to me very good – soulless, legal, harsh, dramatic; when I say I like the Overture to *Die Feen* better, R. observes that the other (*L.-Verb.*) shows more talent. He searches out a few passages, but apart from the '*Salve Regina*' (*Tannhäuser*) he finds it all 'horrible', 'execrable', 'disgusting'. – It is well orchestrated, he says – 'That I could do in my mother's womb' – but the Overture is all thunder and lightning.

Monday, February 3 R. works and says to me, 'Do not expect too much

---

[1] Wagner's second opera (after *Die Feen*), based on Shakespeare's *Measure for Measure*, first performed 1836 in Magdeburg. The nuns' chorus, '*Salve Regina*', uses the so-called '*Dresdner Amen*' that he used again in *Tannhäuser*.

from the meadow – it must of course be short, and it cannot express delight in nonexistence, as in *Tristan*.' Then he laughs and says, 'Rubinstein will ask, "How does it happen that Parsifal recognizes Kundry?" – if indeed he does recognize her.' And he continues: 'It is all unspoken ecstasy, as Parsifal returns home and gazes upon this poor woman.' Oh, if I could only reproduce the expression on his face and the sound of his voice as he describes the state of Parsifal's soul! – Then he tells me once more something I forgot to note down on Saturday: when he was walking beside the pond he heard a curious horn sounding, very absurd, and it was probably blown by the watchman on the ice; everyone vanished from the pond and he continued his walk alone; suddenly he saw on the snow the very faint shadow of himself and the two dogs, and, glancing up at the sky, he saw the moon in its first quarter. It had been a very mysterious moment; probably as a child he would have laughed heartily at the horn, but nobody had laughed. – R. goes out, is pleased with his room, which I help to arrange, calls it his shaman, and then goes down to his work. But suddenly he is upstairs with me again: 'I shouted to the children from the hall, asking them to call you, but nobody heard; I have come upstairs to tell you that the entry of the kettledrum in G is the finest thing I have ever done!' I accompany him downstairs and he plays to me the anointment of Parsifal by Gurnemanz, with its wonderful canon, and the baptism of Kundry with the annihilating sound of the kettledrum[1]: 'Obliteration of the whole being, of all earthly desire,' says R. – In the evening we come back to a declaration by Herr R. which yesterday astonished us – that on his first encounter with them (when he was a student at the Vienna Conservatoire) *Tannhäuser* and *Lohengrin* made no impression on him at all! – It is intellect which has brought this poor man to his feeling for these works. . . . Later R. discusses with me the inner loneliness of such a piteous character, and says this makes Rubinstein interesting in his eyes, he has found his way back to him in spite of the gulf which divides one from such a person. At the end of the conversation R. says to him gently, 'We are trying to explain a phenomenon to ourselves; it is not dislike but liking that sets us on this path.' And he concludes jokingly, 'You'll probably take that again as an affront.'

Wednesday-Saturday, February 5–15 Have not written in my book. I felt unwell during the night of 5–6 and had to stay in bed for three days, till Sunday; R. kept a loyal watch beside me, full of divine love, read to me Plutarch's glorious discussion of Socrates's guardian spirit and also his own still more beautiful letter to the King about Fidi. In the meantime he fully completes the *meadow*. Arrival of 'Scheherazade', the new dress which R. has given me and which I put on! – Saturday the 15th, R. well, returns to his work, tells me at lunch

---

[1] In the full score the kettledrum was replaced by cello and double bass.

that I must write some words for him – he already has the melody, which conveys the sense of the matter, but the words are lacking.

Monday, February 17 R. joyfully informs me that he has words enough – he had overlooked one verse (*'der liess sie so gedeihen'*). He takes pride in not having had to alter his words: yesterday he recalled the melody of the 'Prize Song', which came to him before the words, and was pleased with it. – Referring to what he is doing now, he says he is taking care not to put in too many figurations – something he has sometimes done, as when Brünnhilde pleads to Wotan on Siegmund's behalf; I remark that this was just because Frau Materna did not have the personality to act it – she was overshadowed by the music, as it were. (Fidi brought me the first flowers of the year; on the very day of Eva's birth – she herself one of life's blossoms!)

Tuesday, February 18 Towards noon R. comes to me and says, 'I have found a transition which is worthy of you,' leads me into his room and plays to me this divine transition from *'will ihr Gebet ihm weihen'* to *'ihn selbst am Kreuze.'* 'The main thing,' R. says, 'is that it doesn't cause a shock – there must be no feeling of shock.' – This morning he said he would like to compare his works with those of other composers and see whether his do not contain ten times as much music – that is something which has never been acknowledged. And for this reason he was willing to believe that his works would have a great future. He is so well and cheerful that today seems like a really sunny day. Snow flurries, but he goes out for a while with Brange, who, having run after him, touches him by demanding to return to her newborn puppies.

Friday, February 21 My wish to give him my picture for his birthday coincides with earache and toothache; I ask to be allowed to go to Munich. He wants to come, too; my anxiety about his health does not permit it. A sad evening – disconsolate mood –

Saturday, February 22 Journey! No diary until Tuesday the 25th, when my return takes R. by surprise; travelled in the night. R. not entirely well, he had bad dreams about me. He did not come to join me because he also dreamed all the children were ill. Was I wrong to inflict all this on us just to bring him pleasure? A difficult question!

Wednesday, February 26 I feel as if the heavens have re-opened when I hear his sounds, the only music in the world for me! R. laughs and says he does not know what to make of it: when I went away, music abandoned him entirely, but now he has his head full of themes again!

Saturday, March 1 In the morning R. tells me that he considers it very important for everything to sound well, including the subsidiary voices, and that is why he likes to have a piano at hand, he is not satisfied until it all sounds right. He works, and around lunchtime he fetches me and sings to me *'Du weinest, sieh! es lacht die Aue'* ...

Sunday, March 2 At noon he fetches me and plays to me the wonderful transition to the bells. In the evening conclusion of the 48 Preludes and Fugues.

Monday, March 3 In the morning we talk a lot about *Der F[liegende] H[olländer]*, which he intends to revise slightly.

Friday, March 7 R. had a good night, and he works. At lunch he suddenly exclaims, 'That is a good idea! I must write it down at once.' We bring him a pencil and some music paper, and he writes a harmonic passage to accompany the bells. Afterwards he asks me if I know what the 6/4 time means while the bells are sounding. It shows Gurnemanz and Parsifal in the act of listening; one hears the bells from a distance. He is completely absorbed in his creative work, and I am permitted to share it with him! . . . Otherwise we talk of hardly anything except Naples.

Sunday, March 9 In the evening we go through the 'Good Friday Music', up to the bells, and celebrate in tears, tears of bliss, the salvation of mankind.

Thursday, March 20 At lunch R. said that he would allow himself plenty of time to complete *Parsifal*, this final realization of a series of images which had arisen in his mind. He says he does not believe he will presume to create anything more that is new; the symphonies are different, but he wants to complete everything in peace and contentment. Before supper he comes up to my room, talks to me about the 'elegy',[1] and says he would like to play it to me; and he does so – this unique elegy, the process within Parsifal's soul when he becomes once again 'an ordinary mortal' before he becomes a king. . . . 'You have no idea of all the things in it,' he says. I: 'I believe I have.' He: 'Yes, of course.'

Monday, March 24 From *Parsifal* the consecration of the King and the meadow, then R. looks for his new sketches and plays to us the responses up to Amfortas's first outburst. He feels that his interpretations from the pencilled sketches cannot have made things clear to us, but when I go to him upstairs, as he is putting the pages away, I tell him what a wonderful picture they had conjured up, how lifeless these singing and marching knights seemed, the whole thing working on one like a ghostly parade, until the tender and sorrowful laments of Amfortas enter suddenly like a living experience and move one profoundly. R. observes that I am the only person who could get such clear impressions from these 'muddled pages' – ah, it is the inspiration of being permitted to follow him that gives me the power to do it!

Tuesday, March 25 R. goes out in the afternoon, discovers that the *Bayreuther Blätter* has arrived, and when I come down to supper, he embraces me in great excitement; Glasenapp's article, the reports of the

---

[1] The final bars of the 'Good Friday Music' (*'Du weinest, sieh! es lacht die Aue'*)

growth of the Society have moved him greatly and instilled in him a sense of obligation, since nothing like this has ever happened before. He remains in this state of excitement all evening and is also preoccupied with his composing. I do not know how he suddenly comes to the idea – though of course in a joking way – that Fidi may turn out to be a practical man of the world, who will find his papa and his mama terribly old-fashioned. If that were to be the case, all the papers would have to be left to one of the girls. But R. adds that it is a good thing Fidi has not yet betrayed any signs of knowing what sort of person his father really is.

Saturday, March 29 At breakfast R. and I discuss the positioning of Titurel's catafalque and decide that it should be placed high up in the arch from which Titurel's voice is heard in the first act, thus leaving the middle of the stage free for Amfortas's outburst, Parsifal's act of healing, and the blessing.

Thursday, April 3 Herr Jäger calls at coffee-time and tells us about the great success of the final performances of *Götterdämmerung*, but says all other opera performances remained constantly empty. R. laughs and says: 'So Herr von Hülsen is quite right when he says I am ruining the theatre – where the *Ring* is being performed people will go to see nothing else! – At lunch he tells me about Carlyle's 'Voltaire'[1], which pleases him so much that he would like to send Carlyle something of his own. The fact that he is a theist hardly bothers him; he says this is what gives him his peculiar character.

Friday, April 4 R. works and is satisfied with it. He says to me: 'You do not even notice how I keep all my melodies in a certain style, so that it all looks the same but is in fact different. Just to string one melody to another, splish-splash – there's no art in that.' Over coffee he tells me about his plan for arranging some concerts here with the patrons' money, spread over two months, with the aim of showing conductors how to interpret the classics. Is my reaction due to concern for his health (though I hardly think so, since what he wishes is good for him), or to fear of once more having closer contacts with the world and having again to concern myself with so many things I have put behind me? In any case the news hardly pleases me, and I betray my apprehension, but when R. says to me, 'You would surely like to hear these things again,' my gratitude for his kindness makes up for the lack of pleasure I derive from undertakings of any sort. – We play with the children, and then R. reads to me Carlyle's 'Voltaire', excellent characterization, so just, so subtle. 'For him, in all matters the first question is, not what is true, but what is false' – R. finds this particularly excellent.

Sunday, April 6 R. has several things to vex him, as always when he comes into contact with the outside world; the dogs have killed a cat, Brange is accused of spoiling the local hunting of hares, and appeals are made to R.,

---

[1] In *Critical and Miscellaneous Essays.*

both in person and in writing; to one man he says in reply, among other things, 'I did not wish to do harm to the Bayreuth population by settling here.' On top of that, the gas is not burning well, and other such domestic troubles. All this irritates him, but he soon recovers, and after a short game of whist we read *The Winter's Tale*, the unique shepherd's scene! 'What, art so near?' – the old shepherd's question which shows all of Shakespeare's immediacy, how he hears the raging of the storm, which prevents the old man's hearing his son's voice, and which accounts for his surprise – it is this immediacy which R. again singles out.

Thursday, April 10 For lunch Herr Levi, who stays all day. In the evening *Parsifal*. While Rubinstein is playing, even singing quietly, and Levi listening with great emotion, R. says softly to me, 'What touching figures they are!'

Saturday, April 12 R. is pleased with the return to normal routine; he says it had been a veritable flood of holiness. At breakfast he tells me how yesterday he imagined the Crucifixion to himself – 'not possible in our climate, the wounds need the hot rays of the sun'; he pictured in his mind the languishing, then the cry, and he felt very moved. He explains that it was not Christ's death but his resurrection which gave rise to the religion; the death all but destroyed the poor disciples, but the women's not finding the body in the morning, and seeing Christ in their exaltation, created the community: 'In the disappearance of the corpse a strange and subtle fate was at work.' He quotes Renan, who sees the foundation of Christianity in a woman's love. R. works; after lunch he speaks to me about the strange compulsion exerted by a poetic conception, which restricts all one's freedom, and he says one cannot create many such dramatic works, or work on other things at the same time. 'Children,' he says at lunch, 'you see what a man looks like who is writing his last opera.'

Thursday, April 17 When we withdraw upstairs, R. talks about his *Parsifal*, saying it has not been possible to avoid a certain restriction of feeling; this does not mean that it is churchlike in tone, he says, indeed there is even a divine wildness in it, but such affecting emotions as in *Tristan* or even the *Nibelungen* would be entirely out of place. 'You will see – diminished sevenths were just not possible!'

Friday, April 18 Snow, and yesterday I noticed the first hints of green in our garden! – R. works, tells me he will probably be happy with his conception by the end of April, and then he will take some time off: 'If it weren't for my love for you, no God would ever induce me to orchestrate *Parsifal*.'

Monday, April 21 Confusion everywhere; Wahnfried is to be spring-cleaned, and we begin with the *salon*. R. works, now in ink, in my room; his reading matter in between still Carlyle, who is becoming a real friend; he likes the study of Jean Paul[1], and quotes me bits from it.

---

[1] 'J.P.F.Richter' in *Critical and Miscellaneous Essays*.

Friday, April 25 R. tells me that at a quarter to six he went downstairs and altered a passage in his sketches: 'I have got rid of those stupid syncopations.' He shows me the passage and tells me that while he was doing it, a bird tapped on the window and demanded to be let in. Hardly has he said this when Georg announces the sudden death of Herr v. Staff during a hunt in the forest. I take leave of R., look in on Fidi, who is still unwell, and then go to the poor wife. When I return around noon, R. greets me with the news that *Parsifal* is finished, he has been working very strenuously! Though our conversation at lunch revolves around the sad blow in the neighbouring house, it does not affect the mood arising from this event. And when, after lunch, R. sings to me Amfortas's last lament and Parsifal's words, and plays the ending, I once more feel that pain and mourning make the soul even more vulnerable to music – I breathe in this blessing deeply, and tears of joy follow on the tears of sympathy I shed in the morning like transfigured sisters. Bless you, dear heavens! – R. says that never before has he been permitted to work so uninterruptedly. I: 'Oh, that I have lived to see it!'

Saturday, April 26 It is decided to celebrate the completion of *Parsifal* today, since it is not until today that he can sort out and arrange the pages to present to me; I lay my very modest return gift at his feet, and the lamp holder is fixed to the table. At lunch we drink to the 26th. Meanwhile I go to the house of mourning and accompany my poor friend to the station, seeing her off on her very sad journey. Yet all deep things are akin to one another, today I can both weep and feel joy, in my heart a single harmony. I am somewhat overcome by the wealth of my emotions, and over coffee I fall asleep without being aware of it; I am woken by a slight noise, and find R.'s blessing! [*Enclosed is a piece of paper containing, in Wagner's handwriting, the words:* 'My dearest wife! Sleep well!'] All weariness is swept away, and I take the cherished sketches and arrange them, thinking of the children, who will one day find them. – Evening of chat, then something from *Rienzi*.

Sunday, April 27 R. slept well. I tell him he will not know now what to do with his time! . . . I write in my diary and read Malwida's book[1] just arrived. Silence, no more sounds of music in Wahnfried – instead, a hideous military band! – In the evening we ask Wol. to join us, so that we may congratulate him on the periodical [*Bayreuther Blätter*]. The very numerous performances in Cologne (mostly of *Holländer*) have brought in new members. We go through *Parsifal*, from the second entrance into the Temple up to the end; R. said yesterday what he has said before: that the orchestration would be completely different from the *Ring*, no figurations of that kind; it would be like cloud layers, dispersing and then forming again. The naïveté which had

---

[1] *Stimmungsbilder (Impressions).*

kept sentimentality at bay in the 'Forest Murmurs' would also keep it at bay in *Parsifal*; in the former it was the naïveté of Nature, here it would be the naïveté of holiness, 'which is free of the dross of sentimentality.' He plays certain intervals to us, saying, 'That would be absolutely impossible in *Parsifal*.' 'And so that you can see what a foolish fellow I am,' he tells Wolzogen, 'I'll show you what I intend to alter in the first act.' He looks for the chord in the first act, but cannot find it: 'Yes, of course, it is in the Prelude; when I heard it, I said to myself, "Not bad on the whole, but this chord must go."'' He thinks it is too sentimental. Discussion of the final, wordless scene. R. says he will cut some of the music if the action on stage is insufficient, but it gave him pleasure to be able to show that he was not wearied. Talk of Amfortas, his weakness, his exhaustion, and just the one terrible moment when he tries to force them to kill him. Perhaps the most wonderful thing about the work is its divine simplicity, comparable to the Gospels – 'the pure fool' who dominates everything.... As R. himself said, 'It is all so *direct*!' ...

Monday, April 28 R. had a good rest. He is using these quiet days for correspondence. He does not wish to read Malwida's recently published book; he says at lunch, 'I shall not read any book by a woman until you write one.' He does glance through one chapter but soon puts the book down, finding all the philosophizing distasteful.

Tuesday, April 29 He was up once, at four o'clock, but he is not unwell, it is just, as he says, a curious feeling when a work like this has been completed. He goes through it in the morning and tells me at lunch that he has already made several pencil marks in it; several things were too abrupt, leaving the listener too much to fill in as far as music was concerned, and that could be put right.

Tuesday, May 6 This morning a letter arrived from the King. The letter makes a pleasant impression on R., as does a letter from Heckel in Mannheim, enclosing one from Herr Schön[1]; this gentleman from Worms wants to make an annual contribution to the school and inquires about the situation in a serious, understanding manner.

Thursday, May 8 R. says how strange he feels when he regards his completed *Parsifal* – the time spent on it seems to have passed in a flash. He works on his article and says at lunch that he has written only one page. – In the afternoon we follow in each other's footsteps, R. and I: first of all to see friend Gross, then to various shops! R. buys little rakes for the bank he has planned for this evening! All our neighbours come along, six in total, and the Jägers as well, and R. revives 'youthful memories'; sets up the bank, taking great trouble in and getting much enjoyment from arranging things

[1] Friedrich Schön (b.1850), a factory owner, is regarded as the founder of the Bayreuth Festival Scholarship Fund (*Stipendienstiftung*) set up in 1882; he contributed 10,000 marks.

properly, then initiates all of us ignoramuses into the secrets of a 'gambling hell'! Lusch and Boni are his *croupiers,* he calls them Hugin and Munin. Great amusement, and R. sets it up so that winnings shall be valid only for our guests.

Saturday, May 17 In the evening whist with Rubinstein and a dummy. – Then something in passing from *Parsifal* ('*sah ihn und lachte*' and the page after that). Afterwards I recall that some days ago R. told me that Kundry was his most original female character; when he had realized that the servant of the Grail was the same woman who seduced Amfortas, he said, everything fell into place, and after that, however many years might elapse, he knew how it would turn out.

Monday, May 19 In the evening I had the task of informing R. of Semper's death[1]. Solemn mood, silence. – R. recalled the supper given by Semper in honour of *Tannhäuser,* Herr v. Birk was invited, also Meyerbeer, who did not come; a very violent argument between R. and S. Semper: 'I am not the only one who thinks like this, there is Birk, too –' They look at him, find him snoring, whereupon much laughter!

Wednesday, May 21 Final rehearsal of pantomime and festival play, all in excellent shape, the good children dedicated heart and soul. – Mimi arrives, along with Prince Liechtenstein and his wife. Greetings. A splendid thunderstorm, Donner cleaning things up thoroughly for tomorrow, it is now warm. R. stands at the door of Wahnfried, impatiently awaiting me, I tell him about the guests. In the afternoon R. corrects his article, and we spend a very pleasant evening with the Ls., Mimi and Frau v. Wöhrmann[2].

Thursday, May 22 The day of days! . . . It is also Ascension Day! Bells pealing and glorious weather. – Setting up the stands; everything has arrived in time except for the *Parsifal* sketches. At ten o'clock I am able to fetch R., and he is greeted by the Pilgrim[3]! Everything comes off well – Fidi indescribably moving as he sits before my picture[4] in the costume and hairstyle of Ludwig Geyer, painting it. We gaze at each other as if in a dream – thank you, my children! – All the gifts have the good fortune to please R., from my picture down to the glasses – after he has gone, one of the Moorish bowls falls down and breaks; go thy ways, Klingsor's glory! R. takes a rest, I receive the birthday guests, and we then go for a walk in the palace gardens, where extracts from R.'s works are being played. At two o'clock lunch, the guests from outside, among whom is also friend Lenbach – Wolz. provides a dinner for the Bayreuth colony. Fidi proposes the toast to his father, R. is pleased with the song, '*An den Geliebten*' ['To My

[1] Semper died on May 15 in Rome.
[2] Baroness Emma Wöhrmann, a friend of Marie von Schleinitz.
[3] A character (played by one of the children) in the birthday play written by the Wolzogen family.
[4] Lenbach's new portrait of Cosima.

Beloved']¹, tells me he has found the right ending for it, since he has not slept! After lunch he leads the children in song, and slips into '*Wer ein holdes Weib errungen*' (from *Fidelio*)². 'Oh, if I could die!' . . . Around six o'clock R. goes to Angermann's with friends Levi, Lenbach and Liechtenstein, and when he returns home we are able to perform our pantomime³, which is so successful that R. thanks us with tears for our little bit of nonsense. Oh, my splendid children! In the evening R. has the dance repeated for our guests. When I appear to receive the guests, R. greets me with the same song from *Fidelio*, but this time just played on the piano.

Friday, May 23 R. had a somewhat restless night, but he is looking well. He goes off for his morning rest, I do a bit of straightening up and await the guests whom R. invited to listen to *Parsifal*. We play it through in his absence – he comes in only at the finish. Lunch with our friends (only Lenbach has left) – we come together again at six o'clock for the second act. Most unfortunately, R. allows himself to be stirred by it into singing; this puts a great strain on him, and in consequence there is a gloomy shadow over the evening for me.

Saturday, May 24 R. had a very restless night! . . . At 10.30 the guests arrive for the third act; R. there at the end, saying goodbye to Mimi, amid all the emotion caused by *Parsifal*!

Friday, May 30 Towards evening a drive to the Riedelsberg, where our children have been spending the day; R. well enough to enjoy the journey home in the sunset. He is also pleased with our children. Previously Loldi reminded him of his ideal sister, and she also reminds me of family things, of mystical relationships, and we are moved to see ourselves reflected like this in our child.

Sunday, June 1 R. is reading Carlyle's *Fr[ench] Revolution* with great enjoyment. Frl. Uhlig has sent a copy of part of his letters, and we read them in the summerhouse in the afternoon. Much delight in them. R. mentions at lunch that the King is now having novels written for him about the times of Louis XIV and XV; this raises sad thoughts!

Monday, June 2 R. had a good night. Our conversation turns to the letters; R. is pleased with them, and I always come back to feeling how splendid it is that his character appears so consistent at all periods of his life. As then, he is still expecting socialism to take over, the only difference being that he does not foresee its happening at any particular time.

Thursday, June 5 I read to R. a circular written by W. to the patrons,

¹ Possibly Beethoven's '*An den fernen Geliebten*'.
² 'Who has won a noble wife': Beethoven's *Fidelio*, Act II finale.
³ Choreographed by Richard Fricke, it depicted a schoolroom in which, after the teacher (Fricke) has left, the children throw books around and dance a tarantella; the teacher returns and threatens the children, but Columbine (played by Daniela) enters and persuades him to join in the dance; the music was provided by Rubinstein at the piano.

declaring that *Parsifal* will not be performed next year, describing the plan for the school, and inviting contributions. R. very much against it – he says he is here, and if people care to approach him, he will not be found lacking, but he cannot commit himself to anything or offer his services for anything. A drive to the Fantaisie, R. a little put out by certain happenings, in me just the feeling that I am to blame when everything is not exactly as he wants and needs it. Everything – worries, intentions, feelings of helplessness, the overwhelming burden of loving thoughts – I leave to my star, begging it to take charge and to exert its influence, to punish me when I am remiss, not to praise me when I succeed, but simply to shine on me. My star! How often does my spirit gaze upon it! It is my good wish, my good yearning, that I see in the invisible heavens in the form of a star, which shines on me and comforts me when the waves of my heart break darkly and stormily over the depths from which it came – at times in their ferocity they obscure its light, but only now and again and for short periods; my call sounds to it from the depths: Let me be good, as my fate has been good!

Friday, June 6 Fidi's day – when we recently recalled R.'s past life, R. exclaimed, 'How different, how different!' Today R. writes to Vreneli, inquiring whether we might be able to spend a few days in Tribschen. Devout thoughts of that blessed day! Presentation of gifts at one o'clock; the main present, the aquarium, causes great delight, and R. says Fidi should always be given something which gives pleasure to all. At lunch R. proposes the toast – 'Let Fidi be buried today – long live Siegfried, Siegfried the First!' – and it is decided that from now on he shall be given his full name. Spent part of the afternoon with R. in the summerhouse, R. then pleased when the ten boys, Siegfried's guests, shoot towards him like arrows and bid him good day.

Sunday, June 8 The snake in the aquarium has disappeared, and we feared it might crawl into Siegfried's bed; we both go there, one after another, but all is quiet – just a silent gulping in the aquarium! R. tells me that he saw the two girls, I. and E. sitting on our grave, and when he asked them what they were doing there: 'Looking for worms for the tortoise.' This answer amused him very much.

Tuesday, June 17 R. had a good night, but he still cannot start on his cure, after which he intends to set about the *Parsifal* score, beginning with ruling the lines neatly and carefully: 'I should like work on it to last until my 70th year, and then we would perform it.' He continues, 'On the other hand it would be nice if I could rely on Fidi sufficiently to leave the performance to him.' Today he describes to the children (Lusch) the consequences of the emancipation of the Jews, how the middle classes have been pushed to the wall by it and the lower classes led into corruption. The Revolution destroyed feudalism, he says, but introduced Mammon in its place – oh, how comforting it is to turn one's back on all that and just gaze at the trees!

A blackbird, hopping before us on the grass, brings from R. the remark, 'Like Materna — birds with good voices are never particularly beautiful.' — To please me, he plays his *Liebesmahl der Apostel*[1]; I asked him for it because I do not know the work, and he tells me I should not expect too much. By recalling to myself the occasion, and by visualizing the Frauenkirche, I come to the conclusion that the work, with all its theatrical, Catholic brilliance, must have given an appearance of pomp. R. laughs at the theatrical entry of the Holy Ghost, and when I tell him my feelings he says, 'Yes, it's a sort of Oberammergau play.' — Putting the music aside, he says, 'There one is fully aware of the composer of *Tristan und Isolde*.' He talks of the plagiarisms of his youth: only recently, when we played M[endelssohn]'s *Calm Sea*, he realized that this was his *Columbus* Overture! He also relates how he wrote his overture, in a room with Minna and Apel[2], and how — since he was jealous of Apel — he kept looking at them, to see whether they were not flirting too much! . . .

Thursday, June 19 At one o'clock R. comes to read me the first part of his article 'On Poetry and Composition'; glorious moments! And then the ensuing discussion about it. R. says, 'If only we had written down all our conversations, for you know it all!'

Saturday, June 21 R. works happily on his article. A close day, but it clears up, and we are able to have our coffee in the summerhouse and enjoy an afternoon rest, both reading the currency debate! . . . Around six o'clock a walk to Birken and beyond through the fields; a glorious evening. The meadows more gaily coloured and lush than I think I have ever seen them, forget-me-nots, marigolds, daisies, woodpinks rising above the rosy blades of grass, which in the sunshine cast a reddish-gold veil over the flowers; a celebration of rebirth — how to express one's gratitude? A lark does it for us, trilling forth our thanks exultantly on high. R. leads us along a narrow path through the middle of a field of grain, and our figures vanish in a sea of grain; lost in it, we espy innumerable cornflowers, like greetings from Heaven — the blue ether transformed into stars, the blue star of the deep. Where Friedrichstrasse ends (and the meadow begins) R. shows me a farmhouse dovecote which has taken his fancy, and then we return home, along paths new to us, amid the scent of elder blossom. During the evening we think frequently of the meadow and the wheatfield. And we see our house, too, with redoubled pleasure. R. loves my picture, says it contains 'a noble reproach'.

Friday, June 27 Coffee in the summerhouse, friend W. joins us, and, speaking of his article, R. says he is going to write once more about religion,

[1] A choral work, performed in 1843 by 1,200 singers and 100 instrumentalists in the Frauenkirche in Dresden.
[2] Theodor Apel, a close friend in Dresden and author of the play for which the *Columbus* Overture was written.

and he develops his idea that the new religion will one day evolve from the working-man, from an industrialist who loves his workers.

Saturday, June 28 It is very hot; around seven o'clock we drive out to the Bürgerreuth, where we have supper by moonlight. Before that we stopped beside the theatre, admired the growth in the surrounding plantations, and recalled the chaotic times when the place was teeming with people. The sight affects me unutterably, my thoughts are filled with sublime melancholy, R.'s greatness depicted here in all its isolation! He says, 'It stands there like a folly, and once I had emperors and princes here.'

Monday, June 30 The night is spent in opening and shutting windows, two thunderstorms in succession, but at last R. falls peacefully asleep and gets up in lively spirits to continue his spa cure. A fine day, the air cooler, R. starts C. Frantz's latest book, which is about federalism, and he is so pleased with it that he wants me to read aloud the first chapter in the evening. R. says C. Frantz bears some resemblance to himself in the way he constantly refashions his basic idea. Before that R. read to me the new ending for his article. In the evening he says it would be a good thing if we could marry off our girls well; certainly it would be a good thing, but one our star will have to take care of, for it is not in our power to do anything about it.

Tuesday, July 1 When I was in my bath, he called out, 'Let's have the curtains,' for he wanted to read something to me; I shut myself in like Beckmesser, and he comes in and reads to me Frantz's description of the attitude of the Jewish socialists towards the stock exchange, which they ignore entirely. Alarming evidence of yet another idea falsified. Some time ago R. pointed out how disastrous this law against the socialists was, he said that a prudent statesman would have seen the advantage to the nation of having representatives of socialism as members of the Reichstag, to learn from them or to reduce them ad absurdum.

Sunday, July 6 Our lighthearted breakfast conversation includes the emancipation of women, a question which is so well treated by C. Frantz. R. says the ladies are always thinking of Portia in *The Merchant of Venice*, but she got a lawyer to tell her what to do. 'What a scene that is!' R. exclaims. At lunch our good mayor; his visit concerns the announcement that it will not be possible to perform *Parsifal* next year, which R. has phrased very succinctly; the management committee is unwilling to sign it, for fear of acting contrary to the agreement and getting into difficulties on that account. R. very much put out, and he says angrily that the declaration must be made, even if he has to go off to America to give concerts. He cannot eat a thing, and leaves the table! The old trouble, always the same kind of cooperation – sufficient to cause obligations, insufficient to be helpful! R. is also unable to take his afternoon rest, he tries a walk, whist in the evening – all under a cloud.

Monday, July 7 In the afternoon I go to see Herr Gross with my letter to Herr Bürkel (in which I ask to have a new paragraph inserted in the contract), learn from him of the difficulties – that the King's end is felt to be nigh, and that Herr Feustel and Herr Gross have been assuring the sceptical bank in Coburg in particular that the contract would be observed without fail. I ask Herr Gross himself to edit the announcement, which everybody feels must be made. When I go to R. to report on the success of my mission, I find him stretched out on the *chaise longue* (the 'Muchanoff') in the *salon*, much upset. The weather, his own position, which in a certain sense remains unaltered, the enormous expenditures revealed by his current account – all this is indeed enough to depress him. Already at lunch he had been talking of emigrating to America. But he rouses himself to write a letter to the King in which he says that he wishes to produce *Parsifal* only when funds are such to ensure that performances can be given every three years, financed from the interest on the capital. After writing these seven pages he looks refreshed, but he explains that, out of joy at having completed them at all, he has drunk too much beer.

Tuesday, July 8 Herr Gross sends us his draft of the announcement, in a form the management committee is willing to sign; R. rejects it, since on no account does he want to commit himself to the year 1881. In the fear that he will now start tormenting himself with new drafts, I quickly write down a few lines[1]; these he accepts and improves, and thus this tiresome intermezzo is disposed of.

Friday, July 11 A restless night for R.; he caught cold yesterday; talked a lot about Naples – to console ourselves for the wild, blustery weather, which robs us of our pleasure in the roses. R. revises his announcement, and immediately afterwards the reply comes from Herr Bürkel, the secretary, granting my request. Satisfaction!

Sunday, July 13 In the evening R. talks admiringly about America and the American war, the only war whose aim was humane, and we jocularly discuss the founding of a new Bayreuth. He believes we are heading for a complete political breakdown, with social problems coming more and more to the fore, held back by wars. – An hour of whist.

Wednesday, July 16 R. works on his article[2], still hoping for the weather to turn fine at last, so that he can begin his cure. In the afternoon friend Levi, coming from Paris – he brings me news of my sister Claire and also has many tales to tell about the capital city *par excellence*. We do nothing else but chat, and in the evening the 'upright men'. Rub., Jäger, Wolzogen, are invited to join the conversation.

Thursday, July 17 The weather is fine; a cheerful meal with our friends Levi

---

[1] The gist of these is that persons who joined the society only in the expectation of festival performances in 1880 could withdraw and claim the return of their subscription.

[2] 'On Opera Poetry and Composition in Particular', *Bayreuther Blätter*, September 1879.

and Cyriax, who has just arrived from London. The latter tells us of
Richter's 'triumphs' as a conductor in London. Herr Cyriax has brought me
a picture of the house in which R. stayed in Boulogne[1]! In the evening the
'upright men' with wives; we make music, Beethoven's *Battle of Vittoria* and
King Stephen, of which the first is R.'s particular favourite, on account of its
popular tone. Then he tells us how he remembers having seen Weber
playing with his son on the balcony of his house as the miners were passing
by, and on the market place there was a man standing before a placard and
singing, 'A new murder story to tell you, my readers.' Years later R. hears
a Weber bassoon concerto being played in the Gewandhaus and recognizes
this same melody he had heard sung so roughly on the market place, now
appearing as a delicate theme on the oboe! 'What does that signify?' R. then
asks, referring to the tremendous popular flavour of Beethoven's themes.

Wednesday, July 23 Towards evening R. tells me I am in for a surprise, but
he will not say what; then I hear him working on *Parsifal.* 'Familiar sounds,'
I say. He: 'And some unfamiliar ones –' (entry into the Temple, third act).
In the evening a very lively game of whist with the children – how children,
with the obligation they impose on one, always help merriness to triumph!
R. says of Lusch, 'She is the cleverest person we know here.'

Thursday, July 24 At breakfast we talk about state aid for our cause. Herr
Schön wants to approach the Federal Council; R. would claim an allowance
of three million marks. In the evening, as we take leave of each other with
an embrace, he says, 'If our union leads to nothing, then I'm at a loss.' We
enlarge upon this theme, and I am constrained to tell him my belief: that
the Will felt the need to manifest itself in the festival theatre, and thus it
came about; what people would then do with it was their affair.

Sunday, July 27 R. has been to Angermann's with Siegfried and laughed
heartily to see Fidi being served in a glass of his own, marked 'Herr
Siegfried Wagner'. In the evening whist.

Monday, July 28 Letters from poor Herr Tappert, wasting away in Berlin –
how to help him? It is unutterably sad, looking at the outside world! R. has
the satisfaction of securing an engagement for Herr Zumpe, the oldest
member of the Nibelungen Kanzlei, in Frankfurt a/M.

Tuesday, July 29 R. slept well and finishes his article. In the evening friend
Feustel; much politics, he entirely for Bismarck, whereupon R. with
splendid vivacity points out to him in what way B. is unequal to the task
Fate has imposed on him.

Thursday, July 31 R. has received a letter from a woman in Wiesbaden who
sends him a book about vivisection and in well-turned phrases asks him to
join in taking steps against such cruelty; she believes that its rapid growth
is due to the great number of Jewish doctors. R. deeply moved and incensed

---

[1] During his visit to Meyerbeer in 1839, a wine merchant's villa.

by it; he says if he were a younger man he would not rest until he had brought about a demonstration against such barbarism. He says religion should be linked with compassion for animals; human beings' treatment of one another is already bad enough, for they are so vindictive they put up a resistance to one another, and the noble teachings of Christianity are scarcely applicable. One should begin with quiet and patient creatures, and people who felt compassion for animals would certainly not be harsh towards human beings. 'We must preach a new religion, you and I.'

Tuesday, August 5 Our morning conversation is devoted to England, R. says he would like to read a witty writer's precise description of that curious country, of which Carlyle had given him some glimpses.

Thursday, August 7 Around lunchtime I find R. engaged on a once familiar task – he is ruling a score! He has 'pinched' my copy of the Prelude, since I would not give it up; he also knows what alterations he made in it. He says he is now going to write the score and keep it in a safe until the world becomes worthy of a performance. – In the evening the mail brings us an appeal to women to demonstrate against vivisection, announcing a meeting of the animal-protection society in Gotha; R. resolves first to go, then to get someone to represent him there and to write an article.

Saturday, August 9 R. had a talk with Dr. Landgraf about vivisection; the latter denies that the animals feel any pain, saying that if they did, one would be unable to make any observations on them. R. is sent a protest against the Jews from Dresden.

Monday, August 11 I am suddenly summoned, and the doctor tells me that Eva, since yesterday slightly unwell, has scarlet fever. Many precautions to be taken, the other children to leave the house, R. goes with them to the Fantaisie and then, since there is no room there, to the Sonne, where they also sleep. Our sick child very quiet and resigned. In the evening R. and I alone in the *salon*, curious feelings. I am particularly concerned by R.'s complaining to the doctor of pains in his chest. Maybe his first shock about Eva did him harm?

Tuesday, August 12 Eva had a restless night, but the doctor is not worried; breakfast with R. in the children's *salon*; the children will be put up at the Riedelsberg through friend Feustel's kindness. In this matter one can see both the difference and the harmony between R.'s character and mine; the Riedelsberg occurred to me because I found it hard to think of the children in a hotel (the Fantaisie), but I should never have requested it; R. wrote at once and arranged it all. While I stay at home with the little invalid, he visits the children and the Feustels at the Riedelsberg and returns home very contented.

Thursday, August 14 We continue to share the children between us, he the healthy ones, I the sick one. He writes to Herr v. Weber[1], sends 100 marks

---

[1] Ernst von Weber (b.1830), founder of an international society against vivisection; Wagner's letter to him was later enlarged into an article in the *B.B.* of October 1879 ('Open Letter to Herr Ernst von Weber').

for the society, and expresses his idea of reviving religion through the love of animals, the love of human beings, particularly with regard to vivisectors, being by comparison somewhat difficult.

Friday, August 15 Eva's condition causing no anxiety. We talk a lot about her, she always has a charming smile but at the same time is very deep and serious and full of wit; she is like R. – I am pleased to find in her eyes the depth and sharpness of R.'s eyes, in Loldi's gaze their ecstasy, and in Fidi's their humour.

Saturday, August 16 In the evening the two of us cosily alone together; R. says, 'I shall always keep a child with scarlet fever on hand, so people will stay away from our house.' It is only the children he wants – he misses Loldi and Fidi in the poultry yard.

Sunday, August 17 R. slept well, but he is tired and complains of tightness in his chest and an inflamed throat; the doctor, whom I question about this, feels it is not good for R. to take such long walks as the one he took yesterday; he talks of overtiring the heart. – Eva's condition good, weather still fine; R. has a bridge put up, so that the children have a direct route to us from the Riedelsberg.

Tuesday, August 19 In the evening, when we are alone in the *salon*, we talk about the King. R. says that this one year which turned him away from utter devotion into vagaries of taste and a complete denial of our cause is incomprehensible; I try to explain it by saying that the King is no normal being: 'The Will wished to help you, and knew no other way of doing it in the present circumstances; an anomaly, such as you are, can be helped only by another anomaly, an additional cause of suffering for you.'

Wednesday, August 20 R. today finishes his letter to the King and tells me that in it he has also touched on the subject of vivisection. Coffee in the garden, a fine day, we walk through the meadows to the Riedelsberg, across the bridge R. had erected. Always creative in the small as well as the large things; and it is a constant source of amazement to me how, in the unsettled conditions of his life, he has always had this urge to found, to build, to achieve permanence! There is a curious connection between the vitality of his inner contemplation and the acuteness of his vision, which allows nothing in the outward appearance to escape him, whereas he soon becomes blind to external circumstances in general.

Thursday-Sunday, August 21–31 My father's visit – R. and he splendid together; R. remarkably patient, even when listening to music which gives him no pleasure. Much talk about vivisection, much whist in the evening, a great deal of joking by R. about the 'old priest' he wants made into a cardinal. – On the 23rd R. starts on the orchestration, but soon breaks off. ... He is greatly stimulated by his reading of Haug's *Old Testament*,[1] and he

---

[1] Transcription by H. Haug 'to make the O.T. understandable for the first time to all lovers of truth,' published 1872.

tells me his ideas on our religion, which he intends to put down in writing again. Pleasure in Eva's patience. On the 25th we go to visit the children at the Riedelsberg with my father. – On Sunday, August 31, at 1.10, my father departs with Lusch; they are spending a day in Munich, from there he goes on to Rome, she to our friends the Bassenheims. Rainy day. We walk from the station to the Riedelsberg with the three children and bring their stay there to an end.

Tuesday, September 2 At lunch R. tells me that he has gone back to work on his score. – Very nice letter from Lusch about the busy world, also a very cheerful one from Judith, and we in our love-enchanted haven of peace! . . .

Wednesday, September 3 R. complains of his left eye, which is watering, and his left ear, which is dull of hearing. He resolves to make no more complaints, but I thank him for doing so, for otherwise I should die of worry.

Saturday, September 6 We have been rewarded with lovely autumn days. Our conversation leads us from the military character in general to Cromwell, the Lord Protector. This naïve title, which R. also chose for his Lohengrin, leads R. to reflect on the character of this 'gigantic' human being, his enormous understanding, his relatively less developed powers of reasoning, a man in whom everything taken to be hypocrisy and dissimulation was in fact naïveté; he could not express himself in any other way. R. also talks about Charles II, who with his black wig was particularly repulsive to him. R. does some orchestration.

Sunday, September 7 Eva's reawakening! – She returns to us after an absence of four weeks! . . . R. not satisfied with the enthusiasm of the other children – they seem to him too casual about their reunion. But he was pleased in the morning to be able to take his bath with Fidi, who told him of a dream in which, while swimming, he rescued several people from the water!

Monday, September 8 R. orchestrates. In the evening we are alone, R. and I, which is a great blessing; R. working in his head, and he at last finds the alteration in the Prelude which he has long been looking for! He plays it to me.

Tuesday, September 9 In the afternoon R. finds the ending to *Parsifal* and plays it to me as he has now finally written it. He says he went through the whole thing some 30 or 40 times in his head before giving it its present form.

Saturday, September 13 At lunch we come to the subject of the letter the Crown Princess sent to Herr v. W[eber], in which she ranges herself fairly clearly on the side of the vivisectionists. When I say to R. that this is a shame, for she has the reputation of being a good and sincere woman, R. replies, 'It is easy to be sincere when one is vindictive and possesses power.' He says he will never forget her 'Oh, no, Fritz' when the Crown Prince was about to take up some certificates of patronage. – Nice weather, R. reads the pamphlets which Herr v. W. brought with him[1]; I beg him not to do so, to participate as much as he can but not to concern himself with the horrors in detail, for then he would find it impossible to work. Herr v. W. has supper with us, shows us some diamonds which he dug up, also petrified animals in amber. The children greatly interested in these. In the morning R. worked on his score, with some vexation over frequently writing things down incorrectly.

Friday, September 19 In the past few days I have been occupying myself with last wishes, a very painful task for me, since my will and fortune consist in having no will of my own. But for the sake of the children let it be done, in R.'s name! My head feels exhausted, weary; old sufferings, old wounds keep breaking open again, and in one's feelings of sorrow one sees the unreality of time; all that one gains from it is a stillness in the suffering, which, as if drugged, ceases to speak, no longer stirs – but it is still there in all its strength, seemingly immortal! 'Calm my thoughts, give light to my needy heart' – in the morning, with this prayer in my head, I stroll with the children to the woods via the Bruckmühle, great peace and pleasure in everything; a glance at the theatre, silent greeting; forget-me-nots on the banks of the Main; a blue, unknown bird – 'king's fisher' in English[2], the '*roi pêcheur*' – arouses wonderful thoughts. Driving home, I realize that death can be a release to us only when we pass into it as from slumber to sleep; when there is peace inside us, when we have achieved ecstasy in suffering, serenity in renunciation. Mere ending does not by itself bring us rest. Not just forgetting, either – a vain endeavour, anyway – but recalling in love what is destroying us. – Why do we find help above all in Nature, in which desire and the will to live are expressed so strongly – why does it bring us peace more readily than all the poets?

Monday, September 22 Herr Schön arrives; a pleasant man who also tells us very pleasant things about his relations with the workers in his factory. R. welcomes him very cordially, and he then goes off with friend Wolzogen to discuss the public campaign.

Tuesday, September 23 In the afternoon I drive with friends Schön and Wolzogen to the theatre. R. comes to join us, delight in the building, in Faf[3], who guards it. Had some beer at the new railway station, which pleases R. very much; impressive entry to the town, due to the view of the theatre[4]. In the evening Herr Schön works out almost all the details regarding a public campaign, a petition to the Reichstag! R. is glad that this

[1] He had arrived on a visit the previous day.
[2] Written thus in English by Cosima.
[3] A Newfoundland dog.
[4] At that time the festival theatre could be seen from the station; the buildings now obscuring it came later.

excellent man is still young. And yesterday, when he was speaking of his workers, R. recommended to him Carlyle's essay on conditions in England. During the evening R. played to us the Prelude to *Parsifal*, which he calls a preamble, like the preamble to a sermon, since the themes are merely laid out side by side.

Wednesday, September 24 I say goodbye to Herr Schön and believe I have discovered in him a friend for Siegfried.

Thursday, September 25 A very good translation of *Parsifal* (so it seems to us) sent by Herr Schott[1]. – In the evening R. occupies himself by drawing lines for his score.

Monday, September 29 Herr Jäger comes, bringing news of Vienna; R. finds his visit, like all visits, disturbing, and I laughingly tell him that he took refuge in his silence, which is so stony that one feels one can never break through it. At times, incidentally, I feel his loquacity to be a complete shutting off of himself, a way of keeping everything at bay which might get inside his defences; very few people understand those turbulent waves of wit, through which I see to the mysterious and fertile depths. – In the evening whist, R., Boni and I. – Recently R. talked about the ruling of his score, which is now keeping him occupied during the afternoon and in which the various instruments are so precisely indicated that, as he maintains, another person could write the score by following it!

Wednesday, October 1 Discussion about the visit of Herr v. Stein[2]; will we really be granted the boon of educating our son according to our own ideas, bringing him to Communion as a devout Christian, in a non-Jewish way? R. says, 'We must wait for a miracle.' When I say that it is too much for me to be able to believe, he advises me not to think of it at all. – Visit from the doctor, he advises against a bath in the evening, which I had recommended to R., recommending camomile tea instead! Whist.

Thursday, October 2 Unfortunately the camomile tea does not work, and though R. calls it *'calmatif'*, I am too sad to laugh from the bottom of my heart. I believe that his preoccupation with vivisection is much to blame for R.'s depression, and there is nothing coming to him from outside to refresh him; he says it is only when I go out that he hears enlivening news; I tell him what I hear in the shops about life in the town, all sorts of funny stories which amuse him.

Friday, October 3 In the evening we play whist with Loldi for the first time, and at eleven o'clock we all go by omnibus to the station to fetch Lusch. The moonlight on the silent streets, the rattling omnibus, which forces us to keep silent, the unaccustomed journey, it is an absurd dream. Alarm caused by a man who suddenly appears at the door, then swings himself

---

[1] By Frederick and Henrietta Louisa Corder, published by Schott in 1879.
[2] Heinrich von Stein (b.1857), from Coburg, was recommended as a tutor for Siegfried by Malwida von Meysenbug; he had just completed his philosophical studies at Halle University.

onto the carriage – all this puts us into the gayest of spirits, and we meet our child amid laughter and bear her home, where we drink champagne in welcome.

Saturday, October 4 At seven o'clock the very fine fireworks display, celebrating Eva's recovery and Lulu's return home.

Tuesday, October 7 R. writes a new page in his article about animals; we talk a lot about the question with which he is wholly occupied. He says man's variety of motives makes him, if he is not fully mature, little superior to an animal in terms of truthfulness and simplicity. The artist is also assailed by too many motives, and the only genuine artist is the one who is able to take them to form a whole. Much about the regard in which ancient civilizations held animals; he says the difficulty of his task lies in not going too far, not putting in too much, for there is no end to the material.

Wednesday, October 8 Some newspaper reports about the scorn with which doctors are treating our movement upset him greatly, and he says he could bring himself to devote all his energies to it and become a socialist in addition.

Thursday, October 9 The evening ended in melancholy mood, I believe vivisection is proving the most dismal of occupations! – All the same, once he has at last managed to get to sleep, R. sleeps well, and he goes off to his work, which today is devoted to additions to his article and, at last, its dispatch.

Friday, October 10 I arrange some little things to celebrate the 10th[1]. R. comes in, and all is spoiled. However, the cup with the façade of the old [Dresden] theatre makes up for everything, and when R. laments my little misfortune, I really feel what a triumph it is that the delights of love have managed to overcome the vexations of chance! R. praises me for still taking such great care to preserve the joys of life – ah, it is my soul's gratitude which finds expression thus. Many memories of that time 26 years ago – also of Weber and L. Geyer on account of the cup. After lunch I return to bed, where these last pages are written. In the evening R. reads *Twelfth Night* to us, to the delight of all. I always live again through these hours as they will appear in the future memories of our children, seen now so blissful before me.

Monday, October 13 In the evening the conclusion of *Twelfth Night* and a story about Minna and her family to the children. Their sympathy; R. says he really does not know how he stood it all: 'It could not have continued, either.' – Of the house in which he was born he says, 'The white lion turned red with rage, and the red one white with alarm.'[2] – He continues ruling his score in the afternoon and says he could now dictate the orchestration, so clear is it in his mind.

[1] Their first meeting, on 10 October 1853 in Paris.
[2] In Leipzig, named '*Roth und Weisse Löwe*' ('Red and White Lion').

Tuesday, October 14 Over coffee we discuss *Twelfth Night*, And R. remarks how right Carlyle was to observe that the English might lose their colonies, but they would still have their Shakespeare. R. regrets that Sh. did not devote more words at the end to the transference of the Duke's love from Olivia to Viola; the comedy has a permanent flaw, he feels, and the happy end seems somewhat contrived. – We then talk about the children's education, and he observes that he himself was never really educated at all – how often did he lie to his mother, and he went around with the wildest and roughest of boys.

Wednesday, October 15 Herr Levi for lunch, and towards evening the first act of *Siegfried* with Herr Jäger! Great delight – indeed, enchantment! R. is also pleased.

Thursday, October 16 At twelve o'clock the second act of *Siegfried*; when R. sings the words accompanying the burial of Fafner, the figure of Siegfried seems to become daemonic, overwhelmingly huge – superhuman! And when he sings of the doe and the human mother, I feel – through the music, as it were – that the connection between human beings and animals, with the human beings' superiority over them, is being movingly proclaimed. – At five o'clock the third act – and this is too much for us poor mortals! R. is worn out, our good conductor completely ill, Herr Jäger somewhat exhausted; so we have a family whist party, the two daughters, R. and I.

Sunday, October 19 Presentation of the picture[1] in memory and celebration of the 19th twenty-three years ago, when I heard the *Tannhäuser* Overture and R.'s music for the first time. R. is pleased with it! – He says the curious thing about Lenbach is that at first sight his pictures strike one like an idea; afterwards one might find this or that not very good, but the overall impression is always a convincing one. R. drapes and hangs the picture himself, and frequently during the day he shows it to me. In the evening the first act of *Coriolanus* for the young people, and whist.

Monday, October 20 The event of the day is the arrival of Herr von Stein, a young, fair-haired, fine-looking man, a true German, very serious, but at the same time friendly. He is indeed willing to undertake Siegfried's education! We still cannot quite believe it; and in the evening friend Wolzogen as well – 'a black one and a white one!'[2]. The only thing that alarms us is the discovery that our new friend is a supporter of Dühring![3] Also an opponent of Christianity – but it all emerges from him in an unaffected and indeed noble manner.

Tuesday, October 21 R. slept well, and with astonishment and amusement

---

[1] A pastel drawing of Cosima by Lenbach, 1879.
[2] Wolzogen's hair was dark, Stein's fair.
[3] Karl Eugen Dühring (b.1833), philosopher, favoured a realistic outlook and opposed religions assuming a life after death.

we discuss the new element in our household; we owe it to Malwida, and when in great satisfaction I tell R. of my walk to the theatre with our new friend, he at once sends her a telegram: 'Devil take me, Münchhausen, you did that well – voice from the clouds.' – But a little booklet of materialistic poems written by our young friend alarms us a little. R. tells him frankly all his ideas about universities, etc. The young mind is assailed from many sides, but holding its own staunchly and well. In the evening the second act of *Coriolanus*; for R. and me the object of unceasing, ever-recurring expressions of astonishment and admiration.

Wednesday, October 22 Much to-ing and fro-ing with Herr v. Weber about the open letter, which is to be published in the *B. Blätter* as well as in separate copies. The Conservative party appears to be supporting the antivivisection movement. First lesson today for Fidi; the elements of geometry, and planing with a cabinet-maker. R. and I feel as if we are dreaming, [Goethe's *Wilhelm Meister's] Apprentice Years and Travels* now being translated into reality here – God grant that the noble spirit of our young teacher and friend will now gradually begin to feel at home with us and abandon all this modern rubbish! He is touchingly zealous in his approach to his task. – 'There is a real devil in you,' R. tells him with a laugh, encouraging him to be merry.

Thursday, October 23 Delight in Herr v. St.; discussion about the problems of socialism, our young friend hopes to see them solved in an amicable way, R. on the other hand feels there are bound to be convulsions. In the evening the last two acts of *Coriolanus*.

Friday, October 24 At lunch we talk about *Coriolanus*, and R. says only the fifth act does not much appeal to him – indeed, all the fifth acts, including that of *Hamlet*, he says the tragic catastrophe has already taken place, and death adds nothing. Discussion with Herr v. St. about Siegfried; in response to R.'s ideas on surgery, he says he would consider it right to have models of the human form, including the internal organs, in the schoolroom we are going to build. R. thinks: Later; first of all, allow him to take pleasure in the outward appearance, the naked body as depicted by the Greeks, which will enchant him, and *only when the daemon begins to stir within him* show him the inner workings. At this stage he would perhaps feel revolted. He then talks of Fidi's willing nature: he is lighthearted but not unthinking, 'the youngster enjoys life.'

Saturday, October 25 A fine October day tempts us to take a walk to the Eremitage, the children, Herr von Stein and I; R. joins us later in the summer carriage, a merry stroll through the park. A visit to the inn, then the drive home, nine people and so many rugs that we have to laugh out loud. At home our guest gets news of the sudden death of Dr. Dühring, his guiding star till now; this seems to us both cruel and significant. – R. says, 'Life is so unseemly,' and indeed, it does do things very drastically.

Sunday, October 26 Letter from Prof. Overbeck about the wretched state of our poor friend Nietzsche's health – and not to be *permitted* to do anything, let alone to be able to!

Tuesday, October 28 We talked about the *B. Blätter*, and I told R. what I had said to friend W. – that with every article a new category is introduced, and it is subsequently expanded by one or several other writers: with Semper's obituary it was sculpture, with Dr. Dühring (Herr v. St. wants to write this), education. R. feels I am right, and we agree that the important thing is not adding to our community, but strengthening its outlook in all directions, by always keeping our artistic ideals in the forefront and observing everything from that point of view.

Wednesday, October 29 R. tells me that now, when he lights his *Lubin*, he finds himself thinking a lot about my mother, since I told him that she too used to fumigate her apartment with it; he talks of her relationship with my father and says he can understand why she was unable to tolerate his unfaithfulness. Much about this dismal relationship between two significant people, then jokingly to us: 'You will also leave me!' Gay memories of that daemonic night in January nearly two years ago; the sudden flaring of the flame which told me, as I sought him in concern about his rest, that paper had been burned here, his return to the *salon* after it had been put out, his surprise over my question whether something had been burning – how pleasant that one can speak gaily of dreadful memories![1]

Sunday, November 2 Put on my white dress for the first time since May 22. R. is pleased. We have sent our friend Stein to Munich to see the *Ring*, we play whist with the two girls.

Tuesday, November 4 Alarming rumours regarding Frau Feustel's health induce us to address an inquiry to Dr. Landgraf; he sends us a short bulletin, so careful and precise that R. breaks out in praise of our good doctor, who has now, he says, replaced the parson. – Hans has resigned his conducting position in Hanover following a dispute with the tenor Herr [Anton] Schott! – So once again homeless! . . .

Wednesday, November 5 R. feels very run down, could do no work either, he stretches out in bed. I stay downstairs, awaiting friend Gersdorff, and Richter comes in, with beaming face and spirits, the old Tribschen youth again. The children overjoyed, R. calls him up to his bedside and then has supper with us on his account, much about the present agitation against the Jews. After an hour R. goes off. (Friend Gersdorff has also arrived, to tell me of many things he has on his mind; R. says to me jokingly that I am Macaria, the All Souls' woman – everyone comes to me.)

Thursday, November 6 R. had a restless night, but he comes down to say

[1] Possibly a reference to Cosima's discovery of Wagner's secret correspondence with Judith Gautier, though her cryptic reference to that in the Diaries was not in January, but on February 12, 1878.

goodbye to Richter. Lunch with friend Gersdorff, during which R. remarks that he has regained his appetite and does not know why! Great concern about Frau Feustel, seriously ill with typhus.

Friday, November 7 R. had a good night, the heavens are bright, his mood also, and he works on his article, which Lusch is copying. A constant stream of jokes with friend Gersdorff, whose amorous affairs enliven our lunch table, and the news that Dr. Dühring is not dead increases our gaiety still further. Herr v. Bürkel writes that the King was very willing to allow Herr v. Stein admittance to the special performances, which, it seems, have turned out very well.

Monday, November 10 R. had a good night, but when he wakes up, his nose is very red and swollen – we fear erysipelas! – He works on his article. His cold is getting worse; he does indeed joke about it, saying his nose is swelling up like a hippopotamus's, but both he and I are worried. The doctor prescribes inhalations of marshmallow tea – these clear his brain a little.

Tuesday, November 11 My mind is taken up almost entirely with the death of Frau Feustel – our best, indeed our only female friend here. When R. asks me about her during the afternoon, I had to tell him of a turn for the worse; he wanted to visit her, and when I tell him that she is unconscious, he replies, 'I shall soon restore her to consciousness.' Now she is dead, and with her the soul of our identification with Bayreuth has gone, as well as a truly good and brave being.

Wednesday, November 12 R. feels severe pains in his brain. Dr. Landgraf comes, and precautions are taken that the steam, passing through a funnel, does not rise too violently into R.'s face; the preparation of the paper cone amuses him, and he says to the doctor, 'We shall have to send this to the next World Exposition.'

Friday, November 14 Siegfried's run-down appearance gives us cause for reflection regarding his present studies.

Saturday, November 15 Siegfried's indisposition causes us to send for the doctor, and when he looks through the exercise book (geometry), he too has his doubts, though he does admit that mathematics is a very necessary subject nowadays, even in medicine, with optics, for example, being applied mathematics. 'Applied mathematics and denied experience,' says R. Before we go to lunch R. shows me the orchestral sketch of *Parsifal* and his ruled score; in the former all the instruments have been written in. These preparations provide his final pleasure in his work, he says, for once it is written down, pleasure vanishes – all that is left is piano arrangement, publication and – worst of all, performance!

Sunday, November 16 R. is somewhat better, though he is still not allowed out of doors. However, he is having good nights, and today he continues ruling according to his method. – *Don Quixote* in the evening, somewhat trying since much of it is not designed for being read aloud to women. However, R. with divine calm continues equably to read, and we put a brave face on it.

Monday, November 17 R. talks again about America, saying that he might still perhaps go there in order to make his fortune, but then he would not come back. He believes that if he had settled there permanently with his family, the Americans would probably have stood by him, but not now, when all he does is demand contributions for this place.

Tuesday, November 18 R. had a good night's rest, which is indeed a miracle, to be gratefully accepted, considering that he is still not allowed out of doors. – Arrival of Herr Schön's appeal! We approve it with a sigh. 'A great honour for me if it does not succeed,' R. exclaims, 'and torture if it is successful, for it will be based on a misunderstanding.'

Monday, November 24 In the evening a letter from Herr Levi, nothing will come of *Tannhäuser* in Munich unless R. writes to Baron Perfall; swift decision: then let it rest. – R., who felt yesterday that I showed too much concern over an indisposition of Herr v. Stein's, tells me that I do not know what men are like; he himself has a low opinion of them all.

Tuesday, November 25 R. goes out for a while and in the afternoon writes to friend Levi, refusing his suggestion and consoling him. Levi has also written to me, asking me to use my influence on R. Reminded that he had once before extended a hand to Baron Perfall, R. says: 'I would not think of it. That time when I was forced by the deficit to visit the man, he was so stiff with me – so now they can do what they like. The least little thing one tries to do only causes unpleasantness.'

Thursday, November 27 At lunch R. told me he was curious whether I should manage in Naples to get him back to the biography; it would get shorter and shorter, he said, for it was only youthful memories one felt the urge to re-create for oneself. With Munich, for example, he would deal very briefly; he could not tell the whole truth, one never knew what would come out of such things, Fidi could buy puff pastry with it. He said he would work on the affinities between religion and art: 'They do exist, as long as the religion is not synthetic.'

Friday, November 28 R. growls in my room, while I am taking my lessons, 'What's this? These eternal celebrations!' He has found the *Rheingold* buttons[1] and is now teasing me in his own peculiar way, only to go around all day with rolled-up sleeves and shower me extravagantly with thanks for the pleasure I gave myself! – Over coffee he says that in Cologne Hans had not wanted to continue playing, since he caught sight of the 'musical Jew' sitting in the front row; our good Lesimple then hit on the idea of turning the piano around, so that Hans could no longer see Herr Hiller. 'Good,

---

[1] Cosima had had them made from melted-down Rhine coins.

now I can play again,' he said when he came on again. – R. often comes up to see me, showing off his buttons!

Thursday, December 4 Departure of friend Gersdorff. Very cold day, packing; letter from Dr. Schrön[1] asking whether we shall want stoves – so it is cold there too!

Friday, December 5 R. wakes up in great concern, his nose is again swollen; he uses the steam bath, it continues to swell, and it soon becomes evident that it is erysipelas!... The cold compresses do him good, he sleeps a lot, around midday he takes some soup and roasted meat, and sends word to me that he enjoyed it; in the afternoon he is cheerful, says he is putting up with the compresses in order to please the doctor. When I tell him that our lunch was gloomy, he says, 'The funny man was missing; you are the poet and the director, but I am the jester.' – Severe snowstorm. This illness of R.'s fills me with gloomy thoughts; it is becoming increasingly clear to me that he cannot stand excitement of any kind, and I feel that his preoccupation with Siegfried and the consequent discussions with Herr v. Stein in this connection were too much for him. I talk about this to our young friend.

Sunday, December 7 R. had a good and tranquil night. His temperature has gone down, but he still has what seem like mild hallucinations, and the inflammation is spreading. But fortunately his appetite is good, and his divine sense of humour is not deserting him.

Tuesday, December 9 The erysipelas seems to be subsiding, though it has now spread to one ear, which is very painful. A little reading and talking, interspersed with sleep. – Interrupted my diary from the 9th to the 20th – I shall now attempt to catch up.

Thursday, December 11 His eyes have now become inflamed! All the children in bed, one after another!

Friday, December 12 The inflammation has got worse, he thinks because of the ice packs which have been prescribed for him, and he becomes very impatient. On top of this, various domestic troubles, the pipes freezing, the bath overflowing, the bells out of order.

Sunday, December 14 In the evening a dose of chloral, which at the beginning of the night from Sunday to Monday gives him the most absurdly horrible dreams – his sister Klara sitting on his neck to make him sink in the water, Frau Wesendonck trying to poison him!... But in the morning he feels better and is able to 'circulate' for the first time; over coffee in my grey room, where he and I had lunch, he receives our whole troop of children, all of them back on their feet! Much gaiety and sunshine, all of us together again in the little room! Also in the evening for tea.

Monday, December 15 Towards eleven o'clock departure of Herr von Stein, who is going home for Christmas, R.'s splendid words to him. –

[1] Otto von Schrön, director of the Pathological Institute in Naples, where Wagner had rented a villa.

Siegfried unwell, Eva too! The winter very cold, but sunny – unbearable, all the same.

Wednesday, December 17 Siegfried still feverish, Eva down with acute rheumatism. – R. is still confined to the upstairs rooms; our imprisonment and above all the illness of the children make us both feel a little melancholy (Eva sobs violently when she sees her father again; during the night she saw us both lying dead!).

Thursday, December 18 R. once more down in the *salon*, feels like Mary Stuart in Fotheringhay, plays some things on the piano, and says: 'What can compare with a melody? What would the world be without these sorrowing, pure, uplifting sounds?' Siegfried gets up too, and at least Eva is no worse. Discussion with friend Gross about our funds, which are not flourishing at the moment.

Saturday, December 20 R. would have liked to write his words for the New Year, but he is still feeling 'stupid' and run down. He spends much time with Beethoven's sonatas; in the evening he plays the first movement of the A Major (Op. 101) and says it is a consummate whole, a spring day, it is the model according to which he writes his *idylls*. This first movement is quite incredible, he says, everything in it is gripping, every link in the chain, it is all melos. – A merry game of whist ends a day which was particularly welcome since Eva had no temperature; in his joy R. gave her a thaler.

Sunday, December 21 First walk, blue spectacles, blue veil, in the palace gardens; R. still vexed by the winter. At lunch his expression is completely changed, the children completely silent, and he hands me Gedon's latter. [*Enclosed a letter from Gedon, giving his reasons for having let Wagner down in a Christmas arrangement.*] R. tells me he has been pursuing this matter since last June, and all his hopes were pinned on it; last year I had been celebrated in music, this year it was to have been the visual arts. My victory today is that, though this mishap is constantly mentioned, we manage in the end to treat it gaily – though with scornful laughter for visual art and its 'lying' ways! 'These people are all enthusiasm but no backbone, and it all gets squandered in beer and silly sensuality!' In the evening I dress myself as nicely as I can (Scheherazade) to celebrate my surprise, which I still have in spite of all the vexation, and our mood is bright and gay.

Tuesday, December 23 Fine weather, but we do not go out, since his nose is again hard and swollen – he puts on the sulphur amulet which old Frau v. Aufsess[1] sent him and writes her a little verse of thanks. – Visit from our friend Feustel, the first since his wife's death . . . 'He is a character,' R. says after he has gone, 'and can be regarded as a true man of the people.' 'Heavens alive, not to have our dear auntie with us any more!' R. says to him.

---

[1] Charlotte von Aufsess (b. 1804), widow of the founder of the Germanic Museum in Nuremberg.

Wednesday, December 24 Presentation of gifts at seven o'clock, Eva there, but very run down. After the gifts R. sits down at the piano and plays pieces from *Tristan* (second act) to me – ah, how wonderful! At our final parting in the evening, when I thank him, he says, 'When I went off to Venice that time, you should have said to me, "I am coming too!"'[1] I was like Tristan, didn't understand you, and – you would have left Hans more easily than I would have given him up. If I had had you with me in Venice, we could have got by with your little property, and nobody would ever have seen me again!' – To the strains of *Tristan* we go to our rest – however great my happiness, that melody is always sounding in my heart.

Thursday, December 25 When I enter my room, I find the splendid garnet-red velvet costume which R., as I discover, has spent months having prepared! As I am gazing at it in emotion, there stands R. beside the portière, scolding me for looking sad!... Dear scolding, cherished sulking! ...A banquet in the hall with our neighbours and the Jägers; R. toasts me just between ourselves, and silence accompanies our tears. Eva present, but very unwell.

Sunday, December 27 A day in bed, and in consequence nothing to report. I am plagued by a severe headache and remain thus in numbed weariness until

Sunday, December 28 towards midday, when we are once more all together, including two cripples! Yesterday evening R. read to me some passages from poor Nietzsche's new book[2], and E. Schuré's saying about '*nihilisme écoeurant*' ['nauseating nihilism'] came into his mind. 'To feel nothing but scorn for such a noble and compelling figure as Jesus Christ!' R. exclaims indignantly. He continues with it today and reads several more things (about *Faust*, for instance) which are horrifying. In the evening R. reads us his article for the New Year, so serene in its melancholy, providing consolation in a way only genius can. – Then he finds a volume of Chopin's preludes on the piano; having played the fourth (in E Minor) he remarks disapprovingly that an ambiguous chord has been interpolated at the end, as if to create a shock. I seek to excuse it by saying that this sketch is an attempt to reproduce something like a strange natural sound, but only long afterwards, when he is lying in bed, does he say, 'A natural sound – that is very good, but it is precisely these which one must try to reconcile with our laws of harmony.'

Monday, December 29 R. slept well, and now we set about locking things up and packing! Travelling the day after tomorrow in a saloon carriage on account of the invalids. – Last lunch with friends Wolz., Rub., Gross; R. indulgent towards Rub., praises his article[3], says he has written a preface

[1] In August 1858, on the day before he left for Venice to write *Tristan*, Hans and Cosima visited him in Zurich.
[2] *The Wanderer and His Shadow*.
[3] 'Musical Style in Modern Germany', *B.B.*, March 1880; Wagner's New Year article, *B.B.*, Jan.-Feb. 1880.

for him in his words for the New Year. Through his kindness a new spirit is created here! Nothing but packing from the afternoon until Wednesday morning. But I find time on Tuesday to convey to friend Feustel the feelings which the memory of his wife arouses in me on our departure from Bayreuth.

Wednesday, December 31 At 1.10 p.m. departure in the saloon carriage. R. and the children in very high spirits; much to eat. The journey, however, gradually coming to seem rather long. In Munich at last. Remarkable New Year's Eve with friend Lenbach, Levi, Bürkel, greeted the New Year with punch in the Hotel Marienbad. For me a particular joy that when L., seeking to excuse his friend Gedon, is describing his character and the circumstances of his life, R. interrupts to tell him how splendidly he is speaking. Afterwards he tells me that no practised speaker could have framed and delivered his speech more beautifully than this man for whom words are not a natural medium. He embraces him with warm emotion, and I experienced the happiness of seeing a friend to whom I have for years been devoted being recognized by him in the way I myself see him.

1880

Thursday, January 1 For me and the children a performance of *Tannhäuser.* Very good in many respects, and for me overwhelmingly impressive; the first scene blissfully relaxing. I do not miss R., inasmuch as a few things would have vexed him greatly, and he was glad to avoid the ovation which would certainly have been given him here in the Munich theatre.

Friday, January 2 Friend Lenbach is kind enough to send us his Bismarck, a wonderful portrait. R. exclaims: 'Terrible! Such a strong will and such narrow-mindedness! For a man like this, you, my dear Herr Lenbach, and I are mere nothings; we can understand him – but he does not understand us.' The sinner Gedon is also received; today I was in his studio, experiencing once again how talent is ignored in Germany. It is disgraceful.

Saturday, January 3 Departure at nine o'clock. Trouble in the carriage, where the lighted stove gives off so much heat that we have to open all the windows, thereby letting in the severe cold; all the same

Sunday, January 4 a fine, sunny day. Whether it is the scenery or the fact that the greater part of the journey is now behind us, all of us are in good spirits anyway, and it seems no time at all before we are in Naples, where friend Gersdorff comes to meet us. First trouble, the trunks not there, second and greater, a whole floor spirited away and all kinds of sharp practice, but on

Monday, January 5 bright sunshine and an indescribable view[1] make up for it all. R. insists on having all the furniture moved around at once, and he supervises the rearrangements with great energy.

Wednesday, January 7 R. had a good night, but the erysipelas is spreading, and Eva has severe pain in her knee. Nothing to do but be patient! – R. is vexed with the ill luck that prevents him from enjoying this magnificent spot in all its glorious light. He explains the mysterious figure of Dr. Schr[ön] by saying that the Germans are such *donkeys* – in foreign lands they set store by pretending to elegance: 'They want to be like the others, but remain stuck in their shabby ways.'

Thursday, January 8 R. had a good night, and the erysipelas is disappearing; Eva is also somewhat better and much more lively. Sunshine in rain! In the

---

[1] The Villa d'Angri, a substantial house in a large garden on the slopes of the Posilipo just outside Naples, had a wide view of the bay.

afternoon I stroll for the first time in the garden, absorbed and oblivious, accompanied by the melody of the three graces in *Tannhäuser*, which R. described to me as 'sensuousness transformed into beauty'. – R. is reading a book (*Thalysia*) by a French vegetarian (Gleizès)[1], which has been sent to him – he likes it very much.

Saturday, January 10 R. feels unwell; though the erysipelas is clearing up, his stomach seems to be upset. I spend the whole day with him, the children go looking for shells on the beach and return home entranced with everything.

Monday, January 12 Arrival of our friend Herr von Stein, a happy reunion. – Prof. Schrön talks about the Camorra[2], with which he claims to be in touch.

Wednesday, January 14 Splendid weather, R.'s first outing as far as the palm tree (with me), which enchants him! Roses and carnations are in bloom, and Dr. Schrön, whom I had summoned, calms all my fears. In the afternoon R. walks to the pavilion and returns home enchanted, though the penetrating cry of a beggarwoman had pierced him with its piteousness: 'One can call it play acting, but it is terrible that such play acting is necessary – need has turned this woman's cry into her second nature.'

Thursday, January 15 Sirocco all day, rain and storms – it is really very sad that R. should be prevented from going out, when he is so much longing for it.

Friday, January 16 I order a carriage and we go for a drive at about 1.30, R. bursting into ecstatic exclamations: 'Naples is the city for me, the D—— take all ruins, here everything is alive! I know only two cities which reflect their countries, London and Naples – Paris belongs to the cosmopolitan rabble.' I fear the open carriage is too much for R. and notice his difficulty in climbing stairs, but he wants the carriage to be kept open and takes delight in everything; all of it interests him, the man adjusting his cap, the ugliest of people, all these tell him something, he says.

Saturday, January 17 In the afternoon R. takes the tram into the city for the first time and returns very content, except that an encounter with a German headmaster somewhat spoiled his mood; he remarks how improper it is for a person he does not know to address him just because he recognizes him; it would be much more proper for people who do not recognize him to speak to him simply as a fellow countryman. In the evening to see [Halévy's] *La Juive*, pleasure in the San Carlo, a genuine opera house, pleasure in the many beauties of the work, pleasure in the orchestra, outstanding, and in the two English-horn players, but dismay over the

---

[1] Jean Antoine Gleizès (1773–1843); *Thalysia*, first published in 1821, was translated into German in 1872.
[2] A secret society in southern Italy akin to the Mafia in Sicily.

singing and acting and the production; continual discrepancies between music and theatrical presentation, continual shouts from the prompter's box. R. remarks how this work, originating in the school of Méhul and Cherubini, is full of life and refinement and is not at all Jewish, even in its treatment of its subject – it is just correctly observed.

Sunday, January 18 R. comes to my bed and reports rain, which persists all day. He goes into the city by tram with our friend Stein and Siegfried, the former is causing us some concern. – R. is looking for a barber, and he tells us very funny things about his experiences. A merry late lunch, I talk about what I have read in the newspaper, among other things that England now seems to be going through a great crisis. R. expresses his annoyance with the Queen, the silly old frump, for not abdicating, for she thereby condemns the Prince of Wales to an absurd life; in earlier times, he says, sons became their mothers' guardians when they came of age. – In the evening we are visited by Herr v. Joukowsky[1], and conversation flows in a pleasant and lively way, causing R. to observe later, 'The Slavs are the people most closely related to us Germans.'

Wednesday, January 21 R. slept well and attributes his good nights to the climate here. It is now fine again, though very windy. A visit from the San Carlo theatre directors, to whom R., in his expressive French, outlines the damage caused by present-day opera, telling them how Rossini always demanded the best from his singers and how his strictness was feared in Vienna, whereas Meyerbeer ruined it all.

Thursday, January 22 We go for a walk together, R. and I, very, very slowly, up as far as the vineyards; everything delights him, the brooms of laurel leaves used for sweeping, a magnificent sheep, workers calling to one another ('Man as a bird,' says R.), the view, the air – his slow pace worries me! – Whist in the evening.

Friday, January 23 Herr Joukowsky introduces his servant to us, a Neapolitan folk singer, who delights us with his singing and his passion; among other things, R. admires his breath control, and the things he sings are unique in their wild tenderness, their ingratiating gaiety and their seductive sensuousness. But what feelings come over me when the singer tries to remember the Rhinemaidens' theme (he has seen the *Ring*)! R. plays it, and all the beauty of Nature rises before us; where before we had seen the lustful animal, now we have the innocent human being! . . . Pepino himself very remarkable, sturdy, thickset, simple and proud – a lovely experience!

Tuesday, January 27 R. has erysipelas and remains in bed in a state of

---

[1] Paul von Joukowsky (b.1845), painter, son of a Russian poet and a German mother; first met Cosima in Munich, then in Bayreuth during the 1876 festival; having a studio in Naples, he called on Cosima and was introduced to Wagner; he quickly became a friend to both.

lethargy, broken only by expressions of ill humour. His condition deteriorates in the evening to the extent that he can eat nothing.

Saturday, January 31 R. had a better night, and the rash is subsiding more and more, but he remarks sadly that, though it is going away, the catarrhal rheumatic troubles are returning with renewed force. I am made sadly aware of the depth of his depression through the way he chides me for wearing the dress he gave me at Christmas; he says it distorts my gait, which he loves. Though hurt, I say nothing, and soon see how far his thoughts have taken him. He whispers in my ear that he will tell me his plan, and he tells it to me in detail when we are alone, on

Sunday, February 1 after a tolerable night. He wants to move to America (Minnesota) and there, for a subscription of one million dollars, build a drama school and a house. He would dedicate *Parsifal* to them and stage it there, for he can no longer tolerate the situation here in Germany. It is years since I have seen him as he was yesterday. Today the eye inflammation is worse, and it is tormenting him. – Again and again he keeps coming back to America, says it is the only place on the whole map which he can gaze upon with any pleasure: 'What the Greeks were among the peoples of this earth, this continent is among its countries.' He works out his whole plan while we are sitting in the room darkened for the sake of his eyes.

Tuesday, February 3 R. slept well, and his eye is somewhat better; indeed, he goes out on the terrace and delights in all the beauty. Still many thoughts about America, he asks friend Stein to bring him a map of North America, proclaims his intention of writing to Dr. Jenkins, and says, 'Yes, they will outstrip us, and we professors will be left behind with our *polyphonic spectacles.*' – 'We are a sinking crew.'

Thursday, February 5 At one o'clock we drive with the children in two carriages to the Toledo for the flower throwing. During our drive there great pleasure in the city, the people, the sun and the sky: 'The only big city for me!' R. repeatedly exclaims in his delight. But on the homeward journey the traffic becomes congested, long waits, the throwing becomes violent, R. very annoyed, for those of us with him indescribable anxiety on his account. But the children in the carriage behind see only the fun, and when they tell us about it in the Villa d'Angri, our feverish mood soon resolves into merriment.

Sunday, February 8 R. had a somewhat restless night and is impatient with taking all this medicine. He wants to stay here for a year, then return to Bayreuth for a year to see whether there have been any developments; if not, move to America in his 70th year. 'Escape from these 15-mark contributions! But what horrifies me above all is having to live on bad performances of my works, even urging theatre directors to give them!'

Wednesday, February 11 Lusch goes to bed with a temperature.

Thursday, February 12 Typhoid fever, which is a worry and calls for careful nursing. Diary laid aside until Eva's birthday, on the 17th. Lusch still in bed, but all danger past. During these days R.'s main preoccupation has been Renan's book[1], from which it emerges that the church, even in the second century after its foundation, was already showing all the wretched characteristics of later times.

Tuesday, February 17 Eva's birthday, the 'Prize Song' played to her by R. at early breakfast. – With the children in the afternoon to Herr Joukowsky's studio, Pepino sings in honour of the birthday and delights us all once more. R. plays something from the *Ring* which he thinks Pepino may have remembered, then the bridal procession from *Lohengrin* – a lovely hour, wondering what will become of the passionate Pepino. Will he continue in this existence, out of love for his master, who rescued him from the gutter? ... When R. talked at length yesterday about the wickedness and mendacity of the present world, I asked him, for the sake of the children, to broach this topic less frequently; he says I am right, for how else can the poor creatures find the courage to go on living?

Thursday, February 19 Glorious weather. Lusch gets up for an hour. R. occupies himself with his biography and tells us he cannot believe that after such a terrible life he now has me and the children!

Friday, February 20 Lovely weather still, sunshine and blossom. In the afternoon Herr Joukowsky comes and starts work on my portrait, in the evening R. tells us some things from his 'delightful' Gleizès, and we conclude the evening with a game of whist.

Saturday, February 21 R. continues going through our biography. Friend Wolzogen sends us details concerning Hans's concert in Bayreuth!!² ... After the sitting for Herr J., R. says to him jokingly that his picture will be a 'Stabat *mater colorosa*', for the amiable painter wishes to paint me in the Marajah! ... R. goes to join the children on the sea front, and he improvises a boat ride around the Donna Anna, which gives him great pleasure.

Thursday, February 26 R. and I drive with Herr Joukowsky and Herr Stein to secondhand shops to look for old materials. We come to an Israelite dealer on the Strada di Constantinopoli, where we see very fine materials at a price we can afford. From there R. goes to the brewery, and I with Herr J. to even seedier dealers, who let down blankets in baskets from upper stories onto the square, a square which is indescribably Neapolitan and where I buy several rugs for R. I find it great fun when, on the larger square where the carriage has been obliged to wait, I meet Prince Our[oussoff][3], show him my booty, spreading it out amid an ever-growing crowd of onlookers, then go to fetch R. from the brewery and tell him all

---

[1] *L'Église chrétienne (The Christian Church)*, 1878.
[2] Bülow gave two piano recitals in Bayreuth at this time, part of his self-imposed effort to raise 40,000 marks for Wagner's cause.
[3] A Russian provincial governor.

about it. One of the joys of the experience, imparting it to him. Splendid journey home, and in the evening such curious moonlight and cloud formations that one has the feeling of being part of the ether itself; layers of cloud cover all the mountains, the countryside has suddenly become a completely different one, the sea is like a blue sky, and we, on our balcony, seem to be hovering in the clouds. I invoke all the blessings of Creation on the cherished head my hand is touching.

Friday, February 27 After lunch, since his quotations from Gleizès have led us to India, R. relates to us the story underlying his *Sieger*, wonderful and moving. He says he will write it in his ripe old age, it will be gentler than *Parsifal*, where everything is abrupt, the Saviour on the cross, blood everywhere.

Saturday, February 28 First drive out with Lusch, on the Posilipo, always a delight. – When I tell R. that I find it hard to reconcile Schopenhauer's philosophy with the idea that human beings are made better or worse by what they eat, R. says, 'One does not have to assume for a fact that Nature made men evil, but as we see them, they are evil, and this is due to their habit of eating meat.' – In the evening *H[enry] IV.*

Saturday, March 6 We breakfast together cheerfully, and he then settles down to read Gleizès. R. feels that, with his aversion to fruit, nothing would suit him so well as a diet of milk and vegetables, and he thinks many of his violent upsets come from eating meat.

Tuesday, March 9 Before Lusch departs for Rome R. talks to her warmly and kindly and movingly, as is his way. – Today Vesuvius is not to be seen for dust storms, nor are Sorrento and Capri. R.'s indisposition is in line with his reading material, and his thoughts are tending more and more towards vegetarianism. In the evening he tells us many things about lions and wolves, ingenious hypotheses and inspirations thought up by his delightful Frenchman, including hopes for a uniform climate throughout the world, and that the lion's young look like lambs and the wolf's like rats, and they are frequently consumed by their parents. – Our whist (I again with R.) is cheerful, R. calls Herr v. Stein 'Virtue' and Gersdorff 'Vice', and he arouses much merriment.

Wednesday, March 10 The weather is glorious, but everything is thirsting for rain – when I returned home yesterday I saw flowering plants lying on the ground, uprooted by the storm, and it reminded me of the end of the second act in *Parsifal.* – After lunch (we have returned to our German mealtimes) we once more attempt to reconcile Gleizès's optimism with Schopenhauer's view of the world; R. thinks that degeneracy set in during a period of change on earth, but it is not absolutely necessary for the Will just to consume itself; Nature is injudicious, he says, but it has no wish to be sheerly destructive; how otherwise to explain the Will's delight in genius, in which it sees itself reflected? The possibility exists for a gentler kind of tolerance, for desire not utterly uncontrolled; in India, for example, human beings during a period of adversity could calmly starve along with their domestic animals, without ever thinking of consuming them.

Thursday, March 11 Letters from Bayreuth, differences of opinion among the committee members, friend Wolz. wants the Emperor's patronage, others are afraid of offending the King. R. is of the opinion that everything should be laid before the King. What happens when one *wants* something can be seen from this example, when the only pillar of our enterprise can be almost forgotten! We, who want nothing, feel this very strongly; the Emperor, who has never done anything for our cause, is to be approached and the King ignored, for him we have already. – R. is arranging another little room for himself, the light is very dazzling, he says he could do with the Franconian woods on these rocks!

Tuesday, March 16 His room is finished, and he plays pieces from *Parsifal* to us to celebrate his domestic comfort!

Thursday, March 18 R. gets up with a headache, is already in an ill humour when a letter from Dr. Jauner and the unavoidable reply complete his misery. In the evening he says, 'I have lost all my illusions now. When we left Switzerland, I thought it a remarkable coincidence, the victories and the culmination of my work, I asked whether there were not 1,000 people in Germany who would be prepared to give 300 marks for such an undertaking. How miserable was the reply! I have coincided with the most miserable time Germany has ever known, with this beastly agitator at its head. But all the same I brought it off. No one else in the whole history of art has ever succeeded as I did in building a big theatre, bringing together through the strength of my personality the best artists we have and staging such performances. And what was my reward for it all? Baa baa! I thought they would simply make up the deficit for me – oh, yes, they came along, the women with their trains, the men with their moustaches, enjoyed themselves, and, since emperors and kings were also there, people ask: My God, what more does Wagner want? Does he want something else? – I believe that 25 years ago I could have done it better.'

Saturday, March 20 Boni's birthday, R. extremely kind; I, elevated and sustained by him, embark with great fervour on this day, whose great event is – the resumption of the biography! Dressed in the Marajah I sit in his little room, to which he has added a skylight, as if in Heaven; R. feels everything is too lovely for such a life, but I am blissful at being his right hand again. – Watching a glorious sunset above Vesuvius: 'Beautiful,' says R., 'but where can I grasp you, Nature without end?' – 'Grasp me,' I say to him, and we put our arms around each other as we stroll.

Tuesday, March 23 Cheerful rising, caused by a minor incident yesterday: I heard a moan and rushed to R., thinking he had called out; R. later discovered that it was some cats up to their tricks on the terrace! Early this morning he was still laughing about it and, remembering how I rushed to his side though I am not supposed to walk[1], he says, 'When you are alarmed, you could dance a ballet.' – A vegetarian pamphlet leads R. to that subject over coffee, he describes what things would be like if we stopped murdering animals: 'Perhaps we should have no more art, but if we were morally more secure, that would be no hardship.' But he does not wish to have anything to do with vegetarians, since they always have the utility principle in mind. – In the evening he talks about Weissheimer[2], Cornelius; I am glad that these things are being preserved in the biography – a true book of justice! – How touched I was to devote to the memory of Serov the fine words which he dictated to me today!

Thursday, March 25 Letters from Bayreuth; friend Wolz. wants after all to present concerts in Bayreuth under Hans's direction this summer. R. very saddened by his friends, even the best of them; says, 'I am in fact just in the way, without me everything would be all right.' I have the task of conveying his 'no' to our friend. 'Oh,' says R., 'if only I could find myself a pleasant wilderness!' – He almost decides to drop the school idea entirely and to consider presenting *Parsifal* with the Munich company, on condition that the King appoint another opera director, perhaps Herr v. Bürkel. – In the afternoon Frau Lucca appears with [Pietro] Cossa, the poet, to invite R. on behalf of the syndic of Rome to attend the performance of *Lohengrin* there. Frau Lucca imprudently noisy, but the poet listens intelligently to R.'s expatiations, which grow more and more heated with the urgings of this turbulent woman! – Great concern over R.'s allowing himself to be goaded by such nonsense. They leave at last, R. tries to sleep but cannot! He comes out onto the terrace and after some grumbling calms down. I want to cancel the carriage, but he says he wishes to go to the church to hear the *Miserere*. – Long drive to the Conservatoire – 'The moon is flirting with Vesuvius.' – Arrive in a splendid courtyard along a narrow alley, then enter a lovely vaulted chapel. Received by the charming Duchess of Bagnara[3]; wailing of psalms, worshippers passing in and out, R. is led off by the Duke and the other gentlemen from the Conservatoire, since the service still has an hour to run. He returns, and in the darkness the choir begins to sing. – 'What an awesomely noble impression the music makes!' says R.; then, 'This is true music, which makes everything else look like child's play.' The work (by Leo) rears up like a mighty cathedral, severe in outline, noble and essential; every modulation of tremendous effect, since dictated by the logic of the part writing. The performance suffers because of the pauses the conductor feels impelled to make in the interests of security. But the boys' voices sound touchingly naïve. – We think of *Parsifal*! Afterwards R.

---

[1] She was incapacitated by pains in her knees.

[2] Wendelin Weissheimer, a composer friend from the Biebrich years with whom he had now fallen out.

[3] Wife of the president of the Conservatorio di Musica in Naples.

accompanies the delightful Duchess, who, surrounded by her lovely children, pleases him immensely, while the friendly Duke escorts me to our carriage. We drive through a tumultuous crowd; driving is not permitted today, one must go to church on foot, and the people hiss at us; moonlight, the houses like palaces from *The Arabian Nights.*

Tuesday, March 30 R. is still very run down, I hope it is the sirocco which is to blame, but above all it is his mood. He gives expression to it in a letter to the King – reply to a letter received today. In it he talks about his thoughts of America and desires Herr v. Perfall's removal if he is to produce *Parsifal.*

Thursday, April 1 Joyfully I greet April, which enters in bright sunshine, for R. had a good night, he jokes with the children and laughs at me when I tearfully beg him to be patient with life! He dictates to me our second meeting in Berlin! 'We were like children.' – He is so well that he is able to talk with Jenkins about his thoughts of emigrating. In the evening a visit from the Liechtensteins, whom R. invites to spend the night with us. Much merry chat.

Saturday, April 3 There is some dictation, although R. says at first that he is not enjoying it, but during work his spirits revive and he finds it pleasurable.

Sunday, April 4 Biography around noon; the Goethe-like flavour of certain descriptions (for example, of the relations with Mathilde [Maier] and Friederike Meyer) gives me great delight. – Gladstone's campaign against Disraeli, which will probably be successful, delights us. R. says: 'If only they would keep pointing out that he is a Jew. – And he does not know his country, either, or he would not have dissolved Parliament and called for a general election.'

Thursday, April 8 Letters about the success of *Lohengrin* in Rome arrive, and when we talk jokingly about them, he says: 'Lord, how ungrateful we are! It reminds me of Gaspérini, who told me how impossible I am to satisfy: "When Rossini is given a good beefsteak, he is delighted and gives thanks to God for it, but you despise such things."' (Unpleasant experience with Herr v. Stein, whose severity towards Siegfried is very embarrassing to us.)

Friday, April 9 In the evening much about Gladstone, who has won Midlothian. A great deal, too, about *Lohengrin* in Rome, photographs, enclosures, expressions of gratitude, etc.! ... Then whist. R. wishes not to do any more dictating, but to settle down to some work. He wants to put off the dictation until after the production of *Parsifal,* when he wants also to take Siegfried's education in hand and revise *Der Fl. Holländer.*

Sunday, April 11 The mail arrives and brings me news of the death of our dear Brange! I am able with the aid of another death notice to conceal this from R. If only I could remember whether I received a sign on the day of her death! So that the dear faithful creature did not leave us unnoticed. The day passes as in a gloomy dream, unheeded R.'s conversation with Liechtenstein, all other callers, Lusch's homecoming.

Monday, April 12 Woke up in a fever during the night, thought of Brange – oh, how to tell him, and how to bear it that I must tell him? – R. is delighted with Lusch's return, much merriment between them. And when he tells me of his delight in Lusch's development, my overflowing feelings burst forth, and I have to tell him that all, all of it is his doing, that to each of us he is the salvation and the blessing (yesterday, at dictation, I was privileged to hear him giving expression to our feelings at a time of deep distress).

Wednesday, April 14 R. slept well, gets up early and walks to the palm tree drinking Aqua di Leone. In the vineyards he meets Siegfried with the gardener, and they whistle to each other: 'How nice it is, previously it was a parrot who answered me, now it is a son!' – Today we work together on the biography. – In the evening friend Rubinstein, straight from Bayreuth.

Sunday, April 18 After dictation the Duke of Meiningen and his wife are announced. R. is pleased to see him again and welcomes him very warmly. – In the evening our Posilipine friends and, besides them, the Duke and his wife. R. plays the Prelude to *Parsifal* for the Duke, with explanations. When the Duke says he is curious about the production, R. replies, 'I have called my work a stage *dedication* play; it would be unthinkable in our ordinary theatres, and it is very bold; but, if our sweet secrets can be taken so lightly, I do not see why one should not also deal with them in the noblest way.' The Duke once more pleases R. with his personality: 'He looks like Wotan, like Barbarossa, there is nothing in the least modern about him – he is the only German prince who makes one think of his origin, completely heathen.' – The musicians strike up, and R. again does his duet with Pepino.

Friday, April 23 R. still somewhat weary, but he goes for a walk in the morning. He dictates to me, up to the arrival in his life of the King of Bavaria, at which point he intends for the time being to conclude![1]

Saturday, April 24 Visit from the Duke of Meiningen and his wife. Shortly before that a nice letter from the Cabinet secretary, saying that the King is following R.'s suggestion of changing the theatre director[2]. – Much consideration, no one to suggest for this position! ... Thoughts of going back to the Vienna pamphlet[3] and desiring no director at all. Somewhat to my surprise, R. discusses the matter with the Duke and asks him whether, together with the dukedom of Franconia, he would not take over the directorship.

---

[1] This in fact marks the conclusion of *My Life*: Wagner never took his autobiography further.

[2] The King was, however, unwilling to adopt Wagner's suggestion of giving the post to Bürkel, who asked for other ideas.

[3] The brochure entitled *Das Wiener Operntheater* (*The Vienna Operahouse*), published in 1863.

Wednesday, April 28 A letter from the conductor Levi evokes the remark: 'I cannot allow him to conduct *Parsifal* unbaptized, but I shall baptize them both, and we shall all take Communion together.' He says he will find a way around the difficulty. We go for a walk in the garden, and when I tell him that I was deeply upset by a passage in L.'s letter about Lenbach, who was painting a still life of a freshly slaughtered chicken: 'Painters are like that, to them all things are there to be looked at, to feast their eyes on.'

Thursday, April 29 At lunch he tells me he has been communing with me, reading *Measure for Measure* – I am Isabella, down to the last detail! – Yesterday he spoke of his *final work*, the long one about religion and art. This he still wants to write, though he approaches the subject with a feeling of real trepidation, but otherwise he finds the thought of literary work utterly repulsive.

Sunday, May 2 Some visitors, including professors from the Conservatoire. – Then, beneath grey skies, R. and I stroll together through the villa; when we come upon a cactus of unusually rugged appearance, R. says, 'That looks like an ox, which is really what it wanted to be.' – In the evening farewell visit from the Liechtensteins, sad in many ways. As they depart, I hear from the street, hoarse and high-pitched, a prolonged sorrowful cry.

Monday, May 3 Fine weather, a good night for R. – I have some business to do with secondhand merchants in the morning. On my return I find him ruling lines and in good spirits. Final sitting for my picture. In the evening R. reads to us the three main scenes of *Measure for Measure*; an indescribable impression, the noblest and artistically most perfect of works. R. and I in tears, justice and mercy in their fairest forms.

Tuesday, May 4 I have again some things to do in town, and I find R. completely absorbed in preparing his lines, so that he cannot at first eat any lunch, having overexerted himself. He says, 'I could be like the young men of today, not bother my head about the outward appearance of my score, but it leaves me no peace – I must set it out so that it is nice to look at.'

Wednesday, May 5 Lunch starts very gaily but ends on quite a serious note, when R. relates what he actually intended to keep to himself, that a decision had been made in Berlin on the question of vivisection: that it is a necessity. R. wants to leave the Reich and take out American citizenship. He asks what his art has to do with these cruel and indifferent people. Deep distress.

Thursday, May 6 R. spent the morning on his score. In the afternoon he writes to friend Wolz. and sends the biography off to the printers. In the evening a curious visit from three English Wagnerites, whose imposing manner permits no conversation. The second act of *Tristan* played by Rubinstein; R. sleeps, Joukowsky and Stein too, only the English people and the children and I awake: Lusch and I moved, the English people holding out nobly. Much amusement about it and discussion of the English character in all its steadfastness – enduring things in the assumption that they are special, but without in fact having the slightest idea.

Friday, May 7 Yesterday evening brings back to R. the idea of making some cuts in *Tristan*; he says it demands too much of the audience as well as the singers, and he would do this in both the second and third acts, reserving the full work for performances in Bayreuth, for he wishes *Tristan* to be staged there too. – At lunch he announces that he intends to arrange the choruses from the first act of *Parsifal* for our children; he says he will not be able to prepare it as a surprise for me, for it would have to be practised 'mercilessly'. – Delight in Siegfried, his cheerful temperament, which will make things easy for him.

Whitmonday, May 17 Arrival of Malwida, in the evening the Knights of the Grail[1]; too much for him. He goes to bed in an ill humour.

Wednesday, May 19 The whole company has to laugh heartily when R. says, 'It would be my greatest triumph if I were to make you all laugh in my final hour.' – We reflect gladly that in the biography we now have only four more years to write down, and R. earnestly resolves to write these, so as to throw light on our personal destinies. He rehearses the choruses from *Parsifal* with the children (already begun yesterday) – so lovely, so touching, his dear hand strews blessings over them with every movement indicating rhythm and stress! Much rehearsal necessary, and intertwined with it the delight of the children – every movement an outburst of laughter. R. says, 'Now the children are unhappy again!'

Saturday, May 22 A shining morning brings him my greeting! At about eight o'clock the children bring him theirs, a greeting from the stars, and amid tears and sobs our souls intermingle, while the children hear from their father things they will never forget. He rests, we move the festivities from the hall to the *salon* and arrange roses, picture and fabrics, so that R., entering the salon around eleven o'clock, is delighted; he spends an hour there, looks at Loldi's drawings[2], and when I go to greet him, I am permitted to see his happiness in his transfigured appearance and hear it in his very moving words. – Lunch at one o'clock. R. was not in favour of the number 13, to which I had linked the Last Supper and *Parsifal*, the suns and the letters of his name, also the year '13 of this century[3]; we invite a 14th guest and change the form. All spoke well and with deep emotion, and R. replied, repeating what he had already told me in the morning – why he is

[1] These were Engelbert Humperdinck (b.1854), the composer who was to become Wagner's assitant in the preparation of *Parsifal*, and two composers and music critics, Martin Plüddemann (b.1854) and Ludwig Hartmann (b.1836).
[2] For Wagner's 67th birthday 67 flower pots containing roses had been wrapped in paper on which Isolde had made drawings, each depicting some event in his life.
[3] *Parsifal* as his 13th opera (starting from *Die Feen*); the suns a reference to a dream he had had in April, and [18]13 the year of his birth.

now superstitious, whereas previously he had always liked to think of himself as the 13th! He does not wish to spite his good fortune, he says, and he mentions seven as the number which means everything to him, the children and the two of us – all that is well disposed towards him derives from that; about this relationship he says many things which you, my children, have certainly noted, and which were accompanied by the tears of all present. Over coffee we hear '*Mignonne*', sung by Pepino. Then a rest, a walk to the palm tree, and finally a trip on the sea. Five boats rock their way along the blessed shores, bathed in a moonlight which seems to wrap us in gentle warmth, Naples glittering in the distance, Vesuvius like a dream image behind it; yet more blissful than all outward appearances the harmony of souls binding us all together. – We return home to the illumined *salon*, and the day and the evening are brought to a close with the choruses from *Parsifal*, sung by our children, our friends Plüddemann, Rubinstein, Humperdinck, and R.

Monday, May 24 Heavenly journey to Amalfi, visit to the cathedral, which vexes R. somewhat, but the evening, spent on the terrace of the Hôtel des Capucins, restores his good spirits.

Wednesday, May 26 Merry breakfast and drive to Ravello, lovely beyond description. Discovered Klingsor's garden in Ravello[1]. Late breakfast at the Villa . . . (?), then coffee with Mr. Reed's manager, whose wife, a Swiss, pleases us very much with her serious air – she reminds us of Vreneli. (In the book in Ravello R. wrote, 'Have found the second act of *Pars*.')

Thursday, May 27 Corpus Christi Day, much noise and banging, brutish affair which would shock anybody of a humanitarian or religious turn of mind. Siegfried full of it, six times to the cathedral, back and forth! Sea trip to the grotto in two boats, really splendid, as also the return journey to the beautiful Vietri and after that the journey by train, during which R. becomes increasingly exuberant. As we arrive, Naples exercises all its powerful and imperious magic. – In the evening, as if to celebrate our return, Vesuvius keeps sending up its flares, so regularly that one feels an eruption is nigh.

Saturday, May 29 In the afternoon by boat to the Villa Postiglione, where our good friend Joukowsky, kept indoors by a fever, has nevertheless managed to work out a sketch for the second act of *Parsifal*. Return by boat with R. and Malwida; the children also returning from the Villa Post., on the Polilipo road above, constantly waving to us!

Tuesday, June 1 R. is not entirely well, he had a somewhat restless night, but he settles down to his big work and says we will be amazed by what he is producing[2]. In the evening friend Joukowsky brings his sketch for the second act of *Parsifal*. Several things have to be altered, but occupation with it is in itself a pure delight, as is also the zeal of our friend.

[1] The park of the Palazzo Rufalo, whose owner was an Englishman, Neville Reed.
[2] The lengthy essay 'Religion and Art'.

Friday, June 4 R. did not have too bad a night, and he is able to work on his long article, the outline of which he described to me at breakfast; with such a subject, he says, one must be more circumspect – it is not like a review of an opera. When I return from town with Malwida, I find a heap of popping pods on my dressing table, for me to burst! This is now his and the children's main amusement.

Monday, June 7 A letter arrives from Herr v. Bürkel, a petition to the King which occupies our entire afternoon conversation. R. writes down some points, which I am to set out for Herr v. B.[1]

Tuesday, June 8 I wrote to Herr v. Bürkel and add to R.'s notes, at his request, the remark that what would be best of all would be a director of good will and understanding. R. says: 'Though the Court theatres are bad institutions, all it would need to have things put right would be a few well-disposed theatre directors, as well as a princess on the throne with sympathy for my cause. But the princes all have other ideas in their heads!' – The children tell me that R. said to them, 'I know that Brange is dead.' – We did not speak of it – he understands my inability to tell him sad news.

Thursday, June 10 R. is very put out that there is no level walk here. Malwida mentions the botanical gardens to us, and we decide to go there. At five o'clock all nine of us take the tram, to R.'s great joy. He says one feels like part of some great element, and indeed one does have the pleasant sense that reputation, power, position mean nothing here – one is 'a man among the rest'. A most delightful journey through lively working-class districts; R. jokes, 'Just as in London, everything here takes place in the streets.' All of it picturesque, and the botanical gardens truly enchanting. The streets become more and more lively, and, to crown it all, the gracious Queen of Italy drives past our tram. On R., who salutes her, she makes a very charming impression, and this gives our expedition its first happy conclusion, which is soon followed by another. R. presses my hand, cries, 'See you again at the Torretta,' and swiftly leaves the tram. He literally runs to Dreher's! We ride on, and at the Torretta there he is again. I send the children ahead and walk slowly after them with Malwida in almost total darkness, wave to a *carrozzella* which I first took to be empty, though in the very same moment I cry, 'R. is in it!,' and, quite true, he is in it, and amid much merriment all three of us squeeze ourselves into the little carriage! Quite an incomparable journey, from beginning to end a vista of palm trees

---

[1] Set down in telegraphic style in Wagner's handwriting as follows: 'Protectorate – royal decision acceptable to us, German Reich idea of friends rejected, unfruitful. *Earlier:* Only raised because of difficulties in Bavaria. Therefore director question so important. No candidate yet, Bürkel in better position to find one. Perhaps take up my Vienna plan with economic control (Bürkel, remaining secretary). Difficult, not impossible to find right way. Desired goal regular festivals in Bayreuth, to provide at same time model productions of all works for Munich and for German audiences everywhere in a German location (outside theatre framework), Society of Patrons always covering extra costs. Start with *Parsifal* 1882. Consequently no unduly heavy expenditure for the King.'

against the evening sky, the Chiaia[1] softly illuminated. R. concludes the evening with a vehement apostrophe to Malwida, reproaching her for her pseudo-relationships and saying that she should come to us and let the others come to her, not she to them. He mentions my father with 'his three flagpoles,' Pest, Rome, Weimar, and all the important faces, and he says it is quite worthless and betrays an emptiness which has to be filled out with pseudo-obligations of this kind. 'Cosima did it differently – you marry Liszt!' With this joking remark he concludes his very earnest and vehement address in which the extent of his passionate truthfulness once again enchants and moves me.

Saturday, June 12 After our friends have gone, Lulu brings me the domestic-accounts book; I exhort her to thriftiness, since her father has twice told me that the housekeeping is costing a lot of money. A violent outburst of anger from R. on this account, he completely misunderstands everything I say. The night begins for me in great sorrow. Was some god giving me warning? Was he punishing insufficient strength, or was it just a demon tormenting me? I believe that R. was upset by his memories. However, he goes off to sleep. While I am seeking and finding the reason for this trial, I hear a moaning sound; anxiety about Loldi[2], who is still occupying Lulu's room; I rush to her side; but she is asleep; then I hear the sound again, it is coming from the sea, a musical instrument or a human voice; the lament fills the silence, and what my heart does not utter I hear sounding from outside!

Sunday, June 13 R. looks quite indisposed. He heard the sound too, and thought it was an unusually powerful female voice; we are told later that it is ships' sirens announcing their presence at sea during the night. Perhaps from the English ship the children visited and on which they today attend divine service – R. is pleased that they have inherited such a facility for languages. Towards noon I explain to R. that my exhortation to Lusch was not meant in an offensive way, and today he listens to me and my explanation. Fear of the demon who makes sport of us poor mortals!

Tuesday, June 15 R. went out of doors in the morning, saw Fidi with the gardener's boy, and was so delighted with the latter that he decided we should take him with us as Fidi's Kurwenal.

Wednesday, June 16 R. is well. And at eleven o'clock he calls me in to dictate to me, making jokes throughout about our work for posterity![3]

Sunday, June 20 I say goodbye to Malwida in great sorrow. R. says that he always feels in a state of suppressed rage with her for not staying with us permanently. – In the evening Sgambati with wife and child; he plays to us his new concerto, in a fine and masterly way.

---

[1] The main coastal thoroughfare in Naples.
[2] She had become unwell on the previous day.
[3] Wagner was now dictating 'Religion and Art' to Cosima.

Monday, June 21 At breakfast R. and I exchange impressions of the concerto yesterday. R. says, 'Music has taken a bad turn; these young people have no idea how to write a melody, they just give us shavings, which they dress up to look like a lion's mane and shake at us!' 'It's as if they avoid melodies, for fear of having perhaps stolen them from someone else.'

Wednesday, June 23 R. remembers a long unexpressed desire of ours and calls for Aeschylus's *Agamemnon*. He then reads it, and I feel as if I have never before seen him like this, transfigured, inspired, completely at once with what he is reading; no stage performance could have a more sublime effect than this recital.

Thursday, June 24 We luxuriate in memories of yesterday. R. says, 'I declare that to be the most perfect thing in every way, religious, philosophic, poetic, artistic.' – 'One can put Shakespeare's histories beside it, but he had no Athenian state, no Areopagus as final resort.' – I say I would put only the *Ring* beside it. R. says, 'But that stands outside time, it is something thought up by an individual, only to be made a mess of immediately, as happened with newly established religions.' – In the evening *The Suppliants*, just as moving as *Agamemnon*.

Saturday, June 26 R. gets up early, goes for a walk, enjoys the air, which, he tells me, was like milk of roses. Much at breakfast about his work, he is pleased with the curious relevance of *Parsifal* – of his conception of sanctity, which makes seduction, conflicts, etc., impossible. – He goes to Dreher's in the tram, and on the Piazza dei Martiri he feels a hand on his arm – Fidi had seen him from a house he happened to be in and ran swiftly to catch up with him: 'What a feeling that gives me! I, who for two whole generations was like the Tannhäuser I wrote about, that is to say, a completely finished man! You, Joukowsky, were not even born then. Sometimes I feel like the Flying Dutchman – and then to see this boy before me!' – Herr Rub. plays us some fugues from the 48 Preludes and Fugues: 'They are like the roots of words,' R. says, and later, 'In relation to other music it is like Sanskrit to other languages.'

Friday, July 2 Delight on our arrival in Sorrento; R. is pleased for Lusch, who was not with us on the previous occasion. While the children go for a walk on the road to Massa, we sit on the main loggia and rest. Then Rub. light-heartedly plays to us some passages from Hummel's septet, some Strauss waltzes. Lunch is a success, R. drinks meaningfully to Lusch's health, recalling to himself why she was not with us before, and how well things have now turned out. Return journey at four o'clock on the upper deck, the children and our guests in very merry mood. And when we arrive back at the Villa d'Angri, we recall our previous visit to Sorrento and how much better things are now: 'We are no longer deceiving ourselves.'

Sunday, July 4 The Schröns and Rubinstein to lunch; the latter refuses to eat fish, so as not to return to earth as a fish, and R. criticizes so personal and literal an interpretation of symbols. Talk at lunch about the Germans, their addiction to beer, their beer halls and tobacco-smoke arguments: 'In beer halls, that's where they discover their wit.' – Also about our accursed climate, which he says makes us so materialistic, so immoderate. After lunch R. talks of the human being's finest achievement: the dog; this act occurred before recorded history, he says, but now they are being chained up, virtually turned back into wild animals.

Monday, July 5 When I talk of my diaries and the trouble Fidi will perhaps have with them, R. says, 'Yes, perhaps it is not such a good thing to drag such a father around with one' – whereupon I explain to him my desire to allow my children as much freedom of outlook as possible. – Before dictating he tells me that wherever he turns he hears Nietzsche speaking; his judgment on Beethoven is a disgrace, he says, and also on the Jews.

Tuesday, July 6 R. is annoyed by a renewed request to sign a petition against the Jews addressed to Prince Bismarck. He reads aloud the ridiculously servile phrases and the dubiously expressed concern: 'And I am supposed to sign that!' he exclaims. He writes to Dr. Förster[1], saying that in view of what happened to the petition regarding vivisection he has resolved never again to sign a petition. Arrival of the Swiss painter, M. de Pury, R. sits for him for a quarter of an hour.

Wednesday, July 7 R. talks with a certain amount of bitterness about Munich and Bayreuth and says, 'Should one really sacrifice to these matters the few years one still has to live?' He takes a bath in the sea, and since his movements are too violent, it has a bad effect on him, and he spits up a little blood! . . . But he feels that on the whole the bath did him good.

Thursday, July 8 He is not feeling very well, and that overshadows our day; he frequently spits up blood, and he complains to the doctor that he always has some irritation, like a heat rash, etc. When I return from visiting a boarding school, I find him much occupied with thoughts of America; his earnings, reported on by friend Gross, have not been very good, and at the same time there arrive greetings from America and news from Dr. Jenkins which he finds very affecting.

Friday, July 9 Throughout the day discussions about our friend Stein's departure[2]; R. recommends looking on the bright side, saying that their friendship represents a gain: 'You are young, I am old, and yet we have come close to each other.' – Sea bath for R. and for me! Amusement over who is first in the water!

Thursday, July 15 R. took a bran bath for his heat blisters and went to sleep in it, had some wild dreams and now talks about the 'unlimited possibilities' of dreams. – He warns our younger friends against drinking cognac and

---

[1] Bernhard Förster (b.1843), schoolteacher, anti-Semitic agitator, later married Nietzsche's sister Elisabeth.

[2] He had been called back to the family estate by his father.

says it is a bad habit which he himself took up only late in life. Before lunch he brought me some 'Eau de Richard', his latest perfume concoction, and, when I smilingly reflect that, though previously I did not care at all for essence of roses, it has now, through him, become my favourite scent, I find myself wishing that my whole self might be changed in the same way and nothing remain except what he himself has created.

Monday, July 19 In the afternoon he reads his work to me (conclusion), and I am enchanted by it. Before that he had read my words about the Wittelsbach celebration[1], and he praises them so highly that it would be coldness in me to describe myself merely as happy on this afternoon during which he confides to me the richness, profundity and greatness of his thoughts and at the same time welcomes my few words as a melody! 'Mine is a fugue, yours a melody.' Thus in defiance of all that is bad or evil we pass as if in a trance into the evening; a flaming meteor, as it falls, takes with it the single wish (*'wahnlos hold bewusst'*!)[2] I cherish – eternity will fulfil it for me. – Around eleven o'clock we go to bed, after R. has taken a coal-tar bath, but all too soon he leaves his bed, and since he does not return, I follow him; in silence we sit on the terrace, bathed in light, hear strange sounds, a woman whose call is reminiscent of Hungarian melodies; then we leave the terrace and stroll in the garden before the door, exchanging words and lost in contemplation. The loveliest night, perhaps, that we have ever experienced! My whole being immersed in his, in the richly consoling sea of his thoughts, and both of us silently lost in the still, mild glory. He laughs at the idea of wanting to sleep when one cannot! – Between two and three we go to bed, and at nine o'clock on

Tuesday, July 20 we are having breakfast and thinking of the night, so rich and significant! At seven o'clock he dictates to me, and when, while we are working, cannons roar to signal the arrival of the King, R. remarks that here people celebrate more than the whole of Nature, and, 'It would be nice if one could assume that the entire population were really glad when the King arrived.' – He receives a pleasant surprise from Leipzig, a larger payment than he was expecting.

Sunday, July 25 R. slept so soundly that he did not notice an earth tremor which I and others in the household felt very strongly. – Lengthy dictation, conclusion of the much-loved work. Yesterday R. exclaimed to me, 'Brahms is advertising in the newspapers for an opera libretto; I have described my views on composition in the *Blätter*, and now he thinks he has got a recipe.'

Tuesday, July 27 R. is pleased by a letter from Berlin: a Herr Oelten offers a large plot of ground in Berlin for the erection of a Wagner theatre. In

[1] The seventh centennial of the Wittelsbach dynasty in Bavaria was to be celebrated on August 25, 1880 (Ludwig II's birthday); Cosima's piece about the occasion was published anonymously in the August issue of the *B.B.*

[2] Quotation from the love duet in Act II of *Tristan und Isolde*.

view of the attitude of the Court theatre, this would be quite acceptable to R., and he instructs me to ask friend Feustel to look into both the offer and the man. He laughs and says, 'The Emperor will surely come when I stage my *Ring* there, he will not consider it beneath his dignity.' – Evening on the terrace: he yearns for the Villa *Angermann* and a glass of good Rhine wine; but when I suggest that we return home, he will not hear of it.

Wednesday, July 28 R. has erysipelas! Brought on yesterday by a draughty room (at Loldi's bedside) . . .

Friday, August 6 No complications, but the most dismal of spirits! Since the heat rash gets no better, resolve to leave. The children are staying here, we pack our things. Curious feelings about Naples – though it is still nice, I too feel as if all this splendour were poisoned. – During the six days of his illness, particularly at the beginning, R. had many wild dreams. He finds all the medical treatments repulsive – 'All doctors are vivisectors.' – We decide on Gräfenberg[1]. His bed by day was in the *salon*, so this brightest of places also a sickroom.

Sunday, August 8 R. slept, with the aid of bromine. Breakfast at twelve and then taking leave of the children. Under what circumstances shall we see one another again? Lusch, Boni, Eva in tears, Loldi and Fidi composed. – In Rome at ten in the evening, Hôtel Quirinal, run by Herr Guggenbühl, a Swiss. Able to talk German even with the chambermaid.

Monday, August 9 Tuscany, with all its flowers and cultivated fields, delights R. Nice memories of Naples, of which he always says, 'That is Africa, this is Italy, the southern tip of Europe.' – Between eight and nine in the evening arrive in heavy rain in dark Pistoia. A nice apartment in the Hotel London and a pleasant Italian supper. R. very tired, however, his head feels hot.

Tuesday, August 10 R. had a tolerable night, at ten o'clock we set out for San Marcello; uphill journey of three and a half hours, at first very hot, but then noticeably cooler. Curious accommodations in the village, where fleeing Ghibellines once settled. The road was reminiscent of French Switzerland, the village is something like Berneck. – Gay mood to begin with, but R. becoming increasingly irritable; in the evening his skin is even redder, and he has fits of shivering, extreme anxiety; helpless and powerless as I am, I beseech the heavens, ecstatically accept a night of violent toothache, and pray, pray, pray that he be allowed rest, which on

Wednesday, August 11 he is, he looks better, and we laugh more over the incredible place in which we are staying, without a garden, without a view. We decide to go back to Pistoia, where we once again arrive in black night after a drive of nearly six hours.

Thursday, August 12 Decision to go on to Perugia. In Florence put up at the Hôtel de Rome, where friend Buonamici visits us.

---

[1] A resort in Silesia, North Germany.

Friday, August 13 Early departure. – We like Perugia, also the Albergo Perugia, we decide to enjoy rest and fresh air here. At last! After six days. R. calls to me on my balcony, 'Do you want to see something nice?' He empties a bottle; in reply to my question he says that it is his cognac – he feels that it is bad for his rash. – Around six o'clock I leave him to visit the Helbigs, who booked our apartment in the hotel. Strange impression of the place, darkly gleaming, powerful! I tell R. about it – also the comical fact that he is famous here as Morlacchi's successor!¹

Saturday, August 14 R. was restless early in the night, but it got better, and he woke up refreshed. We go for a drive through the city, which pleases R. greatly, then go via the Helbigs' house, S. Erminica, to the Tiber valley. A letter from Lulu tells us that Antonio² has been stealing in our house, and R. at once decides to abandon the adoption.

Monday, August 16 R. regrets having left Naples, since his rash is not improving.

Thursday, August 19 A very strict diet does him good, and around four o'clock we set off on a drive round and through Perugia, which at sunset and moonrise has a decided effect – on me a very heartening and inspiring one because of R.'s delight in everything, which delights me, and the fact that he is better. In the evening he declares in the most humorous way that he will not go to Gräfenberg – he laughs over pine trees, spa guests, spa music, in fact the complete prospectus, which has much alarmed him. He keeps exclaiming, 'What an ass I should be to leave Italy during the loveliest months for – pine trees and rain and a thick winter paletot!' Much sending of telegrams cancelling everything, with R. in high good humour.

Friday, August 20 I go straight to the Helbigs' in the morning to ask about Siena, where R. has resolved to live. I myself should like to stay here, where there is a villa which is recommended, in order to save R. further upset, but he does not wish it. He wants first of all to wait for the children in Florence. – At two o'clock departure from Perugia. R. delights in the countryside and keeps exclaiming with a laugh, 'Pine trees, indeed!' He says he will hang the prospectus on a wall. In Florence at seven in the evening.

Saturday, August 21 Decision to wait for the children not in Florence, but in Siena. Departure at 6.30, the air fresh, the scenery makes a good impression on R. Since I did not sleep during the night, I doze off, and awake in R.'s embrace. – He says he has been writing to my father in his thoughts – and now I hesitate to write down what he said – though I should like to show you his love for me, my children, I just cannot; such things one may scarcely even acknowledge as having been spoken! – Arrival in Siena around 10 o'clock, immediate inspection of villas, great heat, the

¹ Francesco Morlacchi had been a conductor in Dresden until his death in 1841.
² The boy Wagner wanted to adopt as Siegfried's 'Kurwenal'.

position not very pleasant, for me at least Perugia still standing very much in the way of proper appreciation. But then a visit to the cathedral! R. moved to tears, the greatest impression he has ever received from a building. How I should love to hear the Prelude to *Parsifal* beneath this dome![1]

Sunday, August 22 The children with us again, all of them good, healthy, affectionate, happy! Siegfried very tender.

Tuesday, August 24 I arrange things in *Torre di Fiorentina*, go back to the hotel at one o'clock for lunch, drive to the villa at four in order to welcome the children there permanently. In the meantime R. and the children look over the cathedral and its *libreria*. And so in the space of four days we have once again set up a household in this completely unknown town! Merry first supper (salami and risotto) in the tower!

Wednesday, August 25 Most unfortunately, R.'s night was not a good one – probably the food somewhat indigestible! But he is utterly delighted with my little present[2]. For me the day passes in household arrangements, but he makes corrections – in the copy of his article.

Friday, August 27 A fairly good night, and in the early morning a cold pack, which seems to lead to great exhaustion and irritability. He is extremely vexed by the very unfriendly manner of the German servants. I take the children to go and look at several things, including the lovely *Three Graces* on their pedestal. – R. sends off his article.

Saturday, August 28 R. plays *Parsifal* (the 'Good Friday Music') before breakfast. He works, and at lunch says jokingly that he is not obliged to say on what. In the afternoon we go for a walk in the little wood opposite, but R. finds the steep paths all the more of a strain since he was not able to sleep in the afternoon. But the site pleases him, and in the evening we experience a few happy hours, made unforgettable by the fact that R. plays to us the beginning of the Adagio from the Ninth, and [Schubert's] *'Sei mir gegrüsst'* is also played.

Sunday, August 29 Mosquitoes ruin the night for us! ...

Monday, August 30 With the help of ventilation, *sogni tranquille*, net curtains around the beds, etc., we procure ourselves a very good night, and, relieved, I set out in the morning with the children on a quest for art treasures. – In the noble and simple spaces of S. Domenico we discover in the *Saint Catherine* with the stigmata a full manifestation of inspiration. After this I find it difficult to look at anything else, and the three female figures remain in my mind as an eternal exhortation to nobility.

Tuesday, August 31 Friend Rubinstein comes to visit us, and we show him the cathedral, the *libreria*. I show R. the *Saint Catherine*, and it seems to me

---

[1] The interior of this cathedral was used as a model for the Temple of the Grail in the 1882 production of *Parsifal*.

[2] Some fabric bought the day before.

that it makes some impression on him, though he says it is not ascetic enough, too round, too colourful; it is precisely this unimpassioned mildness which I find so moving, her gentle resignation is uplifting. – I have to listen to much joking from R. over the fact that I was so extraordinarily moved at seeing the *Saint Catherine* again! ...

Wednesday, September 1 Friend Rub.'s departure brings him to the subject of his own situation. He says he is sick to death of the *Nibelungen*; now that he has released it to all the theatres, a manager in Königsberg is demanding it; instead of simply refusing, he has to negotiate with him, since he needs the money. This is why he wants to go to America, he says, to earn money and at least to keep *Parsifal* unencumbered.

Sunday, September 5 Not a good night, R. got up five times and was running a temperature! – He spends the whole day quietly lying down, I with him, finally reading to him a story by Tieck which the children begged from the clergyman who says Mass in our house and talks to them and welcomes them in a very friendly manner. A former tutor with the Strozzis[1], he has been without occupation since the dissolution of the monasteries, has built himself a house with a chapel in the vicinity of our house, lives there with a weak-minded abbot, and now travels around (Spain, England, Egypt); he knows Bavaria well, possesses, among other things, the collected *Fl [iegende] Blätter*,[2] knows all of R.'s works, and would have come to Bayreuth if he had had sufficient means. We laugh over this acquaintanceship of the children's and make use of his richly variegated and, it seems, rather unusual, library.

Monday, September 6 R. slept well and is feeling better. We rest together side by side in the papal bed[3] until eleven o'clock. – R. is amused by Rothschild's request for an audience with the Emperor in order to explain to him to what extent the Jews in Germany are endangered, and he says with a certain satisfaction, 'I have played some part in that.' However, he does not see much significance in the movement. R. is not yet taking his meals with us, but in the afternoon he feels well enough to sit in the garden, and in the evening he has supper with us, and once again we are all together in gay spirits. The children show us their drawings of the cathedral – Fidi will become an architect and Loldi a painter!

Monday, September 13 R. rises in cheerful spirits and settles down to some ruling even before breakfast. When I greet him, he says, 'I have the strength to work on it only because I have made up my mind to go to America and thus achieve what I want – to free the work, to stage it only in Bayreuth, and to become completely independent.' He intends to take all the children. – He is hurt by the King's failure to reply to him about replacing the theatre

---

[1] A noble family in Florence.
[2] A humorous weekly periodical in Munich.
[3] Pope Pius VI was said to have spent a night at the villa in 1775.

director, hopes nevertheless to get from him the promise that, if *Parsifal* is performed in the Munich Court theatre, it will be for himself alone.

Thursday, September 16 At four o'clock arrival of my father from Rome. We all go to fetch him, in splendid weather. R. very sweet: 'They can't get rid of the gay old sparks,' he says.

Friday, September 17 We drive (without R., who is ruling lines) with my father to view the cathedral, and here I become aware how different R. is, how youthfully energetic he has remained. My father is all but unmoved.

Monday, September 20 A wet cold day. This adds very much to our resolve to leave here. R. rules lines industriously and ruminates on his American plan. My father has acquainted me with three Petrarch sonnets he set to music: '*Pace non trovo*', '*Benedetto*' and [*left blank*]'. '*Benedetto*' in particular pleases me greatly, I tell R. about it, and he gets my father to play it to him; then he says to him with much warmth, 'I am glad to see something of your worldly side once again.' – In the evening R. and my father play so the children can dance; R. is delighted with the skill with which Siegfried dances (particularly the mazurka). After that whist, with many remarks on R.'s part, he keeps teasing me about Saint Catherine of Siena.

Tuesday, September 21 R. is pleased, not only by the sun, but by an inspiration for the third act of *Parsifal*, the prolonging of the clarinet after the violin, he writes it down and is very cheerful.

Wednesday, September 22 R. had a cold and restless night, Italian beds annoy him; and he is vexed that today we cannot have our cosy breakfast room to ourselves. 'With me it is always paroxysms,' he says, 'indifference is unknown to me, and everything is a paroxysm, either of joy or of pain.' In the evening my father plays his 'Dante' to us, R. has serious reservations with regard to the material. – We then play whist.

Friday, September 24 R. finishes ruling his lines today, thus has completed what is actually the most important preliminary work in his score, and what remains, he says, is just the pleasant part – and the final joy. But on the whole he is not in the best of moods, and he does not come to supper – nevertheless, my father, through what he says about *Parsifal*, gives him the urge to play something from it, and after supper almost the whole of the third act is played by my father and divinely sung by R. – 'Scarcely have I discovered a sensible wife when she must turn out to be your daughter and for that reason placed beyond my reach –' R. says jokingly to my father.

Saturday, September 25 R. again had a bad night; having to rise early for my father's departure, then the hasty final corrections to his article – all this puts him out of humour. All the same, he gaily brings me the ruled score, 334 pages. – Thought of Fidi (who is now in Orvieto) and his talent for

---

[1] '*Io vidi in terra angelici costumi.*' These three songs were first published with Italian text 1846–47; arranged for piano, 1857; German texts had now been added.

architecture; R. feels one should not allow this too much nourishment, as happened with my father's virtuosity, otherwise the other aspects would be too much neglected.

Sunday, September 26 Decision to save *Parsifal* at all costs, to allow Schott to publish only the piano score, for a payment of 50,000 marks. We gaily welcome Fidchen and Joukowsky, who have much to relate concerning Orvieto.

Tuesday, September 28 R. wakes up cheerfully with the remark, 'In this bed there could have slept not only a pope, but the whole schism as well' (Pius VI once occupied our bedroom). He reads his biography to us, which leads to a discussion of Friederike Meyer; he agrees with me when I call her the most interesting of his female acquaintances. – Pleasure in Ferry[1] and the fact that a minister of education was made minister for foreign affairs: 'I should like to see matters dealt with here as they are in France, and I should gladly give them Metz. They are going about things in the right way.'

Thursday, September 30 R. had a good rest but is in poor spirits, and a suggestion I make to him – to allow Siegfried to see Ravenna with Jouk. – unfortunately irritates him greatly. He then observes that everything is making him melancholy, all his thoughts, the fact that he is not feeling well, the view from our rooms, and the remoteness of the town, indeed even the town itself, which has little to offer him – all this depresses him. He longs for Venice, and we pack and settle the inventory in haste.

Friday, October 1 Up early; R. lively, plays the finale of the C Minor Symphony as a farewell! Glorious sunny day; six oxen pull our luggage, at ten o'clock in Florence.

Monday, October 4 At four o'clock in Venice.

Wednesday, October 6 Arrival of our friend Wolzogen. In the evening we move into Contarini[2].

Saturday, October 9 Glorious weather, which R. enjoys with all his heart; his delight in the city is unbounded, whether going by boat or on foot. Reunion with Mimi, still the same friendly person.

Tuesday, October 12 Lusch's birthday. The Schleinitzes in the evening; R. takes Mimi aside and begs her to give some thought to Lulu's fate, because in our seclusion we can do nothing for her. Though I was of the opinion that his star would take care of everything, nevertheless it must be given every opportunity.

Friday, October 15 In the evening a pleasant hour at Princess Hatzfeldt's with all the children[3]; while Rub. plays the *Msinger* Prelude, R. acts out the

---

[1] Wagner had become friends with the journalist Jules Ferry in Paris in 1859; Ferry was now prime minister.

[2] Palazzo Contarini on the Grand Canal.

[3] Marie von Schleinitz's mother, widow of Prince Friedrich von Hatzfeldt-Trachenberg (her second husband); Marie was the daughter of her first husband.

scene between Walther and Eva with Mimi. When we return home, he tells me he cannot bear listening to his own music.

Saturday, October 16 Excellent letter from Herr von Bürkel, saying that our matter is now settled, *Parsifal* assured for 1882, orchestra and chorus from Munich at our disposal.

Monday, October 18 R. had a good night. But the weather is rough, R. works on his article 'What Boots This Knowledge?'[1]

Friday, October 22 In the evening Count Gobineau comes to visit us, undoubtedly an interesting and significant man; but the French language is causing R. increasing difficulties – not only speaking it, but also listening to it; he finds it 'horribly hard'.

Wednesday, October 27 A letter from the King, requesting us to come to Munich in the second part of Nov., causes dejection. Is it that he does not wish to see R., or that he does not want him to know about his private performances (*Aida*, Louis XIV plays)[2]? R. sends Herr v. Bürkel a telegram, saying he has to be in Munich during the first half of the month.

Saturday, October 30 Departure at six o'clock, after bidding a warm farewell to Mimi, so touching in her friendliness. The singers who had so often upset R. arrive, and this time they really please us and rouse our spirits as, singing all the while, they precede our gondola and accompany us as far as the station. Farewell, Venice! Departure at six o'clock.

Sunday, October 31 We all more or less slept and are merry, glorious sunshine greets us in Germany. – We arrive in Munich at six o'clock in very good spirits; met by Lenbach and Bürkel, Levi comes along later. Lodging at Jungfer Schmidt's house, Briennerstrasse 8c – strange, but full of feeling!

Monday, November 1 A good night, though arrangements to be made once more; thoughts of moving to the hotel, but the friendly Frl. Schmidt proves the decisive factor in our staying where we are. R. is pleased that I make all the arrangements with good humour – the King sends some flowers. At last, in the evening, Beethoven's *Mass*. Fine, if somewhat mixed impression.

Tuesday, November 2 R. writes a few lines of verse to the King for the flowers, and in the evening we see quite a good performance of [Méhul's] *Joseph*, a work which both moves and delights us. That is style.

Wednesday, November 3 In Berlin Herr v. Hülsen is inquiring about the *Nibelungen*, having heard that Herr Neumann is to stage it at the Viktoria Theater. R. sends a telegram to Tappert, saying he does not intend to release any of his works to the Berlin theatre. Around noon we visit

---

[1] A supplement to 'Religion and Art', *B.B.* December 1880.

[2] In a letter to the King from Siena, Wagner had asked him to arrange performances of *Lohengrin* and *Die Meistersinger* in Munich in the first two weeks of November, when he intended to be there, so that the children could see them; Ludwig in his reply, now received, agreed to do so, but added that it would cause less difficulty if the performances were to be in the second half of November. (Verdi's *Aida*, unlike the Louis XIV plays, would not be a private performance: it was in the Court opera's normal repertoire.)

Lenbach, R. sits for him but says in the course of it that he is tired and would like best to close his eyes. – Herr v. Bürkel visits R. Reports concerning the King arouse melancholy – among other things, the King does not travel around, because he fears for his life (assassinations).

Thursday, November 4 Continued negotiations with the Leipzig director [Neumann] about the *Nibelungen* in Berlin. In the evening a performance of *Der Fl. Holländer*, R. affected in spite of the shortcomings of the perform- ance, he frequently bursts into tears.

Friday, November 5 R. asks me which I would prefer – correct singers without any great talent or the other way around; he says he prefers the former; I observe that there can be no artistic correctness – that is to say, no living performance – without great talent. Bad weather, R. does not go out; for me and the children *The Merchant of Venice*; R. goes to bed.

Saturday, November 6 Morning discussion about *The Merchant*, which completely fills my being, in spite of the dismal performance. – Then much vacillation about spending the evening at Lenbach's, R. wants not to go, then to go, in the end we do go and have a nice party, which does not tire R. But at the conclusion there is so much agitation and fury on his part, and as a result such a terrible night, that the miseries of life and original sin trouble my soul almost more than ever before!

Sunday, November 7 Only in the early hours does R. fall asleep, and he has a wild dream about Fidi falling in the water. We rouse ourselves to a sort of conversation about the previous evening. But the saddest of days, on which even what R. likes to call my beauty becomes a source of sorrow, for he tells me that I stand in the way of my children. *Tristan* in the evening, probably never before heard in such sorrow; R. very affected, tells us that he feels with every character, with Marke, with Kurwenal, he feels he is each one of them. – The orchestra very good. The second act the crowning glory.

Monday, November 8 A kind God lends me words which satisfy R., he tells me that I can see from his madness that I mean everything to him, excluding all others. I: 'But you are my salvation.' – Our lunch is then a very cheerful one, and when there is mention of Lenbach's remark that in life we are like the donkey, always following the bundle of hay retreating in front of its nose, then of his loyal and not exactly requited love for Marie D[önhoff], R. says, 'Now I know how I should address the Countess: "Honoured bundle of hay," whether she understands it or not.' Whereupon someone adds, 'At any rate she would understand that the donkey is L.' We part amid great laughter. The evening was spent at home with friends (Heckel, Pohl, Levi). But when R. advises Heckel and Pohl of the altered situation of the Society of Patrons, refers to the deficit and says that no one has yet thought of returning to the children the sum of money that belongs to them, Heckel says, 'That is the difficulty.' Then R. explodes:

'The difficulty! While I abandon my whole idea, charge admission for the performances! – What are you there for, you Societies of Patrons?' He gradually calms down, excuses Heckel in particular, who has done all he can and performed real miracles.

Tuesday, November 9 R. slept well but is nevertheless still very tired. First of all we have a sitting for him with Gedon, who with boundless excitement is starting on a bust[1], then with Lenbach, who seems to be on the best way to painting a magnificent picture. R. is pleased, when Jouk. joins us and draws Lenbach's attention to various things, that L. simply gets him to sit down in his place and paint, and this gives rise to all kinds of friendly jokes. Feustel with us, for lunch, warmly welcomed.

Wednesday, November 10 A magnificent bouquet from the King inaugurates the *Lohengrin* performance, R. watches it from the royal box, we from below. Otherwise a completely empty theatre. On me it is the tragedy in particular which makes an impact – R. dissatisfied with the tempi, tells Levi that conductor and producer deserve to be sent God knows where. But he got much pleasure from his meeting with the King, whom he found completely unchanged.

Thursday, November 11 R. and I up very late, for the performance lasted until midnight, and R. wanted to chat a little afterwards. He works out the programme for *Parsifal*[2], and we talk a lot about the tragic element in *Lohengrin*, which offers no reconciliation. – Love produces faith, life produces doubt, which is punished unatoned. The lovingly faithful Elsa has to die, since the living Elsa must put the question to him. And all the scenic splendour, all the glory of the music, seem to be built up to throw light on the unique value of this one heart. – Drove with R. to the town hall, in Lenbach's portrait of the King he does not see the King as he knows him. Sitting for Lenbach. We dine at five o'clock and then go to see *Die Zauberflöte*. – R. describes this work as the genesis of the German character, and he draws our attention especially to Pamina's aria (G minor).

Friday, November 12 I visit the painter and costumier R. Seitz in order to discuss with him the costumes for *Parsifal*. At three o'clock rehearsal and [*Parsifal*] Prelude in the Court theatre. The orchestra's pleasure in seeing R. once more in their midst; a flourish, he very cheerful, friendly, pleased among other things by the expression on the face of the violist Toms. The Prelude is played twice, then the King demands the Prelude to *Lohengrin*. R. very put out by this.[3] He summons me to his dressing room, where he is cheerful in spite of it all. But at home he is tired, and when Lenbach makes some unfortunate remarks about Bismarck, R. loses his temper about this bulldog face which is always being painted. – Lenbach takes his leave after

---

[1] A bronze bust that was not cast till 1883, after Wagner's death.
[2] Programme note for the King about the *Parsifal* Prelude.
[3] He sent Levi to conduct it.

R. has sought to explain to him the reasons for his anger. Late in the evening he goes for a walk on the Dultplatz with Jouk.; on his return he says merely that he has an antipathy towards Lenbach, who irritates him.

Saturday, November 13 R. had a wild and restless night, he cries out 'Joukowsky' and 'My son,' but he soon recovers from his fatigue. He is now reading Count Gobineau's *La Renaissance*[1] with much interest.

Sunday, November 14 R. slept well, and a fine sunny day puts him in good spirits. He writes to the King, then goes for a walk with Jouk., meets Frau Vogl, and says teasingly to me that he embraced her. – Members of the orchestra, singers, Knights of the Grail in the Orlando Lasso,[2] where it was very cheerful and companionable, he says. We meet again in the theatre; *As You Like It* is being performed, and the first scene grips us at once with all Shakespeare's usual power; unfortunately the performance then gets so bad that we leave after the second act. We return home in lovely moonlight, stop to look at the Kleine Residenz garden, then, back at home, forget the performance, thank goodness, and think only of the play.

Monday, November 15 R. has a cold, has to keep to his room and miss today's performance of *Die Meistersinger*. He receives Herr v. Bürkel, who makes a very good impression on him and who, among other things, tells him that he must not imagine that 'beneath this fleshy bulk' there does not dwell a warm sympathy and understanding for his ideas. – But R. remains in poor spirits, and my reports on the very good *Msinger* performance do little to cheer him up.

Tuesday, November 16 We see Lenbach for the first time since the explosion; I had also been avoiding him, but Lusch told us that he had been downright ill on account of it. R. explains his feelings to him, and we then drive with him to his studio, where quite an agreeable conversation develops. At lunch R. is completely cheerful, and he says we do not admire him enough for having sacrificed *Die Msinger*, to which he had been particularly looking forward. And today I am able to tell him all my feelings about this divine work, and what a triumph of ideality I see in his ability, amid all the dreary realities of his situation at the time, to conjure up such a vision of a lovely reality and a noble fatherland. That he fled from disagreeableness into the worldlessness and night of *Tristan* seems to me less wonderful than this creation of a 'daytime', and this affirmation amid the very worst of experiences. He goes out, meets the whole world in the street, and is much fatigued. However, he is pleased by Herr v. Ziegler's visit; this influential man, whose task is to keep the King informed on all political matters, professes to be a grateful devotee of R.'s, intends to recommend everything (in the matter of the rail connection to Bayreuth,

[1] A series of dialogues involving figures from the Renaissance period, first published in 1877.
[2] A restaurant favoured by Munich's artistic community.

for instance), and, on leaving, kisses R.'s hand. In this place in which we previously experienced nothing but hostility, we now have two loyal and enthusiastic men. – Before supper R. goes through *Lohengrin* with the conductor, and at table he talks about the dismal influence of the Jews on our present conditions, and warns Levi against the implications for him, which Levi accepts good-humouredly but nevertheless with some melancholy. We also talk about Gedon and the lack of recognition for his talents, and finally Lenbach enlarges interestingly upon the state of technique in painting. R. had said to him that painters were lucky in comparison with composers – all they had to do was to create their works, then they were dependent on nobody. L. says that, on the contrary, technique in painting has got into such an appalling state and been passed down to them by such bad predecessors that there is still everything to search for. – Very friendly parting from this peculiar man, of great stature, certainly, but nervy and highly-strung.

Wednesday, November 17 Friend Levi at the station to see us off. First greetings from our beflagged theatre, Moritz and Fuchs[1] wave to us. In Bayreuth we are met by our doughty friends Feustel, Gross and the mayor's wife, the mayor being ill. – Marke at Wahnfried. – Everything in good order, a curious feeling: Have we been away? Are we back? – Neither seems real. –

Thursday, November 18 Towards evening friend Wolzogen; all kinds of Society of Patrons affairs, which rather tire R.; but he is touched by such evidence of good will as renewed gifts from Herr Irwine (a Scot in Leipzig)[2] and from Herr Rosenlehner[3], who still does not wish to be named – last month brought in about 8,000 marks.

Friday, November 19 In the mornings R. is now reading *La Renaissance* with ever-increasing interest. Talking of Italy, he says, 'Naples is an intoxication, Venice a dream.' Here, beneath these grey skies, he says, the sad tune[4] is sounding. – He invites our friend Jouk. to stay with us until his studio is built. – A biography of my father by a lady called Ramann[5] has arrived here. Two pages about my father's life with my mother in Como before my birth catch my attention; I show them to R., and he is pleased. 'There must have been something like that,' he exclaims, and now everything friendly in relation to me is called 'Bellagio' – even the expression on Loldi's face.

Sunday, November 21 R. finishes *La Renaissance* and comes to me around noon, the book in his hand, much affected by the final scene between

---

[1] Jacob Moritz, inspector, and Konrad Fuchs, caretaker at the Bayreuth festival theatre.

[2] David Irwine wrote several books about Wagner, e.g., *A Wagnerian's Midsummer Madness*.

[3] Rudolph Rosenlehner, Munich, who was in fact cited in the *B.B.* in 1880 for a special contribution of 400 marks.

[4] The shepherd's tune in *Tristan und Isolde*.

[5] Lina Ramann; the 1st volume of her well-known biography of Liszt appeared in 1880; Bellagio is the village on Lake Como where Cosima was born.

M[ichel]angelo and V[ittoria] Colonna. He gives it to me to read, and it makes a quite wonderful impression on me. How many of his characteristics can be seen in M., too, and he says he was reminded of himself when M. talks of the inordinate violence of his temperament, combined with great energy. We discuss M.'s attitude towards the Renaissance, very perceptively described by Gobineau. R. says of himself that he is the plenipotentiary of downfall (this he sees increasingly): 'If my ideas were to strike root, all these great men would be listened to as teachers and would not, as it were, have lived in vain.' – In the evening Jouk. tells us that Pepino is feeling homesick, which is only too understandable.

Tuesday, November 23 Skies still grey. R. settles down to his score but is dissatisfied. He goes out for a while, then returns to his work. He is not happy with the brass music on stage, he seeks and, he believes, finds what he wants.

Thursday, November 25 R. had a good night, but he is in no mood for work, makes writing mistakes, is absent-minded, has great feelings of anxiety, and when the Voltz and Batz affair crops up (they want to sell back to him their rights in his works for 60,000 marks), he is quite beside himself with rage. – Frl. Uhlig has sent the final copies of R.'s letters to her father.

Friday, November 26 R. does some work and then goes for a little walk, but it takes hold of him again – what he calls the *crab* in his chest. – Our friends the Grosses, whose warm friendliness does us good. Feustel's idea of publishing the piano score of *Parsifal* on subscription, which would perhaps make America unnecessary.

Sunday, November 28 Herr Neumann comes and reports that Herr v. Hülsen has offered him the opera house in Berlin, together with the orchestra and chorus and whatever singers he wants, for the *Ring*. R. much against it, wants to see it all done in the Viktoria Theater, though he leaves the decision up to the promoter; however, he promises to make a visit to the Viktoria Theater, but not to the opera house. Our good theatre director could not understand at all that R. should think nothing at all of the Emperor and royal family's attending the performance of the *Ring*! – We compare Neumann's energy and resourcefulness with Hülsen's narrow-mindedness and vindictiveness and have to laugh over Israel's predominance.

Monday, November 29 Voltz & Batz seem to have calmed down. In the evening there are discussions with Wolzogen about the extended *Blätter*, the basis of which R. wishes to be his own view of the decline of the human race and the need for the establishment of a system of ethics: intellectually, he says, people will always remain unequal, but one could aim for a greater moral equality. We might not achieve anything, but we could prepare the ground.

Tuesday, November 30 R. works, then goes out for a little while, but without any pleasure; indeed, the dampness makes him feel as if he were at the mercy of those hostile beings who are sometimes revealed to him in dreams. However, since I wish to do some shopping in the afternoon, he goes out again with me, I abandon my shopping, and we stroll in the palace gardens, very merry, though it is a rather macabre kind of humour. – In a climate like this, he observes, the only possible life is in taverns by lamplight, though, to be sure, it spells ruin for everybody. The Philistine figures passing by, the old maids, annoy him, but when we speak of them we remain merry. He works in the evening, but says he had to do a lot of erasing. His best-written score, he adds, was *Lohengrin*. In the evening read the letters to Uhlig, still with great interest. Even at that time he was finished with everything, all things vain and worldly. We talk of Fidi's publishing these letters after our death, also those to his wife Minna, to A[lwine] Fromann, to my father. But our own, those between R. and me, must never on any account be presented to the public. I solemnly pronounce this here as their sacred duty.

Thursday, December 2 Telegram from Hans, whom I had asked on Lulu's account whether she might see him and at the same time hear the 9th. [*Bülow's telegram from Meiningen, in French, states that he finds it impossible to answer at once; he was laid up for several days and is still indisposed.*] – This reply brings R. back to the idea of adopting all the children, which is his wish.

Sunday, December 5 Wolz. has sent his plan for the enlarged *Blätter*, I read it with some misgivings; I find it hard to envisage the possibility of R.'s far-reaching ideas being propounded by his pupils. I show R. the MS. over coffee, R. makes a few deletions, we experience the same feelings of embarrassment without, however, going more deeply into the matter. He takes a walk, returns to me after a while, and says, 'I believe I shall be complying with a growing thought in you if I decide to leave the whole thing as it is.' I am very much in favour.

Monday, December 6 At one o'clock friend Stein, great joy at seeing him again, particularly because of Fidi; hopes that it will after all be possible to maintain the connection, that Stein will come to us for a few months each year and later Fidi go to him in Halle.

Tuesday, December 7 Our conversation leads us to life, I say that to me it seems to be just. R. says, 'Certainly, and when we look at the difficulties in a life such as that of Cervantes, we can tell ourselves that the world's will had quite other things in mind than just providing him with honours and riches.' I feel that if that had been what he wanted, he could also have achieved it, and I see a streak of nobility in his gaiety, his contempt for despair. One has what one *wills* (not what one desires). – He says that Will had required him to perserve, and that is why it had given him a good little wife and a king (recently he pointed out how unusual their relationship was, since the King demanded nothing at all from him).

Thursday, December 9 R. now has a new volume of the General Staff's report [on the Franco-Prussian War], and he tells us of the heroic deeds at Belfort: 'It is impossible not to admire such things, but what was the point of putting all these forces in danger?' He talks of his intention of staging a mourning ceremony and says he still wants to write some funeral music, for which he would take as motto the reply of a dying sergeant to his officer: 'Sir, I die for Germany.' – ' "I die for Germany," ' he exclaims, 'what a state of ecstasy!' I observe that this was our mood in Tribschen, and he says, 'True – and what came of it?'

Saturday, December 11 R. works on his score, leads Amfortas to his bath. – Yesterday, watching Marke happily sniffing around in the palace gardens, he said: 'What a poet he is – Ossian in the mists of the past! He is utterly immersed in the ecstasy of scenting things out.'

Sunday, December 12 R. goes to his work but complains that he requires instruments he does not have, and he would need to invent some – not in order to make more noise, but to express what he had in mind. Later he tells me he has decided on trombones and trumpets (it concerns the exit to the lake): strange as it might seem it should prove as successful as previously the trumpets and flutes in the *Faust* Overture. – At lunch our friend Stein's views on the right to sacrifice lives for the sake of an idea (Marat) results in R.'s adopting Carlyle's opinion that revolution is a triviality run mad; and he says if the idea is such that it must be sealed by human blood, one must in that case sacrifice oneself.

Tuesday, December 14 R. did not have an utterly bad night, but he got out of bed. – In the morning he tells me that the water dripping in the cistern made such a pleasant noise that it was just like listening to a piece by Chopin. – He does some work in the evening and says he did something good today and is in exuberant mood, as always when satisfied with his work.

Wednesday, December 15 At midday we took leave of our friend Stein, looking forward to seeing him again. Talking of his still imperfect manner of reading aloud, R. says he throws the verses out like rogues from some tavern: Here, you – I know you, and you too – etc . . . In the evening a visit from our friend Feustel, who tells us in the most comical way of the quarrel between Voltz and Batz, which has led to their books' now being deposited on neutral ground. The two wives (sisters) could not get along together, neither was willing for her husband to visit the other! And Batz, cut off from his father, is now reconciled with him again, having quarrelled with his mother, who is separated from her husband, leaseholder of a *prison.* Balzac!

Thursday, December 16 A subject of conversation is the adoption of vegetarianism by our friends the Wolzogens; with this R. sees his ideas reflected back to him as in a distorting mirror, a great perception mistakenly converted into a petty practical act. – Perceivers and followers, perhaps the most deeply divided of natures! In the one, everything is great, free, tranquil; in the other, narrow, agitated, restricted; the one exerting its powers for the world, the other just for a sect.

Friday, December 17 At breakfast R. recalls his orchestrations and says he has never misjudged his effects – he may previously have overloaded the accompaniment for the singers, but he made no mistakes with the instruments. In the afternoon we again go for a walk in the palace gardens, and R. tells me of his desire to know once and for all what is genuine in the Gospels and what has been inserted. He says he recently glanced through the Bhavagad-Gita and was dismayed by the chaos of additions; if only one could be shown what the original was! – He works on his score but complains of lack of concentration. In the evening he talks to friend Wolz. in an earnest and fatherly way about vegetarianism, and the latter listens – but will it be of any use?

Saturday, December 18 R. looks run down – was he not pleased with his work? He is also easily irritated, as by the subject of Siegfried's education; I hoped to have arranged things satisfactorily with Herr Vogler, the head teacher, but R. wants a house tutor and is annoyed at always being surrounded by incompetent people who are unable to help him. – I suggest a reading, and we choose Cervantes's 'Rimorete and Contado', which gives us tremendous enjoyment. – The evening passes, we go upstairs, and when we are alone in R.'s little room, he begins to talk about Hans, with indignation on account of his behaviour towards Lusch[1]. He recapitulates the whole relationship and wants to write to him. I advise him that it would be better to state his feelings to Hans's cousin Frege[2], along with a repayment of the Bülow fund. A sad conversation; R. tells me this was the reason for his irritation – to hear about the performance of the Ninth from friends who went to hear it (Gross, etc.) this cut him to the heart. – His decision calms him somewhat, we go to bed – but soon he starts again, asks me many thing about the past, and thus the night is a very restless one. R. gets up and reads; at last he falls asleep!

Sunday, December 19 At midday he reads to me the draft of his letter to Herr Frege for Hans. Solemn feelings.

Monday, December 20 In the evening R. works on his score and shows me how carefully he has erased one passage. I receive friend Feustel, who tells me that his son-in-law was received in Meiningen by Hans with a flood of complaints about Bayreuth, and particularly about Wolz., who had misled him into signing the Jewish petition, whereas he sees that R. abstained and now stands well with the Jews. He, Hans, made the sacrifice and was hissed, etc.

[1] Bülow had curtly turned down Cosima's request to allow Daniela to go to Meiningen to hear him conduct Beethoven's Ninth symphony.

[2] Arnold Frege, son of a maternal aunt; the Bülow fund: the 40,000 marks produced by Hans's concert tour in aid of the festival earlier in 1880.

Tuesday, December 21 Some things said about Lusch upset us. We wonder whether Hans's attitude might not have an oppressive effect on the girls and disturb the even course of their development. If so, the blame is primarily mine. Conference at five – on friend Feustel's advice R. decides not to send his letter to Frege, lest it appear that the letter was the consequence of the altercation between Bülow and Gross.

Friday, December 24 Over coffee R. tells us something funny which he heard from Schnappauf: the knacker here said to him that since R. was in such good standing with the King, he might procure him the executioner's post, which has just fallen vacant. – The *tableau vivant*, splendidly posed and held by the children, delights and moves him, and he wants Joukowsky to paint it. Marke's Christmas present also pleases him, and the evening, lit right up to the end by the tree, passes merrily. The portrait of Fidi, presented by Jouk. to R., also delights him. But above all the dear children, who looked splendid in the *tableau* (three angels playing musical instruments: *Boni, Loldi, Eva*; Fidi, planing, as the young Jesus; Lulu as Madonna, praying; off to one side Pepino as Saint Joseph[1]). During the *tableau* Rubinstein plays the first chorale from *Die Msinger*.

Saturday, December 25 How to describe, how indeed to write? . . . The children strike up their song after the first embraces and sing it splendidly – then they bring me 'the locker', and what things there are in it! . . . The Ninth Symphony, copied out by R. 50 years ago – he coaxed it out of Frl. Uhlig for me! Splendidly written, pleasing him too with its painstaking thoroughness, which, when I think of all the things that must have been going on in that 17-year-old head, seems incredible to me. Then a lovely old necklace, which R. calls 'Frau Vogl's kiss', because, when he was choosing it in the antiquarian's shop, Frau Vogl rushed in and embraced him passionately. 'You will never see anything like that again,' R. said to the dealer. 'You should let me have it 100 marks cheaper.' 'That's true,' the man said, and R. remarks that much more and he would have given it to him for nothing. Then a gold heart, an old saltcellar, and many little things from the children, which I took out one by one out of the drawers, with comments from R. and the children. In my room I discover a table carpentered for me by Fidi, and lovely sketches by Joukowsky, full of associations. The morning passes in friendly felicitations, and R. says he would like to go on drinking without a break, he can do or write nothing. – Since the King kindly remembers me in a telegram, R. thanks him, sending birthday bliss to the sun! At lunch R. proposes my health, I have difficulty in replying, for what exists between us cannot be expressed in words before others, not even those nearest to us. After lunch he says to me, 'Forgive me for speaking like that.' – Ah, he is well and in good spirits

[1] In the subsequent painting Joukowsky, and not Pepino, is shown as Joseph.

– how can I have any other feeling than overwhelming gratitude? – In the evening the *tableau vivant* is repeated, and it moves R. to tears. Then R. plays the *Euryanthe* Overture with Rub., and after playing it he embraces me, exclaiming, 'Oh, Weber! I love him as much as I do you!' and then adds, 'No, not quite as much.' He then becomes immersed in memories of W., whom the Dresdeners called 'Humpelmarie' ['Hobbling Mary'], he recalls his walk, his expression, somewhat weary, and attributes his earnest application to so neglected a genre as opera to forebodings of his early death. R. is moved as he expresses this thought, and it is very affecting. Then he says to the children, 'Now I am going to sing something for Mama,' and he sings the passage in the first act where Lysiart comes to fetch Eur[yanthe], turning to me on the words 'When thou appearest.' – Then we start discussing *Fidelio*, which R. describes as unworthy of the composer of the symphonies in spite of splendid individual passages, and the finale of *Fidelio* is played. – The evening ends, I kneel in prayer before Him whose blessing can alone make me worthy of him. And as we lie quietly in bed, I hear his voice softly saying, 'I am happy, I am happy, now I could die, for it has all been fulfilled – what is still to come is a bonus.'

Monday, December 27 I occupy myself arranging the nice, dear things I was given, and delight in my little room, whose every corner arouses pleasant feelings. R. receives a nice letter from the King, who is sending him a Renaissance cabinet and a bronze model of his new castle near Hohen-schwangau[1]. R. once again feels his chest pains, but his afternoon rest restores him, and in the evening a magician delights him and us and a multitude of children in the hall. – Some Batz affairs disturb him, but he is pleasantly stimulated by a telegram from Herr Neumann, announcing further ventures with the *Ring* in America, London, St. Petersburg [*enclosed a telegram from Angelo Neumann in Leipzig, requesting exclusive rights to stage the* Ring *for three years against a royalty of ten percent of gross receipts*]. Since the director asks for an immediate answer, R. replies something like this: 'Somewhat tempestuous; confident that your intentions are upright, I give my consent.' – It would certainly be a good thing if the *Ring* itself were to bring R.'s finances back in order.

Wednesday, December 29 Seidl with us, which leads our conversation primarily to the Berlin venture. We go for a walk in the palace gardens, and R. has the idea of surprising Seidl at a rehearsal he is good-naturedly holding for the amateur concert. After the concert in the evening, R. reproaches him for having done it, saying: 'When one is under an obligation, as you are to Gross, one should discharge it in a homophonous way, but not with one's soul. Mount guard in front of Gross's bank, but do not conduct a concert. If Rothschild offered me a million to set a poem to

[1] Neuschwanstein.

music for him, do you think I would do it?' – He tells him that he went to the rehearsal in order to surprise him, take the baton from him, and beat time in such a way that they came to grief – but unfortunately, he says, the rehearsal was already over.

Thursday, December 30 Our friend Seidl has departed with instructions for Neumann, also equipped with cuts for *Tristan*.

Friday, December 31 We go for a walk in the palace gardens at one o'clock and again later in the afternoon, when, however, our walk was 'washed clean', as R. puts it, for it was raining. Over coffee we discuss Siegfried's development, and since R. talks about the importance of having a companion for his studies and his games, I have to laugh when he irritably exclaims, 'These boys are all so precious!' – He feels that the parents, such as the Giessels[1], etc., will not let us have one; his instinctively felt right to demand whatever he wants is here expressed so clearly, and is so different from anyone else, that I find it a joy to observe.

---

[1] Carl Giessel was a Bayreuth bookseller and publisher of the newspaper *Bayreuther Tagblatt*.

1881

Saturday, January 1 In the evening R. tells us feelingly about a blind starling, which a flock of starlings are looking after, feeding, taking with them on their migrations. His final word in bed is an exclamation over the stupidity of Gladstone, who is practising the policies of the former government, though he himself previously stood up for the Boers. – Before that he expressed a wish to see Carlyle.

Monday, January 2 Departure of Lusch, who is going to Mimi in Berlin.

Tuesday, January 4 A sketch of Kundry, brought along by Jouk., pleases us a lot. 'Actually,' says R., 'she ought to be lying there naked, like a Titian Venus.' – Now this has to be replaced by finery.

Wednesday, January 5 In the evening R. works a little on the orchestration of *Parsifal* and says how curious it was that, while orchestrating '*in heilig ernster Nacht nahten sich des Heilands holde Boten*,' he happened to open the book at that passage and saw that in his sketch he had left out the word *dereinst*; this he immediately put back in, for rhythmically it was very welcome to him; words like *Heiland* should never be extended, he says.

Thursday, January 6 While still in bed, R. says, 'If you look after me well, clothe me well, feed me well, then I shall still compose *Die Sieger*.' – 'My difficulty there is the locality and the speech. Christianity is all noble simplicity, but in Buddhism there is so much education, and education is very inartistic.' We talk of the fact that in both, *Parsifal* and *Sieger*, more or less the same theme (the redemption of a woman) is treated. 'It is impossible to judge what an effect the third act of *P*. will have if it is well done.' – That is why for Kundry he wants some other singer than Materna, whose face does not appeal to him, for she should be capable of deep and noble expressions. – He highly praises Gobineau's stories[1]. – Countess La Tour's[2] action in sending us the Count's picture starts a discussion over coffee about relationships of this kind. When I say that the Countess would be very shocked if one were to assume anything beyond friendship, R. says: 'But what is that – spending their evenings in intellectual conversations together? In such cases it always turns out that she is a goose and he a silly

---

[1] *Nouvelles asiatiques*, a series of stories on Asian themes, 1876.
[2] Wife of the Italian ambassador in Stockholm, where she met Gobineau; she was an artist, and she painted his portrait.

fool, for if one assumes that such contacts are not at the same time – how shall I put it? – physically beneficial, then all this homage to Plato is ridiculous.' – He works in the afternoon, three bars cause him trouble. – The question of costumes and decorations is discussed in the evening.

Saturday, January 8 R. is not entirely pleased by our friends' coming here for a conference, he says he feels no great eagerness to stage the work, though it gave him much joy to write it. – At twelve R. calls me and shows me how he has placed his nice slippers beneath his big chair; things like that give him pleasure, he says, when he enters the room. When I tell him I can understand that, he says, 'Yes, but your way of making your room pleasant is just to put up nasty pictures of me.' – In the evening Herr Schön, Pohl and Heckel; R. annoyed, first because, not wishing to retain his informal clothes, he feels uncomfortable, and second because he has no desire to talk about these things. He finds the good people all too unsatisfactory and insignificant, and the first moment of meeting is tart on his side and rather off-putting. But he soon recovers, makes jokes with and about Pohl, and when Rub. plays my father's arrangement of the Hummel septet, R. is in high spirits and finds much amusement in this old-fashioned, worthy piece, with all its padding.

Sunday, January 9 The conclusions of the conference are discussed, as well as the present relationship of the Society of Patrons to the performances, seats for which are now after all to be put on sale[1].

Monday, January 10 Molle[2] arrives from Bremen, a good and handsome creature. Also a letter from Herr Neumann enclosing very large announcements.

Tuesday, January 11 At breakfast and also at lunch we talked about Empress Augusta, who appears to have directed some malicious remarks at Lusch. R. says, 'These creatures are such utter nobodies, they cannot even make people happy, for when they bring someone into their entourage, they then find it a bother, and all that's left to them is to make malicious remarks.' – He expresses his happy feelings of certitude that nothing can happen to our children, and so foolish am I that, instead of being pleased, I am gripped by a kind of fear; I betray this only through a movement and an exclamation, but how unjust of me, how lacking in self-discipline, not simply to be pleased when he expresses pleasure!

Thursday, January 13 At four o'clock our old comrade-in-arms Karl Brandt! Against Feustel's advice R. has turned to him and invited him here to discuss the staging of *Parsifal*. Many memories, but above all much good sense, all conceivable technical questions; the music for the walk to the Temple listened to in order to assess the time needed for the transformation

---

[1] This was contrary to Wagner's wish, followed in 1876, that seats in his festival theatre be confined to subscribers, not sold directly through a box office.

[2] A Newfoundland bitch; her name was soon changed to Molly.

scene. – On the one hand R. regrets, but on the other he is glad, that things are now beginning in earnest. And that means Brandt. It is truly curious to hear the spear now being discussed – how it is to be held up with wires – whereas up till now it was only his soul that mattered. – R. is still taking great pleasure in Gobineau; he exclaims, 'What a shame that I find the only original writer so late in life!'

Friday, January 14 A good night, good work, and much Brandt. Our old friend has been to the theatre and pleases us with his delight at the way everything has been preserved. Maquettes are brought down so that he can show friend Jouk. what he wants. – In the afternoon, while the expert and the amateur are deliberating, R. and I go for a walk, watch Fidi tracing curves for the first time, delight in the two dogs, who look very funny in all the snow and come bounding towards us over the bridge. The cold is severe. R. takes delight in the full moon, standing very proudly in the sky 'as if Gottlieb had put it there.' (He tells us that during a theatrical performance a voice was suddenly heard saying, 'Gottlieb, pull out the moon.')

Saturday, January 15 Friend Feustel has sent me the minutes of the committee meeting, and I am pleased to see an alteration in the final paragraph which will enable R.'s wish to be fulfilled, namely, that the Bülow fund should go to his children.

Sunday, January 16 R. works and is pleased that the 30 pages of his score already look imposing. But before he goes to work, immediately after our parting, he comes to me wearing my old fox fur, which he has had covered in black velvet in a single day as a surprise for me. He is happy to have brought it off and reproaches me for denying everything, the cold and all the rest – as exuberant again now as ever before! We go for a walk in the palace gardens, I in my new furs – this time just with Molly, since Marke has a glass splinter in his paw; she is very obedient.

Tuesday, January 18 In the evening, stretched out in his big chair in his dressing room, he says, 'And now I am supposed to be looking forward to *Parsifal,* to coaching Jäger.' – But when, to distract him from all solemn thoughts, I admire his robe, which is pink, he says, 'Yes, this is what makes me feel good, something Feustel would find it completely impossible to understand.'

Wednesday, January 19 Friend Levi arrives towards evening, and music is played. Then R. announces to Herr Levi, to his astonishment, that he is to conduct *Parsifal*: 'Beforehand, we shall go through a ceremonial act with you. I hope I shall succeed in finding a formula which will make you feel completely one of us.' – The veiled expression on our friend's face induces R. to change the subject, but when we are alone, we discuss this question further. I tell R. that what seems to me to be the difficulty here is that the community into which the Israelite would be accepted has itself abandoned

Christ, though it might write about him, whereas previously blood was shed and everything sacrificed on his behalf. R. says he himself has certainly remained true to him, and in his last essay he more or less outlined what the formula would be. 'The trouble is,' he exclaims, 'that all great personalities reveal themselves to us in time and space, and are thus subject to change.' When we have our first parting, he exclaims jokingly, 'What an accursed subject you have brought up here!' and when we come together again, he raises it once more, and we agree that this alien race can never be wholly absorbed into our own. R. tells me (and I write it down here, for he has repeatedly said it to me, with very great earnestness and not a trace of mockery) that when our friend modestly approached him and kissed his hand, R. embraced him with great inner warmth, and from what emanated between them, he came to feel with extraordinary precision what a difference of race and separateness really mean. And thus the good Jew always suffers a melancholy lot in our midst.

Thursday, January 20 R. criticizes the conductor's gloominess and says: 'I should think that being taken up in such a friendly way by people like us would be enough to make anyone cheerful. Or are you all superstitious, having trouble with your souls?' He then speaks of Rub., how he is always preoccupied with himself, and in spite of his good qualities can never throw this off. He compares him with Levi, who is much more fortunate, since he has his own field of activity. He advises 'a carefree expansiveness.' – R. calls me Flower Mother, since at present I am frequently wearing asters, but he chides me for dressing *à la vieille*, is unwilling to admit that I am old! R. talks of the new version he made of the ballade in *Der Fl. Holländer*, which he has unfortunately lost. The same thing happened with the '*ich sank in süssen Schlaf*' passage in *Lohengrin*[1], he says: he had it quite wonderfully but never found it again; as it now stands, it is an approximation.

Friday, January 21 We go out, the dogs almost knock R. over in their joy, and in this devotion of animals to him I see one of the signs of R.'s wonderful connection with Nature. Animals like me very much too, but it seems to me that they greet him as if no division had ever taken place. When we return home, R. feels Marke's ear and finds that it is still stiff: 'Things like this don't just go away,' he says. 'It is like my finger, but he puts up with it better.' – I: 'He has no *Parsifal* to compose.' 'That's true,' says R., 'and every page calls for some new invention.'

Saturday, January 22 He works in the evening and reaches Parsifal's arrow shot. – In the evening we turn to Gobineau. (Yesterday, when I informed him that Gobin. had a malicious wife, R. exclaims how terrible it is that a youthful urge to find fulfilment must then be dragged in misery through one's whole life. He says how wrong the woman's place is in our society –

---

[1] Elsa in Act I, Scene 1 (conclusion of '*Einsam in trüben Tagen*').

on the one hand making a show of chivalrous devotion, yet on the other, holding her in contempt.) – R. has written to Lilli Lehmann about engaging the Flower Maidens.

Sunday, January 23 His royalties from Vienna seem very good; now that *Die Msinger* is beginning to make an impact, he says, he hopes things will get better and better.

Thursday, January 27 When we are alone in his dressing room, R. tells me he has received a telegram from Prof. Frege, saying he is returning the letters without passing them on. – After we remark with a fleeting smile on such courageousness, long discussion about what to do. I end by saying to R. that everything he wishes or does is acceptable to me.

Friday, January 28 R. slept well, and though our morning conversation returns anxiously to the subject which is foremost in our thoughts, it does so in such a way that at lunch R. can refer to it jokingly through the story of a man who spoke of obstacles in a horse race. 'What was the obstacle?' 'I didn't have a horse.' – R. observes that he also has no horse – that is to say, Hans will not read the letters. But he does some work, and even though he says, '*Parsifal* bores me, I should like to do something else,' his spirits are raised by some good work.

Tuesday, February 1 In the evening friend Feustel, whom R. instructs to reimburse the 40,000 marks to Hans, telling him that he can discover the reasons for this reimbursement in letters to Prof. Frege. Friend Feustel very understanding.

Wednesday, February 2 In the evening we read Gobineau's story '*La Vie de voyage*' with great interest. R. feels that the Count must be unhappy; his companion, Countess La Tour, seems to him to be insufficiently equipped to make a man happy, for, 'A woman who paints –!' he exclaims.

Friday, February 4 Boni at her first ball yesterday, the two girls preparing themselves for confirmation, Lusch out in the wide world, sending us melancholy reports! Fidi the only one still displaying childhood in all its innocence. – At supper joking with Loldi about the major and minor prophets and with Boni about her experiences at the ball. After that our friends; an attempt with [Spontini's] *La Vestale* miscarries somewhat, but then Beeth.'s last quartet – ours! R. summarizes our feelings during the playing thus: 'It seems something like an act of grace that one is allowed in one's stupidity to listen to such a being.' – When all have gone, we 'wash down the evening' with champagne, R. and I, and talk of Beeth.: 'If only one had known, had seen a being like that! He would not have put up with us, but what tremendous outbursts there would have been – cries of bliss and ecstasy! He would then have gone his own way, rather like your father. It is quite unimaginable. I have seen both him and Shakespeare in my dreams – towards me always gently consoling.'

Monday, February 7 In the evening he writes his score, though he keeps saying how much he would rather be writing symphonies: 'All the time I am putting aside themes for the sake of the drama – I cannot do things as, for example, even Weber did, when he introduced his hermit with a dance tune because it happened to occur to him just at that moment.'

Wednesday, February 9 We talk of Wolz.'s manner, of his eyebrows, which give one the feeling that he could turn the world upside down. 'And I, who am energy personified, have none at all,' R. adds, in such a humorous tone of voice that we all burst out laughing. We go for a walk in the palace gardens. 'That would be nice,' I suddenly hear him say. 'What?' 'I can't say just now,' and then: 'If one melody were to accompany another, the first one were to disappear, and its accompaniment be turned by the cellos into the main melody, and so on alternately. I have got something of that sort in the "*Kaisermarsch.*" ' He adds, 'The "*Kaisermarsch*" is probably the nicest of my instrumental compositions; it shows what one can still place beside Beeth.' In the evening we chat together about all sorts of things, my father, the Israelites – and finally [Wilhelmine] Schröder-Devrient. Jouk. asked whether she was beautiful. R.: 'How shall I reply to that? Everything about her was life, soul, warmth, and an expression of delight such as I have otherwise seen only in Cosima. – A face easily expresses suffering, but true delight – I once saw such an expression in Grisi[1], when she uttered the word "*gioia*" ["joy"], and there was something of it in Judith.' Of the latter he said, 'At that time, in 1876, I found her natural warmth very pleasant in contrast to all the prevailing stiffness.'

Thursday, February 10 Towards lunchtime he calls me and reads to me his new article, 'Know Thyself'.[2] – Whether the Jews can ever be redeemed is the question which, in connection with it, occupies our thoughts – their nature condemns them to the world's reality. They have profaned Christianity, that is to say, adapted it to this world, and from our art, which can only be a refuge from prevailing conditions, they also expect world conquest.

Friday, February 11 R. reads to me the revised ending of his article, which seems to me more fitting than the first, and R. himself says that he always meant to write about us, not about the Jews. And yet I have to tell him what strange feelings it arouses in me when he alters anything at my instigation; I say that for me every idea he has is sacred. – 'You foolish girl,' he says. 'As if we were not always in harmony!'

Monday, February 14 R. allows me to cut off one of his eyebrow hairs which has grown too long and to place it in my locket. In the evening I read his article out loud; R. listens, standing, interrupts me now and again with signs of approval, and then embraces me. The loving intensity with which he listened and watched did, I believe, increase my powers of

---

[1] Giulia Grisi, Italian soprano whom Wagner saw and praised as Donna Anna in *Don Giovanni* in 1840 during his time in Paris; her sister was Judith Gautier's mother.

[2] A supplement to 'Religion and Art', *B.B.* February-March 1881.

interpretation, and if he was satisfied with the way I imparted his ideas, to me it was bliss to express them.

Thursday, February 17 R. observes that Hans has never got beyond the age of 15–17, never become a man, whereas Fidi would reach fulfilment only as an adult man – I observe that for R. himself this age of fulfilment would be old age, since only then would all that he is become apparent. – Yesterday he said to me jokingly, 'You must have a very bad conscience towards me, since you always give in and adapt yourself to me' – and this makes me feel very solemn, as if I have no right even to the happiness of being permitted to obey him! And for me the main burden of my life is that, though I should like to surrender myself utterly all the time, I still hold firm, desist even from expressing many things, in order not to disturb the tranquillity which is better for him than ecstasy. . . . But yesterday I had to tell him that on the night of Eva's birth he spoke a word to me which transported me beyond all the sufferings of mind and body; he wanted to know what it was, I could not say it – for you, my Eva, let it be written down here, as a blessing on you: 'I have never loved before.' – This is what he said, showing me the full extent of his love. . . . 'Good night, you big and pretty girls,' he said tonight to these two beings who have so flourished beneath his star.

Friday, February 18 In the evening we receive a visit from Herr Irwine, the donor who wishes to remain anonymous, a quiet and serious Scotsman. R. gets Rub. to play [Mendelssohn's] *Hebrides* Overture and delights in this beautiful work, though he feels it requires a programme, for when he heard it for the first time, in Leipzig, under the title of *Hebrides* Overture – which meant nothing to him – he did not understand it at all. The Scotsman made a good impression on him, but he remarks that Nature is now no longer producing beautiful mouths!

Saturday, February 19 R. recalls the *Hebrides* Overture and Mendelssohn, that uncanny man, silently lying in wait, then suddenly breaking into violent speech. – After lunch he tells us how handsome he was, and how at the age of 30 he became so Jewish.

Sunday, February 20 Yesterday, in our conversation about Mendelssohn, R. recalled Disraeli's *Tancred*, in which it is asserted that all significant people are Jews. R. says, 'Most of them are German Jews, and Disraeli overlooks the fact that it is German talent which is being used in this way.' When we return home from our walk, R. recalls the passage in *Parsifal* which he is just orchestrating, '*Waren die Menschen, die mir wehrten, bös?*'[1] He is pleased with Gurnemanz's laughter in reply, and he says it was necessary in order to show the childlike qualities which make Gurnemanz believe that this is the creature for whom they have been waiting.

---

[1] Correctly, '*Die mich bedrohten, waren sie bös?*' ('Those who hindered me, were they wicked?'), Act I.

Monday, February 21 When I come downstairs for lunch, I find R. very cheerful; the rubber fingers recommended by Dr. Hess[1] have arrived, and they do him good, take away the irritation, and that is enough to restore him to the most splendid of spirits.

Wednesday, February 23 Herr Neumann writes to me to say that there is a growing danger of the Jews' staying away from the *Ring* in Berlin; R. is advising him to abandon Berlin and go straight to London; the ordinary citizens have no money, the aristocracy and the Court will stay away on account of Hülsen, and the Jews on account of the agitation. But all of this is unpleasant to a high degree, like everything else outside!

Thursday, February 24 R. had a bad night, his fingers are tormenting him, and today he cannot even write. He does have a moment of gaiety before lunch, but it soon passes, everything pains and upsets him. Dr. Landgraf, who joins us for coffee, thinks that the rubber fingers have overheated him, he takes them off. – in the evening friend Wolz. visits us; R. tells him that we cannot champion special causes such as vegetarianism in our *Blätter*, but must always confine ourselves to defining and demonstrating the ideal, leaving those outside to fight for their special cause; for the same reason we cannot join in the anti-Jewish agitation.

Friday, February 25 A telegram from Herr Neumann says that Berlin cannot be abandoned. After lunch Jouk.'s relationship with Pepino discussed in much detail, brought up by a sad amorous incident. I allow myself to be provoked into describing it as *silly*, and I regret that. We talk about it with R. as we go for a walk together amid snowflakes to the Birk, and for R.'s sake I almost prefer this subject to the anti-Jewish agitation, Berlin, etc. About the relationship with P., R. said: 'It is something for which I have understanding, but no inclination. In any case, with all relationships, what matters most is what we ourselves put into them. It is all illusion.'

Sunday, February 27 R. works on his score, and when I come downstairs around lunchtime, he shows me a letter from the Société des Amis du Divorce [Society of the Friends of Divorce], appointing him an honorary member. At lunch a telegram arrives, reporting the success of *Lohengrin* in Naples. Our guest is Prof. Toussaint[2], who is giving Siegfried Latin lessons and who seems quite bright . . .

Monday, February 28 R. works and with a smile signs the letter of thanks to the Friends of Divorce. He is still not content with his fingers.

Tuesday, March 1 The boys, Fidi's friends, skylark in the gallery, celebrating Shrovetide. R. then corrects the proofs of 'Know Thyself'.

Thursday, March 3 Over coffee R. talks about the Boers and says he has joined the committee set up to support them – at present looking after the

---

[1] Otto Hess, a physician in Bayreuth; Wagner had been having some (unidentified) trouble with his fingers for the past 3 weeks.
[2] Maximilian Toussaint, teacher at the Lateinschule, Bayreuth.

wounded. And he talks of a recent perfidious act on the part of the English, though it has been of no help to them, for they were beaten by the Boers in spite of their superior numbers[1]. – When we are alone and talking about the unfathomably deep wisdom of the Indians, I ask R. whether he does not feel that they are nevertheless at a disadvantage compared with Christians, appear indeed even petty: they sought to arrange and regulate the world, whereas Christianity leads us away from it. He agrees with me.

Friday, March 4 Though the weather is not good, we go for a walk in the palace gardens. As we are happily watching Fidi, alone on the ice, and the dogs chase after him, he is suddenly shouted at by the keeper to take the dogs off the ice; R. very angry – he cannot bear such admonishments – and his anger at once gives him chest spasms. – He writes to the palace gardener, and by supper has overcome his vexation.

Saturday, March 5 The palace gardener has sent him a polite reply; R. is pleased and says, 'So you see these people do not regard one merely as trash.' – When we are alone together, we lose ourselves in the remotest regions of religion and philosophy. He still holds out hope of man's regeneration, believes in the establishment of a community, but will hear nothing of it when, speaking of Loldi, I say that I believe she has a leaning towards a withdrawal from the world.

Sunday, March 6 R. writes some additional music for *Parsifal – 4 minutes of music*[2].

Friday, March 11 R. is having trouble with the Magic Garden, which friend Jouk. still cannot get right. He drives off with the latter and with Fidi and takes a walk on the station platform, since the weather does not permit anything else. – R. then works before supper and afterwards we look with great enjoyment at H. Burgkmair's splendid work, *Der Weisskunig*[3], lent me by the royal library in Munich. 'The power in these robes!' R. exclaims. At ten o'clock, when we were still all assembled in the *salon*, I heard a distant sound, we open the door into the hall and hear Isolde and Eva singing his '*Gruss seiner Treuen*'[4] in bed to themselves. It touches us greatly.

Sunday, March 13 In the evening Rub. plays us the music from the Paris *Tannhäuser*, and I see R., actually for the first time, taking great pleasure in it: 'If someone were to tell me to do such a thing, I should find it impossible.' He is pleased with its fullness, for he says it is no easy matter to write such an extended allegro. He also asks himself, when we are alone, what it is that makes the old *Tannhäuser* Overture so significant, for from a

---

[1] At Majuba Hill on 27 February in the war concerning the independence of Transvaal.

[2] For the transformation scene in Act I.

[3] Hans Burgkmair (1473–1531), German painter and engraver; the original of *Der Weisskunig*, done for Emperor Maximilian I, is in Graz, Austria.

[4] A choral work by Wagner, composed for the King of Saxony and performed in Pillnitz on August 12, 1844.

musical point of view it is in many ways much inferior to Weber's, and Mendelssohn would certainly have looked down on it in scorn. It is the vividness of the motives, he thinks: 'I have never been grudging.' – It consists entirely of motives, he continues, and his theme for Tannhäuser, for instance, broke with the usual custom of making the second subject a graceful one; he believes that, placed beside preceding works of greater musical accomplishment, it nevertheless looks new. – And in conclusion he says he enjoys watching me while his music is being played; he will stage performances and seat himself with his glasses so that he can watch me, for that is something worth seeing – and he blesses me, and blissfully we go off to bed!

Monday, March 14 'So they have got him at last,' R. says in the morning, and he reads me the dispatch reporting the assassination of the Tsar[1]. I am very shocked; but R. ponders with great calm on the forces which have been unleashed here, and he is particularly struck by the fact that a second bomb was thrown. Our poor friend Jouk. utterly downcast; at lunch we talk a lot about Tsar Alexander, whose limited outlook, combined with good intentions, led to this tragic conclusion. – R. replies on a postcard to an appeal from an anti-Jewish newspaper – does not wish to have anything to do with this affair, or indeed with the German Reich at all, after its behaviour in the vivisection matter.

Tuesday, March 15 Count Gobineau has sent us a piece about India for the *Blätter.* Concerning the assassination, R. says there was madness on both sides – two bombs of stupidity which burst against each other. The Tsar, who did not wish to have any contacts with the Liberals, leaving such matters to his son but not abdicating – as if events would wait! 'Oh, the madness of rulers!' R. exclaims. And now his successor, who out of filial piety must hang, banish and imprison, and cannot be humane. 'You would need a genius in this post,' he says. – We ask Rub. to play the Venusberg music again. – R. tells me that during the rehearsals in Paris Wesendonck said to him, 'What utterly voluptuous sounds these are!' 'I suppose he was afraid I had been dancing something like that in front of his wife,' R. says!

Wednesday, March 16 Bright sunshine persuades R. to arrange a drive to the theatre. The dog Faf, offspring of Marke, enchants us with his beauty. And letters to me from Count Gobineau, expressing a half-spoken wish to settle here, and from Herr Levi, affected by 'Know Thyself', have on the whole a pleasant effect on R. Today he bubbles over with humour as seldom before! He maintains that it is because he does not wish to make me speak, on account of my cough. His good spirits and his wit also extend to Hans, of whom, over coffee, he says quite simply that he is unbearable! Which, in my depressed state of mind on this subject, causes me great amusement.

---

[1] Tsar Alexander II in St. Petersburg on March 13.

Monday, March 21 Towards evening I wish to greet R. before he goes downstairs to work; I go into his little room, he is already in his dressing room; I wait on the spiral staircase and hear him say, 'I should prefer cures to newspaper reports – well, all right, he knows the child has relations in Brazil –' and, after a pause, 'It's as if it were predestined, they occupy all the southern countries.' I ask him what all this means, tell him what I heard, he reflects, laughs and says: 'When I looked at my finger, I was reminded of the doctor; he has gone into the country on account of the murder of a child, the girl has disappeared, and within me arose a romance about Schnappauf having concealed the girl in his home (knowing of rich relations in Brazil) in order to marry her off to his son! And, as regards Brazil, it occurred to me that all immigrations there are in the hands of the Catholics, and all that remains for the Protestants is the North.' – We laugh heartily over this spoken monologue. – At supper he complains humorously of our having so many girls – there are no men around, and they will become old maids. – (As evidence of his hard work he shows me page 80 of his score, which he completed today, and particularly the bassoon passage in it.)

Tuesday, March 22 When R. wishes me good morning, I tell him how beautiful he is; he replies gaily, in the tone of Bottom, 'Not so, neither,' which leads us to talk about this scene in Shakespeare. – Then he goes off, first to his reading (Gobineau), later to his score. – Towards four o'clock Brandt and the Brückner brothers; much of a technical nature; Brandt excellent as always.

Sunday, March 27 R. annoyed by Feustel's accounts to me of the impossibility of getting hold of Hans. But he gradually recovers his spirits. – Walk to the Birk after Jouk.'s costume designs have been accepted. A strong wind is blowing, proving very troublesome, constant thoughts of Italy. – Whether to give up here entirely – but in that case R. would want to burn everything down, for he would find it too painful to see alien, common furnishings here, as in Tribschen.

Wednesday, March 30 At lunch, talking of Count Gobineau's book[1], R. remarks that distinguished Frenchmen seem able to understand all the peoples of the earth with the exception of the Germans. 'When the right man appears among us, we produce what are probably the only completely universal and unprejudiced minds.' He feels that even Carlyle is prejudiced in many ways. 'But,' he says, 'we do not present ourselves well, we are thoroughly unpleasant.'

Thursday, March 31 R. had a somewhat restless night; he read a lot of Gobineau, who annoys him with his Celts and various other things, but he retains his satisfaction with this intelligent man. He works. Our Friedel is hoarse, and it looks as if it may be something serious. Rough weather.

[1] *The Inequality of the Human Races.*

Before supper R. goes to Fidi, but he admits to me that he does not really know how to speak to him, he felt he was being so affected when he tried to play the piano to him.

Saturday, April 2 Our morning conversation touches on how ill-natured musicians are (Brahms, Berlioz); R. says they are perhaps more irritable than other people. I realize ever more deeply that when he (R.) sometimes says things which are offensive and deeply wounding, he does it with complete innocence, and he has a daemonic instinct for being right. The fact that one is so defenceless against it is what makes one feel so uncomfortable. Today he writes three pages of his score and shows me that he has arrived at the '*mein Sohn Amfortas*' passage.

Sunday, April 3 I spend most of my time with Fidi, pleased by his patience and amiability. Letters from Lusch and Countess La Tour enliven our coffee-time. Speaking of Count G.'s book, R. observes that one becomes conscious of his immaturity, and really people should not write long books. In the morning R. had counted up how many English governments he had already lived through, and he talked of Canning's head, which as a child he had seen on pipes with the inscription '*Liberté civile et religieuse pour tous*' ['Civil and religious liberty for all'].

Thursday, April 7 Towards evening Herr Francke[1] from London comes to see R. about *Tristan* and *Meistersinger*: the project, it seems, is assured. – R. praises the English in comparison with the Germans; when they think there is something they do not know, they become all attention, and on this it is then possible to build. 'But we – we know it all, we are horrible! I can say that, because: *J'en suis* [I am one of them]!' . . . When Herr Francke remarked that Hanslick was just a gnat, R. became very vexed and demonstrated to him what such a man can do in the way of creating obstacles for existing talents and destroying means.

Saturday, April 9 At the conclusion of the evening R. reads aloud the first scenes from Aristophanes's *The Frogs*, to our great amusement. R. sees it all before him, the people, the poet, the actors, and he delights in its freedom and its genius. Afterwards he points out to me how much more genuine this kind of comedy is, however difficult for women's ears in its bluntness, than our own kind, which shows human beings only as they seem, their positions and other things of that sort. Whereas this turns its attention to the generic animality of the human being, shows it in conflict with his qualities as a god, and this, in the middle of a ceremony in honour of this very god, with all the invocations of his priests who are sitting there, must have produced inimitable comic effects.

Sunday, April 10 Our conversation turns to tenors, etc., and telegrams

---

[1] Hermann Francke, violinist and concert promoter in London, who was planning with Pollini, Hamburg, to stage *Tristan* and *Die Meistersinger* at the Drury Lane Theatre.

from Herr Neumann, alarmed on account of the Francke project[1], also provide things from the outside world – and thoroughly unpleasant ones – to talk about! R. laments that among musicians he has only the most primitive handymen to represent him! Now we are returning to the old miseries, and both of us are apprehensive, in our own ways.

Wednesday, April 13 Herr Seitz's costume sketches reveal to us in their 'masterliness' all the wretchedness which divides us from all others – Flower Maidens like cabaret Valkyries – yet all of it lovely. – Deep gloom hangs over R. in consequence – at times he looks just like Siegfried! At lunch [Levi] talks about the bells to be obtained for *Parsifal* and about the glass bells in the Munich theatre. R. laughs and says such Cyclopean cheese-covers would be just the thing.

Thursday, April 14 At meals our talk revolves mainly about casting. In the evening R. tells our friends about his disappointment with the costume designs – 'shopworn women' where all should be innocence: 'Everything in my art is chaste,' he can say with pride!

Saturday, April 16 Spring is here. All kinds of things for me, including the newly arrived Herr Köhler[2] – a wild sort of creature – can he be tamed?

Tuesday, April 19 Our first conversation leads us – I do not know how – to the ancient world; I say to R. that clothing seems to give life a particular flavour, because, as it were, it leads one to expect the movement which these copious folds would encourage; nakedness, rather, arouses feelings of stillness. – R. agrees with me and says that painting in particular is on the wrong path when it depicts the nude female figure, which, from an aesthetic point of view, is not really beautiful. Then we part and are reunited in the church, to which R. comes after the sermon for the holy act[3]. He too is moved, deeply moved. He wishes to baptize Levi and to admit no Jews to Holy Communion. In the evening he plays for me parts of *Parsifal*.

Wednesday, April 20 Herr Köhler at lunch, rather heavy going. In the evening Feustel, bringing important news about Batz & Voltz, and much joking as well. The evening ends with great agitation on R.'s part, since friend Feustel starts, in his usual wordy style, to sing the praises of the German Reich. R. tries to point out to him how little wisdom there is to be found in it, and to what completely different uses the situation and potentialities could have been put.

Saturday, April 23 A letter from Loulou tells us that my father is leaving [Berlin] on the very day of our arrival! That ferments inside R., and he writes to my father with utter frankness! I tell him I myself would not write

[1] He was alarmed at the prospect of his *Ring* performances at Her Majesty's Theatre in London coinciding with the Francke-Pollini productions of *Tristan und Isolde, Die Meistersinger, Tannhäuser* and *Lohengrin* in Drury Lane; they did in fact overlap.
[2] A School teacher from Cologne, engaged as tutor for Siegfried.
[3] Confirmation of Isolde and Eva.

this letter, he keeps it back, then demands it again from me and sends it off! He is so indignant over my father's passing us by. He keeps talking about it all evening, but without anger, because there is nobody to contradict him, and he goes to bed pacified.

Monday, April 25 R. had a tolerable night but is nevertheless indisposed and later out of humour. The matter of the contract with London, the journey to Berlin, Hans's behaviour, it all weighs on him, and he complains that all he is conscious of nowadays is a state of either exaltation or deep depression. The weather is also vexing him – that probably most of all. To distract him a little, I tell him about the picture (a surprise) and the sittings[1]. The Jägers at lunch, he arousing confidence in me. No walk, I arranging the little house for Herr Köhler; while I am there, R. comes in search of me to give me back the sketch of the first act – his first act is now completely orchestrated!

Wednesday, April 27 A better night for R., and a better mood, as always when he sees nobody. Feustel's telegram causes concern, Lusch's a sort of satisfaction. [*Enclosed Daniela's telegram from Berlin*: 'Indescribably moved by today's reunion[2], I beg for your thoughts. Would it be possible to put off your arrival for one day on account of hotel and other considerations, await answer – Lulu.'] – We postpone our journey. We try taking a walk in the garden, but rain and snow drive us back indoors.

Thursday, April 28 All morning R. is agog to hear details. Letters from Lusch and from Feustel provide little information, except that Lusch was much moved by the reunion. R. thinks it natural that she should now find it difficult to approach him – Nature is powerful, he says. My feeling, however, is that she might rather turn against me. At lunch some aggressive remarks of Loldi's cause him to comment on the peculiarity of the female character.

Friday, April 29 At noon I receive a letter from Hans – four explosive lines of thanks! – At one o'clock departure with M[arie] Gross. R. soon in good spirits, keeps wishing for Jouk. to admire the scenery of Saxony. Sad arrival after a cheerful journey. Feustel all alone on the platform! – Lusch not even at the hotel! When it gets late and I have written to the children (two postcards) I fall asleep, and when I awake, I find R. deeply moved – and about me. – Once, when I opened my eyes and moved my hands, he placed them together again and then said to me, 'Go on sleeping, you are so beautiful!' And thus I feel his blessing on me and feel that it was he who brought about the reunion which has made me so happy. Gentle tears fall from our eyes – how blissful we are in this unblissful life!

Saturday, April 30 A good night. – At ten o'clock Lusch! Many reports of

[1] Joukowsky's *The Holy Family*, based on the Christmas *tableau vivant*.
[2] With her father; Feustel's presence in Berlin was also connected with this event.

the emotional reunion with her father – that he spoke constantly of me; R. somewhat dejected. Feustel's initial mediation very clumsily done. Visits to Mimi, then to the singers, L[illi] Lehmann – meal at the Schleinitzes', who cannot praise Lusch too highly. The Count very original, friendly and interesting. In the evening Lusch with us again. The poor child wildly excited; R. in his truthfulness speaks his thoughts concerning her father – it pains me, for she is in such a state of turbulence, both physically and morally!

Monday, May 2 The rehearsal begins (first and second acts *Walküre*), R. not with me at first, but then he comes; it goes reasonably well – the orchestra amazing – and when Frau Vogl [as Sieglinde], in fetching the utensils, does not match the action with the music, R. is still sufficiently good-humoured to interrupt and call out, 'We must do that again, or Herr v. Hülsen will run away.' – And during another passage, 'This will please even Herr v. Hülsen.' The orchestra fills us with astonishment, and in our friend Seidl we are able to take genuine delight. Scaria confronts us with certain Viennese cuts. R. points out how absurd they are – for example, the entry of the Wanderer – whereas it would be easier to make slight cuts in the course of the scene. This happened on the following day. The tone in which Herr Scaria [Wotan] speaks is reminiscent of earlier, painful experiences. We eat alone together, R. and I, then drive to the rehearsal (third act *Walküre*) – much trouble with machinery and lighting. We drive home, not too late, and are alone together. Lusch rushes in from a *soirée* at the Crown Prince's – her accounts of it are not enlivening!

Tuesday, May 3 Lilli Lehmann visited in the morning; discussion about the Flower Maidens. Letters from the children! At eleven o'clock we drive to the rehearsals, R. with Mimi, I with Lusch. First act *Siegfried*. Mime 'a Jewish dwarf,' R. says, but excellent¹, Vogl [Siegfried] also very good, clear and assured. But Seidl is greeted by R. as a pearl. He dines with us, at six o'clock Herr Niemann in a mood of enthusiastic excitement, we drive with him to the rehearsals (second and third acts *Siegfried*), Scaria overwhelming in the scene with the Wala – Materna [Brünnhilde] unfortunately gesticulating very strongly, making a cut (*'dort sehe ich Grane'*) which throws Vogl off, R. indignant and provoked into a very loud exclamation. Vexation during the rehearsal, at the end much weeping and lamenting in the corridor. Herr Niemann thinks it was all because of Vogl's gratified expression! . . . Seidl quite composed.

Wednesday, May 4 I write letters. R. goes to see Materna, who starts to cry again, R. cuts her short by saying he has not come to hear all yesterday's twaddle over again. I also visit the singers. We come together again at three o'clock and eat cosily alone. Then to the *Rheingold* rehearsal, which is held

¹ Julius Lieban (b.1857), son of a Jewish cantor.

with piano; the first scene just about all right, but everything else, lighting, scenery, etc., is very poor. R., depressed, says that he experienced such things in Magdeburg 50 years ago and never thought to see them repeated!

Thursday, May 5 We drive to the theatre with Lusch. R. is received with a flourish and applauded enthusiastically. The performance [*Das Rheingold*] is on the whole so excellent that R. has the desire to acknowledge the applause from the stage with the singers. He makes a little speech and indicates the artists – the merit is theirs and they deserve the applause. Scaria excellent as Wotan and the whole performance extraordinarily lively. R. thought it not bad that an intermission was inserted. Unfortunately it was necessary to use steam between the Rhine scene and Valhalla in order to drown out the sounds of the scene changing – an embarrassing absurdity. A letter from Count Gobineau, he is at Wahnfried and seems to be quite happy with the children.

Friday, May 6 R. slept well, but he has caught a cold. Friend Stein is here, always welcome. We drive to the theatre, R. stages the fight in *Walküre* with incredible agility. (Twice during a rehearsal he frightened me by climbing from one first-floor proscenium box to the other.) He is tired, goes straight to bed when we arrive home, and at our meal around four o'clock he is again in good spirits, declares it is due to Stein. But he wonders whether or not to attend the performance, decides he will. Reception, flourish; for us the first act something of a failure, he goes on stage, talks with the singers. The acting better in the second act, the fight very successful. At the conclusion R. is all but exhausted and very irritable; he acknowledges the applause from the box.

Saturday, May 7 A bad night, R. sends for the doctor, he has a slight sore throat. Dr. Zwingenberg prescribes something for him, bows deferentially low, and says: 'Now, having seen you, I feel a few inches taller. I first read *Opera and Drama* in 1851.' – A letter from Frau v. Heldburg reports Hans's emotion over his reunion with his daughter.

Sunday, May 8 We remain at home, R. reading Gobineau. Herr Neumann full of misgivings about the rehearsal. And in the evening the dream comes true: Jäger as Siegfried utterly unsuccessful, he actually provokes the audience to demonstrations. R. does not appear at the end.

Monday, May 9 *Götterdämmerung* in the evening; despite all the deficiencies in the acting, R. and I are very moved by it; with Brünnhilde's last words we are leaning against each other, my head on his arm, and he exclaims to me, 'What we go through together!' – He goes on stage and makes a speech. We stay up together for a long time. (The Crown Prince wished to see R. in his box, R. begs to be excused.)

Tuesday, May 10 R. writes to friend Wolz. about Jäger and tells Neumann that in this case an amputation will be necessary. – Lusch's and Boni's first nursemaid visits me, many memories – very touching that she joined the crowd lining the street to see us drive up for *Rheingold*. Then for me Dr. Herrig[1] and poor, oblivious Herr Jäger! – We breakfast with Seidl at the Schleinitzes', after which R. goes to an artists' dinner in the Hôtel de Rome, which to his annoyance turns out to be a Jewish family-hotel dinner. In the evening we receive old Prof. Werder[2], whom R. holds in most cordial memory. – At last, at eleven o'clock, we are at the station with Lusch and take our departure.

Wednesday, May 11 Arrival at one thirty – all the dear children, Count Gobineau and friend Paul [Joukowsky] as well, Siegfried gazing fixedly at his father with radiant eyes. – In the evening R. very tired, we break up early. –

Thursday, May 12 To work at once, that is to say, a sitting with Joukowsky, the Count reading aloud his *Amadis* and endless discussions with the Count about everything.

Tuesday, May 17 In the afternoon the Brückners and Herr Brandt show us the maquettes of the temple and the Magic Garden, which are thoroughly satisfactory.

Wednesday, May 18 We drive up to the theatre with the Count, R. looks at it with cheerful pride; and in the evening, when he reads that many people in Berlin find the *Nibelungen* tiring, he is extremely glad to see this mentioned, because he thinks it is correct. – In the evening a quarrel develops between the Count and him about the Irish, whom Gob. declares to be incapable of working. R. becomes very angry, says he would not work under such conditions either, and he castigates the English aristocracy. The Count goes so far in his ideas as to reproach the Gospels for interceding on behalf of the poor. But it all ends very amicably, R. admits that he does not know the problem in detail, and the Count says to him, '*Vous voyez la chose en philosophe et moi en homme d'affaires*' ['You view the matter like a philosopher and I like a businessman'].

Friday, May 20 The Ritter children arrive, most welcome at the rehearsals, which we begin immediately.

Saturday, May 21 There is nowhere for him to go – the Eyssers[3] are working on the surprise, and in the hall we are holding rehearsals! At lunch he says merrily that he wishes he could be given his presents right away! At coffee-time the Standhartners appear, father and daughter.

Sunday, May 22 The Flower Greeting[4] takes place at eight o'clock and is very successful, the clock presented by Fidi-Parsifal delights R., and he is

[1] Hans Herrig (b.1845), poet and playwright, first approached Wagner in 1870.

[2] Karl Friedrich Werder, poet; he gave Wagner encouragement when *Der Fliegende Holländer* was hissed in Berlin in 1844.

[3] Decorators who had come to paint the coats of arms of all towns with Wagner Societies on the ceiling of the *salon*.

[4] Written by Wolzogen, with Siegfried as Parsifal and the girls as Flower Maidens.

pleased with the flower costumes. The coats of arms of the Wagner Society towns genuinely surprise him, and he is pleased with the ceiling. In a mood of divine happiness he strolls to the summerhouse with me in the blue robe, and we exchange gold pens and little poems! Our lunch table consists of; Standhartners three (with Gustav!)[1], Ritters (the parents), the Count, Jouk., Boni, Lusch and Fidi; in the hall Eva, Loldi, Ferdi Jäger, Julchen and Elsa [Ritter]; the latter two have to slip away unnoticed, so that the singing of the verse will float down from the gallery. Siegfried speaks Stein's poem very well, splendidly proposing the health of eternal youth, and then in a full voice Elsa movingly sings '*Nicht Gut noch Pracht*,' etc.,[2] from above. – Over coffee Faf from the Festival Theatre appears with the programme for this evening on his back. The dear good children act out the little farces by Lope and Sachs magnificently, and Lusch speaks Wolz.'s linking epilogue particularly well[3]. To the conclusion of the Sachs play J. Rub. linked the Prelude to *Die Msinger*, and when R. went into the *salon*, the children, in different costumes, sang his '*Gruss der Getreuen*'; at the conclusion of the evening, after the meal, came the '*Kaisermarsch*' with altered text. All splendidly done by the children, though we are not entirely successful in sustaining the mood. Before lunch R. was upset by the military band[4], which he – somewhat to my concern – had allowed to take part, and it required Siegfried's toast to raise his spirits again. In the evening he was irked by the dullness of our friends, he asked Standhartner to remain behind, without considering that the stepson would also then remain, and the presence of this man whom he cannot bear kept him from expressing all that was in his heart, and that made him almost painfully unhappy!

Tuesday, May 24 A telegram from Herr Neumann inquiring whether we are coming to the fourth cycle. I think it is in order to express his thanks to the children that R. decides to do so, and when I am a bit startled, he exclaims, 'Let us not be Philistines.' Great turmoil, hither and thither with friend Gross, saloon carriage reserved, I timidly ask whether I might not be allowed to stay here with the Count, who is very tired, but it is no use, a special train to Neuenmarkt is ordered, and to friend Gross he says humorously, 'When it comes to throwing away money, you can always rely on me!' – At midnight we are all sitting ready in the dining room, at one o'clock we leave, and on

Wednesday, May 25 at one o'clock in the afternoon, after a merry and exuberant journey, we are in Berlin, installed with our two friends in the

---

[1] Gustav Schönaich, Standhartner's stepson, a journalist whom Wagner disliked.

[2] Brünnhilde's concluding words in *Götterdämmerung*, omitted from the music drama, but composed at King Ludwig's request (with piano accompaniment) in 1876.

[3] *The Man with His Throat Cut* by Lope de Vega and *The Horse Thief from Fünsing* by Hans Sachs.

[4] According to Glasenapp's biography, the band outstayed its welcome by playing for a full hour and a half in the palace gardens.

Hôtel du Nord. At 7.30 p.m. we are all sitting in *Das Rheingold!* During which a few things unfortunately cause R. vexation. But the row of children's heads cheers him up.

Thursday, May 26 In the evening to *Die Walküre*, the Count in a hat borrowed from Jouk., which amuses us greatly. The performance both good and bad, Frau Hofmeister[1] effective as Sieglinde, Frau Vogl less so as Brünnhilde, many crass errors of production which upset R., and when afterwards he has to stand in the middle of a gaping crowd awaiting our carriages, he loses patience entirely. Concern for Lusch, the great and sublime effect of the work on me and R.'s mood of vexation form a complicated whole to which my humour cannot measure up, and I wake up on

Friday, May 27 with my head in a whirl, preventing me from adapting myself to R.'s unconstrained mood as completely as I should like. I take the children to the museum (yesterday to the palace); returning home, I find R. unwilling to go to the breakfast arranged with the Countess for all the children together. The misery of finding myself in the 'outside world' comes over me in full force, and I burst into tears! R. promises to come, and he does so; if to begin with he is much out of humour in the home of the friendliest of our friends, he soon recovers.

Saturday, May 28 Lunch in the hotel with our good Seidl. Then to *Siegfried*, some of it good, much not, the enthusiasm still as great as ever. R. sad, says he is gradually being made to lose confidence in his work.

Sunday, May 29 With R. to see our friend Kathi Eckert, whom I found the day before yesterday very ill. The poor woman is almost paralyzed, but she stammers out the words 'Dear master.' My poor child again so unsettled here that I have to reproach myself for not having brought her up in a more Christian spirit of resignation. R. tells me sharply not to worry, I withdraw into myself and feel something like bliss in the midst of my pain. – At lunch in the hotel Lusch, whom I ask for some wine, thinks her father has finished speaking and asks him on my behalf; R. becomes violently annoyed, and violent too are my little one's tears, overtired as she is by all the things happening to her. Not exactly well prepared, but with our spirits restored, we go off to *Götterdämmerung*. Various things again upset R., and when Herr Neumann starts an ovation for him according to his own taste, he rushes away[2]. I notice that he is very agitated, follow him, and prevail upon him to acknowledge the audience for the last time from the box. – Luckily we manage to laugh merrily about it on the homeward journey, for

[1] Anna Sachse-Hofmeister, Berlin.
[2] Neumann invited Wagner to join the singers on the stage at the end, and from there made a speech of thanks, during which Wagner left the stage, afterwards taking a bow from his box; to Neumann, who was greatly offended by this act, he later made the excuse that he had felt one of his 'chest spasms' coming on, but it is significant that Cosima makes no mention of that in her entry.

truly there is something disconcerting about this Israelite affair. In laughter and melancholy we go off to bed!

Monday, May 30 At eleven o'clock we depart, after Herr Neumann, in a second letter, has asked R. to make public amends, that is to say, attendance at *Die Walküre* with some kind of 'theatrical participation'.

Tuesday, May 31 Delight in being back at home.

Wednesday, June 1 All slept well, and the weather is glorious. In the morning R. reads [Gobineau's] *Dogme et philosophie* in the summerhouse and feels content; we spend a long time in the garden. Molly presents us with some puppies and abandons them to follow R.

Saturday, June 4 We all drive to the Fantasie and take enormous delight in the lovely blossom time. R. presents his collected writings to the Count, with a dedication extolling the bond between Normans and Saxons. (Blandine brought us the news of K. Eckert's death!)

Sunday, June 5 R. tells me of a ghost which Siegfried and Georg saw at ten o'clock last night – we connect it with Rausch, who is very ill in hospital. At twelve o'clock Rausch comes to the house in a high fever, half dressed and looking terrible and asks for his room! The topic of our conversation is ghost stories!

Tuesday, June 7 Farewell to the Count very cordial.

Sunday, June 12 A letter from Seidl brings news of Herr Neumann, unfortunately in a rather brutal way, and in consequence R. writes to Herr Förster. At lunch he says how embarrassing he finds such relationships, when he is obliged to write to untruthful, narrow-minded, phrase-making people who are nevertheless devotees. Over coffee he reads aloud his letter, in which he complains in particular about Herr Neumann's stage directing and demands changes in it; he laughs about it, saying he knows of no single person whom he could recommend.

Wednesday, June 15 Each morning now I have a sitting at friend Jouk.'s with Lusch, since she dearly wishes to take a picture of herself to Weimar for her father. R. works on his score.

Thursday, June 16 Today I allow Lusch to attend the sitting without me. R. works on his score and tells me that the aversion he feels for magicians and evil beings will perhaps induce him to write *Die Sieger*, since in that everything remains gentle.

Monday, June 20 We have breakfast in the garden, and I read to R. a nice letter from Count Gob., after which R., reflecting on him, says, 'He is my only *contemporary*.' – A letter from Herr Neumann indicates that the conflict is as good as over. R. replies to him, and he will probably visit us in mid-July. Herr Brandt is here, and we spend an hour with him 'in the treetops.' Unfortunately R. again feels a chest spasm, and I cannot think of the preparations for next year without misgivings.

Tuesday, June 21 R. starts on his cure, drinks two glasses of Rakoczy water, and we have breakfast in the summerhouse. He then works on his score, and we spend virtually the whole afternoon in the garden. Herr Köhler, Siegfried's tutor, comes; R. counters his singular, abstruse manner with a calm, attentive earnestness, and then exhorts him in the most splendid words to be cheerful, to look around himself and stop brooding.

Friday, June 24 Midsummer's Day! Up very early, listened to the birds, great melancholy. Departure of Daniela, who is going to see her father in Weimar. Then to the hospital on account of our good Rausch, who died last night.

Saturday, June 25 In the afternoon our good Rausch's funeral, moving in its simplicity; the superiority of Protestantism over the Catholic church in terms of its detachment and lack of power symbols.

Monday, June 27 Letter from Lusch – dismal reflections, R. mentions how difficult his position has become through the attitude taken by Hans, who talks about me but avoids mentioning him. At lunch discussion on finding a cast for the chorus.

Wednesday, June 29 Around lunchtime R. comes to me in a state of some excitement: 'Here's a nice letter.' I: 'Something bad?' 'Oh, you'll see.' I read it, am at first astonished, but then join in R.'s lively merriment. But when the letter is shown to the poor conductor, he cannot master his feelings, it seems that such instances of baseness are something new to him!...[1] Marianne Brandt comes, R. offers her the role of Kundry.

Thursday, June 30 Toothache for me, the doctor diagnoses an abscess on the gum; I would like to stay in bed, but there is Hans Richter with all his sunny good humour to receive, and poor friend Levi – who cannot recover his composure – to take leave of! – Lunch much enlivened by Richter's countless anecdotes. He also talks about the unparalleled success of the new Venusberg music in London. He is confident about the theatrical venture[2]. R. sends a telegram to friend Levi.

Friday, July 1 Around lunchtime R. brings me a letter from our poor conductor, who asks to be released from his obligations. R. writes to him, asking him to take courage and not to make things so difficult for him[3]. – Letter from Lusch, saying that Hans wants to see me! R. upset about it; I feel that for my children it will be better if I comply. R. says he regrets having brought about Daniela's reunion with her father. In the evening

---

[1] An anonymous letter in which, as Cosima wrote to Daniela on July 1, 'poor Levi was so scandalously accused (and in connection with me!) that he could not get over it'; in the letter Wagner is also exhorted not to allow his work to be conducted by a Jew; Cosima's account in the Diaries of this incident and Levi's reaction to it correct previous accounts in some details: Levi did not leave Wahnfried at once, but on the following day, and remained away for only two days (see July 2).

[2] Richter was engaged as conductor in the forthcoming Francke-Pollini season in London.

[3] 'For God's sake, come back at once and get to know us properly! Lose nothing of your faith, but find some courage and strength for it! Perhaps there will be a great turning in your life – but in any case, you are my *Parsifal* conductor!'

Kundry's second act gone through with Marianne Brandt. R. despondent about the discrepancy between the tasks he sets and the people who carry them out.

Saturday, July 2 Richter's departure. At one o'clock return of our poor friend Levi as a result of R.'s splendid reply to his letter. Very relaxed, indeed even very cheerful mood at lunch. In the afternoon I write to Lusch, telling her my reasons for agreeing to a meeting, and I inform R. of it. He indicates to Levi that he has been thinking of having him baptized and of accompanying him to Holy Communion.

Monday, July 4 R. says goodbye to the conductor, telling him jokingly to stick to his telegram and remain 'ruefully resolute'. I receive a letter from Lusch: her father insists on a meeting. I discuss it with R., who is vexed when I tell him that I should like to spare Hans a discussion after a long hot journey, and I myself would therefore travel as far as possible in his direction. I am overcome by an overwhelming sadness; R. bemoans the fact that in this matter he can only be silent; and that, consciously or unconsciously, Hans is using the situation maliciously.

Tuesday, July 5 We have breakfast in the garden pavilion, R. curses his score, but he does some work on it. In the afternoon our friend Jouk. returns and is given a jokingly hostile reception by R.[1] – A telegram from Lusch puts my mind at rest about my father[2], but saddens me at the same time; she says his weakness is persisting. R. suggests that I travel to Weimar, since he notices my mood. – In the morning, when I say to him, 'Think well of me,' he replies, 'Only too well – otherwise I should be less perturbed.'

Thursday, July 7 Letter from Lusch, who tells me that Weimar would suit her father for our meeting; however, I decide on Nuremberg, since I can travel there and back in a single day, and R. is content with that!

Sunday, July 10 R. calls me at eight o'clock, I make haste, he and Siegfried take me to the station. Parting! Oh, how strong the feeling that we should die together! Journey as in a dream, and dreamy delight in lark song and villages. At one o'clock Lusch at the station, very, very good, the poor dear child! Sad accounts of her father's state of health. She leaves me at two o'clock. The sad tune! Who could, who would wish to be happy? Hans with me from 4 to 6.30. Attempt to quell the violent outbursts on his part and overcome his unfairness towards Daniela. Unsolvable task! He begs me to stay here till tomorrow morning, since he has not, as he intended, explained to me what he wants. I consent.

Monday, July 11 Second interview, Hans tells me he does not know when white is white or black is black, he no longer has a guiding star. He is overcome by a nervous twitch, we take leave of each other. I go to fetch

---

[1] He had gone off to Baden on June 19 'without saying goodbye'.
[2] Liszt had fallen down a flight of steps.

Daniela, would like to speak to him again, but he does not wish it. Journey home in tears with Daniela. Arrival in port; R. happy to have us back again. He says that last night he organized a whist party but was in a disgracefully bad mood. What I have to report is all sad, but still the feeling of being at home together comes over us, and we can discuss it all without embarrassment. However, one thing is clear to me – that I should and can only be with him and the children, that all other contacts, with strangers and also with friends, are a trial and an injustice! ... I enter this house after this meeting as if a new life were beginning for me, unconsoled and yet in peace, made happy entirely through his happiness, and deep in my heart the knowledge of my unatonable guilt. To enjoy the one, never to forget the other – may God help me to achieve this! – For Lusch R. plays Kurwenal's theme, '*auf eigner Weid und Wonne*', for me he recalls – joking, yet all the same moved – the finale from [Weigl's] *Die Schweizerfamilie*: 'He's mine again!' – Kurwenal's melody is for me a reflection of my feelings in Wahnfried, pain and misery everywhere; sorrow deep within my heart, and yet the possibility of recovery. But only here, and by confining myself to those I love.

Tuesday, July 12 Cosy breakfast in the pavilion with Lusch. R. asks her if she thinks her father would come to *Parsifal* and whether he would see him. R. feels a meeting would not be possible in the house, for what would be their words on parting? – But perhaps in the theatre.

Wednesday, July 13 We again come to the subject of Hans, and R. says, 'I could be helped – he could not be helped.' – I tell R. that this case makes me so clearly aware of the tragedy of life and the unatonable guilt of existence – that is to say, *my* guilt; for nobody had been better equipped than Hans to follow R., nobody more in need of guidance than he, and then I came between them – how can one ever close one's eyes to my sin? And when R. tells me, 'Your crime was a beneficial folly,' I may be enabled thereby to give him a look of serene contentment, but never to deceive myself about the misery of having ever been born!

Thursday, July 14 Still fine weather and spa cure. – He is longing to return to his score and be finished with the cure. We have supper in the pavilion. The conversation turns to my father and his relationships, and R. says it speaks badly for a man when he cannot live happily with a beautiful and noble woman, yet on the other hand remains faithful to ugly ones out of complaisance. He adds that it does tell one something about a man to see the kind of woman he can live with; he finds an ugly woman terrible, unless her face radiates kindness. In the evening the Jägers, Wolz., Porges. Once again R. exclaims, 'My God, what bores you are!'

Saturday, July 16 I come upon R. in the garden turret with Dr. Landgraf. The cure is finished, and for his convulsive cough R. will need sea air. – R. does not work today, but is all the same in good spirits. Some talk about

Levi, who has become distasteful to R. (Dannreuther reports the purchase of a tom-tom for the bells.[1])

Tuesday, July 19 At one o'clock Herr Neumann, whom R. does not dislike. We drive up to the theatre, great pleasure in the work going on there, a splendid sight, this stage teeming with good workmen! The whole thing a source of pride. How it rears up, huge and simple, dedicated wholly to the sublime! – Herr Neumann inspects the machinery with a view towards purchasing it. Supper in the garden, the scent of linden trees. Departure of Herr N., who asks R. whether he has forgiven him, whereupon R.: 'You did nothing to me, you just didn't appreciate who I was. I could not have remained, not at any price, though I admit that it was a horrible situation for you.'

Tuesday, July 26 At lunchtime Herr Brandt reports that we can now inspect the Magic Garden scenery. We set off for the theatre, and a storm greets us before we have even got beyond the foot of the hill. Inside everything in darkness; also rain is falling on the stage. Much vexation, but we decide to wait. Afternoon snack in the artists' room, beer, rye bread and butter offered us by the friendly foreman, Kranich; R. very mild and cheerful, he recalls our moods in the year 1876, we feel a similar kind of enthusiasm, the children play tag with Marie Gross and Jouk. The sun shines, Kranich calls, the Magic Garden is set up and the tom-toms are tried out; fine bell-like sound. R. goes on stage, he speaks the words '*Du weisst, wo du mich wieder siehst,*'[2] and points to the spot, feelings of unreality, life a dream, happiness!

Wednesday, July 27 In the evening our friends Rub. and Hump. R. somewhat vexed by the latter's lack of energy. I remind R. of the idea he expressed earlier in the day to read to us the scenes with the fairies and the artisans in *A Midsummer Night's Dream*, and to our delight he does so.

Thursday, July 28 Our morning conversation revolves around *A Midsummer Night's Dream*, and we find ourselves still laughing heartily at Bottom's 'Not a word of me,' which shows him to be a complete original, a being such as only Nature and Shakespeare can bring forth. And how individual all his comedies are, whereas in Calderón the characters are always the same! We surrender entirely to the magic of Oberon and Titania in our memories. R. works. Jouk. brings a Flower Maiden; the costume problem worries me a little. – Towards five o'clock conference with the management committee; after the men have been together for a while, R. comes to fetch me, telling me that he does not know what to say to them. We discuss the building of the King's box, copyists, and also the subject of

---

[1] For the temple bells in *Parsifal* Wagner first made use of tom-toms (gongs), which he ordered in London through Dannreuther.

[2] Correctly, '*...wieder finden kannst*' ['You know where you can find me again'], Parsifal's final words to Kundry in Act II.

N[athalie] Planer (which makes R. smile incredulously at his first wife for finding it in her heart to conceal from her daughter that she was her mother!)[1].

Saturday, July 30 R. works on his score. After lunch we drive via the Rollwenzel to Aichig, he delighting in the charming countryside. During our drive we talked of the possibility of our all being descended from animals, because Evchen suddenly looked to R. like a tortoise, with her long neck, small head and glittering eyes. R. joked of having been a flea, Loldi thought I was an elephant, R. said, 'A pelican, or an ostrich with me the Moor sitting on its back.' –

Monday, August 1 I play excerpts from *Götterdämmerung*, arranged for piano duet, with Loldi. R. says he is pleased with the work. Unfortunately in this edition there are a lot of markings such as 'wanderlust motive', 'disaster motive', etc. R. says, 'And perhaps people will think all this nonsense is done at my request!' During the evening R. reads to us his article 'Art and Climate'[2]; while we are discussing it, he says, 'It was supposed to say something like "Stop talking about art," but in fact I myself did not believe in a future, all I wanted was to have nothing to do with this world and its art institutes; I planned the *Ring*, and in it I have remained true to myself: there may have been some deviations, but no concessions.'

Tuesday, August 2 Resuming our discussion from yesterday, R. says, 'Need is the spur to activity; if the spur is of an ideal kind, it soon yields to insight, and activity continues, as it were, just as a means of sustaining existence, since we lack a community of noble beings.' – We discuss the subject of supporters; one can share in sanctity, but can one in genius? Very questionable. Schopenhauer's true supporter is R., who went his own way, was himself productive, and could have given Sch. at least as much as he took from him.

Wednesday, August 3 He works, and since we are expecting our friend Stein, he writes a poem about him. Cordial general delight at this dear friend's arrival in our home. Supper in the garden by moonlight. 'I am a happy man,' R. exclaims. – When Molly comes into the *salon*, R. says that during the afternoon, as he was reflecting on and singing the allegro theme in the first movement of the A Major Symphony, the two dogs had leapt around him, licking him, as if saying, 'What's the matter with him?'

Friday, August 5 We are in the theatre from twelve to one and see not only the Magic Garden scenery, but also its transformation into a desert. All of it magnificent – I find this technical work in the service of the imagination very affecting. For me much discussion with Stein regarding

---

[1] Minna had always passed off her illegitimate daughter Nathalie as her sister; Nathalie had now written to Wagner, appealing for financial help.
[2] Written in 1850.

Siegfried. In the evening a singer – Carrie Pringle[1] – who sings Agathe's aria very tolerably (R. observed recently that some people one could only refer to approvingly as 'tolerable', 'bearable').

Saturday, August 6 At lunch R. spoke about Kundry – how she should look in the desert; he thinks I may be right when I suggest that she should not fade like the flowers, but during the dramatic action should appear to be tearing her clothes, casting off her jewellery. – The fact that our friend Humperdinck has won the Meyerbeer Prize (4,500 marks)[2] gives rise to many jokes.

Sunday, August 7 R. works on his score, he is now doing two pages every day. – The newspaper contains an article, 'Kant and Darwin', and R. points out how much superior Schopenhauer's interpretation of instinct is to that of Darwin. The day brings us Herr Francke with requests for London; R. little pleased by it, the participation of Herr Pollini is particularly distasteful to him. In the evening the gathering of our acquaintances is a downright torture to him, and a piece of tactlessness on the part of the prizewinner puts him into a real rage. Concertmaster Francke offers to play Beeth.'s Sonata Opus 96, and does so; R. comically finds fault with the squeaking of the violin, which cannot play a melody and sounds like a Nuremberg toy. However, he asks to have the trio of the Scherzo repeated. Of the final movement he says: 'Curious! One can hardly call that civilized music.' – When our friends have all departed, R. complains most bitterly about all this company, and since speaking about it does not calm him down, I leave the room. A few moments later I hear him singing 'O Mathilde' beneath my window, along with Jouk. He had fetched him and Stein, and he invites me to go for a walk. The four of us stroll through the deserted palace gardens by moonlight, and a lovely mood of gaiety takes hold of us.

Monday, August 8 R. is still laughing over his serenade and Stein's excuse for not singing – that Jouk. has such a good voice. In the afternoon R. signs the contract with Herr Francke and in so doing again shows his great grasp of business. In the evening Ernst von Weber, much about the antivivisection movement – that the Crown Princess attended an experiment carried out by Herr [Emil] Du Bois-Reymond and declared herself to be thoroughly satisfied.

Friday, August 12 Towards noon Jouk. brings along a picture which gives us pleasure; yesterday evening, when R. withdrew for a brief rest, Lusch had surrounded me in my chair with Oriental rugs, Jouk. brought out the globe, and, getting the children to work it, I asked Stein to name the places to which one might emigrate, pointing to them with a finger. Our friend has now charmingly recaptured this moment. R. is delighted with it.

Saturday, August 13 R. is busy with his work, with which he is thoroughly

[1] An English singer who sang one of the solo Flower Maidens in 1882.
[2] Meyerbeer bequeathed money to set up a scholarship for German students in Berlin and Cologne, enabling them to spend 18 months studying in Italy, Paris, Vienna, Munich and Dresden.

pleased. In the evening our friend Cyriax; in his cheerful, frank way R. asks him about his income from his business, and thinks it rather small. A letter from Herr Vogl about the role of Kundry for his wife reminds R. all too clearly of the whole dreary theatrical scene, and he bemoans having to work with such vain people.

Thursday, August 18 The costume designer from Frankfurt-an-Main[1] visits us and pleases us with his liveliness and understanding; we feel we might do very well with him. Jouk. gives him the sketches.

Friday, August 19 Another grey day; we take leave of our friend Rub. as from an unsolvable but affecting enigma. – Towards five o'clock, after R. had written his page, we drive to Bürgerreuth, to which the children have gone ahead; he is worried about the preparations for *Pars.* – the singers, etc. – he feels there is a lack of true enthusiasm. On our return we take delight in the playing puppies, which R. recently compared to his heap of cupids (*Tannhäuser*), telling me that he had wanted a heap like that resting on the ground and then suddenly shooting up to fly in the air and dispatch their arrows from there.

Sunday, August 21 In the evening the tenor Winkelmann[2], who had already presented himself during the afternoon. He sings a few things from *Rienzi*.

Tuesday, August 23 R. begins his article and says gaily that he went through his old ones and is scribbling a new one from them![3] J. brings along the Grail's chalice, and it is accepted by R. Telegram after telegram on account of Seidl, who, enchained by Frau [Reicher-]Kindermann,[4] is reluctant to come, which seems to me to mean that we must dispense with him. As we are going into the garden in the afternoon, R. recalls the beginning of *Henry V* and exclaims: 'How utterly and incomparably inexplicable Shakespeare is! The way he allows the death of Falstaff to be related by a boy, who then dies a heroic death! – And how the ground is prepared, as it were, for the subsequent shallowness of the King, as revealed in the French wooing – all of it unspoken, but it is all there. Nowhere else can one get to know the world as one can through him.'

Wednesday, August 24 R. coaches Herr Winkelmann, who proves teachable; but R., as he tells me, is very tired of always having to begin again from the beginning and having to work with bricks instead of marble blocks.

Thursday, August 25 Ludwig Day![5] To church, but beforehand set out roses

---

[1] Johann Georg Plettung, whose firm (Schwab und Plettung) prepared costumes and props for *Parsifal.*
[2] Hermann Winkelmann (b. 1849), recommended by Richter after he had sung Tannhäuser and Lohengrin in Vienna; he was one of the singers of Parsifal in 1882.
[3] 'Herodom and Christianity' (thus in W. Ashton Ellis's translation), a supplement to 'Religion and Art', *B.B.*, September 1881.
[4] Hedwig Reicher-Kindermann (b. 1853) sang a Valkyrie and (at one performance) Erda in the 1876 Bayreuth *Ring* and Brünnhilde in Neumann's touring company; Wagner seems to have been blind to her much acclaimed talents in a career cut short by her death in 1883.
[5] The King's birthday and their wedding day.

and boxes for R. He is delighted, and when I return home, it is to a heavenly atmosphere. He takes the cover downstairs to show our friends, telling them that it is the children's work. Seidl has now joined them, and R. makes the merriest jokes about his relationship with Frau H. Kindermann. In the evening Herr Winkelmann sings the 'Forging Songs', and Seidl plays the 'Entrance into the Temple of the Grail' to the delight of us all and to R.'s complete satisfaction. – Today R. sings the melody from *Die Msinger* and says, 'When a melody leaves no place to draw a breath, then it is beautiful.'

Saturday, August 27 First rehearsal between Kundry[1] and Parsifal! R. divine in all his instructions, in his identification with, his clear understanding of his characters, down to their slightest movement. But unfortunately little hope that he will be followed. Lunch with the entire small company, the weather overcast, but R. is in good spirits. In the evening he brings out on the spur of the moment the piano score of [Rossini's] *Otello*, and with Seidl and M. Brandt he sings the trio from the first act with unbelievably comic effect. Because of this the evening takes on a very gay colour, but our feelings with regard to the production of *Parsifal* are subdued.

Sunday, August 28 The weather still dull. R. concentrates all the objections he has against the appearance and the singing of M. Brandt on the fact that she cannot pronounce the letter *s*. He said very emphatically at lunch yesterday that she would have to consult a 'mouth doctor'. But he admits with a sigh that not a single member of the public would hear an *s*! – Again today at one o'clock rehearsal of half of the scene between P. and K.; in the evening, from Herr Wink., bits of the conclusion and the third act. Weariness amounting almost to despair. But his rendering of the third act of *Siegfried*, that is to say, Siegfried's entrance and awakening of Brünnhilde, brings us out of our ill-humour. The evening concludes with Neapolitan songs, sung by Pepino. R. praises P. highly and tells me he felt as if a Greek sky were opening above him.

Wednesday, August 31 A good night for R.; he calls out to me in bed, 'Anyone who finds you comparable will have to reckon with me!' Early in the morning an idyllic scene pleased him greatly: two ducks, which the cook bought, bathing while the whole poultry yard looked on; R. gives orders that the happy birds are not to be used in the kitchen. Only a piece of inconsiderate behaviour on the part of Herr Köhler, which strengthens the decision to dismiss him, causes me serious concern – a dismal experience! – In the evening R. goes through 'Hagen's Watch' – to see, as he says, what he has stolen – and he then links Waltraute's scene onto it; our good Brandt sings it – beautifully, in spite of her hoarseness, making an indescribable

[1] Marianne Brandt, who had arrived the previous day.

impression. R. calls our good Brandt, whom I like very much, pure animal, but in a positive sense: there is nothing in any way false about her.

Thursday, September 1 R. had a good night's rest and faces the day, apart from the bad weather, cheerfully. He works on his article and also on the score. In the latter he makes a small harmonic change in '*holde süsse Mutter*' and says, 'One could spend a lifetime working on a thing like this.' Our good Brandt does some studying in our house; R. turns to Handel, takes out the 'Ode for Saint Cecilia's Day' and asks M. Br. to sing his favourite piece from it, 'The soft complaining flute'; she does not know how to sing it and R. demonstrates it to her. He also plays the march from *Judas Maccabaeus*, which he likes enormously, and at supper he maintains that Handel must surely have composed 'God Save the King': 'The fellow was a scoundrel, but a genius as well.'

Friday, September 2 The day brings the very pleasant assurance that Marianne Brandt will be able to sing Kundry well. R. summons me downstairs, since he is so pleased with her, and she touches us very deeply with her first words to Parsifal. Her outward appearance, we feel, can be overcome, since, as R. tells us, 'Everything about Kundry is costume – her ugliness, her beauty – all of it a mask.'

Tuesday, September 6 A good night at the Hôtel Bellevue;[1] the children's first walk is to the dentist's; I leave them there and visit the gallery alone, afterwards going with R. to Dr. Jenkins and then back with all of them to the gallery. While I was in the gallery by myself, R. heard the chorus rehearsing the *Holländer* in the theatre as he was shaving, and he was as pleased by the good voices as he was annoyed by the tempi. He sends word to the chorus master, asking to have it taken a bit slower. In the evening *Holländer*. – For me much emotion, for R. a good impression of the singer [Therese] Malten,[2] and he tells her so immediately afterwards in her dressing room.

Thursday, September 8 At two o'clock we have lunch on the terrace with Dr. Strecker, to whom R. says, 'My dentist has advised me to demand a lot of money from the house of Schott for *Parsifal*.' After arranging with Dr. S. to have another conference with him in the evening, we drive out to Pillnitz. R. shows me the courtyard in which he performed the music for the returning King. We then drive to Gross-Graupen, where *Lohengrin* was first sketched. From such a cramped and indigent place did this world of brilliance and beauty shine forth! R. shows us the paths he often walked, and we come to the romantic Lochner mill, where we stop for refreshments. In darkness, late in the evening, we return home. Dr. Str. arrives; to

[1] Richard and Cosima had left Bayreuth for a visit to Dresden with Eva and Siegfried on the previous day.
[2] Soprano (b. 1855); she sang Kundry in 1882 and in subsequent festivals up to 1894, also Isolde and Eva.

begin with, R. speaks to him very severely for having imagined that he had him in his power, having published the text; then, when Dr. Str. apologizes, R. accepts his explanation that, in spite of their great success, his works are still not a good business proposition, and the terms of the contract are agreed upon. R. trusts this man, who behaves with great propriety, and he reduces some of his demands. – And so great is R.'s sense of justice that, when we are alone, he regrets having made an additional demand for 15,000 marks.

Saturday, September 10 We drive to the churchyard to visit Weber's grave. R. shows us all his familiar places, and thus Dresden has become virtually a second home to me!

Sunday, September 11 In the evening *Der Freischütz*, a joy, a solace, fragrant as a forest. But one thing greatly astonishes R. – that the traditional manner of performing these works has been forgotten to such an extent that the Ännchen did not even know the characteristic movements (with her apron, to the accompaniment of the clarinet). R. draws my attention to the use of the bass register of the oboe, also of the flute – all Weber's own inventions.

Tuesday, September 13 Many bills to pay! . . . And a final appointment with Dr. Jenkins for R. Departure at two o'clock.

Wednesday, September 14 We are welcomed at Neuenmarkt with a hailstorm. In Bayreuth, however, the children and our friends. Unfortunately R. immediately has a chest spasm!

Tuesday, September 20 At five o'clock R. has a conference; just before it he feels greatly indisposed, goes to sit in the garden. But the discussion goes smoothly, agreement is reached on advertisements, prices of seats, etc. R. expresses his wish to have a '*strapontin*',[1] as he calls a coupé, amused by the name of the little seat inside it. In the evening the contracts with London cause him vexation, he makes certain stipulations to Herr Francke and sends the contracts back.

Wednesday, September 21 R. busy on his score. We drive to the theatre, inspect the construction of the royal box. – Then the workshop, in which the rollers for the transformation scenery are being planed. R. is much pleased by all this activity, all this effort in the service of an ideal aim.

Thursday, September 22 R. receives 40,000 marks from Dr. Strecker today and offers us all money! At three o'clock my father arrives; R., I and everyone else at the station; he looks much better than we had anticipated; R. tries very cordially to persuade him to remain with us permanently, and concludes, 'But you are exactly like Köhler – you must have your freedom.'

Friday, September 23 In the morning R. has to swear an affidavit for Herr Fürstner,[2] much to his displeasure, and we discuss the dismal necessity over

[1] A coach with collapsible seats.
[2] In connection with their dispute over the *Tannhäuser* rights.

lunch. – Then we come to the subject of vegetarianism, and my father amuses us greatly by singing to us in English the words the Temperance Society sings to the melody from *Norma*: 'We belong, we belong, we belong to the Temperance, the Temperance Society!' Over coffee R. talks about the American war. 'Very well,' he says, 'one says all these things about America, but all the same this war is the only one to have been waged for the sake of humanity and an idea.'

Saturday, September 24 In the evening all sorts of things arise – our manservant drunk, for R. bad luck at cards, which he then abandons, but above all, I fear, the *Mephisto-Walzer*, played by my father, along with a conversation with Porges while the rest of us are playing whist – quite an appalling atmosphere. He flares up, and everybody goes away in some alarm. I stand at the top of his spiral staircase listening to him in order to decide what to do, and to my joy I hear him say: 'Still so-and-so many pages to do! I shall be glad when I have finished my score.' – I then go to him, and together we pour out our hearts over, oh, so many things, among which the *tête-à-tête* with Porges and the tipsy Georg with the guitar (Pepino had been singing) provide the moments of light relief.

Sunday, September 25 R. works, complaining of lack of concentration. At lunch we have the mayor's family, it all goes quite well, and at half past four the *strapontin* arrives! ... R. and I ride in it together, everything amuses him, even the way the people stare, the coachman, the horses – and the weather is fine, too. I had been offered the carriage just for inspection, but he wants to keep it, if only for the reason that a man here built it at his own risk, and who will otherwise support him?

Monday, September 26 At lunch our friend Judith Gautier; I do not yet know whether this is pleasing to R., or just embarrassing, as he says. He goes for a drive with me. – Strange evening with Mme Gautier – when the others sit down to a game of whist, R. says, 'This is Porges all over again!' – My feelings are strange, I leave the room; when I return, R. is reading aloud his material for *Die Sieger* from Burnouf. – For me Loldi, now returned,[1] is everything today – indeed, all the children, who show me the point of living. What do children ever owe to their parents, compared with what they give to their parents?

Tuesday, September 27 Saint Cosmas! ... Yesterday I desisted from responding to R.'s remarks about Judith's character, which he finds embarrassing; instead, I kept bringing the conversation back to the children. He is sad today about that, weeps, and says that, if anything were to come between us, it would be all over with him; I seek to explain to him in all mildness the feeling which makes me so intensely aware of this strange woman in our house that yesterday I had to leave the room for a moment. We part

---

[1] She had been away, staying with friends, since September 5.

in good spirits, I blissful that I have been able to account for something that could so easily have been presented in the wrong way. Even before I went to my bath, he appeared in my room: 'What shall we make our coffin of? Which do you want – lead or wood? For until death comes this nonsense will never cease – death is all that remains to us.' – I arrange my little gifts and lay them in his room while he is dressing. He then comes to me: 'Again I have forgotten your name day! – Oh, yes, you live for me more than I do for you, and that explains why I get so little joy from my work.' – When I go to greet him as he is working on his score, he observes, 'Art and love don't go together,' but he is using the new snuffbox with much pleasure. At lunch he praises my father for having given me Cosmas, the healer, as my guardian angel. But then he comes to *Faust* and the thousand antics which disfigure life – how well Goethe expressed that! – Mention is made of cuttlefish and the way they save their lives by disappearing, and R. says, 'That's what God did after creating the world – He disappeared.' – Previously he said to my father, 'You invented me, and then you were obliged to push your wares.' – We drive with Loldi along the avenue from the Eremitage to the theatre and then home, much contented. Then he works and pastes over two bars in Parsifal's reply to Kundry which he felt to be Meyerbeerish – one works towards something like *grace* and then does not know how to handle it. – When I come downstairs, I discover R. at the piano and our friend Judith in rich, rather revealing finery: 'I was taken by surprise,' he tells me; he plays the *Prelude* and later some other things.

Wednesday, September 28 R. complains loudly that everything, everything is a lie! He feels, for instance, that since my father played the waltz, the innocence of our relationships has vanished. 'The Prussian state also consists of lies, of which they are unaware.' He works both morning and afternoon and tells us that he has inserted a solo violin in place of a clarinet at the words '*so schüttelte sie die Locken.*' R. and I drive out to Mistelbach, and he feels that all is well when we are together. – In the evening he plays whist, the beautiful Judith sits down beside him and then declares that she wishes to play with him, and the group (Lusch with my father) makes a charming and merry picture. – Eva causes much amusement with her talent for mimicry.

Thursday, September 29 R. returns from his little walk with a chest spasm. At lunch Judith and her friend Herr Benediktus[1] – Israel, R.'s remark about the smooth, somewhat oily voice of the Israelite. R. somewhat beside himself over the growing numbers of Israel. In the evening he feels pains in his side and sends for the doctor. At supper he is still cheerful. But he is vexed at having to speak French and he soon withdraws, after the doctor

---

[1] Correctly, Ludwig Benedictus, Judith's companion since the break-up of her marriage with Catulle Mendès; he was the son of a Dutch diamond merchant, and an amateur composer.

has seen him, diagnosed his trouble as rheumatism and prescribed a compress. '*Ma chère enthousiaste, prenez pitié de moi*' ['My dear devotee, have pity on me'], he says to Judith as he takes leave of her and makes his excuses.

Friday, September 30 R. had a restless night, the doctor's treatment has only made things worse. Three leeches are applied – R. calls them the Three Graces – and he has to stay in bed.

Sunday, October 2 R. had a comparatively quiet night, he works; writes a few lines to Marianne Brandt – a variant on '*fühlst du im Herzen nur andrer Schmerzen*' to facilitate the breathing. Our lunch is harmonious. My father is also somewhat better[1], but we do not venture on a walk.

Monday, October 3 Whist in the evening; between games R. goes to his desk and asks my father whether he has ever used the kettledrum below F. My father says no, since it does not sound right, but R. says he will use it all the same, and he whispers in my ear the passage for which he needs it: '*ich sah ihn – ihn.*'

Thursday, October 6 Brandt arrives, with him the Brückners; when we return from our drive to the theatre, where we inspect the box, the maquettes are displayed, to R.'s very great satisfaction; the transformation scenery in particular pleases us all very much.

Friday, October 7 R. has another massage and goes to his work in good spirits, but when he takes a walk in the garden and sees Marke catching a little fish in the fountain, he gets very upset and tries in vain to rescue the creature. At lunch afterwards he is unwell and very depressed. And everything, every conversation, is a burden to him; he leaves the supper table, with my father's permission I follow him, calm him down, and the day ends with an amicable game of whist. At the request of the Princesses Hohenlohe and Wittgenstein it is decided that Daniela will accompany her grandfather. R. consents, though he is annoyed that commands should be given from outside, as he puts it.

Saturday, October 8 I very downcast, since Daniela did not take well the news that she should go with her grandfather, and it also means much work for me to prepare for her sudden departure. Misunderstandings occur, melancholy discord prevails, R. leaves his bed, but I follow him at once and calm him down and beg him, if I have said something unkind to him, to put it down to my overtiredness!

Monday, October 10 Departure! Dismal weather – very dismal feelings. R. takes leave of father and child here, the other children and I accompany them. At lunch talk about my father's fate, also Carolyne W.'s, and since I recall only her good features and say that, when she became angry with us and goaded my father, it was only because R. had once offended her by

---

[1] He had been in pain from an 'inflamed gland' the day before.

forbidding a visit from her, R. replies, 'All right, but if she had any nobility, she would have forgiven, sought an explanation, instead of just making trouble.' At seven o'clock it is exactly 28 years since I saw R. for the first time; I bring him the little compass, and he gives me the ring he had meant for Christmas, a wonderfully beautiful opal!

Tuesday, October 11 R.'s chest constrictions start again, and our table conversation consists in imagining a journey up the Nile.

Saturday, October 15 Dreadful stormy night, and R. again had his chest spasms in the morning. But he works, and figures that he now has 90 pages of the score still to do. We drive out in a gale: to friend Gross, then home via the Eremitage, and once again to our friend, since 20,000 marks have arrived from Herr Neumann. When the postman delivers them, R. says to him, 'I expect you wouldn't mind having these.' 'Oh, if I only had a quarter of them!' the good man exclaims merrily!

Monday, October 17 The billiard table arrives, R. finds it already set up when he comes downstairs, and he is much taken with it – after every page he goes back to practise with the cues. He also comes upstairs to me, commiserating with me for having such a restless husband! Then he sends the children to tell me he is in the garden. He says that Neumann seems to him thoroughly eudaemonic, to him he now owes his highest income from the theatre. He said that Berlin would bring in about 900 marks, and true enough, that is how it happened. The family gathers around the billiard table before and after lunch.

Wednesday, October 19 I receive a very lively letter from my good Lusch in Rome, which greatly entertains R. as well.

Thursday, October 20 The Nile journey usurps everything. R. sees himself and us in turbans, will have himself fanned all day long – in short, the plan serves at least to distract him thoroughly from other thoughts.

Friday, October 21 We get up late, since R. had a somewhat restless night. In the course of the day he confesses to me that when he awoke, he wondered where he was, and the thought of the Nile journey suddenly seemed like madness, let alone writing his third act there.

Saturday, October 22 R. requests that the toast to my father[1] be drunk soon, since he is not feeling well. Friend Wolzogen proposes it, but the atmosphere remains subdued, and when R. learns of the death of Councillor Kraussold, he says, 'He was my forerunner – now I shall live another ten years.' He recalls his speech at the concert on my birthday and says he feels that a cordial word of encouragement could keep such a person alive, whereas when he was left in a state of both moral and physical debility, life was bound to end. In the evening farewell chat with Stein.

Sunday, October 23 I consult Dr. Landgraf, who advises that R. should leave

---

[1] On his 70th birthday.

here as soon as possible. I book the rooms in Palermo, and R. seems content with the arrangement.

Tuesday, October 25 R. had a restless night, he says goodbye to our friend Jouk., whose servant Pepino has preferred to remain here, out of fear of being left behind in Italy. We talk a lot about this singular case. Today R. attempts to go out alone, but he returns home in great distress. He says people in the palace gardens must have thought he was drunk, he leaned for support on every tree; he will not take one further step here.

Wednesday, October 26 At 3.30 Prof. Leube from Erlangen. Long consultation, the best of results – R.'s organs completely healthy; only strict diet and much fresh air necessary. Abundant – indeed, super-abundant – joy following silent fears!

Friday, October 28 We drive to the theatre, inspect the royal box, and then visit friend Feustel, who talks with great confidence about the performances next year.

Sunday, October 30 Brandt writes very nicely and takes on the management of the whole thing. A cold wind, R. attempts to go out, but soon returns home for fear of erysipelas. Herr Humperdinck shows us his neat copy of the score; R. looks at the '*die Klage, die furchtbare Klage*' passage and fears he may have orchestrated it too heavily, particularly in the wind instruments. When I venture to remark that, since the actors would certainly not be able to convey the whole situation, it is a good thing for it to be carried by the orchestra, and that a powerful orchestra never disturbs, but enhances (as in the awakening of the Wala), he agrees with me.

Tuesday, November 1 Departure at seven o'clock in the evening. Siegfried weeping! When we are in our saloon carriage, R. says he can now see Georg spending all day playing billiards with his wife.

Wednesday, November 2 In Munich around eight o'clock. Herr Levi awaits us with breakfast. Severe cold, the enormous station means a long walk for R., during which his chest spasms recur. Departure around nine o'clock. We are soon in the mountains, snow scenes. We look at patterns for the *Pars.* costumes. In Bolzano friend Jouk., who accompanies us as far as Verona; discussed costumes and many other things.

Thursday, November 3 Around eleven o'clock in Naples. Moonlight and silence. Arrival at the Hôtel Bristol, all tired.

Friday, November 4 Prof. Schrön comes to greet us, and then we drive, R., I and Fidi (the others having gone ahead), to the Villa d'Angri. Reunion with our good gardeners. At five, to the ship. Departure in moonlight at six o'clock. R. soon goes down to the cabin, I settle the children on the deck and sit beside them. R., who comes up at the crack of dawn, says I looked like Hecuba with the corpses! He tells me that the chloral pills Jouk. gave him against seasickness had worked as *agents provocateurs*! Gradually we discover all the things we have on our ship: horses, oxen, chickens, convicts, soldiers and other Italians; it has been the first fine day for weeks, and now everyone is travelling.

Saturday, November 5 Arrival in sunshine at eleven o'clock. Much waving from boats, and the waiting people storming on board, which, since it hinders our leaving the ship, makes R. very indignant. But then he joins in our laughter. Arrival at the Hôtel des Palmes, rooms 24, 25, 26, with a conservatory terrace overlooking the garden, the children on the ground floor opposite; everything nice and homely and green. Rub. welcomes us, we have breakfast, unpack, and drive through the town, which makes little appeal after Naples.

Sunday, November 6 Quite a good night in spite of some deficiencies in the beds. The sun smiles upon us, and we smile back. Our first deed is to rescue birds, which are hunted with lures and cages smeared with birdlime. Drive to the Flora, which pleases R. greatly. Spent a long time in the evening sitting on the terrace (conservatory) in moonlight. The idyllic aspect of Palermo is beginning to captivate us.

Monday, November 7 R. arranges his worktable in the *salon*, and the situation pleases him. In the afternoon we drive to Monreale. Sublime impression: 'What people they must have been to build such a thing!' R. exclaims. We are enchanted by the cloisters. The valley of oranges is like a fairy tale, and when we return home we feel that nothing less than Shakespeare will do. – We begin H[enry] VI, Act I, the children showing great interest. As he reads, R. looks so wonderfully young that I have to tell him so.

Tuesday, November 8 R. settles down to his score, page one of the third act, and he calls out to me, 'I have made no mistakes.' We have lunch with the children in a cheerful and harmonious mood and then go for a walk in the Via Maqueda, looking at the shops. The air is very mild. – In the evening R. reads to us the second act of *H. VI Part I*, again making an indescribable impact, especially the scene involving the brawl with the roses. It is impossible to speak of anything else. When I say to R. that the play with the symbolic roses reminds one of *Tr. und Isolde* (the torch), he says, 'Yes, it is musical.'

Wednesday, November 9 Battle with mosquitoes for R., I suggest changing beds, and that enables him to get some sleep. It is stormy in the morning, but at noon the sun comes out. We go for a drive, R. and I, and visit the Cappella Palatina, which makes a splendid impression on us. I have feelings of anxiety when I hear that Siegfried has been climbing Monte Pellegrino with Herr Türk[1].

Thursday, November 10 A stormy morning prevents our having breakfast in the conservatory. R. works and shows me the completed page of his score. We do not go out but are able to stroll on the terrace, where, among other

[1] Siegfried's tutor, engaged just before leaving Bayreuth.

things, R. is much amused by the monkeys; he goes to give one of them a tap, but it anticipates him and hits R. In the evening delight in Siegfried, who is again drawing ceaselessly here.

Friday, November 11 Lovely sunshine, cheerful breakfast. Work for R., he is pleased to have overcome a bad passage at the end of the third act. After lunch we, he and I, take a lovely drive to the Villa Giulia, delighting in all the blooming vegetation.

Saturday, November 12 At twelve Dr. Berlin[1] arrives, making some changes in R.'s diet. – We take a two-hour walk which enchants R., in the English Gardens [*Giardino Inglese*], heavenly air and indescribable colours. Returning home, R. writes his score, and in then evening we finish *Part I*.

Monday, November 14 R. spoke of the two pages he has written and mentions how much he dislikes harsh effects, how he always tries to anticipate them, to make them understandable, prevent their sounding abrupt; and he points to the Gurnemanz passage, '*kalt und starr*', pleased that today he has given it an accompaniment of muted horns. He says this is what pleased him when he heard the *Nibelungen* – that even the very boldest of the sounds to which he had had to resort did not come in unanticipated. With subjects such as his, he says, it is necessary to make use of eccentric colours, but the art lies in not allowing them to sound like eccentricities. He points out how effective in *H. VI* mild and resigned words are in their wild environment. – A letter from Count Gobineau gives him the idea of summoning him here.

Wednesday, November 16 In the afternoon a walk to the marina, where we take much delight in the sea, the mountains and the sunshine. Before supper our time is taken up in discussion of a letter from Herr Neumann and various things derived from it in connection with Paris and London. Difficulties appear to be arising. – In the evening the fourth act of *H. VI* makes us forget all these troubles!

Friday, November 18 I look at some apartments, and R. speaks to the landlord about alterations; I do not know whether it is just this that makes him so agitated, but during our walk he is bothered by all his old complaints, we have to rest frequently on benches, and he arrives home very tired. – At lunch he talks about *Parsifal*, saying it will amaze us all; he particularly mentions the prayer, which reveals all, things impossible to put into words, for they are concepts and must be seen as such. He tells me that I cannot imagine what this prayer is like. I observe that I already know it: 'Oh, yes, on the piano, but that is nothing, it is the instrumentation that matters.'

Saturday, November 19 We finally agree on terms with the landlord and now arrange things as we wish them to be; it costs much effort, but at the same

---

[1] Physician in Palermo.

time – because of the result – gives us pleasure. The prefect[1] calls on R. and turns out to be a clever and well-informed man with a clear idea of whom he is talking to. In the evening R. reads to us the first act and half of the second of *H. VI, Part III.*

Sunday, November 20 One of the monkeys has died through the carelessness of a boy who gave it a cactus to eat; the other one is grieving for its companion! 'What else can one expect from these creatures who go about on their two legs?' R. exclaims in disgust, and we leave the terrace, which has now been spoiled for us.

Wednesday, November 23 At half past twelve we drive with the children to the Villa Camastra, Count [Almerita-] Tasca's home; a very nice, lavish *déjeuner* in charming rooms of ancient style. Our hosts extremely friendly and natural, the elderly wife knows Germany, and she shows R. his photograph. The weather is splendid, and the garden enchants us again. All the same, R. is rather tired on our return. We finish *H. VI*, horrified by the picture of the world Sh. gives us.

Saturday, November 26 Before breakfast R. writes to Frl. Malten in Dresden to tell her that he would like to have her for Isolde as well as for Kundry. We drive to the Flora and delight in the fantastic avenue of palms. In the evening the first act of *R[ichard] III* . . . Before that R. spoke of how anxious he is to complete his score; he says he is afraid of dying before it is done, and that he has felt this anxiety with every work of his.

Sunday, November 27 A letter from friend Wolz. about the *B. Blätter* arouses R.'s displeasure, and he bemoans all he has encountered in the way of assistance and understanding. He says he will sell Wahnfried, hand over the performances of *Pars.* to Neumann, settle down here.

Tuesday, November 29 A very restless night for R., a sort of crisis which he himself regards as not unsalutary, but which wears him out – and on top of that a battle with mosquitoes. At the first light of dawn he sees a young girl in the street, a baby on one arm and a basket on the other, picking over the garbage and having at the same time to reprimand a naughty little brother. R. says he wishes he had had some money to give to this very lovely girl, and at the same time that he could have punished the little boy. – He is much amused to see my father being cited as a Jew-baiter: a very drastic extract from *Des Bohémiens* is now being prominently featured in the newspapers[2].

Wednesday, November 30 News from London about the Neumann affair is more unpleasant than otherwise. At three o'clock R. and I visit a villa close

[1] Count Bardessone; Wagner's letter of November 22 to Ludwig shows that the king had asked that Wagner be given the prefect's especial protection.

[2] Liszt's book (translated into English as *The Gypsy in Music*) had recently appeared in a second edition, and certain passages were severely criticized, particularly those in which Liszt compared gypsies with Jews, describing the latter as sullen, servile, cruel and avaricious.

to the Favorita; the air, the countryside continue to delight us, R. feels decidedly well here. He is also working regularly. – Boni told us that, when she was looking for gloves for me in a shop and chose a pair on the spot, she was told to take them all away without paying, since our name is so well known!

Thursday, December 1 Fidi tells us at lunch that yesterday the whole street gathered around him while he was drawing a church (S. Domenico); this amuses R. – At supper he talks about his page, saying he made a lot of writing mistakes. – We continue to speak of this world, and he says that never again can he bring himself to write another word about politics or even mention such a name as Bismarck. In the evening he reads *R. III* to us up to the end of the fourth act. When Fidi says good night before the reading, R. says, 'You are right, my boy, to go off to bed! And yet,' he adds afterwards, 'when I was his age, wild horses could not have dragged me away. God, how these things gripped me!' – Later, when Fidi's teacher praises his diligence, R. says, referring to his passion for architecture, 'That is just how I want it – I should have no use for a composer son.'

Friday, December 2 It is raining gently, but it is still clear, and R. shows me how transfigured Monte Pellegrino looks. We go for a walk through narrow lanes. Everything entertains him, the life in the streets, various views such as the one above the splendid towers of the cathedral, unusual peacocks; we go into a church (S. Oliva) and pay a short visit to friend Rub. In the evening we finish *R. III*.

Sunday, December 4 R. had a good night and rises early to have a cold sponge bath. He tells me that he has prescribed this for himself, knows very well what he is doing, is vexed when he is treated as a delicate person to be cosseted by artificial means. Exactly the opposite of what he said in Bayr. when he was feeling ill! He is looking well, and he tells me over afternoon coffee that here it gives him tremendous pleasure to sit down at his writing desk. He is glad not to need a fire – and then the lovely plants. 'How lovely it is,' he thinks to himself, 'that you are able to write such a score without sweat or anxiety, completely at ease!' He says everything here seems homely – quite different from Naples, where there is so much excitement.... Today he speaks to me of the beauty of S.'s eyes: 'The lad is all eyes.'

Tuesday, December 6 R. goes to his work early, even before our family breakfast. – 'Oh,' he suddenly exclaims over coffee, 'why do I need to have the bassoon blowing low notes?' – I: 'Where?' He: 'In the baptism. Anyway, I can't bear the bassoon.' Then he says he ruled his score lines wrongly in Siena: 'It's terrible when one has been given pedantry and inspiration inside the same skin – a real torment.' Today, when R. mentioned the girls' situation, it stabbed my heart, so much melancholy does it cause me to think of the children in our state of isolation and estrangement. Then I call upon God, the Silent One, and plead for the strength to dispel all these gloomy thoughts which weigh me down, and I do believe, my children, that by quietly accepting things as they come I shall bring down upon your heads more blessings than if I were to attempt, at the cost of peace, to win for you some other lot. Let the blessings which are certainly yours persist undisturbed by my worries, and everything be entrusted to God – and, dear Lord, give me, preserve in me the strength of serenity! – We conclude the evening with a discussion of the *B. Blätter*; R. feels that it should be allowed to die, though he is concerned about Wolz.'s fate.

Wednesday, December 7 The great success of *Tristan und Isolde* in Berlin, of which our friend Mimi has told us, both pleases and surprises him, and he speaks appreciatively of Niemann's ambition, which keeps him alert.

Saturday, December 10 In the Florio Gardens, which are very beautiful, a magnificent owl arouses admiration in R. and all the rest of us. 'That is Nature,' R. exclaims in the evening, 'without disguise, terrible but truthful; and that fellow looked like a lion – more beautiful than a lion.' The town pleases him more and more; its dissection by the two great arteries as a means of controlling the confusion of the narrow streets seems to him completely right, and it gives great delight to see the sea through the Porta Nuova across the roofs of the town. In the evening he loses his temper again, this time in connection with the theatre fire in Vienna[1], about which he was asked. He replies that the most useless people frequented such an opera house; if poor workers are buried in a coal mine, that both moves and angers him, but a case like this scarcely affects him at all.

Sunday, December 11 A stormy night, and the day remains overcast most of the time. Before lunch, when I go to greet him, he is still erasing the lines he ruled wrongly in Siena. In the evening he works again, but he is so tired that he has to take a short nap after supper. The concentration and exertion of his work are proving a strain on him. When we are alone together – after he has encouraged young Türk, Siegfried's tutor, to regard our stay here with a bit more enjoyment – I tell him that I can well understand what he said yesterday, that in *Pars.* he will have none of the 'polyphonic playing about' which he used in the *Nibel.* – the 'Forest Murmurs', for instance. It is all too solemn, he says, too concentrated, there is none of the luxuriating in suffering that there is in *Tristan*. He continues: 'God, when one thinks how I started, a Magdeburg conductor with four first violins, what a joy it is to write for twelve and to do oneself justice! I went furthest in the *Ring*, in order to reproduce effects of Nature.'

Monday, December 12 At supper he became absorbed in reflections as to whether the sum of existence, which has already developed so nobly in

---

[1] On December 8 a fire had broken out in the Ring-Theater, just as the curtain was about to rise on Offenbach's *The Tales of Hoffmann*, and more than 400 people lost their lives.

some heads and even in some hearts, might not in fact have an ethical purpose, as has indeed been finely surmised. 'Or are we really just here to eat grass? It's possible.' – At breakfast yesterday we reflected on immortality, that is to say, living on in the memory of others, and how questionable this is, since even a being like Goethe was so vague and indeed almost conventional in his judgments of the deceased.

Tuesday, December 13 R. had a restless night and chest spasms both morning and afternoon. He forces himself to do his page. But we succeed in spending a very quiet and peaceful evening.

Thursday, December 15 R. does some work; he still has 30 pages of score to finish, and thinks of them with a sigh! We drive to the sea, which is wild and raging, a sight which keeps us entertained.

Saturday, December 17 Letters at coffee-time, a very nice one from Herr Vogl about *Tristan* [*enclosed in Diaries*: 'Königsberg did not shame your miraculous work!']¹, then another calendar 'with good wishes' – we joke about the recognition now coming to R. from all sides. – We hear from Lusch that my father's condition alternates between apathy and irritability. 'It must be particularly painful to him,' R. says, 'that he is completely ignored even in Paris, whereas my things, which are not at all suitable for concerts, are being played – and above all in Paris. Both time and place have let him down.'

Sunday, December 18 Rub. asks R. various questions in connection with his piano score², and this leads R. to show us his last page and its orchestration. Of the worshipping of the spear he says, 'Here I have done something which will earn me praise even from my wife,' and further, 'For Parsifal's entrance I have horns and trumpets; horns alone would have been too soft, not ceremonious enough, trumpets alone too clattery, brassy – such things one must go in search of, and then I expect people to play them well.' – When we are alone, I say to him, 'Tristan and Parsifal, one dies because of his will to live, the other lives because of his dying will.' R.: 'You must always have a *mot*,' then, after a pause, 'Parsifal sees Tristan' (in Amfortas), and after another pause, 'Something has come between them – the blood of Christ.' –

Tuesday, December 20 In the afternoon we drive with Count Tasca to see Princess Butera³, whose *palazzo* shows great splendour and opulence. The Princess herself a curious, cheerfully abrupt person who keeps us much amused. But R. soon tires, and we return home. He works again in the evening. The second part of the first act in the piano score – Rub. plays it, it seems satisfactory to R. (except for the triplets, at which he exclaims,

¹ The production in Königsberg had been on December 10.
² J. Rubinstein was preparing the piano score of *Parsifal*.
³ Or Buttera, Count Tasca's sister-in-law.

'Only Liszt and I know how to play triplets!'), but the whole thing bores and vexes him, he says it seems to him so stale.

Wednesday, December 21 Again a very, very restless night for R., and it is as if his digestion were completely blocked. He does not work. He attempts to go out but has a chest spasm in the street and returns home in a state of violent agitation. In the evening we play whist, after I have tried to keep the conversation as light as possible. Nevertheless his cheerfulness still continues to break through.

Thursday, December 22 R. finds his new reading[1] entertaining, and he tells me many bits about Nap[oleon] and Talleyrand. He works. Unfortunately his anger is aroused over coffee by Lusch's fate and the arrangements being made by my father, whose rules of life are repugnant to him. But after going off for his siesta, he returns to tell me the new idea he has had: after the glowing of the blood he will bring down the curtain, darken the auditorium, and allow the music to play thus to the end. – We drive to the Villa Camastra. We meet Count T., and he conducts us around his enchanting estate. – But R. makes an error of diet (lobster at lunch), and there are many complaints in the evening; only gradually do we manage to get a conversation going. – Rub. tells me of difficulties with his father and feels that a letter to his father from R. would improve matters; R., to whom I impart this, starts to write it right away, but the idea soon begins to worry him, and he even jumps out of bed in order to forget this task, which makes him feel rather uneasy.

Saturday, December 24 A good night, and R. gets up in good spirits. Schnappauf is sent several times to the post office, but nothing seems to have arrived. – At eleven o'clock, as I am at my writing desk, R. comes in, followed by somebody I take to be Schnappauf, and he says, 'Nothing has arrived.' I: 'An excellent thing that my birthday should turn into a calamity for you!' He continues to approach with his companion, and at last I recognize Joukowsky!...When the astonished laughter has subsided, I manage to learn that he has come bringing some things for R., in order to ensure they are here in time! I had been told that there would be no tree this year, and now I find a little fir standing there [in the conservatory] – so for the first time a Christmas tree shines on us quite unexpectedly!

Sunday, December 25 'Gratel, gratel,' I hear in the morning beside me, and his mighty head appears to me like the head of a child as he merrily wishes me many happy returns. But soon things get serious, he calls me in, and with the children hands to me all my fair gifts – *Polonia*[2], the *Parsifal* sketches, the talisman ring, and – *pia fraus* [pious deception]! – the

---

[1] He was reading the memoirs or the letters of Countess Claire Elisabeth Jeanne de Rémusat, who had been lady-in-waiting to Empress Josephine.

[2] An overture by Wagner written in 1836; thought to have been lost, it was recovered and returned to him in 1869 by the French conductor Jean Pasdeloup.

completed score![1] ... The weather keeps us from going out but does not spoil our high spirits. At lunch R. proposes a toast to me, but he breaks off and afterwards tells me that mists gather around his soul whenever he tries to talk about me. – We bemoan the grey weather for the sake of our dear friend. In the evening *Polonia* is played and all kinds of things from his life linked to it. When I say that *Polonia* seems to me to be exactly what it was meant to be, R. says, 'Oh, with a military band for the people, as I thought of everything at that time, it would have sounded splendid and produced a great effect.'

Monday, December 26 Grey skies still. Today's joke is the news that *Lohengrin* has been banned in Paris, which in fact delights us. R. says with a laugh that it makes him look very important.

Wednesday, December 28 The sun smiles down upon us again. Unfortunately R. is not feeling very well, and – God knows through what combination of events – when we are sitting together in the evening and he starts talking about Munich and among other things about the coach the King had built at that time, he flies into a rage over the visual arts and artists. He describes how childishly they – Gedon, Lenbach – expressed their delight in this golden coach, whereas he and his plans were abandoned. They are only a little worse than courtesans, these painters, he says, and adds, 'But my mama, too – she is not far off from taking delight in such things as that coach, either.' – So well do I know, when he gets so angry and violent and tries to hurt someone or other, that his malaise takes complete possession of him and any reply, however conciliatory, only pours more oil on the flames, that I leave the room for a while. He follows me out, is soon pacified, and explains his all-too-justified grounds for bitterness, and we play whist, after I have made excuses for my attitude towards people by saying that I lack the ability to keep bad experiences constantly in mind; with Nietzsche, for instance, I can think only of his friendly aspects, and the same with Lenbach, Gedon, etc. R. says this is the result of my education, the influence of my father confessor, subsequently a bishop, to whom I owe what he calls my 'pious serenity'.

Thursday, December 29 A good night for R., but all the same a chest spasm on rising. At lunch Herr Ragusa [the hotel manager] brings Jouk. a telegram, remarking that it must contain good news, or he would not have brought it. Jouk. reads it, does not understand it, and hands it to me, and I have to impart what is in it[2]. – After the first sombre surprise there follow reflections on this stroke of fate. 'He has fallen into practically the same grave as Offenbach,'[3] R. remarks bitterly, and in the course of further

---

[1] 'Pious fraud' because in fact the orchestral score was not yet quite complete: in order to present it to Cosima on her birthday Wagner completed the final page, leaving some of the preceding ones blank.
[2] News of the death of Karl Brandt, who died on December 27 of pneumonia at the age of 53.
[3] Offenbach had died in October.

observations he says, 'I know that his son will be able to take over, indeed I was even advised to entrust things to him in the first place, but he was the only reliable man I had.' And we go through all our experiences with Brandt. 'It is all so stupid!' he exclaims. Before that, despondently, 'It was not necessary.' It reminds me of Schnorr's death, and R. says to me, 'I too was thinking of that.' We go for a drive after he has had a short rest; before that, over coffee, his thoughts turned to the uncertainties of life: 'I shall consider carefully how things can be brought to a swift close.' – He thinks of Fidi in this connection, and that there could be a sudden disaster. – 'It is all so depressing!' We drive to the Villa Florio to see the owl, then the Strada della libertà, and R. returns in somewhat better spirits, even receives two calls with me. And in the evening we play whist, and when we are alone and think of his dying in harness but not in pursuit of his vocation in Bayreuth, R. says, 'Oh, one can look at it in whatever way one likes, it is still terrible.'

Saturday, December 31 The sun is not quite loyal to us, it fights through only now and then, and R. again has a chest spasm. All too many things vex him – struggles with an ink which will not flow and a thousand other petty things of which he tells me vexedly at lunch, for which he arrives late; but his mood then changes to one of great merriment when I agree with him that life is terrible, in the little as well as the big things. After lunch we drive to the Orto Botanico and delight in the splendid trees there. He works in the evening, and when I ask him at table how much he still has to do, he says mournfully, 'Fifteen pages,' and then with quiet satisfaction, 'Fourteen.' Our Bonus[1] goes to a ball, taken to Princess Butera's by Princess Filangieri; we enter the New Year sleeping.

---

[1] A new nickname for Blandine.

1882

Sunday, January 1 We drive with the children to the Tascas' for a kind of New Year court, of which R. quickly becomes weary. We soon make our way home, where we are then obliged to receive the prefect and his wife, and are glad when we can sit down to a game of whist, after a lengthy talk about the world situation!

Monday, January 2 R. says he has written only a quarter of a page, and altogether he has now decided to work only when everything else bores him. At lunch he is very cheerful and full of fun. His talk alternates between jest and earnest; he suddenly stops; we ask him what is the matter: 'Well, when all I see after my jokes is puzzled faces . . .' (Apparently some joke he made had not been understood.) I: 'But who is making puzzled faces?' Whereupon from the far end of the table, quite calmly, Fidi: 'I am,' which amuses us indescribably. – We go for a drive, R. recalls Fidi's reply, expresses delight in the boy and his character, so harmonious in his development, quiet, but in no way afraid of adversity, not at all soft. From the English Gardens we go on to the sea, which, bathed in a wonderful light, always has such a liberating effect on me! – In the evening R. reads the first two acts of *H[enry] IV Part I*. 'It is terrible,' he exclaims in the middle of it, 'for after this nothing else seems worth bothering about; even ironic dialogues, as in *Faust* – what are they in comparison with these authentic characters, of whom, but for Shak., we should know nothing, yet who now come before our eyes like living beings?'

Thursday, January 5 We drive, he and I, via the English Gardens to the Favorita. When I tell him I have just been thinking of *Parsifal* and am pleased that this last work of his is also his masterpiece, he replies, or rather interrupts me very excitedly, 'No, no, I was telling myself today that it is quite remarkable that I held this work back for my fullest maturity; I know what I know and what is in it; and the new school, Wolz. and the others, can take their lead from it.' He then hints at, rather than expresses, the contents of this work, 'salvation to the saviour' – and we are silent after he has added, 'Good that we are alone.' – Then he suddenly mentions Brandt, saying very earnestly, 'Oh, that this profoundly loyal person – for that he was to me – had to die!' And he recalls all his remarkable talents.

Saturday, January 7 R. goes through the Stein pieces of which I had spoken

– 'Saint Catherine', 'Luther', 'Homeless' – and is thoroughly delighted with them; he says he feels in some way implicated, seeing his ideas bearing such fruit, and he considers Stein to have a definite vocation. In the evening, when Rub. plays us one of his 'Pictures', R. does not at first recognize the awakening of Brünnhilde, but then he is pleased with it, even though he does not at the moment enjoy hearing music.

Friday, January 13 Today is Jouk.'s birthday. After lunch we visit a house which has been offered us. R. then works, and in the evening, in honour of Jouk., the chorus from *Die Feen* is played, then the witch's ballad (sung by R.) and the Overture to *Die Feen*. During the last of these R. goes out, I go to see what he is doing – he is putting the finishing touches on his score: 'It gave me no rest,' he says. The splendid sounds of the *Tannhäuser* march ring out, he comes in, and – all is completed! With this, as with all his other works, he had feared being interrupted by death – that is what he told us at lunch today! As he is talking, I place the Monreale bowl on his desk, and when he goes to fetch something from his room, he discovers it, stays out for a while, then comes in with the heavy box. He likes it! He recognized Eva first, also Fidi. Then everything is told – how the theme of Monreale was adapted in this way by Jouk. at my request. We drink to *Parsifal*. Our friends depart later than usual, we stay up, R. and I, and talk of the various completions (*Tristan, Msinger* –), and of life in general, and go off to bed in a mood of exaltation and peace.

Saturday, January 14 R. writes to Fritz Brandt, entrusting the supervision of the machinery to him. He then goes for a walk with the girls, and at one o'clock we have our meal in celebration of *Parsifal*, though R. insists that the work was finished on December 25, and this was the afterbirth. We go for a short walk, and as we are returning, we hear some long, sustained, solemn tones; the sounds come closer, arousing feelings of earnestness and exaltation in us; we listen; a funeral procession passes by, the music simple but not vulgar, extremely beautiful, expressively played; R. is completely entranced: 'Oh, what a divine thing music is – how it transforms everything!' he exclaims. In the evening, after Rub. has played part of my father's arrangement of the *Tannh.* Overture, he says he was influenced by a passage in the first part of Berlioz's *Harold* Symphony; in youth one borrows from others, he says; he likes this symphony, the first movement in particular, also the serenade and the pilgrims' march.

Sunday, January 15 At twelve o'clock a sitting for the French painter Renoir, whom R. jokingly claims to have mistaken for Victor Noir[1]. This artist, belonging to the Impressionists, who paint everything bright and in full sunlight, amuses R. with his excitement and his many grimaces as he

---

[1] Auguste Renoir (1841–1919) made a portrait sketch of Wagner in Palermo, completing it later in full colour; Victor Noir was a French journalist shot dead in 1870 by Prince Pierre Napoleon Bonaparte.

works, so much so that R. tells him he is the painter from the *Fl. Blätter.* Of the very curious blue-and-pink result R. says that it makes him look like the embryo of an angel, an oyster swallowed by an epicure.

Thursday, January 19 R. had a good night, but he is much annoyed by the exorbitant demands of our landlord. – A letter from the publishers [Breitkopf &] Härtel announces that *Lohengrin* is at last to be engraved, also a new edition of *Tristan.* R. considers whether he should make some simplifications in this, but then abandons the idea.

Friday, January 20 Today Lusch's letter about marriage prospects arrived.

Sunday, January 22 We accompany Jouk. to the ship and take leave of him there with much waving. At supper Fidi pleases us with his efforts to take over from our friend in our conversations; he talks about a conspiracy in Constantinople, mining disasters, etc. R. says, 'He is saying, "Please put me in his place." ' – We play whist and Chopin! The latter pleases even R. with his melodic refinement, which is indeed downright astonishing in one who, as a virtuoso, as R. says, had to provide scope for rhetorical brilliance. When we are alone, we come to the subject of Hans, his remarks against Lulu, his attitude towards me; we comment on the ability to say the most terrible things lightly. (The letter to Rub.'s father has put something of a strain on him, he complains about having things of this sort demanded of him, but – according to his account – he spoke very warmly of our friend.)

Monday, January 23 At twelve o'clock Prince Gangi appears with Count Tasca and offers us the former's villa in the country, which we then visit; it pleases us very much, and we accept it with much gratitude.[1]

Tuesday, January 24 Now all our thoughts are directed towards the new house. Unfortunately R. does not feel well, we drive to the Favorita, get out in the Via [della] libertà, and frequently have to sit down for a rest. He notices an old and ragged man dragging himself along laboriously with a rake and a spade: 'Always the aged who have the hard work!' R. exclaims. I: 'Let's give him something.' R. approaches him with our gift, the old man at first regards him with solemn surprise, then understands him, smiles, and continues laboriously on his way. 'The earnestness of that look!' R. exclaims. I had felt it too – the withdrawal from everything, from the whole world, which was expressed in this look. – We return home slowly, and R. has much vexation with the proofs of the piano score. (Fritz Brandt writes very reassuringly.)

Thursday, January 26 In the afternoon R. goes to the new villa with Siegfried, meets Count Tasca there, and brings him back; Fidi tells me that Papa was satisfied, but soon afterwards I notice that R. is much out of humour, and then it comes out – to our dismay – that he dislikes the villa and would sooner remain in the hotel.

---

[1] A summer villa with terrace and large garden in Piazza dei Porrazzi on the road to Monreale.

Saturday, January 28 I drive out to Porrazzi, and since the sky is wonderful and the mountains make a glorious impression on me, I am able to give him a cheerful report and get him to regard our move favourably. Though he first of all feels my equanimity regarding Lulu's visit [to Rome] ('When the witch interferes,' he says, meaning Princess W., 'everywhere is Hell') to be stiff and cold, he gradually comes around to my way of seeing things, after I have assured him that, difficult as I may sometimes find certain things, I can never forget how much happier I am than others. A look from Siegfried, the sweet faces of the girls, even my ability to feel the greatness and sublimity of Nature as I did today – all this fills me with gratitude. And even some disquiet concerning how differently the elder girls have turned out – this, too, tells me in the mighty language of Nature that it was right to dissolve my first marriage, and teaches me patience and timid, though joyful, resignation.

Monday, January 30 I go off to Porrazzi, return home in good spirits; although some things there seem to me somewhat primitive when I consider R.'s tastes, I tell him of the fine carriage we shall have – Prince Gangi had just shown it to me – and the lovely location. But after lunch R. drives out to Porrazzi and is so struck by the simplicity of the house that he wants to make as many alterations and additions as possible; when I ask him to stop worrying on my account, since I should soon get things to my liking and do not like offending people who have been so friendly towards us, however alien they may seem, R. is at first angry, but then he jokes about what he calls my pride on the one hand and my aspirations towards sainthood on the other. When we are alone, we read Stein's article on Rousseau in the *B. Bl.* and find it quite outstanding.

January 31 Earlier than expected, as we are still chatting in bed, Lusch is announced. 'With Lusch there must always be some excitement,' R. says gaily. How much, how much is there to say, with never a pause! Once again the dear child has been looking into life's ugly countenance. R. immediately drives with her to the Via libertà and the Villa Trabia and returns thoroughly satisfied with her – 'a splendid child'.

Thursday, February 2 Candlemas, moving today, packing, amid many difficulties; it is reported that some English people in San Martino have been set upon and robbed, and we are advised to notify the prefect of our moving. Our final lunch goes off merrily, though what Lusch has told me about my father's condition, and the torments he is having to undergo, leaves me in melancholy mood; he is being told that R. and I are complaining about his visits to us and that with R. he is exposed to ridicule! When I am alone with R. after lunch, I have to shed some bitter tears. A man of such talents and a life so miserably squandered, as if in the clutches of an evil witch! While we are talking with R. about it, we suddenly realize to what an extent his gift of virtuosity has condemned him to worldliness, and this is the dismal explanation for the whole thing. We resolve, when the moment seems right, to make a final onslaught on him, in an attempt to persuade him to make a complete break and remain with us. . . . We leave the room, remembering that here *Parsifal* was completed. Arrival at 3 o'clock, much confusion! But in the end a merry supper and a merry evening, for which Rub. joins us.

Friday, February 3 Luckily the sun is shining, but it is very cold! . . . R. drives into town to pick out carpets while we arrange the furniture. The children go off at once on a walk. After lunch R. takes a long rest, but on waking he feels very hot, and the simultaneous arrival of paper hangers, piano tuner and Count Tasca upsets him greatly. The Count himself is anxious when he learns that the girls have gone off to the left for a walk without being accompanied, and, after sending the *facchino* [carrier] away, he sets out on foot to meet them. Once R. has calmed down, we also drive towards them, meeting the Count first and then the children, accompanied by Antonio with a powerful shotgun on his back! Much amusement.

Saturday, February 4 A good night for R., but the cold is severe. However, we are cheerful in the morning. At 12 o'clock we stroll with R. to the Villa Camastra and return home very pleased with Nature, but amused by our escort of two security guards, lent to us by an anxious Count Tasca! In the afternoon I pay some calls with Lusch, and when I return home, I see R., returning from Camastra, still flanked by his two guards, and now very annoyed by it all. To conclude our outing I had decided to visit our owl with Lusch, we looked for it, could not find it, and were told that the fine bird is now dead. 'He must have been pining for us,' R. says at first on hearing about it; then we tell ourselves how miserable the beautiful creature must have been in captivity. Fidi has a slight chill, I put him to bed right away. The evening passes harmoniously, but we are beset by uneasy feelings of having been rash in moving here, and I go to bed in a state of indescribable anxiety about R.

Sunday, February 5 Worry! I sent to Dr. Berlin to ask whether it is advisable to stay on here. Above all R. wants the bodyguard removed!

Monday, February 6 R. is unwell! Probably a cold; a stove is brought in, and it helps a little. He remains all day in his room. I purchase carpets in town, eat with the children, and in the evening put my Siegfried to bed with a temperature! . . .

Tuesday, February 7 I start the day hopefully, since at any rate things seem no worse, either with him or with Fidi. – When I go into R.'s room in the evening and find it comfortably warm and nicely furnished, I tell him that every time I come to him I feel as if I am entering harbour; it is a reflection in miniature of my fate, although outsiders probably imagine life with him is all misery and unrest, as it indeed might appear from the outside. – He regrets that I have not furnished my own rooms like his, so that he could come to me in the same way, but he understands when I explain to him that I have no life of my own, and the children and everyone else in the house must be allowed to keep their share of me.

Wednesday, February 8 R. had a good night, but his cough is very persistent. He is in quite good spirits; lying in bed, he is overcome by the thought of how beautiful it is in music when one instrument joins in with another; one frequently has to deny oneself something, he says, in order to achieve a climax or to ensure that a new theme makes a maximum effect; these are things of which people like Marschner and Schumann have no notion. I observe that this is because they probably never saw a melody as a living form, and consequently never felt the need to give it special clothing. He spends the morning quietly, reading [George Sand's] *Le Piccinino*. But Fidi's temperature is rising, and when R. meets the doctor and the latter shakes his head dubiously, R. gets into such a state that his spasms return; a short walk with me does nothing to help him, and an anxious evening leads to a wild night for him. (Siegfried's temperature has risen to 40 degrees!) – Since there is a parade ground in front of the house, we are constantly hearing the blaring of trumpets: 'Nobody here but the sons of Nimrod!' jokes R., who finds these childish toy-trumpet sounds quite absurd – he would prefer drums.

Friday, February 10 Our dear son is ill, and the nature of his illness cannot be denied – it is typhoid fever! . . . I stay beside him and go now and again to R. In the afternoon, when the boy has quietened down and I go across to R., I find him reading the dialogue which Stein has sent us, dissatisfied with it and with the whole house, complaining about boredom, about bad country houses; very annoyed at having come to live here. Sorrowfully I leave him, after begging him to be a little patient. Whether this irritability is the cause of his illness or the result of it I do not know. When, in the evening, the doctor prescribes a cold compress to counter the fever, R. flies into a rage about the way the doctor wants this compress applied, and he becomes so violent that the doctor afterwards asks me to see that he is no longer present during his visits, since he gets so excited about everything. Since Schnap. has spent two nights beside the sickbed, I take over for tonight the continual moistening of the linen; and our boy has a good night, he quietens down, his breathing becomes more regular, and when he opened his eyes once as I was pouring out the tepid water, he looked at me and softly cried, 'How nice!' – But at half past two R. appears and is beside himself that I have not asked Schnappauf to relieve me; I have to speak to him vigorously and at length try to convince him that it is better for our child and for everyone else that I stay with him. R. goes off to bed, and at about a quarter to seven, after Siegfried has slept soundly and well, I lie down beside him.

Saturday, February 11 R. has a slight sore throat and keeps to his room, complaining greatly about our stay here. He also does not care for his reading – Stein's dialogues on the Revolution – and he decides not to write a preface, since these pieces seem to him very juvenile[1]. He transfers his attention to Shakespeare and in the evening reads to me the great scene between Beatrice and Benedict, pleased that in it the hollow wit and the cruel cynicism of the princes and counts are emphasized, thus allowing one to feel that Shakespeare took no pleasure in depicting these trivialities, but brought these Renaissance figures back to life only out of his sense of truthfulness. Then he talks to me about the Society of Patrons and what he might do to ensure that after our death the cause does not fall into the hands of petty people, hindering Siegfried in all he undertakes. He asks himself whether he will retain enough strength and desire to stage his other works, besides *Parsifal*, there; he says he ought to take them all up again, with close attention to detail – *Tannhäuser*, for instance.

Sunday, February 12 Friedel had a good night, and the doctor is very satisfied with his condition! R. has a cough, against which he is advised to take opium drops. – Around twelve o'clock I go for a walk with him; the lovely air once again revives his desire to make a second home in Sicily.

Monday, February 13 Fidi quiet during the night, but very listless during the day . . . R. is very depressed and out of humour in the afternoon, his revision of the third act [of the *Parsifal* piano score] gives him no pleasure, and the material difficulties of our life, such as the unsatisfactory furniture, arouse his anger. But in between, much laughter (before lunch). I had made inquiries about the owl, in order to have it stuffed as a memento for R. if possible. Then I receive the news that it was not the owl, but Herr Florio's mother-in-law who had died! '*Mi dispiace molto*' ['I am very sorry'], the servant said in conveying this correction!

Saturday, February 18 R. had the good night he hoped for, the girls enjoyed themselves[2], things are going in the right direction for Fidi, and so there would be reason enough for satisfaction. But R.'s mood does not improve, and lunch, along with a discussion with a paper hanger, upsets him extremely. I sink into sleep – very tired after many sleepless nights – Count Tasca's visit awakens me, R. comes in, very irritable, saying that strangers always make me wake up. We go for a drive to Parco, through glorious scenery, R. is sombre, shut up inside himself, an almond tree offers him its blossom, which Eva, whom we have taken with us, plucks for me. On the homeward journey he reproaches himself, saying he can feel what a burden he must be on those around him.

Sunday, February 19 The departure of Herr Türk, whom we are sending home, gives rise to much merriment, since Siegf., in his concern for

---

[1] Wagner had promised to write a foreword to a book of Stein's dialogues, and it did eventually appear in the *B.B.* in 1883.
[2] They had been to a ball under Count Tasca's protection.

economy, looks through Baedeker for all the cheaper hotels. In the evening I am obliged to go to a ball at Prince Gangi's, R. insists that I go and looks on as I dress. However, on

Monday, February 20 I find him still awake at 4 a.m.! On my departure he had gone straight to bed but was unable to sleep, and so he waited up for me! But he then goes off to sleep, and at around eleven o'clock I describe to him all the little happenings, which appear to amuse him. When, in the evening, I ask whether the girls might go to Princess Butera's for the final and most glittering ball, since I had been pressed to send them there with the Tascas, and Blandine in particular was very anxious to go, he flies into a great rage and says that he feels nothing but contempt for a girl who wishes to gad about 4 nights in a row, and if he were head of the family, he would forbid it. This final remark decides us, but also causes great dismay among the children. Many tears are shed; Lusch behaves splendidly, understanding her father's and my feelings completely, and that we are of the same opinion, but Loldi is beside herself, while Boni sheds a few silent tears for her lost enjoyment (she has both given and received much pleasure here). For R. and me also the night is much disturbed, but after shedding hot tears myself, I hear him getting into bed. After a few quiet words he gets up again, goes off to read, comes back, and says, 'The Duke of Augustenburg is still laying claim to the throne [of Denmark].' – Gladly would I have laughed at the change of subject, but my strength deserted me; some time later he falls into a half-drowsing state: 'Here, take my foot,' I hear him say; I lay mine on his. 'Oh, you are good!' he says, and after a tender and silent embrace I take his hand, and he sinks into a deep sleep.

Tuesday, February 21 In the morning he tells me that, half asleep, he had really wished to sacrifice his foot as a penance, like the fakir, and when I touched him, he had felt comforted – that was what he meant by 'you are good.' We merrily welcome Lusch, the 'angel of death', and then, with a joyful shock, Siegfried, who, allowed up for an hour, comes to greet us! – As we are having breakfast in bed, we decide merrily that, as far as peace and quiet are concerned, the children might just as well have danced the whole night through. It is cold, with snow and hailstorms.

Sunday, February 26 The mood today is very good, at twelve o'clock we stroll in the garden with Fidi, and in the afternoon I walk with R. to Camastra, where the red aloes are in flower. Though we often have to sit down, R. is not too worn out. Before that the appearance of Dr. Berlin with some bottles of beer cheered R. greatly. The great event of the day is the completion of the tent on the terrace, and beneath it we enjoy our coffee and also the beer. The air is wonderful. R. humorously scolds the children, the many 'useless girls' who constantly want to be entertained, and in the evening he hospitably receives our good landlords Tasca and Gangi and rails amusingly, if energetically, against Chevalier Guccia's *monocle*, recommending that he wear an 'honest' pair of spectacles.

Monday, February 27 In the evening we begin [Turgenev's] novel *Fathers and Sons* with the children; I do the reading; at half past nine we break up, and R. and I spend a long time in his room in intimate conversation, in effusions of love! R. pays tribute to what he calls my courage and my sufferings, and when I tell him that it is only because of him that I was able to do it, he denies that and says no, he is not even permitted to advise me, for in matters of love the woman must take precedence; when I still maintain that it was him inside me and not myself, he exclaims: 'Oh, no! To have any sense of himself, a man must be loved – the life-giving power is female. And things began to work again when you were with me – people had been saying that I would never do anything more, and then it all started again. One can live for a while on one's inner resources, but then one must be shown a picture of oneself in a mirror to know what one really is.' And he recalls the terrible circumstances in which I showed my belief in him, and also the good King, who stood by us loyally, 'and for that reason one can say a few flattering things to him.' And his final words before going off to sleep: 'It is now as it was on the first day, only better! ...'

Tuesday, February 28 R. tells me with some annoyance that the first sight of the *Parsifal* music the general public has had is in the correspondence columns of a newspaper (concluding bars of the first act). The impatience with which the piano score is being awaited reminds him of his own impatience for the piano score of *Oberon* following Weber's death. – The day ends in a regrettable outburst, since the supplement to the *B. Blätter* – an advertisement for books on vegetarianism, the description of the *Blätter* itself ('monthly periodical for the propagation of a German culture') – upsets him extremely. He reflects on how he might put an end to this relationship.

Thursday, March 2 R. had a restless night, and he keeps returning to his dislike of our present house. – He strolls up and down for a while on the terrace and in the little garden, then I hear him improvising downstairs, he writes down a melody[1], then shows it to me, saying that he has at last found the line he was looking for. He plays it to me and calls it an antidote – he had been reading my father's second 'Mephisto-Walzer', and we agree that silence is our only proper response to so dismal a production. But I feel this apparition as a sort of renewed blessing on my existence – perhaps I might call it a reward for never having allowed my hopes to diminish – these sounds blossom before me like a water lily rooted in the depths of our being – how, dear God, shall I thank Thee?

---

[1] The so-called 'Porrazzi Melody' rounds off an idea that came to Wagner while composing Act II of *Tristan und Isolde*.

Sunday, March 5 After supper R. plays the new melody, which he has altered a little, and can I permit myself to say that in it I see the present state of my soul fully reflected? I should not dare, were I not to feel that the yearning gaze of a worm seems to bear some relationship to the shining blessings of a star. – In the evening, in the presence of some acquaintances, R. gets Rub. to play the first movement of 106, and he takes tremendous delight in it, kissing me as it is being played and then telling me he was pleased by the way I was listening.

Wednesday, March 8 At breakfast we have serious thoughts about whether we should not after all send Siegfried to school, since he has no contact with other boys. Yesterday, for a joke, Fidi arranged his elder sisters' hair, and that alarmed R. greatly.

Thursday, March 9 Around lunchtime R. breaks out in a fury over the shooting practice on the parade ground, he fears it will go on and on. Yesterday he gave our host to understand in almost unmistakable words that he does not like the house and its situation, and he even said that the bedroom was responsible for S.'s illness. Since we are here dealing with a very well meant act of kindness, it pains me to think that our departure might take place in a spirit of vexation.

Sunday, March 12 Since the Grand Duke of Mecklenburg's heir paid us a first call yesterday, R. instructed me to make an appointment with the good people for today[1]; we are received, very graciously, at 4.30; R. is very pleased with the friendly gentleman's free and open character, but he finds Her Imperial Highness thoroughly disagreeable: in her features he discerns a Phryne-like cruelty, and he feels that only extreme measure would be of any avail against such a character.

Monday, March 13 We talk of Hans's character, and R. admits to me that from the beginning there was always something alien about it for him, amounting almost to repulsion. He remarks how Lusch, for all her great resemblance to her father, nevertheless presents a completely transfigured image of his character. – At the conclusion of the evening R. is still very vexed to think of Jouk.'s having shown his sketches to the King in Munich, since R. feels they are by no means sufficiently advanced for that. He is always complaining of being surrounded by 'bunglers', and he takes this relatively trivial matter terribly to heart.

Tuesday, March 14 A letter from Levi brings all the difficulty with singers before his eyes; he replies in humorous vein, but he is not satisfied with our conductor's methods, he thinks of Richter's practical ways. Wolz.'s clinging to Jäger also arouses his displeasure. And I fear the whole thing is becoming a burden to him. (Packing for Acireale.)[2]

Wednesday, March 15 Today I am much preoccupied with the news,

---

[1] Friedrich Franz and his wife, formerly Grand Duchess Anastasia Michailova.
[2] A spa on the slopes of Mount Etna.

conveyed to me by Count Tasca, that Count Gravina[1] is asking for Boni's hand. I tell R. first, then together we tell Boni, who appears very surprised. R. and I then dine with the Grand Duke's heir and family. He talks to the Grand Duke's heir about Fidi's education, and he tells me afterwards how it felt to be talking in this way about a son!

Thursday, March 16 Our talk is devoted to Boni, and with some concern. At twelve o'clock I drive to see Countess Tasca, who has taken over from Countess Mazzarino the office of go-between! The condition I make, in view of the Count's unsettled financial situation, is that he take up some occupation. In the afternoon, since we have decided to round off our stay in Porrazzi with a musical reception for our friends, there is a rehearsal of the *Idyll*. A horrible orchestra, and yet delight in the work.

Friday, March 17 News of the Count's financial condition causes us increasing concern, but their feelings for each other appear to be mutual! – In the afternoon rehearsal with the military band; the marches for King and Emperor, both of them splendid, go very well, R. wonderfully cheerful and kind with the players, he tells them that Garibaldi is coming and makes one joke after another, so that they say, 'If only we had a conductor like that!'

Saturday, March 18 Our guests appear at two o'clock, and the concert begins. Unfortunately the people do not play the *Idyll* well, even when it is repeated, and even the '*Kaisermarsch*' gives R. no pleasure. When it is all over, we laugh at our rashness in letting ourselves in for such a venture.

Sunday, March 19 For me a day of packing and shopping, also a conversation with Count Gr[avina], about whom R. says he should come to Acireale, so that we can get to know him better. The reports of him are good, and his behaviour was excellent. Around seven in the evening we go to bed, at one o'clock we are up again, and towards three o'clock, amid much turmoil, we leave Porrazzi, which R. could no longer stand. At the station the prefect, Count Tasca, Gravina, Guccia, Rubinstein. Friendly farewells and then sleep till sunrise.

Wednesday, March 22 R. had a good night [in Acireale], and he is extremely pleased that we have come here. The weather is very hot, and R. feels it severely when he walks in the garden around midday.

Thursday, March 23 We discuss Blandine's character and fate and agree that for her marriage is a good thing. Then R. expresses his delight in the refined tranquillity of this place. – At one o'clock the arrival of Count Gravina, who will now of course have to be regarded as our son-in-law, and whose natural talents speak highly for him.

Friday, March 24 We are nine at table for lunch, our conversation half in German, half in Italian, half in French. R. decides on an outing. When we part and he goes off for a rest, I hear him exclaim loudly, 'Alas!' I go in to

[1] Count Biagio Gravina (b. 1850), second son of the Prince of Ramacca, Catania, Sicily.

ask him about it, and he tells me, 'I was wondering when we – you and I – would be in that other world to which we belong; there is nothing for us in this one – it was there just to produce us both.' – Ah, how blissful is my feeling that life can give us nothing! Nor can it harm us. . . . After our little concert in Porrazzi I went upstairs to speak to Blandine about her future; after a while Daniela came in and told me that they, the children, had had such a fine conversation with their father downstairs. And I learned that he had spoken about me, even about my appearance, in fact; and he himself hints jokingly about it to me. I, however, feel the ecstasies of eternity; to have the image of myself planted in the children's hearts by him! It will live in their hearts as the image of our love. – A peaceful evening; the six children play and chat, R. plays some Beeth. themes to start with. Then he reads *The Tempest* and talks to me about the wonderful things in it, also about the peculiar vitality of Prospero's character, the fullness of his first scene with Ariel. R. also remarks on the way Prosp. makes the young prince chop wood, and we immerse ourselves in this wonderful creation.

Sunday, March 26 We drive out to Belvedere, having heard that Gar[ibaldi] is expected today, but he does not arrive.

Monday, March 27 We go for a drive to a coastal village, whose prettiness pleases R. Returning, we wait for Garibaldi, who does in fact pass through around eight o'clock. A wonderful sight, almost the entire population at the station, the train approaches slowly, first a ripple of movement as it is announced, then silence; at last, when the hero's carriage is recognized, hearty cries of welcome, lovely to hear, ceremonious procession of the sick man, whom no one can see, since he has to lie still; the white kerchiefs and the flowers give the children the impression of a funeral, Gravina bursts into tears, it makes a profound impression on R. and me as we stand on the balcony; when the locomotive, quietly moving off, lets out a long whistle, it sounds to me like Earth's lament for its finest sons. Bengal lights and moonlight illumine the scene, the people buzz like a gigantic bird's nest, making harmonious sounds, which pleases R. – Our conversation, when the children return, is devoted to the aged hero; R. praises him from the bottom of his heart and mentions the tragic fate which gave him, without his knowledge, a part to play in the comedy of Nap. III and Palmerston, but this time it was in a good cause; he became a nuisance in the politics he began by serving – 'all these frightful politics which lead to the abyss.' R. says that what he most admired was Garibaldi at Capua[1] – there he appeared to have supplied the greatest proofs of his indefatigability and his persistence. But he lays stress on all his deeds, the retreat from Rome, etc., and it does one good to listen to him. While we were on the balcony, he considered how it would be if they were to meet: they would have nothing

---

[1] The main seat of Neapolitan resistance to Garibaldi in 1860.

to say to each other; he, G., would ask R. whether he was a democrat, a Liberal. It is the deeds of such a person which one must recognize, in all else there was a gulf between. I observe that G. would surely admire the greatness and independence of his character. 'Yes,' says R., 'but in what way would that come through to him?' We wonder whether the cheers of the crowd do not disturb the sick man. 'Oh,' says R., 'he remembers how he was torn to pieces, how he had to send most of them away, it can't bring him much joy.' – Before going off to bed, R. improvises on the Porrazzi melody, which once more reveals to me the most secret aspects of my soul, and I go to rest in a mood of bliss.

Tuesday, March 28 As I am writing my letter to Hans, the maid tells me that R. is having a severe attack, I hasten to him and am confronted with a sight which so affects me that I faint. I soon pull myself together again and return to R. from the bed on which I have been laid; his condition gradually becomes calmer, he is given electric treatment, starts joking again: 'My intestines are tying themselves in knots, so as to remind themselves of something.' But he is very run down. – Only yesterday we were talking about our end, I wished to do everything I could to be worthy of dying with him. He said that we must live, and this is much more difficult. My fainting today has now given me hope. The doctors say attacks like this are not dangerous, but when I see him in such a condition, see him suffering, groaning, and there is nothing anyone can do, then, dear God, my strength deserts me!

Friday, March 31 Discussion about the engagement; letters yesterday from the Tascas raise some doubts in us. R. laughs over our amateurishness in such matters! It will be a hard task to find the right occupation for our future son-in-law, his education has not equipped him for anything! – R. writes to Materna about the role of Kundry and tells her not to worry about the low notes, what is needed is less a voice than a good heart, and that she has shown in the second act of *Die Walküre*. For Klingsor, he feels, he requires more viciousness than voice.

Sunday, April 2 Our breakfast conversation revolves around the children, mainly Blandine, with some apprehension! The laconic tone of Hans's telegram[1] says a very great deal!

Monday, April 3 The beauty here could drive one out of one's mind; we visit Taormina and are rewarded with a unique view! – We met S.'s Latin teacher, Herr Toussaint, in the Hôtel Timeo, concerning which R. says we should have fled there in 1858 and spared ourselves many, many torments. The children could have lived on prickly pears! – But the meeting with Herr T. and also a letter from Stein bring up the education problem again. R. is

---

[1] Bülow's reply to Cosima's request for his formal consent to Blandine's proposed marriage had been 'You have full powers madame.'

against high school and says that what might have been all right for the Grand Duke's heir is not suitable for Siegfried. He believes that at school he would lose his innocence; he feels that everything will turn out all right for him; having in our home become sensible while still remaining childlike, he requires no further education.

Wednesday, April 5 In the evening, between R. and me a long conversation about love and, from there, the realization of ideas. It begins with R.'s pointing out to me the moonlight on the sea and adding how little such a sight now means to him; he mentions Schop.'s similar remark and stresses how wise he was to confine himself to criticism; invention leads to foolishness. We then go on to Christianity, which in its pure form was too fragile to gain ground and, in accommodating itself to the world, could only give rise to inconsequentiality. We come to see how this realization – that an idea cannot give rise to a corresponding deed, that such a deed can only be released by an urge – which appears to be such a bitter one, can nevertheless lead to serenity: it draws one away from the outside world and bids one dig deeper within oneself. We see that the Saviour had no community in the true sense of the word, and that he allowed himself to be crucified for the few who committed themselves to him. 'That is sublime,' R. exclaims. But the need to inform, to show others the truth one has perceived, that exists, he says – but it means monasteries! Feelings and thoughts pass to and fro between us, until it is just glances we are exchanging, and we go off to bed. – 'I did the right thing, another the wrong,' he says in our bedroom, thinking of Hans and his marriage. He mentions often during the day that, on account of the wrong done to him, Hans now expects to be absolved from responsibility.

Good Friday, April 7 We go to church, the children and I, in very bad weather; it is quiet and empty, I am able to read the Gospel, and through its veil the cross speaks to me. And today I was in need of it. After an hour we return home. R. then plays parts of *Parsifal* and finally the new melody. When I go to take a rest, Lusch shows me a letter from her father which in offensiveness transcends everything so far experienced[1]. However, under the influence of my hour of prayer and R.'s playing, I am able to accept it calmly and to dictate to Lusch a good letter to her father; I then try to forget it, but when we are alone I give R. a summary of the scornful attitude Hans is adopting in the matter of Blandine. R. wishes me, in the name of the children, to repudiate everything he has set aside for them and to forbid any further interference, and he wants to dictate it to me right away. I hesitate and promise to do it tomorrow, and we continue to reflect on it –

[1] In his letter Hans wrote: 'Fearing to compromise your sister's plans (I like to hope that she is playing an *active* role in them) by a reply in which I should not be able to conceal my *displeasure*, I shall follow the sage's advice that in matters of doubt it is better to abstain. . . . My dear Daniela, I appoint you my plenipotentiary in this affair. Justify my confidence in you.'

for a long, a very long time! R. is violent in his expressions of repugnance and contempt, I tell both him and myself that, if I am to blame for such a deterioration, then may God protect me! – Along with this most serious of matters, the mail also brought the news that L. Lehmann has declined to take part, something I do not tell R., but which affects me greatly, for she is all but indispensable[1].

Saturday, April 8 R. had a somewhat restless night, I compose in my mind a letter to Lusch, a copy of which I would send to Hans; but today R. is for 'letting it go', and so let it be forgotten and – to the extent that I have the right to say it – forgiven! – We receive Marquis San Giuliano and Prince Ramacca, Blandine's future father-in-law. R. very, very charming and kind.

Wednesday, April 12[2] We learn that the ship we were counting on has no room for us, since the ex-Khedive, turned away from Alexandria with his wives, has taken it over. In the afternoon R. and I set out on a drive to the temple of Neptune, the sea is showing the most remarkable colours, mauve and green, and the shores are beautiful. But rain forces us to turn back.

Thursday, April 13 Departure at five o'clock. The weather is bright, but very windy, and after a few glances at the coast R. withdraws to his cabin. I remain on the upper deck, first with the children, then at last alone, gazing upon a starry night beyond compare, softly glittering, and a phosphorescent sea, till my gazing turns into a prayer. Sailing past Stromboli, Loldi even sees flames. It is after ten o'clock when I join R. in the cabin; he is not actually sick, but feeling the strain, and he sleeps with interruptions.

Friday, April 14 We arrive in Naples at 8 o'clock, Dr. Schrön to greet us; parting from our friend and son [Gravina], made very moving by R.'s words. '*Soyez homme et vous nous avez pour amis*' ['Be a man and you will have us as your friends'], he says, and expresses his appreciation of his good and honourable character – and what lies in its power to achieve – in such a wonderful way that all pain is dissolved in blissful melancholy. – We leave the city, which R. declares to be the loveliest of all (we had once more enjoyed the drive down the Posilipo), and now hasten away. The country-side beyond the Naples coast does not interest R. very much (I am fascinated by the sunset over Monte Cassino), but Tuscany on

Saturday April 15 enchants us with its cultivation. It is raining when we arrive in Venice, whereas in Naples we had the brightest weather, as always. R. very tired, can scarcely eat a thing, goes straight off to bed.

Sunday, April 16 Following a good night, delight in Venice, and a walk he takes to San Marco around midday utterly enchants him; we are in no doubt that this is the loveliest place of all.

---

[1] Lilli Lehmann had declined to take charge of the Flower Maidens in *Parsifal* because of reluctance to come into contact again with Fritz Brandt, with whom she had had an unhappy love affair.
[2] Written in Messina, to which they had moved in order to board a ship to Naples.

Monday, April 17 Yesterday R. took the news of L. Lehmann's desertion very calmly, but something from Batz has annoyed him. I go out in search of palazzos, but without success today. On my return I find a letter to Lusch from Hans, from which I see that my mood of resignation has been rewarded, for he writes in a very proper manner, to Gravina as well. In the evening I write at R.'s request to Herr Neumann, saying he will not be coming to London, and to a Herr Schulz-Curtius[1], who has inquired whether R. would accept an honorary doctorate from Oxford, saying that he considers the time for his accepting such honours is now past.

Wednesday, April 19 I set out on my searches, and R. goes on his own to the Belle Arti.

Saturday, April 22 Sirocco and a certain amount of confusion today, various letters and requests. R. tells me the news of Hans's engagement[2]. Is this perhaps the resolution of the discords Hans hinted at in his most recent letter? . . . I feel very apprehensive on the children's account.

Sunday, April 23 R. has remembered a Verdi theme which he heard sung yesterday on the Grand Canal as a duet; he sings it to me, laughing at the way this outburst of rage was bellowed out yesterday; he made a note of its broken rhythm – 'And *that* one is asked to call a natural line!' – there is nothing like it in Rossini.

Tuesday, April 25 We discuss Italian melody, and I tell R. that here it seems at times to be curiously effective, in spite of all its banalities – in some way in harmony with the air and the sky. R. agrees with me and says, 'In our country everything must be locked in, and that produces a sound which has nothing to do with the visual world; it must all be locked in.'

Saturday, April 29 A good night, nice weather, packing. R. goes out around noon and tells me he went to visit K[arl] Ritter[3], whose address he came upon by chance in the bookshop; given at first a wrong direction on the Riva, he sees a grey-haired gentleman at the window, asks himself, 'Has Karl really altered so much?' Then, led into a room in which a lot of pictures are standing, he again asks himself, 'Does he paint, too?' At last he sees his mistake, makes further inquiries, and comes to the right door, where a woman with a baby in her arms tells him that Herr Ritter is not at home; whereupon R.: 'I think he is at home.' The woman, embarrassed, asks if he is indeed Herr Wagner. 'Yes, I am,' R. says, writes on a scrap of paper, 'What sort of a person are you?' and goes away. All the same, he is greatly upset by this experience; even before it, the feeling that he would

---

[1] A Wagner supporter in London, where (according to a letter from him preserved in the Wahnfried archives) he wished to see a special Wagner theatre built.

[2] He had become engaged to the actress Marie Schanzer (b. 1857) and married her later in the year.

[3] Son of Wagner's benefactress Julie Ritter and brother of Alexander, Karl Gottlieb Ritter (b. 1830) had been very close to Wagner in the Zurich years, when he had ambitions of a musical career; their subsequent estrangement was possibly due, as Wagner himself suspected, to *Judaism in Music*.

have to take K.R. more or less by surprise in order to see him had brought on a prolonged chest spasm. – We also learn that our old friend Gersdorff is here and has not visited us! We leave the hotel at one o'clock, accompanied by the singers, a sight which draws people onto all the bridges, and we leave Venice, after having once again inspected the *entresol* of the P. Vendramin.

Monday, May 1 Nice impression of the countryside between Nuremberg and Bayreuth, woods and meadows. Constant waving as we approach, at the station a large crowd, our friends, Gross! Wahnfried at last, Jouk. Wolz. there. Reunion with the dogs, entry into the *salon*, R. thanks me for our home, birds twittering – for me it is like coming into a haven of rest!

Tuesday, May 2 R. had a good night, and while I am in my bath, I hear him playing the Porrazzi melody! – There is a lot of chat with friend Jouk., then a walk in the palace gardens, where the swans from the Fantaisie both please and sadden us, since their water is not very nice. We stop at the poultry yard, the turkey amuses R.: 'A butcher's shop in front, a fashion magazine behind,' he says.

Thursday, May 4 R. slept well and wakes from a comical dream in which he was kicking the children! The Grosses and Feustel have lunch with us. The piano score of *Parsifal* has arrived!

Friday-Saturday, May 5–6 Nothing written down, because busy with the start of rehearsals and other little preparations. Herr Levi and Herr Heckel are here for discussions about the performances.

Sunday, May 7 A warm day, and I go to the school to listen to the boys' choir, which I wish to have sing on his birthday. It moves me greatly!

Monday, May 8 Siegfried is ill – muscular rheumatism, it seems. I hold a rehearsal with the girls. In the evening we see Fritz Brandt, the son! . . .

Tuesday, May 9 In the afternoon we drive up to the theatre, the bells are effective, but R. is beset by great misgivings about it all as we drive home. In the evening various technical problems are discussed with Fritz Brandt.

Thursday, May 11 R. is not well. However, he makes an effort to pull himself together when our friend Count Gobineau arrives unexpectedly. We chat about all his travel adventures, and the ill-humoured mood is overcome to some extent.

Sunday, May 21 At lunch R. declares that he will now read only Gobineau, Schopenhauer and himself. The first of these, he tells me, possesses much acuteness, but no real profundity.

Monday, May 22 Happy awakening; then, unfortunately, a chest spasm, so that the children have to wait before bringing their greetings. During this delay, sudden arrival of Gravina, joy and shock, I hide him with our Count, make signs to the children, who have all seen him, except for Blandine! At last the 'Thespis Cart'[1] can be held. R. comes downstairs, receives his

---

[1] A *tableau* devised by the children, showing the beginnings of art.

congratulations. After embracing the children in tears, he goes away; Boni, still in her costume, is sobbing in the knowledge that this will be her last festival, we call her, she keeps her hands over her face, at last she hears Gravina's voice, and we withdraw! – Now our task is to surprise R. with the new arrival. The hangings[1] are arranged in the *salon*, and after I have shown R. the little gifts in the garden – fish, golden pheasant and roses – we enter the newly decorated room, the bell for lunch is sounded, Biagino is the first to enter. R.'s joy is very great, and he tells us the arrival has put new spirit into him, for he had been feeling very run down. A look from Else [Ritter] tells me that the boys have arrived. Blandine rises and speaks her toast very beautifully[2] (R. tells me she looked completely transfigured). Else succeeds in disappearing without R.'s noticing, and, supported by her, the choir starts to sing quite wonderfully[3], greatly affecting us all. R. hopes that his performances will go off as well as these little festival offerings! At coffee Fidi, dressed as a page, brings in the telegrams and the programme for the evening, and while R. is resting and the children having a musical session at Jouk.'s, I decorate the hall for the performance. Then R. and I go off to see the black swans[4], which give him very great delight, and, returning home, we and the 50 boys who, looked after by Siegfried, fill Wahnfried with the sounds of *Parsifal* and other merry noises. At 8 o'clock the company of players is ready! The first play, by Cervantes, is done in a very lively manner, but there is some nervousness with *Liebes-Not*[5] – between the two plays Herr Humperdinck and Herr Hausburg[6] play the Scherzo from [Wagner's] symphony – but it all goes as it should, and Daniela really distinguishes herself! The scenery arrangements also function without a hitch, and we have every reason to be satisfied with our success. R. remains in the best of spirits; nothing happened to spoil the day, and everything was allowed to succeed and to give R. a little pleasure.

Tuesday, May 23 R. slept well, and when I tell him merrily that I am not at all tired, he calls me a 'splendid fellow'! But we are not allowed to remain in this gay mood; he is vexed by the hotelkeeper Herr Albert[7], whose arrival prevents his looking at the hangings [of embroidered silk] from the King, just received, which I have put up. But above all he is vexed by a letter from Seidl reporting on [the *Ring* in] London. However, he cheers up in the evening, and Herr Albert's gift, a lantern attached to a pole, gives him the

---

[1] A 50m. length of pale blue satin material on which Joukowsky had painted an old Chinese pattern of trees, flowers and birds.
[2] Thanking him for his loving care.
[3] The boys' chorus from *Parsifal*, rehearsed by Humperdinck.
[4] A present from King Ludwig.
[5] *Love's Distress*, a little play by Cosima, in which Daniela played the main role.
[6] Ernst Hausburg, *Parsifal* copyist since August 1881, musical assistant at the 1882 festival and later Siegfried's tutor.
[7] He had come to Bayreuth to look after the restaurant during the festival.

idea of marching through the garden 'like glowworms', surrounded by the children, and surprising our neighbours.

Wednesday, May 24 In the afternoon we drive up to the theatre, where the scenery for the Temple of the Grail and the singing of the boys give us great delight. Unfortunately, however, the tom-toms (bells) have not been tuned, and since there is a misunderstanding with the coachman on the return journey (the Count and I are driven home, the others to the Eremitage), R. is put into an ill humour, which Pepino, requested to sing in the evening, aggravates rather than diverts. But the principal reason is probably Lulu's departure.

Friday, May 26 When I come down to the *salon* around six o'clock, I find R. in earnest conversation with the Count; he has been asking him how he came to study such things as the Persian language, and he is pleased that I join them. He praises the Count's writings, saying that such work is the finest product of a lifetime. – In the evening R. reads to us the beginning of [Shakespeare's] *R[ichard] II*, to our enchantment.

Tuesday, May 30 In the afternoon we go to Jouk.'s to see the cover for the Grail, which has turned out too opulent-looking. R. expresses his dislike for all Israelite pomp and says that, if people even begin to observe details such as the shrine, etc., then his aim as a dramatist is lost. We return to our garden and delight in our lovely surroundings. We also delight in Isolde and Eva, who are looking particularly pretty today. R. had a dark moment this morning when he read the address on a letter from Lusch, 'Frl. I. von Bülow'[1], but the black fit passed, and he never ceases to delight in the children and to praise the womb which put its stamp on them!

Friday, June 2 R. receives a letter from Herr Vogl, who declares himself unwilling to sing without his wife. R. sends the letter via Levi to Herr v. Bürkel. Meanwhile I have a consultation with the doctor about our friend – it is not at all encouraging! I resolve to do all I can to keep our friend here with us. – We drive up to the theatre, the Temple of the Grail, Flower Garden, wilderness, highly delight us.

Saturday, June 3 R. is somewhat indisposed, the Vogl affair is upsetting him, and the expected arrival of Herr Batz is a burden on him. He had hoped to see this gentleman only in friend Gross's office, but then he comes along with his wife and throws R. into a fury with his way of behaving. Nothing is accomplished today, and a conference is arranged for tomorrow with friend Gross at the mayor's. A nice letter from Richter reports the great success of *Die Msinger* in London and tells us, just at the right moment, how excellent the tenor Winkelmann was. At the same time we receive a French newspaper which describes the encoring of [the] *Tr.*

---

[1] Officially Isolde was always treated as Hans's child.

und Isolde [Prelude] in Aachen[1] as a sign of the times. After all these somewhat varied news items, R. tells us of Garibaldi's death.

Tuesday, June 6 In the evening R. plays us the Prelude to *T. und I.* and moves us all deeply, with the exception of our good Count, who, the minute it ends, gets up to tell R. the Swedish verb we were searching for when R. asked where the English '*I am*' could have come from. – Much amusement over this!

Wednesday, June 7 R. and I drive up to the theatre, summoned by Herr Brandt, and inspect the tower, meadow and transformation scenery with satisfaction; R. is very pleased with it all. He talks about the use of painting on the stage, saying it is like the use of music in drama; people may hold it in contempt, but in fact it provides the living element; and he puts machinists above architects, who nowadays can only imitate. – Returning home, we say goodbye to Biagino. Then a letter from Daniela claims our sorrowful attention – oh, Lord! . . . R. reproaches himself for having restored the link between the child and her father.

Saturday, June 10 I encounter difficulties with Dean Caselmann on the subject of duplicate weddings[2].

Monday, June 12 I have the same difficulties with the Catholic parson as with the Protestant one! A letter from Lusch in Nuremberg deeply affects me, but the girl is conducting herself well[3]. We drive up to the theatre, where R. unfortunately gets very annoyed, since work on the King's box is making hardly any progress. In the evening we are faced with the problem of how to receive the Grand Duke of [Mecklenburg-]Schwerin, and it is indeed a difficult problem, since it seems the King will this time be offering no hospitality, and indeed the King is making the need to receive foreign princes his excuse for not coming at all.

Wednesday, June 14 We have many Batz problems, R. extricates himself by sending a telegram to Voltz, saying he wishes to deal only with him, and surrenders a fourth share of the royalties. He summons us to lunch with the tom-tom which has just arrived from London, but he himself comes in later, since his vexation over these Batz affairs has quite spoiled his appetite. He welcomes Herr Levi, just arrived.

Saturday, June 17 Severe cold, and departure of the Count, which fills us with gloomy thoughts. – After supper the distribution of the roles is discussed, and R. is firmly resolved to reject all the singers' pretensions (about 'creating' the roles).

Sunday, June 18 The costumier from Frankfurt, Herr Schwab, is here, also

[1] In the music festival at which Hans von Bülow was conducting; Daniela was there with him.
[2] Ceremonies in both Catholic and Protestant churches – desired by Blandine (Protestant) and Gravina (Catholic).
[3] In Nuremberg Daniela had met Marie Schanzer, who was acting in a play performed there by the Meiningen company.

Fritz Brandt, and so we set out on a drive to the theatre via the Eremitage with the entire 'art of the future'. R. is very merry. On stage he climbs right up to the rigging loft and tries out the tom-tom. But already the sky is clouding over! . . . In the evening I put on the Kundry costume, which does not entirely come up to our expectations.

Monday, June 19 Around four o'clock R. and I drive up to the theatre in the *strapontin*, which always pleases him; costume session, which can be divided into three stages: (1) horror; (2) absurd comicality of the figures demonstrating the things to us; (3) earnest and worried efforts to alter them! However, in the end I feel we shall be able to save the day. But, oh, our feelings of having been let down! – In the evening we have some music, and Herr Humperdinck plays a pretty song of his own, the only thing to criticize being the tremendous amount of modulation underlying a fairly unremarkable theme.

Tuesday, June 20 Our first conversation concerns the Flower Maidens' costumes. Loldi makes us a drawing, and we decide on naturally wavy hair with no headdress. – The evening produces some vexation for R.: he dislikes the 'authentic' helmets of the Knights, would prefer a cap with a cloth veil, and since Jouk. does not understand him properly, he loses his temper and leaves the table, then does a drawing himself and returns. He gradually calms down, and the evening passes in friendly conversation.

Wednesday, June 21 We drive up to the theatre. The discrepancy between the transformation scenes and the music provided for them becomes clearly apparent; R. at first jokes about it, saying that usually conductors make cuts, now they have to compose additional music for him. But it saddens him to see that even here his ideas are not realized in practice. The forest scenery in the first transformation is not at all the way he wanted it, and it is also bad that at the end the rocks sink into the ground. . . . Return of our good Lusch – great excitement everywhere! . . .

Thursday, June 22 In the evening the cap for the Knights of the Grail is decided on – a cap with a veil, to be made as much unlike a fez as possible. – Our friend Stein arrives, having walked all the way from Nuremberg – great, unmitigated delight.

Friday, June 23 We have breakfast in the summerhouse, and our conversation leads us to Hans; yesterday I received news that he wishes the 40,000 marks to be used to pay back my 40,000 francs, which Boni will then receive. I find this a good solution, but R. is not satisfied, he does not wish any of the 40,000 marks to be put to use. The impossibility of obtaining permission to adopt Isolde and Eva is also a matter of great concern to him! – As regards practical problems, R. has decided that the Flower Maidens should appear in their costumes from the start, leaving only the headdress to be attended to. Around noon I drive up to the theatre and select flowers, with which I adorn the children at home, and R. is satisfied.

Saturday, June 24 We are very pleased with the Temple of the Grail and its new cupola. It is decided that Amfortas shall be given no special mark as king, that his cloak will be his blanket and his head left bare (only, in the forest, a light silk scarf). R. is very pleasantly affected by the way things are gradually emerging and by the decision. After returning home we sit in the garden, where we also have supper. Unfortunately R. learns that a Herr Strauss[1], who is connected with some of the most distressing memories of our life in Munich, is to take part in the performances. This throws him into a fury, which dies down, however, when he hears how zealous Strauss has been in the interests of *Parsifal*.

Sunday, June 25 R. is overcome by a very severe spasm and remains in a tortured mood all day long.

Monday, June 26 R. had a good night, but he takes medicine in the hope of avoiding a repetition of yesterday's state. We talk about Siegfried's education; R. does not agree with my plan of sending him to Stein in Halle for a year, and he suggests we look among the young people to whom free seats are to be given, to see whether a good house tutor cannot be found among them. As we were strolling in the garden before our drive, thinking of all the unpleasant things connected with the performances, R. swore this would be the last thing he would ever stage.

Tuesday, June 27 In the afternoon we drive up to the theatre, the forest is dressed with foliage, and I am overcome by strange feelings of contentment in the midst of this industrious quiet, with people devoting all their will and energies to an illusion. In this artificial forest thoughts flutter around me like friendly birds, and the work of art itself seems scarcely more enchanting than watching it emerge tirelessly into being! – At supper we at first discuss the positioning of the orchestra, and R. again argues heatedly against the practice of placing string and wind instruments side by side; he says the orchestra must form a complete whole, the wind instruments giving the effect of lights; he had managed to reproduce the magnificent sound of the orchestra in Paris by adopting positions he had learned from Spontini. The strings must also be divided up, in order to provide more '*points de départ*' ['starting points'], as Berlioz expressed it.

Wednesday, June 28 The transformation scenery for the third act is rehearsed again, there seems not to be enough music, but finally it all fits, and R. willingly accepts a suggestion made by Humperdinck[2]. Then the positioning of Titurel is tried out, the placing of the benches, the

---

[1] Franz Strauss, horn player at the Munich opera and father of Richard Strauss the composer; he had upset both Wagner and Bülow by his boorish behaviour during rehearsals of *Die Meistersinger* in 1868.

[2] This presumably refers to the bars of connecting music that Humperdinck wrote of his own accord and showed to Wagner (according to Humperdinck's own reminiscences) on June 22; Wagner approved them, and they were incorporated in the score for the 1882 performances, then dropped in succeeding years, when ways were found of changing the scenery more swiftly.

arrangement of the orchestra – all kinds of things, in fact! 'What a fantastic place to be, a theatre like this!' says R., who is enjoying all the activity, in spite of the difficulties. I feel as if I am in a dream, and cannot understand how I came to be granted the good fortune of being permitted to stand beside him and share it with him! On our return home we find Herr Winkelmann's assurance that he will be here in time, and Herr Gudehus[1] also announces his arrival. R. is pleased that, despite Vogl's withdrawal, he has three tenors, 'each one better than the last – or at any rate two better than the one!'

Thursday, June 29 R. goes through the role of Parsifal with poor Jäger and finds him completely unsuitable!...At four o'clock we drive up to the theatre, lighting rehearsal. The need to repeat the mournful music is a real grief to R.!

Friday, June 30 The transformation scenery for the first act is tried out and things take a turn for the better. In the afternoon we walk in the garden, also in the palace gardens, delight in the swans, the roses too, gaze in concern at our silver pheasant, now grown weak with age, though we still hope to save it, look after the dogs and enjoy a few peaceful hours!

Sunday, July 2 Start! Orchestral sounds heard again, R. says some friendly words to the orchestra[2], but dealing with masses of people wears him out. Materna and many others as well. The orchestra entirely lacks style, the players are unschooled, R. feels that very strongly, but there is no embarrassing hitch, the first act is played through satisfactorily. At home I find the news that the King is not coming!... At five o'clock rehearsal of the first act with piano, the entire company on stage! (In the morning, after the orchestra rehearsal, we saw all the Flower Maidens assembled in one room – they made a charming sight.) A glorious impression!... Celestial, in fact – blessedness brought to life! Herr Scaria wonderful as Gurnemanz, Herr Reichmann[3] very moving as Amfortas, and everyone without exception so earnest, so absorbed in it, a unique occasion. We return home around ten o'clock in pouring rain, R. satisfied, I deeply, deeply moved! I believe it was the divine will that he should refine his art to this expression of it.

Monday, July 3 In the morning R. discusses with me the King's decision not to come, and he says he intends to write to Herr v. Bürkel. However, he does not find time; first of all a visit from Herr Winkelmann, and then a conference with the poor little ballet master (Fricke), greatly aged! Lunch with the two Kundrys and Klingsor[4]. – Rehearsal at five o'clock (voice and

---

[1] Heinrich Gudehus (b. 1845), tenor in Dresden since 1880.
[2] The orchestra was that of the Munich opera, reinforced by players from Berlin, Meiningen, Karlsruhe, Darmstadt, etc.; 107 instrumentalists in all.
[3] Theodor Reichmann (b. 1849), baritone in Hamburg and Berlin before joining Vienna in 1882.
[4] Amalie Materna, Marianne Brandt and Karl Hill.

piano); R. asks the people to pay attention to his rhythms: 'I think I have got them right; I may have composed badly, but my rhythm is good.' – He is extraordinarily merry and keeps putting new heart into his singers with his high spirits. At supper we are all merry together, he talks about his previous life, the revolution in Dresden, the happiness for him of no longer being a conductor – 'no wine is as intoxicating as this feeling of freedom.' While we are cosily chatting together after the meal, Herr Winkelmann's letter arrives[1]. After having written a few lines to Herr Wink., R. sets out, and surprises the good and simple man, whom R. soon brings around by telling him that all he wanted was to return his call, and was obliged to come so late since he would be leaving in the morning!

Tuesday, July 4 R. goes off to the scenery rehearsal of the first act, which lasts from 9.30 to 2.30 and causes R. great, great vexation and much exertion. The props are missing, the chorus leaders know nothing, the poor lady choristers have to stand in the rigging loft in the most terrible heat. We put off the little dinner we had arranged. R. takes a short rest, and at five o'clock there is an orchestra rehearsal (first act) with the singers; this does not tire R., since he has had a slot inserted in the hood over the orchestra and is thus able to converse with the conductor in comfort; he is satisfied with the sound of the invisible orchestra. We spend the evening with Jouk., Stein and Levi, and R. tries to show the latter how to wield the baton, since he finds that he conducts much too much with his arm, whereas it should all be done with the wrist!

Wednesday, July 5 He had a good night's rest, but he feels he has caught cold. We go to an orchestra rehearsal with singers, still the first act. The need to raise his voice tires him, but it all goes well. R. is pleased that his first act is not boring! In the afternoon another scenery rehearsal with piano accompaniment, the orchestra is permitted to look on, and breaks into hearty applause after the transformation scene, which does R. good, though he has many difficulties to contend with: the bells are not right, and our good ballet master is not much help! Much agitation in the evening, but no real indisposition, thank goodness! . . . (M. Brandt very expressive as Kundry today.)

Thursday, July 6 R. spends the morning quietly, and at twelve o'clock we drive together to the theatre to try the bells, which are much improved this time. At one o'clock we give a dinner for the tenors, the fine Amfortas (Reichmann) is also present. At five o'clock rehearsal of the first act. Trouble with the choral singers, the ladies do not wish to go aloft, and R. finds they do not sound right if they stay below. R. and I climb up and find that it is indeed very hot, but the trouble can be cured with lighter clothing.

Friday, July 7 At around twelve o'clock we go to the theatre to rehearse

[1] Threatening to leave Bayreuth at once, having heard that Gudehus would sing the first performance.

the choruses, everything runs smoothly, and they climb to positions halfway up. On our way there R. told me that he is giving up the idea of allowing the boys to come down and take part in the Communion ceremony, since they have not yet been confirmed and he does not wish to give any offence. In the afternoon rehearsal Herr Siehr sings Gurnemanz, and the choruses stand up above; Fischer takes over the conducting. The effect increases as it all gains in depth.

Saturday, July 8 R. had a restless night; in the morning he writes to the King about his decision not to attend the performances, and he tells me he has done what Luther did to the Lord in connection with Melanchthon's illness – thrown his club at his feet[1]! – Costume fittings. The swords are missing and various things have to be modified, but the overall impression is lovely, and the effect as powerful as any theatre can produce. R. is disappointed that the Knights' accolade does not fill the time required by the music written for it; this music is still being played as they start marching, but there is nothing that can be done about it, and for me this moment of brotherly love is one of the most moving of all.

Sunday, July 9 At lunch we have the three bass singers, and there is much gaiety. R. feels decidedly more at ease with his artists than with people in society. At 4.30 we drive through pouring rain to the first piano and voice rehearsal of the second act. The Flowers (R. wishes them to be called that and not Fl. Maidens, since this reminds one of flower sellers) are enchanting. The big scene between Kundry and Pars. will almost certainly never be done in the way he created it. R. complains about how insensitive the singers are to all there is in it, and he thinks of Schröder-Devr., how she would have uttered the words '*So war es mein Kuss, der hellsichtig dich machte*' ['So it was my kiss that gave thee understanding']. Now the music has to do it all. – As we were driving to the theatre, he told me that, when he thought of his times in Zurich and Paris and then looked at all the life going on around him now, he felt literally like a magician.

Wednesday, July 12 In the morning I express to R. my misgivings about Parsifal and Kundry's having to play out their tragic scene amid all the luxuriant flowers, and observe that, at any rate next year, a large expanse of foliage might screen them off during Kundry's approach. As we are about to drive off to the morning rehearsal, we meet Fräulein Malten, who has just arrived; she is very nice to look at, and she reminds R. of Wilh. Schr.-Devr., even in the way she looks at one. The rehearsal causes M. Brandt much trouble; the Flower Maidens are excellent. In the afternoon scenery rehearsal with piano (M. Brandt, Gudehus), the orchestra looks on

---

[1] 'I could not have received a bitterer blow than the news that my noble benefactor had decided to attend none of the performances of my stage dedication play.... It is the last thing I shall write. The tremendous over-exertion, which leaves me only enough strength for these few lines today, tells me how things stand with my powers. From me *nothing* more can be expected....'

and again breaks out in applause at the transformation. But the exertion for R. is endless! . . . In the evening, after we return home, the weather clears up, and I sit at the *salon* door, listening to the birds; R. discovers me there and comes to listen with me – a moment (the only one) of recuperation.

Friday, July 14 R. feels weak and takes medicine. At around ten o'clock Georg brings me the news that our lovely dear dog [Molly] has died – and you know, my children, what she meant to us! . . . After paying my final respects to the good creature, who suffered in such silence, I drive up to the theatre to inspect the Flower costumes. There is a rehearsal in the afternoon, I tell R. that the children have caught cold; they stay at home (the younger ones), and after the dissection they bury our dear Molly.

Saturday, July 15 R. asks after Molle, Georg tells him that we must be prepared for the worst, he goes into the garden around lunchtime, sits down in the arbour, notices Marke sniffing at the grave! At table, where we are alone, he utters the name, and we burst into tears, realizing that he knows all. He thanks us for not having told him. . . . Towards two o'clock my father arrives, met by the children and looking well – we are overjoyed to see him! While the children and I are keeping him company during his meal, R. joins us, stands for a while unnoticed behind my father's chair and whispers to me, '*Die Mutter!*'[1] – Our dog came into my mind too yesterday when I heard those words! – When I return to my room as my father is resting, I hear R. calling out 'Molle!' in the garden and sobbing. I rush to him, and we weep together in the arbour. . . . Then we go to the costume session for the first and second acts. R. is so delighted by my father's presence that he hurries to me from the stage and says this is his only genuine relationship!

Sunday, July 16 R. fell asleep last night on his big dressing chair, I watched over him and prayed. Alas, we are both so tired, and our wish is to live for the children, only for the children! . . . He then goes cheerfully to bed and has a good night. Towards eleven o'clock we drive up to the orchestra rehearsal of the third act, in which R. particularly notices how the orchestra just bangs away, no longer playing with feeling, but just ignoring the sensitive, the passing notes. We return home feeling sad; R. accuses himself of having scored too heavily at times! In one passage he cuts out the woodwinds.

Monday, July 17 At five o'clock a rehearsal (of the third act, reading, with piano). R. very thorough on the various points of significance, among them Parsifal's blissful smile, Gurnemanz's rapture and his folklike simplicity. The impossibility of his being understood causes great depression. In silence we drive home by a roundabout route; the drive does R. good; now and again we exchange a word about the work. Arriving home, R. goes off to bed. I only wish I could take him in my arms and carry him far, far away from it all!

---

[1] 'My mother!': Parsifal's exclamation on hearing from Kundry how his mother Herzeleide died.

Tuesday, July 18 R. had a good night's sleep, and he tells me in the morning that the Grail processions in the third act are now in order (in his head). At 10.30 we go to the rehearsal, the violincellos, which so annoyed him the day before yesterday, play better today, but there is still much which is not as he wants it. His main trial now is not knowing what he should let pass, what comment on. He adds a drum roll to the crowning of Parsifal, but he is very tired. All the same, the presence of our friend Malwida at lunch pleases him. At five o'clock a rehearsal with piano to fix stage positions, much trouble for R.! No one to help him. Concern about the transformation scenery. We return home in silence. But he has supper with us, and when I pass on to him Herr Scaria's suggestion of cutting the second transformation entirely, he is pleased with it, sends for our young friend Brandt late in the evening, and arranges it with him.

Wednesday, July 19 R. is feeling unwell. The doctor has given him something to calm him down, he looks in during the evening and finds him well, reassures me by finding all his organs completely sound. Herr Scaria comes and gives a good report of the rehearsal. – After I have already said good night to him, R. comes into my dressing room and says, 'The nicest thing of all is when we are sitting side by side in silence, as in the turret today.'

Thursday, July 20 Over breakfast in the turret we read the King's letter, which arrived yesterday and which R. put aside. The news of the wretched state of his health is all too easy to believe. R. wanted to have lunch with us (me and four children, my father and Lusch invited out), but he got upset about something, and instead of broth he enjoyed Humperdinck, he says, then the ballet master, who did in fact put him in a good humour, but he is tired. He sleeps in the *salon,* and on awaking discovers me asleep in the hall; my watching over him amuses him greatly, he says I am turning him into the Emperor of Siam, who has a female bodyguard. At five o'clock rehearsal of the third act (orchestra, Winkelmann, Materna), R. is satisfied with the orchestra. We are pleased that the curtain now falls and no transformation scenery disturbs the music.

Sunday, July 23 We have breakfast together in the turret in nice weather. He then stays in the summerhouse and lunches there alone, keeping himself amused with E.T.A. Hoffmann. At five o'clock we go to the rehearsal, Mar. Brandt (whom I had to console yesterday after an imagined slight by R.), Herr Gudehus. But we spend only a very little time there. The foliage to screen off Pars. and Kundr. is tried out, but it does not entirely meet R.'s wishes. The tempi also dissatisfy him. We soon return home. The evening begins in a very cosy and humorous way, R. tells Fidi the story of *Pars.* after asking him how much of it he had understood; while he is doing this, my father explains the *Almanach de Gotha* to Boni. But towards the end R. becomes irritable with Malw. and taunts her about her many friendships with vivisectors.

Monday, July 24 I have all sorts of purchases to make in town; in the meantime R. strolls in the garden and, catching sight on Jouk.'s balcony of someone he takes to be Malwida, makes all kinds of gestures of humility and apology. On inquiry, it turns out that the woman was Judith Gautier. At four o'clock we have the dress rehearsal. R. finds the tempi in the first act drawn out rather too long; he is also not satisfied with the lighting. The second act goes better. Between the second and third acts we have our supper. In the third act he is very touched; since my father and Daniela leave in order to meet our friends the Schleinitzes, R. exclaims bitterly, 'More of this obsequiousness – D—— take you all!' There are many strangers present; since there is applause at the end, he acknowledges it ironically from our gallery. – To me he makes the remark that as a member of the orchestra he would not like to be conducted by a Jew!

Tuesday, July 25 We have lunch with my father and Herr Levi, with whom R. once more goes through the tempi. Judith visits us after lunch, I receive her in my room, since R. is rather tired.

Wednesday, July 26 R. had a restless night, I hear him saying softly in a dream, 'Children, I am going, suffering.' We leave home at half past three, the weather unfortunately not good. The first act goes more or less according to his wishes [*the entries broken off here, the resumption, on September 18 in Venice, being indicated in a footnote*], it is just the large amount of 'play acting' he finds displeasing. When, after the second act, there is much noise and calling, R. comes to the balustrade, says that though the applause is very welcome to his artists and to himself, they had agreed, in order not to impinge on the impression, not to take a bow, so that there would be no 'curtain calls'. After our meal R. and I are together in our box! Great emotion overwhelms us. But at the end R. is vexed by the silent audience, which has misunderstood him; he once again addresses it from the gallery, and when the applause then breaks out and there are continual calls, R. appears in front of the curtain and says that he tried to assemble his artists, but they were by now half undressed. The journey home, taken up with this subject, is a vexed one. Once we are home, it takes a very long time to calm R. down, since a host of different impressions are mixed up inside him, Even the fact that Schnapp. talks to him of Dr. *von* Liszt annoys him. At last I am able to hand over my little gift (a cushion), and gradually his thoughts are diverted; at twenty to one we go off to bed[1].

[1] This was the first performance of *Parsifal*, of which 16 performances were given, the first two being for members of the Society of Patrons, the remainder for the general public; the chief conductor was Hermann Levi, though some performances were conducted by Franz Fischer; the role of Parsifal was sung by Hermann Winkelmann (9 performances, including first and last), Heinrich Gudehus (5) and Ferdinand Jäger (2); Kundry by Amalie Materna (8, including first and last), Marianne Brandt (5) and Therese Malten (3); Gurnemanz by Emil Scaria (10, including first and last) and Gustav Siehr (6); Amfortas by Theodor Reichmann; Klingsor by Karl Hill (12, including first and last) and Anton Fuchs (4); Titurel by August Kindermann; there were 29 Flower Maidens (6 solo, 23 chorus), 31 Knights of the Grail, 29 singers behind the scenes (12 female, 17 male) and 50 boys' voices.

Thursday, July 27 The subject of our first conversation is once again the audience, and how to deal with it in such a way that the artists are not put out of humour by the absence of applause. We have a very merry lunch with the children. In the evening a reception at Wahnfried – Herr Schnappauf thinks 300 people, I think 200.

Friday, July 28 At lunch R. is amused by the children's accounts of all kinds of experiences with our guests. We drive up to the theatre early. The Prelude is dragged out. After the first act there is a reverent silence, which has a pleasant effect. But when, after the second, the applauders are again hissed, it becomes embarrassing. At the end, believing himself to be in the presence of his patrons only, R. makes a short speech, presenting his artists and asking the audience to express its gratitude to them, after having himself first expressed to them – and particularly to the conductor – his own appreciation and emotion. (Between the second and third acts Herr v. Bürkel visited us.) In connection with his singers, he said to me that they moved and vexed him at one and the same time. However, the impression is a much more harmonious one than on the first occasion.

Saturday, July 29 At lunch we have the singers (Materna, Winkelmann, Scaria), to whom R. imparts some rules of enunciation and much else besides. At three o'clock we have a rehearsal in the theatre with Frl. Malten and Herr Jäger; the former makes a surprisingly good impression on R. He is very tired in the evening. Today I had to deal consolingly with the complaints of our restaurant manager, who wants to give up on account of the lack of customers.

Sunday, July 30 The performance is good, Frau Materna indeed very good, and R. asks me to congratulate her in her dressing room. Again silence after the first act, great applause after the second act; calls after the third act, and the curtain rises on the final tableau. R. expresses thanks on behalf of his artists from our box. 'This is how I want it,' he says. Business is said not to be good, on account of the bad weather; we also hear all sorts of bad things about the way the visitors are being looked after. Very disturbed about this, R. writes – at nearly midnight – to our excellent mayor.

Tuesday, August 1 The performance turns out only moderately well, the transformation scenery goes wrong because of a draught, the chorus wavers at the end, and several other things of that sort.

Wednesday, August 2 Constant rain. R. and I are in the theatre from five to nine on account of a rehearsal with Frl. Malten and Herr Jäger. The rehearsal wears R. out but also satisfies him; it is truly moving how indefatigable and how unshakably earnest all our participants are, down to the least of them!

Friday, August 4 At four o'clock the performance with Herr Jäger and Frl. Malten, the latter with very lovely, lively accents, but still somewhat immature. R.'s mood is one of great excitability, but he is always pleased with the diligence of his singers. He proclaims his thesis: 'Here on my stage anarchy reigns: everyone does as he wishes, but each wishes well.'

Saturday, August 5 R. is very tired and is troubled by a chest spasm. Between three and four in the morning he wrote to friend Gross, having read a report in Herr Lessman's music periodical about the poor distribution of tickets, which upsets him greatly. My father's departure also arouses very great anger in him, and I am obliged to have both breakfast and lunch today without him. Friend Gross comes in great agitation to defend himself, R. has already half forgotten what he wrote during the night.

Sunday, August 6 The persistence of the bad weather makes him curse ever having settled here. I cannot in all sincerity do other than stand up for our little town – and Germany – and I consider the drawbacks of our life here to be far less significant than the advantages. We are alone for lunch, and then we drive to the theatre, where today Frau Materna and Herr Gudehus (Herr Winkelmann being ill) are singing. R. criticizes some things he finds not at all good – for example, Kundry's advances to Parsifal after the great outburst – but the eagerness of the singers as always touches him anew. However, the day is dominated by ill-humour. In the gallery he misses Siegfried, whom I have left at home for his own good, also Daniela, whom I have surrendered to the Schleinitzes, because I no longer dare ask them to our house, since recently he felt uneasy in their presence. But these concessions of mine do not meet with his approval, and I resolve to revert to my former ways. When he is in such an excitable state he makes errors in his diet, and late this evening he was still wandering excitedly in the garden.

Monday, August 7 First thing in the morning R. begs my pardon in his touchingly humble way for yesterday's irritable mood. He begins by asking me very gently how I am, whether I am still alive! Wilhelmj comes for lunch, very refreshing, with all sorts of stories and accounts, Malwida and Stein are also our guests. The conductor appears for coffee, and the casts for the next performances are determined.

Wednesday, August 9 In the evening R. is in a somewhat irritable mood, and the necessity of talking French with Biag. is a torture to him. He sends for Malwid. – who never disturbs him – and Stein.

Friday, August 11 R. feels so languid that he does not attend the performance, just appears during the intermissions, and the only thing he hears all through is the flower scene, since the excellence of the performance always refreshes him. From our box he calls out, 'Bravo!,' whereupon he is hissed. Countess Tasca attends this performance, and we have her and our dear friends the Schl.'s in our home. – R.'s mood is changeable, but on the whole biased against Bayreuth – indeed he even talks of handing over *Parsifal* and the festival theatre to Herr Neumann!

Sunday, August 13 R. has a cold and spends the morning in bed. Scaria and

Materna pleased R. today, particularly the latter, by paying attention to his hints.

Monday, August 14 R. feels somewhat better. Unfortunately tuna is served at lunch, R. eats some and suffers all day from indigestion! During the night his pains increase, I make hot compresses for him, and in the joy of seeing him gradually recover and of being permitted to perform this humble little service for him, my soul sinks down in grateful prayer.

Tuesday, August 15 He is still not feeling well, and he has some soup in the *salon* while I lunch with the children. He and I then drive to the theatre with Loldi, and R. is so pleased with the success of his exhortations to Herr Reichmann (first scene, '*Habt Dank*', etc.) that he goes to him and gives him a 10-mark piece.

Thursday, August 17 At five o'clock a rehearsal with Frau Materna and Herr Winkelmann, during which R. lays down the main points to be observed in the scene in the second act. He divides up the character of Kundry: first the temptress, who has no recollection of what has gone before; then, after '*so flatterten die Locken*', remembering in wild horror and desiring loving pity from her redeemer; and, finally, blazing with fury. He also arranges the stage positions of Kundry and Pars. in this scene. In the evening we hold our reception, and R. is unusually hospitable despite his exhausting work in the afternoon.

Friday, August 18 Herr Levi sits with us throughout the performance, during which R. has much to say to him about incorrect tempi, and in particular the insensitive playing of the orchestra.

Saturday, August 19 In the afternoon we experience all sorts of difficulties with regard to the wedding. I propose to R. an outing to the Fantaisie; but when he learns something of these difficulties, he insists on turning back halfway to visit the mayor. The Catholic parish priest happens to be standing in front of the town hall. R. promises to restrain himself (we have heard that the priest – angry that Blandine is not being converted – has written to Palermo saying that she will be no asset to the Catholic church; he also added that she is a baptized Protestant, and the parish priest cannot publish the banns of a mixed marriage without a dispensation, which in Italy can be given only by the Pope, not the archbishop). When we declare that we intend to wait quietly until all this has been cleared up, the priest says the Archbishop of Bamberg can give the dispensation!

Sunday, August 20 Rain! At breakfast Rub. with his father, who looks entirely un-Semitic, and this makes R. suspect that his family, like so many heathen ones in Russia, assumed Judaism, and the men then married Jewesses. At four o'clock to the theatre, where unfortunately R. is faced with vexations, Herr Scaria curtly insisting that the casting problem should be decided in his favour, and Herr Siehr not prepared to give way. But he is pleased with Frl. Brandt's truly enraptured look in the second act, and during the third act he is in the orchestra and also on stage, where he is pleased to see everyone, even those who at the moment have nothing to do, following it all with keen attention. At home Biag. has received a telegram from his brother, saying that the marriage will be null and void if no public notice is given in Palermo, something which has not yet been done – deliberately, it seems.

Monday, August 21 We are living in a whirl of telegrams in both directions, since great misunderstandings still prevail.

Tuesday, August 22 At four o'clock we drive to the theatre, where R. again finds things to vex him in the rivalry of the two Gurnemanzes, and also an appeal from Frau Materna, from whom, it seems, Vienna is trying to withdraw the role of Isolde. But she pleases R. with her correct grasp of the turning point for Kundry (second act).

Wednesday, August 23 The vexation over Scaria and Siehr continues, the latter intends to leave if he is not permitted to alternate on a regular basis. Herr Gudehus also writes from Dresden that it would be incompatible with his honour as an artist not to take part in the final performance! – At five o'clock Richter arrives, and he absolutely denies having been put in an awkward position in London by Francke's bankruptcy[1]. Friend Gross came with him to see me; the general has suddenly withdrawn the military band for *Pars.*, which was promised for the whole period – impossible to find out why. We send a telegram to Herr von Bürkel – without telling R. about it – and he immediately sets things right. From Palermo comes the news that the wedding may proceed.

Thursday, August 24 At last I am able to make my arrangements for Boni's wedding; R. writes a telegram to the King and also a little verse for Boni (to be spoken by Fidi). My father arrives, we hold a reception in the evening. In the afternoon I utter my final words to Boni!

Friday, August 25 At 11.30 the civil marriage ceremony at Wahnfried; around eleven o'clock the town councillors bring Blandine a pretty table centrepiece. The mayor's speech very dignified; at 12.30 lunch, 27 people at table. R. makes the first speech, turns to Blandine, recalling the poem she recited to him on May 22; he speaks of the crises of his life and describes that which led him to me as the crisis of salvation, remarks how lovely it is for him in this life of crises to see something so natural and so simple as the relationship between her and Biagino; then he comes to the King and calls him the good guardian angel of our lives! – Then Count Schleinitz toasts the Gravina family in a charming speech, whereupon the mayor proposes the health of Count and Countess Schleinitz, and the minister rises once more to toast the geniuses of the family in the most graceful and at the same time moving way. At four o'clock we drive to the theatre, where

[1] He had got into financial difficulties as a result of the Wagner performances at the Drury Lane Theatre.

Mar. Brandt plays Kundry. In the intermissions there is a fireworks display in honour of the day, and on our return home electrical illuminations.

Saturday, August 26 Much turmoil. The young bride very moved and touching. At eleven o'clock the church wedding, the priest, it seems, not very favourably disposed and keeping just within the bounds of personal propriety; his address, with all its sacristan trimmings and impertinent indiscretions, has an embarrassing effect. Biagio conducts himself splendidly, and when, gazing earnestly at Blandine, he places the ring on her finger, we feel that this was the truly sacred act! – The music literally acts on us like balm, an *a cappella* Mass conducted by Herr Levi and sung by our chorus. Then we see them off at the station. It so happens that R. and my father, who remained at home at my request, suddenly appear, to the surprise and joy of all on the platform! The children get in the saloon carriage provided by the railway management and are borne away. Their departure for me a more than usually serious occasion! –

Sunday, August 27 R. sends a telegram to Herr v. Bürkel, expressing his concern at having received no word from the King. In the evening we have a performance in the presence of the German Crown Prince.

Monday, August 28 Herr v. Bürkel has sent a reassuring reply[1].

Tuesday, August 29 At four o'clock I drive with my father to the theatre. Frl. Malten and Herr Siehr watch the performance from my box, 'heaping coals of fire on the heads of the others,'[2] as R. says when he appears during the intermission between Acts I and II. – Everything on the stage satisfies him, and in the third act, after the transformation music, he takes the baton himself and conducts to the end![3] Then from the orchestra he says farewell to his artists, after a storm of applause which threatens never to end. Not many of his words could be heard in the auditorium, and he himself tells me that he never knows what he has said. – Our drive home is quiet and solemn, I observe that we can be grateful, even if the achievement was bought at great cost and meant the sacrifice of almost our entire domestic tranquillity. But without a doubt such activity is a necessity for R., and the right thing for him in spite of all difficulties. – Late in the evening we talk with the children about what we have just been experiencing, and it is remarked how differently the orchestra played under his direction, how incomparably different Herr Reichmann as he sang his '*Sterben, einz'ge Gnade.*' – I tell how I discovered Papa drinking grog in his dressing room with the conductor, while some of the Flower Maidens were waiting outside

---

[1] Reiterating that the King's absence was due solely to ill health, and there was not the slightest ground for concern.

[2] Both having accepted his invitation to be present at the final performance despite not having been chosen to sing.

[3] From the 23rd bar of the transformation music in Act III to the end of the work.

to see him once more. – Unfortunately the news of my father's departure tomorrow produces a great outburst of anger.

Wednesday, August 30 Rain! Leave-takings on all sides. For me from my father. For R., who gets up late, from Reichmann, Hill, Frl. Galfy[1]. Herr Neumann annoys him by asking for *Parsifal*! A visit from our friends the Schöns cheers him up at coffee-time, in the evening he also enjoys seeing our friends Mimi, Malwida, and with them Count Wolkenstein[2] and Stein; he talks at length about the performances and remarks how much the singers have learned. He says that Materna completely astonished him, and she had told him that it was all quite different when he was standing with them in the wings! He also talks jokingly of Levi's concern that he might upset the performance[3]. We, on the other hand, maintain that almost all of us heard what was happening in the orchestra, even if we could not exactly explain it at the time. He tells us that when he indicated the fifth quarter note for Herr Reichmann's benefit, he received a 'Bravo' from the conductor for this recognition of the singer's weakness. And so these sixteen performances have come to an end, and never once did the spirit of eagerness and dedication desert the artists! And the audience too had the feeling of something out of the ordinary, indeed in the highest sense of the word. I think we can be satisfied.

Friday, September 1 R. feels uneasy about the King, particularly the fact that Herr v. Bürkel, present at the last performance, did not visit us. The *Fl. Blätter* cheers him up, and a very nice letter from Blandine gives us great delight. At lunch we have our excellent machinist Fritz Brandt, who cannot be praised too highly.

Saturday, September 2 We take a drive with the children in the direction of the theatre, via the road to the Eremitage. The packing of the restaurant equipment and Herr Albert's complaints leave a sad impression. But it is always a joy to see the dogs again[4]. In the evening R. bursts out in bitter complaint about Bayreuth, saying that nobody has followed him and settled down here, and that the town itself has shown him not the slightest understanding. With the exception of a few friends, everyone has remained aloof; we had made an effort with all classes of society, he had joined the historic Thursday gathering, but nowhere had he gained an influence, and at his performances it stabbed him to the heart to see the army officers lounging around, the Bayr. citizens looking on as if it were all just a spectacle – to none of them did it ever occur to buy a seat. (Departures: Malw., Mimi.)

Monday, September 4 At lunch we have our friends the Grosses; Adolf

---

[1] Hermine Galfy, Vienna; she sang 1st Squire and a solo Flower Maiden.
[2] The Austrian ambassador in St. Petersburg.
[3] When he took the baton from Levi's hand.
[4] Faf had been given a mate, Freia.

crowned indeed with fame, since his activities during the festival were quite beyond compare. Herr von Ziegler (secretary) writes to me on behalf of the King, on whom R.'s telegram seems to have had some effect[1]. – We receive the thoroughly satisfactory accounts of the festival performances[2].

Sunday, September 10 R. receives a letter from Fidi[3], I tell R. my worries, and since he can never bear to see suffering without doing something about it, he writes to friend Glasenapp, asking him to move here with his whole family in order to take over Siegfried's education. – The question of the W. Society, brought up again by Wolz. and Schön, is distasteful to him, he wants the utmost simplicity. In the evening we go through the various relationships we have had with people. 'Alas,' R. exclaims, 'we are as full of experiences as a dog is of fleas!'

Monday, September 11 R. is kept busy signing the many photographs he is sending to his artists. His delight in his artists grows ever greater in recollection, and thoughts of the consistency of the performances have a very beneficial effect on him.

Tuesday, September 12 Siegfried returns today, delights us with his lively eyes, and Dr. Jenkins's report on him is extremely encouraging. But we are soon concerned about his pale face.

Thursday, September 14 R. gets down to clearing things up, a task we began a few days ago. Several business matters have to be settled. Hardest of all R. finds the parting from the dogs, Marke in particular, whom he feels he will not see again! – Siegfried's appearance is also worrying us, and me the unsettled nature of his young existence, also the sorrow he experienced in finding on his return that the large theatre he had laboriously built for himself in the little garden had been destroyed on his father's instructions. We depart at seven in the evening. In Nuremberg we say goodbye to our friend Joukowsky. R. sleeps but is restless, frequently talking aloud. When there is mention on the train of the Wagnerites' preference for *T. und I.* even over *Parsifal*, R. says: 'Oh, what do they know? One might say that Kundry already experienced Isolde's *Liebestod* a hundred times in her various reincarnations.'

Friday, September 15 At eight in the morning we are in Munich; the station inspector, who travelled to Bayreuth four times to see *Parsifal*, offers us breakfast. In Bolzano we are greeted in pouring rain by our dear and honoured friends the Schleinitzes. At eleven in the evening we are in Verona.

Saturday, September 16 Much noise during the night. We soon learn that

---

[1] Wagner's reproach to the King for 'spurning' the Grail stung Ludwig into replying through his secretary that he greatly regretted the illness that had prevented him from coming to Bayreuth.

[2] These (enclosed in the Diaries) showed total receipts – from the Patrons' contributions, sale of tickets and sale of the *Ring* scenery – of 438,025 marks, and outgoings of 293,885 marks, thus leaving a healthy surplus.

[3] On a visit to the Jenkins family in Dresden.

Verona is flooded, and to reach the station we have to make detours and drive through water. There is a real threat of danger, and the noise during the night was made by soldiers leaving their barracks. At half past two we are in Venice; the town pleases us in spite of the grey weather, and the P[alazzo] Vendramin, which we inspect immediately, greatly appeals to us. Our lunch around 4 o'clock is very cheerful.

Sunday, September 17 A terrible storm in the night! In the morning we go to the Vendramin and arrange things there. When we return home at one o'clock, there is such a huge thunder-storm that we feel it will not be possible to ride in a gondola, but the gondoliers reassure us and perform a real masterpiece.

Monday, September 18 In spite of the rain R. and I go out around midday to look at furniture, and in the afternoon we move into the Vendramin, worried about S.'s pallor! In the evening the singers appear; R. gives them a substantial gift, along with a request never to come again.

Tuesday-Wednesday, September 19–20 R. has now decided either to find contentment here or, failing that, to return to Wahnfried for ever. Over our breakfast together he talks about the book on Buddha[1] and says that by giving much attention to B. one learns to understand Christianity, and people were surely now beginning to realize that the greatest heroic power lies in resignation. A telegram from Glasenapp[2] consenting to R.'s proposal touches us greatly.

Thursday, September 21 Our night was disturbed by thunder-storms and mosquitoes. In the house a little 70-year-old paper hanger is working with quiet, but frantic zeal. The weather is fine.

Monday, September 25 R.'s delight in Venice and our dwelling grows daily. The palazzo opposite, single-storied, as he likes it, pleases him immensely, and to watch the gondolas across the garden, 'flitting past like elves', is for him the ultimate charm.

Thursday, September 28 We stay up late in the evening. We read parts of the Anti-Semitic Society's manifesto, which seems to us both sad and comical, and R. makes jokes about the German passion for 'committees' in particular! Then, more seriously, he remarks that nobody has paid any attention at all to what he wrote in 'Know Thyself' about our own blame for our situation. When we go off to bed, he shows me the Cosmas portières which our little 75-year-old paper hanger put up for him with tremendous dexterity! . . . Yesterday he told me merrily that he was thinking of having his 'extravagances' in Wahnfried gradually removed, so that after our death certain Wagnerites – R. mentions Dr. Schemann – cannot laugh at them.

Friday, September 29 R. goes out with the children while I copy his letter

[1] *Buddha, His Life, Teaching and Community* by Hermann Oldenberg, first published 1881.
[2] Accepting the invitation to take over Siegfried's education.

to Herr Neumann. They tell me at supper about their visit to Bauer's, where they enjoyed beer and chocolate, then about the rude waiters, all very lighthearted. In the evening Herr Wolkoff[1] visits us and entertains R. with his lively conversation about the present problems of science, among them experiments with hypnosis. Then he amuses us with stories about the present-day painters called Impressionists, who paint 'nocturne symphonies' in ten minutes!

Saturday, September 30 A basilica designed by Siegf. astonishes R. We go out together, Stein, Siegf., R. and I, and R. leads us to S. Zaccaria; the church itself, the exterior, which he finds too effeminate, as well as the interior, which does not appeal to him, leave him indifferent, but Bellini's painting fascinates him. 'It is good to live close to something like this,' he says. – We sit down between the pillars of the portal on Saint Mark's Square, R.'s favourite place. We return home in a glorious sunset.

Sunday, October 1 Around eleven o'clock we are surprised by the young bridal couple, very happy, it seems. At lunch much chatter in all languages; we go out for a ride around four o'clock; because of my bad foot I remain in the gondola. R. lets the children go into S. Marco and climb the tower, while he sits down again between the pillars. 'I was Hagen on the Wasgenstein[2],' he says, adding that it is so lovely that he will one day be found dead lying there. – In the evening R. talks to Stein and me about the book on Buddha, which he praises highly. Buddhism itself he declares to be a flowering of the human spirit, against which everything that followed was decadence. It exerts no compulsion of any sort, in consequence it has no church; the monk could return to the world if he no longer cared for the monastic life; no divine service, just atonement and good works. But it was this happy lack of organization which made it so easy for such a highly organized power as Brahmanism to oust it. – For him, R. says, the whole of Christianity is contained in Holy Communion. But it is the fact that it was possible to found a church, and that so gloriously gentle a character as Saint Francis had humbly to bow before its leader, that makes Christianity so questionable.

Monday, October 2 We go out with Siegfried, get out at the colonnades. On the homeward journey R. is amused by the man in the gondola who, accompanied by a barrel organ, imitates opera singers and conducts. R. says he is without doubt a destitute orchestra player. In the evening friend Rub. arrives and at our request plays us the conclusion of *Götterdämmerung*, R. joins in and sings Brünnhilde's last words, is pleased with it all, so heathen and Germanic! 'It is so free,' he says, 'yet at the same time so tender.' – 'I am glad that I had the ability to paint in variegated colours.' – He recalls Gobineau and the Germanic world which came to an end with this work, and says he wishes for strength to stage the *Ring* once more and do it well.

---

[1] Correctly, Vassili Alexeivich Volkov (b.1842), a Russian portrait painter.
[2] A reference to Act II of *Götterdämmerung*.

Tuesday, October 3 Friend Levi visits us, by no means unwelcome to R., who, sitting in the smoking niche, is content looking back on the *Parsifal* days, and his only regret is not having spent enough time with his artists. In the evening he withdraws early, I follow him and lie down beside him. He cannot get to sleep and complains about the boring company he is keeping; indeed, he is even disturbed by all the bustle of the children, which he usually enjoys: 'Oh, if only I were dead!'

Friday, October 6 R. had a good night's rest, and at breakfast he thinks about the festivals; says he would like to stage *Tannhäuser*, which he regards as a consummate drama, but then again not, since he feels that musically some things are insufficiently expressed. He observes that *Tannhäuser*, *Tristan* and *Parsifal* belong together. – The news I have just received that Jouk. has sent Pepino home stimulates R. into writing him a congratulatory message. Biag. buys a sheet of illuminated paper, R. writes, 'We congratulate you from the bottom of our hearts,' and we all sign it.

Sunday, October 8 Around midday we visit our friends the Schl[einitzes], who have at last arrived here safe and sound. Yesterday, when he heard about the popularity in Munich of Schumann's *Manfred*[1], he said, 'They feel about it exactly what they felt about *Tristan*, a sort of emotional tipsiness, but there is not a trace of artistic appreciation.'

Tuesday, October 10 In the afternoon R. and I take a gondola to Saint Mark's Square. R. then leaves me at the Palazzo Malipiero[2], where Siegfried and Eva come to fetch me at the very moment I am about to leave. The journey home with these two dear, good, sensible children is like a blessing on me – we three are Wahnfried, wandering abroad in foreign lands! At home I find R. reading, and I embrace him at the very hour I first set eyes on him[3]! 'That was an encounter which has proved its worth,' he says. – Herr Hausburg arrives to replace Stein with S. temporarily, until Glasenapp takes over.

Thursday, October 12 When he was riding with me in the gondola today, R. told me he was still toying with the idea of asking the King of Bavaria to show him no more favours; the news that the King is also having a deer park laid out in the style of L[ouis] XV at his newly built castle has truly appalled R.!

Saturday, October 14 Around noon, when I go to fetch him, R. is having a spasm. However, he soon recovers and goes out with me. When I contemplate my happiness directly, realize what it is to be with him like this, undisturbed, unconcerned, then I take fright; my unworthiness threatens to destroy me, I become conscious that in all legends the divine can be seen only through a veil, and I feel like holding back every breath I take on my own so that he, and he alone, can reign supreme. And pray that the world, alas, may not cast its shadow over us! Towards four o'clock our

---

[1] A staging of Byron's dramatic poem with Schumann's overture and incidental music.

[2] Where the Schleinitzes were staying with Marie's mother, Princess Hatzfeldt.

[3] On the anniversary of their first meeting in 1853.

friend [Mimi] Schleinitz pays us a visit, which R. finds very agreeable. In the evening we are visited by Dr. Thode[1].

Sunday, October 15 The wet weather is worse than ever before. We say goodbye to our poor friend Stein, who takes his departure so sadly[2]. But R. feels oppressed all day long, and he is thinking of moving permanently to warmer climes, 'so as to live to see Siegfried's maturity!' – Yesterday, when we were discussing Sicily with Dr. Thode, he was led to the subject of the Romans and their terrible treatment of this country, in the interior of which no tree was permitted to grow.

Friday, October 20 Since R. is feeling run down, we sit under the archway of the Doge's Palace and talk about W. Scott, whom he greatly esteems, even though he admits that one never exactly warms to his characters, and that Carlyle was right when he said they act their characters and do not live them. R. says, 'He is the theatre director who sets it all in motion; he himself is always interesting, but his characters much less so.'

Sunday, October 22 Lunch with friend Rubinstein, a toast to my father, departure of Rub.

Tuesday, October 24 In the evening Voltz and Batz crop up[3], R. talks of the spirit in trade today, which consists simply in trying to buy up cheap something one thinks valuable, then selling it dear; all business people, he says, are in fact united in their adherence to this principle.

Wednesday, October 25 The mail arrives, R. comes in to find out if there is news from V. and Batz, discovers me reading, I am unable to conceal from him that our friend [Gobineau], the dearest of them all, has died[4]. . . . This dominates our day – we would find it impossible to talk to others about it. . . . I go out with Siegfr.; some time after one o'clock I come upon him on the path outside our house. 'When one has at last encountered something, it slips like water through one's fingers,' is what he says after a while, and we retrace together the signs which pointed towards this death, the restlessness, the haste, wherever he might be, to get away, and in the end this utterly solitary death. When we met R. on the broad path,[5] R.'s nerves were so on edge, probably because of the news, that he was quite unable to bear the tapping of the women's clogs, which he compared to castanets. He also dislikes the sirocco air. . . . At lunch R. suddenly strokes his nose, in the way our friend did when he was enjoying a private joke! In the afternoon he brings home for me a lovely promenade fan and a notebook with a swallow. The day is spent in efforts to bear up against the blow. 'One feels so useless, so superfluous!' R. exclaims as we are talking of

[1] Henry Thode (b.1857), German art historian, professor in Heidelberg; he married Daniela in 1886.
[2] He left to take up residence and qualify at the University of Halle.
[3] They were withholding payments because of a dispute about *Tristan*, for which Wagner claimed the right to sanction or veto all performances.
[4] He died of heart failure in Turin on October 13.
[5] Leading from their house to the church of S. Felice.

Gob.'s indifference towards his works. . . . And again and again during the day we keep coming back to this incomparable man, until in the evening R. plays the first bars of 'Siegfr.'s Funeral March'!

Thursday, October 26 R. dreamed of Gob., that he was telling many anecdotes, as was his way. I begin writing the piece about G. which R. wants me to do for the *Blätter*. Over coffee I read to R. a lively letter from Wolz. and a report from Malwida about the performance of the *Pars.* Prelude in Paris. We then meet R. in St. M.'s Square, where he gives me a second notebook. He had gone there with Loldi and told her of Gob.'s death. At the whist table he says to me: 'How silent you can be! It is enough to drive one mad.' – And indeed I find talking impossible, and when the children, having been told the news, come to me to talk about it, I have to leave the room. In my room I pace up and down, then hear that R. is in his, and some time later I find him there sitting in silence. Our thoughts are without a doubt on the same thing. After a while he wonders where Nietzsche is now – Wolz. told me about his latest book, *Die fröhliche Wissenschaft* [*The Joyful Wisdom*]. 'The terrible thing is,' he adds, 'that the people who reply to these absurdities also seem to be fools.' After the whist he suggested a game of lansquenet, but it all ends dismally! At lansquenet Lusch takes a lucky coin from her father and says she will have a bracelet made of all the things he has already given her. 'You will soon be getting other things from me, dear girl,' he replies to her sadly. He also complains of the fact that we cannot be alone: 'Sublime Spirit, thou gav'st me everything – gav'st me Cosima – and we cannot be by ourselves.' He says he never feels the desire to visit anyone, but I do have contacts outside; declares that there is something of my father in me. I tell him that, if now and again I do pay a visit, I do it for the children's sake.

Saturday, October 28 Georg comes in and tells R. that people are riding in gondolas over Saint Mark's Square. During the night there was heavy thunder, and as we are sitting over breakfast, lightning strikes in La Giudecca, and all day long there is a downpour of warm rain.

Sunday, October 29 R. is greatly vexed by a letter from friend Feustel, who, it seems, tells him rather carelessly that V. and Batz have submitted their accounts, but without the earnings from *Tristan*. Quite beside himself with rage, he goes with me to the post office and sends off a telegram to Herr Voltz saying that he will withhold his signature if the money from *Tristan* is not paid to him. At home he finds news of good receipts in Vienna, he writes to Feustel and, now calmed down, goes with us in the evening to our friends at the Pal. Malipiero.

Monday, October 30 In the morning we say goodbye to our children the Gravinas. In spite of the persistent rain R. is in good spirits.

Sunday, November 5 Since he wishes me to complete my obituary [for Gobineau], R. goes to the Piazzetta by himself in the morning and meets the children there. In the afternoon we arrange to meet in Saint Mark's

Square, but I find him in Lavena's shop, having had a spasm. Riding in the gondola, he and the girls had heard strains of *Lohengrin*, he then tried to hurry, and that brought on the trouble!...Hardly is the spasm over, however, when he beckons Tesarini and invites him and the music director to our house in the evening on account of the wrong tempi!...But he then says to me, 'I ought to forget who I am, make no sudden movements, and turn into a boring donkey!'

Tuesday, November 7 The Ibach grand piano arrives and pleases R. with its gentle tone, he writes to Herr I.[1] that from now on he will write only soft music. – As the evening ends, our conversation turns to Hans, R. taking the lead in very animated fashion! Each of us has the sickness he deserves, he says: 'I too – I have the sickness of my lack of breeding.'

Wednesday, November 8 In the morning he talks to me at length about his complaint and explains to me what an unduly active part the imagination plays in it. Then, at breakfast, he talks again about Hans; he deplores my marriage, then says Nature had never given him anything completely his own, he had always taken things over from someone else, and he mentions Minna and myself! Oh, how I wish from the very depths of my soul that a being without taint had devoted herself to him! – Hurt as I of course am by such a statement, my dominant feeling is happiness that he can make it, that he feels so free, is so certain of me, that he can let it all pour out, and everything that emanates from him is good!

Friday, November 10 R. had a tolerable night, but in the morning he has a spasm in bed, and today he has four in all!

Saturday, November 11 Gobineau's history of the Persians[2] – that interests him greatly. We talk a lot about our friend, and he continues writing out my article in the morning and afternoon, also praising me for it! – Before supper he called me from my reading with the children to listen to Fidi, who, accompanying himself on the piano, was whistling all kinds of themes and variations. After supper he has to repeat the performance to us. R. says this is just the way he himself treated music in his youth.

Wednesday, November 15 The expected arrival of my father and of Joukowsky keeps us busy. Towards four o'clock we go out, R., Fidi and I; it cheers R. up to stroll through the arcades, and our short stop at Lavena's he also finds entertaining. There his attention is caught by a handsome tomcat, who sits motionless on the sweets counter watching the movement made by the gas flame on the ceiling. We ride home through the narrow canals, Fidi rows and calls while Luigi [the gondolier] prompts him – but it makes us laugh heartily to see that, when it really matters, Luigi always calls out himself.

Thursday, November 16 Today he did not have a spasm! From *Lohengrin*

---

[1] Rudolf Ibach was a member of the Patrons' Society in Barmen, where his pianoforte factory was situated.

[2] *Histoire des Perses*, 1869.

(third act) he plays me the march and sings the final narration. We talk about Lohengrin, his naïveté: 'Since it is never in doubt that he will have to leave, it is possible for him to be so naïve and simple.' We remark how few people understand this commandment or even recognize its necessity; and now they talk about the loving woman, for whose sake he should have been permitted to reveal his secret, stay with her, and possibly even have children. But the folk tale accepts without question that he will have to depart. – (As we were leaving Saint Mark's today, R. said he would like to stage all his works in Bayreuth, then bring Siegfried to the point where he could assume control; that would mean living another ten years, 'for at the age of 23 a man already shows what he has in him.')

Saturday, November 18 R. finishes his letter to the King and tells me that in it he has spoken about the necessity of staging nothing but *Pars.* during the next two years, in order to keep down expenses. – In the evening I read aloud my letters from Rub. and Humperdinck; R. remarks on how extraordinarily cultured the former is; the latter, which pleases him greatly, makes him reflective. What Bayreuth could be if we were there! How gladly he would stay there if the town itself, and not only the weather, had something more to offer! – He goes through *Siegfried* and says he is glad some people have noticed that there is music in the first act.

Sunday, November 19 R. stays in the palazzo while we go to meet my father, whom he welcomes on the steps of Vendramin. He would dearly have liked to have lighted torches, but in the absence of these, many gas lamps are burning. My father is somewhat tired but better in health than we feared. Yet, for all the cordiality on both sides, it is hard to get a conversation going.

Tuesday, November 21 R. is much vexed around lunchtime by over-strong heating, rudeness of the servant, intimidation of the children. Gradually, with the help of time, I manage to raise his spirits, and he himself suggests a visit to my father[1]. There he is delighted with the second window, which offers such a pleasant view over the canal.

Wednesday, November 22 R. tells me in the morning that during the night he mixed up his pills and took five of a sort of which he should only take one! To counter it, he is now taking opium drops again!

Thursday, November 23 R. visits my father upstairs, and relations between them seem to become easier, rather than more difficult. Since the paper hanger is working in his room, R. occupies himself with pastimes which distract him, and in consequence he spends most of his time in the anterooms, reading, listening to the children, even playing on the piano some arias from the new collection. Schubert's '*Ständchen*'[2] arouses great feelings of warmth in us; R. finds this uniquely beautiful song full of invention, and indeed dramatic (somewhat like the turn in the *Walküre*

---

[1] Liszt was staying in a different apartment in Vendramin.
[2] 'Serenade', from *Schwanengesang*.

'Spring Song' at the words '*mit leichten Waffen bezwingt er die Welt*'). – As we are chatting together, talking of Fidi and his studies, R. asks himself if he had ever been diligent. He thinks he was at times, but he cannot remember ever having put anything he had learned to any use. Things just came into his head. The 'Sailors' Song' in *Tristan*, for example – that just came into his head; he never pondered or said to himself he must do this or that, and this is probably what gives his things their naïveté and will keep them alive.

Friday, November 24 In the afternoon we walk to Saint Mark's Square, which R. enjoys. At around 7 o'clock my father plays various things to us, the E Major Sonata and Schubert's '*Ständchen*', the latter so wonderfully that it affords R. the very greatest delight. In the evening we play whist, and during a pause R. – who has the dummy hand – plays his 'Porrazzi Melody'; after only the first two bars my father stops to listen and says, 'That is beautiful.' This so surprises R. that he feels I must already have acquainted my father with it. When we deny it, he is very pleased and praises my father's acuteness of perception.

Monday, November 27 The mail brings a proposal from Voltz-Batz! – In the afternoon, in spite of the mist and dampness, R. walks in Saint Mark's Square, buys lottery tickets with the children, and very much enjoys life, as he tells me, particularly the children's pleasure and excitement. Unfortunately the evening brings him much vexation; my father wishes to keep Lusch company – she is in bed; this makes R. thoroughly indignant, and he breaks out in a rage. I remain silent, and later too, when alone with him, sad from the depths of my heart at being unable to respond to his usual tendernesses, assuring him that I am not at all angry, yet able only to wish him a sorrowful good night.

Thursday, November 30 R. had a restless night, the V. and Batz affair torments him and causes him anxiety – for how long now? Years! But in bed in the morning he gives me instructions to prepare a nice Christmas for the children. Then he observes that my father was not looking well yesterday. I: 'He isn't well.' He wonders whether we should not consult a doctor. I say he has consulted Brehm and is living according to his instructions, whereupon R. disputes that very violently. When I tell him that I saw him drinking only Marsala and water, R. reproaches me for contradicting him; that arouses great annoyance in me, I angrily declare to R. that my entire efforts are always directed at not opposing him in anything, whereupon he jumps angrily out of bed with the remark that I obviously think I am virtue itself. Hardly has he gone when I sorrowfully tell myself that I should have kept silent after he contradicted my statement that my father is living according to doctor's orders; his remark about my opinion of myself seemed at first a bitter and painful punishment, but in the very next moment, though still in tears, I accept it with all my heart – if it is just, as a salutary punishment, if unjust (I am not aware of having any good opinion of myself, for I have never felt myself to be above anyone else), then as a blessing! May the blessings of suffering prevail! Certainly I have deserved my sorrow on account of my anger. – R. comes to breakfast; a nice letter has arrived from the King, we talk amicably about it. Before he goes, he tells me that it is unfair of him to talk to me so freely about my father, he realizes that and regrets it. Certainly it is not that; I keep silent, however, in the way I know he prefers when he has explained something, and I kiss him with a heart wholly free of rancour; but the fact that he returns my kiss without warmth pains the violently trembling self within me; however, I have no love for this self, and I know that the present flood of tears will give way to happiness. (As I am writing this, still under the immediate influence of it all, the sun shines silver and gold and smiles on me for a moment; otherwise it is a grey day. – In the evening R. writes to Voltz; Eva copies it. I send it to friend Gross. Unfortunately this subject gives R. no respite. The only distraction is provided by Siegfried, who is writing a play, *Catilina*! Yesterday he delighted us with his first piano production (theme from the Andante of the A Major Symphony). The fact that the King wants to see *Pars.* in Munich also disturbs R.! . . .

Monday, December 4 At breakfast we talk about yesterday's rehearsal of [Goethe's] *Die Geschwister*[1], and I tell R. my father's remark to the effect that he has no feeling for drama, and even in Shakespeare is interested only in the ideas. R. thinks, as do I, that this is the result of a French upbringing. – Lusch joins us, is praised for her acting yesterday, R. jokingly offers himself for the part of Fabrice. – The conversation at lunch is very cheerful; R. is continuing to read the Russian novel[2] with great interest.

Wednesday, December 6 Around midday our dear friends the Grosses appear on the doorstep! Several things: the King is eager to have *Parsifal* staged for him with our scenery; Holtzendorff is giving good and encouraging advice about how to deal with V. & B. Friend Gr. tells me there are reports that Neumann is going bankrupt (we keep this from R.).

Thursday, December 7 Towards six o'clock, after meeting in Saint Mark's Square, R. discusses with friend Adolf [Gross] the performances, our attitude towards the King, who is insisting on having a performance given in Munich; R. is at first violently against it, but then accepts my suggestion of offering the King our decorations and costumes in the autumn instead of the spring, since there is work to be done on them, and there will have to be rehearsals in the spring.

Friday, December 8 R. had a wretched night, and our breakfast time is not as amicable as usual – complaints about life gain the upper hand, and even the thought of the children does not cheer R. up, their merriness seems to him like triviality. Friend Jouk. arrives around eight o'clock, received by R.

---

[1] *Brother and Sister*, an amateur production in the Palazzo Malipiero.
[2] Tolstoy's *War and Peace*.

with a mixture of gaiety and gruffness; he tells him his greeting must take this form if he is to avoid looking like the biggest of hypocrites. – His humour keeps on breaking through his vexation.

Saturday, December 9 This morning was very bad indeed; the fact that Feustel lost the contract and then made no copy of it when it was recovered upsets R. so much that I become extremely worried. R. sends a telegram to the lawyer. In the afternoon the lawyer's reply is received: Batz refuses to produce the contract, which deprives us of any chance of making headway in court! . . . R. quite beside himself; he also says that on account of all this he finds it impossible to work. However, to my surprise, he disciplines himself in the evening to be friendly, spending part of the time playing whist with my father and part talking to Jouk., Marie Gr. and me, mainly about Tolstoy's novel, in which he particularly praises old Kutusov.

Sunday, December 10 To my surprise and delight, R. slept well, and our breakfast is cheerful, despite news of floods. When we hear friend Gross whistling Siegfried's call through the window, he becomes very high-spirited and goes for a little walk with him, during which, however, he is again beset by a chest spasm. In the evening we are at Princess Hatzf.'s, where Lusch plays Marianne in *Die Geschwister.* The play itself once again moves R. to tears, but he feels that Lulu's portrayal should have been more naïve. The rest of the *soirée,* however, the introductions, etc., R. finds more than ever unbearable, though he very patiently takes it in good part. The presence of our dear Grosses is of help to him in this; we say goodbye to one another, and R. allows me to give Marie the fan I got from him.

Monday, December 11 In the afternoon R. receives Count Contin, founder and president of the Conservatoire[1], R. describes correctness of tempo as the alpha and omega of what should be taught. (My father is very, very unwell, has to take to his bed!)

Wednesday, December 13 Today is payday, and our expenses are always very, very great, but R. will not hear of economizing!

Thursday, December 14 R. says he will never again speak about religion, explain his ideas, for instance, regarding the blood of Christ; these are things one all of a sudden grasps – let those who can understand them, one cannot explain them. – Suddenly he smiles to himself, and I ask why; he feels he should not tell me, but then he talks about the little grace note my father occasionally adds, on the same note, to make the melody sound more expressive; he says this reminds him of the wrong way certain singers sing. Our lunch is somewhat delayed by my father, R. very vexed about it, since he had promised to go with my father to the Lyceo. At supper he tells me that he had some spasms there. But when he says he must go again tomorrow, since they have no conductor, and notes my slight surprise, it

---

[1] The Società Benedetto Marcello, founded in 1877 to perform music both old and new.

bursts out of him that on my birthday he is going to play his symphony to me! ... Great laughter from Loldi and Fidi (Eva in bed, Lusch with her grandpa at Princess Hatzfeldt's). He tells me all the difficulties he has been having at rehearsals, with missing parts, with Seidl's absence; now he has sent a telegram to Humperdinck in Paris, hoping to get him here for the occasion. It moves me to complete silence! ...

Friday, December 15 We eat early, since he is going to the rehearsal; the open secret of the 'surprise' provides table conversation of the merriest kind. My mood remains subdued throughout, since the doctor is not satisfied with Eva's condition, but he does not say precisely what it is! – Around four o'clock R. goes to the rehearsal (yesterday Frontali, the first violinist, told Lusch that the players were all enraptured with R.). He returns home very content, saying it all went well! He told the players that it was an old piece, written 50 years ago, and they would find nothing new in it – if they wanted something new they had better choose a symphony by Beethoven or Haydn. – Talking to me about his symphony, R. says contentedly that it is not at all sentimental, striving throughout towards nobility.

Saturday, December 16 R. is in good spirits, I try as much as possible to play down Eva's illness. In the afternoon he goes to rehearsal; the children go there, too, and return home in raptures, R. also pleased and excited: he recalls the performance 50 years ago, after only one rehearsal, and says the present one will be much better. Since I am not allowed to attend the rehearsals, I find it only a melancholy consolation that I cannot in any case leave Eva's bedroom at present! ... R. complains that he and my father are now such strangers to each other. (Fidi wrote a hymn today, R. sat correcting it for him in the smoking niche, having gone there, first, because he had been dealt very bad cards, and then because my father played with such seriousness, not allowing himself to be distracted. I soon followed R. and left Loldi to take my place.)

Sunday, December 17 At lunch my father says jokingly that he feels humiliated – he has been told that all he is now good for is playing whist! When R. hears that, he greatly regrets what he has been saying, and he tries in every conceivable way to make up for it, just as he is wonderfully kind towards Jouk., having been somewhat curt with him on the previous day. Since the doctor has ordered Eva to be kept very quiet, I remain alone with her; R. goes out with the children, and they tell me he was very cheerful and sprightly and walked along swiftly and briskly; he himself is conscious of it and says it does him good to be back in his *métier* (conducting). We play whist with much merriment, R. has good cards, and he also tells my father that the game is nothing if one does not take it seriously. But in the end, when R. tries to explain cadential form with examples from *Die Schweizerfamilie* or *Das unterbrochene Opferfest*[1], and my father, after comparing the

---

[1] Two popular German *Singspiele*.

beginning with the '*Marseillaise*', stops listening, a comical situation arises which at first causes great laughter, but then R. becomes extremely annoyed. We go to bed, but R. continues for a long time talking to himself in his room, severely criticizing my father. I try to make him see that my father is very tired and not fully aware of what is going on, but he will only half accept it. I go off to bed; it is a long time before he follows me; he comes in quietly, looks to see if I am asleep; when I say good night to him, he exclaims, 'You best of all creatures!' and a very tender embrace delivers us lovingly into the arms of the friendliest of gods! – During whist R. talks about his symphony and says that it could be placed between Beeth.'s Second and Third, and it sounds very droll when he adds, 'If one really thought that, one would be surprised at the advanced state of preparations for the *Eroica*!' – Then to my father: 'If we write symphonies, Franz, then let us stop contrasting one theme with another, a method Beeth. has exhausted. We should just spin a melodic line until it can be spun no farther; but on no account drama!'

Monday, December 18 Herr Humperdinck has arrived. R. explains several things to him, and in the middle of the conversation Jouk. comes in to greet H. This so annoys R. that he packs J. off home. After a while he appears at Jouk.'s and kneels down in the middle of the room! Rehearsal in the afternoon, unfortunately very upsetting for R. First, he does not care for his Scherzo, second, a number of gentlemen staying with Herr Bassani[1], invited along on my father's account, have to leave early, and then he is angry with me for allowing Daniela to dine at Bassani's with her grand-father. Then, since by nearly ten o'clock my father has not returned, R. becomes very, very annoyed, saying that this dinner ruined his rehearsal, that if Lusch joins in such things, she no longer belongs to him, his star, in which I put my trust, cannot exert its influence. – He says all this in the angriest of tones, pacing up and down! – Then he returns and loudly throws out the news which even now, after its harshness has been softened, I cannot bring myself to write down! I cannot stay with him any longer, I flee to my room and see Hans before me, alone in that institution, and I feel like screaming, screaming to some god to help me![2] R. does not come to bed. I go to him, find him asleep, he wakes up, I ask his pardon, and he – he replies that I have done him a favour by waking him up. We go off to bed, but not for a moment does the picture leave me, I go through my whole life and get up in great misery. I do not believe that I shall ever have, or deserve to have, another happy moment.

Tuesday, December 19 What we talked about at breakfast I do not know – oh, God, God, always this picture in my soul! I do not wish to wipe it out – what

---

[1] An agent.

[2] Wagner and Cosima seem to have assumed – probably because of the institution to which he was admitted – that Bülow had gone insane; in fact, he had sustained an injury to his head and concussion in a fall.

help is there in such misery? ... That I can sit beside Eva's sickbed, that is a great help to me. But lunch – I see my daughter and ask myself how to tell her, how to plunge the knife into her youthful happiness ... The sun is shining, R. wishes me to go out with him, I beg to be allowed to remain at home, this arouses his anger, we go out. He then goes to rehearsal, I return home to Eva, my gentle support, but I struggle to find comfort, to find God – oh, children, may you never go through hours such as these! – R. and the children return from the rehearsal, say it went very well. Shortly before supper R. comes to me in Eva's room with moist eyes; I have not the strength to respond to his expansive words, and I fear the effect his agitation may have on Eva; he goes off – in an ill-humour, it seems to me. At table he says, and I feel only partly in fun, that I hate him; when I pick up his napkin, he says I do it only out of hate. I can scarcely look at Lusch, and in my heart sits the constant companion of all feeling. R. says that Goethe is the greatest of all poets and that he had wished to say something about him to me, but I had not been in the right mood to listen. Supper is spent in talk about the rehearsal, afterwards R. is vexed by conversations with Herr Hausburg and Hump. He leaves the room, I follow him and ask him to tell me now what he wished to say to me; at first he refuses, then he says he has been reading the end of the first and the second part of Faust. I leave him and say good night to my father, and we go to bed. I do not know why – I should have to ask life's daemons – but bitterness impelled me to say that no poet now means anything at all to me, that poetry seems to me like some wretched plaything. R. is very angry, accuses me of not understanding him; I immediately follow him into his room and beg his pardon, saying that perhaps, if he were to see inside my heart, he would excuse me. Very emotionally he tells me that I mean everything to him, that without me he is nothing. He says he came home from the rehearsal worn out, forced himself to read these two scenes in order to shut out everything, all feeling, all suffering, and tell himself that the highest being is one transfigured through suffering, is myself! He asked himself, he says, whether he is a bad person, but he is not, and for several days he had kept this news to himself. I beg him for forgiveness and God for mercy! He calms down, goes to bed, falls asleep, while I lie and lie there with this dreadful picture which has haunted me ever since yesterday; at last sleep comes to me, too!

Wednesday, December 20 We get up late, and at breakfast I pluck up courage to speak to R. about Hans's condition. R. observes that it was after all to be expected. But not by me – not that! And, even if feared, the advent of what one fears still splits open a precipice which nothing can hide! – R. is much more resigned than I am. However, I make the resolve, whatever my inner feelings, to regain my self-control. I embrace R. with all my heart and tell myself that God will have mercy, He will! – After coffee and his afternoon rest R. brings me the news, which is better! ... He had already told me in the morning that the dreadful name of the illness had not been mentioned in the report, he had just deduced it from the description. And I feel as if I have been restored to life as I set out with R. on this afternoon walk. The light outside is glorious, and the sunshine in my heart matches it. R. gazes at the sea and describes the ebb and flow as its breathing in and out. Then he goes off to rehearsal; on his return I go to see him, and he tells me – after saying that I should ask the children to tell me about it – that the rehearsal began very stormily because two players were absent and the others tried to make excuses for them! R. made a speech in French which had a great effect; after that, apparently, they played excellently, and altogether the players seem to be full of enthusiasm for R., they repeat his jokes to one another and understand him quite well. – R. reports in the evening that Hans has indeed been put in an institution, but there are hopes of an improvement. R. adds that Hans will outlive us all! – I feel that God has had mercy on me.... (At the start of the terrible night of Monday R. cried out from his bed, 'I hate all pianists – they are my Antichrist!')

Thursday, December 21 The *B. Blätter* arrives, R. gets it first, opens the door to the *salon*, where I am talking with the children, and cries that he knows what he will read to begin with. And round lunchtime he again praises my modest lines, adding, 'Only a woman could have done it like that; a man would have made it look pedantic!' – In the afternoon he shows me two extra bars which he has composed for the Scherzo, and he says he is curious to see whether the children will spot them.

Friday, December 22 Today Eva gets up. R. brings her to the lunch table, where she is greeted! In the afternoon she returns to bed, and around four o'clock we go to the rehearsal, which I am allowed to attend, hidden from sight! First we stroll in Saint Mark's Square, then enter the Teatro La Fenice. It is very cold! R. has a spasm, but he conducts the first movement, then, after quite a long pause, the others. I sit in concealment far away from him and am touched to think that 50 years ago he performed this work for his mother, now for me. Then I take delight in the straightforward, courageous work, and I tell R., 'That was written by someone who knew no fear.' We ride home, R. and I, in the moonlight with Loldi, forbearing to speak. He spends the evening by himself, and unfortunately has a very restless night.

Sunday, December 24 The morning is spent in preparations; R. says my face so often wears an expression of delicate sorrow, and that is why he is so pleased to hear me 'singing like a lark.' – He brings me better news of Hans.

Towards six o'clock the tree is lit in the *sala*, and there is a very merry presentation of gifts in which our Italian servants join with great delight. My father too, whom we imagined to be quite above such things, is with us heart and soul. Around 7.30 we set off in three gondolas, with the moon shining and bells chiming, for La Fenice. Eva is allowed to come with us! The hall festively lit; my father, the children and I go in first, a friendly reception[1]. Somewhat later R., received with cheers. The two first movements are played fairly quickly in succession, then there is a pause; R. comes to me and my father, talks to me very gaily. I send thanks to the orchestra players, which earns me an '*evviva*'. At the end the players come to join us, and my health is toasted. Then R. murmurs in my father's ear, 'Do you love your daughter?' My father looks startled. 'Then sit down at the piano and play.' My father does so at once, to everybody's cheering delight. Then in French R. relates the history of his symphony. Towards eleven o'clock we ride home, Venice transfigured in a blue light. The children enchanted with the evening, R. very content!

Monday, December 25 Towards nine o'clock I am given my presents. R. has his 'dear God' robe on – everything very touching and harmonious! There is no toast to me at lunch, since nothing was prepared, but R. gets up and plays to me from the *salon* 'Who has found so good a wife'[2]. – Before whist in the evening, I am telling my father about Gob. when R. sticks a notice on the door: '*Ici on parle français*'.[3]

Wednesday, December 27 Blandine's inexplicable silence causes very embarrassing upset. But at last, as around lunchtime I am attending my father's sitting for Herr Wolkoff, Fidi comes to tell me that Bl. has received everything, but the telegraph lines were cut. R. came in at first, but when he saw that my father was at the piano and being drawn at the same time, he went away at once, and later told me how disagreeable he found this sight. – In the evening R. does not feel well, he has been drinking beer and champagne. I think that all the disturbance of the moving – we have installed my father on this side of the house – upset him, too.

Thursday, December 28 Around lunchtime we stroll on the Piazzetta in the most glorious sunshine. R. is also in a particularly good mood, since he was able to begin his work – a report on the symphony[4]. That always washes away all his irritation. – My second Christmas gown has arrived, I put it on in the evening for R. and the children. But the day ends dismally: R. tells me that he gave Georg 100 francs as a reward for six years in his service; since Christmas has just gone by and there seems no real justification for it, and also our expenses are not matched by our income, I am stupid enough to make a remark about it to R. This annoys him extremely, and it takes me a long time and many confessions of remorse to pacify him.

---

[1] Besides these, the audience consisted only of Count Contin, Joukowsky, Hausburg and the governess; public and press were rigidly excluded.

[2] '*Wer ein holdes Weib errungen*': in both Beethoven's Ninth Symphony and his opera *Fidelio*.

[3] 'French spoken here': the piece of paper in Wagner's handwriting enclosed in the Diaries.

[4] 'A Youthful Symphony', first published in the *Musikalisches Wochenblatt* and reprinted in vol. 10 of the collected writings.

1883

Thursday, January 4 Marie Dönhoff puts in an appearance, charming and friendly; even R. finds her pleasant, though he is usually harsh in his judgment against her, and he recently said, 'What sort of a human being is that, who thinks society more important than anything else?' She wins him over by talking very earnestly about Malwida's influence on her mother in persuading her to regard things from the standpoint of ideals. In the evening R. and I are alone together, all the rest at Princess H.'s. We talk as we always do when we are alone. Unfortunately, however, his attitude towards my father is becoming increasingly difficult and incensed!

Friday, January 5 Makart's portrait of the Countess [Dönhoff] has been put on display in our apartment – something R. finds distasteful. But our friend herself is received by him in a very friendly fashion; he exclaims to the children at lunch that, since they always imitate everybody, they should imitate the Countess! – In the evening, while the others are playing whist, we are alone with Marie; she tells us her situation, R. responds by describing our fate to her. He speaks the following beautiful words: 'It took Nature a very long time to produce passion; this is what can lead one to the heights; music is its transfiguration, is, alone among all the arts, directly connected with it.' After and during this expansive conversation R. is infinitely kind towards me, lovingly animated. At supper, sitting opposite me, he cries out, 'I love you!' – Today he was not at all pleased by having a number of society people come to our home at my father's invitation to inspect Makart's picture.

Saturday, January 6 Yesterday a telegram from Herr Neumann came, announcing that he is sending 10,000 francs. But at lunch R. is very serious, I think his sympathy for our friend is somewhat exhausted; he is taciturn, and it falls to me to keep the conversation going. My father's manners and customs offend him, he says he is just like King Lear, his acquaintances the 100 knights, and his arrangements the Learisms. (In our evening conversation yesterday the Countess spoke about the performances of the *Ring* in Vienna and praised them very highly, particularly Winkelm., Scaria, Materna. R. then talks about the subjects of his works, calling *Lohengrin* the saddest of them all; he also tells us about Lüttichau's suggestion that Tannhäuser should be pardoned in Rome and should marry Elisabeth.)

Monday, January 8 Hans's birthday – on which day it is given to me to learn that he has been holding a rehearsal! ... R. had a good night, he is cheerful and comes frequently to my room during the morning to read me bits of his letter to Levi. Our lunch passes without the little Countess, who is indisposed. We visit her, first I alone, then R. comes to fetch me, and, friendly though he is towards the charming lady, the impression all her elegance in bed makes on him is a very dismal one! And so these days bear the stamp of sadness! – While my father is playing whist, R. reads *Lear* to me and Eva, the scene in which Kent is put in the stocks, and we come to the conclusion that one ought to read Shakespeare scene by scene, for otherwise one never really gets to know him. My father and the others come in unnoticed to listen, which surprises and pleases R. – In recent days R.'s face has had a wonderful radiance, and when his eyes fell on me, I felt 'gladness and woe in one.' Today I felt it indescribably! ...

Tuesday, January 9 R. slept well, but he is in a disturbed state of mind, and I must feel glad that our friend stays away! Everything upsets him. He has a spasm in the morning and at lunch is all but silent. He starts a letter to the King. In the afternoon he goes out, I wait in the antechamber to greet him, but he is in an ill-humour, and in the evening this turns into anger. My father's manners and customs, the whist table, the constriction of our living space, all the disturbance arising from his visit – this makes him furious, and long, long after it is past he gives way to his anger, which I can only assuage by suffering with him in silence! – As a curiosity I might note down that R. considers the black eyes and hair of our friend to be unwomanly.

Wednesday, January 10 R. thinks I am looking worn out and says it is impossible for me to regain my strength as long as he is the way he is. When I tell him that even to suffer with him is happiness, and if in words and manners he prefers me to others, this is something I owe entirely to him, such lovely feelings take possession of us that they give me wings to surmount the day's troubles! These consist of R.'s health, his spasms, then his vexation – about the various things from which he has to dissuade the King, for instance; he says that in his rage he has added only one sentence to the letter during the whole afternoon. He is also oppressed by the smallness of the rooms, he misses books and music, but when I suggest we return to Wahnfried, he cannot make up his mind to do so.

Thursday, January 11 I hear R. saying in his dreams: 'If He created me, who asked Him to? And if I am made in His image, the question remains whether I am pleased about that.' – Today R. finishes his letter to the King, I take our friend to the station. In the afternoon he pays a visit to my father, and proposes to him that he remain with us. There was a report in a newspaper to the effect that we were living in a sumptuously furnished 1st-floor apartment, whereas my father had only a modestly equipped one on the mezzanine floor; this annoys R. In the evening, before going off with the younger girls to Malip., Siegfried reads to us the first scenes of his comedy, *Die Lügner!* . . . We take delight in the boy, he is good-looking and talented. When we are alone together, we read *Hamlet* with ever-increasing astonishment and emotion; we are indeed carried right out of ourselves, and I feel as if Richard, Hamlet, Shakespeare have become one, as if I can comprehend the one only through the other, as if Hamlet could never be understood except with R.'s voice, R.'s character except with Shakespeare's genius, and neither except through this creation of Hamlet. The goodness of Hamlet's veracity – how could I feel this so deeply if I had not experienced it through R.?

Friday, January 12 R.'s spasms start today first thing in the morning and last for more than two hours! He does not eat with us – in fact not at all. Dr. Keppler[1] comes at last at five o'clock and proposes massage, which he begins at once, promising R. alleviation within a month! R. is greatly encouraged by this, whereas I, alas . . .!

Saturday, January 13 R.'s night was a good one, and today he is massaged twice. Arrival of our friend Gross. A request has come from Munich (on account of the exhibition[2]) that we give only ten performances this year, and these in July. R. is at first very annoyed, but then he gives way, though not before saying that the best thing would be to give it up entirely – though he then thinks of the children and feels one ought to set them an example of constancy. At two o'clock my father takes his departure – R. claims frequently to have discerned in him a mood of sadness about himself. When he is in his room, I hear him playing softly on the piano. Today he frequently plays a melody of his own which has come into his mind, in the manner of an English folk song.

Sunday, January 14 R. had a good night, and I believe that massage is really doing him good. A letter from Lenbach announcing a visit causes R. to pull my leg about my enthusiasm for this artist, and when I protest he says, 'When one has someone like you to tease, one doesn't often let the chance slip.' Sirocco storm, no outing possible.

Tuesday, January 16 A consultation with Dr. Keppler reveals that my heartbeat is the strongest imaginable, and since he is also completely satisfied with R.'s condition, we joke at breakfast that neither of us will ever die! It is raining again, consequently no outing.

Wednesday, January 17 Since the sun is shining, we ride in an open gondola via the Cannaregio into the open sea, and from there to the Rialto, where we get out. Since R. was on the verge of a spasm, he would have found the walk home difficult if he had not been distracted by everything he saw

---

[1] Friedrich Keppler, surgeon and physician in Venice.
[2] A Bavarian show in Munich.

along the way – two men, for example, talking to each other, one of them standing motionless wearing a large round hat, a cycling cape, around his waist an apron of blue rags stitched together, black-bearded; the other grey, beardless, with a yellow-brown jacket, trousers and cap, violently gesticulating. He plays the piano in the evening. I recall that music usually seems to produce ill-humour or irritability in him, and I speak to him about it, pointing out how much more tranquil his mood is when he has been occupying himself with books. He says I am talking in a casual tone about something of great importance, but I am right; then he pleases me by declaring that he will be quite satisfied with the ten performances. Today he goes so far as to ask himself whether the whole thing should not be given up entirely and he should instead try to make as much money as possible, so that we could live independently! . . . Then he goes through our disloyal friendships – Nietzsche, Gersdorff – and feels we should be downright ashamed of not having been able to keep a better grip on them.

Friday, January 19 He slept well and is in such a merry mood that the doctor is unable to massage him for a while. He told him that the stomach tube was an invasion of his personal rights! R. talks to the doctor about vegetarianism and deplores the stupidity of vegetarians who despise milk, which is after all the food Nature gave us.

Saturday, January 20 Our breakfast brings up the subject of the children's life, whether one can and should cut them right off from the community, whether we are not asking too much of them in our isolation. Eva, for example, is curiously irritable, and the doctor has forbidden reading material such as [Schiller's] *D. Carlos*. A difficulty which I leave to my good star!

Sunday, January 21 R. is skipping the massage on Sundays, and I beg him to give up the stomach tube entirely, believing that it must upset his nerves. He has arranged an outing for today, we are to have lunch in Saint Mark's Square, and, sure enough, Venice is enveloped in fog! Today he started his preface for Stein's book, and that puts him in a good mood. But it is cold, the meal is not ready in the Cappello Nero; I read aloud a nice letter from our dear Ponsch[1], and that helps, but the mood almost threatens to turn sour; however, since we are entirely by ourselves except for Jouk., R. does not become irritable, and gradually a very good atmosphere is achieved. We wish to go home but are forced back by the crush, and from the restaurant we watch the masked procession, in which a cook keeps greeting R.; and R. replies. It is estimated that there are 20,000 people in the square; the children – who went off at R.'s bidding but then returned – watch the seething crowds with us, 'a black mass in which patches of flesh colour emerge,' a strange, uncanny impression. As R. and I are riding home together, he talks about the sight and the impression, both so sad. 'And

---

[1] Blandine.

yet,' he says, 'a person who does not try to make closer contact with the masses is not worth much!' In the evening he plays things by Weber, from *Euryanthe* and again, at my request, from *Der Freischütz*. We are pleased that after Beethoven such utterly new things should have been written, which in no way detract from Beeth.'s greatness.

Monday, January 22 R. is restless almost throughout the night, is also unable to work. Yesterday was too much for him. We ride to the Square, he sits down under the portal but spends only a little time there. I receive a letter from Herr v. Bürkel, but I refrain from telling him about it; he says that the King is holding to his order for a performance of *Parsifal* in May (in Munich). – He feels the outing yesterday was a success, and he says we should always just let him grouse properly – in him imprecations are the heralds of a good mood.

Tuesday, January 23 R. has decided to have a massage only once a day. At breakfast we chat quietly together, and I make a firm resolve to tell him as little as I possibly can, in order not to thwart or overburden the cherished workings of his mind. He does a little work, and at 12.30 we ride to the Piazzetta in glorious weather, walk almost as far as the arsenal, sit down for a while in the Giardinetto, and return at three o'clock. On the trip out R. mentioned Bach's fugues – 'In these, chaos is turned into harmony' – he finds all other forms trivial in comparison, and yesterday he expressed his regret that music is so much the slave of its time, except perhaps only in its use of drama. Chat in the evening, brought to an end by R. with the 'Shepherd's Song' and 'Pilgrims' Chorus' from *Tannhäuser*. He says he still owes the world *Tannhäuser*.

Wednesday, January 24 We are much concerned about Lusch's condition, she is in bed. I consult Dr. Keppler. In consequence, a conversation with him about the present position of women, which R. describes as an unnatural one. Many, many great worries, alas! – R. tells me about a young couple who committed suicide for love, and he adds, 'This is still the main tragedy of life.' We are diverted from these dismal thoughts by my remarking how pretty his room (blue grotto) is, and this leads us to his desire for colours, for perfumes, the latter having to be very strong, since he takes snuff. 'Taking snuff is really my soul,' he says very drolly. At the start, he describes how gently glowing colours influence his mood, but later in the conversation he denies any connection and says very emphatically, 'These are weaknesses.' – Then we recall the roof-raising ceremony in Bayreuth (1873), and he expresses his amazement about the theatre, 'that it is there, that I brought it into being with my scores!'

Thursday, January 25 R. has a massage and seems to be well, but he complains that life is an eternal winter, the short days are a torment to him. – In the evening I have at last to tell him the contents of Bürkel's letter; he is very agitated by it, though he shows no anger, decides to engage an orchestra of his own, and tells me I should write and say that the state of his health does not permit such communications to be sent to him.

Friday, January 26 R. has calmed down. He goes to his work and is satisfied with what he does. But around lunchtime, when I have to inform him of the passage in Herr v. B.'s letter (he did not wish to read the letter yesterday), he gets very upset, even though the prospect of not having to do the performance until the spring of '84 is a welcome one. We then ride to the Square in nice sunshine, but he feels indisposed, and even after our return home his 'heaviness' does not vanish; he comes to our meal late, having abandoned it earlier. – The evening is spent quietly and cosily in chat about all sorts of things, R. somewhat taciturn but listening with enjoyment. Just now and again he flares up like a half-extinguished fire about what the King is doing to him in ordering this separate performance.

Saturday, January 27 R. told me his dream: wearing the mauve nightgown which he has on now, he went with me into a box in a theatre; there people behaved improperly towards him, but he did not wish to show himself, though he could hardly avoid it, while I became very embarrassed, whereupon he woke up. R. slept well, and he works, jokingly remarking that he is no longer capable of producing an article as long as mine was. Towards one o'clock we take a trip to S. Moisè; but R. is somewhat agitated and remains so throughout the day, all the more so since the doctor does not come today.

Monday, January 29 No morning conversation today, since I have to remain in bed with a cold, but instead, at lunchtime, a reading of the fine preface to Stein's dialogues! R. goes out, meets the children in Saint Mark's Square, and returns in good spirits with Lusch. Much joking at lunch about a letter to me from Herr Levi, and it comes out that, whereas I dictated my letter to him, I wrote to Lenbach in my own hand. In the afternoon R. has a massage, and it seems to me that this treatment is certainly doing him good. And R. takes delight in the children, particularly Fidi, who is writing poetry in the lobby in a very neat handwriting – not because he feels inspired, just as a routine! (Of Loldi he said yesterday, 'She lands in one's soul with a thud.')

Tuesday, January 30 R. copies out his article and then goes for a walk by himself, since I still have a cold. He returns home much delighted with the sight of the lively lanes, and observes that it is better for him to go out without me, however silly that sounds, but he is ashamed of his attacks when he is with me, the need to walk so slowly. He is afraid of offending me with this remark, seems unaware that the only thing which pleases me is what seems right to him! He has brought me a lovely coffee service, and he returned home in high spirits in anticipation of my surprise. – At coffeetime we receive a visit from the two friendly painters Passini and

Ruben[1], but they make an arid impression on R. and produce from him the merriest jokes. Otherwise he is in a subdued mood, as so often now in the hours of dusk; he regrets that our palace is so far from the Square, feels we have no luck with our arrangements (a statement he tries to take back at once, fearing that it will make me sad); he says this will probably be our last stay in Italy – in future we shall just make a long journey every year. At supper a great disturbance was caused by the news that Herr Neumann is to bring the *Ring* to Venice after all, though R. specifically advised Count Contin against it. R. sends Neumann a very emphatic telegram of disapproval. – R. asks Lusch to play the piano with him, but unfortunately she behaves childishly and refuses. So R. plays by himself, first the Andante from the Fourth Symphony, then '*froh, froh, wie seine Sonnen*' from the Ninth. – At the end of the evening he tells me that he can still imagine a type of symphonic work, like the '*Kaisermarsch*', for example, in which themes are not contrasted, but each emerges out of another. However, he says he will make no more music – it excites him too much.

Wednesday, January 31 In the morning all kinds of reflections about the children. Then R. turns to the subject of the King of Bavaria, and we reflect on the ways of life, which has turned the relationship which appeared to solve everything into an unforeseeable source of bitterness! – Herr Neumann cables that the performance in Venice will not take place – a relief! R. was very pleased today that Hoffmann's valerian drops were such a help and allowed him to get on with his work by allaying his spasms. He is also very cheerful during his indoor walk in the afternoon; before that I hear him improvising, the blessed spirit of music is stirring in him.

Thursday, February 1 Restless night for R., at any rate much talking aloud during it. He also complains of earache, and I put a few drops of tepid milk in his ear. We have both sirocco and rain, but all the same I suggest a short outing. It does not cheer R. up, however, and in the evening he eats no supper, complaining a lot about his heaviness. But he becomes more cheerful as the evening goes on and also feels somewhat better. A letter from Boni is a real balm to us; so I have really been granted the boon of seeing this child pursuing the paths to which I directed her!

Friday, February 2 In glorious weather we ride to the Piazzetta, but the crowds milling around on account of the festival are repugnant to him, we stroll through the Merceria to the Rialto, where we embark at the side, avoiding the butcher's shop which made such a terrible impression on R. the day before yesterday. – A letter from Malw. Meys. vexes him because of the remarks it contains about Gobineau. R. then plays various things by Weber, but at last we come to *Die Msinger*, and he plays a lot of things from it, pleased with this enchanting work. 'Cobble your shoes' – that had been

[1] Ludwig Johann Passini (b.1832) and Franz Leo Ruben (b.1842); Ruben, who lived in Venice, produced the Lohengrin paintings in King Ludwig's castle Hohenschwangau.

his mood at the time, he says. As we are going to bed, he wonders whether he will ever see Marke again – he says he has the feeling that we hide various things from him. I reassure him.

Saturday, February 3 There is an article about Nietzsche's *Fröhliche Wissenschaft* in Schmeitzner's monthly [*Internationale Monatsschrift*]; I talk about it, and R. glances through it, only then to express his utter disgust with it. The things in it of any value, he says, have all been borrowed from Schopenhauer, and he dislikes everything about the man. Late in the evening, as we are going to bed, R. mentions that *Fl[ick] und Flock* has been performed in Berlin for the 500th time, always in the presence of the Emperor! To this I add the King of B. with his Versailles – and there you have Germany.

Sunday, February 4 R. tells me the nice dream he had: he was with Schopenhauer, who was extraordinarily cheerful and friendly (and completely white, causing R. to ask himself, 'Who would ever think that this is the great philosopher?'). – Then R. comes back to Nietzsche, observes that the one photograph is enough to show what a fop he is, and declares him to be a complete nonentity, a true example of the inability to see. Sirocco, R. does not go out. Levi arrives towards four o'clock, most welcome to all of us. The evening passes in chat; Levi tells us that Nietzsche recommended to him a 'young Mozart', actually a thoroughly incompetent musician[1]! This gives us food for thought! R. says to me eventually that Nietzsche has no ideas of his own, no blood of his own, it is all foreign blood which has been poured into him.

Monday, February 5 At lunch much with the conductor about the preparations for *Pars.* Over coffee we discuss the King's deficit, he is spending 500,000 marks annually on the theatre (excluding the special performances). In the evening the casting of *Parsifal* is discussed, as well as the pleasure R. got from Materna's Kundry; he also declares his wish to do *Tannhäuser* in Bayreuth first; he says that if he can get this settled, he will have achieved more than by staging *Tristan*. – For the past two days he has been thinking of the Villa d'Angri, he would not be disinclined to rent it again. As I go to sleep I hear him speaking divine words to me, words I may not repeat, words which wrap me around like guardian angels and settle deep, deep in my heart like the most sacred of my treasures. 'Good night, my angel,' I said to him yesterday. 'Good night, my dear wife – that means much more.'

Tuesday, February 6 I go with Lusch and the conductor to see Moretto's picture; on our way home I hear amid all the crush and noise 'Psst!' and I know at once that it is R.; I tell my companions, who look around, and true enough, there he is sitting on the bench beside the Doge's Palace and in very good spirits; the air is splendid, and he has been happily watching two lovely boys of five and seven playing with sand on the bench; he put some

---

[1] Peter Gast, pseudonym of Heinrich Köselitz (b.1854).

money in the sand pit for them. At around nine o'clock we set out to the Square for the Shrovetide celebrations. R. does this to please the children, who reward him with their gaiety. The impression is mixed; R. finds something touching about the procession carrying carnival to the grave, with its melody which he thinks to be an old one, but after going to the podium with the children, he returns to me in the Cappello Nero looking sad. He says poor artisans were hopping around there without really understanding why. But the midnight bells and the extinguishing of the flames produce another fine effect. – We return home towards one o'clock. R. not entirely dissatisfied, but as I go to sleep, I hear him say, 'I am like Othello, the long day's task is done.' He asked me earlier whether I still cared for him – he is so difficult!

Thursday, February 8 I have breakfast at R.'s bedside, since he is not feeling well. He gets up towards 10 o'clock, but he does not come to lunch, in order not to excite himself; shortly before lunch he shows me the newspaper report of our friend Dohm's death[1]. As we are finishing our meal, we hear him loudly singing '*Don Giovanni tu m'invitasti!*'[2]. He comes in to us for a moment but soon leaves us, so as not to excite himself. Towards four o'clock he comes into the *salon*, and we chat about all kinds of things, though I refrain from telling him that Scaria is causing difficulties! ... In the evening, after the doctor has given him a massage, R. has supper with us and stays with us for a while. At the start of the evening he was in somewhat low spirits, but he gradually cheers up and is merry and unconstrained, suddenly expressing delight in my 'clever face'!

Friday, February 9 R. plays a melody which sounds very beautiful, he then comes and shows it to me, neatly written on a nice sheet of paper; he says he found it while sorting out his musical scraps and wondered how it came to be there. ... At last he remembers that it was to be attached to *Parsifal* as a dedication page! I joke about it, saying that I had indeed been disappointed at finding nothing! Now it lies in the book. He declares, incidentally, that he will never make any use of these musical scraps. In the gondola he tells me that he will still do his article about masculine and feminine, then write symphonies, but nothing more on the literary side, though he still intends to finish the biography. While he was arranging his papers, mine also came into his hands; they breathe upon him like a swarm of All Souls, he says! He considers his article 'Herodom and Christianity', which he read again today, to be his best; this leads us to Gob., whose vision was so broad and so acute, but who did not look deep enough. We ride as far as the Bacino, then stroll beneath the arcades to S. Moisè to look at some blue satin fabric which has caught R.'s eye. Lunch with the

[1] Ernst Dohm died on February 5.
[2] 'Don Giovanni, thou hast invited me': the Commendatore in Act II of Mozart's opera.

children; the conductor is ill, Jouk. keeping him company! In the evening R. talks about his supporters – how they seem to be designed to make all the ideas he expresses look ridiculous. (He excepts Stein.) He tells Jouk. that he never expected the *Blätter* to last more than two years; he is considering what is to become of Wolz. And finally he loudly regrets having built Wahnfried, the festivals also seem to him absurd! ... With our friend Jouk., who comes around in the evening, we discuss the health of our poor conductor! R. observes that Jewishness is a terrible curse; no possibility, for example, of marrying an Christian woman; recently, he says, he had been thinking about Dr. Markus, a Israelite who once admitted to him amid tears that he loved R.'s sister (Cäcilie) but would never be permitted to marry her, for, were he to be baptized, he would lose his practice! R. says he told this story in front of Levi, and it must have affected him deeply – the Jews, the good ones, are 'condemned to a gently resigned asceticism'. ... After Joukowsky has left, the children show us their little preparations for tomorrow (the 100th birthday of Jouk.'s father). Loldi's drawing arouses R.'s utter admiration!

Saturday, February 10 R. dreamed about his mother; he met her at the Brockhauses', but she was very pretty and young – as he could only at best recall her from her portrait – and also very elegant. – But R. is not feeling well and he is very depressed; as we are finishing breakfast he says he hates himself because he is such a nuisance to me! – I rehearse Fidi in a speech for lunch, R. thinks it too long, goes to his room and writes a verse. We come to lunch late, since he had a spasm. But he is in good spirits, tells us various things from the *Fl. Blätter*; then mention is made of his 100th birthday, which we will surely live to see and hope to celebrate! R. leaves the table for a moment, then returns, the champagne is poured out, Fidi rises to his feet – but he has forgotten it all! – Our poor conductor is very ill, and when in the evening the doctor lets fall the words 'emotional disturbance', we realize that his friendship with us must in the end make him melancholy. R. almost regrets having recently told him the story of Dr. Markus! He is overworked, the victim of intrigues in his profession – also on our account! – After a sad discussion of this case (the conductor is staying in bed with us here), R. withdraws for a while, and when he returns we talk of other things, the city of Paris, its various beauties and its boring aspects, then we come to the S[istine] Chapel, which R. calls a monstrosity; he says he would like to know if it was admired when it was first opened. I bring him M[ichel]a[ngelo]'s poem about this chapel, and it pleases him greatly.

Sunday, February 11 R. saw Schröder-Devrient in his dreams; telling me of it, he says, 'All my women are now passing before my eyes.' We then talk about my father, in connection with a letter he has written excusing himself for not playing for the flood victims; we talk of my father's misfortune in always being regarded as a pianist, and about the difficulties of his career, which always caused such upsets that he could not help taking counter-measures of an extreme kind; but we end by observing that, as a person of greatness, he has risen above his difficult situation. – At twelve o'clock R. comes to me and reports that he has begun his work[1], and it is so heavily salted that not even Wolz. will be willing to print it. He reads the first page to me and observes that the motives have been set out clearly enough! Our poor conductor is causing much concern. In R. it shows itself indeed as ill-humour, he observes that one should really have nothing to do with Israelites – either it causes them emotional disturbance, or it finds expression in arrogance, as with J. Rub. This theme is discussed over lunch, R. almost angry about it. – In the evening we are alone together, R. and I, the dear children with the Princess. We read *Undine* (discovered among the papers belonging to Jouk.'s father, which we looked through), and we take pleasure in the very good portrayal of this figure[2]. – Around noon he came into my room. 'I have a letter from Cyriax.' 'Is there anything in it?' 'You'll soon see.' When I have dried my hands, I look: it is a scherzo theme, written down on an envelope from Cyriax – he then plays it on his piano.

Monday, February 12 R. got up once during the night and looked among his papers for his cheque book, which he did not find, and that disturbs him somewhat. He tells me gaily at breakfast that his barber has been complimenting him on his progress in Italian. R. had spoken of the rain as '*piova fruttuosa*' ['fruitful rain']. And indeed a sirocco is blowing; we say goodbye to the poor conductor, who is still very run down. R. worked on his article. At lunch the children and Jouk. tell us all sorts of droll things about the *soirée* yesterday, which amuse R. and tempt him into relating some very drastic jokes and anecdotes. In the afternoon he goes out with Eva – since I am expecting Princess Hatzf. – and he tells me on his return that he gave Eva some chocolate. Before supper he shows me in the newspaper a letter from my father, in which he quasi justifies his attitude towards the Jewish problem; the letter is very well written, but we regret that he felt the need to write it. R. recalls that it was the Princess who landed him in all these difficulties, and he says, 'Your father goes to his ruin out of pure chivalry!' At supper we discuss with the children the sea and its creatures; before that, prisons, penalties (the treadmill), all there to protect property. (Yesterday R. read to me some very fine and frank statements by Bismarck about his longing to withdraw from affairs.) He reads *Undine*, of which he prefers the first part. He makes many jokes about the fact that the copy Jouk.'s father used for his translation is full of ink blots, and he quotes the

---

[1] His article 'On the Womanly in the Human'.
[2] Joukowsky's father had translated this novel by the German writer Friedrich de la Motte-Fouqué into Russian, and Wagner was reading it in the copy in which his translation was written.

joke from the *Fl. Blätter* in which a boy makes excuses for all the ink blots in his schoolbook by saying that the nose of his neighbour, a little Moor, had been bleeding. – When I am already lying in bed, I hear him talking volubly and loudly; I get up and go into his room. 'I was talking to you,' he says, and embraces me tenderly and long. 'Once in 5,000 years it succeeds!' 'I was talking about Undine, the being who longed for a soul.' He goes to the piano, plays the mournful theme '*Rheingold, Rheingold*', continues with 'False and base all those who dwell up above'. 'Extraordinary that I saw this so clearly at that time!' – And as he is lying in bed, he says, 'I feel loving towards them, these subservient creatures of the deep, with all their yearning.'

These were the last words Cosima wrote in her Diaries. On the following day Wagner suffered a heart attack and died in her arms at about 3.30 in the afternoon.

The simultaneous death for which she had always longed did not come to pass. She lived for another forty-seven years before dying on April 1, 1930, having taken full charge of the festivals in Bayreuth until 1906, when she handed the responsibility over to her son Siegfried. From the date of Wagner's death to her own she wrote no further diaries.

Index